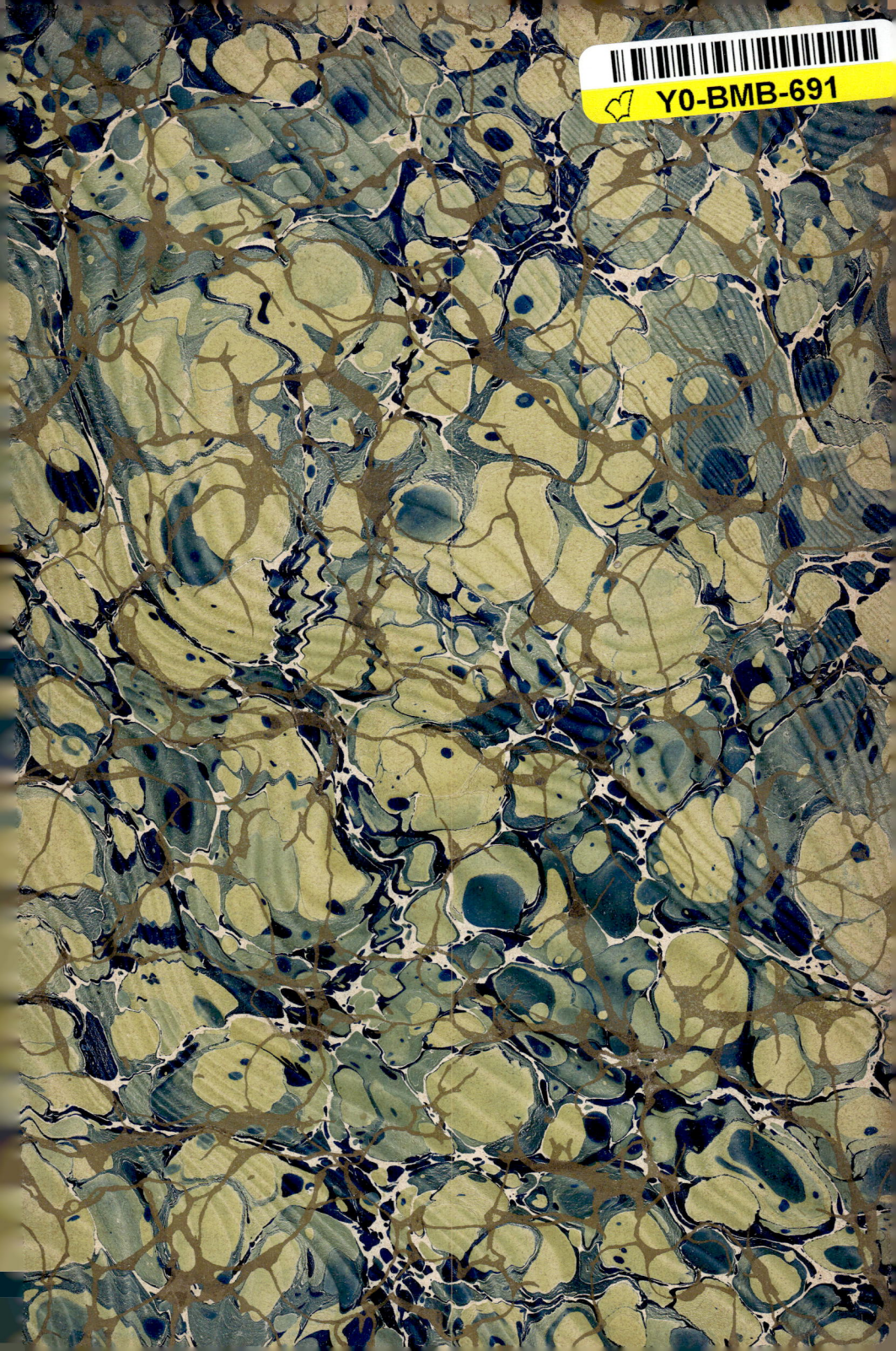

THE HISTORY OF ENGLAND

FROM THE

ACCESSION OF JAMES THE SECOND

BY

LORD MACAULAY

VOLUME II

NEW YORK
HARPER & BROTHERS, PUBLISHERS
FRANKLIN SQUARE

CONTENTS

OF

THE SECOND VOLUME.

CHAPTER VI.

	PAGE
The Power of James at the height	13
His Foreign Policy	14
His Plans of domestic Government; the Habeas Corpus Act; the standing Army	15
Designs in favor of the Roman Catholic Religion	17
Violation of the Test Act; Disgrace of Halifax	22
General Discontent	23
Persecution of the French Huguenots	24
Effect of that Persecution in England	27
Meeting of Parliament; Speech of the King; an Opposition formed in the House of Commons	28
Sentiments of Foreign Governments	30
Committee of the Commons on the King's Speech	32
Defeat of the Government	35
Second Defeat of the Government; the King reprimands the Commons	37
Coke committed by the Commons for Disrespect to the King	38
Opposition to the Government in the Lords; the Earl of Devonshire	39
The Bishop of London	40
Viscount Mordaunt	41
Prorogation	43
Trials of Lord Gerard and of Hampden	44
Trial of Delamere	45
Effect of his Acquittal	48
Parties in the Court; Feeling of the Protestant Tories	49

CONTENTS.

	PAGE
Publication of Papers found in the Strong-box of Charles II.	51
Feeling of the respectable Roman Catholics	52
Cabal of violent Roman Catholics	53
Castelmaine; Jermyn; White; Tyrconnel	54
Feeling of the Ministers of Foreign Governments	57
The Pope and the Order of Jesus opposed to each other	59
The Order of Jesus	60
Father Petre; the King's Temper and Opinions	66
The King encouraged in his Errors by Sunderland	68
Perfidy of Jeffreys; Godolphin	71
The Queen; Amours of the King; Catharine Sedley	72
Intrigues of Rochester in favor of Catharine Sedley	74
Decline of Rochester's Influence	77
Castelmaine sent to Rome; the Huguenots ill-treated by James	80
The Dispensing Power	83
Dismission of refractory Judges	84
Case of Sir Edward Hales	86
Roman Catholics authorized to hold ecclesiastical Benefices; Sclater	87
Walker	88
The Deanery of Christ Church given to a Roman Catholic	89
Disposal of Bishoprics; Resolution of James to use his ecclesiastical Supremacy against the Church	90
His Difficulties	91
He creates a new Court of High Commission	94
Proceedings against the Bishop of London	98
Discontent excited by the public Display of Roman Catholic Rites and Vestments	99
Riots	100
A Camp formed at Hounslow	102
Samuel Johnson	104
Hugh Speke	105
Proceedings against Johnson	106
Zeal of the Anglican Clergy against Popery	107
The Roman Catholic Divines overmatched	109
State of Scotland	111
Queensberry; Perth and Melfort	112
Favor shown to the Roman Catholic Religion in Scotland; Riots at Edinburgh	114

CONTENTS.

	PAGE
Anger of the King	115
His Plans concerning Scotland; Deputation of Scotch Privy Councillors sent to London	116
Their Negotiations with the King	117
Meeting of the Scotch Estates; they prove refractory	118
They are adjourned; arbitrary System of Government in Scotland	122
Ireland; State of the Law on the Subject of Religion	124
Hostility of Races	125
Aboriginal Peasantry	126
Aboriginal Aristocracy	127
State of the English Colony	128
Course which James ought to have followed	130
His Errors	133
Clarendon arrives in Ireland as Lord-lieutenant; his Mortifications	135
Panic among the Colonists	136
Arrival of Tyrconnel at Dublin as General	138
His Partiality and Violence	139
He is bent on the Repeal of the Act of Settlement; he returns to England	141
The King displeased with Clarendon; Rochester attacked by the Jesuitical Cabal	142
Attempts of James to convert Rochester	144
Dismission of Rochester	149
Dismission of Clarendon; Tyrconnel Lord Deputy	151
Dismay of the English Colonists in Ireland	153
Effect of the Fall of the Hydes	154

CHAPTER VII.

William, Prince of Orange; his Appearance	155
His early Life and Education	156
His Theological Opinions	157
His Military Qualifications	159
His Love of Danger; his bad Health	161
Coldness of his Manners and Strength of his Emotions; his Friendship for Bentinck	162
Mary, Princess of Orange	165
Gilbert Burnet	167

CONTENTS.

	PAGE
He brings about a good Understanding between the Prince and Princess	171
Relations between William and English Parties	172
His Feelings toward England; his Feelings toward Holland and France	173
His Policy consistent throughout	178
Treaty of Augsburg	181
William becomes the Head of the English Opposition	182
Mordaunt proposes to William a Descent on England; William rejects the Advice	183
Discontent in England after the Fall of the Hydes	184
Conversions to Popery; Peterborough; Salisbury	185
Wycherley; Tindal; Haines	186
Dryden	187
The Hind and Panther	190
Change in the Policy of the Court toward the Puritans	192
Partial Toleration granted in Scotland	196
Closeting	197
It is unsuccessful; Admiral Herbert	198
Declaration of Indulgence	199
Feeling of the Protestant Dissenters	201
Feeling of the Church of England	202
The Court and the Church	203
Letter to a Dissenter	206
Conduct of the Dissenters	207
Some of the Dissenters side with the Court; Care	209
Alsop; Rosewell; Lobb	210
Penn; the Majority of the Puritans are against the Court	211
Baxter; Howe	212
Bunyan	213
Kiffin	215
The Prince and Princess of Orange hostile to the Declaration of Indulgence	220
Their Views respecting the English Roman Catholics vindicated	222
Enmity of James to Burnet	228
Mission of Dykvelt to England	230
Negotiations of Dykvelt with English Statesmen; Danby	231
Nottingham	232
Halifax	233

CONTENTS.

	PAGE
Devonshire	234
Edward Russell	237
Compton; Herbert; Churchill	238
Lady Churchill and the Princess Anne	240
Dykvelt returns to the Hague with Letters from many eminent Englishmen	243
Zulestein's Mission	244
Growing Enmity between James and William	245
Influence of the Dutch Press	246
Correspondence of Stewart and Fagel	247
Castelmaine's Embassy to Rome	248

CHAPTER VIII.

Consecration of the Nuncio at Saint James's Palace; his public Reception	253
The Duke of Somerset	254
Dissolution of the Parliament; Military Offences illegally punished	255
Proceedings of the High Commission; the Universities	258
Proceedings against the University of Cambridge	261
The Earl of Mulgrave	262
State of Oxford	264
Magdalene College, Oxford	267
Anthony Farmer recommended by the King for President	270
Election of the President	271
The Fellows of Magdalene cited before the High Commission; Parker recommended as President	272
The Charter-house	273
The royal Progress	274
The King at Oxford; he reprimands the Fellows of Magdalene	276
Penn attempts to mediate	277
Special Ecclesiastical Commissioners sent to Oxford	281
Protest of Hough; Parker	282
Ejection of the Fellows	284
Magdalene College turned into a Popish Seminary	285
Resentment of the Clergy	286
Schemes of the Jesuitical Cabal respecting the Succession	288

CONTENTS.

	PAGE
Scheme of James and Tyrconnel for preventing the Princess of Orange from succeeding to the Kingdom of Ireland	290
The Queen pregnant; general Incredulity	291
Feeling of the Constituent Bodies, and of the Peers	294
James determines to pack a Parliament	295
The Board of Regulators	297
Many Lords-lieutenants dismissed; the Earl of Oxford	298
The Earl of Shrewsbury	299
The Earl of Dorset	301
Questions put to the Magistrates	304
Their Answers; Failure of the King's Plans	305
List of Sheriffs; Character of the Roman Catholic Country Gentlemen	309
Feeling of the Dissenters; Regulation of Corporations	312
Inquisition in all the Public Departments	316
Dismission of Sawyer	318
Williams Solicitor-general	319
Second Declaration of Indulgence; the Clergy ordered to read it	320
They hesitate; Patriotism of the Protestant Non-conformists of London	322
Consultation of the London Clergy	323
Consultation at Lambeth Palace	325
Petition of the Seven Bishops presented to the King	326
The London Clergy disobey the royal Order	329
Hesitation of the Government	331
It is determined to prosecute the Bishops for a Libel	332
They are examined by the Privy Council	333
They are committed to the Tower	335
Birth of the Pretender	336
He is generally believed to be supposititious	337
The Bishops brought before the King's Bench and bailed	341
Agitation of the Public Mind	344
Uneasiness of Sunderland	345
He professes himself a Roman Catholic; Trial of the Bishops	346
The Verdict; Joy of the People	357
Peculiar State of Public Feeling at this Time	362

CHAPTER IX.

	PAGE
Change in the Opinion of the Tories concerning the Lawfulness of Resistance	366
Russell proposes to the Prince of Orange a Descent on England; Henry Sidney	374
Devonshire; Shrewsbury; Halifax; Danby	376
Bishop Compton; Nottingham	378
Lumley; Invitation to William despatched	379
Conduct of Mary	380
Difficulties of William's Enterprise	382
Conduct of James after the Trial of the Bishops	386
Dismissions and Promotions	387
Proceedings of the High Commission. Sprat resigns his Seat	389
Discontent of the Clergy; Transactions at Oxford	390
Discontent of the Gentry	391
Discontent of the Army	392
Irish Troops brought over; public Indignation	394
Lillibullero	399
Politics of the United Provinces; Errors of the French King	400
His Quarrel with the Pope concerning Franchises	403
The Archbishopric of Cologne	404
Skilful Management of William	405
His military and naval Preparations	406
He receives numerous Assurances of Support from England	408
Sunderland	409
Anxiety of William	413
Warnings conveyed to James	414
Exertions of Lewis to save James	415
James frustrates them	416
The French Armies invade Germany	419
William obtains the Sanction of the States-general to his Expedition	420
Schomberg	421
British Adventurers at the Hague	422
William's Declaration	423
James roused to a Sense of his Danger; his naval Means	426
His military Means	427
He attempts to conciliate his Subjects	428

CONTENTS.

	PAGE
He gives Audience to the Bishops	429
His Concessions ill received	431
Proofs of the Birth of the Prince of Wales submitted to the Privy Council	434
Disgrace of Sunderland	435
William takes leave of the States of Holland	437
He embarks and sails; he is driven back by a Storm	438
His Declaration arrives in England; James questions the Lords	439
William sets sail the second Time	441
He passes the Straits	443
He lands at Torbay	444
He enters Exeter	448
Conversation of the King with the Bishops	453
Disturbances in London	456
Men of Rank begin to repair to the Prince	457
Lovelace	458
Colchester; Abingdon	459
Desertion of Cornbury	460
Petition of the Lords for a Parliament	464
The King goes to Salisbury	466
Seymour; Court of William at Exeter	467
Northern Insurrection	469
Skirmish at Wincanton	471
Desertion of Churchill and Grafton	473
Retreat of the Royal Army from Salisbury	475
Desertion of Prince George and Ormond	476
Flight of the Princess Anne	477
Council of Lords held by James	479
He appoints Commissioners to treat with William	483
The Negotiation a Feint	484
Dartmouth refuses to send the Prince of Wales into France	486
Agitation of London; forged Proclamation	487
Risings in various Parts of the Country	489
Clarendon joins the Prince at Salisbury	491
Dissension in the Prince's Camp	492
The Prince reaches Hungerford; Skirmish at Reading; the King's Commissioners arrive at Hungerford	495
Negotiation	496
The Queen and the Prince of Wales sent to France	501

CONTENTS.

	PAGE
Lauzun	502
The King's Preparations for Flight	505
His Flight	506

CHAPTER X.

The Flight of James known; great Agitation	507
The Lords meet at Guildhall	508
Riots in London	511
The Spanish Ambassador's House sacked	513
Arrest of Jeffreys	514
The Irish Night	516
The King detained near Sheerness	520
The Lords order him to be set at liberty	525
William's Embarrassment	526
Arrest of Feversham	527
Arrival of James in London	528
Consultation at Windsor	530
The Dutch Troops occupy Whitehall	533
Message from the Prince delivered to James; James sets out for Rochester	534
Arrival of William at St. James's	535
He is advised to assume the Crown by right of Conquest	537
He calls together the Lords and the Members of the Parliaments of Charles II.	539
Flight of James from Rochester	542
Debates and Resolutions of the Lords	543
Debates and Resolutions of the Commoners summoned by the Prince	544
A Convention called; Exertions of the Prince to restore Order	545
His tolerant Policy	546
Satisfaction of the Roman Catholic Powers; State of Feeling in France	548
Reception of the Queen of England in France	550
Arrival of James at Saint Germains	551
State of Feeling in the United Provinces	553
Election of Members to serve in the Convention	554
Affairs of Scotland	555
State of Parties in England	558

	PAGE
Sherlock's Plan	561
Sancroft's Plan	562
Danby's Plan	564
The Whig Plan	566
Meeting of the Convention; leading Members of the House of Commons	568
Choice of a Speaker	570
Debate on the State of the Nation	572
Resolution declaring the Throne vacant	574
It is sent up to the Lords; Debate in the Lords on the Plan of Regency	576
Schism between the Whigs and Followers of Danby	583
Meeting at the Earl of Devonshire's	585
Debate in the Lords on the Question whether the Throne was vacant; Majority for the Negative; Agitation in London	587
Letter of James to the Convention	588
Debates; Negotiations; Letter of the Princess of Orange to Danby	589
The Princess Anne acquiesces in the Whig Plan	590
William explains his Views	591
The Conference between the Houses	593
The Lords yield; new Laws proposed for the Security of Liberty	595
Disputes and Compromise	597
The Declaration of Right	599
Arrival of Mary	600
Tender and Acceptance of the Crown	601
William and Mary proclaimed	602
Peculiar Character of the English Revolution	603

HISTORY OF ENGLAND.

CHAPTER VI.

The power of James at the height.

JAMES was now at the height of power and prosperity. Both in England and in Scotland he had vanquished his enemies, and had punished them with a severity which had indeed excited their bitterest hatred, but had, at the same time, effectually quelled their courage. The Whig party seemed extinct. The name of Whig was never used except as a term of reproach. The Parliament was devoted to the King; and it was in his power to keep that Parliament to the end of his reign. The Church was louder than ever in professions of attachment to him, and had, during the late insurrection, acted up to those professions. The Judges were his tools; and, if they ceased to be so, it was in his power to remove them. The corporations were filled with his creatures. His revenues far exceeded those of his predecessors. His pride rose high. He was not the same man who, a few months before, in doubt whether his throne might not be overturned in an hour, had implored foreign help with unkingly supplications, and had accepted it with tears of gratitude. Visions of dominion and glory rose before him. He already saw himself, in imagination, the umpire of Europe, the champion of many states oppressed by one too powerful monarchy. So early as the month of June he had assured the United Provinces that, as soon as the affairs of England were settled, he would show the world how little he feared France. In conformity with these assurances, he, within a month after the battle of Sedgemoor, concluded with the States-general a defensive treaty, framed in the very spirit of the Triple League. It was regarded, both at the

Hague and at Versailles, as a most significant circumstance that Halifax, who was the constant and mortal enemy of French ascendency, and who had scarcely ever before been consulted on any grave affair since the beginning of the reign, took the lead on this occasion, and seemed to have the royal ear. It was a circumstance not less significant that no previous communication was made to Barillon. Both he and his master were taken by surprise. Lewis was much troubled, and expressed great, and not unreasonable, anxiety as to the ulterior designs of the prince who had lately been his pensioner and vassal. There were strong rumors that William of Orange was busied in organizing a great confederacy, which was to include both branches of the House of Austria, the United Provinces, the kingdom of Sweden, and the electorate of Brandenburg. It now seemed that this confederacy would have at its head the King and Parliament of England.*

In fact, negotiations tending to such a result were actually opened. Spain proposed to form a close alliance with James; His foreign policy. and he listened to the proposition with favor, though it was evident that such an alliance would be little less than a declaration of war against France. But he postponed his final decision till after the Parliament should have reassembled. The fate of Christendom depended on the temper in which he might then find the Commons. If they were disposed to acquiesce in his plans of domestic government, there would be nothing to prevent him from interfering with vigor and authority in the great dispute which must soon be brought to an issue on the Continent. If they were refractory, he must relinquish all thought of arbitrating between contending nations, must again implore French assistance, must again submit to French dictation, must sink into a potentate of the third or fourth class, and must indemnify himself for the contempt with which he would be regarded abroad by triumphs over law and public opinion at home.

It seemed, indeed, that it would not be easy for him to de-

---

* Avaux Neg., Aug. $\frac{6}{16}$, 1685; Despatch of Van Citters and his colleagues, enclosing the treaty, Aug. $\frac{14}{24}$; Lewis to Barillon, Aug. $\frac{14}{24}$, $\frac{20}{30}$.

mand more than the Commons were disposed to give. Already they had abundantly proved that they were desirous to maintain his prerogatives unimpaired, and that they were by no means extreme to mark his encroachments on the rights of the people. Indeed, eleven-twelfths of the members were either dependents of the court or zealous Cavaliers from the country. There were few things which such an assembly could pertinaciously refuse to the Sovereign; but, happily for the nation, those few things were the very things on which James had set his heart.

His plans of domestic government.

One of his objects was to obtain a repeal of the Habeas Corpus Act, which he hated, as it was natural that a tyrant should hate the most stringent curb that ever legislation imposed on tyranny. This feeling remained deeply fixed in his mind to the last, and appears in the instructions which he drew up, in exile, for the guidance of his son.* But the Habeas Corpus Act, though passed during the ascendency of the Whigs, was not more dear to the Whigs than to the Tories. It is indeed not wonderful that this great law should be highly prized by all Englishmen without distinction of party: for it is a law which, not by circuitous, but by direct operation, adds to the security and happiness of every inhabitant of the realm.†

The Habeas Corpus Act.

James had yet another design, odious to the party which had set him on the throne and which had upheld him there. He wished to form a great standing army. He had taken advantage of the late insurrection to make large additions to the military force which his brother had left. The bodies now designated as the first six regiments of dragoon guards, the third and fourth regiments of dragoons, and the nine regiments of infantry of the line, from the seventh to the fifteenth inclusive, had just been raised.‡

The standing army.

---

* Instructions headed, "For my son the Prince of Wales, 1692," among the Stuart Papers.

† "The Habeas Corpus," said Johnson, the most bigoted of Tories, to Boswell, "is the single advantage which our government has over that of other countries."

‡ See the Historical Records of Regiments, published under the supervision of the Adjutant-general.

The effect of these augmentations, and of the recall of the garrison of Tangier, was that the number of regular troops in England had, in a few months, been increased from six thousand to near twenty thousand. No English King had ever, in time of peace, had such a force at his command. Yet even with this force James was not content. He often repeated that no confidence could be placed in the fidelity of the trainbands, that they sympathized with all the passions of the class to which they belonged, that, at Sedgemoor, there had been more militia-men in the rebel army than in the royal encampment, and that, if the throne had been defended only by the array of the counties, Monmouth would have marched in triumph from Lyme to London.

The revenue, large as it was when compared with that of former kings, barely sufficed to meet this new charge. A great part of the produce of the new taxes was absorbed by the naval expenditure. At the close of the late reign the whole cost of the army, the Tangier regiments included, had been under three hundred thousand pounds a year. Six hundred thousand pounds a year would not now suffice.* If any further augmentation were made, it would be necessary to demand a supply from Parliament; and it was not likely that Parliament would be in a complying mood. The very name of standing army was hateful to the whole nation, and to no part of the nation more hateful than to the Cavalier gentlemen who filled the Lower House. In their minds a standing army was inseparably associated with the Rump, with the Protector, with the spoliation of the Church, with the purgation of the Universities, with the abolition of the peerage, with the murder of the King, with the sullen reign of the Saints, with cant and asceticism, with fines and sequestrations, with the insults which major-generals, sprung from the dregs of the people, had offered to the oldest and most honorable families of the kingdom. There was, moreover, scarcely a

* Barillon, Dec. $\frac{3}{13}$, 1685. He had studied the subject much. "C'est un détail," he says, "dont j'ai connoissance." It appears from the Treasury Warrant Book that the charge of the army for the year 1687 was fixed on the first of January at 623,104*l*. 9*s*. 11*d*.

baronet or a squire in the Parliament who did not owe part of his importance in his own county to his rank in the militia. If that national force were set aside, the gentry of England must lose much of their dignity and influence. It was therefore probable that the King would find it more difficult to obtain funds for the support of his army than even to obtain the repeal of the Habeas Corpus Act.

But both the designs which have been mentioned were subordinate to one great design on which the King's whole soul Designs in favor of the Roman Catholic religion. was bent, but which was abhorred by those Tory gentlemen who were ready to shed their blood for his rights, abhorred by that Church which had never, during three generations of civil discord, wavered in fidelity to his house, abhorred even by that army on which, in the last extremity, he must rely.

His religion was still under proscription. Many rigorous laws against Roman Catholics appeared on the Statute-book, and had, within no long time, been rigorously executed. The Test Act excluded from civil and military office all who dissented from the Church of England; and, by a subsequent Act, passed when the fictions of Oates had driven the nation wild, it had been provided that no person should sit in either House of Parliament without solemnly abjuring the doctrine of transubstantiation. That the King should wish to obtain for the Church to which he belonged a complete toleration was natural and right; nor is there any reason to doubt that, by a little patience, prudence, and justice, such a toleration might have been obtained.

The extreme antipathy and dread with which the English people regarded his religion was not to be ascribed solely or chiefly to theological animosity. That salvation might be found in the Church of Rome, nay, that some members of that Church had been among the brightest examples of Christian virtue, was admitted by all divines of the Anglican communion and by the most illustrious Non-conformists. It is notorious that the penal laws against Popery were strenuously defended by many who thought Arianism, Quakerism, and Judaism more dangerous, in a spiritual point of view, than

II.—2

Popery, and who yet showed no disposition to enact similar laws against Arians, Quakers, or Jews.

It is easy to explain why the Roman Catholic was treated with less indulgence than was shown to men who renounced the doctrine of the Nicene fathers, and even to men who had not been admitted by baptism within the Christian pale. There was among the English a strong conviction that the Roman Catholic, where the interests of his religion were concerned, thought himself free from all the ordinary rules of morality, nay, that he thought it meritorious to violate those rules if, by so doing, he could avert injury or reproach from the Church of which he was a member.

Nor was this opinion destitute of a show of reason. It was impossible to deny that Roman Catholic casuists of great eminence had written in defence of equivocation, of mental reservation, of perjury, and even of assassination. Nor, it was said, had the speculations of this odious school of sophists been barren of results. The massacre of Saint Bartholomew, the murder of the first William of Orange, the murder of Henry the Third of France, the numerous conspiracies which had been formed against the life of Elizabeth, and, above all, the gunpowder treason, were constantly cited as instances of the close connection between vicious theory and vicious practice. It was alleged that every one of these crimes had been prompted or applauded by Roman Catholic divines. The letters which Everard Digby wrote in lemon-juice from the Tower to his wife had recently been published, and were often quoted. He was a scholar and a gentleman, upright in all ordinary dealings, and strongly impressed with a sense of duty to God. Yet he had been deeply concerned in the plot for blowing up King, Lords, and Commons, and had, on the brink of eternity, declared that it was incomprehensible to him how any Roman Catholic should think such a design sinful. The inference popularly drawn from these things was that, however fair the general character of a Papist might be, there was no excess of fraud or cruelty of which he was not capable when the safety and honor of his Church were at stake.

The extraordinary success of the fables of Oates is to be

chiefly ascribed to the prevalence of this opinion. It was to no purpose that the accused Roman Catholic appealed to the integrity, humanity, and loyalty which he had shown through the whole course of his life. It was to no purpose that he called crowds of respectable witnesses, of his own persuasion, to contradict monstrous romances invented by the most infamous of mankind. It was to no purpose that, with the halter round his neck, he invoked on himself the whole vengeance of the God before whom, in a few moments, he must appear, if he had been guilty of meditating any ill to his prince or to his Protestant fellow-countrymen. The evidence which he produced in his favor proved only how little Popish oaths were worth. His very virtues raised a presumption of his guilt. That he had before him death and judgment in immediate prospect only made it more likely that he would deny what, without injury to the holiest of causes, he could not confess. Among the unhappy men who were convicted of the murder of Godfrey was one Protestant of no high character, Henry Berry. It is a remarkable and well attested circumstance, that Berry's last words did more to shake the credit of the plot than the dying declarations of pious and honorable Roman Catholics who underwent the same fate.*

It was not only by the ignorant populace, it was not only by zealots in whom fanaticism had extinguished all reason and charity, that the Roman Catholic was regarded as a man the very tenderness of whose conscience might make him a false witness, an incendiary, or a murderer, as a man who, where his Church was concerned, shrank from no atrocity and could be bound by no oath. If there were in that age two persons inclined by their judgment and by their temper to toleration, those persons were Tillotson and Locke. Yet Tillotson, whose indulgence for various kinds of schismatics and heretics brought on him the reproach of heterodoxy, told the House of Commons from the pulpit that it was their duty to make effectual provision against the propagation of a religion more mischievous than irreligion itself, of a religion

---

* Burnet, i., 447.

which demanded from its followers services directly opposed to the first principles of morality. His temper, he truly said, was prone to lenity; but his duty to the community forced him to be, in this one instance, severe. He declared that, in his judgment, Pagans who had never heard the name of Christ, and who were guided only by the light of nature, were more trustworthy members of civil society than men who had been formed in the schools of the Popish casuists.* Locke, in the celebrated treatise in which he labored to show that even the grossest forms of idolatry ought not to be prohibited under penal sanctions, contended that the Church which taught men not to keep faith with heretics had no claim to toleration.†

It is evident that, in such circumstances, the greatest service which an English Roman Catholic could render to his brethren in the faith was to convince the public that, whatever some too subtle theorists might have written, whatever some rash men might, in times of violent excitement, have done, his Church did not hold that any end could sanctify means inconsistent with morality. And this great service it was in the power of James to render. He was king. He was more powerful than any English king had been within the memory of the oldest man. It depended on him whether the reproach which lay on his religion should be taken away or should be made permanent.

Had he conformed to the laws, had he kept his promises, had he abstained from employing any unrighteous methods for the propagation of his own theological tenets, had he suspended the operation of the penal statutes by a large exercise of his unquestionable prerogative of mercy, but, at the same time, carefully abstained from violating the civil or ecclesiastical constitution of the realm, the feeling of his people must have undergone a rapid change. So conspicuous an example of good faith punctiliously observed by a Popish prince toward a Protestant nation would have quieted the public

---

* Tillotson's Sermon, preached before the House of Commons, Nov. 5, 1678.
† Locke, First Letter on Toleration.

apprehensions. Men who saw that a Roman Catholic might safely be suffered to direct the whole executive administration, to command the army and navy, to convoke and dissolve the legislature, to appoint the Bishops and Deans of the Church of England, would soon have ceased to fear that any great evil would arise from allowing a Roman Catholic to be captain of a company or alderman of a borough. It is probable that, in a few years, the sect so long detested by the nation would, with general applause, have been admitted to office and to Parliament.

If, on the other hand, James should attempt to promote the interest of his Church by violating the fundamental laws of his kingdom and the solemn promises which he had repeatedly made in the face of the whole world, it could hardly be doubted that the charges which it had been the fashion to bring against the Roman Catholic religion would be considered by all Protestants as fully established. For, if ever a Roman Catholic could be expected to keep faith with heretics, James might have been expected to keep faith with the Anglican clergy. To them he owed his crown. But for their strenuous opposition to the Exclusion Bill he would have been a banished man. He had repeatedly and emphatically acknowledged the debt which he owed to them, and had vowed to maintain them in all their legal rights. If he could not be bound by ties like these, it must be evident that, where his superstition was concerned, no tie of gratitude or of honor could bind him. To trust him would thenceforth be impossible; and, if his people could not trust him, what member of his Church could they trust? He was not supposed to be constitutionally or habitually treacherous. To his blunt manner, and to his want of consideration for the feelings of others, he owed a much higher reputation for sincerity than he at all deserved. His eulogists affected to call him James the Just. If then it should appear that, in turning Papist, he had also turned dissembler and promise-breaker, what conclusion was likely to be drawn by a nation already disposed to believe that Popery had a pernicious influence on the moral character?

For these reasons many of the most eminent Roman Catholics of that age, and among them the Supreme Pontiff, were of opinion that the interest of their Church in our island would be most effectually promoted by a moderate and constitutional policy. But such considerations had no effect on the slow understanding and imperious temper of James. In his eagerness to remove the disabilities under which the professors of his religion lay, he took a course which convinced the most enlightened and tolerant Protestants of his time that those disabilities were essential to the safety of the state. To his policy the English Roman Catholics owed three years of lawless and insolent triumph, and a hundred and forty years of subjection and degradation.

Many members of his Church held commissions in the newly raised regiments. This breach of the law for a time Violation of the Test Act. passed uncensured: for men were not disposed to note every irregularity which was committed by a King suddenly called upon to defend his crown and his life against rebels. But the danger was now over. The insurgents had been vanquished and punished. Their unsuccessful attempt had strengthened the government which they had hoped to overthrow. Yet still James continued to grant commissions to unqualified persons; and speedily it was announced that he was determined to be no longer bound by the Test Act, that he hoped to induce the Parliament to repeal that Act, but that, if the Parliament proved refractory, he would not the less have his own way.

As soon as this was known, a deep murmur, the forerunner of a tempest, gave him warning that the spirit before which Disgrace of Halifax. his grandfather, his father, and his brother had been compelled to recede, though dormant, was not extinct. Opposition appeared first in the cabinet. Halifax did not attempt to conceal his disgust and alarm. At the Council board he courageously gave utterance to those feelings which, as it soon appeared, pervaded the whole nation. None of his colleagues seconded him, and the subject dropped. He was summoned to the royal closet, and had two long conferences with his master. James tried the effect of compliments and blandishments, but to no purpose. Halifax positively refused to promise that he would give his vote in the House of Lords for the repeal either of the Test Act or of the Habeas Corpus Act.

Some of those who were about the King advised him not, on the eve of the meeting of Parliament, to drive the most eloquent and accomplished statesman of the age into opposition. They represented that Halifax loved the dignity of office, that, while he continued to be Lord President, it would be hardly possible for him to put forth his whole strength against the government, and that to dismiss him from his high post was to emancipate him from all restraint. The King was peremptory. Halifax was informed that his services were no longer needed, and his name was struck out of the Council Book.*

<small>General discontent.</small> His dismission produced a great sensation not only in England, but also at Paris, at Vienna, and at the Hague: for it was well known that he had always labored to counteract the influence exercised by the court of Versailles on English affairs. Lewis expressed much pleasure at the news. The ministers of the United Provinces and of the House of Austria, on the other hand, extolled the wisdom and virtue of the discarded statesman in a manner which gave serious offence at Whitehall. James was particularly angry with the secretary of the imperial legation, who did not scruple to say that the eminent service which Halifax had performed in the debate on the Exclusion Bill had been requited with gross ingratitude.†

It soon became clear that Halifax would have many followers. A portion of the Tories, with their old leader, Danby, at their head, began to hold Whiggish language. Even the prelates hinted that there was a point at which the loyalty due to the prince must yield to higher considerations. The discontent of the chiefs of the army was still more extraordinary and still more formidable. Already began to appear the first

---

* Council Book. The erasure is dated Oct. 21, 1685. Barillon, Oct. $\frac{19}{29}$.

† Barillon, $\frac{\text{Oct. 26,}}{\text{Nov. 5,}}$ 1685; Lewis to Barillon, $\frac{\text{Oct. 27}}{\text{Nov. 6}}$; Nov. $\frac{6}{16}$.

symptoms of that feeling which, three years later, impelled so many officers of high rank to desert the royal standard. Men who had never before had a scruple had on a sudden become strangely scrupulous. Churchill gently whispered that the King was going too far. Kirke, just returned from his Western butchery, swore to stand by the Protestant religion. Even if he abjured the faith in which he had been bred, he would never, he said, become a Papist. He was already bespoken. If ever he did apostatize, he was bound by a solemn promise to the Emperor of Morocco to turn Mussulman.*

Persecution of the French Huguenots.

While the nation, agitated by many strong emotions, looked anxiously forward to the re-assembling of the Houses, tidings, which increased the prevailing excitement, arrived from France.

The long and heroic struggle which the Huguenots had maintained against the French government had been brought to a final close by the ability and vigor of Richelieu. That great statesman vanquished them; but he confirmed to them the liberty of conscience which had been bestowed on them by the edict of Nantes. They were suffered, under some restraints of no galling kind, to worship God according to their own ritual, and to write in defence of their own doctrine. They were admissible to political and military employment; nor did their heresy, during a considerable time, practically impede their rise in the world. Some of them commanded the armies of the state; and others presided over important departments of the civil administration. At length a change took place. Lewis the Fourteenth had, from an early age, regarded the Calvinists with an aversion at once religious and political. As a zealous Roman Catholic, he detested their theological dogmas. As a prince fond of arbitrary power, he detested those republican theories which were intermingled with the Genevese divinity. He gradually retrenched all the privileges which the schismatics enjoyed. He interfered with the education of Protestant children, confiscated property

* There is a remarkable account of the first appearance of the symptoms of discontent among the Tories in a letter of Halifax to Chesterfield, written in October, 1685. Burnet, i., 684.

bequeathed to Protestant consistories, and on frivolous pretexts shut up Protestant churches. The Protestant ministers were harassed by the tax-gatherers. The Protestant magistrates were deprived of the honor of nobility. The Protestant officers of the royal household were informed that His Majesty dispensed with their services. Orders were given that no Protestant should be admitted into the legal profession. The oppressed sect showed some faint signs of that spirit which in the preceding century had bidden defiance to the whole power of the House of Valois. Massacres and executions followed. Dragoons were quartered in the towns where the heretics were numerous, and in the country-seats of the heretic gentry; and the cruelty and licentiousness of these rude missionaries was sanctioned or leniently censured by the government. Still, however, the edict of Nantes, though practically violated in its most essential provisions, had not been formally rescinded; and the King repeatedly declared in solemn public acts that he was resolved to maintain it. But the bigots and flatterers who had his ear gave him advice which he was but too willing to take. They represented to him that his rigorous policy had been eminently successful, that little or no resistance had been made to his will, that thousands of Huguenots had already been converted, that, if he would take the one decisive step which yet remained, those who were still obstinate would speedily submit, France would be purged from the taint of heresy, and her prince would have earned a heavenly crown not less glorious than that of Saint Lewis. These arguments prevailed. The final blow was struck. The edict of Nantes was revoked; and a crowd of decrees against the sectaries appeared in rapid succession. Boys and girls were torn from their parents and sent to be educated in convents. All Calvinistic ministers were commanded either to abjure their religion or to quit their country within a fortnight. The other professors of the reformed faith were forbidden to leave the kingdom; and, in order to prevent them from making their escape, the outports and frontiers were strictly guarded. It was thought that the flocks, thus separated from the evil shepherds, would soon return to the true fold. But in spite of all the vigilance of the military police there was a vast emigration. It was calculated that, in a few months, fifty thousand families quitted France forever. Nor were the refugees such as a country can well spare. They were generally persons of intelligent minds, of industrious habits, and of austere morals. In the list are to be found names eminent in war, in science, in literature, and in art. Some of the exiles offered their swords to William of Orange, and distinguished themselves by the fury with which they fought against their persecutor. Others avenged themselves with weapons still more formidable, and, by means of the presses of Holland, England, and Germany, inflamed, during thirty years, the public mind of Europe against the French government. A more peaceful class erected silk manufactories in the eastern suburb of London. One detachment of emigrants taught the Saxons to make the stuffs and hats of which France had hitherto enjoyed a monopoly. Another planted the first vines in the neighborhood of the Cape of Good Hope.*

In ordinary circumstances the courts of Spain and of Rome would have eagerly applauded a prince who had made vigorous war on heresy. But such was the hatred inspired by the injustice and haughtiness of Lewis that, when he became a persecutor, the courts of Spain and Rome took the side of religious liberty, and loudly reprobated the cruelty of turning a savage and licentious soldiery loose on an unoffending people.† One cry of grief and rage rose from the whole of Protestant Europe. The tidings of the revocation of the edict of Nantes reached England about a week before the day to which the Parliament stood adjourned. It was clear then that the spirit of Gardiner and of Alva was still the spirit of the Roman Catholic Church. Lewis was not inferior to James in

---

* The contemporary tracts in various languages on the subject of this persecution are innumerable. An eminently clear, terse, and spirited summary will be found in Voltaire's Siècle de Louis XIV.

† "Misionarios embotados," says Ronquillo. "Apostoli armati," says Innocent. There is, in the Mackintosh Collection, a remarkable letter on this subject from Ronquillo, dated $\frac{\text{March 26,}}{\text{April 5,}}$ 1686. See Venier, Relatione di Francia, 1689, quoted by Professor Ranke in his Römischen Päpste, Book VIII.

generosity and humanity, and was certainly far superior to James in all the abilities and acquirements of a statesman. Lewis had, like James, repeatedly promised to respect the privileges of his Protestant subjects. Yet Lewis was now avowedly a persecutor of the reformed religion. What reason was there, then, to doubt that James waited only for an opportunity to follow the example? He was already forming, in defiance of the law, a military force officered to a great extent by Roman Catholics. Was there anything unreasonable in the apprehension that this force might be employed to do what the French dragoons had done?

James was almost as much disturbed as his subjects by the conduct of the court of Versailles. In truth, that court Effect of that persecution in England. had acted as if it had meant to embarrass and annoy him. He was about to ask from a Protestant legislature a full toleration for Roman Catholics. Nothing, therefore, could be more unwelcome to him than the intelligence that, in a neighboring country, toleration had just been withdrawn by a Roman Catholic government from Protestants. His vexation was increased by a speech which the Bishop of Valence, in the name of the Gallican clergy, addressed at this time to Lewis the Fourteenth. The pious Sovereign of England, the orator said, looked to the most Christian King for support against a heretical nation. It was remarked that the members of the House of Commons showed particular anxiety to procure copies of this harangue, and that it was read by all Englishmen with indignation and alarm.* James was desirous to counteract the impression which these things had made, and was also at that moment by no means unwilling to let all Europe see that he was not the slave of France. He therefore declared publicly that he disapproved of the manner in which the Huguenots had been treated, granted to the exiles some relief from his privy purse, and, by letters under his great seal, invited his subjects to imitate his liberality. In a very few months it became clear that all this

---

* "Mi dicono che tutti questi parlamentarii ne hanno voluto copia, il che assolutamente avrà causate pessime impressioni."—Adda, Nov. $\frac{9}{19}$, 1685. See Evelyn's Diary, Nov. 3.

compassion was feigned for the purpose of cajoling his Parliament, that he regarded the refugees with mortal hatred, and that he regretted nothing so much as his own inability to do what Lewis had done.

On the ninth of November the Houses met. The Commons were summoned to the bar of the Lords; and the King spoke from the throne. His speech had been composed by himself. He congratulated his loving subjects on the suppression of the rebellion in the West: but he added that the speed with which that rebellion had risen to a formidable height, and the length of time during which it had continued to rage, must convince all men how little dependence could be placed on the militia. He had, therefore, made additions to the regular army. The charge of that army would henceforth be more than double of what it had been; and he trusted that the Commons would grant him the means of defraying the increased expense. He then informed his hearers that he had employed some officers who had not taken the test; but he knew those officers to be fit for public trust. He feared that artful men might avail themselves of this irregularity to disturb the harmony which existed between himself and his Parliament. But he would speak out. He was determined not to part with servants on whose fidelity he could rely, and whose help he might perhaps soon need.*

Meeting of Parliament; speech of the King.

This explicit declaration that he had broken the laws which were regarded by the nation as the chief safeguards of the established religion, and that he was resolved to persist in breaking those laws, was not likely to soothe the excited feelings of his subjects. The Lords, seldom disposed to take the lead in opposition to a government, consented to vote him formal thanks for what he had said. But the Commons were in a less complying mood. When they had returned to their own House there was a long silence; and the faces of many of the most respectable mem-

An opposition formed in the House of Commons.

---

* Lords' Journals, Nov. 9, 1685. "Vengo assicurato," says Adda, "che S. M. stessa abbia composto il discorso."—Despatch of Nov. $\frac{19}{28}$, 1685.

bers expressed deep concern. At length Middleton rose and moved the House to go instantly into committee on the King's speech: but Sir Edmund Jennings, a zealous Tory from Yorkshire, who was supposed to speak the sentiments of Danby, protested against this course, and demanded time for consideration. Sir Thomas Clarges, maternal uncle of the Duke of Albemarle, and long distinguished in Parliament as a man of business and a vigilant steward of the public money, took the same side. The feeling of the House could not be mistaken. Sir John Ernley, Chancellor of the Exchequer, insisted that the delay should not exceed forty-eight hours; but he was overruled; and it was resolved that the discussion should be postponed for three days.*

The interval was well employed by those who took the lead against the Court. They had indeed no light work to perform. In three days a country party was to be organized. The difficulty of the task is in our age not easy to be appreciated; for in our age all the nation assists at every deliberation of the Lords and Commons. What is said by the leaders of the ministry and of the opposition after midnight is read by the whole metropolis at dawn, by the inhabitants of Northumberland and Cornwall in the afternoon, and in Ireland and the Highlands of Scotland on the morrow. In our age, therefore, the stages of legislation, the rules of debate, the tactics of faction, the opinions, temper, and style of every active member of either House, are familiar to hundreds of thousands. Every man who now enters Parliament possesses what, in the seventeenth century, would have been called a great stock of parliamentary knowledge. Such knowledge was then to be obtained only by actual parliamentary service. The difference between an old and a new member was as great as the difference between a veteran soldier and a recruit just taken from the plough; and James's Parliament contained a most unusual proportion of new members, who had brought from

* Commons' Journals; Bramston's Memoirs; James Van Leeuwen to the States-general, Nov. $\frac{10}{20}$, 1685. Van Leeuwen was secretary of the Dutch embassy, and conducted the correspondence in the absence of Van Citters. As to Clarges, see Burnet, i., 98.

their country seats to Westminster no political knowledge and many violent prejudices. These gentlemen hated the Papists, but hated the Whigs not less intensely, and regarded the King with superstitious veneration. To form an opposition out of such materials was a feat which required the most skilful and delicate management. Some men of great weight, however, undertook the work, and performed it with success. Several experienced Whig politicians, who had not seats in that Parliament, gave useful advice and information. On the day preceding that which had been fixed for the debate, many meetings were held at which the leaders instructed the novices; and it soon appeared that these exertions had not been thrown away.*

The foreign embassies were all in a ferment. It was well understood that a few days would now decide the great question, whether the King of England was or was not to be the vassal of the King of France. The ministers of the House of Austria were most anxious that James should give satisfaction to his Parliament. Innocent had sent to London two persons charged to inculcate moderation, both by admonition and by example. One of them was John Leyburn, an English Dominican, who had been secretary to Cardinal Howard, and who, with some learning and a rich vein of natural humor, was the most cautious, dexterous, and taciturn of men. He had recently been consecrated Bishop of Adrumetum, and named Vicar Apostolic in Great Britain. Ferdinand, Count of Adda, an Italian of no eminent abilities, but of mild temper and courtly manners, had been appointed Nuncio. These functionaries were eagerly welcomed by James. No Roman Catholic bishop had exercised spiritual functions in the island during more than half a century. No Nuncio had been received here during the hundred and twenty-seven years which had elapsed since the death of Mary. Leyburn was lodged in Whitehall, and received a pension of a thousand pounds a year. Adda did not yet assume a public character. He

<small>Sentiments of foreign governments.</small>

---

* Barillon, Nov. $\frac{16}{26}$, 1685.

passed for a foreigner of rank whom curiosity had brought to London, appeared daily at court, and was treated with high consideration. Both the Papal emissaries did their best to diminish, as much as possible, the odium inseparable from the offices which they filled, and to restrain the rash zeal of James. The Nuncio, in particular, declared that nothing could be more injurious to the interests of the Church of Rome than a rupture between the King and the Parliament.*

Barillon was active on the other side. The instructions which he received from Versailles on this occasion well deserve to be studied; for they furnish a key to the policy systematically pursued by his master toward England during the twenty years which preceded our revolution. The advices from Madrid, Lewis wrote, were alarming. Strong hopes were entertained there that James would ally himself closely with the House of Austria, as soon as he should be assured that his Parliament would give him no trouble. In these circumstances, it was evidently the interest of France that the Parliament should prove refractory. Barillon was therefore directed to act, with all possible precautions against detection, the part of a makebate. At court he was to omit no opportunity of stimulating the religious zeal and the kingly pride of James; but at the same time it might be desirable to have some secret communication with the malcontents. Such communication would indeed be hazardous, and would require the utmost adroitness: yet it might perhaps be in the power of the Ambassador, without committing himself or his government, to animate the zeal of the opposition for the laws and liberties of England, and to let it be understood that those laws and liberties were not regarded by his master with an unfriendly eye.†

---

* Dodd's Church History; Van Leeuwen, Nov. $\frac{17}{27}$, 1685; Barillon, Dec. 24, 1685. Barillon says of Adda, "On l'avoit fait prévenir que la sureté et l'avantage des Catholiques consistoient dans une réunion entière de sa Majesté Britannique et de son parlement." Letters of Innocent to James, dated $\frac{\text{July 27}}{\text{Aug. 6}}$, and $\frac{\text{Sept. 25}}{\text{Oct. 3}}$, 1685; Despatches of Adda, Nov. $\frac{9}{19}$, and Nov. $\frac{16}{26}$, 1685. The very interesting correspondence of Adda, copied from the Papal archives, is in the British Museum.

† This most remarkable despatch bears date the $\frac{9}{19}$th of November, 1685, and will be found in the Appendix to Mr. Fox's History.

Lewis, when he dictated these instructions, did not foresee how speedily and how completely his uneasiness would be removed by the obstinacy and stupidity of James. On the twelfth of November the House of Commons resolved itself into a committee on the royal speech. The Solicitor-general, Heneage Finch, was in the chair. The debate was conducted by the chiefs of the new country party with rare tact and address. No expression indicating disrespect to the Sovereign or sympathy for rebels was suffered to escape. The Western insurrection was always mentioned with abhorrence. Nothing was said of the barbarities of Kirke and Jeffreys. It was admitted that the heavy expenditure which had been occasioned by the late troubles justified the King in asking some further supply: but strong objections were made to the augmentation of the army and to the infraction of the Test Act.

Committee of the Commons on the King's speech.

The subject of the Test Act the courtiers appear to have carefully avoided. They harangued, however, with some force on the great superiority of a regular army to a militia. One of them tauntingly asked whether the defence of the kingdom was to be entrusted to the beef-eaters. Another said that he should be glad to know how the Devonshire trainbands, who had fled in confusion before Monmouth's scythemen, would have faced the household troops of Lewis. But these arguments had little effect on Cavaliers who still remembered with bitterness the stern rule of the Protector. The general feeling was forcibly expressed by the first of the Tory country gentlemen of England, Edward Seymour. He admitted that the militia was not in a satisfactory state, but maintained that it might be remodelled. The remodelling might require money: but, for his own part, he would rather give a million to keep up a force from which he had nothing to fear, than half a million to keep up a force of which he must ever be afraid. Let the trainbands be disciplined: let the navy be strengthened; and the country would be secure. A standing army was at best a mere drain on the public resources. The soldier was withdrawn from all useful labor. He produced nothing: he consumed the fruits of the industry of other men; and he domineered over those by whom he was supported. But the nation was now threatened, not only with a standing army, but with a Popish standing army, with a standing army officered by men who might be very amiable and honorable, but who were on principle enemies to the constitution of the realm. Sir William Twisden, member for the county of Kent, spoke on the same side with great keenness and loud applause. Sir Richard Temple, one of the few Whigs who had a seat in that Parliament, dexterously accommodating his speech to the temper of his audience, reminded the House that a standing army had been found, by experience, to be as dangerous to the just authority of princes as to the liberty of nations. Sir John Maynard, the most learned lawyer of his time, took part in the debate. He was now more than eighty years old, and could well remember the political contests of the reign of James the First. He had sat in the Long Parliament, and had taken part with the Roundheads, but had always been for lenient counsels, and had labored to bring about a general reconciliation. His abilities, which age had not impaired, and his professional knowledge, which had long overawed all Westminster Hall, commanded the ear of the House of Commons. He, too, declared himself against the augmentation of the regular forces.

After much debate it was resolved that a supply should be granted to the crown; but it was also resolved that a bill should be brought in for making the militia more efficient. This last resolution was tantamount to a declaration against the standing army. The King was greatly displeased; and it was whispered that, if things went on thus, the session would not be of long duration.*

---

* Commons' Journals, Nov. 12, 1685; Van Leeuwen, Nov. $\frac{13}{23}$; Barillon, Nov. $\frac{16}{26}$; Sir John Bramston's Memoirs. The best report of the debates of the Commons in November, 1685, is one of which the history is somewhat curious. There are two manuscript copies of it in the British Museum, Harl., 7187; Lans., 253. In these copies the names of the speakers are given at length. The author of the Life of James, published in 1702, transcribed this report, but gave only the initials of the speakers. The editors of Chandler's Debates and of the Parliamentary History guessed from these initials at the names, and sometimes guessed wrong. They ascribe to Waller a very remarkable speech, which will hereafter be mentioned,

II.—3

On the morrow the contention was renewed. The language of the country party was perceptibly bolder and sharper than on the preceding day. That paragraph of the King's speech which related to supply preceded the paragraph which related to the test. On this ground Middleton proposed that the paragraph relating to supply should be first considered in committee. The opposition moved the previous question. They contended that the reasonable and constitutional practice was to grant no money till grievances had been redressed, and that there would be an end of this practice if the House thought itself bound servilely to follow the order in which matters were mentioned by the King from the throne.

The division was taken on the question whether Middleton's motion should be put. The Noes were ordered by the Speaker to go forth into the lobby. They resented this much, and complained loudly of his servility and partiality: for they conceived that, according to the intricate and subtle rule which was then in force, and which, in our time, was superseded by a more rational and convenient practice, they were entitled to keep their seats; and it was held by all the parliamentary tacticians of that age that the party which stayed in the House had an advantage over the party which went out; for the accommodation on the benches was then so deficient that no person who had been fortunate enough to get a good seat was willing to lose it. Nevertheless, to the dismay of the ministers, many persons on whose votes the Court had absolutely depended were seen moving toward the door. Among them was Charles Fox, Paymaster of the Forces, and son of Sir Stephen Fox, Clerk of the Green Cloth. The Paymaster had been induced by his friends to absent himself during part of the discussion. But his anxiety had become insupportable. He came down to the Speaker's chamber, heard part of the debate, withdrew, and, after hesitating for an hour or two between conscience and five thousand pounds a year, took a manly resolution and rushed into the House just in time to

---

and which was really made by Windham, member for Salisbury. It was with some concern that I found myself forced to give up the belief that the last words uttered in public by Waller were so honorable to him.

vote. Two officers of the army, Colonel John Darcy, son of the Lord Conyers, and Captain James Kendall, withdrew to the lobby. Middleton went down to the bar and expostulated warmly with them. He particularly addressed himself to Kendall, a needy retainer of the Court, who had, in obedience to the royal mandate, been sent to Parliament by a packed corporation in Cornwall, and who had recently obtained a grant of a hundred head of rebels sentenced to transportation. "Sir," said Middleton, "have not you a troop of horse in His Majesty's service?" "Yes, my Lord," answered Kendall: "but my elder brother is just dead, and has left me seven hundred a year."

When the tellers had done their office, it appeared that the Ayes were one hundred and eighty-two, and the Noes one hundred and eighty-three. In that House of Commons which had been brought together by the unscrupulous use of chicanery, of corruption, and of violence, in that House of Commons of which James had said that more than eleven-twelfths of the members were such as he would himself have nominated, the Court had sustained a defeat on a vital question.*

Defeat of the government.

In consequence of this vote, the expressions which the King had used respecting the test were taken into consideration. It was resolved, after much discussion, that an address should be presented to him, reminding him that he could not legally continue to employ officers who refused to qualify, and pressing him to give such directions as might quiet the apprehensions and jealousies of his people.†

A motion was then made that the Lords should be requested to join in the address. Whether this motion was honestly made by the opposition, in the hope that the concurrence of the peers would add weight to the remonstrance, or artfully made by the courtiers, in the hope that a breach

---

* Commons' Journals, Nov. 13, 1685; Bramston's Memoirs; Reresby's Memoirs; Barillon, Nov. $\frac{16}{26}$; Van Leeuwen, Nov. $\frac{13}{23}$; Memoirs of Sir Stephen Fox, 1717; The Case of the Church of England fairly stated; Burnet, i., 666, and Speaker Onslow's note.

† Commons' Journals, Nov. 13, 1685; Harl. MS., 7187; Lansdowne MS., 253.

between the Houses might be the consequence, it is now impossible to discover. The proposition was rejected.*

The House then resolved itself into a committee, for the purpose of considering the amount of supply to be granted. The King wanted fourteen hundred thousand pounds: but the ministers saw that it would be vain to ask for so large a sum. The Chancellor of the Exchequer mentioned twelve hundred thousand pounds. The chiefs of the opposition replied that to vote for such a grant would be to vote for the permanence of the present military establishment: they were disposed to give only so much as might suffice to keep the regular troops on foot till the militia could be remodelled; and they therefore proposed four hundred thousand pounds. The courtiers exclaimed against this motion as unworthy of the House, and disrespectful to the King: but they were manfully encountered. One of the western members, John Windham, who sat for Salisbury, especially distinguished himself. He had always, he said, looked with dread and aversion on standing armies; and recent experience had strengthened those feelings. He then ventured to touch on a theme which had hitherto been studiously avoided. He described the desolation of the western counties. The people, he said, were weary of the oppression of the troops, weary of free quarters, of depredations, of still fouler crimes which the law called felonies, but for which, when perpetrated by

---

* The conflict of testimony on this subject is most extraordinary; and, after long consideration, I must own that the balance seems to me to be exactly poised. In the Life of James (1702), the motion is represented as a court motion. This account is confirmed by a remarkable passage in the Stuart Papers, which was corrected by the Pretender himself. (Life of James the Second, ii., 55.) On the other hand, Reresby, who was present, and Barillon, who ought to have been well informed, represent the motion as an opposition motion. The Harleian and Lansdowne manuscripts differ in the single word on which the whole depends. Unfortunately Bramston was not at the House that day. James Van Leeuwen mentions the motion and the division, but does not add a word which can throw the smallest light on the state of parties. I must own myself unable to draw with confidence any inference from the names of the tellers, Sir Joseph Williamson and Sir Francis Russell for the majority, and Lord Ancram and Sir Henry Goodricke for the minority. I should have thought Lord Ancram likely to go with the Court, and Sir Henry Goodricke likely to go with the opposition.

this class of felons, no redress could be obtained. The King's servants had indeed told the House that excellent rules had been laid down for the government of the army; but none could venture to say that these rules had been observed. What, then, was the inevitable inference? Did not the contrast between the paternal injunctions issued from the throne and the insupportable tyranny of the soldiers prove that the army was even now too strong for the prince as well as for the people? The Commons might surely, with perfect consistency, while they reposed entire confidence in the intentions of His Majesty, refuse to make any addition to a force which it was clear that His Majesty could not manage.

The motion that the sum to be granted should not exceed four hundred thousand pounds was lost by twelve votes. Second defeat of the government. This victory of the ministers was little better than a defeat. The leaders of the country party, nothing disheartened, retreated a little, made another stand, and proposed the sum of seven hundred thousand pounds. The committee divided again, and the courtiers were beaten by two hundred and twelve votes to one hundred and seventy.*

On the following day the Commons went in procession to Whitehall with their address on the subject of the test. The The King reprimands the Commons. King received them on his throne. The address was drawn up in respectful and affectionate language; for the great majority of those who had voted for it were zealously and even superstitiously loyal, and had readily agreed to insert some complimentary phrases, and to omit every word which the courtiers thought offensive. The answer of James was a cold and sullen reprimand. He declared himself greatly displeased and amazed that the Commons should have profited so little by the admonition which he had given them. "But," said he, "however you may proceed on your part, I will be very steady in all the promises which I have made to you."†

The Commons reassembled in their chamber, discontented,

---

* Commons' Journals, Nov. 16, 1685; Harl. MS., 7187; Lansdowne MS., 235.
† Commons' Journals, Nov. 17, 18, 1685.

yet somewhat overawed. To most of them the King was still an object of filial reverence. Three more years filled with bitter injuries, and with not less bitter insults, were scarcely sufficient to dissolve the ties which bound the Cavalier gentry to the throne.

The Speaker repeated the substance of the King's reply. There was, for some time, a solemn stillness: then the order of the day was read in regular course; and the House went into committee on the bill for remodelling the militia.

In a few hours, however, the spirit of the opposition revived. When, at the close of the day, the Speaker resumed the chair, Wharton, the boldest and most active of the Whigs, proposed that a time should be appointed for taking His Majesty's answer into consideration. John Coke, member for Derby, though a noted Tory, seconded Wharton. "I hope," he said, "that we are all Englishmen, and that we shall not be frightened from our duty by a few high words."

<small>Coke committed by the Commons for disrespect to the King.</small>

It was manfully, but not wisely, spoken. The whole House was in a tempest. "Take down his words," "To the bar," "To the Tower," resounded from every side. Those who were most lenient proposed that the offender should be reprimanded: but the ministers vehemently insisted that he should be sent to prison. The House might pardon, they said, offences committed against itself, but had no right to pardon an insult offered to the Crown. Coke was sent to the Tower. The indiscretion of one man had deranged the whole system of tactics which had been so ably concerted by the chiefs of the opposition. It was in vain that, at that moment, Edward Seymour attempted to rally his followers, exhorted them to fix a day for discussing the King's answer, and expressed his confidence that the discussion would be conducted with the respect due from subjects to the sovereign. The members were so much cowed by the royal displeasure, and so much incensed by the rudeness of Coke, that it would not have been safe to divide.*

---

* Commons' Journals, Nov. 18, 1685; Harl. MS., 7187; Lansdowne MS., 253; Burnet, i., 667.

The House adjourned; and the ministers flattered themselves that the spirit of opposition was quelled. But on the morrow, the nineteenth of November, new and alarming symptoms appeared. The time had arrived for taking into consideration the petitions which had been presented from all parts of England against the late elections. When, on the first meeting of the Parliament, Seymour had complained of the force and fraud by which the government had prevented the sense of constituent bodies from being fairly taken, he had found no seconder. But many who had then flinched from his side had subsequently taken heart, and, with Sir John Lowther, member for Cumberland, at their head, had, before the recess, suggested that there ought to be an inquiry into the abuses which had so much excited the public mind. The House was now in a much more angry temper; and many voices were boldly raised in menace and accusation. The ministers were told that the nation expected, and should have, signal redress. Meanwhile it was dexterously intimated that the best atonement which a gentleman who had been brought into the House by irregular means could make to the public was to use his ill-acquired power in defence of the religion and liberties of his country. No member who, in that crisis, did his duty had anything to fear. It might be necessary to unseat him; but the whole influence of the opposition should be employed to procure his re-election.*

Opposition to the government in the Lords. The Earl of Devonshire.

On the same day it became clear that the spirit of opposition had spread from the Commons to the Lords, and even to the episcopal bench. William Cavendish, Earl of Devonshire, took the lead in the Upper House; and he was well qualified to do so. In wealth and influence he was second to none of the English nobles; and the general voice designated him as the finest gen-

---

* Lonsdale's Memoirs. Burnet tells us (i., 667) that a sharp debate about elections took place in the House of Commons after Coke's committal. It must therefore have been on the 19th of November; for Coke was committed late on the 18th, and the Parliament was prorogued on the 20th. Burnet's narrative is confirmed by the Journals, from which it appears that several elections were under discussion on the 19th.

tleman of his time. His magnificence, his taste, his talents, his classical learning, his high spirit, the grace and urbanity of his manners, were admitted by his enemies. His eulogists, unhappily, could not pretend that his morals had escaped untainted from the wide-spread contagion of that age. Though an enemy of Popery and of arbitrary power, he had been averse to extreme courses, had been willing, when the Exclusion Bill was lost, to agree to a compromise, and had never been concerned in the illegal and imprudent schemes which had brought discredit on the Whig party. But, while blaming part of the conduct of his friends, he had not failed to perform zealously the most arduous and perilous duties of friendship. He had stood near Russell at the bar, had parted from him on the sad morning of the execution with close embraces and with many bitter tears, nay, had offered to manage an escape at the hazard of his own life.* This great nobleman now proposed that a day should be fixed for considering the royal speech. It was contended, on the other side, that the Lords, by voting thanks for the speech, had precluded themselves from complaining of it. But this objection was treated with contempt by Halifax. "Such thanks," he said, with the sarcastic pleasantry in which he excelled, "imply no approbation. We are thankful whenever our gracious Sovereign deigns to speak to us. Especially thankful are we when, as on the present occasion, he speaks out, and gives us fair warning of what we are to suffer."† Doctor Henry Compton, Bishop of London, spoke strongly for the motion. Though not gifted with eminent abilities, nor deeply versed in the learning of his profession, he was always heard by the House with respect; for he was one of the few clergymen who could, in that age, boast of noble blood. His own

The Bishop of London.

---

* Burnet, i., 560; Funeral Sermon of the Duke of Devonshire, preached by Kennet, 1708; Travels of Cosmo III. in England; The Hazard of a Death-bed Repentance argued from the Remorse of Conscience of W——, late D—— of D——, when dying; a most absurd pamphlet by John Dunton, which reached a tenth edition.

† Bramston's Memoirs. Burnet is incorrect both as to the time when the remark was made and as to the person who made it. In Halifax's Letter to a Dissenter will be found a remarkable allusion to this discussion.

loyalty, and the loyalty of his family, had been signally proved. His father, the second Earl of Northampton, had fought bravely for King Charles the First, and, surrounded by the parliamentary soldiers, had fallen, sword in hand, refusing to give or take quarter. The Bishop himself, before he was ordained, had borne arms in the Guards; and, though he generally did his best to preserve the gravity and sobriety befitting a prelate, some flashes of his military spirit would, to the last, occasionally break forth. He had been intrusted with the religious education of the two princesses, and had acquitted himself of that important duty in a manner which had satisfied all good Protestants, and had secured to him considerable influence over the minds of his pupils, especially of the Lady Anne.* He now declared that he was empowered to speak the sense of his brethren, and that, in their opinion and in his own, the whole civil and ecclesiastical constitution of the realm was in danger.

One of the most remarkable speeches of that day was made by a young man, whose eccentric career was destined to amaze Europe. This was Charles Mordaunt, Viscount Mordaunt, widely renowned, many years later, as Earl of Peterborough. Already he had given abundant proofs of his courage, of his capacity, and of that strange unsoundness of mind which made his courage and capacity almost useless to his country. Already he had distinguished himself as a wit and a scholar, as a soldier and a sailor. He had even set his heart on rivalling Bourdaloue and Bossuet. Though an avowed freethinker, he had sat up all night at sea to compose sermons, and had with great difficulty been prevented from edifying the crew of a man-of-war with his pious oratory.† He now addressed the House of Peers, for the first time, with characteristic eloquence, sprightliness, and audacity. He blamed the Commons for not having taken a bolder line. "They have been afraid," he said, "to speak out. They have talked of apprehensions and jealousies. What have appre-

<small>Viscount Mordaunt.</small>

---

* Wood, Ath. Ox.; Gooch's Funeral Sermon on Bishop Compton.
† Teonge's Diary.

hension and jealousy to do here? Apprehension and jealousy are the feelings with which we regard future and uncertain evils. The evil which we are considering is neither future nor uncertain. A standing army exists. It is officered by Papists. We have no foreign enemy. There is no rebellion in the land. For what, then, is this force maintained, except for the purpose of subverting our laws, and establishing that arbitrary power which is so justly abhorred by Englishmen?"*

Jeffreys spoke against the motion in the coarse and savage style of which he was a master; but he soon found that it was not quite so easy to browbeat the proud and powerful barons of England in their own hall as to intimidate advocates whose bread depended on his favor or prisoners whose necks were at his mercy. A man whose life has been passed in attacking and domineering, whatever may be his talents and courage, generally makes a poor figure when he is vigorously assailed: for, being unaccustomed to stand on the defensive, he becomes confused; and the knowledge that all those whom he has insulted are enjoying his confusion confuses him still more. Jeffreys was now, for the first time since he had become a great man, encountered on equal terms by adversaries who did not fear him. To the general delight, he passed at once from the extreme of insolence to the extreme of meanness, and could not refrain from weeping with rage and vexation.† Nothing, indeed, was wanting to his humiliation; for

---

* Barillon has given the best account of this debate. I will extract his report of Mordaunt's speech. "Milord Mordaunt, quoique jeune, parla avec éloquence et force. Il dit que la question n'étoit pas réduite, comme la Chambre des Communes le prétendoit, à guérir des jalousies et défiances, qui avoient lieu dans les choses incertaines; mais que ce qui se passoit ne l'étoit pas, qu'il y avoit une armée sur pied qui subsistoit, et qui étoit remplie d'officiers Catholiques, qui ne pouvoit être conservée que pour le renversement des loix, et que la subsistance de l'armée, quand il n'y a aucune guerre ni au dedans ni au dehors, étoit l'établissement du gouvernement arbitraire, pour lequel les Anglois ont une aversion si bien fondée."

† He was very easily moved to tears. "He could not," says the author of the Panegyric, "refrain from weeping on bold affronts." And again: "They talk of his hectoring and proud carriage; what could be more humble than for a man in his great post to cry and sob?" In the Answer to the Panegyric it is said that "his having no command of his tears spoiled him for a hypocrite."

the House was crowded by about a hundred peers, a larger number than had voted even on the great day of the Exclusion Bill. The King, too, was present. His brother had been in the habit of attending the sittings of the Lords for amusement, and used often to say that a debate was as entertaining as a comedy. James came, not to be diverted, but in the hope that his presence might impose some restraint on the discussion. He was disappointed. The sense of the House was so strongly manifested that, after a closing speech, of great keenness, from Halifax, the courtiers did not venture to divide. An early day was fixed for taking the royal speech into consideration; and it was ordered that every peer who was in or near the capital should be in his place.*

On the following morning the King came down, in his robes, to the House of Lords. The Usher of the Black Rod summoned the Commons to the bar; and the Chancellor announced that the Parliament was prorogued to the tenth of February.† The members who had voted against the Court were dismissed from the public service. Charles Fox quitted the Pay-office: the Bishop of London ceased to be Dean of the Chapel Royal; and his name was struck out of the list of Privy Councillors.

Prorogation.

The effect of the prorogation was to put an end to a legal proceeding of the highest importance. Thomas Grey, Earl of Stamford, sprung from one of the most illustrious houses of England, had been recently arrested and committed close prisoner to the Tower on a charge of high-treason. He was accused of having been concerned in the Rye-house Plot. A true bill had been found against him by the grand jury of the City of London, and had been removed into the House of Lords, the only court before which a temporal peer can,

---

* Lords' Journals, Nov. 19, 1685; Barillon, $\frac{\text{Nov. 23}}{\text{Dec. 3}}$; Dutch Despatch, Nov. $\frac{20}{30}$; Luttrell's Diary, Nov. 19; Burnet, i., 665. The closing speech of Halifax is mentioned by the Nuncio in his despatch of Nov. $\frac{16}{26}$. Adda, about a month later, bears strong testimony to Halifax's powers. " Da questo uomo che ha gran credito nel parlamento, e grande eloquenza, non si possono attendere che fiere contradizioni, e nel partito Regio non vi è un uomo da contrapporsi" (Dec. $\frac{21}{31}$).

† Lords' and Commons' Journals, Nov. 20, 1685.

during a session of Parliament, be arraigned for any offence higher than a misdemeanor. The first of December had been fixed for the trial; and orders had been given that Westminster Hall should be fitted up with seats and hangings. In consequence of the prorogation, the hearing of the cause was postponed for an indefinite period; and Stamford soon regained his liberty.*

Three other Whigs of great eminence were in confinement when the session closed, Charles Gerard, Lord Gerard of Brandon, eldest son of the Earl of Macclesfield, John Hampden, grandson of the renowned leader of the Long Parliament, and Henry Booth, Lord Delamere. Gerard and Hampden were accused of having taken part in the Rye-house Plot, Delamere of having abetted the Western insurrection.

It was not the intention of the government to put either Gerard or Hampden to death. Grey had stipulated for their lives before he consented to become a witness against them.† But there was a still stronger reason for sparing them. They were heirs to large property: but their fathers were still living. The Court could therefore get little in the way of forfeiture, and might get much in the way of ransom. Gerard was tried, and, from the very scanty accounts which have come down to us, seems to have defended himself with great spirit and force. He boasted of the exertions and sacrifices made by his family in the cause of Charles the First, and proved Rumsey, the witness who had murdered Russell by telling one story and Cornish by telling another, to be utterly undeserving of credit. The jury, with some hesitation, found a verdict of Guilty. After long imprisonment Gerard was suffered to redeem himself.‡ Hampden had inherited the political opinions and a large share of the abilities of his grandfather, but had degenerated from the uprightness and the courage by which his grandfather had been distinguished. It appears that the prisoner was, with cruel cunning, long kept in an agony of sus-

Trials of Lord Gerard and of Hampden.

---

* Lords' Journals, Nov. 11, 17, 18, 1685.   † Burnet, i., 646.
‡ Bramston's Memoirs; Luttrell's Diary.

pense, in order that his family might be induced to pay largely for mercy. His spirit sank under the terrors of death. When brought to the bar of the Old Bailey, he not only pleaded guilty, but disgraced the illustrious name which he bore by abject submissions and entreaties. He protested that he had not been privy to the design of assassination; but he owned that he had meditated rebellion, professed deep repentance for his offence, implored the intercession of the Judges, and vowed that, if the royal clemency were extended to him, his whole life should be passed in evincing his gratitude for such goodness. The Whigs were furious at his pusillanimity, and loudly declared him to be far more deserving of blame than Grey, who, even in turning King's evidence, had preserved a certain decorum. Hampden's life was spared; but his family paid several thousand pounds to the Chancellor. Some courtiers of less note succeeded in extorting smaller sums. The unhappy man had spirit enough to feel keenly the degradation to which he had stooped. He survived the day of his ignominy several years. He lived to see his party triumphant, to be once more an important member of it, and to make his persecutors tremble in their turn. But his prosperity was embittered by one insupportable recollection. He never regained his cheerfulness, and at length died by his own hand.*

That Delamere, if he had needed the royal mercy, would have found it, is not very probable. It is certain that every
<small>Trial of Delamere.</small> advantage which the letter of the law gave to the government was used against him without scruple or shame. He was in a different situation from that in which Stamford stood. The indictment against Stamford had been removed into the House of Lords during the session of Parliament, and therefore could not be prosecuted till the Parliament should reassemble. All the peers would then have voices, and would be judges as well of law as of fact. But the bill against Delamere was not found till after the proro-

---

* See the trial in the Collection of State Trials; Bramston's Memoirs; Burnet, i., 647; Lords' Journals, Dec. 20, 1689.

gation.* He was therefore within the jurisdiction of the Court to which belongs, during a recess of Parliament, the cognizance of treasons and felonies committed by temporal peers; and this Court was then so constituted that no prisoner charged with a political offence could expect an impartial trial. The King named a Lord High Steward. The Lord High Steward named, at his discretion, certain peers to sit on their accused brother. The number to be summoned was indefinite. No challenge was allowed. A simple majority, provided that it consisted of twelve, was sufficient to convict. The High Steward was sole judge of the law; and the Lords Triers formed merely a jury to pronounce on the question of fact. Jeffreys was appointed High Steward. He selected thirty Triers; and the selection was characteristic of the man and of the times. All the thirty were in politics vehemently opposed to the prisoner. Fifteen of them were colonels of regiments, and might be removed from their lucrative commands at the pleasure of the King. Among the remaining fifteen were the Lord Treasurer, the principal Secretary of State, the Steward of the Household, the Comptroller of the Household, the Captain of the Band of Gentlemen Pensioners, the Queen's Chamberlain, and other persons who were bound by strong ties of interest to the government. Nevertheless, Delamere had some great advantages over the humbler culprits who had been arraigned at the Old Bailey. There the jurymen, violent partisans, taken for a single day by courtly sheriffs from the mass of society and speedily sent back to mingle with that mass, were under no restraint of shame, and being little accustomed to weigh evidence, followed without scruple the directions of the bench. But in the High Steward's Court every Trier was a man of some experience in grave affairs. Every Trier filled a considerable space in the public eye. Every Trier, beginning from the lowest, had to rise separately and to give in his verdict, on his honor, before a great concourse. That verdict, accompanied with his name, would go to every part of the world, and

---

* Lords' Journals, Nov. 9, 10, 16, 1685.

would live in history. Moreover, though the selected nobles were all Tories, and almost all placemen, many of them had begun to look with uneasiness on the King's proceedings, and to doubt whether the case of Delamere might not soon be their own.

Jeffreys conducted himself, as was his wont, insolently and unjustly. He had indeed an old grudge to stimulate his zeal. He had been Chief-justice of Chester when Delamere, then Mr. Booth, represented that county in Parliament. Booth had bitterly complained to the Commons that the dearest interests of his constituents were intrusted to a drunken jackpudding.* The revengeful Judge was now not ashamed to resort to artifices which even in an advocate would have been culpable. He reminded the Lords Triers, in very significant language, that Delamere had, in Parliament, objected to the bill for attainting Monmouth, a fact which was not, and could not be, in evidence. But it was not in the power of Jeffreys to overawe a synod of peers as he had been in the habit of overawing common juries. The evidence for the crown would probably have been thought amply sufficient on the Western Circuit or at the City Sessions, but could not for a moment impose on such men as Rochester, Godolphin, and Churchill; nor were they, with all their faults, depraved enough to condemn a fellow-creature to death against the plainest rules of justice. Grey, Wade, and Goodenough were produced, but could only repeat what they had heard said by Monmouth and by Wildman's emissaries. The principal witness for the prosecution, a miscreant named Saxton, who had been concerned in the rebellion, and who was now laboring to earn his pardon by swearing against all who were obnoxious to the government, was proved by overwhelming evidence to have told a series of falsehoods. All the Triers, from Churchill, who, as junior baron, spoke first, up to the Treasurer, pronounced, on their honor, that Delamere was not guilty. The gravity and pomp of the whole proceeding made a deep impression even on the Nuncio, accustomed as he was to the cer-

---

* Speech on the Corruption of the Judges in Lord Delamere's works, 1694.

emonies of Rome, ceremonies which, in solemnity and splendor, exceed all that the rest of the world can show.* The King, who was present, and was unable to complain of a decision evidently just, went into a rage with Saxton, and vowed that the wretch should first be pilloried before Westminster Hall for perjury, and then sent down to the West to be hanged, drawn, and quartered for treason.†

The public joy at the acquittal of Delamere was great. The reign of terror was over. The innocent began to breathe freely, and false accusers to tremble. One letter written on this occasion is scarcely to be read without tears. The widow of Russell, in her retirement, learned the good news with mingled feelings. "I do bless God," she wrote, "that he has caused some stop to be put to the shedding of blood in this poor land. Yet, when I should rejoice with them that do rejoice, I seek a corner to weep in. I find I am capable of no more gladness; but every new circumstance, the very comparing my night of sorrow, after such a day, with theirs of joy, does, from a reflection of one kind or another, rack my uneasy mind. Though I am far from wishing the close of theirs like mine, yet I cannot refrain giving some time to lament mine was not like theirs."‡

Effect of his acquittal.

And now the tide was on the turn. The death of Stafford, witnessed with signs of tenderness and remorse by the populace to whose rage he was sacrificed, marks the close of one proscription. The acquittal of Delamere marks the close of another. The crimes which had disgraced the stormy tribuneship of Shaftesbury had been fearfully expiated. The blood of innocent Papists had been avenged more than tenfold by the blood of zealous Protestants. Another great reaction had commenced. Factions were fast taking new forms. Old allies were separating. Old enemies were uniting. Discontent was spreading fast through all the ranks of the party lately dominant. A hope, still indeed faint

---

* "Fu una funzione piena di gravità, di ordine, e di gran speciosità."—Adda, Jan. $\frac{15}{25}$, 1686.

† The trial is in the Collection of State Trials. Van Leeuwen, Jan. $\frac{15}{25}, \frac{19}{29}$, 1686.

‡ Lady Russell to Dr. Fitzwilliam, Jan. 15, 1686.

and indefinite, of victory and revenge, animated the party which had lately seemed to be extinct. With such omens the eventful and troubled year 1685 terminated, and the year 1686 began.

The prorogation had relieved the King from the gentle remonstrances of the Houses: but he had still to listen to remonstrances, similar in substance, though uttered in a tone even more cautious and subdued. Some men, who had hitherto served him but too strenuously for their own fame and for the public welfare, had begun to feel painful misgivings, and occasionally ventured to hint a small part of what they felt.

Parties in the court.

During many years the zeal of the English Tory for hereditary monarchy and his zeal for the established religion had grown up together and had strengthened each other. It had never occurred to him that the two sentiments, which seemed inseparable and even identical, might one day be found to be not only distinct, but incompatible. From the commencement of the strife between the Stuarts and the Commons, the cause of the crown and the cause of the hierarchy had, to all appearance, been one. Charles the First was regarded by the Church as her own martyr. If Charles the Second had plotted against her, he had plotted in secret. In public he had ever professed himself her grateful and devoted son, had knelt at her altars, and, in spite of his loose morals, had succeeded in persuading the great body of her adherents that he felt a sincere preference for her. Whatever conflicts, therefore, the honest Cavalier might have had to maintain against Whigs and Roundheads, he had at least been hitherto undisturbed by conflict in his own mind. He had seen the path of duty plain before him. Through good and evil he was to be true to Church and King. But, if those two august and venerable powers, which had hitherto seemed to be so closely connected that those who were true to one could not be false to the other, should be divided by a deadly enmity, what course was the orthodox Royalist to take? What situation could be more trying than that of a man distracted between

Feeling of the Protestant Tories.

II.—4

two duties equally sacred, between two affections equally ardent? How would it be possible to give to Cæsar all that was Cæsar's, and yet to withhold from God no part of what was God's? None who felt thus could have watched, without deep concern and gloomy forebodings, the dispute between the King and the Parliament on the subject of the test. If James could even now be induced to reconsider his course, to let the Houses reassemble, and to comply with their wishes, all might yet be well.

Such were the sentiments of the King's two kinsmen, the Earls of Clarendon and Rochester. The power and favor of these noblemen seemed to be great indeed. The younger brother was Lord Treasurer and prime minister; and the elder, after holding the Privy Seal during some months, had been appointed Lord-lieutenant of Ireland. The venerable Ormond took the same side. Middleton and Preston, who, as managers of the House of Commons, had recently learned by proof how dear the established religion was to the loyal gentry of England, were also for moderate counsels.

At the very beginning of the new year these statesmen and the great party which they represented had to suffer a cruel mortification. That the late King had been at heart a Roman Catholic had been, during some months, suspected and whispered, but not formally announced. The disclosure, indeed, could not be made without great scandal. Charles had, times without number, declared himself a Protestant, and had been in the habit of receiving the Eucharist from the Bishops. Those Churchmen who had stood by him in his difficulties, and who still cherished an affectionate remembrance of him, must be filled with shame and indignation by learning that his whole life had been a lie, that, while he professed to belong to their communion, he had really regarded them as heretics, and that the demagogues who had represented him as a concealed Papist had been the only people who had formed a correct judgment of his character. Even Lewis understood enough of the state of public feeling in England to be aware that the divulging of the truth might do harm, and had, of his own accord, promised to keep the conversion of Charles strictly secret.* James, while his power was still new, had thought that on this point it was advisable to be cautious, and had not ventured to inter his brother with the rites of the Church of Rome. For a time, therefore, every man was at liberty to believe what he wished. The Papists claimed the deceased prince as their proselyte. The Whigs execrated him as a hypocrite and a renegade. The Tories regarded the report of his apostasy as a calumny which Papists and Whigs had, for very different reasons, a common interest in circulating.

<small>Publication of papers found in the strong-box of Charles II.</small> James now took a step which greatly disconcerted the whole Anglican party. Two papers, in which were set forth very concisely the arguments ordinarily used by Roman Catholics against Protestants, had been found in Charles's strong-box, and appeared to be in his handwriting. These papers James showed triumphantly to several Protestants, and declared that, to his knowledge, his brother had lived and died a Roman Catholic.† One of the persons to whom the manuscripts were exhibited was Archbishop Sancroft. He read them with much emotion, and remained silent. Such silence was only the natural effect of a struggle between respect and vexation. But James supposed that the Primate was struck dumb by the irresistible force of reason, and eagerly challenged His Grace to produce, with the help of the whole episcopal bench, a satisfactory reply. "Let me have a solid answer, and in a gentlemanlike style; and it may have the effect which you so much desire of bringing me over to your Church." The Archbishop mildly said that, in his opinion, such an answer might, without much difficulty, be written, but declined the controversy on the plea of reverence for the memory of his deceased master. This plea the King considered as the subterfuge of a vanquished disputant.‡ Had His Majesty been well acquainted with the polemical literature of the preceding century and a half, he would have known that the documents to which he attached so much value might have been composed by any lad of fifteen in the college of

---

* Lewis to Barillon, Feb. $\frac{19}{29}$, 168$\frac{5}{6}$. † Evelyn's Diary, October 2, 1685.
‡ Life of James the Second, ii., 9, Orig. Mem.

Douay, and contained nothing which had not, in the opinion of all Protestant divines, been ten thousand times refuted. In his ignorant exultation, he ordered these tracts to be printed with the utmost pomp of typography, and appended to them a declaration attested by his sign-manual, and certifying that the originals were in his brother's own hand. James himself distributed the whole edition among his courtiers and among the people of humbler rank who crowded round his coach. He gave one copy to a young woman of mean condition whom he supposed to be of his own religious persuasion, and assured her that she would be greatly edified and comforted by the perusal. In requital of his kindness, she delivered to him, a few days later, an epistle adjuring him to come out of the mystical Babylon and to dash from his lips the cup of fornications.*

These things gave great uneasiness to Tory Churchmen. Nor were the most respectable Roman Catholic noblemen much better pleased. They might indeed have been excused if passion had, at this conjuncture, made them deaf to the voice of prudence and justice; for they had suffered much. Protestant jealousy had degraded them from the rank to which they were born, had closed the doors of the Parliament House on the heirs of barons who had signed the Charter, had pronounced the command of a company of foot too high a trust for the descendants of the generals who had conquered at Flodden and Saint Quentin. There was scarcely one eminent peer attached to the old faith whose honor, whose estate, whose life, had not been in jeopardy, who had not passed months in the Tower, who had not often anticipated for himself the fate of Stafford. Men who had been so long and cruelly oppressed might have been pardoned if they had eagerly seized the first opportunity of obtaining at once greatness and revenge. But neither fanaticism nor ambition, neither resentment for past wrongs nor the intoxication produced by sudden good fortune, could prevent the most distinguished Roman Catholics from perceiving

Feeling of the respectable Roman Catholics.

---

* Van Leeuwen, Jan. $\frac{1}{11}$ and $\frac{12}{22}$, 1686. Her letter, though very long and very absurd, was thought worth sending to the States-general as a sign of the times.

that the prosperity which they at length enjoyed was only temporary, and, unless wisely used, might be fatal to them. They had been taught, by a cruel experience, that the antipathy of the nation to their religion was not a fancy which would yield to the mandate of a prince, but a profound sentiment, the growth of five generations, diffused through all ranks and parties, and intertwined not less closely with the principles of the Tory than with the principles of the Whig. It was indeed in the power of the King, by the exercise of his prerogative of mercy, to suspend the operation of the penal laws. It might hereafter be in his power, by discreet management, to obtain from the Parliament a repeal of the acts which imposed civil disabilities on those who professed his religion. But, if he attempted to subdue the Protestant feeling of England by rude means, it was easy to see that the violent compression of so powerful and elastic a spring would be followed by as violent a recoil. The Roman Catholic peers, by prematurely attempting to force their way into the Privy Council and the House of Lords, might lose their mansions and their ample estates, and might end their lives as traitors on Tower Hill, or as beggars at the porches of Italian convents.

Such was the feeling of William Herbert, Earl of Powis, who was generally regarded as the chief of the Roman Catholic aristocracy, and who, according to Oates, was to have been prime minister if the Popish Plot had succeeded. John Lord Bellasyse took the same view of the state of affairs. In his youth he had fought gallantly for Charles the First, had been rewarded after the Restoration with high honors and commands, and had quitted them when the Test Act was passed. With these distinguished leaders all the noblest and most opulent members of their Church concurred, except Lord Arundell of Wardour, an old man fast sinking into second childhood.

But there was at the court a small knot of Roman Catholics whose hearts had been ulcerated by old injuries, whose heads had been turned by recent elevation, who were impatient to climb to the highest honors of the state, and who, having little to lose, were not troubled by thoughts of the day of reckoning. One of these

Cabal of violent Roman Catholics.

was Roger Palmer, Earl of Castelmaine, in Ireland, and husband of the Duchess of Cleveland. His title had notoriously been purchased by his wife's dishonor and his own. His fortune was small. His temper, naturally ungentle, had been exasperated by his domestic vexations, by the public reproaches, and by what he had undergone in the days of the Popish Plot. He had been long a prisoner, and had at length been tried for his life. Happily for him, he was not put to the bar till the first burst of popular rage had spent itself, and till the credit of the false witnesses had been blown upon. He had therefore escaped, though very narrowly.* With Castelmaine was allied one of the most favored of his wife's hundred lovers, Henry Jermyn, whom James had lately created a peer by the title of Lord Dover. Jermyn had been distinguished more than twenty years before by his vagrant amours and his desperate duels. He was now ruined by play, and was eager to retrieve his fallen fortunes by means of lucrative posts from which the laws excluded him.† To the same party belonged an intriguing, pushing Irishman named White, who had been much abroad, who had served the House of Austria as something between an envoy and a spy, and who had been rewarded by that House for his services with the title of Marquess of Albeville.‡

Soon after the prorogation this reckless faction was strengthened by an important re-enforcement. Richard Talbot, Earl of Tyrconnel, the fiercest and most uncompromising of all those who hated the liberties and religion of England, arrived at court from Dublin.

Talbot was descended from an old Norman family which had been long settled in Leinster, which had there sunk into degeneracy, which had adopted the manners of the Celts, which had, like the Celts, adhered to the old religion, and

---

* See his trial in the Collection of State Trials, and his curious manifesto, printed in 1681.

† Mémoires de Grammont; Pepys's Diary, Aug. 19, 1662; Bonrepaux to Seignelay, Feb. $\frac{1}{11}$, 1686.

‡ Bonrepaux to Seignelay, Feb. $\frac{4}{14}$, 1686.

which had taken part with the Celts in the rebellion of 1641. In his youth he had been one of the most noted sharpers and bullies of London. He had been introduced to Charles and James when they were exiles in Flanders, as a man fit and ready for the infamous service of assassinating the Protector. Soon after the Restoration, Talbot attempted to obtain the favor of the royal family by a service more infamous still. A plea was wanted which might justify the Duke of York in breaking that promise of marriage by which he had obtained from Anne Hyde the last proof of female affection. Such a plea Talbot, in concert with some of his dissolute companions, undertook to furnish. They agreed to describe the poor young lady as a creature without virtue, shame, or delicacy, and made up long romances about tender interviews and stolen favors. Talbot in particular related how, in one of his secret visits to her, he had unluckily overturned the Chancellor's inkstand upon a pile of papers, and how cleverly she had averted a discovery by laying the blame of the accident on her monkey. These stories, which, if they had been true, would never have passed the lips of any but the basest of mankind, were pure inventions. Talbot was soon forced to own that they were so; and he owned it without a blush. The injured lady became Duchess of York. Had her husband been a man really upright and honorable, he would have driven from his presence with indignation and contempt the wretches who had slandered her. But one of the peculiarities of James's character was that no act, however wicked and shameful, which had been prompted by a desire to gain his favor ever seemed to him deserving of disapprobation. Talbot continued to frequent the court, appeared daily with brazen front before the princess whose ruin he had plotted, and was installed into the lucrative post of chief pander to her husband. In no long time Whitehall was thrown into confusion by the news that Dick Talbot, as he was commonly called, had laid a plan to murder the Duke of Ormond. The bravo was sent to the Tower: but in a few days he was again swaggering about the galleries, and carrying billets backward and forward between his patron and the ugliest maids of honor.

It was in vain that old and discreet counsellors implored the royal brothers not to countenance this bad man, who had nothing to recommend him except his fine person and his taste in dress. Talbot was not only welcome at the palace when the bottle or the dice-box was going round, but was heard with attention on matters of business. He affected the character of an Irish patriot, and pleaded, with great audacity, and sometimes with success, the cause of his countrymen whose estates had been confiscated. He took care, however, to be well paid for his services, and succeeded in acquiring, partly by the sale of his influence, partly by gambling, and partly by pimping, an estate of three thousand pounds a year. For under an outward show of levity, profusion, improvidence, and eccentric impudence, he was in truth one of the most mercenary and crafty of mankind. He was now no longer young, and was expiating by severe sufferings the dissoluteness of his youth: but age and disease had made no essential change in his character and manners. He still, whenever he opened his mouth, ranted, cursed, and swore with such frantic violence that superficial observers set him down for the wildest of libertines. The multitude was unable to conceive that a man who, even when sober, was more furious and boastful than others when they were drunk, and who seemed utterly incapable of disguising any emotion or keeping any secret, could really be a cold-hearted, far-sighted, scheming sycophant. Yet such a man was Talbot. In truth his hypocrisy was of a far higher and rarer sort than the hypocrisy which had flourished in Barebone's Parliament. For the consummate hypocrite is not he who conceals vice behind the semblance of virtue, but he who makes the vice which he has no objection to show a stalking-horse to cover darker and more profitable vice which it is for his interest to hide.

Talbot, raised by James to the earldom of Tyrconnel, had commanded the troops in Ireland during the nine months which elapsed between the termination of the vice-royalty of Ormond and the commencement of the vice-royalty of Clarendon. When the new Lord-lieutenant was about to leave

London for Dublin, the General was summoned from Dublin to London. Dick Talbot had long been well known on the road which he had now to travel. Between Chester and the capital there was not an inn where he had not been in a brawl. He was now more insolent and turbulent than ever. He pressed horses in defiance of law, swore at the cooks and postilions, and almost raised mobs by his insolent rodomontades. The Reformation, he told the people, had ruined everything. But fine times were coming. The Catholics would soon be uppermost. The heretics should pay for all. Raving and blaspheming incessantly, like a demoniac, he came to the court.* As soon as he was there, he allied himself closely with Castelmaine, Dover, and Albeville. These men called with one voice for war on the constitution of the Church and the State. They told their master that he owed it to his religion and to the dignity of his crown to stand firm against the outcry of heretical demagogues, and exhorted him to let the Parliament see from the first that he would be master in spite of opposition, and that the only effect of opposition would be to make him a hard master.

Each of the two parties into which the Court was divided had zealous foreign allies. The ministers of Spain, of the Empire, and of the States-general were now as anxious to support Rochester as they had formerly been to support Halifax. All the influence of Barillon was employed on the other side; and Barillon was assisted by another French agent, inferior to him in station, but superior in abilities, Bonrepaux. Barillon was not without parts, and possessed in large measure the graces and accomplishments which then distinguished the French gentry. But his capacity was scarcely equal to what his great place required. He had become sluggish and self-indulgent, liked the pleasures of society and of the table better than business, and on great emergencies generally waited for admonitions and even for reprimands from Versailles before he showed

_{Feeling of the ministers of foreign governments.}

---

* Mémoires de Grammont; Life of Edward, Earl of Clarendon; Correspondence of Henry, Earl of Clarendon, *passim*, particularly the letter dated Dec. 29, 1685; Sheridan MS. among the Stuart Papers; Ellis Correspondence, Jan. 12, 1686.

much activity.* Bonrepaux had raised himself from obscurity by the intelligence and industry which he had exhibited as a clerk in the department of the marine, and was esteemed an adept in the mystery of mercantile politics. At the close of the year 1685, he was sent to London charged with several special commissions of high importance. He was to lay the ground for a treaty of commerce; he was to ascertain and report the state of the English fleets and dockyards; and he was to make some overtures to the Huguenot refugees, who, it was supposed, had been so effectually tamed by penury and exile that they would thankfully accept almost any terms of reconciliation. The new Envoy's origin was plebeian: his stature was dwarfish: his countenance was ludicrously ugly; and his accent was that of his native Gascony: but his strong sense, his keen penetration, and his lively wit eminently qualified him for his post. In spite of every disadvantage of birth and figure, he was soon known as a pleasing companion and as a skilful diplomatist. He contrived, while flirting with the Duchess of Mazarin, discussing literary questions with Waller and Saint Evremond, and corresponding with La Fontaine, to acquire a considerable knowledge of English politics. His skill in maritime affairs recommended him to James, who had, during many years, paid close attention to the business of the Admiralty, and understood that business as well as he was capable of understanding anything. They conversed every day long and freely about the state of the shipping and the dock-yards. The result of this intimacy was, as might have been expected, that the keen and vigilant Frenchman conceived a great contempt for the King's abilities and character. The world, he said, had much overrated His Britannic Majesty, who had less capacity than Charles, and not more virtue.†

The two envoys of Lewis, though pursuing one object, very

---

* See his later correspondence, *passim;* Saint Evremond, *passim;* and Madame de Sévigné's Letters in the beginning of 1689. See also the instructions to Tallard after the peace of Ryswick, in the French archives.

† Saint Simon, Mémoires, 1697, 1719; Saint Evremond; La Fontaine; Bonrepaux to Seignelay, $\frac{\text{Jan. 28}}{\text{Feb. 7}}$, Feb. $\frac{8}{18}$, 1686.

judiciously took different paths. They made a partition of the court. Bonrepaux lived chiefly with Rochester and Rochester's adherents. Barillon's connections were chiefly with the opposite faction. The consequence was that they sometimes saw the same event in different points of view. The best account now extant of the contest which at this time agitated Whitehall is to be found in their despatches.

As each of the two parties at the court of James had the support of foreign princes, so each had also the support of an ecclesiastical authority to which the King paid great deference. The Supreme Pontiff was for legal and moderate courses; and his sentiments were expressed by the Nuncio and by the Vicar Apostolic.* On the other side was a body of which the weight balanced even the weight of the Papacy, the mighty Order of Jesus.

The Pope and the Order of Jesus opposed to each other.

That at this juncture these two great spiritual powers, once, as it seemed, inseparably allied, should have been opposed to each other, is a most important and remarkable circumstance. During a period of little less than a thousand years the regular clergy had been the chief support of the Holy See. By that See they had been protected from episcopal interference; and the protection which they had received had been amply repaid. But for their exertions it is probable that the Bishop of Rome would have been merely the honorary president of a vast aristocracy of prelates. It was by the aid of the Benedictines that Gregory the Seventh was enabled to contend at once against the Franconian Cæsars and against the secular priesthood. It was by the aid of the Dominicans and Franciscans that Innocent the Third crushed the Albigensian sectaries. Three centuries later the Pontificate, exposed to new dangers more formidable than had ever before threatened it, was saved by a new religious order,

---

* Adda, Nov. $\frac{16}{26}$, Dec. $\frac{7}{17}$, and Dec. $\frac{21}{31}$, 1685. In these despatches Adda gives strong reasons for compromising matters by abolishing the penal laws and leaving the test. He calls the quarrel with the Parliament a "gran disgrazia." He repeatedly hints that the King might, by a constitutional policy, have obtained much for the Roman Catholics, and that the attempt to relieve them illegally is likely to bring great calamities on them.

which was animated by intense enthusiasm and organized with exquisite skill. When the Jesuits came to the rescue, they found the Papacy in extreme peril: but from that moment the tide of battle turned. Protestantism, which had, during a whole generation, carried all before it, was stopped in its progress, and rapidly beaten back from the foot of the Alps to the shores of the Baltic. Before the Order had existed a hundred years, it had filled the whole world with memorials of great things done and suffered for the faith. No religious community could produce a list of men so variously distinguished: none had extended its operations over so vast a space: yet in none had there ever been such perfect unity of feeling and action. There was no region of the globe, no walk of speculative or of active life, in which Jesuits were not to be found. They guided the counsels of Kings. They deciphered Latin inscriptions. They observed the motions of Jupiter's satellites. They published whole libraries, controversy, casuistry, history, treatises on optics, Alcaic odes, editions of the fathers, madrigals, catechisms, and lampoons. The liberal education of youth passed almost entirely into their hands, and was conducted by them with conspicuous ability. They appear to have discovered the precise point to which intellectual culture can be carried without risk of intellectual emancipation. Enmity itself was compelled to own that, in the art of managing and forming the tender mind, they had no equals. Meanwhile they assiduously and successfully cultivated the eloquence of the pulpit. With still greater assiduity and still greater success they applied themselves to the ministry of the confessional. Throughout Roman Catholic Europe the secrets of every government and of almost every family of note were in their keeping. They glided from one Protestant country to another under innumerable disguises, as gay Cavaliers, as simple rustics, as Puritan preachers. They wandered to countries which neither mercantile avidity nor liberal curiosity had ever impelled any stranger to explore. They were to be found in the garb of Mandarins, superintending the observatory at Pekin. They were to be found, spade in hand, teaching the rudiments of agriculture to the savages of Paraguay. Yet, whatever might be their residence, whatever might be their employment, their spirit was the same, entire devotion to the common cause, unreasoning obedience to the central authority. None of them had chosen his dwelling-place or his vocation for himself. Whether the Jesuit should live under the arctic circle or under the equator, whether he should pass his life in arranging gems and collating manuscripts at the Vatican or in persuading naked barbarians under the Southern Cross not to eat each other, were matters which he left with profound submission to the decision of others. If he was wanted at Lima, he was on the Atlantic in the next fleet. If he was wanted at Bagdad, he was toiling through the desert with the next caravan. If his ministry was needed in some country where his life was more insecure than that of a wolf, where it was a crime to harbor him, where the heads and quarters of his brethren, fixed in the public places, showed him what he had to expect, he went without remonstrance or hesitation to his doom. Nor is this heroic spirit yet extinct. When, in our own time, a new and terrible pestilence passed round the globe, when, in some great cities, fear had dissolved all the ties which hold society together, when the secular clergy had forsaken their flocks, when medical succor was not to be purchased by gold, when the strongest natural affections had yielded to the love of life, even then the Jesuit was found by the pallet which bishop and curate, physician and nurse, father and mother, had deserted, bending over infected lips to catch the faint accents of confession, and holding up to the last, before the expiring penitent, the image of the expiring Redeemer.

But with the admirable energy, disinterestedness, and self-devotion which were characteristic of the Society, great vices were mingled. It was alleged, and not without foundation, that the ardent public spirit which made the Jesuit regardless of his ease, of his liberty, and of his life, made him also regardless of truth and of mercy; that no means which could promote the interest of his religion seemed to him unlawful, and that by the interest of his religion he too often meant the interest of his Society. It was alleged that, in the most atrocious plots recorded in history, his agency could be distinctly traced; that, constant only in attachment to the fraternity to which he belonged, he was in some countries the most dangerous enemy of freedom, and in others the most dangerous enemy of order. The mighty victories which he boasted that he had achieved in the cause of the Church were, in the judgment of many illustrious members of that Church, rather apparent than real. He had indeed labored with a wonderful show of success to reduce the world under her laws; but he had done so by relaxing her laws to suit the temper of the world. Instead of toiling to elevate human nature to the noble standard fixed by divine precept and example, he had lowered the standard till it was beneath the average level of human nature. He gloried in multitudes of converts who had been baptized in the remote regions of the East: but it was reported that from some of those converts the facts on which the whole theology of the Gospel depends had been cunningly concealed, and that others were permitted to avoid persecution by bowing down before the images of false gods, while internally repeating Paters and Aves. Nor was it only in heathen countries that such arts were said to be practised. It was not strange that people of all ranks, and especially of the highest ranks, crowded to the confessionals in the Jesuit temples; for from those confessionals none went discontented away. There the priest was all things to all men. He showed just so much rigor as might not drive those who knelt at his spiritual tribunal to the Dominican or the Franciscan church. If he had to deal with a mind truly devout, he spoke in the saintly tones of the primitive fathers: but with that large part of mankind who have religion enough to make them uneasy when they do wrong, and not religion enough to keep them from doing wrong, he followed a different system. Since he could not reclaim them from vice, it was his business to save them from remorse. He had at his command an immense dispensary of anodynes for wounded consciences. In the books of casuistry which had been written by his brethren, and printed with the approbation of his superiors, were to be found doctrines consolatory to transgressors of every class. There the bankrupt was taught how he might, without sin, secrete his goods from his creditors. The servant was taught how he might, without sin, run off with his master's plate. The pander was assured that a Christian man might innocently earn his living by carrying letters and messages between married women and their gallants. The high-spirited and punctilious gentlemen of France were gratified by a decision in favor of duelling. The Italians, accustomed to darker and baser modes of vengeance, were glad to learn that they might, without any crime, shoot at their enemies from behind hedges. To deceit was given a license sufficient to destroy the whole value of human contracts and of human testimony. In truth, if society continued to hold together, if life and property enjoyed any security, it was because common-sense and common humanity restrained men from doing what the Order of Jesus assured them that they might with a safe conscience do.

So strangely were good and evil intermixed in the character of these celebrated brethren; and the intermixture was the secret of their gigantic power. That power could never have belonged to mere hypocrites. It could never have belonged to rigid moralists. It was to be attained only by men sincerely enthusiastic in the pursuit of a great end, and at the same time unscrupulous as to the choice of means.

From the first the Jesuits had been bound by a peculiar allegiance to the Pope. Their mission had been not less to quell all mutiny within the Church than to repel the hostility of her avowed enemies. Their doctrine was in the highest degree what has been called on our side of the Alps Ultramontane, and differed almost as much from the doctrine of Bossuet as from that of Luther. They condemned the Gallican liberties, the claim of œcumenical councils to control the Holy See, and the claim of Bishops to an independent commission from heaven. Lainez, in the name of the whole fraternity, proclaimed at Trent, amidst the applause of the creatures of Pius the Fourth and the murmurs of French and Spanish prelates, that the government of the faithful had been committed by Christ to the Pope alone, that in the Pope alone all sacerdotal authority was concentrated, and that through the Pope alone priests and bishops derived whatever power they possessed.* During many years the union between the Supreme Pontiffs and the Order had continued unbroken. Had that union been still unbroken when James the Second ascended the English throne, had the influence of the Jesuits as well as the influence of the Pope been exerted in favor of a moderate and constitutional policy, it is probable that the great revolution which in a short time changed the whole state of European affairs would never have taken place. But, even before the middle of the seventeenth century, the Society, proud of its services and confident in its strength, had become impatient of the yoke. A generation of Jesuits sprang up, who looked for protection and guidance rather to the court of France than to the court of Rome; and this disposition was not a little strengthened when Innocent the Eleventh was raised to the papal throne.

The Jesuits were, at that time, engaged in a war to the death against an enemy whom they had at first disdained, but whom they had at length been forced to regard with respect and fear. Just when their prosperity was at the height, they were braved by a handful of opponents, who had indeed no influence with the rulers of this world, but who were strong in religious faith and intellectual energy. Then followed a long, a strange, a glorious conflict of genius against power. The Jesuit called cabinets, tribunals, universities to his aid; and they responded to the call. Port Royal appealed, not in vain, to the hearts and to the understandings of millions. The dictators of Christendom found themselves, on a sudden, in the position of culprits. They were arraigned on the charge of having systematically debased the standard of evangelical morality, for the purpose of increasing their own influence; and the charge was enforced in a manner which at once arrested the attention of the whole world: for the chief accuser was Blaise Pascal. His powers of mind were such as have

---

* Fra Paolo, lib. vii.; Pallavicino, lib. xviii., cap. 15.

rarely been bestowed on any of the children of men; and the vehemence of the zeal which animated him was but too well proved by the cruel penances and vigils under which his macerated frame sank into an early grave. His spirit was the spirit of Saint Bernard; but the delicacy of his wit, the purity, the energy, the simplicity of his rhetoric, had never been equalled, except by the great masters of Attic eloquence. All Europe read and admired, laughed and wept. The Jesuits attempted to reply; but their feeble answers were received by the public with shouts of mockery. They wanted, it is true, no talent or accomplishment into which men can be drilled by elaborate discipline; but such discipline, though it may bring out the powers of ordinary minds, has a tendency to suffocate, rather than to develop, original genius. It was universally acknowledged that, in the literary contest, the Jansenists were completely victorious. To the Jesuits nothing was left but to oppress the sect which they could not confute. Lewis the Fourteenth was now their chief support. His conscience had, from boyhood, been in their keeping; and he had learned from them to abhor Jansenism quite as much as he abhorred Protestantism, and very much more than he abhorred Atheism. Innocent the Eleventh, on the other hand, leaned to the Jansenist opinions. The consequence was that the Society found itself in a situation never contemplated by its founder. The Jesuits were estranged from the Supreme Pontiff; and they were closely allied with a prince who proclaimed himself the champion of the Gallican liberties and the enemy of Ultramontane pretensions. The Order, therefore, became in England an instrument of the designs of Lewis, and labored, with a success which the Roman Catholics afterward long and bitterly deplored, to widen the breach between the King and the Parliament, to thwart the Nuncio, to undermine the power of the Lord Treasurer, and to support the most desperate schemes of Tyrconnel.

Thus on one side were the Hydes and the whole body of Tory Churchmen, Powis and all the most respectable noblemen and gentlemen of the King's own faith, the States-general, the House of Austria, and the Pope. On the other side

II.—5

were a few Roman Catholic adventurers, of broken fortune and tainted reputation, backed by France and by the Jesuits.

The chief representative of the Jesuits at Whitehall was an English brother of the Order, who had, during some time, acted as Vice-provincial, who had been long regarded by James with peculiar favor, and who had lately been made Clerk of the Closet. This man, named Edward Petre, was descended from an honorable family: his manners were courtly: his speech was flowing and plausible: but he was weak and vain, covetous and ambitious. Of all the evil counsellors who had access to the royal ear, he bore, perhaps, the largest part in the ruin of the House of Stuart.

<small>Father Petre.</small>

The obstinate and imperious nature of the King gave great advantages to those who advised him to be firm, to yield nothing, and to make himself feared. One state maxim had taken possession of his small understanding, and was not to be dislodged by reason. To reason, indeed, he was not in the habit of attending. His mode of arguing, if it is to be so called, was one not uncommon among dull and stubborn persons, who are accustomed to be surrounded by their inferiors. He asserted a proposition; and, as often as wiser people ventured respectfully to show that it was erroneous, he asserted it again, in exactly the same words, and conceived that, by doing so, he at once disposed of all objections.* "I will make no concession," he often repeated; "my father made concessions, and he was beheaded."† Even if it had been true that concession had been fatal to Charles the First, a man of sense would have remembered that a single experiment is not sufficient to establish a general rule even in sciences much less complicated than the science of government; that, since the beginning of the world, no two political experiments were ever made of which all the conditions were exactly alike; and that the only way to learn civil

<small>The King's temper and opinions.</small>

---

* This was the practice of his daughter Anne; and Marlborough said that she had learned it from her father. See the Vindication of the Duchess of Marlborough.

† Down to the time of the trial of the Bishops, James went on telling Adda that all the calamities of Charles the First were "per la troppa indulgenza." Despatch of $\frac{\text{June } 29,}{\text{July } 9,}$ 1688.

prudence from history is to examine and compare an immense number of cases. But, if the single instance on which the King relied proved anything, it proved that he was in the wrong. There can be little doubt that, if Charles had frankly made to the Short Parliament, which met in the spring of 1640, but one half of the concessions which he made, a few months later, to the Long Parliament, he would have lived and died a powerful King. On the other hand, there can be no doubt whatever that, if he had refused to make any concession to the Long Parliament, and had resorted to arms in defence of the Ship-money and of the Star-chamber, he would have seen, in the hostile ranks, Hyde and Falkland side by side with Hollis and Hampden. It would indeed be more correct to say that, if he had refused to make any concession, he would not have been able to resort to arms; for not twenty Cavaliers would have joined his standard. It was to his large concessions alone that he owed the support of that great body of noblemen and gentlemen who fought so long and so gallantly in his cause. But it would have been useless to represent these things to James.

Another fatal delusion had taken possession of his mind, and was never dispelled till it had ruined him. He firmly believed that, do what he might, the members of the Church of England would act up to their principles. It had, he knew, been proclaimed from ten thousand pulpits, it had been solemnly declared by the University of Oxford, that even tyranny as frightful as that of the most depraved of the Cæsars did not justify subjects in resisting the royal authority; and hence he was weak enough to conclude that the whole body of Tory gentlemen and clergymen would let him plunder, oppress, and insult them, without lifting an arm against him. It seems strange that any man should have passed his fiftieth year without discovering that people sometimes do what they think wrong: and James had only to look into his own heart for abundant proof that even a strong sense of religious duty will not always prevent frail human beings from indulging their passions in defiance of divine laws, and at the risk of awful penalties. He must have been conscious that, though he thought adultery sinful, he was an adulterer: but nothing could convince him that any man who professed to think rebellion sinful would ever, in any extremity, be a rebel. The Church of England was, in his view, a passive victim, which he might, without danger, outrage and torture at his pleasure; nor did he ever see his error till the Universities were preparing to coin their plate for the purpose of supplying the military chest of his enemies, and till a Bishop, long renowned for loyalty, had thrown aside the cassock, put on jack-boots, and taken the command of a regiment of insurgents.

In these fatal follies the King was artfully encouraged by a minister who had been an Exclusionist, and who still called himself a Protestant, the Earl of Sunderland. The motives and conduct of this unprincipled politician have often been misrepresented. He was, in his own lifetime, accused by the Jacobites of having, even before the beginning of the reign of James, determined to bring about a revolution in favor of the Prince of Orange, and of having, with that view, recommended a succession of outrages on the civil and ecclesiastical constitution of the realm. This idle story has been repeated down to our own days by ignorant writers. But no well informed historian, whatever might be his prejudices, has condescended to adopt it: for it rests on no evidence whatever; and scarcely any evidence would convince reasonable men that Sunderland deliberately incurred guilt and infamy in order to bring about a change by which it was clear that he could not possibly be a gainer, and by which, in fact, he lost immense wealth and influence. Nor is there the smallest reason for resorting to so strange a hypothesis. For the truth lies on the surface. Crooked as this man's course was, the law which determined it was simple. His conduct is to be ascribed to the alternate influence of cupidity and fear on a mind highly susceptible of both those passions, and quick-sighted rather than far-sighted. He wanted more power and more money. More power he could obtain only at Rochester's expense; and the obvious way to obtain power at Rochester's expense was to encourage the dislike which the King felt for Rochester's moderate counsels.

<small>The King encouraged in his errors by Sunderland.</small>

Money could be most easily and most largely obtained from the court of Versailles; and Sunderland was eager to sell himself to that court. He had no jovial generous vices. He cared little for wine or for beauty: but he desired riches with an ungovernable and insatiable desire. The passion for play raged in him without measure, and had not been tamed by ruinous losses. His hereditary fortune was ample. He had long filled lucrative posts, and had neglected no art which could make them more lucrative: but his ill-luck at the hazard table was such that his estates were daily becoming more and more encumbered. In the hope of extricating himself from his embarrassments, he betrayed to Barillon all the schemes adverse to France which had been meditated in the English cabinet, and hinted that a Secretary of State could in such times render services for which it might be wise in Lewis to pay largely. The Ambassador told his master that six thousand guineas was the smallest gratification that could be offered to so important a minister. Lewis consented to go as high as twenty-five thousand crowns, equivalent to about five thousand six hundred pounds sterling. It was agreed that Sunderland should receive this sum yearly, and that he should, in return, exert all his influence to prevent the reassembling of the Parliament.*

He joined himself, therefore, to the Jesuitical cabal, and made so dexterous a use of the influence of that cabal that he was appointed to succeed Halifax in the high dignity of Lord President without being required to resign the far more active and lucrative post of Secretary.† He felt, however, that he could never hope to obtain paramount influence in the Court while he was supposed to belong to the Established Church. All religions were the same to him. In private

---

* Barillon, Nov. $\frac{16}{26}$, 1685; Lewis to Barillon, $\frac{\text{Nov. 26,}}{\text{Dec. 6.}}$ In a highly curious paper which was written in 1687, almost certainly by Bonrepaux, and which is now in the French archives, Sunderland is described thus: "La passion qu'il a pour le jeu, et les pertes considérables qu'il y fait, incommodent fort ses affaires. Il n'aime pas le vin; et il haït les femmes."

† It appears from the Council Book that he took his place as President on the 4th of December, 1685.

circles, indeed, he was in the habit of talking with profane contempt of the most sacred things. He therefore determined to let the King have the delight and glory of effecting a conversion. Some management, however, was necessary. No man is utterly without regard for the opinion of his fellow-creatures: and even Sunderland, though not very sensible to shame, flinched from the infamy of public apostasy. He played his part with rare adroitness. To the world he showed himself as a Protestant. In the Royal Closet he assumed the character of an earnest inquirer after truth, who was almost persuaded to declare himself a Roman Catholic, and who, while waiting for fuller illumination, was disposed to render every service in his power to the professors of the old faith. James, who was never very discerning, and who in religious matters was absolutely blind, suffered himself, notwithstanding all that he had seen of human knavery, of the knavery of courtiers as a class, and of the knavery of Sunderland in particular, to be duped into the belief that divine grace had touched the most false and callous of human hearts. During many months the wily minister continued to be regarded at court as a promising catechumen, without exhibiting himself to the public in the character of a renegade.*

He early suggested to the King the expediency of appointing a secret committee of Roman Catholics to advise on all matters affecting the interests of their religion. This committee met sometimes at Chiffinch's lodgings, and sometimes at the official apartments of Sunderland, who, though still nominally a Protestant, was admitted to all its deliberations, and soon obtained a decided ascendency over the other members. Every Friday the Jesuitical cabal dined with the Secretary. The conversation at table was free; and the weaknesses of the prince whom the confederates hoped to manage were not spared. To Petre Sunderland promised a Cardinal's

---

* Bonrepaux was not so easily deceived as James. "En son particulier il (Sunderland) n'en professe aucune (religion), et en parle fort librement. Ces sortes de discours seroient en exécration en France. Ici ils sont ordinaires parmi un certain nombre de gens du pais."—Bonrepaux to Seignelay, $\frac{\text{May 25,}}{\text{June 4,}}$ 1687.

hat; to Castelmaine a splendid embassy to Rome; to Dover a lucrative command in the Guards; and to Tyrconnel high employment in Ireland. Thus bound together by the strongest ties of interest, these men addressed themselves to the task of subverting the Treasurer's power.*

There were two Protestant members of the cabinet who took no decided part in the struggle. Jeffreys was at this time tortured by a cruel internal malady which had been aggravated by intemperance. At a dinner which a wealthy Alderman gave to some of the leading members of the government, the Lord Treasurer and the Lord Chancellor were so drunk that they stripped themselves almost stark naked, and were with difficulty prevented from climbing up a sign-post to drink His Majesty's health. The pious Treasurer escaped with nothing but the scandal of the debauch: but the Chancellor brought on a violent fit of his complaint. His life was for some time thought to be in serious danger. James expressed great uneasiness at the thought of losing a minister who suited him so well, and said, with some truth, that the loss of such a man could not be easily repaired. Jeffreys, when he became convalescent, promised his support to both the contending parties, and waited to see which of them would prove victorious. Some curious proofs of his duplicity are still extant. It has been already said that the two French agents who were then resident in London had divided the English court between them. Bonrepaux was constantly with Rochester; and Barillon lived with Sunderland. Lewis was informed in the same week by Bonrepaux that the Chancellor was entirely with the Treasurer, and by Barillon that the Chancellor was in league with the Secretary.†

Perfidy of Jeffreys.

Godolphin, cautious and taciturn, did his best to preserve neutrality. His opinions and wishes were undoubtedly with Rochester: but his office made it necessary for him to be in constant attendance on the Queen; and he

Godolphin.

---

* Life of James the Second, ii., 74, 77, Orig. Mem.; Sheridan MS.; Barillon, March $\frac{1}{2}\frac{9}{9}$, 1686.

† Reresby's Memoirs; Luttrell's Diary, Feb. 2, 168$\frac{5}{6}$; Barillon, Feb. $\frac{4}{14}$, $\frac{Jan. 28}{Feb. 7}$; Bonrepaux, $\frac{Jan. 25}{Feb. 4}$.

was naturally unwilling to be on bad terms with her. There is indeed some reason to believe that he regarded her with an attachment more romantic than often finds place in the hearts of veteran statesmen; and circumstances, which it is now necessary to relate, had thrown her entirely into the hands of the Jesuitical cabal.*

The Queen.

The King, stern as was his temper and grave as was his deportment, was scarcely less under the influence of female attractions than his more lively and amiable brother had been. The beauty, indeed, which distinguished the favorite ladies of Charles was not necessary to James. Barbara Palmer, Eleanor Gwynn, and Louisa de Querouaille were among the finest women of their time. James, when young, had surrendered his liberty, descended below his rank, and incurred the displeasure of his family, for the coarse features of Anne Hyde. He had soon, to the great diversion of the whole court, been drawn away from his plain consort by a plainer mistress, Arabella Churchill. His second wife, though twenty years younger than himself, and of no unpleasing face or figure, had frequent reason to complain of his inconstancy. But of all his illicit attachments the strongest was that which bound him to Catharine Sedley.

Amours of the King.

Catharine Sedley.

This woman was the daughter of Sir Charles Sedley, one of the most brilliant and profligate wits of the Restoration. The licentiousness of his writings is not redeemed by much grace or vivacity; but the charms of his conversation were acknowledged even by sober men who had no esteem for his character. To sit near him at the theatre, and to hear his criticisms on a new play, was regarded as an intellectual treat.† Dryden had done him the honor to make him a principal interlocutor in the Dialogue on Dramatic Poesy. The morals of Sedley were such as, even in that age, gave great scandal. He on one occasion, after a wild

---

* Dartmouth's note on Burnet, i., 621. In a contemporary satire it is remarked that Godolphin
"Beats time with politic head, and all approves,
Pleased with the charge of the Queen's muff and gloves."

† Pepys, Oct. 4, 1664.

revel, exhibited himself without a shred of clothing in the balcony of a tavern near Covent Garden, and harangued the people who were passing in language so indecent and profane that he was driven in by a shower of brick-bats, was prosecuted for a misdemeanor, was sentenced to a heavy fine, and was reprimanded by the Court of King's Bench in the most cutting terms.* His daughter had inherited his abilities and his impudence. Personal charms she had none, with the exception of two brilliant eyes, the lustre of which, to men of delicate taste, seemed fierce and unfeminine. Her form was lean, her countenance haggard. Charles, though he liked her conversation, laughed at her ugliness, and said that the priests must have recommended her to his brother by way of penance. She well knew that she was not handsome, and jested freely on her own homeliness. Yet, with strange inconsistency, she loved to adorn herself magnificently, and drew on herself much keen ridicule by appearing in the theatre and the ring plastered, painted, clad in Brussels lace, glittering with diamonds, and affecting all the graces of eighteen.†

The nature of her influence over James is not easily to be explained. He was no longer young. He was a religious man : at least he was willing to make for his religion exertions and sacrifices from which the great majority of those who are called religious men would shrink. It seems strange that any attraction should have drawn him into a course of life which he must have regarded as highly criminal; and in this case none could understand where the attraction lay. Catharine herself was astonished by the violence of his passion. "It cannot be my beauty," she said ; "for he must see that I have none: and it cannot be my wit; for he has not enough to know that I have any."

At the moment of the King's accession, a sense of the new responsibility which lay on him made his mind for a time peculiarly open to religious impressions. He formed and announced many good resolutions, spoke in public with

---

* Pepys, July 1, 1663. † See Dorset's satirical lines on her.

great severity of the impious and licentious manners of the age, and in private assured his Queen and his confessor that he would see Catharine Sedley no more. He wrote to his mistress entreating her to quit the apartments which she occupied at Whitehall, and to go to a house in Saint James's Square which had been splendidly furnished for her at his expense. He at the same time promised to allow her a large pension from his privy purse. Catharine, clever, strong-minded, intrepid, and conscious of her power, refused to stir. In a few months it began to be whispered that the services of Chiffinch were again employed, and that the mistress frequently passed and repassed through that private door through which Father Huddleston had borne the host to the bedside of Charles. The King's Protestant ministers had, it seems, conceived a hope that their master's infatuation for this woman might cure him of the more pernicious infatuation which impelled him to attack their religion. She had all the talents which could qualify her to play on his feelings, to make game of his scruples, to set before him in a strong light the difficulties and dangers into which he was running headlong. Rochester, the champion of the Church, exerted himself to strengthen her influence. Ormond, who is popularly regarded as the personification of all that is pure and high-minded in the English Cavalier, encouraged the design. Even Lady Rochester was not ashamed to co-operate, and to co-operate in the very worst way. Her office was to direct the jealousy of the injured wife toward a young lady who was perfectly innocent. The whole court took notice of the coldness and rudeness with which the Queen treated the poor girl on whom suspicion had been thrown: but the cause of Her Majesty's ill-humor was a mystery. For a time the intrigue went on prosperously and secretly. Catharine often told the King plainly what the Protestant Lords of the Council only dared to hint in the most delicate phrases. His crown, she said, was at stake: the old dotard Arundell and the blustering Tyrconnel would lead him to his ruin. It is possible that her caresses might have done what the united exhortations of the Lords and the Commons,

<small>Intrigues of Rochester in favor of Catharine Sedley.</small>

of the House of Austria and the Holy See, had failed to do, but for a strange mishap which changed the whole face of affairs. James, in a fit of fondness, determined to make his mistress Countess of Dorchester in her own right. Catharine saw all the peril of such a step, and declined the invidious honor. Her lover was obstinate, and himself forced the patent into her hands. She at last accepted it on one condition, which shows her confidence in her own power and in his weakness. She made him give her a solemn promise, not that he would never quit her, but that if he did so, he would himself announce his resolution to her, and grant her one parting interview.

As soon as the news of her elevation got abroad, the whole palace was in an uproar. The warm blood of Italy boiled in the veins of the Queen. Proud of her youth and of her charms, of her high rank and of her stainless chastity, she could not without agonies of grief and rage see herself deserted and insulted for such a rival. Rochester, perhaps remembering how patiently, after a short struggle, Catharine of Braganza had consented to treat the mistresses of Charles with politeness, had expected that, after a little complaining and pouting, Mary of Modena would be equally submissive. It was not so. She did not even attempt to conceal from the eyes of the world the violence of her emotions. Day after day the courtiers who came to see her dine observed that the dishes were removed untasted from the table. She suffered the tears to stream down her cheeks unconcealed in the presence of the whole circle of ministers and envoys. To the King she spoke with wild vehemence. "Let me go," she cried. "You have made your woman a countess: make her a queen. Put my crown on her head. Only let me hide myself in some convent, where I may never see her more." Then, more soberly, she asked him how he reconciled his conduct to his religious professions. "You are ready," she said, "to put your kingdom to hazard for the sake of your soul; and yet you are throwing away your soul for the sake of that creature." Father Petre, on bended knees, seconded these remonstrances. It was his duty to do so; and his duty was not the less strenuously performed because it coincided with his interest. The King went on for a time sinning and repenting. In his hours of remorse his penances were severe. Mary treasured up to the end of her life, and at her death bequeathed to the convent of Chaillot the scourge with which he had vigorously avenged her wrongs upon his own shoulders. Nothing but Catharine's absence could put an end to this struggle between an ignoble love and an ignoble superstition. James wrote, imploring and commanding her to depart. He owned that he had promised to bid her farewell in person. "But I know too well," he added, "the power which you have over me. I have not strength of mind enough to keep my resolution if I see you." He offered her a yacht to convey her with all dignity and comfort to Flanders, and threatened that if she did not go quietly she should be sent away by force. She at one time worked on his feelings by pretending to be ill. Then she assumed the airs of a martyr, and impudently proclaimed herself a sufferer for the Protestant religion. Then again she adopted the style of John Hampden. She defied the King to remove her. She would try the right with him. While the Great Charter and the Habeas Corpus Act were the law of the land, she would live where she pleased. "And Flanders!" she cried; "never! I have learned one thing from my friend the Duchess of Mazarin; and that is never to trust myself in a country where there are convents." At length she selected Ireland as the place of her exile, probably because the brother of her patron Rochester was viceroy there. After many delays she departed, leaving the victory to the Queen.*

The history of this extraordinary intrigue would be imperfect if it were not added that there is still extant a religious

---

* The chief materials for the history of this intrigue are the despatches of Barillon and Bonrepaux at the beginning of the year 1686. See Barillon, $\frac{\text{Jan. 25,}}{\text{Feb. 4,}}$ $\frac{\text{Jan. 28,}}{\text{Feb. 7,}}$ Feb. $\frac{1}{11}$, Feb. $\frac{8}{18}$, Feb. $\frac{19}{29}$, and Bonrepaux under the first four dates; Evelyn's Diary, January 19; Reresby's Memoirs; Burnet, i., 682; Sheridan MS.; Chaillot MS.; Adda's Despatches, $\frac{\text{Jan. 22,}}{\text{Feb. 1,}}$ and $\frac{\text{Jan. 29,}}{\text{Feb. 8,}}$ 1686. Adda writes like a pious, but weak and ignorant man. He appears to have known nothing of James's past life.

meditation, written by the Treasurer, with his own hand, on the very same day on which the intelligence of his attempt to govern his master by means of a concubine was despatched by Bonrepaux to Versailles. No composition of Ken or Leighton breathes a spirit of more fervent and exalted piety than this effusion. Hypocrisy cannot be suspected: for the paper was evidently meant only for the writer's own eye, and was not published till he had been more than a century in his grave. So much is history stranger than fiction; and so true is it that nature has caprices which art dares not imitate. A dramatist would scarcely venture to bring on the stage a grave prince, in the decline of life, ready to sacrifice his crown in order to serve the interests of his religion, indefatigable in making proselytes, and yet deserting and insulting a virtuous wife who had youth and beauty for the sake of a profligate paramour who had neither. Still less, if possible, would a dramatist venture to introduce a statesman stooping to the wicked and shameful part of a procurer, and calling in his wife to aid him in that dishonorable office, yet, in his moments of leisure, retiring to his closet, and there secretly pouring out his soul to his God in penitent tears and devout ejaculations.*

<small>Decline of Rochester's influence.</small>
The Treasurer soon found that, in using scandalous means for the purpose of obtaining a laudable end, he had committed, not only a crime, but a folly. The Queen was now his enemy. She affected, indeed, to listen with civility while the Hydes excused their recent conduct as well as they could; and she occasionally pretended

---

* The meditation bears date $\frac{\text{Jan. 25,}}{\text{Feb. 4,}}$ 168$\frac{5}{6}$. Bonrepaux, in his despatch of the same day, says, "L'intrigue avoit été conduite par Milord Rochester et sa femme. * * * Leur projet étoit de faire gouverner le Roy d'Angleterre par la nouvelle comtesse. Ils s'étoient assurés d'elle." While Bonrepaux was writing thus, Rochester was writing as follows: "Oh God, teach me so to number my days that I may apply my heart unto wisdom. Teach me to number the days that I have spent in vanity and idleness, and teach me to number those that I have spent in sin and wickedness. Oh God, teach me to number the days of my affliction too, and to give thanks for all that is come to me from thy hand. Teach me likewise to number the days of this world's greatness of which I have so great a share; and teach me to look upon them as vanity and vexation of spirit."

to use her influence in their favor: but she must have been more or less than woman if she had really forgiven the conspiracy which had been formed against her dignity and her domestic happiness by the family of her husband's first wife. The Jesuits strongly represented to the King the danger which he had so narrowly escaped. His reputation, they said, his peace, his soul, had been put in peril by the machinations of his prime-minister. The Nuncio, who would gladly have counteracted the influence of the violent party, and co-operated with the moderate members of the cabinet, could not honestly or decently separate himself on this occasion from Father Petre. James himself, when parted by the sea from the charms which had so strongly fascinated him, could not but regard with resentment and contempt those who had sought to govern him by means of his vices. What had passed must have had the effect of raising his own Church in his esteem, and of lowering the Church of England. The Jesuits, whom it was the fashion to represent as the most unsafe of spiritual guides, as sophists who refined away the whole system of evangelical morality, as sycophants who owed their influence chiefly to the indulgence with which they treated the sins of the great, had reclaimed him from a life of guilt by rebukes as sharp and bold as those which David had heard from Nathan and Herod from the Baptist. On the other hand, zealous Protestants, whose favorite theme was the laxity of Popish casuists and the wickedness of doing evil that good might come, had attempted to obtain advantages for their own Church in a way which all Christians regarded as highly criminal. The victory of the cabal of evil counsellors was therefore complete. The King looked coldly on Rochester. The courtiers and foreign ministers soon perceived that the Lord Treasurer was prime-minister only in name. He continued to offer his advice daily, and had the mortification to find it daily rejected. Yet he could not prevail on himself to relinquish the outward show of power, and the emoluments which he directly and indirectly derived from his great place. He did his best, therefore, to conceal his vexations from the public eye. But his violent passions and his intemperate habits disqualified him for the part of a dissembler. His gloomy looks, when he came out of the Council-chamber, showed how little he was pleased with what had passed at the board; and, when the bottle had gone round freely, words escaped him which betrayed his uneasiness.*

He might, indeed, well be uneasy. Indiscreet and unpopular measures followed one another in rapid succession. All thought of returning to the policy of the Triple Alliance was abandoned. The King explicitly avowed to the ministers of those Continental powers with which he had lately intended to ally himself that all his views had undergone a change, and that England was still to be, as she had been under his grandfather, his father, and his brother, of no account in Europe. "I am in no condition," he said to the Spanish Ambassador, " to trouble myself about what passes abroad. It is my resolution to let foreign affairs take their course, to establish my authority at home, and to do something for my religion." A few days later he announced the same intentions to the States-general.† From that time to the close of his ignominious reign he made no serious effort to escape from vassalage, though, to the last, he could never hear, without transports of rage, that men called him a vassal.

The two events which proved to the public that Sunderland and Sunderland's party were victorious were the prorogation of the Parliament from February to May, and the departure of Castelmaine for Rome with the appointments of an ambassador of the highest rank.‡

Hitherto all the business of the English government at the papal court had been transacted by John Caryl. This gentleman was known to his contemporaries as a man of fortune and fashion, and as the author of two successful plays — a tragedy in rhyme which had been made popular by the action

---

* "Je vis Milord Rochester comme il sortoit du conseil fort chagrin; et, sur la fin du souper, il lui en échappa quelque chose."—Bonrepaux, Feb. $\frac{18}{28}$, 1686. See also Barillon, March $\frac{1}{11}$, $\frac{4}{14}$.

† Barillon, $\frac{\text{March 22,}}{\text{April 1,}}$ April $\frac{12}{22}$, 1686.

‡ London Gazette, Feb. 11, 168$\frac{5}{6}$; Luttrell's Diary, Feb. 8; Van Leeuwen, Feb. $\frac{9}{19}$; Life of James, ii., 75, Orig. Mem.

and recitation of Betterton, and a comedy which owes all its value to scenes borrowed from Molière. These pieces have long been forgotten; but what Caryl could not do for himself has been done for him by a more powerful genius. Half a line in the Rape of the Lock has made his name immortal.

Caryl, who was, like all the other respectable Roman Catholics, an enemy to violent courses, had acquitted himself of Castelmaine sent to Rome. his delicate errand at Rome with good sense and good feeling. The business confided to him was well done; but he assumed no public character, and carefully avoided all display. His mission, therefore, put the government to scarcely any charge, and excited scarcely any murmurs. His place was now most unwisely supplied by a costly and ostentatious embassy, offensive in the highest degree to the people of England, and by no means welcome to the court of Rome. Castelmaine had it in charge to demand a Cardinal's hat for his confederate Petre.

About the same time the King began to show, in an unequivocal manner, the feeling which he really entertained toward the banished Huguenots. While he had The Huguenots ill-treated by James. still hoped to cajole his Parliament into submission, and to become the head of a European coalition against France, he had affected to blame the revocation of the Edict of Nantes, and to pity the unhappy men whom persecution had driven from their country. He had caused it to be announced that, at every church in the kingdom, a collection would be made under his sanction for their benefit. A proclamation on this subject had been drawn up in terms which might have wounded the pride of a sovereign less sensitive and vainglorious than Lewis. But all was now changed. The principles of the treaty of Dover were again the principles of the foreign policy of England. Ample apologies were therefore made for the discourtesy with which the English government had acted toward France in showing favor to exiled Frenchmen. The proclamation which had displeased Lewis was recalled.* The Huguenot ministers were admon-

---

* Van Leeuwen, $\frac{\text{Feb. 23,}}{\text{Mar. 5,}}$ 1686.

ished to speak with reverence of their oppressor in their public discourses, as they would answer it at their peril. James not only ceased to express commiseration for the sufferers, but declared that he believed them to harbor the worst designs, and owned that he had been guilty of an error in countenancing them. One of the most eminent of the refugees, John Claude, had published on the Continent a small volume in which he described with great force the sufferings of his brethren. Barillon demanded that some opprobrious mark should be put on this book. James complied, and in full council declared it to be his pleasure that Claude's libel should be burned by the hangman before the Royal Exchange. Even Jeffreys was startled, and ventured to represent that such a proceeding was without example, that the book was written in a foreign tongue, that it had been printed at a foreign press, that it related entirely to transactions which had taken place in a foreign country, and that no English government had ever animadverted on such works. James would not suffer the question to be discussed. "My resolution," he said, "is taken. It has become the fashion to treat kings disrespectfully; and they must stand by each other. One King should always take another's part; and I have particular reasons for showing this respect to the King of France." There was silence at the board: the order was forthwith issued; and Claude's pamphlet was committed to the flames, not without the deep murmurs of many who had always been reputed steady loyalists.*

The promised collection was long put off under various pretexts. The King would gladly have broken his word: but it was pledged so solemnly that he could not for very shame retract.† Nothing, however, which could cool the zeal of congregations was omitted. It had been expected that,

---

* Barillon, $\frac{\text{April 26,}}{\text{May 6,}}$ May $\frac{3}{13}$, 1686; Van Citters, May $\frac{7}{17}$; Evelyn's Diary, May 5; Luttrell's Diary of the same date; Privy Council Book, May 2.

† Lady Russell to Dr. Fitzwilliam, Jan. 22, 1686; Barillon, Feb. $\frac{15}{25}$, $\frac{\text{Feb. 22,}}{\text{Mar. 4,}}$ 1686. "Ce prince témoigne," says Barillon, "une grande aversion pour eux, et aurait bien voulu se dispenser de la collecte, qui est ordonnée en leur faveur : mais il n'a pas cru que cela fût possible."

II.—6

according to the practice usual on such occasions, the people would be exhorted to liberality from the pulpits. But James was determined not to tolerate declamations against his religion and his ally. The Archbishop of Canterbury was therefore commanded to inform the clergy that they must merely read the brief, and must not presume to preach on the sufferings of the French Protestants.* Nevertheless the contributions were so large that, after all deductions, the sum of forty thousand pounds was paid into the Chamber of London. Perhaps none of the munificent subscriptions of our own age has borne so great a proportion to the means of the nation.†

The King was bitterly mortified by the large amount of the collection which had been made in obedience to his own call. He knew, he said, what all this liberality meant. It was mere Whiggish spite to himself and his religion.‡ He had already resolved that the money should be of no use to those whom the donors wished to benefit. He had been, during some weeks, in close communication with the French embassy on this subject, and had, with the approbation of the court of Versailles, determined on a course which it is not very easy to reconcile with those principles of toleration to which he afterward pretended to be attached. The refugees were zealous for the Calvinistic discipline and worship. James therefore gave orders that none should receive a crust of bread or a basket of coals who did not first take the sacrament according to the Anglican ritual.§ It is strange that this inhospitable rule should have been devised by a prince who affected to consider the Test Act as an outrage on the rights of conscience; for, however unjustifiable it may be to establish a sacramental test for the purpose of ascertaining

---

* Barillon, $\frac{\text{Feb. 22,}}{\text{Mar. 4,}}$ 1686.

† Account of the Commissioners, dated March 15, 1688.

‡ "Le Roi d'Angleterre connoit bien que les gens mal intentionnés pour lui sont les plus prompts et les plus disposés à donner considérablement. * * * Sa Majesté Britannique connoit bien qu'il auroit été à propos de ne point ordonner de collecte, et que les gens mal intentionnés contre la religion Catholique et contre lui se servent de cette occasion pour témoigner leur zèle."—Barillon, April $\frac{19}{29}$, 1686.

§ Barillon, Feb. $\frac{15}{25}$, $\frac{\text{Feb. 22,}}{\text{Mar. 4,}}$ April $\frac{19}{29}$, 1686; Lewis to Barillon, Mar. $\frac{5}{15}$.

whether men are fit for civil and military office, it is surely much more unjustifiable to establish a sacramental test for the purpose of ascertaining whether, in their extreme distress, they are fit objects of charity. Nor had James the plea which may be urged in extenuation of the guilt of almost all other persecutors: for the religion which he commanded the refugees to profess, on pain of being left to starve, was not his own religion. His conduct toward them was therefore less excusable than that of Lewis: for Lewis oppressed them in the hope of bringing them over from a damnable heresy to the true Church; James oppressed them only for the purpose of forcing them to apostatize from one damnable heresy to another.

Several Commissioners, of whom the Chancellor was one, had been appointed to dispense the public alms. When they met for the first time, Jeffreys announced the royal pleasure. The refugees, he said, were too generally enemies of monarchy and episcopacy. If they wished for relief, they must become members of the Church of England, and must take the sacrament from the hands of his chaplain. Many exiles, who had come full of gratitude and hope to apply for succor, heard their sentence, and went broken-hearted away.*

May was now approaching; and that month had been fixed for the meeting of the Houses: but they were again prorogued to November.† It was not strange that the King did not wish to meet them: for he had determined to adopt a policy which he knew to be, in the highest degree, odious to them. From his predecessors he had inherited two prerogatives, of which the limits had never been defined with strict accuracy, and which, if exerted without any limit, would of themselves have sufficed to overturn the whole polity of the State and of the Church. These were the dispensing power and the ecclesiastical supremacy. By means of the dispensing power, the King purposed to admit Roman Catholics, not merely to civil and military, but to

The dispensing power.

---

* Barillon, April $\frac{19}{29}$, 1686; Lady Russell to Dr. Fitzwilliam, April 14. "He sent away many," she says, "with sad hearts."

† London Gazette of May 13, 1686.

spiritual offices. By means of the ecclesiastical supremacy, he hoped to make the Anglican clergy his instruments for the destruction of their own religion.

This scheme developed itself by degrees. It was not thought safe to begin by granting to the whole Roman Catholic body a dispensation from all statutes imposing penalties and tests. For nothing was more fully established than that such a dispensation was illegal. The Cabal had, in 1672, put forth a general Declaration of Indulgence. The Commons, as soon as they met, had protested against it. Charles the Second had ordered it to be cancelled in his presence, and had, both by his own mouth and by a written message, assured the Houses that the step which had caused so much complaint should never be drawn into precedent. It would have been difficult to find in all the Inns of Court a barrister of reputation to argue in defence of a prerogative which the Sovereign, seated on his throne in full Parliament, had solemnly renounced a few years before. But it was not quite so clear that the King might not, on special grounds, grant exemptions to individuals by name. The first object of James, therefore, was to obtain from the courts of common law an acknowledgment that, to this extent at least, he possessed the dispensing power.

But, though his pretensions were moderate when compared with those which he put forth a few months later, he soon found that he had against him almost the whole sense of Westminster Hall. Four of the Judges gave him to understand that they could not, on this occasion, serve his purpose; and it is remarkable that all the four were violent Tories, and that among them were men who had accompanied Jeffreys on the Bloody Circuit, and who had been consenting to the death of Cornish and of Elizabeth Gaunt. Jones, the Chief-justice of the Common Pleas, a man who had never before shrunk from any drudgery, however cruel or servile, now held in the royal closet language which might have become the lips of the purest magistrates in our history. He was plainly told that he must either give up his opinion or his place. "For my place," he answered,

Dismission of refractory Judges.

"I care little. I am old and worn out in the service of the crown: but I am mortified to find that Your Majesty thinks me capable of giving a judgment which none but an ignorant or a dishonest man could give." "I am determined," said the King, "to have twelve Judges who will be all of my mind as to this matter." "Your Majesty," answered Jones, "may find twelve Judges of your mind, but hardly twelve lawyers."* He was dismissed, together with Montague, Chief Baron of the Exchequer, and two puisne Judges, Neville and Charlton. One of the new Judges was Christopher Milton, younger brother of the great poet. Of Christopher little is known, except that, in the time of the civil war, he had been a Royalist, and that he now, in his old age, leaned toward Popery. It does not appear that he was ever formally reconciled to the Church of Rome: but he certainly had scruples about communicating with the Church of England, and had therefore a strong interest in supporting the dispensing power.†

The King found his counsel as refractory as his Judges. The first barrister who learned that he was expected to defend the dispensing power was the Solicitor-general, Heneage Finch. He peremptorily refused, and was turned out of office on the following day.‡ The Attorney-general, Sawyer, was ordered to draw warrants authorizing members of the Church of Rome to hold benefices belonging to the Church of England. Sawyer had been deeply concerned in some of the harshest and most unjustifiable prosecutions of that age; and the Whigs abhorred him as a man stained with the blood of Russell and Sidney: but on this occasion he showed no want of honesty or of resolution. "Sir," said he, "this is not merely to dispense with a statute: it is to annul the whole statute law from the accession of Elizabeth to the present day. I dare not do it; and I implore Your Majesty to consider whether such an attack upon the rights of the Church be in accordance with your late gracious promises."§ Sawyer

---

* Reresby's Memoirs; Eachard, iii., 797; Kennet, iii., 451.

† London Gazette, April 22 and 29, 1686; Barillon, April $\frac{12}{23}$; Evelyn's Diary, June 2; Luttrell's Diary, June 8; Dodd's Church History.

‡ North's Life of Guildford, 288.   § Reresby's Memoirs.

would have been instantly dismissed, as Finch had been, if the government could have found a successor: but this was no easy matter. It was necessary, for the protection of the rights of the Crown, that one at least of the crown lawyers should be a man of learning, ability, and experience; and no such man was willing to defend the dispensing power. The Attorney-general was therefore permitted to retain his place during some months. Thomas Powis, an obscure barrister, who had no qualification for high employment except servility, was appointed Solicitor.

The preliminary arrangements were now complete. There was a Solicitor-general to argue for the dispensing power, and a bench of Judges to decide in favor of it. The question was therefore speedily brought to a hearing. Sir Edward Hales, a gentleman of Kent, had been converted to Popery in days when it was not safe for any man of note openly to declare himself a Papist. He had kept his secret, and, when questioned, had affirmed that he was a Protestant with a solemnity which did little credit to his principles. When James had ascended the throne, disguise was no longer necessary. Sir Edward publicly apostatized, and was rewarded with the command of a regiment of foot. He had held his commission more than three months without taking the sacrament. He was therefore liable to a penalty of five hundred pounds, which an informer might recover by action of debt. A menial servant was employed to bring a suit for this sum in the Court of King's Bench. Sir Edward did not dispute the facts alleged against him, but pleaded that he had letters-patent authorizing him to hold his commission notwithstanding the Test Act. The plaintiff demurred, that is to say, admitted Sir Edward's plea to be true in fact, but denied that it was a sufficient answer. Thus was raised a simple issue of law to be decided by the court. A barrister, who was notoriously a tool of the government, appeared for the mock plaintiff, and made some feeble objections to the defendant's plea. The new Solicitor-general replied. The Attorney-general took no part in the proceedings. Judgment was given by the Lord Chief-justice, Sir Edward Herbert. He announced that he had submitted the question to all the twelve Judges, and that, in the opinion of eleven of them, the King might lawfully dispense with penal statutes in particular cases, and for special reasons of grave importance. The single dissentient, Baron Street, was not removed from his place. He was a man of morals so bad that his own relations shrank from him, and that the Prince of Orange, at the time of the Revolution, was advised not to see him. The character of Street makes it impossible to believe that he would have been more scrupulous than his brethren. The character of James makes it impossible to believe that a refractory Baron of the Exchequer would have been permitted to retain his post. There can, therefore, be no reasonable doubt that the dissenting Judge was, like the plaintiff and the plaintiff's counsel, acting collusively. It was important that there should be a great preponderance of authority in favor of the dispensing power; yet it was important that the bench, which had been carefully packed for the occasion, should appear to be independent. One judge, therefore, the least respectable of the twelve, was permitted, or more probably commanded, to give his voice against the prerogative.*

The power which the courts of law had thus recognized was not suffered to lie idle. Within a month after the decision of the King's Bench had been pronounced four Roman Catholic Lords were sworn of the Privy Council. Two of them, Powis and Bellasyse, were of the moderate party, and probably took their seats with reluctance and with many sad forebodings. The other two, Arundell and Dover, had no such misgivings.†

Roman Catholics authorized to hold ecclesiastical benefices.

Sclater.

The dispensing power was, at the same time, employed for the purpose of enabling Roman Catholics to hold ecclesiastical preferment. The new Solicitor readily drew the warrants in which Sawyer had refused to be concerned. One of these warrants was in favor of a wretch named Edward Sclater, who had two liv-

---

* See the account of the case in the Collection of State Trials; Van Citters, May $\frac{4}{14}$, $\frac{\text{June } 22}{\text{July } 2}$, 1686; Evelyn's Diary, June 27; Luttrell's Diary, June 21. As to Street, see Clarendon's Diary, Dec. 27, 1688.

† London Gazette, July 19, 1686.

ings which he was determined to keep through all changes. He administered the sacrament to his parishioners according to the rites of the Church of England on Palm-Sunday, 1686. On Easter-Sunday, only seven days later, he was at mass. The royal dispensation authorized him to retain the emoluments of his benefices. To the remonstrances of the patrons from whom he had received his preferment he replied in terms of insolent defiance, and, while the Roman Catholic cause prospered, put forth an absurd treatise in defence of his apostasy. But, a very few weeks after the Revolution, a great congregation assembled at Saint Mary's in the Savoy, to see him received again into the bosom of the Church which he had deserted. He read his recantation with tears flowing from his eyes, and pronounced a bitter invective against the Popish priests whose arts had seduced him.*

Scarcely less infamous was the conduct of Obadiah Walker. He was an aged priest of the Church of England, and was well known in the University of Oxford as a man of learning. He had in the late reign been suspected of leaning toward Popery, but had outwardly conformed to the established religion, and had at length been chosen Master of University College. Soon after the accession of James, Walker determined to throw off the disguise which he had hitherto worn. He absented himself from the public worship of the Church of England, and, with some fellows and undergraduates whom he had perverted, heard mass daily in his own apartments. One of the first acts performed by the new Solicitor-general was to draw up an instrument which authorized Walker and his proselytes to hold their benefices, notwithstanding their apostasy. Builders were immediately employed to turn two sets of rooms into an oratory. In a few weeks the Roman Catholic rites were publicly performed in University College. A Jesuit was quartered there as chaplain. A press was established

Walker.

---

* The letters-patent are in Gutch's Collectanea Curiosa. The date is the 3d of May, 1686. See Sclater's Consensus Veterum; Gee's reply, entitled Veteres Vindicati; Dr. Anthony Horneck's account of Mr. Sclater's recantation of the errors of Popery on the 5th of May, 1689; Dodd's Church History, Part VIII., Book II., art. 3.

there under royal license for the printing of Roman Catholic tracts. During two years and a half, Walker continued to make war on Protestantism with all the rancor of a renegade: but when fortune turned he showed that he wanted the courage of a martyr. He was brought to the bar of the House of Commons to answer for his conduct, and was base enough to protest that he had never changed his religion, that he had never cordially approved of the doctrines of the Church of Rome, and that he had never tried to bring any other person within the pale of that Church. It was hardly worth while to violate the most sacred obligations of law and of plighted faith, for the purpose of making such converts as these.*

In a short time the King went a step further. Sclater and Walker had only been permitted to keep, after they became Papists, the preferment which had been bestowed on them while they passed for Protestants. To confer a high office in the Established Church on an avowed enemy of that Church was a far bolder violation of the laws and of the royal word. But no course was too bold for James. The Deanery of Christ Church became vacant. That office was, both in dignity and in emolument, one of the highest in the University of Oxford. The Dean was charged with the government of a greater number of youths of high connections and of great hopes than could be found in any other college. He was also the head of a Cathedral. In both characters it was necessary that he should be a member of the Church of England. Nevertheless, John Massey, who was notoriously a member of the Church of Rome, and who had not one single recommendation, except that he was a member of the Church of Rome, was appointed by virtue of the dispensing power; and soon, within the walls of Christ Church, an altar was decked, at which mass was daily celebrated.† To the Nuncio the King said that what had been done at Oxford should very soon be done at Cambridge.‡

<small>*margin: The Deanery of Christ Church given to a Roman Catholic.*</small>

---

* Gutch's Collectanea Curiosa; Dodd, viii., ii., 3; Wood, Ath. Ox.; Ellis Correspondence, Feb. 27, 1686; Commons' Journals, Oct. 26, 1689.

† Gutch's Collectanea Curiosa; Wood's Athenæ Oxonienses; Dialogue between a Churchman and a Dissenter, 1689. ‡ Adda, July $\frac{9}{19}$, 1686.

Yet even this was a small evil compared with that which Protestants had good ground to apprehend. It seemed but too probable that the whole government of the Anglican Church would shortly pass into the hands of her deadliest enemies. Three important sees had lately become vacant—that of York, that of Chester, and that of Oxford. The Bishopric of Oxford was given to Samuel Parker, a parasite, whose religion, if he had any religion, was that of Rome, and who called himself a Protestant only because he was encumbered with a wife. "I wished," the King said to Adda, "to appoint an avowed Catholic: but the time is not come. Parker is well inclined to us: he is one of us in feeling; and by degrees he will bring round his clergy."* The Bishopric of Chester, vacant by the death of John Pearson, a great name both in philology and in divinity, was bestowed on Thomas Cartwright, a still viler sycophant than Parker. The Archbishopric of York remained several years vacant. As no good reason could be found for leaving so important a place unfilled, men suspected that the nomination was delayed only till the King could venture to place the mitre on the head of an avowed Papist. It is indeed highly probable that the Church of England was saved from this outrage solely by the good sense and good feeling of the Pope. Without a special dispensation from Rome no Jesuit could be a bishop; and Innocent could not be induced to grant such a dispensation to Petre.

<small>Disposal of bishoprics.</small>

James did not even make any secret of his intention to exert vigorously and systematically for the destruction of the Established Church all the powers which he possessed as her head. He plainly said that, by a wise dispensation of Providence, the Act of Supremacy would be the means of healing the fatal breach which it had caused. Henry and Elizabeth had usurped a dominion which rightfully belonged to the Holy See. That dominion had, in the course of succession, descended to an orthodox prince, and would be held by him in trust for the

<small>Resolution of James to use his ecclesiastical supremacy against the Church.</small>

---

* Adda, $\frac{\text{July 30,}}{\text{Aug. 9,}}$ 1686.

Holy See. He was authorized by law to repress spiritual abuses; and the first spiritual abuse which he would repress should be the liberty which the Anglican clergy assumed of defending their own religion and of attacking the doctrines of Rome.*

But he was met by a great difficulty. The ecclesiastical supremacy which had devolved on him was by no means the same great and terrible prerogative which Elizabeth, James the First, and Charles the First had possessed. The enactment which annexed to the crown an almost boundless visitatorial authority over the Church, though it had never been formally repealed, had really lost a great part of its force. The substantive law remained; but it remained unaccompanied by any formidable sanction or by any efficient system of procedure, and was therefore little more than a dead letter.

<small>His difficulties.</small>

The statute, which restored to Elizabeth the spiritual dominion assumed by her father and resigned by her sister, contained a clause authorizing the sovereign to constitute a tribunal which might investigate, reform, and punish all ecclesiastical delinquencies. Under the authority given by this clause, the Court of High Commission was created. That court was, during many years, the terror of Non-conformists, and, under the harsh administration of Laud, became an object of fear and hatred even to those who most loved the Established Church. When the Long Parliament met, the High Commission was generally regarded as the most grievous of the many grievances under which the nation labored. An act was therefore somewhat hastily passed, which not only took away from the crown the power of appointing visitors to superin-

---

* "Ce prince m'a dit que Dieu avoit permis que toutes les loix qui ont été faites pour établir la réligion Protestante, et détruire la réligion Catholique, servent présentement de fondement à ce qu'il veut faire pour l'établissement de la vraie réligion, et le mettent en droit d'exercer un pouvoir encore plus grand que celui qu'ont les rois Catholiques sur les affaires ecclésiastiques dans les autres pays."— Barillon, July $\frac{12}{22}$, 1686. To Adda His Majesty said, a few days later, "Che l'autorità concessale dal parlamento sopra l'Ecclesiastico senza alcun limite con fine contrario fosse adesso per servire al vantaggio de' medesimi Cattolici." $\frac{\text{July 23}}{\text{Aug. 2}}$.

tend the Church, but abolished all ecclesiastical courts without distinction.

After the Restoration, the Cavaliers who filled the House of Commons, zealous as they were for the prerogative, still remembered with bitterness the tyranny of the High Commission, and were by no means disposed to revive an institution so odious. They at the same time thought, and with reason, that the statute which had swept away all the courts Christian of the realm, without providing any substitute, was open to grave objection. They accordingly repealed that statute, with the exception of the part which related to the High Commission. Thus, the Archidiaconal Courts, the Consistory Courts, the Court of Arches, the Court of Peculiars, and the Court of Delegates were revived: but the enactment by which Elizabeth and her successors had been empowered to appoint commissioners with visitatorial authority over the Church was not only not revived, but was declared, with the utmost strength of language, to be completely abrogated. It is therefore as clear as any point of constitutional law can be that James the Second was not competent to appoint a commission with power to visit and govern the Church of England.* But, if this were so, it was to little purpose that the Act of Supremacy, in high-sounding words, empowered him to amend what was amiss in that Church. Nothing but a machinery as stringent as that which the Long Parliament had destroyed could force the Anglican clergy to become his agents for the destruction of the Anglican doctrine and discipline. He therefore, as early as the month of April, 1686, determined to revive the Court of High Commission. This design was not immediately executed. It encountered the opposition of every minister who was not devoted to France and to the Jesuits. It was regarded by lawyers as an outrageous violation of the law, and by Churchmen as a direct attack upon the Church. Perhaps the contest might have lasted longer, but for an event

---

* The whole question is lucidly and unanswerably argued in a little contemporary tract, entitled "The King's Power in Matters Ecclesiastical fairly stated." See also a concise but forcible argument by Archbishop Sancroft, Doyly's Life of Sancroft, i., 92.

which wounded the pride and inflamed the rage of the King. He had, as supreme ordinary, put forth directions, charging the clergy of the establishment to abstain from touching in their discourses on controverted points of doctrine. Thus, while sermons in defence of the Roman Catholic religion were preached on every Sunday and holiday within the precincts of the royal palaces, the Church of the state, the Church of the great majority of the nation, was forbidden to explain and vindicate her own principles. The spirit of the whole clerical order rose against this injustice. William Sherlock, a divine of distinguished abilities, who had written with sharpness against Whigs and Dissenters, and had been rewarded by the government with the Mastership of the Temple and with a pension, was one of the first who incurred the royal displeasure. His pension was stopped; and he was severely reprimanded.* John Sharp, Dean of Norwich and Rector of Saint Giles's in the Fields, soon gave still greater offence. He was a man of learning and fervent piety, a preacher of great fame, and an exemplary parish priest. In politics he was, like most of his brethren, a Tory, and had just been appointed one of the royal chaplains. He received an anonymous letter which purported to come from one of his parishioners, who had been staggered by the arguments of Roman Catholic theologians, and who was anxious to be satisfied that the Church of England was a branch of the true Church of Christ. No divine, not utterly lost to all sense of religious duty and of professional honor, could refuse to answer such a call. On the following Sunday Sharp delivered an animated discourse against the high pretensions of the see of Rome. Some of his expressions were exaggerated, distorted, and carried by tale-bearers to Whitehall. It was falsely said that he had spoken with contumely of the theological disquisitions which had been found in the strong-box of the late King, and which the present King had published. Compton, the Bishop of London, received orders from Sunderland to suspend Sharp till the royal pleasure should be further known. The Bishop was in

---

* Letter from James to Clarendon, Feb. 18, 168$\frac{5}{6}$.

great perplexity. His recent conduct in the House of Lords had given deep offence to the Court. Already his name had been struck out of the list of Privy Councillors. Already he had been dismissed from his office in the royal chapel. He was unwilling to give fresh provocation: but the act which he was directed to perform was a judicial act. He felt that it was unjust, and he was assured by the best advisers that it was also illegal, to inflict punishment without giving any opportunity for defence. He accordingly, in the humblest terms, represented his difficulties to the King, and privately requested Sharp not to appear in the pulpit for the present. Reasonable as were Compton's scruples, obsequious as were his apologies, James was greatly incensed. What insolence to plead either natural justice or positive law in opposition to an express command of the Sovereign! Sharp was forgotten. The Bishop became a mark for the whole vengeance of the government.* He creates a new Court of High Commission. The King felt more painfully than ever the want of that tremendous engine which had once coerced refractory ecclesiastics. He probably knew that, for a few angry words uttered against his father's government, Bishop Williams had been suspended by the High Commission from all ecclesiastical dignities and functions. The design of reviving that formidable tribunal was pushed on more eagerly than ever. In July, London was alarmed by the news that the King had, in direct defiance of two Acts of Parliament drawn in the strongest terms, intrusted the whole government of the Church to seven Commissioners.† The words in which the jurisdiction of these officers was described were loose, and might be stretched to almost any extent. All colleges and grammar-schools, even those which had been founded by the liberality of private benefactors, were placed under the authority of the new

---

* The best account of these transactions is in the Life of Sharp, by his son. Van Citters, $\frac{\text{June 29,}}{\text{July 9,}}$ 1686.

† Barillon, $\frac{\text{July 21,}}{\text{Aug. 1,}}$ 1686. Van Citters, July $\frac{16}{26}$; Privy Council Book, July 17; Ellis Correspondence, July 17; Evelyn's Diary, July 14; Luttrell's Diary, August 5, 6.

board. All who depended for bread on situations in the Church, or in academical institutions, from the Primate down to the youngest curate, from the Vice-chancellors of Oxford and Cambridge down to the humblest pedagogue who taught Corderius, were subjected to this despotic tribunal. If any one of those many thousands was suspected of doing or saying anything distasteful to the government, the Commissioners might cite him before them. In their mode of dealing with him they were fettered by no rule. They were themselves at once prosecutors and judges. The accused party was to be furnished with no copy of the charge. He was to be examined and cross-examined. If his answers did not give satisfaction, he was liable to be suspended from his office, to be ejected from it, to be pronounced incapable of holding any preferment in future. If he were contumacious, he might be excommunicated, or, in other words, be deprived of all civil rights and imprisoned for life. He might also, at the discretion of the Court, be loaded with all the costs of the proceeding by which he had been reduced to beggary. No appeal was given. The Commissioners were directed to execute their office notwithstanding any law which might be, or might seem to be, inconsistent with these regulations. Lastly, lest any person should doubt that it was intended to revive that terrible court from which the Long Parliament had freed the nation, the new visitors were directed to use a seal bearing exactly the same device and the same superscription with the seal of the old High Commission.*

The chief commissioner was the Chancellor. His presence and assent were declared necessary to every proceeding. All men knew how unjustly, insolently, and barbarously he had acted in courts where he had been, to a certain extent, restrained by the known laws of England. It was, therefore, not difficult to foresee how he would conduct himself in a situation in which he was at entire liberty to make forms of procedure and rules of evidence for himself.

* The device was a rose and crown. Before the device was the initial letter of the Sovereign's name; after it the letter R. Round the seal was this inscription, "Sigillum commissariorum regiæ majestatis ad causas ecclesiasticas."

Of the other six Commissioners, three were prelates and three laymen. The name of Archbishop Sancroft stood first. But he was fully convinced that the Court was illegal, that all its judgments would be null, and that by sitting in it he should incur a serious responsibility. He therefore determined not to comply with the royal mandate. He did not, however, act on this occasion with that courage and sincerity which he showed when driven to extremity two years later. He begged to be excused on the plea of business and ill health. The other members of the board, he added, were men of too much ability to need his assistance. These disingenuous apologies ill became the Primate of all England at such a crisis; nor did they avert the royal displeasure. Sancroft's name was not, indeed, struck out of the list of Privy Councillors: but, to the bitter mortification of the friends of the Church, he was no longer summoned on Council days. "If," said the King, "he is too sick or too busy to go to the Commission, it is a kindness to relieve him from attendance at Council."*

The government found no similar difficulty with Nathaniel Crewe, Bishop of the great and opulent see of Durham, a man nobly born, and raised so high in his profession that he could scarcely wish to rise higher, but mean, vain, and cowardly. He had been made Dean of the Chapel Royal when the Bishop of London was banished from the palace. The honor of being an ecclesiastical commissioner turned Crewe's head. It was to no purpose that some of his friends represented to him the risk which he ran by sitting in an illegal tribunal. He was not ashamed to answer that he could not live out of the royal smile, and exultingly expressed his hope that his name would appear in history, a hope which has not been altogether disappointed.†

Thomas Sprat, Bishop of Rochester, was the third clerical Commissioner. He was a man to whose talents posterity has scarcely done justice. Unhappily for his fame, it has been usual to print his verses in collections of the British poets;

---

* Append. to Clarendon's Diary; Van Citters, Oct. $\frac{8}{18}$, 1686; Barillon, Oct. $\frac{11}{21}$; Doyly's Life of Sancroft.

† Burnet, i., 676.

and those who judge of him by his verses must consider him as a servile imitator, who, without one spark of Cowley's admirable genius, mimicked whatever was least commendable in Cowley's manner: but those who are acquainted with Sprat's prose writings will form a very different estimate of his powers. He was indeed a great master of our language, and possessed at once the eloquence of the preacher, of the controversialist, and of the historian. His moral character might have passed with little censure had he belonged to a less sacred profession; for the worst that can be said of him is that he was indolent, luxurious, and worldly: but such failings, though not commonly regarded as very heinous in men of secular callings, are scandalous in a prelate. The Archbishopric of York was vacant: Sprat hoped to obtain it, and therefore accepted a seat at the ecclesiastical board: but he was too good-natured a man to behave harshly; and he was too sensible a man not to know that he might at some future time be called to a serious account by a Parliament. He therefore, though he consented to act, tried to do as little mischief, and to make as few enemies, as possible.*

The three remaining Commissioners were the Lord Treasurer, the Lord President, and the Chief-justice of the King's Bench. Rochester, disapproving and murmuring, consented to serve. Much as he had to endure at the Court, he could not bear to quit it. Much as he loved the Church, he could not bring himself to sacrifice for her sake his white staff, his patronage, his salary of eight thousand pounds a year, and the far larger indirect emoluments of his office. He excused his conduct to others, and perhaps to himself, by pleading that, as a commissioner, he might be able to prevent much evil, and that, if he refused to act, some person less attached to the Protestant religion would be found to fill the vacant place. Sunderland was the representative of the Jesuitical cabal. Herbert's recent decision on the question of the dispensing power seemed to prove that he would not flinch from any service which the King might require.

---

* Burnet, i., 675; ii., 629; Sprat's Letters to Dorset.

As soon as the Commission had been opened, the Bishop of London was cited before the new tribunal. He appeared. "I demand of you," said Jeffreys, "a direct and positive answer. Why did not you suspend Dr. Sharp?"

Proceedings against the Bishop of London.

The Bishop requested a copy of the Commission in order that he might know by what authority he was thus interrogated. "If you mean," said Jeffreys, "to dispute our authority, I shall take another course with you. As to the Commission, I do not doubt that you have seen it. At all events you may see it in any coffee-house for a penny." The insolence of the Chancellor's reply appears to have shocked the other Commissioners; and he was forced to make some awkward apologies. He then returned to the point from which he had started. "This," he said, "is not a court in which written charges are exhibited. Our proceedings are summary, and by word of mouth. The question is a plain one. Why did you not obey the King?" With some difficulty Compton obtained a brief delay, and the assistance of counsel. When the case had been heard, it was evident to all men that the Bishop had done only what he was bound to do. The Treasurer, the Chief-justice, and Sprat were for acquittal. The King's wrath was moved. It seemed that his Ecclesiastical Commission would fail him as his Tory Parliament had failed him. He offered Rochester a simple choice, to pronounce the Bishop guilty, or to quit the Treasury. Rochester was base enough to yield. Compton was suspended from all spiritual functions; and the charge of his great diocese was committed to his judges, Sprat and Crewe. He continued, however, to reside in his palace and to receive his revenues; for it was known that, had any attempt been made to deprive him of his temporalities, he would have put himself under the protection of the common law; and Herbert himself declared that, at common law, judgment must be given against the crown. This consideration induced the King to pause. Only a few weeks had elapsed since he had packed the courts of Westminster Hall in order to obtain a decision in favor of his dispensing power. He now found that, unless he packed them again, he should not be able to obtain a decision in favor of the proceedings of his Ecclesiastical Commission. He determined, therefore, to postpone for a short time the confiscation of the freehold property of refractory clergymen.*

<small>Discontent excited by the public display of Roman Catholic rites and vestments.</small> The temper of the nation was indeed such as might well make him hesitate. During some months discontent had been steadily and rapidly increasing. The celebration of the Roman Catholic worship had long been prohibited by Act of Parliament. During several generations no Roman Catholic clergyman had dared to exhibit himself in any public place with the badges of his office. Against the regular clergy, and against the restless and subtle Jesuits by name, had been enacted a succession of rigorous statutes. Every Jesuit who set foot in this country was liable to be hanged, drawn, and quartered. A reward was offered for his detection. He was not allowed to take advantage of the general rule, that men are not bound to accuse themselves. Whoever was suspected of being a Jesuit might be interrogated, and, if he refused to answer, might be sent to prison for life.† These laws, though they had not, except when there was supposed to be some peculiar danger, been strictly executed, and though they had never prevented Jesuits from resorting to England, had made disguise necessary. But all disguise was now thrown off. Injudicious members of the King's Church, encouraged by him, took a pride in defying statutes which were still of undoubted validity, and feelings which had a stronger hold of the national mind than at any former period. Roman Catholic chapels rose all over the country. Cowls, girdles of ropes, and strings of beads constantly appeared in the streets, and astonished a population, the oldest of whom had never seen a conventual garb except on the stage. A convent rose at Clerkenwell, on the site of the ancient cloister of Saint John. The Franciscans occupied a mansion in Lincoln's Inn Fields. The Carmelites were quartered in the City. A society of Benedic-

---

* Burnet, i., 677; Barillon, Sept. $\frac{6}{16}$, 1686. The public proceedings are in the Collection of State Trials.

† 27 Eliz., c. 2; 2 Jac. I., c. 34; 3 Jac. I., c. 5.

tine monks was lodged in Saint James's Palace. In the Savoy a spacious house, including a church and a school, was built for the Jesuits.* The skill and care with which those fathers had, during several generations, conducted the education of youth, had drawn forth reluctant praises from the wisest Protestants. Bacon had pronounced the mode of instruction followed in the Jesuit colleges to be the best yet known in the world, and had warmly expressed his regret that so admirable a system of intellectual and moral discipline should be employed on the side of error.† It was not improbable that the new academy in the Savoy might, under royal patronage, prove a formidable rival to the great foundations of Eton, Westminster, and Winchester. Indeed, soon after the school was opened, the classes consisted of four hundred boys, about one half of whom were Protestants. The Protestant pupils were not required to attend mass: but there could be no doubt that the influence of able preceptors, devoted to the Roman Catholic Church, and versed in all the arts which win the confidence and affection of youth, would make many converts.

These things produced great excitement among the populace, which is always more moved by what impresses the senses than by what is addressed to the reason. Thousands of rude and ignorant men, to whom the dispensing power and the Ecclesiastical Commission were words without a meaning, saw with dismay and indignation a Jesuit college rising on the banks of the Thames, friars in hoods and gowns walking in the Strand, and crowds of devotees pressing in at the doors of temples where homage was paid to graven images. Riots broke out in several parts of the country. At Coventry and Worcester the Roman Catholic worship was violently interrupted.‡ At Bristol the rabble, countenanced, it was said, by the magistrates, exhibited a profane and indecent pageant, in which the Virgin Mary was represented by a buffoon, and in which a mock host was

<small>Riots.</small>

---

* Life of James the Second, ii., 79, 80, Orig. Mem.
† De Augmentis, i., vi., 4.   ‡ Van Citters, May $\frac{14}{24}$, 1686.

carried in procession. Soldiers were called out to disperse the mob. The mob, then and ever since one of the fiercest in the kingdom, resisted. Blows were exchanged, and serious hurts inflicted.* The agitation was great in the capital, and greater in the City, properly so called, than at Westminster. For the people of Westminster had been accustomed to see among them the private chapels of Roman Catholic ambassadors; but the City had not, within living memory, been polluted by any idolatrous exhibition. Now, however, the resident of the Elector Palatine, encouraged by the King, fitted up a chapel in Lime Street. The heads of the corporation, though men selected for office on account of their known Toryism, protested against this proceeding, which, as they said, the ablest gentlemen of the long robe regarded as illegal. The Lord Mayor was ordered to appear before the Privy Council. "Take heed what you do," said the King. "Obey me; and do not trouble yourself either about gentlemen of the long robe or gentlemen of the short robe." The Chancellor took up the word, and reprimanded the unfortunate magistrate with the genuine eloquence of the Old Bailey bar. The chapel was opened. All the neighborhood was soon in commotion. Great crowds assembled in Cheapside to attack the new mass house. The priests were insulted. A crucifix was taken out of the building and set up on the parish pump. The Lord Mayor came to quell the tumult, but was received with cries of "No wooden gods." The trainbands were ordered to disperse the crowd: but the trainbands shared in the popular feeling; and murmurs were heard from the ranks: "We cannot in conscience fight for Popery."†

The Elector Palatine was, like James, a sincere and zealous Catholic, and was, like James, the ruler of a Protestant people; but the two princes resembled each other little in temper and understanding. The Elector had promised to respect

---

* Van Citters, May $\frac{18}{28}$, 1686; Adda, May $\frac{19}{29}$.

† Ellis Correspondence, April 27, 1686; Barillon, April $\frac{19}{29}$; Van Citters, April $\frac{20}{30}$; Privy Council Book, March 26; Luttrell's Diary; Adda, $\frac{\text{Feb. 26,}}{\text{Mar. 8,}} \frac{\text{Mar. 26,}}{\text{April 5,}}$ April $\frac{2}{13}$, April 23, May 3.

the rights of the Church which he found established in his dominions. He had strictly kept his word, and had not suffered himself to be provoked to any violence by the indiscretion of preachers who, in their antipathy to his faith, occasionally forgot the respect which they owed to his person.* He learned, with concern, that great offence had been given to the people of London by the injudicious act of his representative, and, much to his honor, declared that he would forego the privilege to which, as a sovereign prince, he was entitled, rather than endanger the peace of a great city. "I, too," he wrote to James, "have Protestant subjects; and I know with how much caution and delicacy it is necessary that a Catholic prince so situated should act." James, instead of expressing gratitude for this humane and considerate conduct, turned the letter into ridicule before the foreign ministers. It was determined that the Elector should have a chapel in the City whether he would or not, and that, if the trainbands refused to do their duty, their place should be supplied by the Guards.†

The effect of these disturbances on trade was serious. The Dutch minister informed the States-general that the business of the Exchange was at a stand. The Commissioners of the Customs reported to the King that, during the month which followed the opening of the Lime Street Chapel, the receipt in the port of the Thames had fallen off by some thousands of pounds.‡ Several Aldermen, who, though zealous royalists appointed under the new charter, were deeply interested in the commercial prosperity of their city, and loved neither Popery nor martial law, tendered their resignations. But the King was resolved not to yield. He formed a camp on Hounslow Heath, and collected there, within a circumference <small>A camp formed at Hounslow.</small> of about two miles and a half, fourteen battalions of foot and thirty-two squadrons of horse, amounting to thirteen thousand fighting men. Twenty-six pieces of artillery, and many wains laden with arms and ammunition,

---

* Burnet's Travels.   † Barillon, $\frac{\text{May 27,}}{\text{June 6,}}$ 1686.
‡ Van Citters, $\frac{\text{May 25}}{\text{June 4,}}$ 1686.

were dragged from the Tower through the City to Hounslow.* The Londoners saw this great force assembled in their neighborhood with a terror which familiarity soon diminished. A visit to Hounslow became their favorite amusement on holidays. The camp presented the appearance of a vast fair. Mingled with the musketeers and dragoons, a multitude of fine gentlemen and ladies from Soho Square, sharpers and painted women from Whitefriars, invalids in sedans, monks in hoods and gowns, lackeys in rich liveries, peddlers, orange girls, mischievous apprentices, and gaping clowns, was constantly passing and repassing through the long lanes of tents. From some pavilions were heard the noises of drunken revelry, from others the curses of gamblers. In truth the place was merely a gay suburb of the capital. The King, as was amply proved two years later, had greatly miscalculated. He had forgotten that vicinity operates in more ways than one. He had hoped that his army would overawe London: but the result of his policy was that the feelings and opinions of London took complete possession of his army.†

Scarcely indeed had the encampment been formed when there were rumors of quarrels between the Protestant and Popish soldiers.‡ A little tract, entitled A humble and hearty Address to all English Protestants in the Army, had been actively circulated through the ranks. The writer vehemently exhorted the troops to use their arms in defence, not of the mass book, but of the Bible, of the Great Charter, and of the Petition of Right. He was a man already under the frown of power. His character was remarkable, and his history not uninstructive.

---

* Ellis Correspondence, June 26, 1686; Van Citters, July $\frac{2}{12}$; Luttrell's Diary, July 19.

† See the contemporary poems, entitled Hounslow Heath and Cæsar's Ghost; Evelyn's Diary, June 2, 1686. A ballad in the Pepysian Collection contains the following lines:
"I liked the place beyond expressing,
I ne'er saw a camp so fine,
Not a maid in a plain dressing,
But might taste a glass of wine."

‡ Luttrell's Diary, June 18, 1686.

His name was Samuel Johnson. He was a priest of the Church of England, and had been chaplain to Lord Russell. Johnson was one of those persons who are mortally hated by their opponents, and less loved than respected by their allies. His morals were pure, his religious feelings ardent, his learning and abilities not contemptible, his judgment weak, his temper acrimonious, turbulent, and unconquerably stubborn. His profession made him peculiarly odious to the zealous supporters of monarchy; for a republican in holy orders was a strange and almost an unnatural being. During the late reign Johnson had published a book entitled Julian the Apostate. The object of this work was to show that the Christians of the fourth century did not hold the doctrine of non-resistance. It was easy to produce passages from Chrysostom and Jerome written in a spirit very different from that of the Anglican divines who preached against the Exclusion Bill. Johnson, however, went further. He attempted to revive the odious imputation which had for very obvious reasons been thrown by Libanius on the Christian soldiers of Julian, and insinuated that the dart which slew the imperial renegade came, not from the enemy, but from some Rumbold or Ferguson in the Roman ranks. A hot controversy followed. Whig and Tory disputants wrangled fiercely about an obscure passage, in which Gregory of Nazianzus praises a pious bishop who was going to bastinado somebody. The Whigs maintained that the holy man was going to bastinado the Emperor; the Tories that, at the worst, he was only going to bastinado a captain of the guard. Johnson wrote a reply to his assailants, in which he drew an elaborate parallel between Julian and James, then Duke of York. Julian had, during many years, pretended to abhor idolatry, while in heart an idolater. Julian had, to serve a turn, occasionally affected respect for the rights of conscience. Julian had punished cities which were zealous for the true religion, by taking away their municipal privileges. Julian had, by his flatterers, been called the Just. James was provoked beyond endurance. Johnson was prosecuted for a libel, convicted, and condemned to a fine which he had no means of paying. He was therefore kept in jail; and it seemed likely that his confinement would end only with his life.*

Over the room which he occupied in the King's Bench prison lodged another offender whose character well deserves to be studied. This was Hugh Speke, a young man of good family, but of a singularly base and depraved nature. His love of mischief and of dark and crooked ways amounted almost to madness. To cause confusion without being found out was his business and his pastime; and he had a rare skill in using honest enthusiasts as the instruments of his cold-blooded malice. He had attempted, by means of one of his puppets, to fasten on Charles and James the crime of murdering Essex in the Tower. On this occasion the agency of Speke had been traced; and, though he succeeded in throwing the greater part of the blame on his dupe, he had not escaped with impunity. He was now a prisoner; but his fortune enabled him to live with comfort; and he was under so little restraint that he was able to keep up regular communication with one of his confederates who managed a secret press.

Hugh Speke.

Johnson was the very man for Speke's purposes, zealous and intrepid, a scholar and a practised controversialist, yet as simple as a child. A close intimacy sprang up between the two fellow-prisoners. Johnson wrote a succession of bitter and vehement treatises which Speke conveyed to the printer. When the camp was formed at Hounslow, Speke urged Johnson to compose an address which might excite the troops to mutiny. The paper was instantly drawn up. Many thousands of copies were struck off and brought to Speke's room, whence they were distributed over the whole country, and especially among the soldiers. A milder government than that which then ruled England would have been moved to high resentment by such a provocation. Strict search was made. A subordinate agent who had been employed to circulate the address saved himself by giving up Johnson; and

---

* See the Memoirs of Johnson, prefixed to the folio edition of his life, his Julian, and his answers to his opponents. See also Hickes's Jovian.

Johnson was not the man to save himself by giving up Speke. An information was filed, and a conviction obtained without difficulty. Julian Johnson, as he was popularly called, was sentenced to stand thrice in the pillory, and to be whipped from Newgate to Tyburn. The Judge, Sir Francis Withins, told the criminal to be thankful for the great lenity of the Attorney-general, who might have treated the case as one of high treason. "I owe him no thanks," answered Johnson, dauntlessly. "Am I, whose only crime is that I have defended the Church and the laws, to be grateful for being scourged like a dog, while Popish scribblers are suffered daily to insult the Church and to violate the laws with impunity?" The energy with which he spoke was such that both the Judges and the crown lawyers thought it necessary to vindicate themselves, and to protest that they knew of no Popish publications such as those to which the prisoner alluded. He instantly drew from his pocket some Roman Catholic books and trinkets which were then freely exposed for sale under the royal patronage, read aloud the titles of the books, and threw a rosary across the table to the King's counsel. "And now," he cried with a loud voice, "I lay this information before God, before this Court, and before the English people. We shall soon see whether Mr. Attorney will do his duty."

Proceedings against Johnson.

It was resolved that, before the punishment was inflicted, Johnson should be degraded from the priesthood. The prelates who had been charged by the Ecclesiastical Commission with the care of the diocese of London cited him before them in the chapter-house of Saint Paul's Cathedral. The manner in which he went through the ceremony made a deep impression on many minds. When he was stripped of his sacred robe, he exclaimed, "You are taking away my gown because I have tried to keep your gowns on your backs." The only part of the formalities which seemed to distress him was the plucking of the Bible out of his hand. He made a faint struggle to retain the sacred book, kissed it, and burst into tears. "You cannot," he said, "deprive me of the hopes which I owe to it." Some attempts were made to obtain a remission of the flogging. A Roman Catholic priest offered to intercede in consideration of a bribe of two hundred pounds. The money was raised; and the priest did his best, but in vain. "Mr. Johnson," said the King, "has the spirit of a martyr; and it is fit that he should be one." William the Third said, a few years later, of one of the most acrimonious and intrepid Jacobites, "He has set his heart on being a martyr; and I have set mine on disappointing him." These two speeches would alone suffice to explain the widely different fates of the two princes.

The day appointed for the flogging came. A whip of nine lashes was used. Three hundred and seventeen stripes were inflicted; but the sufferer never winced. He afterward said that the pain was cruel, but that, as he was dragged at the tail of the cart, he remembered how patiently the cross had been borne up Mount Calvary, and was so much supported by the thought that, but for the fear of incurring the suspicion of vainglory, he would have sung a psalm with as firm and cheerful a voice as if he had been worshipping God in the congregation. It is impossible not to wish that so much heroism had been less alloyed by intemperance and intolerance.*

Among the clergy of the Church of England Johnson found no sympathy. He had attempted to justify rebellion: he had even hinted approbation of regicide; and they still, in spite of much provocation, clung to the doctrine of non-resistance. But they saw with alarm and concern the progress of what they considered as a noxious superstition, and, while they abjured all thought of defending their religion by the sword, betook themselves manfully to weapons of a different kind. To preach against the errors of Popery was now regarded by them as a point of duty and a point of honor. The London clergy, who were then in abilities and influence decidedly at the head of their profession, set an example which was bravely followed by

Zeal of the Anglican clergy against Popery.

---

* Life of Johnson, prefixed to his works; Secret History of the happy Revolution, by Hugh Speke; State Trials; Van Citters, $\frac{\text{Nov. 23,}}{\text{Dec. 3,}}$ 1686. Van Citters gives the best account of the trial. I have seen a broadside which confirms his narrative.

their ruder brethren all over the country. Had only a few bold men taken this freedom, they would probably have been at once cited before the Ecclesiastical Commission; but it was hardly possible to punish an offence which was committed every Sunday by thousands of divines, from Berwick to Penzance. The presses of the capital, of Oxford, and of Cambridge, never rested. The act which subjected literature to a censorship did not seriously impede the exertions of Protestant controversialists; for that act contained a proviso in favor of the two Universities, and authorized the publication of theological works licensed by the Archbishop of Canterbury. It was therefore out of the power of the government to silence the defenders of the established religion. They were a numerous, an intrepid, and a well appointed band of combatants. Among them were eloquent declaimers, expert dialecticians, scholars deeply read in the writings of the fathers and in all parts of ecclesiastical history. Some of them, at a later period, turned against one another the formidable arms which they had wielded against the common enemy, and by their fierce contentions and insolent triumphs brought reproach on the Church which they had saved. But at present they formed a united phalanx. In the van appeared a rank of steady and skilful veterans—Tillotson, Stillingfleet, Sherlock, Prideaux, Whitby, Patrick, Tenison, Wake. The rear was brought up by the most distinguished bachelors of arts who were studying for deacon's orders. Conspicuous among the recruits whom Cambridge sent to the field was a distinguished pupil of the great Newton, Henry Wharton, who had, a few months before, been senior wrangler of his year, and whose early death was soon after deplored by men of all parties as an irreparable loss to letters.* Oxford was not less proud of a youth, whose great powers, first essayed in this conflict, afterward troubled the Church and the State during forty eventful years, Francis Atterbury. By such men as these every question in issue between the Papists and the Protestants was debated, sometimes in a popular style which boys and women

---

* See the preface to Henry Wharton's Posthumous Sermons.

could comprehend, sometimes with the utmost subtlety of logic, and sometimes with an immense display of learning. The pretensions of the Holy See, the authority of tradition, purgatory, transubstantiation, the sacrifice of the mass, the adoration of the host, the denial of the cup to the laity, confession, penance, indulgences, extreme unction, the invocation of saints, the adoration of images, the celibacy of the clergy, the monastic vows, the practice of celebrating public worship in a tongue unknown to the multitude, the corruptions of the court of Rome, the history of the Reformation, the characters of the chief Reformers, were copiously discussed. Great numbers of absurd legends about miracles wrought by saints and relics were translated from the Italian, and published as specimens of the priestcraft by which the greater part of Christendom had been fooled. Of the tracts put forth on these subjects by Anglican divines during the short reign of James the Second many have probably perished. Those which may still be found in our great libraries make up a mass of near twenty thousand pages.*

The Roman Catholics did not yield the victory without a struggle. One of them, named Henry Hills, had been appointed printer to the royal household and chapel, and had been placed by the King at the head of a great office in London from which theological tracts came forth by hundreds. Obadiah Walker's press was not less active at Oxford. But, with the exception of some bad translations of Bossuet's admirable works, these establishments put forth nothing of the smallest value. It was indeed impossible for any intelligent and candid Roman Catholic to deny that the champions of his Church were, in every talent and acquirement, completely overmatched. The ablest of them would not, on the other side, have been considered as of the third rate. Many of them, even when they had something to say, knew not how to say it. They

The Roman Catholic divines overmatched.

---

* This I can attest from my own researches. There is an excellent collection in the British Museum. Birch tells us, in his Life of Tillotson, that Archbishop Wake had not been able to form even a perfect catalogue of all the tracts published in this controversy.

had been excluded by their religion from English schools and universities; nor had they ever, till the accession of James, found England an agreeable, or even a safe residence. They had therefore passed the greater part of their lives on the Continent, and had almost unlearned their mother-tongue. When they preached, their outlandish accent moved the derision of the audience. They spelled like washer-women. Their diction was disfigured by foreign idioms; and, when they meant to be eloquent, they imitated, as well as they could, what was considered as fine writing in those Italian academies where rhetoric had then reached the last stage of corruption. Disputants laboring under these disadvantages would scarcely, even with truth on their side, have been able to make head against men whose style is eminently distinguished by simple purity and grace.*

---

* Cardinal Howard spoke strongly to Burnet at Rome on this subject. Burnet, i., 662. There is a curious passage to the same effect in a despatch of Barillon or Bonrepaux: but I have mislaid the reference.

One of the Roman Catholic divines who engaged in this controversy, a Jesuit named Andrew Pulton, whom Mr. Oliver, in his biography of the Order, pronounces to have been a man of distinguished ability, very frankly owns his deficiencies. "A. P., having been eighteen years out of his own country, pretends not yet to any perfection of the English expression or orthography." His spelling is indeed deplorable. In one of his letters wright is put for write, woed for would. He challenged Tenison to dispute with him in Latin, that they might be on equal terms. In a contemporary satire, entitled the Advice, is the following couplet:

"Send Pulton to be lashed at Busby's school,
That he in print no longer play the fool."

Another Roman Catholic, named William Clench, wrote a treatise on the Pope's supremacy, and dedicated it to the Queen in Italian. The following specimen of his style may suffice. "O del sagro marito fortunata consorte! O dolce alleviamento d' affari alti! O grato ristoro di pensieri noiosi, nel cui petto latteo, lucente specchio d'illibata matronal pudicizia, nel cui seno odorato, come in porto d'amor, si ritira il Giacomo! O beata regia coppia! O felice inserto tra l' invincibil leoni e le candide aquile!"

Clench's English is of a piece with his Tuscan. For example, "Peter signifies an inexpugnable rock, able to evacuate all the plots of hell's divan, and naufragate all the lurid designs of empoisoned heretics."

Another Roman Catholic treatise, entitled "The Church of England truly represented," begins by informing us that "the ignis fatuus of reformation, which had grown to a comet by many acts of spoil and rapine, had been ushered into England, purified of the filth which it had contracted among the lakes of the Alps."

The situation of England in the year 1686 cannot be better described than in the words of the French Ambassador. "The discontent," he wrote, "is great and general: but the fear of incurring still worse evils restrains all who have anything to lose. The King openly expresses his joy at finding himself in a situation to strike bold strokes. He likes to be complimented on this subject. He has talked to me about it, and has assured me that he will not flinch."*

Meanwhile in other parts of the empire events of grave importance had taken place. The situation of the Episcopalian Protestants of Scotland differed widely from that in which their English brethren stood. In the south of the island the religion of the state was the religion of the people, and had a strength altogether independent of the strength derived from the support of the government. The sincere conformists were far more numerous than the Papists and the Protestant Dissenters taken together. The Established Church of Scotland was the Church of a minority. The Lowland population was generally attached to the Presbyterian discipline. Prelacy was abhorred by the great body of Scottish Protestants, both as an unscriptural and as a foreign institution. It was regarded by the disciples of Knox as a relic of the abominations of Babylon the Great. It painfully reminded a people proud of the memory of Wallace and Bruce that Scotland, since her sovereigns had succeeded to a fairer inheritance, had been independent in name only. The episcopal polity was also closely associated in the public mind with all the evils produced by twenty-five years of cruel and corrupt maladministration. Nevertheless this polity stood, though on a narrow basis and amidst fearful storms, tottering indeed, yet upheld by the civil magistrate, and leaning for support, whenever danger became serious, on the power of England. The records of the Scottish Parliament were thick set with laws denouncing vengeance on those who in any direction strayed from the prescribed pale. By an act passed in the time of Knox, and breathing his spirit, it was a high crime to hear

State of Scotland.

---

* Barillon, July $\frac{19}{29}$, 1686.

mass, and the third offence was capital.* An act recently passed, at the instance of James, made it death to preach in any Presbyterian conventicle whatever, and even to attend such a conventicle in the open air.† The Eucharist was not, as in England, degraded into a civil test; but no person could hold any office, could sit in Parliament, or could even vote for a member of Parliament, without subscribing, under the sanction of an oath, a declaration which condemned in the strongest terms the principles both of the Papists and of the Covenanters.‡

In the Privy Council of Scotland there were two parties corresponding to the two parties which were contending against each other at Whitehall. William Douglas, Duke of Queensberry, was Lord Treasurer, and had, during some years, been considered as first minister. He was nearly connected by affinity, by similarity of opinions, and by similarity of temper, with the Treasurer of England. Both were Tories: both were men of hot temper and strong prejudices: both were ready to support their master in any attack on the civil liberties of his people; but both were sincerely attached to the Established Church. Queensberry had early notified to the court that if any innovation affecting that Church were contemplated, to such innovation he could be no party. But among his colleagues were several men not less unprincipled than Sunderland. In truth the Council-chamber at Edinburgh had been, during a quarter of a century, a seminary of all public and all private vices; and some of the politicians whose character had been formed there had a peculiar hardness of heart and forehead to which Westminster, even in that bad age, could hardly show anything quite equal. The Chancellor, James Drummond, Earl of Perth, and his brother, the Secretary of State, John Lord Melfort, were bent on supplanting Queensberry. The Chancellor had already an unquestionable title to the royal favor. He had brought into use a little steel

---

* Act Parl., Aug. 24, 1560; Dec. 15, 1567.   † Ibid., May 8, 1685.
‡ Ibid., Aug. 31, 1681.

thumb-screw which gave such exquisite torment that it had wrung confessions even out of men on whom His Majesty's favorite boot had been tried in vain.* But it was well known that even barbarity was not so sure a way to the heart of James as apostasy. To apostasy, therefore, Perth and Melfort resorted with a certain audacious baseness which no English statesman could hope to emulate. They declared that the papers found in the strong-box of Charles the Second had converted them both to the true faith; and they began to confess and to hear mass.† How little conscience had to do with Perth's change of religion he amply proved by taking to wife, a few weeks later, in direct defiance of the laws of the Church which he had just joined, a lady who was his cousin-german, without waiting for a dispensation. When the good Pope learned this, he said, with scorn and indignation which well became him, that this was a strange sort of conversion.‡ But James was more easily satisfied. The apostates presented themselves at Whitehall, and there received such assurances of his favor, that they ventured to bring direct charges against the Treasurer. Those charges, however, were so evidently frivolous that James was forced to acquit the accused minister; and many thought that the Chancellor had ruined himself by his malignant eagerness to ruin his rival. There were a few, however, who judged more correctly. Halifax, to whom Perth expressed some apprehensions, answered with a sneer that there was no danger. "Be of good cheer, my Lord: thy faith hath made thee whole." The prediction was correct. Perth and Melfort went back to Edinburgh, the real heads of the government of their country.§ Another member of the Scottish Privy Council, Alexander Stuart, Earl of Murray, the descendant and heir of the Regent, abjured the religion of which his illustrious ancestor had been the foremost champion, and declared himself a member of the Church of Rome. Devoted as Queensberry had always been to the cause of prerogative, he could not stand his ground against competitors who were willing to pay such a price for

---

* Burnet, i., 584. † Ibid., i., 652, 653. ‡ Ibid., i., 678. § Ibid., i., 653.

II.—8

the favor of the court. He had to endure a succession of mortifications and humiliations similar to those which, about the same time, began to embitter the life of his friend Rochester. Royal letters came down authorizing Papists to hold offices without taking the test. The clergy were strictly charged not to reflect on the Roman Catholic religion in their discourses. The Chancellor took on himself to send the macers of the Privy Council round to the few printers and booksellers who could then be found in Edinburgh, charging them not to publish any work without his license. It was well understood that this order was intended to prevent the circulation of Protestant treatises. One honest stationer told the messengers that he had in his shop a book which reflected in very coarse terms on Popery, and begged to know whether he might sell it. They asked to see it; and he showed them a copy of the Bible.* A cargo of copes, images, beads, crosses, and censers arrived at Leith directed to Lord Perth. The importation of such articles had long been considered as illegal; but now the officers of the customs allowed the superstitious garments and trinkets to pass.† In a short time it was known that a Popish chapel had been fitted up in the Chancellor's house, and that mass was regularly said there. The mob rose. The mansion where the idolatrous rites were celebrated was fiercely attacked. The iron bars which protected the windows were wrenched off. Lady Perth and some of her female friends were pelted with mud. One rioter was seized, and ordered by the Privy Council to be whipped. His fellows rescued him and beat the hangman. The city was all night in confusion. The students of the University mingled with the crowd and animated the tumult. Zealous burghers drank the health of the college lads and confusion to Papists, and encouraged each other to face the troops. The troops were already under arms. They were received with a shower of stones, which wounded an officer. Orders were given to fire; and several citizens were killed. The

---

* Fountainhall, Jan. 28, 168⅚. † Ibid., Jan. 11, 168⅚.

disturbance was serious; but the Drummonds, inflamed by resentment and ambition, exaggerated it strangely. Queensberry observed that their reports would lead any person, who had not witnessed what had passed, to believe that a sedition as formidable as that of Masaniello had been raging at Edinburgh. The brothers in return accused the Treasurer, not only of extenuating the crime of the insurgents, but of having himself prompted it, and did all in their power to obtain evidence of his guilt. One of the ringleaders, who had been taken, was offered a pardon if he would own that Queensberry had set him on; but the same religious enthusiasm, which had impelled the unhappy prisoner to criminal violence, prevented him from purchasing his life by a calumny. He and several of his accomplices were hanged. A soldier, who was accused of exclaiming, during the affray, that he should like to run his sword through a Papist, was shot; and Edinburgh was again quiet: but the sufferers were regarded as martyrs; and the Popish Chancellor became an object of mortal hatred, which in no long time was largely gratified.*

The King was much incensed. The news of the tumult reached him when the Queen, assisted by the Jesuits, had just triumphed over Lady Dorchester and her Protestant allies. The malcontents should find, he declared, that the only effect of the resistance offered to his will was to make him more and more resolute.† He sent orders to the Scottish Council to punish the guilty with the utmost severity, and to make unsparing use of the boot.‡ He pretended to be fully convinced of the Treasurer's innocence, and wrote to that minister in gracious words; but the gracious words were accompanied by ungracious acts. The Scottish Treasury was put into commission in spite of the earnest remonstrances of Rochester, who probably saw his own fate

Anger of the King.

---

* Fountainhall, Jan. 31, and Feb. 1, 168$\frac{5}{6}$; Burnet, i., 678; Trials of David Mowbray and Alexander Keith, in the Collection of State Trials; Bonrepaux, Feb. $\frac{11}{21}$.

† Lewis to Barillon, Feb. $\frac{18}{28}$, 1686.

‡ Fountainhall, Feb. 16; Wodrow, Book III., Chap. x., sec. 3. "We require," His Majesty graciously wrote, "that you spare no legal trial by torture or otherwise."

prefigured in that of his kinsman.* Queensberry was, indeed, named First Commissioner, and was made President of the Privy Council: but his fall, though thus broken, was still a fall. He was also removed from the government of the castle of Edinburgh, and was succeeded in that confidential post by the Duke of Gordon, a Roman Catholic.†

And now a letter arrived from London, fully explaining to the Scottish Privy Council the intentions of the King.

<small>His plans concerning Scotland.</small> What he wanted was that the Roman Catholics should be exempted from all laws imposing penalties and disabilities on account of non-conformity, but that the persecutions of the Covenanters should go on without mitigation.‡ This scheme encountered strenuous opposition in the Council. Some members were unwilling to see the existing laws relaxed. Others, who were by no means averse to relaxation, felt that it would be monstrous to admit Roman Catholics to the highest honors of the State, and yet to leave unrepealed the act which made it death to attend a Presbyterian conventicle. The answer of the board was, therefore, less obsequious than usual. The King in reply sharply reprimanded his undutiful Councillors, <small>Deputation of Scotch Privy Councillors sent to London.</small> and ordered three of them, the Duke of Hamilton, Sir George Lockhart, and General Drummond, to attend him at Westminster. Hamilton's abilities and knowledge, though by no means such as would have sufficed to raise an obscure man to eminence, appeared highly respectable in one who was premier peer of Scotland. Lockhart had long been regarded as one of the first jurists, logicians, and orators that his country had produced, and enjoyed also that sort of consideration which is derived from large possessions; for his estate was such as at that time very few Scottish nobles possessed.§ He had been lately appointed President of the Court of Session. Drummond, a cousin of Perth and Melfort, was commander of the forces in Scotland. He was a loose and profane man: but a sense of honor which

---

* Bonrepaux, Feb. $\frac{18}{28}$, 1686. † Fountainhall, March 11, 1686; Adda, March $\frac{1}{11}$.
‡ This letter is dated March 4, 1686.
§ Barillon, April $\frac{19}{29}$, 1686; Burnet, i., 370.

his two kinsmen wanted restrained him from public apostasy. He lived and died, in the significant phrase of one of his countrymen, a bad Christian, but a good Protestant.*

James was pleased by the dutiful language which the three Councillors used when first they appeared before him. He spoke highly of them to Barillon, and particularly extolled Lockhart as the ablest and most eloquent Scotchman living. They soon proved, however, less tractable than had been expected; and it was rumored at court that they had been perverted by the company which they had kept in London. Hamilton lived much with zealous Churchmen; and it might be feared that Lockhart, who was related to the Wharton family, had fallen into still worse society. In truth, it was natural that statesmen, fresh from a country where opposition in any other form than that of insurrection and assassination had long been almost unknown, and where all that was not lawless fury was abject submission, should have been struck by the earnest and stubborn, yet sober, discontent which pervaded England, and should have been emboldened to try the experiment of constitutional resistance to the royal will. They indeed declared themselves willing to grant large relief to the Roman Catholics; but on two conditions; first, that similar indulgence should be extended to the Calvinistic sectaries; and, secondly, that the King should bind himself by a solemn promise not to attempt anything to the prejudice of the Protestant religion.

Both conditions were highly distasteful to James. He reluctantly agreed, however, after a dispute which lasted several days, that some indulgence should be granted to the Presbyterians: but he would by no means consent to allow them the full liberty which he demanded for members of his own communion.† To the sec-

Their negotiations with the King.

---

* The words are in a letter of Johnstone of Waristoun.

† Some words of Barillon deserve to be transcribed. They would alone suffice to decide a question which ignorance and party spirit have done much to perplex. "Cette liberté accordée aux non-conformistes a faite une grande difficulté, et a été débattue pendant plusieurs jours. Le Roy d'Angleterre avoit fort envie que les Catholiques eussent seuls la liberté de l'exercice de leur religion."—April $\frac{19}{29}$, 1686.

ond condition proposed by the three Scottish Councillors he positively refused to listen. The Protestant religion, he said, was false; and he would not give any guarantee that he would not use his power to the prejudice of a false religion. The altercation was long, and was not brought to a conclusion satisfactory to either party.*

The time fixed for the meeting of the Scottish Estates drew near; and it was necessary that the three Councillors should leave London to attend their parliamentary duty at Edinburgh. On this occasion another affront was offered to Queensberry. In the late session he had held the office of Lord High Commissioner, and had in that capacity represented the majesty of the absent King. This dignity, the greatest to which a Scottish noble could aspire, was now transferred to the renegade Murray.

Meeting of the Scotch Estates.

On the twenty-ninth of April the Parliament met at Edinburgh. A letter from the King was read. He exhorted the Estates to give relief to his Roman Catholic subjects, and offered in return a free trade with England and an amnesty for political offences. A committee was appointed to draw up an answer. That committee, though named by Murray, and composed of Privy Councillors and courtiers, framed a reply, full indeed of dutiful and respectful expressions, yet clearly indicating a determination to refuse what the King demanded. The Estates, it was said, would go as far as their consciences would allow to meet His Majesty's wishes respecting his subjects of the Roman Catholic religion. These expressions were far from satisfying the Chancellor; yet, such as they were, he was forced to content himself with them, and even had some difficulty in persuading the Parliament to adopt them. Objection was taken by some zealous Protestants to the mention made of the Roman Catholic religion. There was no such religion. There was an idolatrous apostasy, which the laws punished with the halter, and to which it did not become Christian men to give flattering titles. To call such a superstition Catholic was to

They prove refractory.

---

* Barillon, April $\frac{19}{29}$, 1686; Citters, April $\frac{13}{23}$, $\frac{20}{30}$, May $\frac{9}{19}$.

give up the whole question which was at issue between Rome and the reformed churches. The offer of a free trade with England was treated as an insult. "Our fathers," said one orator, "sold their king for Southern gold; and we still lie under the reproach of that foul bargain. Let it not be said of us that we have sold our God!" Sir John Lauder of Fountainhall, one of the Senators of the College of Justice, suggested the words, "the persons commonly called Roman Catholics." "Would you nickname His Majesty?" exclaimed the Chancellor. The answer drawn by the committee was carried; but a large and respectable minority voted against the proposed words as too courtly.* It was remarked that the representatives of the towns were, almost to a man, against the government. Hitherto those members had been of very small account in the Parliament, and had generally been considered as the retainers of powerful noblemen. They now showed, for the first time, an independence, a resolution, and a spirit of combination which alarmed the court.†

The answer was so unpleasing to James that he did not suffer it to be printed in the Gazette. Soon he learned that a law, such as he wished to see passed, would not even be brought in. The Lords of Articles, whose business was to draw up the acts on which the Estates were afterward to deliberate, were virtually nominated by himself. Yet even the Lords of Articles proved refractory. When they met, the three Privy Councillors who had lately returned from London took the lead in opposition to the royal will. Hamilton declared plainly that he could not do what was asked. He was a faithful and loyal subject; but there was a limit imposed by conscience. "Conscience!" said the Chancellor: "conscience is a vague word, which signifies anything or nothing." Lockhart, who sat in Parliament as representative of the great county of Lanark, struck in. "If conscience," he said, "be a word without meaning, we will change it for another phrase which, I hope, means something. For conscience let us put the fundamental laws of Scotland." These words raised a fierce de-

---

* Fountainhall, May 6, 1686. † Ibid., June 15, 1686.

bate. General Drummond, who represented Perthshire, declared that he agreed with Hamilton and Lockhart. Most of the Bishops present took the same side.*

It was plain that, even in the Committee of Articles, James could not command a majority. He was mortified and irritated by the tidings. He held warm and menacing language, and punished some of his mutinous servants, in the hope that the rest would take warning. Several persons were dismissed from the Council-board. Several were deprived of pensions, which formed an important part of their income. Sir George Mackenzie of Rosehaugh was the most distinguished victim. He had long held the office of Lord Advocate, and had taken such a part in the persecution of the Covenanters that to this day he holds, in the estimation of the austere and godly peasantry of Scotland, a place not far removed from the unenviable eminence occupied by Claverhouse. The legal learning of Mackenzie was not profound: but, as a scholar, a wit, and an orator, he stood high in the opinion of his countrymen; and his renown had spread even to the coffee-houses of Lon-

---

* Van Citters, May $\frac{11}{21}$, 1686. Van Citters informed the States that he had his intelligence from a sure hand. I will transcribe part of his narrative. It is an amusing specimen of the piebald dialect in which the Dutch diplomatists of that age corresponded.

"Des konigs missive, boven en behalven den Hoog Commissaris aensprake, aen het parlement afgesonden, gelyck dat altoos gebruyckelyck is, waerby Syne Majesteyt nu in genere versocht hieft de mitigatie der rigoureuse ofte sanglante wetten van het Ryck jegens het Pausdom, in het Generale Comitée des Articles (soo men het daer naemt) na ordre gestelt en gelesen synde, in 't voteren, den Hertog van Hamilton onder anderen klaer uyt seyde dat hy daertoe niet soude verstaen, dat hy anders genegen was den konig in allen voorval getrouw te dienen volgens het dictamen syner conscientie: 't gene reden gaf aen de Lord Cancelier de Grave Perts te seggen dat het woort conscientie niets en beduyde, en alleen een individuum vagum was, waerop der Chevalier Locquard dan verder gingh; wil man niet verstaen de betyckenis van het woordt conscientie, soo sal ik in fortioribus seggen dat wy meynen volgens de fondamentale wetten van het ryck."

There is, in the Hind Let Loose, a curious passage to which I should have given no credit, but for this despatch of Van Citters. "They cannot endure so much as to hear of the name of conscience. One that was well acquaint with the Council's humor in this point told a gentleman that was going before them, 'I beseech you, whatever you do, speak nothing of conscience before the Lords, for they cannot abide to hear that word.'"

don and to the cloisters of Oxford. The remains of his forensic speeches prove him to have been a man of parts, but are somewhat disfigured by what he doubtless considered as Ciceronian graces, interjections which show more art than passion, and elaborate amplifications, in which epithet rises above epithet in wearisome climax. He had now, for the first time, been found scrupulous. He was, therefore, in spite of all his claims on the gratitude of the government, deprived of his office. He retired into the country, and soon after went up to London for the purpose of clearing himself, but was refused admission to the royal presence.* While the King was thus trying to terrify the Lords of Articles into submission, the popular voice encouraged them to persist. The utmost exertions of the Chancellor could not prevent the national sentiment from expressing itself through the pulpit and the press. One tract, written with such boldness and acrimony that no printer dared to put it in type, was widely circulated in manuscript. The papers which appeared on the other side of the question had much less effect, though they were disseminated at the public charge, and though the Scottish defenders of the government were assisted by an English auxiliary of great note, Lestrange, who had been sent down to Edinburgh, and lodged in Holyrood House.†

At length, after three weeks of debate, the Lords of Articles came to a decision. They proposed merely that Roman Catholics should be permitted to worship God in private houses without incurring any penalty; and it soon appeared that, far as this measure was from coming up to the King's demands and expectations, the Estates either would not pass it at all, or would pass it with great restrictions and modifications.

While the contest lasted the anxiety in London was intense. Every report, every line, from Edinburgh was eagerly devoured. One day the story ran that Hamilton had given way, and that the government would carry every point. Then came intelligence that the opposition had rallied, and was more obstinate than ever. At the most critical moment, orders

---

* Fountainhall, May 17, 1686. † Wodrow, III., x., 3.

were sent to the post-office that the bags from Scotland should be transmitted to Whitehall. During a whole week, not a single private letter from beyond the Tweed was delivered in London. In our age, such an interruption of communication would throw the whole island into confusion: but there was then so little trade and correspondence between England and Scotland that the inconvenience was probably much smaller than has been often occasioned in our own time by a short delay in the arrival of the Indian mail. While the ordinary channels of information were thus closed, the crowd in the galleries of Whitehall observed with attention the countenances of the King and his ministers. It was noticed, with great satisfaction, that, after every express from the North, the enemies of the Protestant religion looked more and more gloomy. At length, to the general joy, it was announced that the struggle was over, that the government had been unable to carry its measures, and that the Lord High Commissioner had adjourned the Parliament.*

<small>They are adjourned.</small>

If James had not been proof to all warning, these events would have sufficed to warn him. A few months before this time, the most obsequious of English Parliaments had refused to submit to his pleasure. But the most obsequious of English Parliaments might be regarded as an independent and even as a mutinous assembly when compared with any Parliament that had ever sat in Scotland; and the servile spirit of Scottish Parliaments was always to be found in the highest perfection, extracted and condensed, among the Lords of Articles. Yet even the Lords of Articles had been refractory. It was plain that all those classes, all those institutions, which, up to this year, had been considered as the strongest supports of monarchical power, must, if the King persisted in his insane policy, be reckoned as parts of the strength of the opposition. All these signs, however, were lost upon him. To every expostulation he had one answer: he would never give way; for concession had

<small>Arbitrary system of government in Scotland.</small>

---

* Van Citters, $\frac{\text{May 28,}}{\text{June 7,}}$ June $\frac{1}{11}$, $\frac{4}{14}$, 1686; Fountainhall, June 15; Luttrell's Diary, June 2, 16.

ruined his father; and his unconquerable firmness was loudly applauded by the French embassy and by the Jesuitical cabal.

He now proclaimed that he had been only too gracious when he had condescended to ask the assent of the Scottish Estates to his wishes. His prerogative would enable him, not only to protect those whom he favored, but to punish those who had crossed him. He was confident that, in Scotland, his dispensing power would not be questioned by any court of law. There was a Scottish Act of Supremacy which gave to the sovereign such a control over the Church as might have satisfied Henry the Eighth. Accordingly, Papists were admitted in crowds to offices and honors. The Bishop of Dunkeld, who, as a Lord of Parliament, had opposed the government, was arbitrarily ejected from his see, and a successor was appointed. Queensberry was stripped of all his employments, and was ordered to remain at Edinburgh till the accounts of the Treasury during his administration had been examined and approved.* As the representatives of the towns had been found the most unmanageable part of the Parliament, it was determined to make a revolution in every burgh throughout the kingdom. A similar change had recently been effected in England by judicial sentences: but in Scotland a simple mandate of the prince was thought sufficient. All elections of magistrates and of town councils were prohibited; and the King assumed to himself the right of filling up the chief municipal offices.† In a formal letter to the Privy Council he announced his intention to fit up a Roman Catholic chapel in his palace of Holyrood; and he gave orders that the Judges should be directed to treat all the laws against Papists as null, on pain of his high displeasure. He, however, comforted the Protestant Episcopalians by assuring them that, though he was determined to protect the Roman Catholic Church against them, he was equally determined to protect them against any encroachment on the part of the fanatics. To this communication Perth proposed an answer couched in the most servile terms. The Council now contained many

---

* Fountainhall, June 21, 1686. † Ibid., Sept. 16, 1686.

Papists: the Protestant members who still had seats had been cowed by the King's obstinacy and severity; and only a few faint murmurs were heard. Hamilton threw out against the dispensing power some hints which he made haste to explain away. Lockhart said that he would lose his head rather than sign such a letter as the Chancellor had drawn, but took care to say this in a whisper which was heard only by friends. Perth's words were adopted with inconsiderable modifications; and the royal commands were obeyed; but a sullen discontent spread through that minority of the Scottish nation by the aid of which the government had hitherto held the majority down.*

When the historian of this troubled reign turns to Ireland, his task becomes peculiarly difficult and delicate. His steps, Ireland. to borrow the fine image used on a similar occasion by a Roman poet, are on the thin crust of ashes, beneath which the lava is still glowing. The seventeenth century has, in that unhappy country, left to the nineteenth a fatal heritage of malignant passions. No amnesty for the mutual wrongs inflicted by the Saxon defenders of Londonderry, and by the Celtic defenders of Limerick, has ever been granted from the heart by either race. To this day a more than Spartan haughtiness alloys the many noble qualities which characterize the children of the victors, while a Helot feeling, compounded of awe and hatred, is but too often discernible in the children of the vanquished. Neither of the hostile castes can justly be absolved from blame; but the chief blame is due to that short-sighted and headstrong prince who, placed in a situation in which he might have reconciled them, employed all his power to inflame their animosity, and at length forced them to close in a grapple for life and death.

The grievances under which the members of his Church labored in Ireland differed widely from those which he was State of the law on the subject of religion. attempting to remove in England and Scotland. The Irish Statute Book, afterward polluted by intolerance as barbarous as that of the dark ages, then contained scarcely a single enactment, and not a single strin-

---

* Fountainhall, Sept. 16; Wodrow, III., x., 3.

gent enactment, imposing any penalty on Papists as such. On our side of Saint George's Channel every priest who received a neophyte into the bosom of the Church of Rome was liable to be hanged, drawn, and quartered. On the other side he incurred no such danger. A Jesuit who landed at Dover took his life in his hand; but he walked the streets of Dublin in security. Here no man could hold office, or even earn his livelihood as a barrister or a school-master, without previously taking the oath of supremacy: but in Ireland a public functionary was not held to be under the necessity of taking that oath unless it were formally tendered to him.* It therefore did not exclude from employment any person whom the government wished to promote. The sacramental test and the declaration against transubstantiation were unknown; nor was either House of Parliament closed by law against any religious sect.

It might seem, therefore, that the Irish Roman Catholic was in a situation which his English and Scottish brethren in the faith might well envy. In fact, however, his condition was more pitiable and irritating than theirs. For, though not persecuted as a Roman Catholic, he was oppressed as an Irishman. In his country the same line of demarcation which separated religions separated races; and he was of the conquered, the subjugated, the degraded race. On the same soil dwelt two populations, locally intermixed, morally and politically sundered. The difference of religion was by no means the only difference, or even the chief difference, which existed between them. They sprang from different stocks. They spoke different languages. They had different national characters as strongly opposed as any two national characters in Europe. They were in widely different stages

_{Hostility of races.}

---

* The provisions of the Irish Act of Supremacy, 2 Eliz., Chap. i., are substantially the same with those of the English Act of Supremacy, 1 Eliz., Chap. i.: but the English act was soon found to be defective; and the defect was supplied by a more stringent act, 5 Eliz., Chap. i. No such supplementary law was made in Ireland. That the construction mentioned in the text was put on the Irish Act of Supremacy, we are told by Archbishop King: State of Ireland, Chap. ii., sec. 9. He calls this construction Jesuitical; but I cannot see it in that light.

of civilization. Between two such populations there could be little sympathy; and centuries of calamities and wrongs had generated a strong antipathy. The relation in which the minority stood to the majority resembled the relation in which the followers of William the Conqueror stood to the Saxon churls, or the relation in which the followers of Cortes stood to the Indians of Mexico.

The appeliation of Irish was then given exclusively to the Celts and to those families which, though not of Celtic origin, had in the course of ages degenerated into Celtic manners. These people, probably about a million in number, had, with few exceptions, adhered to the Church of Rome. Among them resided about two hundred thousand colonists, proud of their Saxon blood and of their Protestant faith.*

The great preponderance of numbers on one side was more than compensated by a great superiority of intelligence, vigor, and organization on the other. The English settlers seem to have been, in knowledge, energy, and perseverance, rather above than below the average level of the population of the mother country. The aboriginal peasantry, on the contrary, were in an almost savage state. They never worked till they felt the sting of hunger. They were content with accommodation inferior to that which, in happier countries, was provided for domestic cattle. Already the potato, a root which can be cultivated with scarcely any art, industry, or capital, and which cannot be long stored, had become the food of the common people.† From a people so fed, diligence and forethought were not to be expected. Even within a few miles of Dublin, the traveller, on a soil the richest and most verdant in the world, saw with disgust the miserable burrows out of which squalid and half naked barbarians stared wildly at him as he passed.‡

The aboriginal aristocracy retained in no common measure the pride of birth, but had lost the influence which is derived

---

* Political Anatomy of Ireland.
† Political Anatomy of Ireland, 1672; Irish Hudibras, 1689; John Dunton's Account of Ireland, 1699.
‡ Clarendon to Rochester, May 4, 1686.

from wealth and power. Their lands had been divided by
<small>Aboriginal aristocracy.</small> Cromwell among his followers. A portion, indeed, of the vast territory which he had confiscated had, after the restoration of the House of Stuart, been given back to the ancient proprietors. But much the greater part was still held by English emigrants under the guarantee of an Act of Parliament. This act had been in force a quarter of a century; and under it mortgages, settlements, sales, and leases without number had been made. The old Irish gentry were scattered over the whole world. Descendants of Milesian chieftains swarmed in all the courts and camps of the Continent. Those despoiled proprietors who still remained in their native land brooded gloomily over their losses, pined for the opulence and dignity of which they had been deprived, and cherished wild hopes of another revolution. A person of this class was described by his countrymen as a gentleman who would be rich if justice were done, as a gentleman who had a fine estate if he could only get it.* He seldom betook himself to any peaceful calling. Trade, indeed, he thought a far more disgraceful resource than marauding. Sometimes he turned freebooter. Sometimes he contrived, in defiance of the law, to live by coshering, that is to say, by quartering himself on the old tenants of his family, who, wretched as was their own condition, could not refuse a portion of their pittance to one whom they still regarded as their rightful lord.† The native gentleman who had been so fortunate as to keep or to regain some of his land too often lived like the petty prince of a savage tribe, and indemnified himself for the humiliations which the dominant race made him suffer by governing his vassals despotically, by keeping a rude harem, and by maddening or stupefying himself daily with strong drink.‡ Politically he was insignificant. No

---

* Bishop Malony's Letter to Bishop Tyrrel, March 8, 1689.

† Statute 10 and 11 Charles I., Chap. xvi.; King's State of the Protestants of Ireland, Chap. ii., sec. 8.

‡ King, Chap. ii., sec. 8. Miss Edgeworth's King Corny belongs to a later and much more civilized generation; but whoever has studied that admirable portrait can form some notion of what King Corny's great-grandfather must have been.

statute, indeed, excluded him from the House of Commons; but he had almost as little chance of obtaining a seat there as a man of color has of being chosen a Senator of the United States. In fact, only one Papist had been returned to the Irish Parliament since the Restoration. The whole legislative and executive power was in the hands of the colonists; and the ascendency of the ruling caste was upheld by a standing army of seven thousand men, on whose zeal for what was called the English interest full reliance could be placed.*

On a close scrutiny it would have been found that neither the Irishry nor the Englishry formed a perfectly homogeneous body. The distinction between those Irish who were of Celtic blood, and those Irish who sprang from the followers of Strongbow and De Burgh, was not altogether effaced. The Fitzes sometimes permitted themselves to speak with scorn of the Os and Macs; and the Os and Macs sometimes repaid that scorn with aversion. In the preceding generation one of the most powerful of the O'Neills refused to pay any mark of respect to a Roman Catholic gentleman of old Norman descent. "They say that the family has been here four hundred years. No matter. I hate the clown as if he had come yesterday."† It seems, however, that such feelings were rare, and that the feud which had long raged between the aboriginal Celts and the degenerate English had nearly given place to the fiercer feud which separated both races from the modern and Protestant colony.

That colony had its own internal disputes, both national and religious. The majority was English; but a large minority came from the south of Scotland. One half of the settlers belonged to the Established Church: the other half were Dissenters. But in Ireland Scot and Southron were strongly bound together by their common Saxon origin. Churchman and Presbyterian were strongly bound together by their common Protestantism. All the colonists had a common language and a common pecuniary

State of the English colony.

---

* King, Chap. iii., sec. 2.

† Sheridan MS.; Preface to the first volume of the Hibernia Anglicana, 1690; Secret Consults of the Romish party in Ireland, 1689.

interest. They were surrounded by common enemies, and could be safe only by means of common precautions and exertions. The few penal laws, therefore, which had been made in Ireland against Protestant Non-conformists, were a dead letter.* The bigotry of the most sturdy Churchman would not bear exportation across Saint George's Channel. As soon as the Cavalier arrived in Ireland, and found that, without the hearty and courageous assistance of his Puritan neighbors, he and all his family would run imminent risk of being murdered by Popish marauders, his hatred of Puritanism, in spite of himself, began to languish and die away. It was remarked by eminent men of both parties that a Protestant who, in Ireland, was called a high Tory would in England have been considered as a moderate Whig.†

The Protestant Non-conformists, on their side, endured, with more patience than could have been expected the sight of the most absurd ecclesiastical establishment that the world has ever seen. Four Archbishops and eighteen Bishops were employed in looking after about a fifth part of the number of Churchmen who inhabited the single diocese of London. Of the parochial clergy a large proportion were pluralists, and resided at a distance from their cures. There were some who drew from their benefices incomes of little less than a thousand pounds a year, without ever performing any spiritual function. Yet this monstrous institution was much less disliked by the Puritans settled in Ireland than the Church of England by the English sectaries. For in Ireland religious divisions were subordinate to national divisions; and the Presbyterian, while, as a theologian, he could not but condemn the

---

* "There was a free liberty of conscience by connivance, though not by the law."—King, Chap. iii., sec. 1.

† In a letter to James found among Bishop Tyrrel's papers, and dated Aug. 14, 1686, are some remarkable expressions. "There are few or none Protestants in that country but such as are joined with the Whigs against the common enemy." And again: "Those that passed for Tories here" (that is in England) "publicly espouse the Whig quarrel on the other side of the water." Swift said the same thing to King William a few years later: "I remember when I was last in England I told the King that the highest Tories we had with us would make tolerable Whigs there."—Letter concerning the Sacramental Test.

established hierarchy, yet looked on that hierarchy with a sort of complacency when he considered it as a sumptuous and ostentatious trophy of the victory achieved by the great race from which he sprang.*

Thus the grievances of the Irish Roman Catholic had hardly anything in common with the grievances of the English Roman Catholic. The Roman Catholic of Lancashire or Staffordshire had only to turn Protestant; and he was at once, in all respects, on a level with his neighbors: but, if the Roman Catholics of Munster and Connaught had turned Protestants, they would still have continued to be a subject people. Whatever evils the Roman Catholic suffered in England were the effects of harsh legislation, and might have been remedied by a more liberal legislation. But between the two populations which inhabited Ireland there was an inequality which legislation had not caused and could not remove. The dominion which one of those populations exercised over the other was the dominion of wealth over poverty, of knowledge over ignorance, of civilized over uncivilized man.

James himself seemed, at the commencement of his reign, to be perfectly aware of these truths. The distractions of Ireland, he said, arose, not from the differences between the Catholics and the Protestants, but from the differences between the Irish and the English.†

Course which James ought to have followed.

The consequences which he should have drawn from this just proposition were sufficiently obvious; but, unhappily for himself and for Ireland, he failed to perceive them.

If only national animosity could be allayed, there could be little doubt that religious animosity, not being kept alive, as in England, by cruel penal acts and stringent test acts, would of itself fade away. To allay a national animosity such as that which the two races inhabiting Ireland felt for each other could not be the work of a few years. Yet it was a

---

* The wealth and negligence of the established clergy of Ireland are mentioned in the strongest terms by the Lord-lieutenant Clarendon, a most unexceptionable witness.

† Clarendon reminds the King of this in a letter dated March 14, 168$\frac{5}{6}$. "It certainly is," Clarendon adds, "a most true notion."

work to which a wise and good prince might have contributed much; and James would have undertaken that work with advantages such as none of his predecessors or successors possessed. At once an Englishman and a Roman Catholic, he belonged half to the ruling and half to the subject caste, and was therefore peculiarly qualified to be a mediator between them. Nor is it difficult to trace the course which he ought to have pursued. He ought to have determined that the existing settlement of landed property should be inviolable; and he ought to have announced that determination in such a manner as effectually to quiet the anxiety of the new proprietors, and to extinguish any wild hopes which the old proprietors might entertain. Whether, in the great transfer of estates, injustice had or had not been committed, was immaterial. That transfer, just or unjust, had taken place so long ago, that to reverse it would be to unfix the foundations of society. There must be a time of limitation to all rights. After thirty-five years of actual possession, after twenty-five years of possession solemnly guaranteed by statute, after innumerable leases and releases, mortgages and devises, it was too late to search for flaws in titles. Nevertheless something might have been done to heal the lacerated feelings and to raise the fallen fortunes of the Irish gentry. The colonists were in a thriving condition. They had greatly improved their property by building, planting, and enclosing. The rents had almost doubled within a few years; trade was brisk; and the revenue, amounting to about three hundred thousand pounds a year, more than defrayed all the charges of the local government, and afforded a surplus which was remitted to England. There was no doubt that the next Parliament which should meet at Dublin, though representing almost exclusively the English interest, would, in return for the King's promise to maintain that interest in all its legal rights, willingly grant to him a very considerable sum for the purpose of indemnifying, at least in part, such native families as had been wrongfully despoiled. It was thus that in our own time the French government put an end to the disputes engendered by the most extensive confiscation that ever took place in Europe. And thus, if James had been guided by the advice of his most loyal Protestant counsellors, he would have at least greatly mitigated one of the chief evils which afflicted Ireland.*

Having done this, he should have labored to reconcile the hostile races to each other by impartially defending the rights and restraining the excesses of both. He should have punished with equal severity the native who indulged in the license of barbarism and the colonist who abused the strength of civilization. As far as the legitimate authority of the crown extended—and in Ireland it extended far—no man who was qualified for office by integrity and ability should have been considered as disqualified by extraction or by creed for any public trust. It is probable that a Roman Catholic King, with an ample revenue absolutely at his disposal, would, without much difficulty, have secured the co-operation of the Roman Catholic prelates and priests in the great work of reconciliation. Much, however, must still have been left to the healing influence of time. The native race would still have had to learn from the colonists industry and forethought, the arts of civilized life, and the language of England. There could not be equality between men who lived in houses and men who lived in sties, between men who were fed on bread and men who were fed on potatoes, between men who spoke the noble tongue of great philosophers and poets, and men who, with a perverted pride, boasted that they could not writhe their mouths into chattering such a jargon as that in which the Advancement of Learning and the Paradise Lost were written.† Yet it is not unreasonable to believe that, if the gentle policy which has been described had been steadily followed by the government, all distinctions would gradually have been effaced, and that there would now have been no more trace of the hostility which has been the curse of Ire-

---

* Clarendon strongly recommended this course, and was of opinion that the Irish Parliament would do its part. See his letter to Ormond, Aug. 28, 1686.

† It was an O'Neill of great eminence who said that it did not become him to writhe his mouth to chatter English. Preface to the first volume of the Hibernia Anglicana.

land than there is of the equally deadly hostility which once raged between the Saxons and the Normans in England.

Unhappily James, instead of becoming a mediator, became the fiercest and most reckless of partisans. Instead of allaying the animosity of the two populations, he inflamed it to a height before unknown. He determined to reverse their relative position, and to put the Protestant colonists under the feet of the Popish Celts. To be of the established religion, to be of the English blood, was, in his view, a disqualification for civil and military employment. He meditated the design of again confiscating and again portioning out the soil of half the island, and showed his inclination so clearly that one class was soon agitated by terrors which he afterward vainly wished to soothe, and the other by cupidity which he afterward vainly wished to restrain. But this was the smallest part of his guilt and madness. He deliberately resolved, not merely to give to the aboriginal inhabitants of Ireland the entire dominion of their own country, but also to use them as his instruments for setting up arbitrary government in England. The event was such as might have been foreseen. The colonists turned to bay with the stubborn hardihood of their race. The mother country justly regarded their cause as her own. Then came a desperate struggle for a tremendous stake. Everything dear to nations was wagered on both sides: nor can we justly blame either the Irishman or the Englishman for obeying, in that extremity, the law of self-preservation. The contest was terrible, but short. The weaker went down. His fate was cruel; and yet for the cruelty with which he was treated there was not indeed a defence, but an excuse: for, though he suffered all that tyranny could inflict, he suffered nothing that he would not himself have inflicted. The effect of the insane attempt to subjugate England by means of Ireland was that the Irish became hewers of wood and drawers of water to the English. The old proprietors, by their effort to recover what they had lost, lost the greater part of what they had retained. The momentary ascendency of Popery produced such a series of barbarous laws against Popery as made the statute-book of Ireland a proverb of infamy throughout Christendom. Such were the bitter fruits of the policy of James.

We have seen that one of his first acts, after he became King, was to recall Ormond from Ireland. Ormond was the head of the English interest in that kingdom: he was firmly attached to the Protestant religion; and his power far exceeded that of an ordinary Lord-lieutenant, first, because he was in rank and wealth the greatest of the colonists, and, secondly, because he was not only the chief of the civil administration, but also commander of the forces. The King was not at that time disposed to commit the government wholly to Irish hands. He had indeed been heard to say that a native viceroy would soon become an independent sovereign.* For the present, therefore, he determined to divide the power which Ormond had possessed, to intrust the civil administration to an English and Protestant Lord-lieutenant, and to give the command of the army to an Irish and Roman Catholic General. The Lord-lieutenant was Clarendon: the General was Tyrconnel.

Tyrconnel sprang, as has already been said, from one of those degenerate families of the Pale which were popularly classed with the aboriginal population of Ireland. He sometimes, indeed, in his rants, talked with Norman haughtiness of the Celtic barbarians:† but all his sympathies were really with the natives. The Protestant colonists he hated; and they returned his hatred. Clarendon's inclinations were very different: but he was, from temper, interest, and principle, an obsequious courtier. His spirit was mean: his circumstances were embarrassed; and his mind had been deeply imbued with the political doctrines which the Church of England had in that age too assiduously taught. His abilities,

---

* Sheridan MS. among the Stuart Papers. I ought to acknowledge the courtesy with which Mr. Glover assisted me in my search for this valuable manuscript. James appears, from the instructions which he drew up for his son in 1692, to have retained to the last the notion that Ireland could not without danger be intrusted to an Irish Lord-lieutenant.

† Sheridan MS.

however, were not contemptible, and, under a good king, he would probably have been a respectable viceroy.

About three-quarters of a year elapsed between the recall of Ormond and the arrival of Clarendon at Dublin. During that interval the King was represented by a board of Lords Justices; but the military administration was in Tyrconnel's hands. Already the designs of the court began gradually to unfold themselves. A royal order came from Whitehall for disarming the population. This order Tyrconnel strictly executed as respected the English. Though the country was infested by predatory bands, a Protestant gentleman could scarcely obtain permission to keep a brace of pistols. The native peasantry, on the other hand, were suffered to retain their weapons.* The joy of the colonists was therefore great, when at length, in December, 1685, Tyrconnel went to London, and Clarendon came to Dublin. But it soon appeared that the government was really directed, not at Dublin, but in London. Every mail that crossed Saint George's Channel brought tidings of the boundless influence which Tyrconnel exercised on Irish affairs. It was said that he was to be a marquess, that he was to be a duke, that he was to have the sole command of the forces, that he was to be intrusted with the task of remodelling the army and the courts of justice.† Clarendon was bitterly mortified at finding himself a subordinate member of that administration of which he had expected to be the head. He complained that whatever he did was misrepresented by his detractors, and that the gravest resolutions touching the country which he governed were adopted at Westminster, made known to the public, discussed at coffee-houses, communicated in hundreds of private letters, some weeks before one hint had been given to the Lord-lieutenant. His own personal dignity, he said, mattered little: but it was no light thing that the representative of the majesty of the throne

<small>*Clarendon arrives in Ireland as Lord-lieutenant.*</small>

<small>*His mortifications.*</small>

---

* Clarendon to Rochester, Jan. 19, 168⅚; Secret Consults of the Romish Party in Ireland, 1690.

† Clarendon to Rochester, February 27, 168⅚.

should be made an object of contempt to the people.* Panic spread fast among the English, when they found that the viceroy, their fellow-countryman and fellow-Protestant, was unable to extend to them the protection which they had expected from him. They began to know by bitter experience what it is to be a subject caste. They were harassed by the natives with accusations of treason and sedition. This Protestant had corresponded with Monmouth; that Protestant had said something disrespectful of the King four or five years ago, when the Exclusion Bill was under discussion; and the evidence of the most infamous of mankind was ready to substantiate every charge. The Lord-lieutenant expressed his apprehension that, if these practices were not stopped, there would soon be at Dublin a reign of terror similar to that which he had seen in London, when every man held his life and honor at the mercy of Oates and Bedloe.†

<small>Panic among the colonists.</small>

Clarendon was soon informed, by a concise despatch from Sunderland, that it had been resolved to make without delay a complete change in both the civil and the military government of Ireland, and to bring a large number of Roman Catholics instantly into office. His Majesty, it was most ungraciously added, had taken counsel on these matters with persons more competent to advise him than his inexperienced Lord-lieutenant could possibly be.‡

Before this letter reached the viceroy the intelligence which it contained had, through many channels, arrived in Ireland. The terror of the colonists was extreme. Outnumbered as they were by the native population, their condition would be pitiable indeed if the native population were to be armed against them with the whole power of the state; and nothing less than this was threatened. The English inhabitants of Dublin passed each other in the streets with dejected looks. On the Exchange business was suspended. Land-owners hastened to sell their estates for whatever could be got, and to re-

---

* Clarendon to Rochester and Sunderland, March 2, 168$\frac{5}{6}$; and to Rochester, March 14.   † Clarendon to Sunderland, February 26, 168$\frac{5}{6}$.
‡ Sunderland to Clarendon, March 11, 168$\frac{5}{6}$.

mit the purchase-money to England. Traders began to call in their debts, and to make preparations for retiring from business. The alarm soon affected the revenue.* Clarendon attempted to inspire the dismayed settlers with a confidence which he was himself far from feeling. He assured them that their property would be held sacred, and that, to his certain knowledge, the King was fully determined to maintain the Act of Settlement which guaranteed their right to the soil. But his letters to England were in a very different strain. He ventured even to expostulate with the King, and, without blaming His Majesty's intention of employing Roman Catholics, expressed a strong opinion that the Roman Catholics who might be employed ought to be Englishmen.†

The reply of James was dry and cold. He declared that he had no intention of depriving the English colonists of their land, but that he regarded a large portion of them as his enemies, and that, since he consented to leave so much property in the hands of his enemies, it was the more necessary that the civil and military administration should be in the hands of his friends.‡

Accordingly several Roman Catholics were sworn of the Privy Council; and orders were sent to corporations to admit Roman Catholics to municipal advantages.§ Many officers of the army were arbitrarily deprived of their commissions and of their bread. It was to no purpose that the Lord-lieutenant pleaded the cause of some whom he knew to be good soldiers and loyal subjects. Among them were old Cavaliers, who had fought bravely for monarchy, and who bore the marks of honorable wounds. Their places were supplied by men who had no recommendation but their religion. Of the new captains and lieutenants, it was said, some had been cowherds, some footmen, some noted marauders; some had been so used to wear brogues that they stumbled and shuffled about strangely in their military jack-boots. Not a few of the officers

---

* Clarendon to Rochester, March 14, 168⅚.
† Clarendon to James, March 4, 168⅚. ‡ James to Clarendon, April 6, 1686.
§ Sunderland to Clarendon, May 22, 1686; Clarendon to Ormond, May 30; Clarendon to Sunderland, July 6, 11.

who were discarded took refuge in the Dutch service, and enjoyed, four years later, the pleasure of driving their successors before them in ignominious rout from the margin of the Boyne.*

The distress and alarm of Clarendon were increased by news which reached him through private channels. Without his approbation, without his knowledge, preparations were making for arming and drilling the whole Celtic population of the country of which he was the nominal governor. Tyrconnel from London directed the design; and the prelates of the Roman Catholic Church were his agents. Every priest had been instructed to prepare an exact list of all his male parishioners capable of bearing arms, and to forward it to his bishop.†

It had already been rumored that Tyrconnel would soon return to Dublin armed with extraordinary and independent powers; and the rumor gathered strength daily. The Lord-lieutenant, whom no insult could drive to resign the pomp and emoluments of his place, declared that he should submit cheerfully to the royal pleasure, and approve himself in all things a faithful and obedient subject. He had never, he said, in his life, had any difference with Tyrconnel, and he trusted that no difference would now arise.‡ Clarendon appears not to have recollected that there had once been a plot to ruin the fame of his innocent sister, and that in that plot Tyrconnel had borne a chief part. This is not exactly one of the injuries which high-spirited men most readily pardon. But, in the wicked court where the Hydes had long been pushing their fortunes, such injuries were easily forgiven and forgotten, not from magnanimity or Christian charity, but from mere baseness and want of moral sensibility. In June,

<small>Arrival of Tyrconnel at Dublin as General.</small> 1686, Tyrconnel came. His commission authorized him only to command the troops: but he brought with him royal instructions touching all parts of the administration, and at once took the real government of the island into his own hands. On the day after his arrival

---

* Clarendon to Rochester and Sunderland, June 1, 1686; to Rochester, June 12; King's State of the Protestants of Ireland, Chap. ii., sec. 6, 7; Apology for the Protestants of Ireland, 1689.

† Clarendon to Rochester, May 15, 1686. ‡ Ibid., May 11, 1686.

he explicitly said that commissions must be largely given to Roman Catholic officers, and that room must be made for them by dismissing more Protestants. He pushed on the remodelling of the army eagerly and indefatigably. It was indeed the only part of the functions of a commander-in-chief which he was competent to perform; for, though courageous in brawls and duels, he knew nothing of military duty. At the very first review which he held, it was evident to all who were near him that he did not know how to draw up a regiment.* To turn Englishmen out and to put Irishmen in was, in his view, the beginning and the end of the administration of war. He had the insolence to cashier the Captain of the Lord-lieutenant's own body-guard; nor was Clarendon aware of what had happened till he saw a Roman Catholic, whose face was quite unknown to him, escorting the state coach.† The change was not confined to the officers alone. The ranks were completely broken up and recomposed. Four or five hundred soldiers were turned out of a single regiment chiefly on the ground that they were below the proper stature. Yet the most unpractised eye at once perceived that they were taller and better made men than their successors, whose wild and squalid appearance disgusted the beholders.‡ Orders were given to the new officers that no man of the Protestant religion was to be suffered to enlist. The recruiting-parties, instead of beating their drums for volunteers at fairs and markets, as had been the old practice, repaired to places to which the Roman Catholics were in the habit of making pilgrimages for purposes of devotion. In a few weeks the General had introduced more than two thousand natives into the ranks; and the people about him confidently affirmed that by Christmas-day not a man of English race would be left in the whole army.§

<small>His partiality and violence.</small>

---

* Clarendon to Rochester, June 8, 1686.

† Secret Consults of the Romish Party in Ireland.

‡ Clarendon to Rochester, June 26, and July 4, 1686; Apology for the Protestants of Ireland, 1689.

§ Clarendon to Rochester, July 4, 22, 1686; to Sunderland, July 6; to the King, August 14.

On all questions which arose in the Privy Council, Tyrconnel showed similar violence and partiality. John Keating, Chief-justice of the Common Pleas, a man distinguished by ability, integrity, and loyalty, represented with great mildness that perfect equality was all that the General could reasonably ask for his own Church. The King, he said, evidently meant that no man fit for public trust should be excluded because he was a Roman Catholic, and that no man unfit for public trust should be admitted because he was a Protestant. Tyrconnel immediately began to curse and swear. "I do not know what to say to that; I would have all Catholics in."* The most judicious Irishmen of his own religious persuasion were dismayed at his rashness, and ventured to remonstrate with him; but he drove them from him with imprecations.† His brutality was such that many thought him mad. Yet it was less strange than the shameless volubility with which he uttered falsehoods. He had long before earned the nickname of Lying Dick Talbot; and, at Whitehall, any wild fiction was commonly designated as one of Dick Talbot's truths. He now daily proved that he was well entitled to this unenviable reputation. Indeed in him mendacity was almost a disease. He would, after giving orders for the dismission of English officers, take them into his closet, assure them of his confidence and friendship, and implore Heaven to confound him, sink him, blast him, if he did not take good care of their interests. Sometimes those to whom he had thus perjured himself learned, before the day closed, that he had cashiered them.‡

On his arrival, though he swore savagely at the Act of Settlement, and called the English interest a foul thing, a roguish thing, and a damned thing, he yet pretended to be convinced that the distribution of property could not, after the lapse of so many years, be altered.§ But when he had been a few

---

* Clarendon to Rochester, June 19, 1686. † Ibid., June 22, 1686.

‡ Sheridan MS.; King's State of the Protestants of Ireland, Chap. iii., sec. 3, sec. 8. There is a most striking instance of Tyrconnel's impudent mendacity in Clarendon's Letter to Rochester, July 22, 1686.

§ Clarendon to Rochester, June 8, 1686.

weeks at Dublin, his language changed. He began to ha-
<small>He is bent on the repeal of the Act of Settlement.</small> rangue vehemently at the Council-board on the necessity of giving back the land to the old owners. He had not, however, as yet obtained his master's sanction to this fatal project. National feeling still struggled feebly against superstition in the mind of James. He was an Englishman: he was an English king; and he could not, without some misgivings, consent to the destruction of the greatest colony that England had ever planted. The English Roman Catholics with whom he was in the habit of taking counsel were almost unanimous in favor of the Act of Settlement. Not only the honest and moderate Powis, but the dissolute and headstrong Dover, gave judicious and patriotic advice. Tyrconnel could hardly hope to counteract at a distance the effect which such advice must produce on the royal mind.
<small>He returns to England.</small> He determined to plead the cause of his caste in person; and accordingly he set out, at the end of August, for England.

His presence and his absence were equally dreaded by the Lord-lieutenant. It was, indeed, painful to be daily browbeaten by an enemy: but it was not less painful to know that an enemy was daily breathing calumny and evil counsel in the royal ear. Clarendon was overwhelmed by manifold vexations. He made a progress through the country, and found that he was everywhere treated by the Irish population with contempt. The Roman Catholic priests exhorted their congregations to withhold from him all marks of honor. The native gentry, instead of coming to pay their respects to him, remained at their houses. The native peasantry everywhere sang Celtic ballads in praise of Tyrconnel, who would, they doubted not, soon reappear to complete the humiliation of their oppressors.* The viceroy had scarcely returned to Dublin from his unsatisfactory tour, when he received letters which informed him that he had incurred the King's serious displeasure. His Majesty, so these letters ran, expected his

---

* Clarendon to Rochester, Sept. 23, and Oct. 2, 1686; Secret Consults of the Romish Party in Ireland, 1690.

servants not only to do what he commanded, but to do it from the heart, and with a cheerful countenance. The Lord-lieutenant had not, indeed, refused to co-operate in the reform of the army and of the civil administration: but his co-operation had been reluctant and perfunctory: his looks had betrayed his feelings; and everybody saw that he disapproved of the policy which he was employed to carry into effect.* In great anguish of mind he wrote to defend himself; but he was sternly told that his defence was not satisfactory. He then, in the most abject terms, declared that he would not attempt to justify himself; that he acquiesced in the royal judgment, be it what it might; that he prostrated himself in the dust; that he implored pardon; that of all penitents he was the most sincere; that he should think it glorious to die in his Sovereign's cause, but found it impossible to live under his Sovereign's displeasure. Nor was this mere interested hypocrisy, but, at least in part, unaffected slavishness and poverty of spirit; for in confidential letters, not meant for the royal eye, he bemoaned himself to his family in the same strain. He was miserable: he was crushed: the wrath of the King was insupportable; if that wrath could not be mitigated, life would not be worth having.† The poor man's terror increased when he learned that it had been determined at Whitehall to recall him, and to appoint, as his successor, his rival and calumniator, Tyrconnel.‡ Then for a time the prospect seemed to clear: the King was in better humor; and during a few days Clarendon flattered himself that his brother's intercession had prevailed, and that the crisis was passed.§

The King displeased with Clarendon.

In truth the crisis was only beginning. While Clarendon was trying to lean on Rochester, Rochester was unable longer to support himself. As in Ireland the elder brother, though retaining the guard of honor, the sword of state, and the title of Excellency, had really been superseded by the Commander of the Forces, so in England,

Rochester attacked by the Jesuitical cabal.

---

* Clarendon to Rochester, October 6, 1686.
† Clarendon to the King and to Rochester, October 23, 1686.
‡ Clarendon to Rochester, October 29, 30, 1686. § Ibid., November 27, 1686.

the younger brother, though holding the white staff, and walking, by virtue of his high office, before the greatest hereditary nobles, was fast sinking into a mere financial clerk. The Parliament was again prorogued to a distant day, in opposition to the Treasurer's known wishes. He was not even told that there was to be another prorogation, but was left to learn the news from the Gazette. The real direction of affairs had passed to the cabal which dined with Sunderland on Fridays. The cabinet met only to hear the despatches from foreign courts read; nor did those despatches contain anything which was not known on the Royal Exchange; for all the English Envoys had received orders to put into the official letters only the common talk of antechambers, and to reserve important secrets for private communications which were addressed to James himself, to Sunderland, or to Petre.* Yet the victorious faction was not content. The King was assured by those whom he most trusted that the obstinacy with which the nation opposed his designs was really to be imputed to Rochester. How could the people believe that their Sovereign was unalterably resolved to persevere in the course on which he had entered, when they saw at his right hand, ostensibly first in power and trust among his counsellors, a man who notoriously regarded that course with strong disapprobation? Every step which had been taken with the object of humbling the Church of England and of elevating the Church of Rome, had been opposed by the Treasurer. True it was that, when he had found opposition vain, he had gloomily submitted, nay, that he had sometimes even assisted in carrying into effect the very plans against which he had most earnestly contended. True it was that, though he disliked the Ecclesiastical Commission, he had consented to be a commissioner. True it was that he had, while declaring that he could see nothing blamable in the conduct of the Bishop of London, voted sullenly and reluctantly for the sentence of suspension. But this was not enough. A prince, engaged in an enterprise so important and arduous as that on which

---

* Barillon, Sept. $\frac{13}{23}$, 1686; Life of James the Second, ii., 99.

James was bent, had a right to expect from his first minister, not unwilling and ungracious acquiescence, but zealous and strenuous co-operation. While such advice was daily given to James by those in whom he reposed confidence, he received, by the penny-post, many anonymous letters filled with calumnies against the Lord Treasurer. This mode of attack had been contrived by Tyrconnel, and was in perfect harmony with every part of his infamous life.*

The King hesitated. He seems, indeed, to have really regarded his brother-in-law with personal kindness, the effect of near affinity, of long and familiar intercourse, and of many mutual good offices. It seemed probable that, as long as Rochester continued to submit himself, though tardily and with murmurs, to the royal pleasure, he would continue to be in name prime-minister. Sunderland, therefore, with exquisite cunning, suggested to his master the propriety of asking the only proof of obedience which it was quite certain that Rochester never would give. At present—such was the language of the artful Secretary—it was impossible to consult with the first of the King's servants respecting the object nearest to the King's heart. It was lamentable to think that religious prejudices should, at such a conjuncture, deprive the government of such valuable assistance. Perhaps those prejudices might not prove insurmountable. Then the deceiver whispered that, to his knowledge, Rochester had of late had some misgivings about the points in dispute between the Protestants and Catholics.† This was enough. The King eagerly caught at the hint. He began to flatter himself that he might at once escape from the disagreeable necessity of removing a friend, and secure an able coadjutor for the great work which was in progress. He was also elated by the hope that he might have the merit and the glory of saving a fellow-creature from perdition. He seems, indeed, about this time, to have been seized with an unusually violent fit of zeal for his religion; and this is the more remarkable, because he had just relapsed, after a short interval

Attempts of James to convert Rochester.

---

* Sheridan MS. † Life of James the Second, ii., 100.

of self-restraint, into debauchery which all Christian divines condemn as sinful, and which, in an elderly man married to an agreeable young wife, is regarded even by people of the world as disreputable. Lady Dorchester had returned from Dublin, and was again the King's mistress. Her return was politically of no importance. She had learned by experience the folly of attempting to save her lover from the destruction to which he was running headlong. She therefore suffered the Jesuits to guide his political conduct; and they, in return, suffered her to wheedle him out of money. She was, however, only one of several abandoned women who at this time shared, with his beloved Church, the dominion over his mind.* He seems to have determined to make some amends for neglecting the welfare of his own soul by taking care of the souls of others. He set himself, therefore, to labor with real good-will, but with the good-will of a coarse, stern, and arbitrary mind, for the conversion of his kinsman. Every audience which the Treasurer obtained was spent in arguments about the authority of the Church and the worship of images. Rochester was firmly resolved not to abjure his religion: but he had no scruple about employing in self-defence artifices as discreditable as those which had been used against him. He affected to speak like a man whose mind was not made up, professed himself desirous to be enlightened if he was in error, borrowed Popish books, and listened with civility to Popish divines. He had several interviews with Leyburn, the Vicar Apostolic, with Godden, the chaplain and almoner of the Queen Dowager, and with Bonaventure Giffard, a theologian trained to polemics in the schools of Douay. It was agreed that there should be a formal disputation between these doctors and some Protestant clergymen. The King told Rochester to choose any ministers of the Established Church, with two exceptions. The proscribed persons were Tillotson and Stillingfleet. Tillotson, the most popular preacher of that age, and in manners the most inoffensive of men, had been much connected with some leading

---

* Barillon, Sept. $\frac{13}{23}$, 1686; Bonrepaux, June 4, 1687.

II.—10

Whigs; and Stillingfleet, who was renowned as a consummate master of all the weapons of controversy, had given still deeper offence by publishing an answer to the papers which had been found in the strong-box of Charles the Second. Rochester took the two royal chaplains who happened to be in waiting. One of them was Simon Patrick, whose commentaries on the Bible still form a part of theological libraries: the other was Jane, a vehement Tory, who had assisted in drawing up that decree by which the University of Oxford had solemnly adopted the worst follies of Filmer. The conference took place at Whitehall on the thirtieth of November. Rochester, who did not wish it to be known that he had even consented to hear the arguments of Popish priests, stipulated for secrecy. No auditor was suffered to be present except the King. The subject discussed was the real presence. The Roman Catholic divines took on themselves the burden of the proof. Patrick and Jane said little: nor was it necessary that they should say much; for the Earl himself undertook to defend the doctrine of his Church, and, as was his habit, soon warmed with conflict, lost his temper, and asked with great vehemence whether it was expected that he should change his religion on such frivolous grounds. Then he remembered how much he was risking, began again to dissemble, complimented the disputants on their skill and learning, and asked time to consider what had been said.*

Slow as James was, he could not but see that this was mere trifling. He told Barillon that Rochester's language was not that of a man honestly desirous of arriving at the truth. Still the King did not like to propose directly to his brother-in-law the simple choice, apostasy or dismissal: but, three days after the conference, Barillon waited on the Treasurer, and, with much circumlocution and many expressions of

---

* Barillon, Dec. $\frac{2}{13}$, 1686; Burnet, i., 684; Life of James the Second, ii., 100; Dodd's Church History. I have tried to frame a fair narrative out of these conflicting materials. It seems clear to me, from Rochester's own papers, that he was on this occasion by no means so stubborn as he has been represented by Burnet and by the biographer of James.

friendly concern, broke the unpleasant truth. "Do you mean," said Rochester, bewildered by the involved and ceremonious phrases in which the intimation was made, "that, if I do not turn Catholic, the consequence will be that I shall lose my place?" "I say nothing about consequences," answered the wary diplomatist. "I only come as a friend to express a hope that you will take care to keep your place." "But surely," said Rochester, "the plain meaning of all this is that I must turn Catholic or go out." He put many questions for the purpose of ascertaining whether the communication was made by authority, but could extort only vague and mysterious replies. At last, affecting a confidence which he was far from feeling, he declared that Barillon must have been imposed upon by idle or malicious reports. "I tell you," he said, "that the King will not dismiss me, and I will not resign. I know him: he knows me; and I fear nobody." The Frenchman answered that he was charmed, that he was ravished to hear it, and that his only motive for interfering was a sincere anxiety for the prosperity and dignity of his excellent friend the Treasurer. And thus the two statesmen parted, each flattering himself that he had duped the other.*

Meanwhile, in spite of all injunctions of secrecy, the news that the Lord Treasurer had consented to be instructed in the doctrines of Popery had spread fast through London. Patrick and Jane had been seen going in at that mysterious door which led to Chiffinch's apartments. Some Roman Catholics about the court had, indiscreetly or artfully, told all, and more than all, that they knew. The Tory Churchmen waited anxiously for fuller information. They were mortified to think that their leader should even have pretended to waver in his opinion; but they could not believe that he would stoop to be a renegade. The unfortunate minister, tortured at once by his fierce passions and his low desires, annoyed by the censures of the public, annoyed by the hints which he had received from Barillon, afraid of losing character, afraid of

---

* From Rochester's Minutes, dated Dec. 3, 1686.

losing office, repaired to the royal closet. He was determined to keep his place, if it could be kept by any villany but one. He would pretend to be shaken in his religious opinions, and to be half a convert: he would promise to give strenuous support to that policy which he had hitherto opposed: but, if he were driven to extremity, he would refuse to change his religion. He began, therefore, by telling the King that the business in which His Majesty took so much interest was not sleeping, that Jane and Giffard were engaged in consulting books on the points in dispute between the churches, and that, when these researches were over, it would be desirable to have another conference. Then he complained bitterly that all the town was apprised of what ought to have been carefully concealed, and that some persons, who, from their station, might be supposed to be well informed, reported strange things as to the royal intentions. "It is whispered," he said, "that, if I do not do as Your Majesty would have me, I shall not be suffered to continue in my present station." The King said, with some general expressions of kindness, that it was difficult to prevent people from talking, and that loose reports were not to be regarded. These vague phrases were not likely to quiet the perturbed mind of the minister. His agitation became violent, and he began to plead for his place as if he had been pleading for his life. "Your Majesty sees that I do all in my power to obey you. Indeed, I will do all that I can to obey you in everything. I will serve you in your own way. Nay," he cried, in an agony of baseness, "I will do what I can to believe as you would have me. But do not let me be told, while I am trying to bring my mind to this, that if I find it impossible to comply, I must lose all. For I must needs tell Your Majesty that there are other considerations." "Oh, you must needs!" exclaimed the King with an oath. For a single word of honest and manly sound, escaping in the midst of all this abject supplication, was sufficient to move his anger. "I hope, sir," said poor Rochester, "that I do not offend you. Surely Your Majesty could not think well of me if I did not say so." The King recollected himself, protested that he was not offended, and advised the

Treasurer to disregard idle rumors, and to confer again with Jane and Giffard.*

After this conversation, a fortnight elapsed before the decisive blow fell. That fortnight Rochester passed in intriguing and imploring. He attempted to interest in his favor those Roman Catholics who had the greatest influence at court. He could not, he said, renounce his own religion: but, with that single reservation, he would do all that they could desire. Indeed, if he might only keep his place, they should find that he could be more useful to them as a Protestant than as one of their own communion.† His wife, who was on a sick-bed, had already, it was said, solicited the honor of a visit from the much-injured Queen, and had attempted to work on Her Majesty's feelings of compassion.‡ But the Hydes abased themselves in vain. Petre regarded them with peculiar malevolence, and was bent on their ruin.§ On the evening of the seventeenth of December the Earl was called into the royal closet. James was unusually discomposed, and even shed tears. The occasion, indeed, could not but call up some recollections which might well soften a hard heart. He expressed his regret that his duty made it impossible for him to indulge his private partialities. It was absolutely necessary, he said, that those who had the chief direction of his affairs should partake his opinions and feelings. He owned that he had very great personal obligations to Rochester, and that no fault could be found with the way in which the financial business had lately been done: but the office of Lord Treasurer was of such high importance that, in general, it ought not to be intrusted to a single person, and could not safely be intrusted by a Roman Catholic King to a person zealous for the Church of England. "Think better of it, my Lord," he continued. "Read again the papers from my brother's box. I will give you a little more time for consideration, if you desire it." Rochester saw that all was over, and that the wisest course left to him was

---

* From Rochester's Minutes, Dec. 4, 1686. † Barillon, Dec. $\frac{20}{30}$, 1686.
‡ Burnet, i., 684. § Bonrepaux, $\frac{\text{May 25,}}{\text{June 4,}}$ 1687.

to make his retreat with as much money and as much credit as possible. He succeeded in both objects. He obtained a pension of four thousand pounds a year for two lives on the post-office. He had made great sums out of the estates of traitors, and carried with him in particular Grey's bond for forty thousand pounds, and a grant of all the estate which the crown had in Grey's extensive property.* No person had ever quitted office on terms so advantageous. To the applause of the sincere friends of the Established Church Rochester had, indeed, very slender claims. To save his place he had sat in that tribunal which had been illegally created for the purpose of persecuting her. To save his place he had given a dishonest vote for degrading one of her most eminent ministers, had affected to doubt her orthodoxy, had listened with the outward show of docility to teachers who called her schismatical and heretical, and had offered to co-operate strenuously with her deadliest enemies in their designs against her. The highest praise to which he was entitled was this, that he had shrunk from the exceeding wickedness and baseness of publicly abjuring, for lucre, the religion in which he had been brought up, which he believed to be true, and of which he had long made an ostentatious profession. Yet he was extolled by the great body of Churchmen as if he had been the bravest and purest of martyrs. The Old and New Testaments, the Martyrologies of Eusebius and of Fox, were ransacked to find parallels for his heroic piety. He was Daniel in the den of lions, Shadrach in the fiery furnace, Peter in the dungeon of Herod, Paul at the bar of Nero, Ignatius in the amphitheatre, Latimer at the stake. Among the many facts which prove that the standard of honor and virtue among the public men of that age was low, the admiration excited by Rochester's constancy is, perhaps, the most decisive.

In his fall he dragged down Clarendon. On the seventh of January, 1687, the Gazette announced to the people of Lon-

---

* Rochester's Minutes, Dec. 19, 1686; Barillon, $\frac{\text{Dec. 30,}}{\text{Jan. 9,}}$ 168$\frac{6}{7}$; Burnet, i., 685; Life of James the Second, ii., 102; Treasury Warrant Book, December 29, 1686.

don that the Treasury was put into commission. On the eighth arrived at Dublin a despatch formally signifying that in a month Tyrconnel would assume the government of Ireland. It was not without great difficulty that this man had surmounted the numerous impediments which stood in the way of his ambition. It was well known that the extermination of the English colony in Ireland was the object on which his heart was set. He had, therefore, to overcome some scruples in the royal mind. He had to surmount the opposition, not merely of all the Protestant members of the government, not merely of the moderate and respectable heads of the Roman Catholic body, but even of several members of the Jesuitical cabal.* Sunderland shrank from the thought of an Irish revolution, religious, political, and social. To the Queen Tyrconnel was personally an object of aversion. Powis was therefore suggested as the man best qualified for the viceroyalty. He was of illustrious birth: he was a sincere Roman Catholic; and yet he was generally allowed by candid Protestants to be an honest man and a good Englishman. All opposition, however, yielded to Tyrconnel's energy and cunning. He fawned, bullied, and bribed indefatigably. Petre's help was secured by flattery. Sunderland was plied at once with promises and menaces. An immense price was offered for his support, no less than an annuity of five thousand pounds a year from Ireland, redeemable by payment of fifty thousand pounds down. If this proposal were rejected, Tyrconnel threatened to let the King know that the Lord President had, at the Friday dinners, described His Majesty as a fool who must be governed either by a woman or by a priest. Sunderland, pale and trembling, offered to procure for Tyrconnel supreme military

Dismission of Clarendon.

Tyrconnel Lord Deputy.

---

* Bishop Malony in a letter to Bishop Tyrrel says, "Never a Catholic or other English will ever think or make a step, nor suffer the King to make a step for your restauration, but leave you as you were hitherto, and leave your enemies over your heads: nor is there any Englishman, Catholic or other, of what quality or degree soever alive, that will stick to sacrifice all Ireland for to save the least interest of his own in England, and would as willingly see all Ireland over inhabited by English of whatsoever religion as by the Irish."

command, enormous appointments, anything but the viceroyalty: but all compromise was rejected; and it was necessary to yield. Mary of Modena herself was not free from suspicion of corruption. There was in London a renowned chain of pearls which was valued at ten thousand pounds. It had belonged to Prince Rupert; and by him it had been left to Margaret Hughes, a courtesan who, toward the close of his life, had exercised a boundless empire over him. Tyrconnel loudly boasted that with this chain he had purchased the support of the Queen. There were those, however, who suspected that this story was one of Dick Talbot's truths, and that it had no more foundation than the calumnies which, twenty-six years before, he had invented to blacken the fame of Anne Hyde. To the Roman Catholic courtiers generally he spoke of the uncertain tenure by which they held offices, honors, and emoluments. The King might die to-morrow, and might leave them at the mercy of a hostile government and a hostile rabble. But, if the old faith could be made dominant in Ireland, if the Protestant interest in that country could be destroyed, there would still be, in the worst event, an asylum at hand to which they might retreat, and where they might either negotiate or defend themselves with advantage. A Popish priest was hired with the promise of the mitre of Waterford to preach at Saint James's against the Act of Settlement; and his sermon, though heard with deep disgust by the English part of the auditory, was not without its effect. The struggle which patriotism had for a time maintained against bigotry in the royal mind was at an end. "There is work to be done in Ireland," said James, "which no Englishman will do."*

All obstacles were at length removed; and in February, 1687, Tyrconnel began to rule his native country with the power and appointments of Lord-lieutenant, but with the humbler title of Lord Deputy.

His arrival spread dismay through the whole English population. Clarendon was accompanied, or speedily followed,

---

* The best account of these transactions is in the Sheridan MS.

across Saint George's Channel, by a large proportion of the most respectable inhabitants of Dublin, gentlemen, tradesmen, and artificers. It was said that fifteen hundred families emigrated in a few days. The panic was not unreasonable. The work of putting the colonists down under the feet of the natives went rapidly on. In a short time almost every Privy Councillor, Judge, Sheriff, Mayor, Alderman, and Justice of the Peace was a Celt and a Roman Catholic. It seemed that things would soon be ripe for a general election, and that a House of Commons bent on abrogating the Act of Settlement would easily be assembled.*

<small>Dismay of the English colonists in Ireland.</small>

Those who had lately been the lords of the island now cried out, in the bitterness of their souls, that they had become a prey and a laughing-stock to their own serfs and menials; that houses were burnt and cattle stolen with impunity; that the new soldiers roamed the country, pillaging, insulting, ravishing, maiming, tossing one Protestant in a blanket, tying up another by the hair and scourging him; that to appeal to the law was vain; that Irish Judges, Sheriffs, juries, and witnesses were all in a league to save Irish criminals; and that, even without an Act of Parliament, the whole soil would soon change hands, for that, in every action of ejectment tried under the administration of Tyrconnel, judgment had been given for the native against the Englishman.†

While Clarendon was at Dublin the Privy Seal had been in the hands of Commissioners. His friends hoped that it would, on his return to London, be again delivered to him. But the King and the Jesuitical cabal had determined that the disgrace of the Hydes should be complete. Lord Arundell of Wardour, a Roman Catholic, obtained the Privy Seal. Bellasyse, a Roman Catholic, was made First Lord of the Treasury; and Dover, another Roman Catholic, had a seat at the board. The appointment of a ruined gambler to such a trust would alone have sufficed to disgust the public. The

---

* Sheridan MS.; Oldmixon's Memoirs of Ireland; King's State of the Protestants of Ireland, particularly Chapter iii.; Apology for the Protestants of Ireland, 1689.

† Secret Consults of the Romish Party in Ireland, 1690.

dissolute Etherege, who then resided at Ratisbon as English envoy, could not refrain from expressing, with a sneer, his hope that his old boon companion, Dover, would keep the King's money better than his own. In order that the finances might not be ruined by incapable and inexperienced Papists, the obsequious, diligent, and silent Godolphin was named a Commissioner of the Treasury, but continued to be Chamberlain to the Queen.*

The dismission of the two brothers is a great epoch in the reign of James. From that time it was clear that what he really wanted was not liberty of conscience for the members of his own church, but liberty to persecute the members of other churches. Pretending to abhor tests, he had himself imposed a test. He thought it hard, he thought it monstrous, that able and loyal men should be excluded from the public service solely for being Roman Catholics. Yet he had himself turned out of office a Treasurer, whom he admitted to be both loyal and able, solely for being a Protestant. The cry was that a general proscription was at hand, and that every public functionary must make up his mind to lose his soul or to lose his place.† Who indeed could hope to stand where the Hydes had fallen? They were the brothers-in-law of the King, the uncles and natural guardians of his children, his friends from early youth, his steady adherents in adversity and peril, his obsequious servants since he had been on the throne. Their sole crime was their religion; and for this crime they had been discarded. In great perturbation men began to look round for help; and soon all eyes were fixed on one whom a rare concurrence both of personal qualities and of fortuitous circumstances pointed out as the deliverer.

Effect of the fall of the Hydes.

---

* London Gazette, Jan. 6, and March 14, 168⁶⁄₇; Evelyn's Diary, March 10. Etherege's letter to Dover is in the British Museum.

† "Pare che gli animi sono inaspriti della voce che corre per il popolo, d'esser cacciato il detto ministro per non essere Cattolico, perciò tirarsi al esterminio de' Protestanti."—Adda, $\frac{\text{Dec. 31,}}{\text{Jan. 10,}}$ 1687.

CHAPTER VII.

<small>1687.
William, Prince of Orange.</small>
The place which William Henry, Prince of Orange Nassau, occupies in the history of England and of mankind is so great that it may be desirable to portray with some minuteness the strong lineaments of his character.*

He was now in his thirty-seventh year. But both in body and in mind he was older than other men of the same age. <small>His appearance.</small> Indeed it might be said that he had never been young. His external appearance is almost as well known to us as to his own captains and counsellors. Sculptors, painters, and medallists exerted their utmost skill in the work of transmitting his features to posterity; and his features were such as no artist could fail to seize, and such as, once seen, could never be forgotten. His name at once calls up before us a slender and feeble frame, a lofty and ample forehead, a nose curved like the beak of an eagle, an eye rivalling that of an eagle in brightness and keenness, a thoughtful and somewhat sullen brow, a firm and somewhat peevish mouth, a cheek pale, thin, and deeply furrowed by sickness and by care. That pensive, severe, and solemn aspect could scarcely have belonged to a happy or a good-humored man. But it indicates, in a manner not to be mistaken, capacity equal to the most arduous enterprises, and fortitude not to be shaken by reverses or dangers.

---

* The chief materials from which I have taken my description of the Prince of Orange will be found in Burnet's History, in Temple's and Gourville's Memoirs, in the Negotiations of the Counts of Estrades and Avaux, in Sir George Downing's Letters to Lord Chancellor Clarendon, in Wagenaar's voluminous History, in Van Kamper's Karakterkunde der Vaderlandsche Geschiedenis, and, above all, in William's own confidential correspondence, of which the Duke of Portland permitted Sir James Mackintosh to take a copy.

Nature had largely endowed William with the qualities of a great ruler; and education had developed those qualities in His early life and education. no common degree. With strong natural sense, and rare force of will, he found himself, when first his mind began to open, a fatherless and motherless child, the chief of a great but depressed and disheartened party, and the heir to vast and indefinite pretensions, which excited the dread and aversion of the oligarchy then supreme in the United Provinces. The common people, fondly attached during three generations to his house, indicated, whenever they saw him, in a manner not to be mistaken, that they regarded him as their rightful head. The able and experienced ministers of the republic, mortal enemies of his name, came every day to pay their feigned civilities to him, and to observe the progress of his mind. The first movements of his ambition were carefully watched: every unguarded word uttered by him was noted down; nor had he near him any adviser on whose judgment reliance could be placed. He was scarcely fifteen years old when all the domestics who were attached to his interest, or who enjoyed any share of his confidence, were removed from under his roof by the jealous government. He remonstrated with energy beyond his years, but in vain. Vigilant observers saw the tears more than once rise in the eyes of the young state prisoner. His health, naturally delicate, sank for a time under the emotions which his desolate situation had produced. Such situations bewilder and unnerve the weak, but call forth all the strength of the strong. Surrounded by snares in which an ordinary youth would have perished, William learned to tread at once warily and firmly. Long before he reached manhood he knew how to keep secrets, how to baffle curiosity by dry and guarded answers, how to conceal all passions under the same show of grave tranquillity. Meanwhile he made little proficiency in fashionable or literary accomplishments. The manners of the Dutch nobility of that age wanted the grace which was found in the highest perfection among the gentlemen of France, and which, in an inferior degree, embellished the court of England; and his manners were altogether Dutch. Even his countrymen thought him blunt. To foreigners he often seemed churlish. In his intercourse with the world in general he appeared ignorant or negligent of those arts which double the value of a favor and take away the sting of a refusal. He was little interested in letters or science. The discoveries of Newton and Leibnitz, the poems of Dryden and Boileau, were unknown to him. Dramatic performances tired him; and he was glad to turn away from the stage and to talk about public affairs, while Orestes was raving, or while Tartuffe was pressing Elmira's hand. He had indeed some talent for sarcasm, and not seldom employed, quite unconsciously, a natural rhetoric, quaint, indeed, but vigorous and original. He did not, however, in the least affect the character of a wit or of an orator. His attention had been confined to those studies which form strenuous and sagacious men of business. From a child he listened with interest when high questions of alliance, finance, and war were discussed. Of geometry he learned as much as was necessary for the construction of a ravelin or a hornwork. Of languages, by the help of a memory singularly powerful, he learned as much as was necessary to enable him to comprehend and answer without assistance everything that was said to him, and every letter which he received. The Dutch was his own tongue. With the French he was not less familiar. He understood Latin, Italian, and Spanish. He spoke and wrote English and German, inelegantly, it is true, and inexactly, but fluently and intelligibly. No qualification could be more important to a man whose life was to be passed in organizing great alliances, and in commanding armies assembled from different countries.

One class of philosophical questions had been forced on his attention by circumstances, and seemed to have interested him more than might have been expected from his general character. Among the Protestants of the United Provinces, as among the Protestants of our island, there were two great religious parties which almost exactly coincided with two great political parties. The chiefs of the municipal oligarchy were Arminians, and were commonly regarded by the multitude as little better than Papists. The

His theological opinions.

princes of Orange had generally been the patrons of the Calvinistic divinity, and owed no small part of their popularity to their zeal for the doctrines of election and final perseverance, a zeal not always enlightened by knowledge or tempered by humanity. William had been carefully instructed from a child in the theological system to which his family was attached; and he regarded that system with even more than the partiality which men generally feel for a hereditary faith. He had ruminated on the great enigmas which had been discussed in the Synod of Dort, and had found in the austere and inflexible logic of the Genevese school something which suited his intellect and his temper. That example of intolerance, indeed, which some of his predecessors had set he never imitated. For all persecution he felt a fixed aversion, which he avowed, not only where the avowal was obviously politic, but on occasions where it seemed that his interest would have been promoted by dissimulation or by silence. His theological opinions, however, were even more decided than those of his ancestors. The tenet of predestination was the keystone of his religion. He often declared that, if he were to abandon that tenet, he must abandon with it all belief in a superintending Providence, and must become a mere Epicurean. Except in this single instance, all the sap of his vigorous mind was early drawn away from the speculative to the practical. The faculties which are necessary for the conduct of important business ripened in him at a time of life when they have scarcely begun to blossom in ordinary men. Since Octavius the world had seen no such instance of precocious statesmanship. Skilful diplomatists were surprised to hear the weighty observations which at seventeen the Prince made on public affairs, and still more surprised to see a lad, in situations in which he might have been expected to betray strong passion, preserve a composure as imperturbable as their own. At eighteen he sat among the fathers of the commonwealth, grave, discreet, and judicious as the oldest among them. At twenty-one, in a day of gloom and terror, he was placed at the head of the administration. At twenty-three he was renowned throughout Europe as a soldier and a politician. He had put domestic factions under his feet: he was the soul of a mighty coalition; and he had contended with honor in the field against some of the greatest generals of the age.

His personal tastes were those rather of a warrior than of a statesman: but he, like his great-grandfather, the silent prince who founded the Batavian commonwealth, occupies a far higher place among statesmen than among warriors. The event of battles, indeed, is not an unfailing test of the abilities of a commander; and it would be peculiarly unjust to apply this test to William; for it was his fortune to be almost always opposed to captains who were consummate masters of their art, and to troops far superior in discipline to his own. Yet there is reason to believe that he was by no means equal, as a general in the field, to some who ranked far below him in intellectual powers. To those whom he trusted he spoke on this subject with the magnanimous frankness of a man who had done great things, and who could well afford to acknowledge some deficiencies. He had never, he said, served an apprenticeship to the military profession. He had been placed, while still a boy, at the head of an army. Among his officers there had been none competent to instruct him. His own blunders and their consequences had been his only lessons. "I would give," he once, exclaimed, "a good part of my estates to have served a few campaigns under the Prince of Condé before I had to command against him." It is not improbable that the circumstance which prevented William from attaining any eminent dexterity in strategy may have been favorable to the general vigor of his intellect. If his battles were not those of a great tactician, they entitled him to be called a great man. No disaster could for one moment deprive him of his firmness or of the entire possession of all his faculties. His defeats were repaired with such marvellous celerity that before his enemies had sung the Te Deum, he was again ready for conflict; nor did his adverse fortune ever deprive him of the respect and confidence of his soldiers. That respect and confidence he owed in no small measure to his personal courage. Courage, in the degree which is necessary to carry a soldier without disgrace through a campaign, is possessed, or might, under proper training, be acquired, by the great majority of men. But courage like that of William is rare indeed. He was proved by every test; by war, by wounds, by painful and depressing maladies, by raging seas, by the imminent and constant risk of assassination, a risk which has shaken very strong nerves, a risk which severely tried even the adamantine fortitude of Cromwell. Yet none could ever discover what that thing was which the Prince of Orange feared. His advisers could with difficulty induce him to take any precaution against the pistols and daggers of conspirators.* Old sailors were amazed at the composure which he preserved amidst roaring breakers on a perilous coast. In battle his bravery made him conspicuous even among tens of thousands of brave warriors, drew forth the generous applause of hostile armies, and was scarcely ever questioned even by the injustice of hostile factions. During his first campaigns he exposed himself like a man who sought for death, was almost foremost in the charge and last in the retreat, fought, sword in hand, in the thickest press, and, with a musket ball in his arm and the blood streaming over his cuirass, still stood his ground and waved his hat under the hottest fire. His friends adjured him to take more care of a life invaluable to his country; and his most illustrious antagonist, the great Condé, remarked, after the bloody day of Seneff, that the Prince of Orange had in all things borne himself like an old general, except in exposing himself like a young soldier. William denied that he was guilty of temerity. It was, he said, from a sense of duty, and on a cool calculation of what the public interest required, that he was always at the post of danger. The troops which he commanded had been little used to war, and shrank from a close en-

---

* William was earnestly entreated by his friends, after the peace of Ryswick, to speak seriously to the French ambassador about the schemes of assassination which the Jacobites of Saint Germain's were constantly contriving. The cold magnanimity with which these intimations of danger were received is singularly characteristic. To Bentinck, who had sent from Paris very alarming intelligence, William merely replied, at the end of a long letter of business, "Pour les assasins je ne luy en ay pas voulu parler, croiant que c'étoit au desous de moy." May $\frac{2}{12}$, 1698. I keep the original orthography, if it is to be so called.

counter with the veteran soldiery of France. It was necessary that their leader should show them how battles were to be won. And in truth more than one day which had seemed hopelessly lost was retrieved by the hardihood with which he rallied his broken battalions and cut down the cowards who set the example of flight. Sometimes, however, it seemed that he had a strange pleasure in venturing his person. It was remarked that his spirits were never so high and his manners never so gracious and easy as amidst the tumult and carnage of a battle. Even in his pastimes he liked the excitement of danger. Cards, chess, and billiards gave him no pleasure. The chase was his favorite recreation; and he loved it most when it was most hazardous. His leaps were sometimes such that his boldest companions did not like to follow him. He seems even to have thought the most hardy field sports of England effeminate, and to have pined in the Great Park of Windsor for the game which he had been used to drive to bay in the forests of Guelders — wolves, and wild boars, and huge stags with sixteen antlers.*

The audacity of his spirit was the more remarkable because his physical organization was unusually delicate. From a child he had been weak and sickly. In the prime of manhood his complaints had been aggravated by a severe attack of small-pox. He was asthmatic and consumptive. His slender frame was shaken by a constant hoarse cough. He could not sleep unless his head was propped by several pillows, and could scarcely draw his breath in any but the purest air. Cruel headaches frequently tortured him. Exertion soon fatigued him. The physicians constantly kept up the hopes of his enemies by fixing some date beyond which, if there were anything certain in medical science, it was impossible that his broken constitution could

His love of danger: his bad health.

---

* From Windsor he wrote to Bentinck, then ambassador at Paris. "J'ay pris avant hier un cerf dans la forest avec les chains du Pr. de Denm. et ay fait un assez jolie chasse, autant que ce vilain paiis le permest." $\frac{\text{March 20,}}{\text{April 1,}}$ 1698. The spelling is bad, but not worse than Napoleon's. William wrote in better humor from Loo. "Nous avons pris deux gros cerfs, le premier dans Dorewaert, qui est un des plus gros que je sache avoir jamais pris. Il porte seize." $\frac{\text{Oct. 25,}}{\text{Nov. 4,}}$ 1697.

II.—11

hold out. Yet, through a life which was one long disease, the force of his mind never failed, on any great occasion, to bear up his suffering and languid body.

He was born with violent passions and quick sensibilities: but the strength of his emotions was not suspected by the world. From the multitude his joy and his grief, his affection and his resentment, were hidden by a phlegmatic serenity, which made him pass for the most cold-blooded of mankind. Those who brought him good news could seldom detect any sign of pleasure. Those who saw him after a defeat looked in vain for any trace of vexation. He praised and reprimanded, rewarded and punished, with the stern tranquillity of a Mohawk chief: but those who knew him well and saw him near were aware that under all this ice a fierce fire was constantly burning. It was seldom that anger deprived him of power over himself. But when he was really enraged the first outbreak of his passion was terrible. It was indeed scarcely safe to approach him. On these rare occasions, however, as soon as he regained his self-command, he made such ample reparation to those whom he had wronged as tempted them to wish that he would go into a fury again. His affection was as impetuous as his wrath. Where he loved, he loved with the whole energy of his strong mind. When death separated him from what he loved, the few who witnessed his agonies trembled for his reason and his life. To a very small circle of intimate friends, on whose fidelity and secrecy he could absolutely depend, he was a different man from the reserved and stoical William, whom the multitude supposed to be destitute of human feelings. He was kind, cordial, open, even convivial and jocose, would sit at table many hours, and would bear his full share in festive conversation. Highest in his favor stood a gentleman of his household named Bentinck, sprung from a noble Batavian race, and destined to be the founder of one of the great patrician houses of England. The fidelity of Bentinck had been tried by no common test. It was while the United Provinces were struggling for existence against the French power that the young Prince on whom all their hopes were fixed was seized by the small-pox. That disease had been fatal to many members of his family, and at first wore, in his case, a peculiarly malignant aspect. The public consternation was great. The streets of the Hague were crowded from daybreak to sunset by persons anxiously asking how His Highness was. At length his complaint took a favorable turn. His escape was attributed partly to his own singular equanimity, and partly to the intrepid and indefatigable friendship of Bentinck. From the hands of Bentinck alone William took food and medicine. By Bentinck alone William was lifted from his bed and laid down in it. "Whether Bentinck slept or not while I was ill," said William to Temple, with great tenderness, "I know not. But this I know, that, through sixteen days and nights, I never once called for anything but that Bentinck was instantly at my side." Before the faithful servant had entirely performed his task, he had himself caught the contagion. Still, however, he bore up against drowsiness and fever till his master was pronounced convalescent. Then, at length, Bentinck asked leave to go home. It was time: for his limbs would no longer support him. He was in great danger, but recovered, and, as soon as he left his bed, hastened to the army, where, during many sharp campaigns, he was ever found, as he had been in peril of a different kind, close to William's side.

Such was the origin of a friendship as warm and pure as any that ancient or modern history records. The descendants of Bentinck still preserve many letters written by William to their ancestor: and it is not too much to say that no person who has not studied those letters can form a correct notion of the Prince's character. He, whom even his admirers generally accounted the most distant and frigid of men, here forgets all distinctions of rank, and pours out all his thoughts with the ingenuousness of a school-boy. He imparts without reserve secrets of the highest moment. He explains with perfect simplicity vast designs affecting all the governments of Europe. Mingled with his communications on such subjects are other communications of a very different, but perhaps not of a less interesting kind. All his adventures, all his personal feelings, his long runs after enormous stags, his carousals on Saint Hubert's Day, the growth of his plantations, the failure of his melons, the state of his stud, his wish to procure an easy pad nag for his wife, his vexation at learning that one of his household, after ruining a girl of good family, refused to marry her, his fits of seasickness, his coughs, his headaches, his devotional moods, his gratitude for the divine protection after a great escape, his struggles to submit himself to the divine will after a disaster, are described with an amiable garrulity hardly to have been expected from the most discreet and sedate statesman of the age. Still more remarkable is the careless effusion of his tenderness, and the brotherly interest which he takes in his friend's domestic felicity. When an heir is born to Bentinck, "he will live, I hope," says William, "to be as good a fellow as you are; and, if I should have a son, our children will love each other, I hope, as we have done."* Through life he continues to regard the little Bentincks with paternal kindness. He calls them by endearing diminutives: he takes charge of them in their father's absence, and, though vexed at being forced to refuse them any pleasure, will not suffer them to go on a hunting-party, where there would be risk of a push from a stag's horn, or to sit up late at a riotous supper.† When their mother is taken ill during her husband's absence, William, in the midst of business of the highest moment, finds time to send off several expresses in one day with short notes containing intelligence of her state.‡ On one occasion, when she is pronounced out of danger after a severe attack, the Prince breaks forth into fervent expressions of gratitude to God. "I write," he says, "with tears of joy

---

* March 3, 1679.

† "Voilà en peu de mot le detail de nostre St. Hubert. Et j'ay eu soin que M. Woodstoc" (Bentinck's eldest son) "n'a point esté à la chasse, bien moin au soupé, quoyqu'il fut icy. Vous pouvez pourtant croire que de n'avoir pas chassé l'a un peu mortifié, mais je ne l'ay pas ausé prendre sur moy, puisque vous m'aviez dit que vous ne le souhaitiez' pas." From Loo, Nov. 4, 1679.

‡ On the 15th of June, 1688.

in my eyes."* There is a singular charm in such letters, penned by a man whose irresistible energy and inflexible firmness extorted the respect of his enemies, whose cold and ungracious demeanor repelled the attachment of almost all his partisans, and whose mind was occupied by gigantic schemes which have changed the face of the world.

His kindness was not misplaced. Bentinck was early pronounced by Temple to be the best and truest servant that ever prince had the good fortune to possess, and continued through life to merit that honorable character. The friends were indeed made for each other. William wanted neither a guide nor a flatterer. Having a firm and just reliance on his own judgment, he was not partial to counsellors who dealt much in suggestions and objections. At the same time he had too much discernment, and too much elevation of mind, to be gratified by sycophancy. The confidant of such a prince ought to be a man, not of inventive genius or commanding spirit, but brave and faithful, capable of executing orders punctually, of keeping secrets inviolably, of observing facts vigilantly, and of reporting them truly; and such a man was Bentinck.

William was not less fortunate in marriage than in friendship. Yet his marriage had not at first promised much domestic happiness. His choice had been determined chiefly by political considerations: nor did it seem likely that any strong affection would grow up between a handsome girl of sixteen, well disposed indeed, and naturally intelligent, but ignorant and simple, and a bridegroom who, though he had not completed his twenty-eighth year, was in constitution older than her father, whose manner was chilling, and whose head was constantly occupied by public business or by field sports. For a time William was a negligent husband. He was indeed drawn away from his wife by other women, particularly by one of her ladies, Elizabeth Villiers, who, though destitute of personal attractions, and disfigured by a hideous squint, possessed talents which well fitted her to

_{Mary, Princess of Orange.}

---

* September 6, 1679.

partake his cares.* He was indeed ashamed of his errors, and spared no pains to conceal them: but, in spite of all his precautions, Mary well knew that he was not strictly faithful to her. Spies and tale-bearers, encouraged by her father, did their best to inflame her resentment. A man of a very different character, the excellent Ken, who was her chaplain at the Hague during some months, was so much incensed by her wrongs that he, with more zeal than discretion, threatened to reprimand her husband severely.† She, however, bore her injuries with a meekness and patience which deserved, and gradually obtained, William's esteem and gratitude. Yet there still remained one cause of estrangement. A time would probably come when the Princess, who had been educated only to work embroidery, to play on the spinet, and to read the Bible and the Whole Duty of Man, would be the chief of a great monarchy, and would hold the balance of Europe, while her lord, ambitious, versed in affairs, and bent on great enterprises, would find in the British government no place marked out for him, and would hold power only from her bounty and during her pleasure. It is not strange that a man so fond of authority as William, and so conscious of a genius for command, should have strongly felt that jealousy which, during a few hours of royalty, put dissension between Guildford Dudley and the Lady Jane, and which produced a rupture still more tragical between Darnley and the Queen of Scots. The Princess of Orange had not the faintest suspicion of her husband's feelings. Her preceptor, Bishop Compton, had instructed her carefully in religion, and had especially guarded her mind against the arts of Roman Catholic divines, but had left her profoundly ignorant of the English constitution and of her own position. She knew that her marriage vow bound her to obey her husband; and it had never occurred to her that the relation in which they stood to each other might one day be inverted. She had been nine years married before she discovered the cause of William's discontent; nor would she

---

* See Swift's account of her in the Journal to Stella.
† Henry Sidney's Journal of March 31, 1680, in Mr. Blencowe's interesting collection.

ever have learned it from himself. In general his temper inclined him rather to brood over his griefs than to give utterance to them; and in this particular case his lips were sealed by a very natural delicacy. At length a complete explanation and reconciliation were brought about by the agency of Gilbert Burnet.

The fame of Burnet has been attacked with singular malice and pertinacity. The attack began early in his life, and is still carried on with undiminished vigor, though he has now been more than a century and a quarter in his grave. He is indeed as fair a mark as factious animosity and petulant wit could desire. The faults of his understanding and temper lie on the surface, and cannot be missed. They were not the faults which are ordinarily considered as belonging to his country. Alone among the many Scotchmen who have raised themselves to distinction and prosperity in England, he had that character which satirists, novelists, and dramatists have agreed to ascribe to Irish adventurers. His high animal spirits, his boastfulness, his undissembled vanity, his propensity to blunder, his provoking indiscretion, his unabashed audacity, afforded inexhaustible subjects of ridicule to the Tories. Nor did his enemies omit to compliment him, sometimes with more pleasantry than delicacy, on the breadth of his shoulders, the thickness of his calves, and his success in matrimonial projects on amorous and opulent widows. Yet Burnet, though open in many respects to ridicule, and even to serious censure, was no contemptible man. His parts were quick, his industry unwearied, his reading various and most extensive. He was at once a historian, an antiquary, a theologian, a preacher, a pamphleteer, a debater, and an active political leader; and in every one of these characters he made himself conspicuous among able competitors. The many spirited tracts which he wrote on passing events are now known only to the curious: but his History of his own Times, his History of the Reformation, his Exposition of the Articles, his Discourse of Pastoral Care, his Life of Hale, his Life of Wilmot, are still reprinted, nor is any good private library without them. Against such a fact as this all the

Gilbert Burnet.

efforts of detractors are vain. A writer, whose voluminous works, in several branches of literature, find numerous readers a hundred and thirty years after his death, may have had great faults, but must also have had great merits: and Burnet had great merits, a fertile and vigorous mind, and a style, far indeed removed from faultless purity, but generally clear, often lively, and sometimes rising to solemn and fervid eloquence. In the pulpit the effect of his discourses, which were delivered without any note, was heightened by a noble figure and by pathetic action. He was often interrupted by the deep hum of his audience; and when, after preaching out the hour-glass, which in those days was part of the furniture of the pulpit, he held it up in his hand, the congregation clamorously encouraged him to go on till the sand had run off once more.* In his moral character, as in his intellect, great blemishes were more than compensated by great excellence. Though often misled by prejudice and passion, he was emphatically an honest man. Though he was not secure from the seductions of vanity, his spirit was raised high above the influence both of cupidity and of fear. His nature was kind, generous, grateful, forgiving.† His religious zeal, though steady and ardent, was in general restrained by humanity, and by a respect for the rights of conscience. Strongly attached to what he regarded as the spirit of Christianity, he looked with indifference on rites, names, and forms of ecclesiastical

---

* Speaker Onslow's note on Burnet, i., 596; Johnson's Life of Sprat.

† No person has contradicted Burnet more frequently or with more asperity than Dartmouth. Yet Dartmouth wrote, "I do not think he designedly published anything he believed to be false." At a later period Dartmouth, provoked by some remarks on himself in the second volume of the bishop's history, retracted this praise: but to such a retraction little importance can be attached. Even Swift has the justice to say, "After all, he was a man of generosity and good-nature."— Short Remarks on Bishop Burnet's History.

It is usual to censure Burnet as a singularly inaccurate historian; but I believe the charge to be altogether unjust. He appears to be singularly inaccurate only because his narrative has been subjected to a scrutiny singularly severe and unfriendly. If any Whig thought it worth while to subject Reresby's Memoirs, North's Examen, Mulgrave's Account of the Revolution, or the Life of James the Second, to a similar scrutiny, it would soon appear that Burnet was far indeed from being the most inexact writer of his time.

polity, and was by no means disposed to be severe even on infidels and heretics whose lives were pure, and whose errors appeared to be the effect rather of some perversion of the understanding than of the depravity of the heart. But, like many other good men of that age, he regarded the case of the Church of Rome as an exception to all ordinary rules.

Burnet had during some years enjoyed a European reputation. His History of the Reformation had been received with loud applause by all Protestants, and had been felt by the Roman Catholics as a severe blow. The greatest Doctor that the Church of Rome has produced since the schism of the sixteenth century, Bossuet, Bishop of Meaux, was engaged in framing an elaborate reply. Burnet had been honored by a vote of thanks from one of the zealous Parliaments which had sat during the excitement of the Popish Plot, and had been exhorted, in the name of the Commons of England, to continue his historical researches. He had been admitted to familiar conversation both with Charles and James, had lived on terms of close intimacy with several distinguished statesmen, particularly with Halifax, and had been the spiritual guide of some persons of the highest note. He had reclaimed from atheism and from licentiousness one of the most brilliant libertines of the age, John Wilmot, Earl of Rochester. Lord Stafford, the victim of Oates, had, though a Roman Catholic, been edified in his last hours by Burnet's exhortations touching those points on which all Christians agree. A few years later a more illustrious sufferer, Lord Russell, had been accompanied by Burnet from the Tower to the scaffold in Lincoln's Inn Fields. The court had neglected no means of gaining so active and able a divine. Neither royal blandishments nor promises of valuable preferment had been spared. But Burnet, though infected in early youth by those servile doctrines which were commonly held by the clergy of that age, had become on conviction a Whig; and he firmly adhered through all vicissitudes to his principles. He had, however, no part in that conspiracy which brought so much disgrace and calamity on the Whig party, and not only abhorred the murderous designs of Goodenough and Ferguson, but was of opinion that even his beloved and honored friend Russell had gone to unjustifiable lengths against the government. A time at length arrived when innocence was not a sufficient protection. Burnet, though not guilty of any legal offence, was pursued by the vengeance of the court. He retired to the Continent, and, after passing about a year in those wanderings through Switzerland, Italy, and Germany, of which he has left us an agreeable narrative, reached the Hague in the summer of 1686, and was received there with kindness and respect. He had many free conversations with the Princess on politics and religion, and soon became her spiritual director and confidential adviser. William proved a much more gracious host than could have been expected. Of all faults officiousness and indiscretion were the most offensive to him; and Burnet was allowed even by friends and admirers to be the most officious and indiscreet of mankind. But the sagacious Prince perceived that this pushing, talkative divine, who was always blabbing secrets, putting impertinent questions, obtruding unasked advice, was nevertheless an upright, courageous, and able man, well acquainted with the temper and the views of British sects and factions. The fame of Burnet's eloquence and erudition was also widely spread. William was not himself a reading man. But he had now been many years at the head of the Dutch administration, in an age when the Dutch press was one of the most formidable engines by which the public mind of Europe was moved, and though he had no taste for literary pleasures, was far too wise and too observant to be ignorant of the value of literary assistance. He was aware that a popular pamphlet might sometimes be of as much service as a victory in the field. He also felt the importance of having always near him some person well informed as to the civil and ecclesiastical polity of our island: and Burnet was eminently qualified to be of use as a living dictionary of British affairs. For his knowledge, though not always accurate, was of immense extent; and there were in England and Scotland few eminent men of any political or religious party with whom he had not conversed. He was therefore admitted to as large a share of favor and confidence as was granted to any but those who composed the very small inmost knot of the Prince's private friends. When the Doctor took liberties, which was not seldom the case, his patron became more than usually cold and sullen, and sometimes uttered a short dry sarcasm which would have struck dumb any person of ordinary assurance. In spite of such occurrences, however, the amity between this singular pair continued, with some temporary interruptions, till it was dissolved by death. Indeed, it was not easy to wound Burnet's feelings. His self-complacency, his animal spirits, and his want of tact, were such that, though he frequently gave offence, he never took it.

All the peculiarities of his character fitted him to be the peace-maker between William and Mary. When persons who ought to esteem and love each other are kept asunder, as often happens, by some cause which three words of frank explanation would remove, they are fortunate if they possess an indiscreet friend who blurts out the whole truth. Burnet plainly told the Princess what the feeling was which preyed upon her husband's mind. She learned for the first time, with no small astonishment, that, when she became Queen of England, William would not share her throne. She warmly declared that there was no proof of conjugal submission and affection which she was not ready to give. Burnet, with many apologies and with solemn protestations that no human being had put words into his mouth, informed her that the remedy was in her own hands. She might easily, when the crown devolved on her, induce her Parliament not only to give the regal title to her husband, but even to transfer to him by a legislative act the administration of the government. "But," he added, "your Royal Highness ought to consider well before you announce any such resolution. For it is a resolution which, having once been announced, cannot safely or easily be retracted." "I want no time for consideration," answered Mary. "It is enough that I have an opportunity of showing my regard for the Prince. Tell him what I say; and bring him to me that he may hear it from my own lips." Burnet went in quest of William: but William was many miles off after a stag. It was not till the

[margin: He brings about a good understanding between the Prince and Princess.]

next day that the decisive interview took place. "I did not know till yesterday," said Mary, "that there was such a difference between the laws of England and the laws of God. But I now promise you that you shall always bear rule; and, in return, I ask only this, that, as I shall observe the precept which enjoins wives to obey their husbands, you will observe that which enjoins husbands to love their wives." Her generous affection completely gained the heart of William. From that time till the sad day when he was carried away in fits from her dying bed, there was entire friendship and confidence between them. Many of her letters to him are extant; and they contain abundant evidence that this man, unamiable as he was in the eyes of the multitude, had succeeded in inspiring a beautiful and virtuous woman, born his superior, with a passion fond even to idolatry.

The service which Burnet had rendered to his country was of high moment. A time had arrived at which it was important to the public safety that there should be entire concord between the Prince and Princess.

Till after the suppression of the Western insurrection grave causes of dissension had separated William from both Whigs and Tories. He had seen with displeasure the attempts of the Whigs to strip the executive government of some powers which he thought necessary to its efficiency and dignity. He had seen with still deeper displeasure the countenance given by a large section of that party to the pretensions of Monmouth. The opposition, it seemed, wished first to make the crown of England not worth the wearing, and then to place it on the head of a bastard and impostor. At the same time the Prince's religious system differed widely from that which was the badge of the Tories. They were Arminians and Prelatists. They looked down on the Protestant Churches of the Continent, and regarded every line of their own liturgy and rubric as scarcely less sacred than the gospels. His opinions touching the metaphysics of theology were Calvinistic. His opinions touching ecclesiastical polity and modes of worship were latitudinarian. He owned that episcopacy was a lawful and convenient form of church

Relations between William and English parties.

government; but he spoke with sharpness and scorn of the bigotry of those who thought episcopal ordination essential to a Christian society. He had no scruple about the vestments and gestures prescribed by the Book of Common Prayer. But he avowed that he should like the rites of the Church of England better if they reminded him less of the rites of the Church of Rome. He had been heard to utter an ominous growl when first he saw, in his wife's private chapel, an altar decked after the Anglican fashion, and had not seemed well pleased at finding her with Hooker's Ecclesiastical Polity in her hands.*

He therefore long observed the contest between the English factions attentively, but without feeling a strong predilection for either side. Nor in truth did he ever, to the end of his life, become either a Whig or a Tory. He wanted that which is the common groundwork of both characters; for he never became an Englishman. He saved England, it is true; but he never loved her; and he never obtained her love. To him she was always a land of exile, visited with reluctance and quitted with delight. Even when he rendered to her those services of which, at this day, we feel the happy effects, her welfare was not his chief object. Whatever patriotic feeling he had was for Holland. There was the stately tomb where slept the great politician whose blood, whose name, whose temperament, and whose genius he had inherited. There the very sound of his title was a spell which had, through three generations, called forth the affectionate enthusiasm of boors and artisans. The Dutch language was the language of his nursery. Among the Dutch gentry he had chosen his early friends. The amusements, the architecture, the landscape of his native country, had taken hold on his heart. To her he turned with constant fondness from a prouder and fairer rival. In the gallery of Whitehall he pined for the familiar House in the Wood at the Hague, and never was so

His feelings toward England.

His feelings toward Holland and France.

---

* Dr. Hooper's MS. narrative, published in the Appendix to Lord Dungannon's Life of William.

happy as when he could quit the magnificence of Windsor for his far humbler seat at Loo. During his splendid banishment it was his consolation to create round him, by building, planting, and digging, a scene which might remind him of the formal piles of red brick, of the long canals, and of the symmetrical flower-beds among which his early life had been passed. Yet even his affection for the land of his birth was subordinate to another feeling which early became supreme in his soul, which mixed itself with all his passions, which impelled him to marvellous enterprises, which supported him when sinking under mortification, pain, sickness, and sorrow, which, toward the close of his career, seemed during a short time to languish, but which soon broke forth again fiercer than ever, and continued to animate him even while the prayer for the departing was read at his bedside. That feeling was enmity to France, and to the magnificent King who, in more than one sense, represented France, and who to virtues and accomplishments eminently French joined in large measure that unquiet, unscrupulous, and vainglorious ambition which has repeatedly drawn on France the resentment of Europe.

It is not difficult to trace the progress of the sentiment which gradually possessed itself of William's whole soul. When he was little more than a boy his country had been attacked by Lewis in ostentatious defiance of justice and public law, had been overrun, had been desolated, had been given up to every excess of rapacity, licentiousness, and cruelty. The Dutch had in dismay humbled themselves before the conqueror, and had implored mercy. They had been told in reply that, if they desired peace, they must resign their independence, and do annual homage to the House of Bourbon. The injured nation, driven to despair, had opened its dikes, and had called in the sea as an ally against the French tyranny. It was in the agony of that conflict, when peasants were flying in terror before the invaders, when hundreds of fair gardens and pleasure-houses were buried beneath the waves, when the deliberations of the States were interrupted by the fainting and the loud weeping of ancient senators who could not bear the thought of surviving the freedom and glory of their native land, that William had been called to the head of affairs. For a time it seemed to him that resistance was hopeless. He looked round him for succor, and looked in vain. Spain was unnerved, Germany distracted, England corrupted. Nothing seemed left to the young Stadtholder but to perish sword in hand, or to be the Æneas of a great emigration, and to create another Holland in countries beyond the reach of the tyranny of France. No obstacle would then remain to check the progress of the House of Bourbon. A few years; and that House might add to its dominions Lorraine and Flanders, Castile and Aragon, Naples and Milan, Mexico and Peru. Lewis might wear the imperial crown, might place a prince of his family on the throne of Poland, might be sole master of Europe from the Scythian deserts to the Atlantic Ocean, and of America from regions north of the Tropic of Cancer to regions south of the Tropic of Capricorn. Such was the prospect which lay before William when first he entered on public life, and which never ceased to haunt him till his latest day. The French monarchy was to him what the Roman republic was to Hannibal, what the Ottoman power was to Scanderbeg, what the Southron domination was to Wallace. Religion gave her sanction to that intense and unquenchable animosity. Hundreds of Calvinistic preachers proclaimed that the same power which had set apart Samson from the womb to be the scourge of the Philistine, and which had called Gideon from the threshing-floor to smite the Midianite, had raised up William of Orange to be the champion of all free nations and of all pure Churches; nor was this notion without influence on his own mind. To the confidence which the heroic fatalist placed in his high destiny and in his sacred cause is to be partly attributed his singular indifference to danger. He had a great work to do; and till it was done nothing could harm him. Therefore it was that, in spite of the prognostications of physicians, he recovered from maladies which seemed hopeless, that bands of assassins conspired in vain against his life, that the open skiff to which he trusted himself on a starless night, amidst raging waves, and near a treacherous shore, brought him safe to land, and that, on twenty fields of battle, the cannon-balls passed him by to right and left. The ardor and perseverance with which he devoted himself to his mission have scarcely any parallel in history. In comparison with his great object he held the lives of other men as cheap as his own. It was but too much the habit even of the most humane and generous soldiers of that age to think very lightly of the bloodshed and devastation inseparable from great martial exploits; and the heart of William was steeled, not only by professional insensibility, but by that sterner insensibility which is the effect of a sense of duty. Three great coalitions, three long and bloody wars in which all Europe from the Vistula to the Western Ocean was in arms, are to be ascribed to his unconquerable energy. When in 1678 the States-general, exhausted and disheartened, were desirous of repose, his voice was still against sheathing the sword. If peace was made, it was made only because he could not breathe into other men a spirit as fierce and determined as his own. At the very last moment, in the hope of breaking off the negotiation which he knew to be all but concluded, he fought one of the most bloody and obstinate battles of that age. From the day on which the treaty of Nimeguen was signed, he began to meditate a second coalition. His contest with Lewis, transferred from the field to the cabinet, was soon exasperated by a private feud. In talents, temper, manners, and opinions, the rivals were diametrically opposed to each other. Lewis, polite and dignified, profuse and voluptuous, fond of display and averse from danger, a munificent patron of arts and letters, and a cruel persecutor of Calvinists, presented a remarkable contrast to William, simple in tastes, ungracious in demeanor, indefatigable and intrepid in war, regardless of all the ornamental branches of knowledge, and firmly attached to the theology of Geneva. The enemies did not long observe those courtesies which men of their rank, even when opposed to each other at the head of armies, seldom neglect. William, indeed, went through the form of tendering his best services to Lewis. But this civility was rated at its true value, and requited with a dry reprimand. The great King affected contempt for the petty Prince who was the servant of a confederacy of trading towns; and to every mark of contempt the dauntless Stadtholder replied by a fresh defiance. William took his title, a title which the events of the preceding century had made one of the most illustrious in Europe, from a city which lies on the banks of the Rhone not far from Avignon, and which, like Avignon, though enclosed on every side by the French territory, was properly a fief not of the French but of the Imperial Crown. Lewis, with that ostentatious contempt of public law which was characteristic of him, occupied Orange, dismantled the fortifications, and confiscated the revenues. William declared aloud at his table before many persons that he would make the most Christian King repent the outrage, and when questioned about these words by Lewis's Ambassador, the Count of Avaux, positively refused either to retract them or to explain them away. The quarrel was carried so far that the French minister could not venture to present himself at the drawing-room of the Princess for fear of receiving some affront.*

The feeling with which William regarded France explains the whole of his policy toward England. His public spirit was a European public spirit. The chief object of his care was not our island, not even his native Holland, but the great community of nations threatened with subjugation by one too powerful member. Those who commit the error of considering him as an English statesman must necessarily see his whole life in a false light, and will be unable to discover any principle, good or bad, Whig or Tory, to which some of his most important acts can be referred. But, when we consider him as a man whose especial task was to join a crowd of feeble, divided, and dispirited states in firm and energetic union against a common enemy, when we consider him as a man in whose eyes England was important chiefly because, without her, the great coalition which he projected must be incomplete, we shall be forced to admit that no long career recorded

---

* Avaux, Negotiations, Aug. $\frac{10}{20}$, Sept. $\frac{14}{24}$, $\frac{\text{Sept. 28,}}{\text{Oct. 8.}}$ Dec. $\frac{7}{17}$, 1682.

in history has been more uniform from the beginning to the close than that of this great Prince.*

The clue of which we are now possessed will enable us to track without difficulty the course, in reality consistent, though in appearance sometimes tortuous, which he pursued toward our domestic factions. He clearly saw what had not escaped persons far inferior to him in sagacity—that the enterprise on which his whole soul was intent would probably be successful if England were on his side, would be of uncertain issue if England were neutral, and would be hopeless if England acted as she had acted in the days of the Cabal. He saw not less clearly that between the foreign policy and the domestic policy of the English government there was a close connection; that the sovereign of this country, acting in harmony with the legislature, must always have a great sway in the affairs of Christendom, and must also have an obvious interest in opposing the undue aggrandizement of any Continental potentate; that, on the other hand, the sovereign, distrusted and thwarted by the legislature, could be of little weight in European politics, and that the whole of that little weight would be thrown into the wrong scale. The Prince's first wish, therefore, was that there should be concord between the throne and the Parliament. How that concord should be established, and on which side concessions should be made, were, in his view, questions of secondary importance. He would have been best pleased, no doubt, to see a complete reconciliation effected without the sacrifice of one tittle of the prerogative. For in the integrity of that prerogative he had a reversionary interest; and he was by nature at least as covetous of power and as impatient of restraint as any of the Stuarts. But there was no flower

<small>His policy consistent throughout.</small>

---

* I cannot deny myself the pleasure of quoting Massillon's unfriendly, yet discriminating and noble, character of William: "Un prince profond dans ses vues; habile à former des ligues et à réunir les esprits; plus heureux à exciter les guerres qu'à combattre; plus à craindre encore dans le secret du cabinet, qu'à la tête des armées; un ennemi que la haine du nom Français avoit rendu capable d'imaginer de grandes choses et de les exécuter; un de ces génies qui semblent être nés pour mouvoir à leur gré les peuples et les souverains; un grand homme, s'il n'avoit jamais voulu être roi."—Oraison funèbre de M. le Dauphin.

of the crown which he was not prepared to sacrifice, even after the crown had been placed on his own head, if he could only be convinced that such a sacrifice was indispensably necessary to his great design. In the days of the Popish Plot, therefore, though he disapproved of the violence with which the opposition attacked the royal authority, he exhorted the government to give way. The conduct of the Commons, he said, as respected domestic affairs, was most unreasonable: but while the Commons were discontented the liberties of Europe could never be safe; and to that paramount consideration every other consideration ought to yield. On these principles he acted when the Exclusion Bill had thrown the nation into convulsions. There is no reason to believe that he encouraged the opposition to bring forward that bill or to reject the offers of compromise which were repeatedly made from the throne. But when it became clear that, unless that bill were carried, there would be a serious breach between the Commons and the court, he indicated very intelligibly, though with decorous reserve, his opinion that the representatives of the people ought to be conciliated at any price. When a violent and rapid reflux of public feeling had left the Whig party for a time utterly helpless, he attempted to attain his grand object by a new road perhaps more agreeable to his temper than that which he had previously tried. In the altered temper of the nation there was little chance that any Parliament disposed to cross the wishes of the sovereign would be elected. Charles was for a time master. To gain Charles, therefore, was the Prince's first wish. In the summer of 1683, almost at the moment at which the detection of the Rye-house Plot made the discomfiture of the Whigs and the triumph of the King complete, events took place elsewhere which William could not behold without extreme anxiety and alarm. The Turkish armies advanced to the suburbs of Vienna. The great Austrian monarchy, on the support of which the Prince had reckoned, seemed to be on the point of destruction. Bentinck was therefore sent in haste from the Hague to London, was charged to omit nothing which might be necessary to conciliate the English court, and was particularly instructed to express in the strongest terms the horror with which his master regarded the Whig conspiracy.

During the eighteen months which followed, there was some hope that the influence of Halifax would prevail, and that the court of Whitehall would return to the policy of the Triple Alliance. To that hope William fondly clung. He spared no effort to propitiate Charles. The hospitality which Monmouth found at the Hague is chiefly to be ascribed to the Prince's anxiety to gratify the real wishes of Monmouth's father. As soon as Charles died, William, still adhering unchangeably to his object, again changed his course. He had sheltered Monmouth, to please the late King. That the present King might have no reason to complain, Monmouth was dismissed. We have seen that, when the Western insurrection broke out, the British regiments in the Dutch service were, by the active exertions of the Prince, sent over to their own country on the first requisition. Indeed William even offered to command in person against the rebels; and that the offer was made in perfect sincerity cannot be doubted by those who have perused his confidential letters to Bentinck.*

The Prince was evidently at this time inclined to hope that the great plan, to which in his mind everything else was subordinate, might obtain the approbation and support of his father-in-law. The high tone which James was then holding toward France, the readiness with which he consented to a defensive alliance with the United Provinces, the inclination which he showed to connect himself with the House of Austria, encouraged this expectation. But in a short time the prospect was darkened. The disgrace of Halifax, the breach between James and the Parliament, the prorogation, the announcement distinctly made by the King to the foreign min-

---

* For example, "Je crois M. Feversham un très brave et honeste homme. Mais je doute s'il a assez d'expérience à diriger une si grande affaire qu'il a sur le bras. Dieu lui donne un succès prompt et heureux! Mais je ne suis pas hors d'inquiétude" (July $\frac{7}{17}$, 1685). Again, after he had received the news of the battle of Sedgemoor, "Dieu soit loué du bon succès que les troupes du Roy ont eu contre les rebelles. Je ne doute pas que cette affaire ne soit entièrement assoupie, et que le règne du Roy sera heureux, ce que Dieu veuille" (July $\frac{10}{20}$).

isters that Continental politics should no longer divert his attention from internal measures tending to strengthen his prerogative and to promote the interest of his Church, put an end to the delusion. It was plain that, when the European crisis came, England would, if James were her master, either remain inactive or act in conjunction with France. And the European crisis was drawing near. The House of Austria had, by a succession of victories, been secured from danger on the side of Turkey, and was no longer under the necessity of submitting patiently to the encroachments and insults of Lewis. Accordingly, in July, 1686, a treaty was signed at Augsburg by which the Princes of the Empire bound themselves closely together for the purpose of mutual defence. The Kings of Spain and Sweden were parties to this compact, the King of Spain as sovereign of the provinces contained in the circle of Burgundy, and the King of Sweden as Duke of Pomerania. The confederates declared that they had no intention to attack and no wish to offend any power, but that they were determined to tolerate no infraction of those rights which the Germanic body held under the sanction of public law and public faith. They pledged themselves to stand by each other in case of need, and fixed the amount of force which each member of the league was to furnish if it should be necessary to repel aggression.* The name of William did not appear in this instrument: but all men knew that it was his work, and foresaw that he would in no long time be again the captain of a coalition against France. Between him and the vassal of France there could, in such circumstances, be no cordial good-will. There was no open rupture, no interchange of menaces or reproaches. But the father-in-law and the son-in-law were separated completely and forever.

At the very time at which the Prince was thus estranged from the English court, the causes which had hitherto produced a coolness between him and the two great sections of the English people disappeared. A large portion, perhaps a

---

* The treaty will be found in the Recueil des Traités, iv., No. 209.

numerical majority, of the Whigs had favored the pretensions of Monmouth: but Monmouth was now no more. The Tories, on the other hand, had entertained apprehensions that the interests of the Anglican Church might not be safe under the rule of a man bred among Dutch Presbyterians, and well known to hold latitudinarian opinions about robes, ceremonies, and bishops; but, since that beloved Church had been threatened by far more formidable dangers from a very different quarter, these apprehensions had lost almost all their power. Thus, at the same moment, both the great parties began to fix their hopes and their affections on the same leader. Old republicans could not refuse their confidence to one who had worthily filled, during many years, the highest magistracy of a republic. Old royalists conceived that they acted according to their principles in paying profound respect to a Prince so near to the throne. At this conjuncture it was of the highest moment that there should be entire union between William and Mary. A misunderstanding between the presumptive heiress of the crown and her husband must have produced a schism in that vast mass which was from all quarters gathering round one common rallying-point. Happily all risk of such misunderstanding was averted in the critical instant by the interposition of Burnet; and the Prince became the unquestioned chief of the whole of that party which was opposed to the government, a party almost co-extensive with the nation.

<small>William becomes the head of the English opposition.</small>

There is not the least reason to believe that he at this time meditated the great enterprise to which a stern necessity afterward drove him. He was aware that the public mind of England, though heated by grievances, was by no means ripe for revolution. He would doubtless gladly have avoided the scandal which must be the effect of a mortal quarrel between persons bound together by the closest ties of consanguinity and affinity. Even his ambition made him unwilling to owe to violence that greatness which might soon be his in the ordinary course of nature and of law. For he well knew that if the crown descended to his wife regularly, all its prerogatives would descend unimpaired with it, and that if it were obtained by election, it must be taken subject to such conditions as the electors might think fit to impose. He meant, therefore, as it appears, to wait with patience for the day when he might govern by an undisputed title, and to content himself in the mean time with exercising a great influence on English affairs, as first Prince of the blood, and as head of the party which was decidedly preponderant in the nation, and which was certain, whenever a Parliament should meet, to be decidedly preponderant in both Houses.

Already, it is true, he had been urged by an adviser, less sagacious and more impetuous than himself, to try a bolder course. Mordaunt proposes to William a descent on England. This adviser was the young Lord Mordaunt. That age had produced no more inventive genius, and no more daring spirit. But if a design was splendid, Mordaunt seldom inquired whether it were practicable. His life was a wild romance made up of mysterious intrigues, both political and amorous, of violent and rapid changes of scene and fortune, and of victories resembling those of Amadis and Launcelot rather than those of Luxemburg and Eugene. The episodes interspersed in this strange story were of a piece with the main plot. Among them were midnight encounters with generous robbers, and rescues of noble and beautiful ladies from ravishers. Mordaunt, having distinguished himself by the eloquence and audacity with which, in the House of Lords, he had opposed the court, repaired, soon after the prorogation, to the Hague, and strongly recommended an immediate descent on England. He had persuaded himself that it would be as easy to surprise three great kingdoms as he long afterward found it to surprise Barcelona. William rejects the advice. William listened, meditated, and replied, in general terms, that he took a great interest in English affairs, and would keep his attention fixed on them.* Whatever his purpose had been, it is not likely that he would have chosen a rash and vainglorious knight-errant for his confidant. Between the two men there was nothing

---

* Burnet, i., 762.

in common except personal courage, which rose in both to the height of fabulous heroism. Mordaunt wanted merely to enjoy the excitement of conflict, and to make men stare. William had one great end ever before him. Toward that end he was impelled by a strong passion which appeared to him under the guise of a sacred duty. Toward that end he toiled with a patience resembling, as he once said, the patience with which he had seen a boatman on a canal strain against an adverse eddy, often swept back, but never ceasing to pull, and content if, by the labor of hours, a few yards could be gained.* Exploits which brought the Prince no nearer to his object, however glorious they might be in the estimation of the vulgar, were in his judgment boyish vanities, and no part of the real business of life.

He determined to reject Mordaunt's advice; and there can be no doubt that the determination was wise. Had William, in 1686, or even in 1687, attempted to do what he did with such signal success in 1689, it is probable that many Whigs would have risen in arms at his call. But he would have found that the nation was not yet prepared to welcome a deliverer from a foreign country, and that the Church had not yet been provoked and insulted into forgetfulness of the tenet which had long been her peculiar boast. The old Cavaliers would have flocked to the royal standard. There would probably have been in all the three kingdoms a civil war as long and fierce as that of the preceding generation. While that war was raging in the British Isles, what might not Lewis attempt on the Continent? And what hope would there be for Holland, drained of her troops, and abandoned by her Stadtholder?

William therefore contented himself for the present with taking measures to unite and animate that mighty opposition of which he had become the head. This was not difficult. The fall of the Hydes had excited throughout England extreme alarm and indignation. Men felt that the question now was, not whether Protestantism

Discontent in England after the fall of the Hydes.

---

* Temple's Memoirs.

should be dominant, but whether it should be tolerated. The Treasurer had been succeeded by a board, of which a Papist was the head. The Privy Seal had been intrusted to a Papist. The Lord-lieutenant of Ireland had been succeeded by a man who had absolutely no claim to high place except that he was a Papist. The last person whom a government having in view the general interests of the empire would have sent to Dublin as Deputy was Tyrconnel. His brutal manners made him unfit to represent the majesty of the crown. The feebleness of his understanding and the violence of his temper made him unfit to conduct grave business of state. The deadly animosity which he felt toward the possessors of the greater part of the soil of Ireland made him especially unfit to rule that kingdom. But the intemperance of his bigotry was thought amply to atone for the intemperance of all his other passions; and, in consideration of the hatred which he bore to the reformed faith, he was suffered to indulge without restraint his hatred of the English name. This, then, was the real meaning of His Majesty's respect for the rights of conscience. He wished his Parliament to remove all the disabilities which had been imposed on Papists, merely in order that he might himself impose disabilities equally galling on Protestants. It was plain that, under such a prince, apostasy was the only road to greatness. It was a road, however, which few ventured to take. For the spirit of the nation was thoroughly roused; and every renegade had to endure such an amount of public scorn and detestation as cannot be altogether unfelt even by the most callous natures.

It is true that several remarkable conversions had recently taken place; but they were such as did little credit to the
Conversions to Popery. Peterborough. Salisbury. Church of Rome. Two men of high rank had joined her communion; Henry Mordaunt, Earl of Peterborough, and James Cecil, Earl of Salisbury. But Peterborough, who had been an active soldier, courtier, and negotiator, was now broken down by years and infirmities; and those who saw him totter about the galleries of Whitehall, leaning on a stick and swathed up in flannels and plasters, comforted themselves for his defection by remarking

that he had not changed his religion till he had outlived his faculties.* Salisbury was foolish to a proverb. His figure was so bloated by sensual indulgence as to be almost incapable of moving; and this sluggish body was the abode of an equally sluggish mind. He was represented in popular lampoons as a man made to be duped, as a man who had hitherto been the prey of gamesters, and who might as well be the prey of friars. A pasquinade, which, about the time of Rochester's retirement, was fixed on the door of Salisbury House in the Strand, described in coarse terms the horror with which the wise Robert Cecil, if he could rise from his grave, would see to what a creature his honors had descended.†

These were the highest in station among the proselytes of James. There were other renegades of a very different kind, needy men of parts who were destitute of principle and of all sense of personal dignity. There is reason to believe that among these was William Wycherley, the most licentious and hard-hearted writer of a singularly licentious and hard-hearted school.‡ It is certain that Matthew Tindal, who, at a later period, acquired great notoriety by writing against Christianity, was at this time received into the bosom of the infallible Church, a fact which, as may easily be supposed, the divines with whom he was subsequently engaged in controversy did not suffer to sink into oblivion.§ A still more infamous apostate was Joseph Haines, whose name is now almost forgotten, but who was well known in his own time as an adventurer of versatile parts—sharper, coiner, false witness, sham bail, dancing-master, buffoon, poet, comedian. Some of his prologues and epilogues were much admired by his contemporaries: and his merit as an actor was universally acknowledged. This man professed himself a Roman Catholic, and went to Italy

---

* See the poems entitled The Converts and The Delusion.

† The lines are in the Collection of State Poems.

‡ Our information about Wycherley is very scanty: but two things are certain, that in his later years he called himself a Papist, and that he received money from James. I have very little doubt that he was a hired convert.

§ See the article on him in the Biographia Britannica.

in the retinue of Castelmaine, but was soon dismissed for misconduct. If any credit be due to a tradition which was long preserved in the greenroom, Haines had the impudence to affirm that the Virgin Mary had appeared to him and called him to repentance. After the Revolution, he attempted to make his peace with the town by a penance more scandalous than his offence. One night, before he acted in a farce, he appeared on the stage in a white sheet, with a torch in his hand, and recited some profane and indecent doggerel, which he called his recantation.*

With the name of Haines was joined, in many libels, the name of a more illustrious renegade, John Dryden. Dryden was now approaching the decline of life. After many successes and many failures, he had at length attained, by general consent, the first place among living English poets. His claims on the gratitude of James were superior to those of any man of letters in the kingdom. But James cared little for verses and much for money. From the day of his accession he set himself to make small economical reforms, such as bring on a government the reproach of meanness without producing any perceptible relief to the finances. One of the victims of this injudicious parsimony was Dryden. A pension of a hundred a year, which had been given to him by Charles and had expired with Charles, was not renewed. The demise of the crown made it necessary that the poet-laureate should have a new patent; and orders were given that, in this patent, the annual butt of sack, originally granted to Jonson, and continued to Jonson's successors, should be omitted.† This was the only notice which the King, during the first year of his reign, deigned to bestow on the mighty satirist who, in the very crisis of the great struggle of the Exclusion Bill, had spread terror through the Whig ranks. Dryden was poor and impatient of poverty. He knew little and cared little about religion. If any sentiment was deeply fixed

---

* See James Quin's account of Haines in Davies's Miscellanies; Tom Brown's Works; Lives of Sharpers; Dryden's Epilogue to the Secular Masque.

† This fact, which escaped the minute researches of Malone, appears from the Treasury Letter Book of 1685.

in him, that sentiment was an aversion to priests of all persuasions—Levites, Augurs, Muftis, Roman Catholic divines, Presbyterian divines, divines of the Church of England. He was not naturally a man of high spirit; and his pursuits had been by no means such as were likely to give elevation or delicacy to his mind. He had during many years earned his daily bread by pandering to the vicious taste of the pit, and by grossly flattering rich and noble patrons. Self-respect and a fine sense of the becoming were not to be expected from one who had led a life of mendicancy and adulation. Finding that, if he continued to call himself a Protestant, his services would be overlooked, he declared himself a Papist. The King's parsimony speedily relaxed. Dryden's pension was restored: the arrears were paid up; and he was employed to defend his new religion both in prose and verse.*

Two eminent men, Samuel Johnson and Walter Scott, have done their best to persuade themselves and others that this memorable conversion was sincere. It was natural that they should be desirous to remove a disgraceful stain from the memory of one whose genius they justly admired, and with whose political feelings they strongly sympathized; but the impartial historian must with regret pronounce a very different judgment. There will always be a strong presumption against the sincerity of a conversion by which the convert is directly a gainer. In the case of Dryden there is nothing to countervail this presumption. His theological writings abundantly prove that he had never sought with diligence and anxiety to learn the truth, and that his knowledge both of the Church which he quitted and of the Church which he entered was of the most superficial kind. Nor was his subsequent conduct that of a man whom a strong sense of duty had constrained to take a step of awful importance. Had he been such a man, the same conviction which had led him to join

---

* It has lately been asserted that Dryden's pension was restored long before he turned Papist, and that therefore it ought not to be considered as the price of his apostasy. But this is an entire mistake. Dryden's pension was restored by letters-patent of the 4th of March, 168$\frac{5}{6}$; and his apostasy had been the talk of the town at least six weeks before. See Evelyn's Diary, January 19, 168$\frac{5}{6}$ (1857).

the Church of Rome would surely have prevented him from violating grossly and habitually rules which that Church, in common with every other Christian society, recognizes as binding. There would have been a marked distinction between his earlier and his later compositions. He would have looked back with remorse on a literary life of near thirty years, during which his rare powers of diction and versification had been systematically employed in spreading moral corruption. Not a line tending to make virtue contemptible, or to inflame licentious desire, would thenceforward have proceeded from his pen. The truth unhappily is that the dramas which he wrote after his pretended conversion are in no respect less impure or profane than those of his youth. Even when he professed to translate he constantly wandered from his originals in search of images which, if he had found them in his originals, he ought to have shunned. What was bad became worse in his versions. What was innocent contracted a taint from passing through his mind. He made the grossest satires of Juvenal more gross, interpolated loose descriptions in the tales of Boccaccio, and polluted the sweet and limpid poetry of the Georgics with filth which would have moved the loathing of Virgil.

The help of Dryden was welcome to those Roman Catholic divines who were painfully sustaining a conflict against all that was most illustrious in the Established Church. They could not disguise from themselves the fact that their style, disfigured with foreign idioms which had been picked up at Rome and Douay, appeared to little advantage when compared with the eloquence of Tillotson and Sherlock. It seemed that it was no light thing to have secured the co-operation of the greatest living master of the English language. The first service which he was required to perform in return for his pension was to defend his Church in prose against Stillingfleet. But the art of saying things well is useless to a man who has nothing to say; and this was Dryden's case. He soon found himself unequally paired with an antagonist whose whole life had been one long training for controversy. The veteran gladiator disarmed the novice, inflicted a few contemptuous scratches, and turned away to encounter more formidable combatants. Dryden then betook himself to a weapon at which he was not likely to find his match. He retired for a time from the bustle of coffee-houses and theatres to a quiet retreat in Huntingdonshire, and there composed, with unwonted care and labor, his celebrated poem on the points in dispute between the Churches of Rome and England. The Church of Rome he represented under the similitude of a milk-white hind, ever in peril of death, yet fated not to die. The beasts of the field were bent on her destruction. The quaking hare, indeed, observed a timorous neutrality; but the Socinian fox, the Presbyterian wolf, the Independent bear, the Anabaptist boar, glared fiercely at the spotless creature. Yet she could venture to drink with them at the common watering-place under the protection of her friend, the kingly lion. The Church of England was typified by the panther, spotted indeed, but beautiful, too beautiful for a beast of prey. The hind and the panther, equally hated by the ferocious population of the forest, conferred apart on their common danger. They then proceeded to discuss the points on which they differed, and, while wagging their tails and licking their jaws, held a long dialogue touching the real presence, the authority of Popes and Councils, the penal laws, the Test Act, Oates's perjuries, Butler's unrequited services to the Cavalier party, Stillingfleet's pamphlets, and Burnet's broad shoulders and fortunate matrimonial speculations.

The Hind and Panther.

The absurdity of this plan is obvious. In truth the allegory could not be preserved unbroken through ten lines together. No art of execution could redeem the faults of such a design. Yet the Fable of the Hind and Panther is undoubtedly the most valuable addition which was made to English literature during the short and troubled reign of James the Second. In none of Dryden's works can be found passages more pathetic and magnificent, greater ductility and energy of language, or a more pleasing and various music.

The poem appeared with every advantage which royal patronage could give. A superb edition was printed for Scotland at the Roman Catholic press established in Holyrood House. But men were in no humor to be charmed by the transparent style and melodious numbers of the apostate. The disgust excited by his venality, the alarm excited by the policy of which he was the eulogist, were not to be sung to sleep. The just indignation of the public was inflamed by many who were smarting from his ridicule, and by many who were envious of his renown. In spite of all the restraints under which the press lay, attacks on his life and writings appeared daily. Sometimes he was Bayes, sometimes Poet Squab. He was reminded that in his youth he had paid to the House of Cromwell the same servile court which he was now paying to the House of Stuart. One set of his assailants maliciously reprinted the sarcastic verses which he had written against Popery in days when he could have got nothing by being a Papist. Of the many satirical pieces which appeared on this occasion, the most successful was the joint work of two young men who had lately completed their studies at Cambridge, and had been welcomed as promising novices in the literary coffee-houses of London, Charles Montague and Matthew Prior. Montague was of noble descent: the origin of Prior was so obscure that no biographer has been able to trace it: but both the adventurers were poor and aspiring: both had keen and vigorous minds: both afterward climbed high; and both united in a remarkable degree the love of letters with skill in those departments of business for which men of letters generally have a strong distaste. Of the fifty poets whose lives Johnson has written, Montague and Prior were the only two who were distinguished by an intimate knowledge of trade and finance. Soon their paths diverged widely. Their early friendship was dissolved. One of them became the chief of the Whig party, and was impeached by the Tories. The other was intrusted with all the mysteries of Tory diplomacy, and was long kept close prisoner by the Whigs. At length, after many eventful years, the associates, so long parted, were reunited in Westminster Abbey.

Whoever has read the tale of the Hind and Panther with attention must have perceived that, while that work was in progress, a great alteration took place in the views of those who used Dryden as their interpreter. At first the Church of England is mentioned with tenderness and respect, and is exhorted to ally herself with the Roman Catholics against the Protestant Dissenters: but at the close of the poem, and in the preface, which was written after the poem had been finished, the Protestant Dissenters are invited to make common cause with the Roman Catholics against the Church of England.

Change in the policy of the court toward the Puritans.

This change in the language of the court poet was indicative of a great change in the policy of the court. The original purpose of James had been to obtain for the Church of which he was a member, not only complete immunity from all penalties and from all civil disabilities, but also an ample share of ecclesiastical and academical endowments, and at the same time to enforce with rigor the laws against the Puritan sects. All the special dispensations which he had granted had been granted to Roman Catholics. All the laws which bore hardest on the Presbyterians, Independents, and Baptists, had been executed by him with extraordinary rigor. While Hales commanded a regiment, while Powis sat at the Council-board, while Massey held a deanery, while breviaries and mass-books were printed at Oxford under a royal license, while the host was publicly exposed in London under the protection of the pikes and muskets of the foot-guards, while friars and monks walked the streets of London in their robes, Baxter was in jail; Howe was in exile; the Five Mile Act and the Conventicle Act were in full vigor; Puritan writers were compelled to resort to foreign or to secret presses; Puritan congregrations could meet only by night or in waste places; and Puritan ministers were forced to preach in the garb of colliers or of sailors. In Scotland, the King, while he spared no exertion to extort from the Estates full relief for Roman Catholics, had demanded and obtained new statutes of unprecedented severity against Presbyterians. His conduct to the exiled Huguenots had not less clearly indicated his feelings. We have seen that, when the public munificence had placed in his hands a large sum for the relief of those unhappy men, he, in violation of every law of hospitality and good faith, required them to renounce the Calvinistic ritual to which they were strongly attached, and to conform to the Church of England, before he would dole out to them any portion of the alms which had been intrusted to his care.

Such had been his policy as long as he could cherish any hope that the Church of England would consent to share ascendency with the Church of Rome. That hope at one time amounted to confidence. The enthusiasm with which the Tories hailed his accession, the elections, the dutiful language and ample grants of his Parliament, the suppression of the Western insurrection, the complete prostration of the faction which had attempted to exclude him from the crown, elated him beyond the bounds of reason. He felt an assurance that every obstacle would give way before his power and his resolution. But he was disappointed. His Parliament withstood him. He tried the effects of frowns and menaces. Frowns and menaces failed. He tried the effect of prorogation. From the day of the prorogation the opposition to his designs had been growing stronger and stronger. It seemed clear that, if he effected his purpose, he must effect it in defiance of that great party which had given such signal proofs of fidelity to his office, to his family, and to his person. The whole Anglican priesthood, the whole Cavalier gentry were against him. In vain had he, by virtue of his ecclesiastical supremacy, enjoined the clergy to abstain from discussing controverted points. Every parish in the nation was warned every Sunday against the errors of Rome; and these warnings were only the more effective, because they were accompanied by professions of reverence for the Sovereign, and of a determination to endure with patience whatever it might be his pleasure to inflict. The royalist knights and esquires who, through forty-five years of war and faction, had stood so manfully by the throne, now expressed, in no measured phrase, their resolution to stand as manfully by the Church. Dull as was the intellect of James, despotic as was his temper, he felt that he must change his course. He could not safely venture to outrage all his Protestant subjects at once. If he

II.—13

could bring himself to make concessions to the party which predominated in both Houses, if he could bring himself to leave to the established religion all its dignities, emoluments, and privileges unimpaired, he might still break up Presbyterian meetings, and fill the jails with Baptist preachers. But, if he was determined to plunder the hierarchy, he must make up his mind to forego the luxury of persecuting the Dissenters. If he was henceforward to be at feud with his old friends, he must make a truce with his old enemies. He could overpower the Anglican Church only by forming against her an extensive coalition, including sects which, though they differed in doctrine and government far more widely from each other than from her, might yet be induced, by their common jealousy of her greatness, and by their common dread of her intolerance, to suspend their mutual animosities till she was no longer able to oppress them.

This plan seemed to him to have one strong recommendation. If he could only succeed in conciliating the Protestant Non-conformists he might flatter himself that he was secure against all chance of rebellion. According to the Anglican divines, no subject could by any provocation be justified in withstanding the Lord's anointed by force. The theory of the Puritan sectaries was very different. Those sectaries had no scruple about smiting tyrants with the sword of Gideon. Many of them did not shrink from using the dagger of Ehud. They were probably even now meditating another Western insurrection, or another Rye-house Plot. James, therefore, conceived that he might safely persecute the Church if he could only gain the Dissenters. The party whose principles afforded him no guarantee would be attached to him by interest. The party whose interests he attacked would be restrained from insurrection by principle.

Influenced by such considerations as these, James, from the time at which he parted in anger with his Parliament, began to meditate a general league of all Non-conformists, Catholic and Protestant, against the established religion. So early as Christmas, 1685, the agents of the United Provinces informed the States-general that the plan of a general toleration had been arranged and would soon be disclosed.* The reports which had reached the Dutch embassy proved to be premature. The separatists appear, however, to have been treated with more lenity during the year 1686 than during the year 1685. But it was only by slow degrees and after many struggles that the King could prevail on himself to form an alliance with all that he most abhorred. He had to overcome an animosity not slight or capricious, not of recent origin or hasty growth, but hereditary in his line, strengthened by great wrongs inflicted and suffered through a hundred and twenty eventful years, and intertwined with all his feelings, religious, political, domestic, and personal. Four generations of Stuarts had waged a war to the death with four generations of Puritans; and, through that long war, there had been no Stuart who had hated the Puritans so much, or who had been so much hated by them, as himself. They had tried to blast his honor and to exclude him from his birthright: they had called him incendiary, cutthroat, poisoner: they had driven him from the Admiralty and the Privy Council: they had repeatedly chased him into banishment: they had plotted his assassination: they had risen against him in arms by thousands. He had avenged himself on them by havoc such as England had never before seen. Their heads and quarters were still rotting on poles in all the market-places of Somersetshire and Dorsetshire. Aged women, held in high honor among the sectaries for piety and charity, had, for offences which no good prince would have thought deserving even of a severe reprimand, been beheaded and burned alive. Such had been, even in England, the relations between the King and the Puritans; and in Scotland the tyranny of the King and the fury of the Puritans had been such as Englishmen could hardly conceive. To forget an enmity so long and so deadly was no light task for a nature singularly harsh and implacable.

The conflict in the royal mind did not escape the eye of Barillon. At the end of January, 1687, he sent a remarkable

---

* Van Leeuwen, $\frac{\text{Dec. 25,}}{\text{Jan. 4,}}$ 168$\frac{5}{6}$.

letter to Versailles. The King—such was the substance of this document—had almost convinced himself that he could not obtain entire liberty for Roman Catholics and yet maintain the laws against Protestant Dissenters. He leaned, therefore, to the plan of a general indulgence; but at heart he would be far better pleased if he could, even now, divide his protection and favor between the Church of Rome and the Church of England, to the exclusion of all other religious persuasions.*

A very few days after this despatch had been written, James made his first hesitating and ungracious advances toward the Puritans. He had determined to begin with Scotland, where his power to dispense with Acts of Parliament had been admitted by the obsequious Estates. On the twelfth of February, accordingly, was published at Edinburgh a proclamation granting relief to scrupulous consciences.† This proclamation fully proves the correctness of Barillon's judgment. Even in the very act of making concessions to the Presbyterians, James could not conceal the loathing with which he regarded them. The toleration given to the Catholics was complete. The Quakers had little reason to complain. But the indulgence vouchsafed to the Presbyterians, who constituted the great body of the Scottish people, was clogged by conditions which made it almost worthless. For the old test, which excluded Catholics and Presbyterians alike from office, was substituted a new test, which admitted the Catholics, but excluded most of the Presbyterians. The Catholics were allowed to build chapels, and even to carry the host in procession anywhere except in the high streets of royal burghs; the Quakers were suffered to assemble in public edifices: but the Presbyterians were interdicted from worshipping God anywhere but in private dwellings: they were not to presume to build meeting-houses: they were not even to use a barn or an out-house for

Partial toleration granted in Scotland.

---

* Barillon, $\frac{\text{Jan. 31,}}{\text{Feb. 10,}}$ 168$\frac{6}{7}$. "Je crois que, dans le fond, si on ne pouvoit laisser que la religion Anglicane et la Catholique établies par les loix, le Roy d'Angleterre en seroit bien plus content."

† It will be found in Wodrow, Appendix, vol. ii., No. 129.

religious exercises; and it was distinctly notified to them that, if they dared to hold conventicles in the open air, the law, which denounced death against both preachers and hearers, should be enforced without mercy. Any Catholic priest might say mass: any Quaker might harangue his brethren: but the Privy Council was directed to see that no Presbyterian minister presumed to preach without a special license from the government. Every line of this instrument, and of the letters by which it was accompanied, shows how much it cost the King to relax in the smallest degree the rigor with which he had ever treated the old enemies of his house.*

There is reason, indeed, to believe that, when he published this proclamation, he had by no means fully made up his mind to a coalition with the Puritans, and that his object was to grant just so much favor to them as might suffice to frighten the Churchmen into submission. He therefore waited a month, in order to see what effect the edict put forth at Edinburgh would produce in England. That month he employed assiduously, by Petre's advice, in what was called closeting. London was very full. It was expected that the Parliament would shortly meet for the despatch of business; and many members were in town. The King set himself to canvass them man by man. He flattered himself that zealous Tories — and of such, with few exceptions, the House of Commons consisted — would find it difficult to resist his earnest request, addressed to them, not collectively, but separately, not from the throne, but in the familiarity of conversation. The members, therefore, who came to pay their duty at Whitehall were taken aside, and honored with long private interviews. The King pressed them, as they were loyal gentlemen, to gratify him in the one thing on which his heart was fixed. The question, he said, touched his personal honor. The laws enacted in the late reign by factious Parliaments against the Roman Catholics had really been aimed at himself. Those laws had put a stigma on him, had driven him from the Admiralty, had driven him from the

Closeting.

---

* Wodrow, Appendix, vol. ii., Nos. 128, 129, 132.

Council-board. He had a right to expect that in the repeal of those laws all who loved and reverenced him would concur. When he found his hearers obdurate to exhortation, he resorted to intimidation and corruption. Those who refused to pleasure him in this matter were plainly told that they must not expect any mark of his favor. Penurious as he was, he opened and distributed his hoards. Several of those who had been invited to confer with him left his bedchamber carrying with them money received from the royal hand. The Judges, who were at this time on their spring circuits, were directed by the King to see those members who remained in the country, and to ascertain the intentions of each. The result of this investigation was, that a great majority of the House of Commons seemed fully determined to oppose the measures of the court.*

It is unsuccessful.

Among those whose firmness excited general admiration was Arthur Herbert, brother of the Chief-justice, member for Dover, Master of the Robes, and Rear Admiral of England. Arthur Herbert was much loved by the sailors, and was reputed one of the best of the aristocratical class of naval officers. It had been generally supposed that he would readily comply with the royal wishes: for he was heedless of religion: he was fond of pleasure and expense: he had no private estate: his places brought him in four thousand pounds a year; and he had long been reckoned among the most devoted personal adherents of James. When, however, the Rear Admiral was closeted, and required to promise that he would vote for the repeal of the Test Act, his answer was, that his honor and conscience would not permit him to give any such pledge. "Nobody doubts your honor," said the King; "but a man who lives as you do ought not to talk about his conscience." To this reproach, a reproach which came with a bad grace from the lover of Catherine Sedley, Herbert manfully replied, "I have my faults, sir: but I could name people who talk much more about con-

Admiral Herbert.

---

* Barillon, $\frac{\text{Feb. 28,}}{\text{March 10,}}$ 168$\frac{6}{7}$; Van Citters, Feb. $\frac{15}{25}$; Reresby's Memoirs; Bonrepaux, $\frac{\text{May 25,}}{\text{June 4,}}$ 1687.

science than I am in the habit of doing, and yet lead lives as loose as mine." He was dismissed from all his places; and the account of what he had disbursed and received as Master of the Robes was scrutinized with great and, as he complained, with unjust severity.*

It was now evident that all hope of an alliance between the Churches of England and of Rome, for the purpose of sharing offices and emoluments, and of crushing the Puritan sects, must be abandoned. Nothing remained but to try a coalition between the Church of Rome and the Puritan sects against the Church of England.

On the eighteenth of March the King informed the Privy Council that he had determined to prorogue the Parliament till the end of November, and to grant, by his own authority, entire liberty of conscience to all his subjects.†

Declaration of Indulgence. On the fourth of April appeared the memorable Declaration of Indulgence.

In this Declaration the King avowed that it was his earnest wish to see his people members of that Church to which he himself belonged. But since that could not be, he announced his intention to protect them in the free exercise of their religion. He repeated all those phrases which, eight years before, when he was himself an oppressed man, had been familiar to his lips, but which he had ceased to use from the day on which a turn of fortune had put it into his power to be an oppressor. He had long been convinced, he said, that conscience was not to be forced, that persecution was unfavorable to population and to trade, and that it never attained the ends which persecutors had in view. He repeated his promise, already often repeated and often violated, that he would protect the Established Church in the enjoyment of her legal rights. He then proceeded to annul, by his own sole authority, a long series of statutes. He suspended all penal laws against all classes of Non-conformists. He authorized both Roman

---

* Barillon, March $\frac{14}{24}$, 1687; Lady Russell to Dr. Fitzwilliam, April 1; Burnet, i., 671, 762. The conversation is somewhat differently related in the Life of James, ii., 204. But that passage is not part of the King's own memoirs.

† London Gazette, March 21, 168$\frac{6}{7}$.

Catholics and Protestant Dissenters to perform their worship publicly. He forbade his subjects, on pain of his highest displeasure, to molest any religious assembly. He also abrogated all those acts which imposed any religious test as a qualification for any civil or military office.*

That the Declaration of Indulgence was unconstitutional is a point on which both the great English parties have always been entirely agreed. Every person capable of reasoning on a political question must perceive that a monarch who is competent to issue such a Declaration is nothing less than an absolute monarch. Nor is it possible to urge in defence of this act of James those pleas by which many arbitrary acts of the Stuarts have been vindicated or excused. It cannot be said that he mistook the bounds of his prerogative because they had not been accurately ascertained. For the truth is that he trespassed with a recent landmark full in his view. Fifteen years before that time, a Declaration of Indulgence had been put forth by his brother with the advice of the Cabal. That Declaration, when compared with the Declaration of James, might be called modest and cautious. The Declaration of Charles dispensed only with penal laws. The Declaration of James dispensed also with all religious tests. The Declaration of Charles permitted the Roman Catholics to celebrate their worship in private dwellings only. Under the Declaration of James they might build and decorate temples, and even walk in procession along Fleet Street with crosses, images, and censers. Yet the Declaration of Charles had been pronounced illegal in the most formal manner. The Commons had resolved that the King had no power to dispense with statutes in matters ecclesiastical. Charles had ordered the obnoxious instrument to be cancelled in his presence, had torn off the seal with his own hand, and had, both by message under his sign-manual, and with his own lips from his throne in full Parliament, distinctly promised the two Houses that the step which had given so much offence should never be drawn into precedent. The two Houses had

---

* London Gazette, April 7, 1687.

then, without one dissentient voice, joined in thanking him for this compliance with their wishes. No constitutional question had ever been decided more deliberately, more clearly, or with more harmonious consent.

The defenders of James have frequently pleaded in his excuse the judgment of the Court of King's Bench, on the information collusively laid against Sir Edward Hales; but the plea is of no value. That judgment James had notoriously obtained by solicitation, by threats, by dismissing scrupulous magistrates, and by placing on the bench other magistrates more courtly. And yet that judgment, though generally regarded by the bar and by the nation as unconstitutional, went only to this extent, that the Sovereign might, for special reasons of state, grant to individuals by name exemptions from disabling statutes. That he could by one sweeping edict authorize all his subjects to disobey whole volumes of laws, no tribunal had ventured, in the face of the solemn parliamentary decision of 1673, to affirm.

Such, however, was the position of parties that James's Declaration of Indulgence, though the most audacious of all the attacks made by the Stuarts on public freedom, was well calculated to please that very portion of the community by which all the other attacks of the Stuarts on public freedom had been most strenuously resisted. It could scarcely be hoped that the Protestant Nonconformist, separated from his countrymen by a harsh code harshly enforced, would be inclined to dispute the validity of a decree which relieved him from intolerable grievances. A cool and philosophical observer would undoubtedly have pronounced that all the evil arising from all the intolerant laws which Parliaments had framed was not to be compared to the evil which would be produced by a transfer of the legislative power from the Parliament to the Sovereign. But such coolness and philosophy are not to be expected from men who are smarting under present pain, and who are tempted by the offer of immediate ease. A Puritan divine might not indeed be able to deny that the dispensing power now claimed by the Crown was inconsistent with the fundamental principles

Feeling of the Protestant Dissenters.

of the constitution. But he might perhaps be excused if he asked, What was the constitution to him? The Act of Uniformity had ejected him, in spite of royal promises, from a benefice which was his freehold, and had reduced him to beggary and dependence. The Five-mile Act had banished him from his dwelling, from his relations, from his friends, from almost all places of public resort. Under the Conventicle Act his goods had been distrained; and he had been flung into one noisome jail after another among highwaymen and house-breakers. Out of prison, he had constantly had the officers of justice on his track: he had been forced to pay hush-money to informers: he had stolen, in ignominious disguises, through windows and trap-doors to meet his flock, and had, while pouring the baptismal water, or distributing the eucharistic bread, been anxiously listening for the signal that the tipstaves were approaching. Was it not mockery to call on a man thus plundered and oppressed to suffer martyrdom for the property and liberty of his plunderers and oppressors? The Declaration, despotic as it might seem to his prosperous neighbors, brought deliverance to him. He was called upon to make his choice, not between freedom and slavery, but between two yokes; and he might not unnaturally think the yoke of the King lighter than that of the Church.

While thoughts like these were working in the minds of many Dissenters, the Anglican party was in amazement and terror. This new turn in affairs was indeed alarming. The House of Stuart leagued with republican and regicide sects against the old Cavaliers of England; Popery leagued with Puritanism against an ecclesiastical system with which the Puritans had no quarrel, except that it had retained too much that was Popish; these were portents which confounded all the calculations of statesmen. The Church was then to be attacked at once on every side; and the attack was to be under the direction of him who, by her constitution, was her head. She might well be struck with surprise and dismay. And mingled with surprise and dismay came other bitter feelings; resentment against the perjured Prince whom she had served too well, and re-

Feeling of the Church of England.

morse for the cruelties in which he had been her accomplice, and for which he was now, as it seemed, about to be her punisher. Her chastisement was just. She reaped that which she had sown. After the Restoration, when her power was at the height, she had breathed nothing but vengeance. She had encouraged, urged, almost compelled the Stuarts to requite with perfidious ingratitude the recent services of the Presbyterians. Had she, in that season of her prosperity, pleaded, as became her, for her enemies, she might now, in her distress, have found them her friends. Perhaps it was not yet too late. Perhaps she might still be able to turn the tactics of her faithless oppressor against himself. There was among the Anglican clergy a moderate party which had always felt kindly toward the Protestant Dissenters. That party was not large; but the abilities, acquirements, and virtues of those who belonged to it made it respectable. It had been regarded with little favor by the highest ecclesiastical dignitaries, and had been mercilessly reviled by bigots of the school of Laud: but, from the day on which the Declaration of Indulgence appeared to the day on which the power of James ceased to inspire terror, the whole Church seemed to be animated by the spirit, and guided by the counsels, of the calumniated Latitudinarians.

Then followed an auction, the strangest that history has recorded. On one side the King, on the other the Church, began to bid eagerly against each other for the favor of those whom up to that time King and Church had combined to oppress. The Protestant Dissenters, who, a few months before, had been a despised and proscribed class, now held the balance of power. The harshness with which they had been treated was universally condemned. The court tried to throw all the blame on the hierarchy. The hierarchy flung it back on the court. The King declared that he had unwillingly persecuted the separatists only because his affairs had been in such a state that he could not venture to disoblige the established clergy. The established clergy protested that they had borne a part in severity uncongenial to their feelings only from deference to the authority of the King. The King got together a collection of stories about

The Court and the Church.

rectors and vicars who had by threats of persecution wrung money out of Protestant Dissenters. He talked on this subject much and publicly; he threatened to institute an inquiry which would exhibit the parsons in their true character to the whole world; and he actually issued several commissions empowering agents on whom he thought that he could depend to ascertain the amount of the sums extorted in different parts of the country by professors of the dominant religion from sectaries. The advocates of the Church, on the other hand, cited instances of honest parish priests who had been reprimanded and menaced by the court for recommending toleration in the pulpit, and for refusing to spy out and hunt down little congregations of Non-conformists. The King asserted that some of the Churchmen whom he had closeted had offered to make large concessions to the Catholics, on condition that the persecution of the Puritans might go on. The accused Churchmen vehemently denied the truth of this charge, and alleged that, if they would have complied with what he demanded for his own religion, he would most gladly have suffered them to indemnify themselves by harassing and pillaging Protestant Dissenters.*

The court had changed its face. The scarf and cassock could hardly appear there without calling forth sneers and malicious whispers. Maids of honor forbore to giggle, and Lords of the Bedchamber bowed low, when the Puritanical visage and the Puritanical garb, so long the favorite subjects of mockery in fashionable circles, were seen in the galleries. Taunton, which had been during two generations the stronghold of the Roundhead party in the West, which had twice resolutely repelled the armies of Charles the First, which had risen as one man to support Monmouth, and which had been

---

* Warrant Book of the Treasury. See particularly the instructions dated March 8, 168⅞, Burnet, i., 715; Reflections on His Majesty's Proclamation for a Toleration in Scotland; Letters containing some Reflections on His Majesty's Declaration for Liberty of Conscience; Apology for the Church of England with relation to the spirit of Persecution for which she is accused, 168⅞. But it is impossible for me to cite all the pamphlets from which I have formed my notion of the state of parties at this time.

turned into a shambles by Kirke and Jeffreys, seemed to have suddenly succeeded to the place which Oxford had once occupied in the royal favor.* The King constrained himself to show even fawning courtesy to eminent Dissenters. To some he offered money, to some municipal honors, to some pardons for their relations and friends, who, having been implicated in the Rye-house Plot, or having joined the standard of Monmouth, were now wandering on the Continent, or toiling among the sugar-canes of Barbadoes. He affected even to sympathize with the kindness which the English Puritans felt for their foreign brethren. A second and a third proclamation were published at Edinburgh, which greatly extended the nugatory toleration granted to the Presbyterians by the edict of February.† The banished Huguenots, on whom the King had frowned during many months, and whom he had defrauded of the alms contributed by the nation, were now relieved and caressed. An Order in Council was issued, appealing again in their behalf to the public liberality. The rule which required them to qualify themselves for the receipt of charity, by conforming to the Anglican worship, seems to have been at this time silently abrogated; and the defenders of the King's policy had the effrontery to affirm that this rule, which, as we know from the best evidence, was really devised by himself in concert with Barillon, had been adopted at the instance of the prelates of the Established Church.‡

While the King was thus courting his old adversaries, the friends of the Church were not less active. Of the acrimony and scorn with which prelates and priests had, since the Restoration, been in the habit of treating the sectaries scarcely a trace was discernible. Those who had lately been designated as schismatics and fanatics were now dear fellow-Protestants, weak brethren it might be, but still brethren, whose scruples were entitled to tender regard. If they would but be true at this crisis to the cause of the English constitution and of the reformed religion, their generosity should be speedily and

---

* Letter to a Dissenter. † Wodrow, Appendix, vol. ii., Nos. 132, 134.

‡ London Gazette, April 21, 1687; Animadversions on a late paper entituled A Letter to a Dissenter, by H. C. (Henry Care), 1687.

largely rewarded. They should have, instead of an indulgence which was of no legal validity, a real indulgence, secured by Act of Parliament. Nay, many Churchmen, who had hitherto been distinguished by their inflexible attachment to every gesture and every word prescribed in the Book of Common Prayer, now declared themselves favorable, not only to toleration, but even to comprehension. The dispute, they said, about surplices and attitudes, had too long divided those who were agreed as to the essentials of religion. When the struggle for life and death against the common enemy was over, it would be found that the Anglican clergy would be ready to make every fair concession. If the Dissenters would demand only what was reasonable, not only civil but ecclesiastical dignities would be open to them; and Baxter and Howe would be able, without any stain on their honor or their conscience, to sit on the episcopal bench.

Of the numerous pamphlets in which the cause of the Court and the cause of the Church were at this time eagerly and anxiously pleaded before the Puritan, now, by a strange turn of fortune, the arbiter of the fate of his persecutors, one only is still remembered, the Letter to a Dissenter. In this masterly little tract, all the arguments which could convince a Non-conformist that it was his duty and his interest to prefer an alliance with the Church to an alliance with the Court, were condensed into the smallest compass, arranged in the most perspicuous order, illustrated with lively wit, and enforced by an eloquence earnest indeed, yet never in its utmost vehemence transgressing the limits of exact good-sense and good-breeding. The effect of this paper was immense; for, as it was only a single sheet, more than twenty thousand copies were circulated by the post; and there was no corner of the kingdom in which the effect was not felt. Twenty-four answers were published: but the town pronounced that they were all bad, and that Lestrange's was the worst of the twenty-four.* The government was greatly ir-

_{Letter to a Dissenter.}

* Lestrange's Answer to a Letter to a Dissenter; Care's Animadversions on A Letter to a Dissenter; Dialogue between Harry and Roger; that is to say, Harry Care and Roger Lestrange.

ritated, and spared no pains to discover the author of the Letter: but it was found impossible to procure legal evidence against him. Some imagined that they recognized the sentiments and diction of Temple.* But in truth that amplitude and acuteness of intellect, that vivacity of fancy, that terse and energetic style, that placid dignity, half courtly half philosophical, which the utmost excitement of conflict could not for a moment derange, belonged to Halifax, and to Halifax alone.

The Dissenters wavered; nor is it any reproach to them that they did so. They were suffering; and the King had given them relief. Some eminent pastors had emerged from confinement; and others had ventured to return from exile. Congregations, which had hitherto met only by stealth and in darkness, now assembled at noonday, and sang psalms aloud in the hearing of magistrates, church-wardens, and constables. Modest buildings for the worship of God after the Puritan fashion began to rise all over England. An observant traveller will still remark the date of 1687 on some of the oldest meeting-houses. Nevertheless, the offers of the Church were, to a prudent Dissenter, far more attractive than those of the King. The Declaration was, in the eye of the law, a nullity. It suspended the penal statutes against non-conformity only for so long a time as the fundamental principles of the constitution and the rightful authority of the legislature should remain suspended. What was the value of privileges which must be held by a tenure at once so ignominious and so insecure? There might soon be a demise of the crown. A sovereign attached to the established religion might sit on the throne. A Parliament composed of Churchmen might be assembled. How deplorable would then be the situation of Dissenters who had been in league with Jesuits against the constitution! The Church offered an indulgence very different from that granted by James, an indulgence as valid and as sacred as the Great

Conduct of the Dissenters.

---

* The letter was signed T. W. Care says, in his Animadversions, "This Sir Politic T. W., or W. T.; for some critics think that the truer reading."

Charter. Both the contending parties promised religious liberty to the separatist: but one party required him to purchase it by sacrificing civil liberty; the other party invited him to enjoy civil and religious liberty together.

For these reasons, even if it could have been believed that the court was sincere, a Dissenter might reasonably have determined to cast in his lot with the Church. But what guarantee was there for the sincerity of the court? All men knew what the conduct of James had been up to that very time. It was not impossible, indeed, that a persecutor might be convinced by argument and by experience of the advantages of toleration. But James did not pretend to have been recently convinced. On the contrary, he omitted no opportunity of protesting that he had, during many years, been, on principle, adverse to all intolerance. Yet within a few months he had persecuted men, women, young girls, to the death for their religion. Had he been acting against light and against the convictions of his conscience then? Or was he uttering a deliberate falsehood now? From this dilemma there was no escape; and either of the two suppositions was fatal to the King's character for honesty. It was notorious also that he had been completely subjugated by the Jesuits. Only a few days before the publication of the Indulgence, that Order had been honored, in spite of the well-known wishes of the Holy See, with a new mark of his confidence and approbation. His confessor, Father Mansuete, a Franciscan, whose mild temper and irreproachable life commanded general respect, but who had long been hated by Tyrconnel and Petre, had been discarded. The vacant place had been filled by an Englishman named Warner, who had apostatized from the religion of his country and had turned Jesuit. To the moderate Roman Catholics and to the Nuncio this change was far from agreeable. By every Protestant it was regarded as a proof that the dominion of the Jesuits over the royal mind was absolute.* Whatever praises those fathers might

---

* Ellis Correspondence, March 15, July 27, 1686; Barillon, $\frac{\text{Feb. 28}}{\text{Mar. 10}}$, March $\frac{3}{13}$, $\frac{6}{16}$, 1687; Ronquillo, March $\frac{9}{19}$, 1687, in the Mackintosh Collection.

justly claim, flattery itself could not ascribe to them either wide liberality or strict veracity. That they had never scrupled, when the interest of their Order was at stake, to call in the aid of the civil sword, or to violate the laws of truth and of good faith, had been proclaimed to the world not only by Protestant accusers, but by men whose virtue and genius were the glory of the Church of Rome. It was incredible that a devoted disciple of the Jesuits should be on principle zealous for freedom of conscience: but it was neither incredible nor improbable that he might think himself justified in disguising his real sentiments, in order to render a service to his religion. It was certain that the King at heart preferred the Churchmen to the Puritans. It was certain that, while he had any hope of gaining the Churchmen, he had never shown the smallest kindness to the Puritans. Could it then be doubted that, if the Churchmen would even now comply with his wishes, he would willingly sacrifice the Puritans? His word, repeatedly pledged, had not restrained him from invading the legal rights of that clergy which had given such signal proofs of affection and fidelity to his house. What security then could his word afford to sects divided from him by the recollection of a thousand inexpiable wounds inflicted and endured?

When the first agitation produced by the publication of the Indulgence had subsided, it appeared that a breach had taken place in the Puritan party. The minority, *Some of the Dissenters side with the court.* headed by a few busy men whose judgment was defective or was biassed by interest, supported the King. Henry Care, who had long been the bitterest and most active pamphleteer among the Non-conformists, and *Care.* who had, in the days of the Popish Plot, assailed James with the utmost fury in a weekly journal entitled the Packet of Advice from Rome, was now as loud in adulation as he had formerly been in calumny and insult.* The chief agent who was employed by the government to

---

* Wood's Athenæ Oxonienses; Observator; Heraclitus Ridens, *passim*. But Care's own writings furnish the best materials for an estimate of his character.

II.—14

manage the Presbyterians was Vincent Alsop, a divine of some note both as a preacher and as a writer. His son, who had incurred the penalties of treason, received a pardon; and the whole influence of the father was thus engaged on the side of the court.* With Alsop was joined Thomas Rosewell. Rosewell had, during that persecution of the Dissenters which followed the detection of the Rye-house Plot, been falsely accused of preaching against the government, had been tried for his life by Jeffreys, and had, in defiance of the clearest evidence, been convicted by a packed jury. The injustice of the verdict was so gross that the very courtiers cried shame. One Tory gentleman who had heard the trial went instantly to Charles, and declared that the neck of the most loyal subject in England would not be safe if Rosewell suffered. The jurymen themselves were stung by remorse when they thought over what they had done, and exerted themselves to save the life of the prisoner. At length a pardon was granted: but Rosewell remained bound under heavy recognizances to good behavior during life, and to periodical appearance in the Court of King's Bench. His recognizances were now discharged by the royal command; and in this way his services were secured.†

Alsop.

Rosewell.

The business of gaining the Independents was principally intrusted to one of their ministers named Stephen Lobb. Lobb was a weak, violent, and ambitious man. He had gone such lengths in opposition to the government, that he had been by name proscribed in several proclamations. He now made his peace, and went as far in servility as he had ever done in faction. He joined the Jesuitical cabal, and eagerly recommended measures from which the wisest and most honest Roman Catholics recoiled. It was remarked that he was constantly at the palace and frequently in the closet, that he lived with a splendor to which the Puritan divines were little accustomed, and that he was perpetu-

Lobb.

---

* Calamy's Account of the Ministers ejected or silenced after the Restoration in Northamptonshire; Wood's Athenæ Oxonienses; Biographia Britannica.

† State Trials; Samuel Rosewell's Life of Thomas Rosewell, 1718; Calamy's Account.

ally surrounded by suitors imploring his interest to procure them offices or pardons.*

Penn.

With Lobb was closely connected William Penn. Penn had never been a strong-headed man: the life which he had been leading during two years had not a little impaired his moral sensibility; and if his conscience ever reproached him, he comforted himself by repeating that he had a good and noble end in view, and that he was not paid for his services in money.

By the influence of these men, and of others less conspicuous, addresses of thanks to the King were procured from several bodies of Dissenters. Tory writers have with justice remarked that the language of these compositions was as fulsomely servile as anything that could be found in the most florid eulogies pronounced by bishops on the Stuarts. But, on close inquiry, it will appear that the disgrace belongs to but a small part of the Puritan party. There was scarcely a market-town in England without at least a knot of separatists. No exertion was spared to induce them to express their gratitude for the Indulgence. Circular letters, imploring them to sign, were sent to every corner of the kingdom in such numbers that the mail-bags, it was sportively said, were too heavy for the post-horses. Yet all the addresses which could be obtained from all the Presbyterians, Independents, and Baptists scattered over England did not in six months amount to sixty; nor is there any reason to believe that these addresses were numerously signed.† One of the most adulatory was that of the Quakers; and Penn presented it with a speech more adulatory still.‡

The majority of the Puritans are against the court.

The great body of Protestant Non-conformists, firmly attached to civil liberty, and distrusting the promises of the King and of the Jesuits, steadily refused to return thanks for a favor which, it might well be suspected, concealed a snare. This was the temper of all

---

* London Gazette, March 15, 168⅚; Nichols's Defence of the Church of England; Pierce's Vindication of the Dissenters.

† The Addresses will be found in the London Gazettes.

‡ London Gazette, May 26, 1687; Life of Penn prefixed to his works, 1726.

the most illustrious chiefs of the party. One of these was
Baxter. He had, as we have seen, been brought to
trial soon after the accession of James, had been
brutally insulted by Jeffreys, and had been convicted by a
jury such as the courtly sheriffs of those times were in the
habit of selecting. Baxter had been about a year and a half
in prison when the court began to think seriously of gaining
the Non-conformists. He was not only set at liberty, but was
informed that, if he chose to reside in London, he might do
so without fearing that the Five-mile Act would be enforced
against him. The government probably hoped that the recollection of past sufferings and the sense of present ease
would produce the same effect on him as on Rosewell and
Lobb. The hope was disappointed. Baxter was neither to
be corrupted nor to be deceived. He refused to join in any
address of thanks for the Indulgence, and exerted all his influence to promote good feeling between the Church and the
Presbyterians.*

If any man stood higher than Baxter in the estimation of
the Protestant Dissenters, that man was John Howe. Howe
had, like Baxter, been personally a gainer by the
recent change of policy. The same tyranny which
had flung Baxter into jail had driven Howe into banishment;
and soon after Baxter had been let out of the King's Bench
Prison, Howe returned from Utrecht to England. It was expected at Whitehall that Howe would exert in favor of the
court all the authority which he possessed over his brethren.
The King himself condescended to ask the help of the subject whom he had oppressed. Howe appears to have hesitated: but the influence of the Hampdens, with whom he was
on terms of close intimacy, kept him steady to the cause of the
constitution. A meeting of Presbyterian ministers was held
at his house, to consider the state of affairs, and to determine
on the course to be adopted. There was great anxiety at the
palace to know the result. Two royal messengers were in
attendance during the discussion. They returned with the

---

* Calamy's Life of Baxter.

unwelcome news that Howe had declared himself decidedly adverse to the dispensing power, and that he had, after long debate, carried with him the majority of the assembly.*

To the names of Baxter and Howe must be added the name of a man far below them in station and in acquired knowledge, but in virtue their equal, and in genius their superior, John Bunyan. Bunyan had been bred a tinker, and had served as a private soldier in the parliamentary army. Early in his life he had been fearfully tortured by remorse for his youthful sins, the worst of which seem, however, to have been such as the world thinks venial. His keen sensibility and his powerful imagination made his internal conflicts singularly terrible. He fancied that he was under sentence of reprobation, that he had committed blasphemy against the Holy Ghost, that he had sold Christ, that he was actually possessed by a demon. Sometimes loud voices from heaven cried out to warn him. Sometimes fiends whispered impious suggestions in his ear. He saw visions of distant mountain-tops, on which the sun shone brightly, but from which he was separated by a waste of snow. He felt the Devil behind him pulling his clothes. He thought that the brand of Cain had been set upon him. He feared that he was about to burst asunder like Judas. His mental agony disordered his health. One day he shook like a man in the palsy. On another day he felt a fire within his breast. It is difficult to understand how he survived sufferings so intense, and so long continued. At length the clouds broke. From the depths of despair, the penitent passed to a state of serene felicity. An irresistible impulse now urged him to impart to others the blessing of which he was himself possessed.† He joined the Baptists, and became a preacher and writer. His education had been that of a mechanic. He knew no language but the English, as it was spoken by the common people. He had studied no great model of composition, with the exception, an important exception undoubtedly, of our noble

---

* Calamy's Life of Howe. The share which the Hampden family had in the matter I learned from a letter of Johnstone of Waristoun, dated June 13, 1688.

† Bunyan's Grace Abounding.

translation of the Bible. His spelling was bad. He frequently transgressed the rules of grammar. Yet his native force of genius, and his experimental knowledge of all the religious passions, from despair to ecstasy, amply supplied in him the want of learning. His rude oratory roused and melted hearers who listened without interest to the labored discourses of great logicians and Hebraists. His books were widely circulated among the humbler classes. One of them, the Pilgrim's Progress, was, in his own lifetime, translated into several foreign languages. It was, however, scarcely known to the learned and polite, and had been, during more than a century, the delight of pious cottagers and artisans before it took its proper place, as a classical work, in libraries. At length critics condescended to inquire where the secret of so wide and so durable a popularity lay. They were compelled to own that the ignorant multitude had judged more correctly than the learned, and that the despised little book was really a masterpiece. Bunyan is indeed as decidedly the first of allegorists as Demosthenes is the first of orators, or Shakspeare the first of dramatists. Other allegorists have shown equal ingenuity; but no other allegorist has ever been able to touch the heart and to make abstractions objects of terror, of pity, and of love.*

It may be doubted whether any English Dissenter had suffered more severely under the penal laws than John Bunyan. Of the twenty-seven years which had elapsed since the Restoration, he had passed twelve in confinement. He still persisted in preaching: but, that he might preach, he was under the necessity of disguising himself like a carter. He was often introduced into meetings through back doors, with a smock-frock on his back and a whip in his hand. If he had thought only of his own ease and safety, he would have hailed the Indulgence with delight. He was now, at length, free to

---

* Young classes Bunyan's prose with Durfey's poetry. The people of fashion in the Spiritual Quixote rank the Pilgrim's Progress with Jack the Giant-killer. Late in the eighteenth century Cowper did not venture to do more than allude to the great allegorist:

"I name thee not, lest so despised a name
Should move a sneer at thy deserved fame."

pray and exhort in open day. His congregation rapidly increased: thousands hung upon his words; and at Bedford, where he ordinarily resided, money was plentifully contributed to build a meeting-house for him. His influence among the common people was such that the government would willingly have bestowed on him some municipal office: but his vigorous understanding and his stout English heart were proof against all delusion and all temptation. He felt assured that the proffered toleration was merely a bait intended to lure the Puritan party to destruction; nor would he, by accepting a place for which he was not legally qualified, recognize the validity of the dispensing power. One of the last acts of his virtuous life was to decline an interview to which he was invited by an agent of the government.*

Great as was the authority of Bunyan over the Baptists, that of William Kiffin was still greater. Kiffin was the first man among them in wealth and station. He was in the habit of exercising his spiritual gifts at their meetings: but he did not live by preaching. He traded largely: his credit on the Exchange of London stood high; and he had accumulated an ample fortune. Perhaps no man could, at that conjuncture, have rendered more valuable services to the court. But between him and the court was interposed the remembrance of one terrible event. He was the grandfather of the two Hewlings, those gallant youths who, of all the victims of the Bloody Assizes, had been the most generally lamented. For the sad fate of one of them James was in a peculiar manner responsible. Jeffreys had respited the younger brother. The poor lad's sister had been ushered by Churchill into the royal presence, and had begged for mercy: but the King's heart had been obdurate. The misery of the whole family had been great: but Kiffin was most to be pitied. He was seventy years old when he was left desolate, the survivor of those who should have survived him. The heartless and venal sycophants of Whitehall, judging by themselves, thought that the old man would be easily pro-

Kiffin.

---

* The continuation of Bunyan's Life appended to his Grace Abounding.

pitiated by an alderman's gown, and by some compensation in money for the property which his grandsons had forfeited. Penn was employed in the work of seduction, but to no purpose.* The King determined to try what effect his own civilities would produce. Kiffin was ordered to attend at the palace. He found a brilliant circle of noblemen and gentlemen assembled. James immediately came to him, spoke to him very graciously, and concluded by saying, "I have put you down, Mr. Kiffin, for an Alderman of London." The old man looked fixedly at the King, burst into tears, and made answer, "Sir, I am worn out. I am unfit to serve Your Majesty or the City. And, sir, the death of my poor boys broke my heart. That wound is as fresh as ever. I shall carry it to my grave." The King stood silent for a minute in some confusion, and then said, "Mr. Kiffin, I will find a balsam for that sore." Assuredly James did not mean to say anything cruel or insolent: on the contrary, he seems to have been in an unusually gentle mood. Yet no speech that is recorded of him gives so unfavorable a notion of his character as these few words. They are the words of a hard-hearted and low-minded man, unable to conceive any laceration of the affections for which a place or a pension would not be a full compensation.†

* An attempt has been made to vindicate Penn's conduct on this occasion, and to fasten on me the charge of having calumniated him. It is asserted that, instead of being engaged, on behalf of the government, in the work of seduction, he was really engaged, on behalf of Kiffin, in the work of intercession. In support of this view the following passage is triumphantly quoted from Kiffin's Memoirs of himself. "I used all the means I could to be excused both by some lords near the King, and also by Sir Nicholas Butler, and Mr. Penn. But it was all in vain * * *." There the quotation ends, not at a full stop, but at a semicolon. The remainder of the sentence, which fully bears out all that I have said, is carefully suppressed Kiffin proceeds thus: "I was told that they (Nicholas and Penn) knew I had an interest that might serve the King, and although they knew my sufferings were great, in cutting off my two grandchildren, and losing their estates, yet it should be made up to me, both in their estates, and also in what honor or advantage I could reasonably desire for myself. But I thank the Lord, these proffers were no snare to me."

† Kiffin's Memoirs; Luson's Letter to Brooke, May 11, 1773, in the Hughes Correspondence.

Since Kiffin could not be seduced by blandishments and fair promises, it was determined to try what persecution would effect. He was told that an information would be filed against him in the Crown Office, and he was threatened with a lodging in Newgate. He asked the advice of counsel; and the answer which he received was that, by accepting office without taking the sacrament according to the Anglican ritual, he would make himself legally liable to a fine of five hundred pounds, but that by refusing office he would make himself liable, not legally, but in fact, to whatever fine a servile bench of judges might, in direct defiance of the statutes, think fit to impose. He might be mulcted in ten, twenty, thirty thousand pounds. His family, which had already suffered so cruelly from two confiscations, might be utterly ruined by this third calamity. After holding out many weeks, he so far submitted as to take the title of Alderman: but he abstained from acting either as a Justice of the Peace or as one of the Commission of Lieutenancy which commanded the militia of the City.*

That section of the dissenting body which was favorable to the King's new policy had from the first been a minority, and soon began to diminish. For the Non-conformists perceived in no long time that their spiritual privileges had been abridged rather than extended by the Indulgence. The chief characteristic of the Puritan was abhorrence of the peculiarities of the Church of Rome. He had quitted the Church of England only because he conceived that she too much resembled her superb and voluptuous sister, the sorceress of the golden cup and of the scarlet robe. He now found that one of the implied conditions of that alliance which some of his pastors had formed with the court was that the religion of the court should be respectfully and tenderly treated. He soon began to regret the days of persecution. While the penal laws were enforced, he had heard the words of life in secret and at his peril: but still he had heard them. When the brethren were assembled in the inner chamber, when the

---

* Kiffin's Memoirs.

sentinels had been posted, when the doors had been locked, when the preacher, in the garb of a butcher or a drayman, had come in over the tiles, then at least God was truly worshipped. No portion of divine truth was suppressed or softened down for any worldly object. All the distinctive doctrines of the Puritan theology were fully, and even coarsely, set forth. To the Church of Rome no quarter was given. The Beast, the Antichrist, the Man of Sin, the mystical Jezebel, the mystical Babylon, were the phrases ordinarily employed to describe that august and fascinating superstition. Such had been once the style of Alsop, of Lobb, of Rosewell, and of other ministers who had of late been well received at the palace: but such was now their style no longer. Divines who aspired to a high place in the King's favor and confidence could not venture to speak with asperity of the King's religion. Congregations, therefore, complained loudly that, since the appearance of the Declaration, which purported to give them entire freedom of conscience, they had never once heard the Gospel boldly and faithfully preached. Formerly they had been forced to snatch their spiritual nutriment by stealth; but, when they had snatched it, they had found it seasoned exactly to their taste. They were now at liberty to feed: but their food had lost all its savor. They met by daylight, and in commodious edifices; but they heard discourses far less to their taste than they would have heard from the rector. At the parish church the will-worship and idolatry of Rome were every Sunday attacked with energy: but at the meeting-house the pastor, who had a few months before reviled the established clergy as little better than Papists, now carefully abstained from censuring Popery, or conveyed his censures in language too delicate to shock even the ears of Father Petre. Nor was it possible to assign any creditable reason for this change. The Roman Catholic doctrines had undergone no alteration. Within living memory, never had Roman Catholic priests been so active in the work of making proselytes: never had so many Roman Catholic publications issued from the press: never had the attention of all who cared about religion been so closely fixed on the disputes between the Roman Catholics and the Protestants. What could be thought of the sincerity of theologians who had never been weary of railing at Popery when Popery was comparatively harmless and helpless, and who now, when a time of real danger to the reformed faith had arrived, studiously avoided uttering one word which could give offence to a Jesuit? Their conduct was indeed easily explained. It was known that some of them had obtained pardons. It was suspected that others had obtained money. Their prototype might be found in that weak apostle who from fear denied the Master to whom he had boastfully professed the firmest attachment, or in that baser apostle who sold his Lord for a handful of silver.*

Thus the dissenting ministers who had been gained by the court were rapidly losing the influence which they had once possessed over their brethren. On the other hand, the sectaries found themselves attracted by a strong religious sympathy toward those prelates and priests of the Church of England who, in spite of royal mandates, of threats, and of promises, were waging vigorous war with the Church of Rome. The Anglican body and the Puritan body, so long separated by a mortal enmity, were daily drawing nearer to each other, and every step which they made toward union increased the influence of him who was their common head. William was in all things fitted to be a mediator between these two great sections of the English nation. He could not be said to be a member of either. Yet neither, when in a reasonable mood, could refuse to regard him as a friend. His system of theology agreed with that of the Puritans. At the same time, he regarded episcopacy, not indeed as a divine institution, but as a perfectly lawful and an eminently useful form of church government. Questions respecting postures, robes, festivals, and liturgies he considered as of no vital importance. A simple worship, such as that to which he had been early accustomed, would have been most to his personal taste. But

---

* See, among other contemporary pamphlets, one entitled a Representation of the threatening Dangers impending over Protestants.

he was prepared to conform to any ritual which might be acceptable to the nation, and insisted only that he should not be required to persecute his brother Protestants whose consciences did not permit them to follow his example. Two years earlier he would have been pronounced by numerous bigots on both sides a mere Laodicean, neither cold nor hot, and fit only to be spewed out. But the zeal which had inflamed Churchmen against Dissenters and Dissenters against Churchmen had been so tempered by common adversity and danger that the lukewarmness which had once been imputed to him as a crime was now reckoned among his chief virtues.

All men were anxious to know what he thought of the Declaration of Indulgence. For a time hopes were entertained at Whitehall that his known respect for the rights of conscience would at least prevent him from publicly expressing disapprobation of a policy which had a specious show of liberality. Penn had visited Holland in the summer of 1686, confident that his eloquence, of which he had a high opinion, would prove irresistible. He had harangued on his favorite theme with a copiousness which tired his hearers out. He had assured them that a golden age of religious liberty was approaching: whoever lived three years longer would see strange things: he could not be mistaken; for he had it from a man who had it from an Angel. Penn also hinted that, though he had not come to the Hague with a royal commission, he knew the royal mind. There was nothing, he was confident, which the uncle would not do to gratify the nephew, if only the nephew would, in the matter of the Test Act, gratify the uncle. As oral exhortations and promises produced little effect, Penn returned to England, and thence wrote to the Hague that His Majesty seemed disposed to make large concessions, to live in close amity with the Prince, and to settle a handsome income on the Princess.* There can indeed be little doubt that James would gladly have purchased at a high price the sup-

The Prince and Princess of Orange hostile to the Declaration of Indulgence.

---

* Burnet, i., 693, 694; Avaux, Jan. 10, 1687. Penn's letters were regularly put, by one of his Quaker friends who resided at the Hague, into the Prince's own hand.

port of his eldest daughter and of his son-in-law. But, on the subject of the Test, William's resolution was immutable. "You ask me," he said to one of the King's agents, "to countenance an attack on my own religion. I cannot with a safe conscience do it, and I will not, no, not for the crown of England, nor for the empire of the world." These words were reported to the King, and disturbed him greatly.* He wrote urgent letters with his own hand. Sometimes he took the tone of an injured man. He was the head of the royal family: he was as such entitled to expect the obedience of the younger branches; and it was very hard that he was to be crossed in a matter on which his heart was set. At other times a bait which was thought irresistible was offered. If William would but give way on this one point, the English government would, in return, co-operate with him strenuously against France. He was not to be so deluded. He knew that James, without the support of a Parliament, would, even if not unwilling, be unable to render effectual service to the common cause of Europe; and there could be no doubt that, if a Parliament were assembled, the first demand of both Houses would be that the Declaration should be cancelled.

The Princess assented to all that was suggested by her husband. Their joint opinion was conveyed to the King in firm but temperate terms. They declared that they deeply regretted the course which His Majesty had adopted. They were convinced that he had usurped a prerogative which did not by law belong to him. Against that usurpation they protested, not only as friends to civil liberty, but as members of the royal house, who had a deep interest in maintaining the rights of that crown which they might one day wear. For experience had shown that in England arbitrary government could not fail to produce a reaction even more pernicious

---

* "Le Prince d'Orange, qui avoit éludé jusqu'alors de faire une réponse positive, dit * * * qu'il ne consentiroit jamais à la suppression de ces loix qui avoient été établies pour le maintien et la sureté de la religion Protestante, et que sa conscience ne le lui permettoit point, non seulement pour la succession du royaume d'Angleterre, mais même pour l'empire du monde; en sorte que le roi d'Angleterre est plus aigri contre lui qu'il n'a jamais été."—Bonrepaux, June $\frac{11}{21}$, 1687.

than itself; and it might reasonably be feared that the nation, alarmed and incensed by the prospect of despotism, might conceive a disgust even for constitutional monarchy. The advice, therefore, which they tendered to the King was that he would in all things govern according to law. They readily admitted that the law might with advantage be altered by competent authority, and that some part of his Declaration well deserved to be embodied in an Act of Parliament. They were not persecutors. They should with pleasure see Roman Catholics as well as Protestant Dissenters relieved in a proper manner from all penal statutes. They should with pleasure see Protestant Dissenters admitted in a proper manner to civil office. At that point their Highnesses must stop. They could not but entertain grave apprehensions that, if Roman Catholics were made capable of public trust, great evil would ensue; and it was intimated not obscurely that these apprehensions arose chiefly from the conduct of James.*

The opinion expressed by the Prince and Princess respecting the disabilities to which the Roman Catholics were subject was that of almost all the statesmen and philosophers who were then zealous for political and religious freedom. In our age, on the contrary, enlightened men have often pronounced, with regret, that on this one point William appears to disadvantage when compared to his father-in-law. The truth is that some considerations which are necessary to the forming of a correct judgment seem to have escaped the notice of many writers of the nineteenth century.

<small>Their views respecting the English Roman Catholics vindicated.</small>

There are two opposite errors into which those who study the annals of our country are in constant danger of falling— the error of judging the present by the past, and the error of judging the past by the present. The former is the error of minds prone to reverence whatever is old, the latter of minds readily attracted by whatever is new. The former error may perpetually be observed in the reasonings of conservative politicians on the questions of their own day. The latter error

---

* Burnet, i., 710; Bonrepaux, $\frac{\text{May 24,}}{\text{June 4,}}$ 1687.

perpetually infects the speculations of writers of the liberal school when they discuss the transactions of an earlier age. The former error is the more pernicious in a statesman, and the latter in a historian.

It is not easy for any person who, in our time, undertakes to treat of the revolution which overthrew the Stuarts, to preserve with steadiness the happy mean between these two extremes. The question whether members of the Roman Catholic Church could be safely admitted to Parliament and to office convulsed our country during the reign of James the Second, was set at rest by his downfall, and, having slept during more than a century, was revived by that great stirring of the human mind which followed the meeting of the National Assembly of France. During thirty years the contest went on in both Houses of Parliament, in every constituent body, in every social circle. It destroyed administrations, broke up parties, made all government in one part of the empire impossible, and at length brought us to the verge of civil war. Even when the struggle had terminated, the passions to which it had given birth still continued to rage. It was scarcely possible for any man whose mind was under the influence of those passions to see the events of the years 1687 and 1688 in a perfectly correct light.

One class of politicians, starting from the true proposition that the Revolution had been a great blessing to our country, arrived at the false conclusion that no test which the statesmen of the Revolution had thought necessary for the protection of our religion and our freedom could be safely abolished. Another class, starting from the true proposition that the disabilities imposed on the Roman Catholics had long been productive of nothing but mischief, arrived at the false conclusion that there never could have been a time when those disabilities were useful and necessary. The former fallacy pervaded the speeches of the acute and learned Eldon. The latter was not altogether without influence even on an intellect so calm and philosophical as that of Mackintosh.

Perhaps, however, it will be found on examination that we may vindicate the course which was unanimously approved by all the great English statesmen of the seventeenth century, without questioning the wisdom of the course which was as unanimously approved by all the great English statesmen of our own time.

Undoubtedly it is an evil that any citizen should be excluded from civil employment on account of his religious opinions: but a choice between evils is sometimes all that is left to human wisdom. A nation may be placed in such a situation that the majority must either impose disabilities or submit to them, and that what would, under ordinary circumstances, be justly condemned as persecution, may fall within the bounds of legitimate self-defence; and such was, in the year 1687, the situation of England.

According to the constitution of the realm, James possessed the right of naming almost all public functionaries, political, judicial, ecclesiastical, military, and naval. In the exercise of this right he was not, as our sovereigns now are, under the necessity of acting in conformity with the advice of ministers approved by the House of Commons. It was evident, therefore, that, unless he were strictly bound by law to bestow office on none but Protestants, it would be in his power to bestow office on none but Roman Catholics. The Roman Catholics were few in number; and among them was not a single man whose services could be seriously missed by the commonwealth. The proportion which they bore to the population of England was very much smaller than at present. For at present a constant stream of emigration runs from Ireland to our great towns: but in the seventeenth century there was not even in London an Irish colony. More than forty-nine-fiftieths of the inhabitants of the kingdom, more than forty-nine-fiftieths of the property of the kingdom, almost all the political, legal, and military ability and knowledge to be found in the kingdom, were Protestant. Nevertheless the King, under a strong infatuation, had determined to use his vast patronage as a means of making proselytes. To be of his Church was, in his view, the first of all qualifications for office. To be of the national Church was a positive disqualification. He reprobated, it is true, in language which has been applauded by some credulous friends of religious liberty, the monstrous injustice of that test which excluded a small minority of the nation from public trust: but he was at the same time instituting a test which excluded the majority. He thought it hard that a man who was a good financier and a loyal subject should be excluded from the post of Lord Treasurer merely for being a Papist. But he had himself turned out a Lord Treasurer whom he admitted to be a good financier and a loyal subject merely for being a Protestant. He had repeatedly and distinctly declared his resolution never to put the white staff in the hands of any heretic. With many other great offices of state he had dealt in the same way. Already the Lord President, the Lord Privy Seal, the Lord Chamberlain, the Groom of the Stole, the First Lord of the Treasury, the Principal Secretary of State, the Lord High Commissioner of Scotland, the Chancellor of Scotland, the Secretary of Scotland, were, or pretended to be, Roman Catholics. Most of these functionaries had been bred Churchmen, and had been guilty of apostasy, open or secret, in order to obtain or to keep their high places. Every Protestant who still held an important post in the government held it in constant uncertainty and fear. It would be endless to recount the situations of a lower rank which were filled by the favored class. Roman Catholics already swarmed in every department of the public service. They were Lords Lieutenants, Deputy Lieutenants, Judges, Justices of the Peace, Commissioners of the Customs, Envoys to foreign courts, Colonels of regiments, Governors of fortresses. The share which in a few months they had obtained of the temporal patronage of the crown was much more than ten times as great as they would have had under an impartial system. Yet this was not the worst. They were made rulers of the Church of England. Men who had assured the King that they held his faith sat in the High Commission, and exercised supreme jurisdiction in spiritual things over all the prelates and priests of the established religion. Ecclesiastical benefices of great dignity had been bestowed, some on avowed Papists, and some on half concealed Papists. And all this had been done while the laws against Popery were still

II.—15

unrepealed, and while James had still a strong interest in affecting respect for the rights of conscience. What, then, was his conduct likely to be, if his subjects consented to free him, by a legislative act, from even the shadow of restraint? Is it possible to doubt that Protestants would have been as effectually excluded from employment, by a strictly legal use of the royal prerogative, as ever Roman Catholics had been by Act of Parliament?

How obstinately James was determined to bestow on the members of his own Church a share of patronage altogether out of proportion to their numbers and importance is proved by the instructions which, in exile and old age, he drew up for the guidance of his son. It is impossible to read without mingled pity and derision those effusions of a mind on which all the discipline of experience and adversity had been exhausted in vain. The Pretender is advised, if ever he should reign in England, to make a partition of offices, and carefully to reserve for the members of the Church of Rome a portion which might have sufficed for them if they had been one-half instead of one-fiftieth part of the nation. One Secretary of State, one Commissioner of the Treasury, the Secretary at War, the majority of the great dignitaries of the household, the majority of the officers of the army, are always to be Catholics. Such were the designs of James after his perverse bigotry had drawn on him a punishment which had appalled the whole world. Is it then possible to doubt what his conduct would have been if his people, deluded by the empty name of religious liberty, had suffered him to proceed without any check?

Even Penn, intemperate and undiscerning as was his zeal for the Declaration, seems to have felt that the partiality with which honors and emoluments were heaped on Roman Catholics might not unnaturally excite the jealousy of the nation. He owned that, if the Test Act were repealed, the Protestants were entitled to an equivalent, and went so far as to suggest several equivalents. During some weeks the word equivalent, then lately imported from France, was in the mouths of all the coffee-house orators; but at length a few pages of keen logic and polished sarcasm written by Halifax put an end to these idle projects. One of Penn's schemes was that a law should be passed dividing the patronage of the crown into three equal parts, and that to one only of those parts members of the Church of Rome should be admitted. Even under such an arrangement the members of the Church of Rome would have obtained near twenty times their fair portion of official appointments; and yet there is no reason to believe that even to such an arrangement the King would have consented. But, had he consented, what guarantee could he give that he would adhere to his bargain? The dilemma propounded by Halifax was unanswerable. If laws are binding on you, observe the law which now exists. If laws are not binding on you, it is idle to offer us a law as a security.*

It is clear, therefore, that the point at issue was not whether secular offices should be thrown open to all sects indifferently. While James was King it was inevitable that there should be exclusion; and the only question was who should be excluded, Papists or Protestants, the few or the many, a hundred thousand Englishmen or five millions.

Such are the weighty arguments by which the conduct of the Prince of Orange toward the English Roman Catholics may be reconciled with the principles of religious liberty. These arguments, it will be observed, have no reference to any part of the Roman Catholic theology. It will also be observed that they ceased to have any force when the crown had been settled on a race of Protestant sovereigns, and when the power of the House of Commons in the state had become so decidedly preponderant that no sovereign, whatever might have been his opinions or his inclinations, could have imitated the example of James. The nation, however, after its terrors, its struggles, its narrow escape, was in a suspicious and vindictive mood. Means of defence, therefore, which necessity had once justified, and which necessity alone could justify, were obstinately used long after the necessity had ceased to exist, and were not abandoned till vulgar prejudice had main-

---

* Johnstone, Jan. 13, 1688; Halifax's Anatomy of an Equivalent.

tained a contest of many years against reason. But in the time of James reason and vulgar prejudice were on the same side. The fanatical and ignorant wished to exclude the Roman Catholic from office because he worshipped stocks and stones, because he had the mark of the Beast, because he had burned down London, because he had strangled Sir Edmondsbury Godfrey; and the most judicious and tolerant statesman, while smiling at the delusions which imposed on the populace, was led, by a very different road, to the same conclusion.

The great object of William now was to unite in one body the numerous sections of the community which regarded him as their common head. In this work he had several able and trusty coadjutors, among whom two were pre-eminently useful, Burnet and Dykvelt.

The services of Burnet, indeed, it was necessary to employ with some caution. The kindness with which he had been welcomed at the Hague had excited the rage of James. Mary received from her father two letters filled with invectives against the insolent and seditious divine whom she protected. But these accusations had so little effect on her that she sent back answers dictated by Burnet himself. At length, in January, 1687, the King had recourse to stronger measures. Skelton, who had represented the English government in the United Provinces, was removed to Paris, and was succeeded by Albeville, the weakest and basest of all the members of the Jesuitical cabal. Money was Albeville's one object; and he took it from all who offered it. He was paid at once by France and by Holland. Nay, he stooped below even the miserable dignity of corruption, and accepted bribes so small that they seemed better suited to a porter or a lackey than to an envoy who had been honored with an English baronetcy and a foreign marquisate. On one occasion he pocketed very complacently a gratuity of fifty pistoles as the price of a service which he had rendered to the States-general. This man had it in charge to demand that Burnet should no longer be countenanced at the Hague. William, who was not inclined to part with a

Enmity of James to Burnet.

valuable friend, answered at first with his usual coldness: "I am not aware, sir, that, since the Doctor has been here, he has done or said anything of which His Majesty can justly complain." But James was peremptory: the time for an open rupture had not arrived; and it was necessary to give way. During more than eighteen months Burnet never came into the presence of either the Prince or the Princess: but he resided near them: he was fully informed of all that was passing: his advice was constantly asked: his pen was employed on all important occasions; and many of the sharpest and most effective tracts which about that time appeared in London were justly attributed to him.

The rage of James flamed high. He had always been more than sufficiently prone to the angry passions. But none of his enemies, not even those who had conspired against his life, not even those who had attempted by perjury to load him with the guilt of treason and assassination, had ever been regarded by him with such animosity as he now felt for Burnet. His Majesty railed daily at the Doctor in unkingly language, and meditated plans of unlawful revenge. Even blood would not slake that frantic hatred. The insolent divine must be tortured before he was permitted to die. Fortunately he was by birth a Scot; and in Scotland, before he was gibbeted in the Grassmarket, his legs might be dislocated in the boot. Proceedings were accordingly instituted against him at Edinburgh: but he had been naturalized in Holland: he had married a woman of fortune who was a native of that province; and it was certain that his adopted country would not deliver him up. It was therefore determined to kidnap him. Ruffians were hired with great sums of money to perform this perilous and infamous service. An order for three thousand pounds on this account was actually drawn up for signature in the office of the Secretary of State. Lewis was apprised of the design, and took a warm interest in it. He would lend, he said, his best assistance to convey the villain to England, and would undertake that the ministers of the vengeance of James should find a secure asylum in France. Burnet was well aware of his danger: but timidity was not among his faults. He published a courageous answer to the charges which had been brought against him at Edinburgh. He knew, he said, that it was intended to execute him without a trial: but his trust was in the King of kings, to whom innocent blood would not cry in vain, even against the mightiest princes of the earth. He gave a farewell dinner to some friends, and, after the meal, took solemn leave of them, as a man who was doomed to death, and with whom they could no longer safely converse. Nevertheless he continued to show himself in all the public places of the Hague so boldly that his friends reproached him bitterly with his foolhardiness.*

While Burnet was William's secretary for English affairs in Holland, Dykvelt had been not less usefully employed in London. Dykvelt was one of a remarkable class of public men who, having been bred to politics in the noble school of John De Witt, had, after the fall of that great minister, thought that they should best discharge their duty to the commonwealth by rallying round the Prince of Orange. Of the diplomatists in the service of the United Provinces none was, in dexterity, temper, and manners, superior to Dykvelt. In knowledge of English affairs none seems to have been his equal. A pretence was found for despatching him, early in the year 1687, to England on a special mission with credentials from the States-general. But in truth

Mission of Dykvelt to England.

---

* Burnet, i., 726–731; Answer to the Criminal Letters issued out against Dr. Burnet; Avaux Neg., July $\frac{7}{17}$, $\frac{14}{24}$, $\frac{\text{July 28,}}{\text{Aug. 7,}}$ 1687, Jan. $\frac{19}{29}$, 1688; Lewis to Barillon, $\frac{\text{Dec. 30, 1687}}{\text{Jan. 9, 1688}}$; Johnstone of Waristoun, Feb. 21, 1688; Lady Russell to Dr. Fitzwilliam, Oct. 5, 1687. As it has been suspected that Burnet, who certainly was not in the habit of underrating his own importance, exaggerated the danger to which he was exposed, I will give the words of Lewis and of Johnstone. "Qui que ce soit," says Lewis, "qui entreprenne de l'enlever en Hollande trouvera non seulement une retraite assurée et me entière protection dans mes états, mais aussi toute l'assistance qu'il pourra désirer pour faire conduire surement ce scélérat en Angleterre." "The business of Bamfield (Burnet) is certainly true," says Johnstone. "No man doubts of it here, and some concerned do not deny it. His friends say they hear he takes no care of himself, but out of vanity, to show his courage, shows his folly; so that, if ill happen on it, all people will laugh at it. Pray tell him so much from Jones (Johnstone). If some could be catched making their coup d'essai on him, it will do much to frighten them from making any attempt on Ogle (the Prince)."

his embassy was not to the government, but to the opposition; and his conduct was guided by private instructions which had been drawn by Burnet, and approved by William.*

Dykvelt reported that James was bitterly mortified by the conduct of the Prince and Princess. "My nephew's duty," said the King, "is to strengthen my hands. But he has always taken a pleasure in crossing me." Dykvelt answered that in matters of private concern His Highness had shown, and was ready to show, the greatest deference to the King's wishes; but that it was scarcely reasonable to expect the aid of a Protestant prince against the Protestant religion.† The King was silenced, but not appeased. He saw, with ill-humor which he could not disguise, that Dykvelt was mustering and drilling all the various divisions of the opposition with a skill which would have been creditable to the ablest English statesman, and which was marvellous in a foreigner. The clergy were told that they would find the Prince a friend to episcopacy and to the Book of Common Prayer. The Non-conformists were encouraged to expect from him, not only toleration, but also comprehension. Even the Roman Catholics were conciliated; and some of the most respectable among them declared, to the King's face, that they were satisfied with what Dykvelt proposed, and that they would rather have a toleration, secured by statute, than an illegal and precarious ascendency.‡ The chiefs of all the important sections of the nation had frequent conferences in the presence of the dexterous Envoy. At these meetings the sense of the Tory party was chiefly spoken by the Earls of Danby and Nottingham. Though more than eight years had elapsed since Danby had fallen from power, his name was still great among the old Cavaliers of England; and many even of those Whigs who had for-

Margin notes: Negotiations of Dykvelt with English statesmen. Danby.

---

* Burnet, i., 708; Avaux Neg., Jan. $\frac{8}{15}$, Feb. $\frac{6}{16}$, 1687; Van Kampen, Karakterkunde der Vaderlandsche Geschiedenis.

† Burnet, i., 711. Dykvelt's despatches to the States-general contain, as far as I have seen or can learn, not a word about the real object of his mission. His correspondence with the Prince of Orange was strictly private.

‡ Bonrepaux, Sept. $\frac{12}{22}$, 1687.

merly persecuted him were now disposed to admit that he had suffered for faults not his own, and that his zeal for the prerogative, though it had often misled him, had been tempered by two feelings which did him honor—zeal for the established religion, and zeal for the dignity and independence of his country. He was also highly esteemed at the Hague, where it was never forgotten that he was the person who, in spite of the influence of France and of the Papists, had induced Charles to bestow the hand of the Lady Mary on her cousin.

Daniel Finch, Earl of Nottingham, a nobleman whose name will frequently recur in the history of three eventful reigns, sprang from a family of unrivalled forensic eminence. One of his kinsmen had borne the seal of Charles the First, had prostituted eminent parts and learning to evil purposes, and had been pursued by the vengeance of the Commons of England with Falkland at their head. A more honorable renown had in the succeeding generation been obtained by Heneage Finch. He had immediately after the Restoration been appointed Solicitor-general. He had subsequently risen to be Attorney-general, Lord Keeper, Lord Chancellor, Baron Finch, and Earl of Nottingham. Through this prosperous career he had always held the prerogative as high as he honestly or decently could; but he had never been concerned in any machinations against the fundamental laws of the realm. In the midst of a corrupt court he had kept his personal integrity unsullied. He had enjoyed high fame as an orator, though his diction, formed on models anterior to the civil wars, was, toward the close of his life, pronounced stiff and pedantic by the wits of the rising generation. In Westminster Hall he is still mentioned with respect as the man who first educed out of the chaos anciently called by the name of equity a new system of jurisprudence, as regular and complete as that which is administered by the Judges of the Common Law.* A considerable part of the moral and intellectual character of this great magistrate had descended with the title of Nottingham to his eldest son. This son, Earl

---

* See Lord Campbell's Life of him.

Daniel, was an honorable and virtuous man. Though enslaved by some absurd prejudices, and though liable to strange fits of caprice, he cannot be accused of having deviated from the path of right in search either of unlawful gain or of unlawful pleasure. Like his father he was a distinguished speaker, impressive but prolix, and too monotonously solemn. The person of the orator was in perfect harmony with his oratory. His attitude was rigidly erect: his complexion was so dark that he might have passed for a native of a warmer climate than ours; and his harsh features were composed to an expression resembling that of a chief mourner at a funeral. It was commonly said that he looked rather like a Spanish grandee than like an English gentleman. The nicknames of Dismal, Don Dismallo, and Don Diego, were fastened on him by jesters, and are not yet forgotten. He had paid much attention to the science by which his family had been raised to greatness, and was, for a man born to rank and wealth, wonderfully well read in the laws of his country. He was a devoted son of the Church, and showed his respect for her in two ways not usual among those Lords who in his time boasted that they were her especial friends—by writing tracts in defence of her dogmas, and by shaping his private life according to her precepts. Like other zealous Churchmen, he had, till recently, been a strenuous supporter of monarchical authority. But to the policy which had been pursued since the suppression of the Western insurrection he was bitterly hostile, and not the less so because his younger brother Heneage had been turned out of the office of Solicitor-general for refusing to defend the King's dispensing power.*

With these two great Tory Earls was now united Halifax, the accomplished chief of the Trimmers. Over the mind of Nottingham, indeed, Halifax appears to have had at this time a great ascendency. Between Halifax and Danby there was an enmity which began in the court of Charles, and which, at a later period, disturbed the court of

Halifax.

---

* Johnstone's Correspondence; Mackay's Memoirs; Arbuthnot's John Bull; Swift's writings from 1710 to 1714, *passim;* Whiston's Letter to the Earl of Nottingham, and the Earl's answer.

William, but which, like many other enmities, remained suspended during the tyranny of James. The foes frequently met in the councils held by Dykvelt, and agreed in expressing dislike of the policy of the government and reverence for the Prince of Orange. The different characters of the two statesmen appeared strongly in their dealings with the Dutch envoy. Halifax showed an admirable talent for disquisition, but shrank from coming to any bold and irrevocable decision. Danby, far less subtle and eloquent, displayed more energy, resolution, and practical sagacity.

Several eminent Whigs were in constant communication with Dykvelt: but the heads of the great houses of Cavendish and Russell could not take quite so active and prominent a part as might have been expected from their station and their opinions. The fame and fortunes of Devonshire were at that moment under a cloud. He had an unfortunate quarrel with the court, arising, not from a public and honorable cause, but from a private brawl in which even his warmest friends could not pronounce him altogether blameless. He had gone to Whitehall to pay his duty, and had there been insulted by a man named Colepepper, one of a set of bravoes who infested the purlieus of the court, and attempted to curry favor with the government by affronting members of the opposition. The King himself expressed great indignation at the manner in which one of his most distinguished peers had been treated under the royal roof; and Devonshire was pacified by an intimation that the offender should never again be admitted into the palace. The interdict, however, was soon taken off. The Earl's resentment revived. His servants took up his cause. Hostilities such as seemed to belong to a ruder age disturbed the streets of Westminster. The time of the Privy Council was occupied by the criminations and recriminations of the adverse parties. Colepepper's wife declared that she and her husband went in danger of their lives, and that their house had been assaulted by ruffians in the Cavendish livery. Devonshire replied that he had been fired at from Colepepper's windows. This was vehemently denied. A pistol, it was owned, loaded with gunpowder, had been discharged. But this had been done in a moment of terror merely for the purpose of alarming the Guards. While this feud was at the height the Earl met Colepepper in the drawing-room at Whitehall, and fancied that he saw triumph and defiance in the bully's countenance. Nothing unseemly passed in the royal sight; but, as soon as the enemies had left the presence-chamber, Devonshire proposed that they should instantly decide their dispute with their swords. This challenge was refused. Then the high-spirited peer forgot the respect which he owed to the place where he stood and to his own character, and struck Colepepper in the face with a cane. All classes agreed in condemning this act as most indiscreet and indecent; nor could Devonshire himself, when he had cooled, think of it without vexation and shame. The government, however, with its usual folly, treated him so severely that in a short time the public sympathy was all on his side. A criminal information was filed in the King's Bench. The defendant took his stand on the privileges of the peerage; but on this point a decision was promptly given against him; nor is it possible to deny that the decision, whether it were or were not according to the technical rules of English law, was in strict conformity with the great principles on which all laws ought to be framed. Nothing was then left to him but to plead guilty. The tribunal had, by successive dismissions, been reduced to such complete subjection, that the government which had instituted the prosecution was allowed to prescribe the punishment. The Judges waited in a body on Jeffreys, who insisted that they should impose a fine of not less than thirty thousand pounds. Thirty thousand pounds, when compared with the revenues of the English grandees of that age, may be considered as equivalent to a hundred and fifty thousand pounds in the nineteenth century. In the presence of the Chancellor not a word of disapprobation was uttered: but, when the Judges had retired, Sir John Powell, in whom all the little honesty of the bench was concentrated, muttered that the proposed penalty was enormous, and that one-tenth part would be amply sufficient. His brethren did not agree with him; nor did he, on this occasion, show the courage by which, on a memorable day some months later, he signally retrieved his fame. The Earl was accordingly condemned to a fine of thirty thousand pounds, and to imprisonment till payment should be made. Such a sum could not then be raised at a day's notice even by the greatest of the nobility. The sentence of imprisonment, however, was more easily pronounced than executed. Devonshire had retired to Chatsworth, where he was employed in turning the old Gothic mansion of his family into an edifice worthy of Palladio. The Peak was in those days almost as rude a district as Connemara now is, and the Sheriff found, or pretended, that it was difficult to arrest the lord of so wild a region in the midst of a devoted household and tenantry. Some days were thus gained: but at last both the Earl and the Sheriff were lodged in prison. Meanwhile a crowd of intercessors exerted their influence. The story ran that the Countess Dowager of Devonshire had obtained admittance to the royal closet, that she had reminded James how her brother-in-law, the gallant Charles Cavendish, had fallen at Gainsborough fighting for the crown, and that she had produced notes, written by Charles the First and Charles the Second, in acknowledgment of great sums lent by her Lord during the civil troubles. Those loans had never been repaid, and, with the interest, amounted, it was said, to more even than the immense fine which the Court of King's Bench had imposed. There was another consideration which seems to have had more weight with the King than the memory of former services. It might be necessary to call a Parliament. Whenever that event took place it was believed that Devonshire would bring a writ of error. The point on which he meant to appeal from the judgment of the King's Bench related to the privileges of peerage. The tribunal before which the appeal must come was the House of Peers. On such an occasion the court could not be certain of the support even of the most courtly nobles. There was little doubt that the sentence would be annulled, and that, by grasping at too much, the government would lose all. James was therefore disposed to a compromise. Devonshire was informed that, if he would give a bond for the whole fine, and thus preclude himself from the advantage which he might derive from a writ of error, he should be set at liberty. Whether the bond should be enforced or not would depend on his subsequent conduct. If he would support the dispensing power nothing would be exacted from him. If he was bent on popularity, he must pay thirty thousand pounds for it. He refused, during some time, to consent to these terms; but confinement was insupportable to him. He signed the bond, and was let out of prison: but, though he consented to lay this heavy burden on his estate, nothing could induce him to promise that he would abandon his principles and his party. He was still intrusted with all the secrets of the opposition: but during some months his political friends thought it best for himself and for the good cause that he should remain in the background.*

The Earl of Bedford had never recovered from the effects of the great calamity which, four years before, had almost broken his heart. From private as well as from public feelings he was adverse to the court: but he was not active in concerting measures against it. His place in the meetings of the malcontents was supplied by his nephew. This was the celebrated Edward Russell, a man of undoubted courage and capacity, but of loose principles and turbulent temper. He was a sailor, had distinguished himself in his profession, and had in the late reign held an office in the palace. But all the ties which bound him to the royal family had been sundered by the death of his cousin William. The daring, unquiet, and vindictive seaman now sat in the councils called by the Dutch Envoy as the representative of the boldest and most eager section of the opposition, of those

---

* Kennet's funeral sermon on the Duke of Devonshire, and Memoirs of the family of Cavendish; State Trials; Privy Council Book, March 5, 168⅚; Barillon, $\frac{\text{June 30}}{\text{July 10}}$, 1687; Johnstone, Dec. $\frac{8}{18}$, 1687; Lords' Journals, May 6, 1689. "Ses amis et ses proches," says Barillon, "lui conseillent de prendre le bon parti, mais il persiste jusqu'à présent à ne se point soumettre. S'il vouloit se bien conduire et renoncer à être populaire il ne payeroit pas l'amende, mais s'il opiniâtre, il lui en coûtera trente mille pièces et il demeurera prisonnier jusqu'à l'actuel payement."

men who, under the names of Roundheads, Exclusionists, and Whigs, had maintained with various fortune a contest of five-and-forty years against three successive Kings. This party, lately prostrate and almost extinct, but now again full of life and rapidly rising to ascendency, was troubled by none of the scruples which still impeded the movements of Tories and Trimmers, and was prepared to draw the sword against the tyrant on the first day on which the sword could be drawn with reasonable hope of success.

Three men are yet to be mentioned with whom Dykvelt was in confidential communication, and by whose help he hoped to secure the good-will of three great professions. Bishop Compton was the agent employed to manage the clergy: Admiral Herbert undertook to exert all his influence over the navy; and an interest was established in the army by the instrumentality of Churchill.

Compton.

Herbert.

The conduct of Compton and Herbert requires no explanation. Having, in all things secular, served the crown with zeal and fidelity, they had incurred the royal displeasure by refusing to be employed as tools for the destruction of their own religion. Both of them had learned by experience how soon James forgot obligations, and how bitterly he remembered what it pleased him to consider as wrongs. The Bishop had by an illegal sentence been suspended from his episcopal functions. The Admiral had in one hour been reduced from opulence to penury. The situation of Churchill was widely different. He had been raised by the royal bounty from obscurity to eminence, and from poverty to wealth. Having started in life a needy ensign, he was now, in his thirty-seventh year, a major-general, a peer of Scotland, a peer of England: he commanded a troop of Life Guards: he had been appointed to several honorable and lucrative offices; and as yet there was no sign that he had lost any part of the favor to which he owed so much. He was bound to James, not only by the common obligations of allegiance, but by military honor, by personal gratitude, and, as appeared to superficial observers, by the strongest ties of interest. But

Churchill.

Churchill himself was no superficial observer. He knew exactly what his interest really was. If his master were once at full liberty to employ Papists, not a single Protestant would be employed. For a time a few highly favored servants of the crown might possibly be exempted from the general proscription in the hope that they would be induced to change their religion. But even these would, after a short respite, fall one by one, as Rochester had already fallen. Churchill might indeed secure himself from this danger, and might raise himself still higher in the royal favor, by conforming to the Church of Rome; and it might seem that one who was not less distinguished by avarice and baseness than by capacity and valor was not likely to be shocked at the thought of hearing a mass. But so inconsistent is human nature that there are tender spots even in seared consciences. And thus this man, who had owed his rise to his sister's dishonor, who had been kept by the most profuse, imperious, and shameless of harlots, and whose public life, to those who can look steadily through the dazzling blaze of genius and glory, will appear a prodigy of turpitude, believed implicitly in the religion which he had learned as a boy, and shuddered at the thought of formally abjuring it. A terrible alternative was before him. The earthly evil which he most dreaded was poverty. The one crime from which his heart recoiled was apostasy. And, if the designs of the court succeeded, he could not doubt that between poverty and apostasy he must soon make his choice. He therefore determined to cross those designs; and it soon appeared that there was no guilt and no disgrace which he was not ready to incur in order to escape from the necessity of parting either with his places or with his religion.*

It was not only as a military commander, high in rank, and distinguished by skill and courage, that Churchill was able to

---

* The motive which determined the conduct of the Churchills is shortly and plainly set forth in the Duchess of Marlborough's Vindication. "It was," she says, "evident to all the world that, as things were carried on by King James, everybody, sooner or later, must be ruined who would not become a Roman Catholic. This consideration made me very well pleased at the Prince of Orange's undertaking to rescue us from such slavery."

render services to the opposition. It was, if not absolutely essential, yet most important, to the success of William's plans that his sister-in-law, who, in the order of succession to the English throne, stood between his wife and himself, should act in cordial union with him. All his difficulties would have been greatly augmented if Anne had declared herself favorable to the Indulgence. Which side she might take depended on the will of others. For her understanding was sluggish; and, though there was latent in her character a hereditary wilfulness and stubbornness which, many years later, great power and great provocations developed, she was as yet a willing slave to a nature far more vivacious and imperious than her own. The person by whom she was absolutely governed was the wife of Churchill, a woman who afterward exercised a great influence on the fate of England and of Europe.

Lady Churchill and Princess Anne.

The name of this celebrated favorite was Sarah Jennings. Her eldest sister, Frances, had been distinguished by beauty and levity even among the crowd of beautiful faces and light characters which adorned and disgraced Whitehall during the wild carnival of the Restoration. On one occasion Frances dressed herself like an orange-girl and cried fruit about the streets.* Sober people predicted that a girl of so little discretion and delicacy would not easily find a husband. She was however twice married, and was now the wife of Tyrconnel. Sarah, less regularly beautiful, was perhaps more attractive. Her face was expressive: her form wanted no feminine charm; and the profusion of her fine hair, not yet disguised by powder according to that barbarous fashion which she lived to see introduced, was the delight of numerous admirers. Among the gallants who sued for her favor, Colonel Churchill, young, handsome, graceful, insinuating, eloquent, and brave, obtained the preference. He must have been enamoured indeed. For he had little property except the annuity which he had bought with the infamous wages bestowed on him by the Duchess of Cleveland: he was insatiable of

---

* Grammont's Memoirs; Pepys's Diary, Feb. 21, 168$\frac{4}{5}$.

riches: Sarah was poor; and a plain girl with a large fortune was proposed to him. His love, after a struggle, prevailed over his avarice: marriage only strengthened his passion; and, to the last hour of his life, Sarah enjoyed the pleasure and distinction of being the one human being who was able to mislead that far-sighted and sure-footed judgment, who was fervently loved by that cold heart, and who was servilely feared by that intrepid spirit.

In a wordly sense the fidelity of Churchill's love was amply rewarded. His bride, though slenderly portioned, brought with her a dowry which, judiciously employed, made him at length a Duke of England, a Prince of the Empire, the captain-general of a great coalition, the arbiter between mighty princes, and, what he valued more, the wealthiest subject in Europe. She had been brought up from childhood with the Princess Anne; and a close friendship had arisen between the girls. In character they resembled each other very little. Anne was slow and taciturn. To those whom she loved she was meek. The form which her anger assumed was sullenness. She had a strong sense of religion, and was attached even with bigotry to the rites and government of the Church of England. Sarah was lively and voluble, domineered over those whom she regarded with most kindness, and, when she was offended, vented her rage in tears and tempestuous reproaches. To sanctity she made no pretence, and, indeed, narrowly escaped the imputation of irreligion. She was not yet what she became when one class of vices had been fully developed in her by prosperity, and another by adversity, when her brain had been turned by success and flattery, when her heart had been ulcerated by disasters and mortifications. She lived to be that most odious and miserable of human beings, an ancient crone at war with her whole kind, at war with her own children and grandchildren, great indeed and rich, but valuing greatness and riches chiefly because they enabled her to brave public opinion, and to indulge without restraint her hatred to the living and the dead. In the reign of James she was regarded as nothing worse than a fine high-spirited young

II.—16

woman, who could now and then be cross and arbitrary, but whose flaws of temper might well be pardoned in consideration of her charms.

It is a common observation that differences of taste, understanding, and disposition are no impediments to friendship, and that the closest intimacies often exist between minds each of which supplies what is wanting to the other. Lady Churchill was loved and even worshipped by Anne. The Princess could not live apart from the object of her romantic fondness. She married, and was a faithful and even an affectionate wife. But Prince George, a dull man whose chief pleasures were derived from his dinner and his bottle, acquired over her no influence comparable to that exercised by her female friend, and soon gave himself up with stupid patience to the dominion of the vehement and commanding spirit by which his wife was governed. Children were born to the royal pair; and Anne was by no means without the feelings of a mother. But the tenderness which she felt for her offspring was languid when compared with her devotion to the companion of her early years. At length the Princess became impatient of the restraint which etiquette imposed on her. She could not bear to hear the words Madam and Royal Highness from the lips of one who was more to her than a sister. Such words were indeed necessary in the gallery or the drawing-room: but they were disused in the closet. Anne was Mrs. Morley: Lady Churchill was Mrs. Freeman; and under these childish names was carried on during twenty years a correspondence on which at last the fate of administrations and dynasties depended. But as yet Anne had no political power and little patronage. Her friend attended her as first Lady of the Bedchamber, with a salary of only four hundred pounds a year. There is reason, however, to believe that, even at this time, Churchill was able to gratify his ruling passion by means of his wife's influence. The Princess, though her income was large and her tastes simple, contracted debts which her father, not without some murmurs, discharged; and it was rumored that her embarrassments had been caused by her prodigal bounty to her favorite.*

At length the time had arrived when this singular friendship was to exercise a great influence on public affairs. What part Anne would take in the contest which distracted England was matter of deep anxiety. Filial duty was on one side; and the interests of the religion to which she was sincerely attached were on the other. A less inert nature might well have remained long in suspense when drawn in opposite directions by motives so strong and so respectable. But the influence of the Churchills decided the question; and their patroness became an important member of that extensive league of which the Prince of Orange was the head.

In June, 1687, Dykvelt returned to the Hague. He presented to the States-general a royal epistle filled with eulogies of his conduct during his residence in London. These eulogies, however, were merely formal. James, in private communications written with his own hand, bitterly complained that the Envoy had lived in close intimacy with the most factious men in the realm, and had encouraged them in all their evil purposes. Dykvelt carried with him also a packet of letters from the most eminent of those with whom he had conferred during his stay in England. The writers generally expressed unbounded reverence and affection for William, and referred him to the bearer for fuller information as to their views. Halifax discussed the state and prospects of the country with his usual subtlety and vivacity, but took care not to pledge himself to any perilous line of conduct. Danby wrote in a bolder and more determined tone, and could not refrain from slyly sneering at the fears and scruples of his accomplished rival. But the most remarkable letter was from Churchill. It was written with that natural eloquence which, illiterate as he was, he never wanted on great occasions, and with that air of magnanimity which, perfidious as he was, he

Dykvelt returns to the Hague

with letters from many eminent Englishmen.

---

* It would be endless to recount all the books from which I have formed my estimate of the Duchess's character. Her own letters, her own Vindication, and the replies which it called forth, have been my chief materials.

could with singular dexterity assume. The Princess Anne, he said, had commanded him to assure her illustrious relatives at the Hague that she was fully resolved, by God's help, rather to lose her life than to be guilty of apostasy. As for himself, his places and the royal favor were as nothing to him in comparison with his religion. He concluded by declaring in lofty language that, though he could not pretend to have lived the life of a saint, he should be found ready, on occasion, to die the death of a martyr.*

Dykvelt's mission had succeeded so well that a pretence was soon found for sending another agent to continue the work which had been so auspiciously commenced.

<small>Zulestein's mission.</small>

The new Envoy, afterward the founder of a noble English house which became extinct in our own time, was an illegitimate cousin-german of William; and bore a title taken from the lordship of Zulestein. Zulestein's relationship to the House of Orange gave him importance in the public eye. His bearing was that of a gallant soldier. He was indeed in diplomatic talents and knowledge far inferior to Dykvelt: but even this inferiority had its advantages. A military man, who had never appeared to trouble himself about political affairs, could, without exciting any suspicion, hold with the English aristocracy an intercourse which, if he had been a noted master of statecraft, would have been jealously watched. Zulestein, after a short absence, returned to his country charged with letters and verbal messages not less important than those which had been intrusted to his predecessor. A regular correspondence was from this time established between the Prince and the opposition. Agents of various ranks passed and repassed between the Thames and the Hague. Among these a Scotchman, of some parts and great activity, named Johnstone, was the most useful. He was cousin to Burnet, and son of an eminent Covenanter, who had, soon after the Restoration, been put to death for treason, and who was honored by his party as a martyr.

---

* The formal epistle which Dykvelt carried back to the States is in the Archives at the Hague. The other letters mentioned in this paragraph are given by Dalrymple; Appendix to Book V.

The estrangement between the King of England and the Prince of Orange became daily more complete. A serious dispute had arisen concerning the six British regiments which were in the pay of the United Provinces. The King wished to put these regiments under the command of Roman Catholic officers. The Prince resolutely opposed this design. The King had recourse to his favorite commonplaces about toleration. The Prince replied that he only followed His Majesty's example. It was notorious that loyal and able men had been turned out of office in England merely for being Protestants. It was then surely competent to the Stadtholder and the States-general to withhold high public trusts from Papists. This answer provoked James to such a degree that, in his rage, he lost sight of veracity and common-sense. It was false, he vehemently said, that he had ever turned out any body on religious grounds. And if he had, what was that to the Prince or to the States? Were they his masters? Were they to sit in judgment on the conduct of foreign sovereigns? From that time he became desirous to recall his subjects who were in the Dutch service. By bringing them over to England he should, he conceived, at once strengthen himself, and weaken his worst enemies. But there were financial difficulties which it was impossible for him to overlook. The number of troops already in his pay was as great as his revenue, though large beyond all precedent, and though parsimoniously administered, would support. If the battalions now in Holland were added to the existing establishment, the Treasury would be bankrupt. Perhaps Lewis might be induced to take them into his service. They would in that case be removed from a country where they were exposed to the corrupting influence of a republican government and a Calvinistic worship, and would be placed in a country where none ventured to dispute the mandates of the sovereign or the doctrines of the true Church. The soldiers would soon unlearn every political and religious heresy. Their native prince might always, at short notice, command their help, and would, on any emergency, be able to rely on their fidelity.

Growing enmity between James and William.

A negotiation on this subject was opened between Whitehall and Versailles. Lewis had as many soldiers as he wanted; and, had it been otherwise, he would not have been disposed to take Englishmen into his service; for the pay of England, low as it must seem to our generation, was much higher than the pay of France. At the same time, it was a great object to deprive William of so fine a brigade. After some weeks of correspondence, Barillon was authorized to promise that, if James would recall the British troops from Holland, Lewis would bear the charge of supporting two thousand of them in England. This offer was accepted by James with warm expressions of gratitude. Having made these arrangements, he requested the States-general to send back the six regiments. The States-general, completely governed by William, answered that such a demand, in such circumstances, was not authorized by the existing treaties, and positively refused to comply. It is remarkable that Amsterdam, which had voted for keeping these troops in Holland when James needed their help against the Western insurgents, now contended vehemently that his request ought to be granted. On both occasions, the sole object of those who ruled that great city was to cross the Prince of Orange.*

Influence of the Dutch press.

The Dutch arms, however, were scarcely so formidable to James as the Dutch presses. English books and pamphlets against his government were daily printed at the Hague; nor could any vigilance prevent copies from being smuggled, by tens of thousands, into the counties bordering on the German Ocean. Among these publications, one was distinguished by its importance, and by the immense effect which it produced. The opinion which the Prince and Princess of Orange held respecting the Indulgence was well known to all who were conversant with public affairs. But, as no official announcement of that opinion had

---

* Sunderland to William, Aug. 24, 1686; William to Sunderland, Sept. $\frac{2}{12}$, 1686; Barillon, May $\frac{6}{16}$, $\frac{\text{May } 26}{\text{June } 5}$, Oct. $\frac{3}{13}$, $\frac{\text{Nov. } 28}{\text{Dec. } 8}$, 1687; Lewis to Barillon, Oct. $\frac{14}{24}$, 1687; Memorial of Albeville, Dec. $\frac{15}{25}$, 1687; James to William, Jan. 17, Feb. 16, March 2, 13, 1688; Avaux Neg., March $\frac{1}{11}$, $\frac{6}{16}$, $\frac{8}{18}$, $\frac{\text{March } 22}{\text{April } 1}$, 1688.

appeared, many persons who had not access to good private sources of information were deceived or perplexed by the confidence with which the partisans of the court asserted that their Highnesses approved of the King's late acts. To contradict those assertions publicly would have been a simple and obvious course, if the sole object of William had been to strengthen his interest in England. But he considered England chiefly as an instrument necessary to the execution of his great European design. Toward that design he hoped to obtain the co-operation of both branches of the House of Austria, of the Italian princes, and even of the Sovereign Pontiff. There was reason to fear that any declaration which was satisfactory to British Protestants would excite alarm and disgust at Madrid, Vienna, Turin, and Rome. For this reason the Prince long abstained from formally expressing his sentiments. At length it was represented to him that his continued silence had excited much uneasiness and distrust among his well-wishers, and that it was time to speak out. He therefore determined to explain himself.

A Scotch Whig, named James Stewart, had fled, some years before, to Holland, in order to avoid the boot and the gallows, and had become intimate with the Grand Pensionary Fagel, who enjoyed a large share of the Stadtholder's confidence and favor. By Stewart had been drawn up the violent and acrimonious manifesto of Argyle. When the Indulgence appeared, Stewart conceived that he had an opportunity of obtaining, not only pardon, but reward. He offered his services to the government of which he had been the enemy: they were accepted; and he addressed to Fagel a letter, purporting to have been written by the direction of James. In that letter the Pensionary was exhorted to use all his influence with the Prince and Princess, for the purpose of inducing them to support their father's policy. After some delay Fagel transmitted a reply, deeply meditated, and drawn up with exquisite art. No person who studies that remarkable document can fail to perceive that, though it is framed in a manner well calculated to reassure and delight English Protestants, it contains not a word which

Correspondence of Stewart and Fagel.

could give offence, even at the Vatican. It was announced that William and Mary would, with pleasure, assist in abolishing every law which made any Englishman liable to punishment for his religious opinions. But between punishments and disabilities a distinction was taken. To admit Roman Catholics to office would, in the judgment of their Highnesses, be neither for the general interest of England nor even for the interest of the Roman Catholics themselves. This manifesto was translated into several languages, and circulated widely on the Continent. Of the English version, carefully prepared by Burnet, near fifty thousand copies were introduced into the eastern shires, and rapidly distributed over the whole kingdom. No state paper was ever more completely successful. The Protestants of our island applauded the manly firmness with which William declared that he could not consent to intrust Papists with any share in the government. The Roman Catholic princes, on the other hand, were pleased by the mild and temperate style in which his resolution was expressed, and by the hope which he held out that, under his administration, no member of their Church would be molested on account of religion.

It is probable that the Pope himself was among those who read this celebrated letter with pleasure. He had some months before dismissed Castelmaine in a manner which showed little regard for the feelings of Castelmaine's master. Innocent thoroughly disliked the whole domestic and foreign policy of the English government. He saw that the unjust and impolitic measures of the Jesuitical cabal were far more likely to make the penal laws perpetual than to bring about an abolition of the test. His quarrel with the court of Versailles was every day becoming more and more serious; nor could he, either in his character of temporal prince or in his character of Sovereign Pontiff, feel cordial friendship for a vassal of that court. Castelmaine was ill-qualified to remove these disgusts. He was indeed well acquainted with Rome, and was, for a layman, deeply read in theological controversy.* But he had none of the ad-

<small>Castelmaine's embassy to Rome.</small>

---

* Adda, Nov. $\frac{9}{19}$, 1685.

dress which his post required; and, even had he been a diplomatist of the greatest ability, there was a circumstance which would have disqualified him for the particular mission on which he had been sent. He was known all over Europe as the husband of the most shameless of women; and he was known in no other way. It was impossible to speak to him or of him without remembering in what manner the very title by which he was called had been acquired. This circumstance would have mattered little if he had been accredited to some dissolute court, such as that in which the Marchioness of Montespan had lately been dominant. But there was an obvious impropriety in sending him on an embassy rather of a spiritual than of a secular nature to a pontiff of primitive austerity. The Protestants all over Europe sneered; and Innocent, already unfavorably disposed to the English government, considered the compliment which had been paid him, at so much risk and at so heavy a cost, as little better than an affront. The salary of the Ambassador was fixed at a hundred pounds a week. Castelmaine complained that this was too little. Thrice the sum, he said, would hardly suffice. For at Rome the ministers of all the great Continental powers exerted themselves to surpass one another in splendor, under the eyes of a people whom the habit of seeing magnificent buildings, decorations, and ceremonies had made fastidious. He always declared that he had been a loser by his mission. He was accompanied by several young gentlemen of the best Roman Catholic families in England—Ratcliffes, Arundells, and Tichbornes. At Rome he was lodged in the palace of the house of Pamfili, on the south of the stately Place of Navona. He was early admitted to a private interview with Innocent: but the public audience was long delayed. Indeed Castelmaine's preparations for that great occasion were so sumptuous that, though commenced at Easter, 1686, they were not complete till the following November; and in November the Pope had, or pretended to have, an attack of gout which caused another postponement. In January, 1687, at length, the solemn introduction and homage were performed with unusual pomp. The state coaches, which had been built at

Rome for the pageant, were so superb that they were thought worthy to be transmitted to posterity in fine engravings and to be celebrated by poets in several languages.* The front of the Ambassador's palace was decorated on this great day with absurd allegorical paintings of gigantic size. There was Saint George with his foot on the neck of Titus Oates, and Hercules with his club crushing College, the Protestant joiner, who in vain attempted to defend himself with his flail. After this public appearance Castelmaine invited all the persons of note then assembled at Rome to a banquet in that gay and splendid gallery which is adorned with paintings of subjects from the Æneid by Peter of Cortona. The whole city crowded to the show; and it was with difficulty that a company of Swiss guards could keep order among the spectators. The nobles of the Pontifical state in return gave costly entertainments to the Ambassador; and poets and wits were employed to lavish on him and on his master insipid hyperbolical adulation such as flourishes most when genius and taste are in the deepest decay. Foremost among the flatterers was a crowned head. More than thirty years had elapsed since Christina, the daughter of the great Gustavus, had voluntarily descended from the Swedish throne. After long wanderings, in the course of which she had committed many follies and crimes, she had finally taken up her abode at Rome, where she busied herself with astrological calculations and with the intrigues of the conclave, and amused herself with pictures, gems, manuscripts, and medals. She now composed some Italian stanzas in honor of the English prince,

---

* The Professor of Greek in the College De Propaganda Fide expressed his admiration in some detestable hexameters and pentameters, of which the following specimen may suffice:

'Ρωγερίου δὴ σκεψόμενος λαμπροῖο θρίαμβον,
ὦκα μάλ' ἤισσεν καὶ θέεν ὄχλος ἅπας·
θαυμάζουσα δὲ τὴν πομπὴν, παγχρύσεα τ' αὐτοῦ
ἅρματα, τοὺς θ' ἵππους, τοιάδε 'Ρώμη ἔφη.

The Latin verses are a little better. Nahum Tate responded in English:

"His glorious train and passing pomp to view,
A pomp that even to Rome itself was new,
Each age, each sex, the Latian turrets filled,
Each age and sex in tears of joy distilled."

who, sprung, like herself, from a race of Kings heretofore regarded as the champions of the Reformation, had, like herself, been reconciled to the ancient Church. A splendid assembly met in her palace. Her verses, set to music, were sung with universal applause: and one of her literary dependents pronounced an oration on the same subject in a style so florid that it seems to have offended the taste of the English hearers. The Jesuits, hostile to the Pope, devoted to the interests of France, and disposed to pay every honor to James, received the English embassy with the utmost pomp in that princely house where the remains of Ignatius Loyola lie enshrined in lazulite and gold. Sculpture, painting, poetry, and eloquence were employed to compliment the strangers: but all these arts had sunk into deep degeneracy. There was a great display of turgid and impure Latinity unworthy of so erudite an order; and some of the inscriptions which adorned the walls had a fault more serious than even a bad style. It was said in one place that James had sent his brother as his messenger to heaven, and in another that James had furnished the wings with which his brother had soared to a higher region. There was a still more unfortunate distich, which at the time attracted little notice, but which, a few months later, was remembered and malignantly interpreted. "O King," said the poet, "cease to sigh for a son. Though nature may refuse your wish, the stars will find a way to grant it."

In the midst of these festivities Castelmaine had to suffer cruel mortifications and humiliations. The Pope treated him with extreme coldness and reserve. As often as the Ambassador pressed for an answer to the request which he had been instructed to make in favor of Petre, Innocent was taken with a violent fit of coughing, which put an end to the conversation. The fame of these singular audiences spread over Rome. Pasquin was not silent. All the curious and tattling population of the idlest of cities, the Jesuits and the prelates of the French faction only excepted, laughed at Castelmaine's discomfiture. His temper, naturally unamiable, was soon exasperated to violence; and he circulated a memorial reflecting on the Pope. He had now put himself in the wrong. The sagacious Italian had got the advantage, and took care to keep it. He positively declared that the rule which excluded Jesuits from ecclesiastical preferment should not be relaxed in favor of Father Petre. Castelmaine, much provoked, threatened to leave Rome. Innocent replied, with a meek impertinence which was the more provoking because it could scarcely be distinguished from simplicity, that His Excellency might go if he liked. "But if we must lose him," added the venerable Pontiff, "I hope that he will take care of his health on the road. English people do not know how dangerous it is in this country to travel in the heat of the day. The best way is to start before dawn, and to take some rest at noon." With this salutary advice, and with a string of beads, the unfortunate Ambassador was dismissed. In a few months appeared, both in the Italian and in the English tongue, a pompous history of the mission, magnificently printed in folio, and illustrated with plates. The frontispiece, to the great scandal of all Protestants, represented Castelmaine, in the robes of a Peer, with his coronet in his hand, kissing the toe of Innocent.*

---

* Correspondence of James and Innocent, in the British Museum; Burnet, i., 703–705; Welwood's Memoirs; Commons' Journals, Oct. 28, 1689; An Account of his Excellency Roger Earl of Castelmaine's Embassy, by Michael Wright, chief steward of His Excellency's house at Rome, 1688.

CHAPTER VIII.

THE marked discourtesy of the Pope might well have irritated the meekest of princes. But the only effect which it produced on James was to make him more lavish of caresses and compliments. While Castelmaine, his whole soul festering with angry passions, was on the road back to England, Consecration of the Nuncio at Saint James's Palace. the Nuncio was loaded with honors which his own judgment would have led him to reject. He had, by a fiction often used in the Church of Rome, been lately raised to the episcopal dignity without having the charge of any see. He was called Archbishop of Amasia, a city of Pontus, the birthplace of Strabo and Mithridates. James insisted that the ceremony of consecration should be performed in the chapel of Saint James's Palace. The Vicar Apostolic Leyburn and two Irish prelates officiated. The doors were thrown open to the public; and it was remarked that some of those Puritans who had recently turned courtiers were among the spectators. In the evening Adda, wearing the robes of his new office, joined the circle in the Queen's apartments. James fell on his knees in the presence of the whole court and implored a blessing. In spite of the restraint imposed by etiquette, the astonishment and disgust of the bystanders could not be concealed.* It was long indeed since an English sovereign had knelt to mortal man; and those who saw the strange sight could not but think of that day of shame when John did homage for his crown between the hands of Pandolph.

In a short time a still more ostentatious pageant was performed in honor of the Holy See. It was deter- His public reception. mined that the Nuncio should go to court in solemn procession. Some persons on whose obedience the King had

---

* Barillon, May $\frac{2}{12}$, 1687.

counted showed, on this occasion, for the first time, signs of a mutinous spirit. Among these the most conspicuous was the second temporal peer of the realm, Charles Seymour, commonly called the proud Duke of Somerset. He was in truth a man in whom the pride of birth and rank amounted almost to a disease. The fortune which he had inherited was not adequate to the high place which he held among the English aristocracy: but he had become possessed of the greatest estate in England by his marriage with the daughter and heiress of the last Percy who wore the ancient coronet of Northumberland. Somerset was only in his twenty-fifth year, and was very little known to the public. He was a Lord of the King's Bedchamber, and colonel of one of the regiments which had been raised at the time of the Western insurrection. He had not scrupled to carry the sword of state into the royal chapel on days of festival: but he now resolutely refused to swell the pomp of the Nuncio. Some members of his family implored him not to draw on himself the royal displeasure: but their entreaties produced no effect. The King himself expostulated. "I thought, my Lord," said he, "that I was doing you a great honor in appointing you to escort the minister of the first of all crowned heads." "Sir," said the Duke, "I am advised that I cannot obey Your Majesty without breaking the law." "I will make you fear me as well as the law," answered the King, insolently. "Do you not know that I am above the law?" "Your Majesty may be above the law," replied Somerset: "but I am not; and, while I obey the law, I fear nothing." The King turned away in high displeasure; and Somerset was instantly dismissed from his posts in the household and in the army.*

On one point, however, James showed some prudence. He did not venture to parade the Papal Envoy in state before the vast population of the capital. The ceremony was performed, on the third of July, 1687, at Windsor. Great mul-

* Memoirs of the Duke of Somerset; Van Citters, July $\frac{5}{15}$, 1687; Eachard's History of the Revolution; Life of James the Second, ii., 116, 117, 118; Lord Lonsdale's Memoirs.

titudes flocked to the little town. The visitors were so numerous that there was neither food nor lodging for them; and many persons of quality sat the whole day in their carriages waiting for the exhibition. At length, late in the afternoon, the Knight Marshal's men appeared on horseback. Then came a long train of running footmen; and then, in a royal coach, was seen Adda, robed in purple, with a brilliant cross on his breast. He was followed by the equipages of the principal courtiers and ministers of state. In his train the crowd recognized with disgust the arms and liveries of Crewe, Bishop of Durham, and of Cartwright, Bishop of Chester.*

On the following day appeared in the Gazette a proclama-
Dissolution of the Parliament. tion dissolving that Parliament which of all the fifteen Parliaments held by the Stuarts had been the most obsequious.†

Meanwhile new difficulties had arisen in Westminster Hall. Only a few months had elapsed since some Judges had been turned out and others put in for the purpose of obtaining a decision favorable to the crown in the case of Sir Edward Hales; and already fresh changes were necessary.

The King had scarcely formed that army on which he chiefly depended for the accomplishing of his
Military offences illegally punished. designs when he found that he could not himself control it. When war was actually raging in the kingdom, a mutineer or a deserter might be tried by a military tribunal, and executed by the Provost Marshal. But there was now profound peace. The common law of England, having sprung up in an age when all men bore arms occasionally and none constantly, recognized no distinction, in time of peace, between a soldier and any other subject; nor was there any act resembling that by which the authority necessary for the government of regular troops is now annually confided to the Sovereign. Some old statutes, indeed, made desertion felony in certain specified cases. But those statutes were applicable only to soldiers serving the King in actual war, and

---

* London Gazette, July 7, 1687; Van Citters, July $\frac{7}{17}$. Account of the ceremony reprinted among the Somers Tracts.

† London Gazette, July 4, 1687.

could not without the grossest disingenuousness be so strained as to include the case of a man who, in a time of tranquillity, should become tired of the camp at Hounslow, and should go back to his native village. The government appears to have had no hold on such a man, except the hold which master-bakers and master-tailors have on their journeymen. He and his officers were, in the eye of the law, on a level. If he swore at them, he might be fined for an oath. If he struck them, he might be prosecuted for assault and battery. In truth, the regular army was under less restraint than the militia. For the militia was a body established by an Act of Parliament; and it had been provided by that Act that slight punishments might be summarily inflicted for breaches of discipline.

It does not appear that, during the reign of Charles the Second, the practical inconvenience arising from this state of the law had been much felt. The explanation may perhaps be that, till the last year of his reign, the force which he maintained in England consisted chiefly of household troops, whose pay was so high that dismission from the service would have been felt by most of them as a great calamity. The stipend of a private in the Life Guards was a provision for the younger son of a gentleman. Even the Foot Guards were paid about as high as manufacturers in a prosperous season, and were therefore in a situation which the great body of the laboring population might regard with envy. The return of the garrison of Tangier and the raising of the new regiments had made a great change. There were now in England many thousands of soldiers, each of whom received only eight-pence a day. The dread of dismission was not sufficient to keep them to their duty; and corporal punishment their officers could not legally inflict. James had therefore one plain choice before him, to let his army dissolve itself, or to induce the Judges to pronounce that the law was what every barrister in the Temple knew that it was not.

It was peculiarly important to secure the co-operation of two courts—the Court of King's Bench, which was the first criminal tribunal in the realm, and the court of jail delivery, which sat at the Old Bailey, and which had jurisdiction over offences committed in the capital. In both these courts there were great difficulties. Herbert, Chief-justice of the King's Bench, servile as he had hitherto been, would go no farther. Resistance still more sturdy was to be expected from Sir John Holt, who, as Recorder of the City of London, occupied the Bench at the Old Bailey. Holt was an eminently learned and clear-headed lawyer: he was an upright and courageous man; and, though he had never been factious, his political opinions had a tinge of Whiggism. All obstacles, however, disappeared before the royal will. Holt was turned out of the recordership: Herbert and another Judge were removed from the King's Bench; and the vacant places were filled by persons in whom the government could confide. It was indeed necessary to go very low down in the legal profession before men could be found willing to render such services as were now required. The new Chief-justice, Sir Robert Wright, was ignorant to a proverb; yet ignorance was not his worst fault. His vices had ruined him. He had resorted to infamous ways of raising money, and had, on one occasion, made a false affidavit in order to obtain possession of five hundred pounds. Poor, dissolute, and shameless, he had become one of the parasites of Jeffreys, who promoted him and insulted him. Such was the man who was now selected by James to be Lord Chief-justice of England. One Richard Allibone, who was even more ignorant of the law than Wright, and who, as a Roman Catholic, was incapable of holding office, was appointed a puisne Judge of the King's Bench. Sir Bartholomew Shower, equally notorious as a servile Tory and a tedious orator, became Recorder of London. When these changes had been made, several deserters were brought to trial. They were convicted in the face of the letter and of the spirit of the law. Some received sentence of death at the bar of the King's Bench, and some at the Old Bailey. They were hanged in sight of the regiments to which they had belonged; and care was taken that the executions should

II.—17

be announced in the London Gazette, which very seldom noticed such events.*

It may well be believed that the law, so grossly insulted by courts which derived from it all their authority, and which were in the habit of looking to it as their guide, would be little respected by a tribunal which had originated in tyrannical caprice. The new High Commission had, during the first months of its existence, merely inhibited clergymen from exercising spiritual functions. The rights of property had remained untouched. But, early in the year 1687, it was determined to strike at freehold interests, and to impress on every Anglican priest and prelate the conviction that, if he refused to lend his aid for the purpose of destroying the Church of which he was a minister, he would in an hour be reduced to beggary.

<small>Proceedings of the High Commission.</small>

It would have been prudent to try the first experiment on some obscure individual. But the government was under an infatuation such as, in a more simple age, would have been called judicial. War was therefore at once declared against the two most venerable corporations of the realm, the Universities of Oxford and Cambridge.

<small>The Universities.</small>

The power of those bodies has during many ages been great; but it was at the height during the latter part of the seventeenth century. None of the neighboring countries could boast of such splendid and opulent seats of learning. The schools of Edinburgh and Glasgow, of Leyden and Utrecht, of Louvain and Leipsic, of Padua and Bologna, seemed mean to scholars who had been educated in the magnificent foundations of Wykeham and Wolsey, of Henry the Sixth and Henry the Eighth. Literature and science were, in the academical system of England, surrounded with pomp, armed with magistracy, and closely allied with all the most august institutions of the state. To be the Chancellor of a University was a distinction eagerly sought by the magnates of the realm. To represent a University in Parliament was a favorite ob-

---

* See the statutes 18 Henry 6, c. 19; 2 & 3 Ed. 6, c. 2; Eachard's History of the Revolution; Kennet, iii., 68; North's Life of Guildford, 247; London Gazette, April 18, May 23, 1687; Vindication of the E. of R. (Earl of Rochester).

ject of the ambition of statesmen. Nobles and even princes were proud to receive from a University the privilege of wearing the doctoral scarlet. The curious were attracted to the Universities by ancient buildings rich with the tracery of the Middle Ages, by modern buildings which exhibited the highest skill of Jones and Wren, by noble halls and chapels, by museums, by botanical gardens, and by the only great public libraries which the kingdom then contained. The state which Oxford especially displayed on solemn occasions rivalled that of sovereign princes. When her Chancellor, the venerable Duke of Ormond, sat in his embroidered mantle on his throne under the painted ceiling of the Sheldonian theatre, surrounded by hundreds of graduates robed according to their rank, while the noblest youths of England were solemnly presented to him as candidates for academical honors, he made an appearance scarcely less regal than that which his master made in the Banqueting House of Whitehall. At the Universities had been formed the minds of almost all the eminent clergymen, lawyers, physicians, wits, poets, and orators of the land, and of a large proportion of the nobility and of the opulent gentry. It is also to be observed that the connection between the scholar and the school did not terminate with his residence. He often continued to be through life a member of the academical body, and to vote as such at all important elections. He therefore regarded his old haunts by the Cam and the Isis with even more than the affection which educated men ordinarily feel for the place of their education. There was no corner of England in which both Universities had not grateful and zealous sons. Any attack on the honor or interests of either Cambridge or Oxford was certain to excite the resentment of a powerful, active, and intelligent class, scattered over every county from Northumberland to Cornwall.

The resident graduates, as a body, were perhaps not superior positively to the resident graduates of our time: but they occupy a far higher position as compared with the rest of the community. For Cambridge and Oxford were then the only two provincial towns in the kingdom in which could be found a large number of men whose understandings had been highly cultivated. Even the capital felt great respect for the authority of the Universities, not only on questions of divinity, of natural philosophy, and of classical antiquity, but also on points which capitals generally claim the right of deciding in the last resort. From Will's coffee-house, and from the pit of the theatre royal in Drury Lane, an appeal lay to the two great national seats of taste and learning. Plays which had been enthusiastically applauded in London were not thought out of danger till they had undergone the more severe judgment of audiences familiar with Sophocles and Terence.*

The great moral and intellectual influence of the English Universities had been strenuously exerted on the side of the crown. The head-quarters of Charles the First had been at Oxford; and the silver tankards and salvers of all the colleges had been melted down to supply his military chest. Cambridge was not less loyally disposed. She had sent a large part of her plate to the royal camp; and the rest would have followed had not the town been seized by the troops of the Parliament. Both Universities had been treated with extreme severity by the victorious Puritans. Both had hailed the Restoration with delight. Both had steadily opposed the Exclusion Bill. Both had expressed the deepest horror at the Rye-house Plot. Cambridge had not only deposed her Chancellor Monmouth, but had marked her abhorrence of his treason in a manner unworthy of a seat of learning, by committing to the flames the canvas on which his pleasing face and figure had been portrayed by the utmost skill of Kneller.† Oxford, which lay nearer to the Western insurgents, had given still stronger proofs of loyalty. The students, under the sanction of their preceptors, had taken arms by hundreds in defence of hereditary right. Such were the bodies which

---

* Dryden's Prologues and Cibber's Memoirs contain abundant proofs of the estimation in which the taste of the Oxonians was held by the most admired poets and actors.

† See the poem called Advice to the Painter upon the Defeat of the Rebels in the West. See also another poem, a most detestable one, on the same subject by Stepney, who was then studying at Trinity College.

James now determined to insult and plunder in direct defiance of the laws and of his plighted faith.

Several Acts of Parliament, as clear as any that were to be found in the statute-book, had provided that no person should
<small>Proceedings against the University of Cambridge.</small> be admitted to any degree in either University without taking the oath of supremacy, and another oath of similar character called the oath of obedience. Nevertheless, in February, 1687, a royal letter was sent to Cambridge directing that a Benedictine monk, named Alban Francis, should be admitted a Master of Arts.

The academical functionaries, divided between reverence for the King and reverence for the law, were in great distress. Messengers were despatched in all haste to the Duke of Albemarle, who had succeeded Monmouth as Chancellor of the University. He was requested to represent the matter properly to the King. Meanwhile the Registrar and Bedells waited on Francis, and informed him that, if he would take the oaths according to law, he should instantly be admitted. He refused to be sworn, remonstrated with the officers of the University on their disregard of the royal mandate, and, finding them resolute, took horse, and hastened to relate his grievances at Whitehall.

The heads of the colleges now assembled in council. The best legal opinions were taken, and were decidedly in favor of the course which had been pursued. But a second letter from Sunderland, in high and menacing terms, was already on the road. Albemarle informed the University, with many expressions of concern, that he had done his best, but that he had been coldly and ungraciously received by the King. The academical body, alarmed by the royal displeasure, and conscientiously desirous to meet the royal wishes, but determined not to violate the clear law of the land, submitted the humblest and most respectful explanations, but to no purpose. In a short time came down a summons citing the Vice-chancellor and the Senate to appear before the new High Commission at Westminster on the twenty-first of April. The Vice-chancellor was to attend in person: the Senate, which consists of all the Doctors and Masters of the University, was to send deputies.

When the appointed day arrived, a great concourse filled the Council-chamber. Jeffreys sat at the head of the board. Rochester, since the white staff had been taken from him, was no longer a member. In his stead appeared the Lord Chamberlain, John Sheffield, Earl of Mulgrave. The fate of this nobleman has, in one respect, resembled the fate of his colleague Sprat. Mulgrave wrote verses which scarcely ever rose above absolute mediocrity; but as he was a man of high note in the political and fashionable world, these verses found admirers. Time dissolved the charm, but, unfortunately for him, not until his lines had acquired a prescriptive right to a place in all collections of the works of English poets. To this day, accordingly, his insipid essays in rhyme and his paltry songs to Amoretta and Gloriana are reprinted in company with Comus and Alexander's Feast. The consequence is that our generation knows Mulgrave chiefly as a poetaster, and despises him as such. In truth, however, he was, by the acknowledgment of those who neither loved nor esteemed him, a man distinguished by fine parts, and in parliamentary eloquence inferior to scarcely any orator of his time. His moral character was entitled to no respect. He was a libertine without that openness of heart and hand which sometimes makes libertinism amiable, and a haughty aristocrat without that elevation of sentiment which sometimes makes aristocratical haughtiness respectable. The satirists of the age nicknamed him Lord Allpride, and pronounced it strange that a man who had so exalted a sense of his dignity should be so hard and niggardly in all pecuniary dealings. He had given deep offence to the royal family by venturing to entertain the hope that he might win the heart and hand of the Princess Anne. Disappointed in this attempt, he had exerted himself to regain by meanness the favor which he had forfeited by presumption. His epitaph, written by himself, still informs all who pass through Westminster Abbey that he lived and died a sceptic in religion; and we learn from his memoirs, written by himself, that one of his favorite subjects of mirth was the Romish superstition. Yet he began, as soon as James was on the throne, to express a strong inclination toward Popery, and at length in private affected to be a convert. This abject hypocrisy had been rewarded by a place in the Ecclesiastical Commission.*

Before that formidable tribunal now appeared the Vice-chancellor of the University of Cambridge, Doctor John Pechell. He was a man of no great ability or vigor; but he was accompanied by eight distinguished academicians, elected by the Senate. One of these was Isaac Newton, Fellow of Trinity College, and Professor of mathematics. His genius was then in the fullest vigor. The great work, which entitles him to the highest place among the geometricians and natural philosophers of all ages and of all nations, had been some time printing under the sanction of the Royal Society, and was almost ready for publication. He was the steady friend of civil liberty and of the Protestant religion: but his habits by no means fitted him for the conflicts of active life. He therefore stood modestly silent among the delegates, and left to men more versed in practical business the task of pleading the cause of his beloved University.

Never was there a clearer case. The law was express. The practice had been almost invariably in conformity with the law. It might perhaps have happened that, on a day of great solemnity, when many honorary degrees were conferred, a person who had not taken the oaths might have passed in the crowd. But such an irregularity, the effect of mere haste and inadvertence, could not be cited as a precedent. Foreign ambassadors of various religions, and in particular one Mussulman, had been admitted without the oaths. But it might well be doubted whether such cases fell within the reason and spirit of the Acts of Parliament. It was not even pretended that any person to whom the oaths had been tendered and who had refused them had ever taken a degree;

---

* Mackay's character of Sheffield, with Swift's note; the Satire on the Deponents, 1688; Life of John, Duke of Buckinghamshire, 1729; Barillon, Aug. 30, 1687. I have a manuscript lampoon on Mulgrave, dated 1690. It is not destitute of spirit. The most remarkable lines are these:

"Peters (Petre) to-day and Burnet to-morrow,
Knaves of all sides and religions he'll woo."

and this was the situation in which Francis stood. The delegates offered to prove that, in the late reign, several royal mandates had been treated as nullities because the persons recommended had not chosen to qualify according to law, and that on such occasions the government had always acquiesced in the propriety of the course taken by the University. But Jeffreys would hear nothing. He soon found out that the Vice-chancellor was weak, ignorant, and timid, and therefore gave a loose to all that insolence which had long been the terror of the Old Bailey. The unfortunate Doctor, unaccustomed to such a presence and to such treatment, was soon harassed and scared into helpless agitation. When other academicians who were more capable of defending their cause attempted to speak they were rudely silenced. "You are not Vice-chancellor. When you are, you may talk. Till then it will become you to hold your peace." The defendants were thrust out of the court without a hearing. In a short time they were called in again, and informed that the Commissioners had determined to deprive Pechell of the Vice-chancellorship, and to suspend him from all the emoluments to which he was entitled as Master of a college, emoluments which were strictly of the nature of freehold property. "As for you," said Jeffreys to the delegates, "most of you are divines. I will therefore send you home with a text of Scripture, 'Go your way and sin no more, lest a worse thing happen to you.'"*

State of Oxford.

These proceedings might seem sufficiently unjust and violent. But the King had already begun to treat Oxford with such rigor that the rigor shown toward Cambridge might, by comparison, be called lenity. Already University College had been turned by Obadiah Walker into a Roman Catholic seminary. Already Christ Church was governed by a Roman Catholic Dean. Mass was already said daily in both those colleges. The tranquil and majestic city, so long the stronghold of monarchical principles, was agitated

---

* See the proceedings against the University of Cambridge in the collection of State Trials.

by passions which it had never before known. The undergraduates, with the connivance of those who were in authority over them, hooted the members of Walker's congregation, and chanted satirical ditties under his windows. Some fragments of the serenades which then disturbed the High Street have been preserved. The burden of one ballad was this:

" Old Obadiah
Sings Ave Maria."

When the actors came down to Oxford, the public feeling was expressed still more strongly. Howard's Committee was performed. This play, written soon after the Restoration, exhibited the Puritans in an odious and contemptible light, and had therefore been, during a quarter of a century, a favorite with Oxonian audiences. It was now a greater favorite than ever; for, by a lucky coincidence, one of the most conspicuous characters was an old hypocrite named Obadiah. The audience shouted with delight when, in the last scene, Obadiah was dragged in with a halter round his neck; and the acclamations redoubled when one of the players, departing from the written text of the comedy, proclaimed that Obadiah should be hanged because he had changed his religion. The King was much provoked by this insult. So mutinous, indeed, was the temper of the University that one of the newly raised regiments, the same which is now called the Second Dragoon Guards, was quartered at Oxford for the purpose of preventing an outbreak.*

These events ought to have convinced James that he had entered on a course which must lead him to his ruin. To the clamors of London he had been long accustomed. They had been raised against him, sometimes unjustly, and sometimes vainly. He had repeatedly braved them, and might brave them still. But that Oxford, the seat of loyalty, the headquarters of the Cavalier army, the place where his father and brother had held their court when they thought themselves

---

* Wood's Athenæ Oxonienses; Apology for the Life of Colley Cibber; Van Citters, March $\frac{2}{12}$, 1686.

insecure in their stormy capital, the place where the writings of the great Republican teachers had recently been committed to the flames, should now be in a ferment of discontent, that those high-spirited youths who a few months before had eagerly volunteered to march against the Western insurgents should now be with difficulty kept down by sword and carbine, these were signs full of evil omen to the House of Stuart. The warning, however, was lost on the dull, stubborn, self-willed tyrant. He was resolved to transfer to his own Church all the wealthiest and most splendid foundations of England. It was to no purpose that the best and wisest of his Roman Catholic counsellors remonstrated. They represented to him that he had it in his power to render a great service to the cause of his religion without violating the rights of property. A grant of two thousand pounds a year from his privy purse would support a Jesuit college at Oxford. Such a sum he might easily spare. Such a college, provided with able, learned, and zealous teachers, would be a formidable rival to the old academical institutions, which exhibited but too many symptoms of the languor almost inseparable from opulence and security. King James's College would soon be, by the confession even of Protestants, the first place of education in the island, as respected both science and moral discipline. This would be the most effectual and the least invidious method by which the Church of England could be humbled and the Church of Rome exalted. The Earl of Ailesbury, one of the most devoted servants of the royal family, declared that, though a Protestant, and by no means rich, he would himself contribute a thousand pounds toward this design, rather than that his master should violate the rights of property, and break faith with the Established Church.* The scheme, however, found no favor in the sight of the King. It was indeed ill suited, in more ways than one, to his ungentle nature. For to bend and break the spirits of men gave him pleasure; and to part with his money gave him

---

* Burnet, i., 697; Letter of Lord Ailesbury printed in the European Magazine for April, 1795.

pain. What he had not the generosity to do at his own expense he determined to do at the expense of others. When once he was engaged, pride and obstinacy prevented him from receding; and he was at length led, step by step, to acts of Turkish tyranny, to acts which impressed the nation with a conviction that the estate of a Protestant English freeholder under a Roman Catholic king must be as insecure as that of a Greek under Moslem domination.

Magdalene College at Oxford, founded in the fifteenth century by William of Waynflete, Bishop of Winchester and Lord High Chancellor, was one of the most remarkable of our academical institutions. A graceful tower, on the summit of which a Latin hymn was annually chanted by choristers at the dawn of May-day, caught far off the eye of the traveller who came from London. As he approached, he found that this tower rose from an embattled pile, low and irregular, yet singularly venerable, which, embowered in verdure, overhung the sluggish waters of the Cherwell. He passed through a gate-way beneath a noble oriel,* and found himself in a spacious cloister adorned with emblems of virtues and vices, rudely carved in gray stone by the masons of the fifteenth century. The table of the society was plentifully spread in a stately refectory hung with paintings and rich with fantastic carving. The service of the Church was performed morning and evening in a chapel which had suffered much violence from the Reformers, and much from the Puritans, but which was, under every disadvantage, a building of eminent beauty, and which has, in our own time, been restored with rare taste and skill. The spacious gardens along the river-side were remarkable for the size of the trees, among which towered conspicuous one of the vegetable wonders of the island, a gigantic oak, older by a century, men said, than the oldest college in the University.

The statutes of the society ordained that the Kings of England and the Princes of Wales should be lodged at Magdalene. Edward the Fourth had inhabited the building while it was

---

* This gate-way is now closed.

still unfinished. Richard the Third had held his court there, had heard disputations in the hall, had feasted there royally, and had mended the cheer of his hosts by a present of fat bucks from his forests. Two heirs-apparent of the crown who had been prematurely snatched away, Arthur, the elder brother of Henry the Eighth, and Henry, the elder brother of Charles the First, had been members of the college. Another prince of the blood, the last and best of the Roman Catholic Archbishops of Canterbury, the gentle Reginald Pole, had studied there. In the time of the civil war Magdalene had been true to the cause of the Crown. There Rupert had fixed his quarters; and, before some of his most daring enterprises, his trumpets had been heard sounding to horse through those quiet cloisters. Most of the Fellows were divines, and could aid King Charles only by their prayers and their pecuniary contributions. But one member of the body, a Doctor of Civil Law, raised a troop of undergraduates, and fell fighting bravely at their head against the soldiers of Essex. When hostilities had terminated, and the Roundheads were masters of England, six-sevenths of the members of the foundation refused to make any submission to usurped authority. They were consequently ejected from their dwellings and deprived of their revenues. After the Restoration the survivors returned to their pleasant abode. They had now been succeeded by a new generation which inherited their opinions and their spirit. During the Western rebellion such Magdalene men as were not disqualified by their age or profession for the use of arms had eagerly volunteered to fight for the crown. It would be difficult to name any corporation in the kingdom which had higher claims to the gratitude of the House of Stuart.*

The society consisted of a President, of forty Fellows, of thirty scholars called Demies, and of a train of chaplains, clerks, and choristers. At the time of the general visitation in the reign of Henry the Eighth the revenues were far larger than those of any similar institution in the realm, larger by

---

* Wood's Athenæ Oxonienses; Walker's Sufferings of the Clergy.

nearly one-half than those of the magnificent foundation of Henry the Sixth at Cambridge, and considerably more than twice as large as those which William of Wykeham had settled on his college at Oxford. In the days of James the Second the riches of Magdalene were immense, and were exaggerated by report. The college was popularly said to be wealthier than the wealthiest abbeys of the Continent. When the leases fell in—so ran the vulgar rumor—the rents would be raised to the prodigious sum of forty thousand pounds a year.*

The Fellows were, by the statutes which their founder had drawn up, empowered to select their own President from among persons who were, or had been, Fellows either of their society or of New College. This power had generally been exercised with freedom. But in some instances royal letters had been received recommending to the choice of the corporation qualified persons who were in favor at court; and on such occasions it had been the practice to show respect to the wishes of the sovereign.

In March, 1687, the President of the college died. One of the Fellows, Doctor Thomas Smith, popularly nicknamed Rabbi Smith, a distinguished traveller, book collector, antiquary, and orientalist, who had been chaplain to the embassy at Constantinople, and had been employed to collate the Alexandrian manuscript, aspired to the vacant post. He conceived that he had some claims on the favor of the government as a man of learning and as a zealous Tory. His loyalty was in truth as fervent and as steadfast as was to be found in the whole Church of England. He had long been intimately acquainted with Parker, Bishop of Oxford, and hoped to obtain by the interest of that prelate a royal letter to the college. Parker promised to do his best, but soon reported that he had found difficulties. "The King," he said, "will recommend no person who is not a friend to His Majesty's religion. What can you do to pleasure him as to that matter?"

---

* Burnet, i., 697; Tanner's Notitia Monastica. At the visitation in the twenty-sixth year of Henry the Eighth it appeared that the annual revenue of King's College was 751*l.*; of New College, 487*l.*; of Magdalene, 1076*l.*

Smith answered that, if he became President, he would exert himself to promote learning, true Christianity, and loyalty. "That will not do," said the Bishop. "If so," said Smith, manfully, "let who will be President: I can promise nothing more."

The election had been fixed for the thirteenth of April; and the Fellows had been summoned to attend. It was rumored that a royal letter would come down recommending one Anthony Farmer to the vacant place. This man's life had been a series of shameful acts. He had been a member of the University of Cambridge, and had escaped expulsion only by a timely retreat. He had then joined the Dissenters. Then he had gone to Oxford, had entered himself at Magdalene, and had soon become notorious there for every kind of vice. He generally reeled into his college at night speechless with liquor. He was celebrated for having headed a disgraceful riot at Abingdon. He had been a constant frequenter of noted haunts of libertines. At length he had turned pander, had exceeded even the ordinary vileness of his vile calling, and had received money from dissolute young gentlemen commoners for services such as it is not good that history should record. This wretch, however, had pretended to turn Papist. His apostasy atoned for all his vices; and, though still a youth, he was selected to rule a grave and religious society in which the scandal given by his depravity was still fresh.

Anthony Farmer recommended by the King for President.

As a Roman Catholic, he was disqualified for academical office by the general law of the land. Never having been a Fellow of Magdalene College or of New College, he was disqualified for the vacant Presidency by a special ordinance of William of Waynflete. William of Waynflete had also enjoined those who partook of his bounty to have a particular regard to moral character in choosing their head; and, even if he had left no such injunction, a body chiefly composed of divines could not with decency intrust such a man as Farmer with the government of a place of education.

The Fellows respectfully represented to the King the difficulty in which they should be placed, if, as was rumored,

Farmer should be recommended to them, and begged that, if it were His Majesty's pleasure to interfere in the election, some person for whom they could legally and conscientiously vote might be proposed. Of this dutiful request no notice was taken. The royal letter arrived. It was brought down by one of the Fellows who had lately turned Papist, Robert Charnock, a man of parts and spirit, but of a violent and restless temper, which impelled him a few years later to an atrocious crime and to a terrible fate. On the thirteenth of April the society met in the chapel. Some hope was still entertained that the King might be moved by the remonstrance which had been addressed to him. The assembly therefore adjourned till the fifteenth, which was the last day on which, by the constitution of the college, the election could take place.

The fifteenth of April came. Again the Fellows repaired to their chapel. No answer had arrived from Whitehall. *Election of the President.* Two or three of the Seniors, among whom was Smith, were inclined to postpone the election once more rather than take a step which might give offence to the King. But the language of the statutes was clear. Those statutes the members of the foundation had sworn to observe. The general opinion was that there ought to be no further delay. There was a hot debate. The electors were too much excited to take their seats; and the whole choir was in a tumult. Those who were for proceeding appealed to their oaths and to the rules laid down by the founder whose bread they had eaten. The King, they truly said, had no right to force on them even a qualified candidate. Some expressions unpleasing to Tory ears were dropped in the course of the dispute; and Smith was provoked into exclaiming that the spirit of Ferguson had possessed his brethren. It was at length resolved by a great majority that it was necessary to proceed immediately to the election. Charnock left the chapel. The other Fellows, having first received the sacrament, proceeded to give their voices. The choice fell on John Hough, a man of eminent virtue and prudence, who, having borne persecution with fortitude and prosperity with meekness, having risen to high honors, and having modestly declined honors higher still, died in extreme old age, yet in full vigor of mind, more than fifty-six years after this eventful day.

The society hastened to acquaint the King with the circumstances which had made it necessary to elect a President without further delay, and requested the Duke of Ormond, as patron of the whole University, and the Bishop of Winchester, as visitor of Magdalene College, to undertake the office of intercessors: but the King was far too angry and too dull to listen to explanations.

Early in June the Fellows were cited to appear before the High Commission at Whitehall. Five of them, deputed by the rest, obeyed the summons. Jeffreys treated them after his usual fashion. When one of them, a grave Doctor named Fairfax, hinted some doubt as to the validity of the Commission, the Chancellor began to roar like a wild beast. "Who is this man? What commission has he to be impudent here? Seize him. Put him into a dark room. What does he do without a keeper? He is under my care as a lunatic. I wonder that nobody has applied to me for the custody of him." But when this storm had spent its force, and the depositions concerning the moral character of the King's nominee had been read, none of the Commissioners had the front to pronounce that such a man could properly be made the head of a great college. Obadiah Walker and the other Oxonian Papists who were in attendance to support their proselyte were utterly confounded. The Commission pronounced Hough's election void, and suspended Fairfax from his fellowship: but about Farmer no more was said; and, in the month of August, arrived a royal letter recommending Parker, Bishop of Oxford, to the Fellows.

The Fellows of Magdalene cited before the High Commission.

Parker recommended as President.

Parker was not an avowed Papist. Still there was an objection to him which, even if the presidency had been vacant, would have been decisive: for he had never been a Fellow of either New College or Magdalene. But the presidency was not vacant: Hough had been duly elected; and all the members of the college were bound by oath to support him in his office. They therefore, with many expressions of loyalty and concern, excused themselves from complying with the King's mandate.

While Oxford was thus opposing a firm resistance to tyranny, a stand not less resolute was made in another quarter.

<small>The Charter-house.</small> James had, some time before, commanded the trustees of the Charter-house, men of the first rank and consideration in the kingdom, to admit a Roman Catholic named Popham into the hospital which was under their care. The Master of the house, Thomas Burnet, a clergyman of distinguished genius, learning, and virtue, had the courage to represent to them, though the ferocious Jeffreys sat at the board, that what was required of them was contrary both to the will of the founder and to an Act of Parliament. "What is that to the purpose?" said a courtier who was one of the governors. "It is very much to the purpose, I think," answered a voice, feeble with age and sorrow, yet not to be heard without respect by any assembly, the voice of the venerable Ormond. "An Act of Parliament," continued the patriarch of the Cavalier party, "is, in my judgment, no light thing." The question was put whether Popham should be admitted; and it was determined to reject him. The Chancellor, who could not well ease himself by cursing and swearing at Ormond, flung away in a rage, and was followed by some of the minority. The consequence was, that there was not a quorum left, and that no formal reply could be made to the royal mandate.

The next meeting took place only two days after the High Commission had pronounced sentence of deprivation against Hough, and of suspension against Fairfax. A second mandate under the Great Seal was laid before the trustees; but the tyrannical manner in which Magdalene College had been treated had roused instead of subduing their spirit. They drew up a letter to Sunderland in which they requested him to inform the King that they could not, in this matter, obey His Majesty without breaking the law and betraying their trust.

There can be little doubt that, had ordinary signatures been
II.—18

appended to this document, the King would have taken some violent course. But even he was daunted by the opposition of Ormond, Halifax, Danby, and Nottingham, the chiefs of all the sections of that great party to which he owed his crown. He therefore contented himself with directing Jeffreys to consider what course ought to be taken. It was announced at one time that a proceeding would be instituted in the King's Bench, at another that the Ecclesiastical Commission would take up the case: but these threats gradually died away.*

The summer was now far advanced; and the King set out on a progress, the longest and the most splendid that had been known during many years. From Windsor he went on the sixteenth of August to Portsmouth, walked round the fortifications, touched some scrofulous people, and then proceeded in one of his yachts to Southampton. From Southampton he travelled to Bath, where he remained a few days, and where he left the Queen. When he departed, he was attended by the High Sheriff of Somersetshire and by a large body of gentlemen to the frontier of the county, where the High Sheriff of Gloucestershire, with a not less splendid retinue, was in attendance. The Duke of Beaufort soon met the royal coaches, and conducted them to Badminton, where a banquet worthy of the fame which his splendid housekeeping had won for him was prepared. In the afternoon the cavalcade proceeded to Gloucester. It was greeted two miles from the city by the Bishop and clergy. At the South Gate the Mayor waited with the keys. The bells rang and the conduits flowed with wine as the King passed through the streets to the close which encircles the venerable Cathedral. He lay that night at the deanery, and on the following morning set out for Worcester. From Worcester he went to Ludlow, Shrewsbury, and Chester, and was everywhere received with outward signs of joy and respect, which he was weak enough to consider as proofs that the discontent excited by his measures had subsided, and that an easy victory was

The royal progress.

---

* A Relation of Proceedings at the Charter-house, 1689.

before him. Barillon, more sagacious, informed Lewis that the King of England was under a delusion, that the progress had done no real good, and that those very gentlemen of Worcestershire and Shropshire who had thought it their duty to receive their Sovereign and their guests with every mark of honor would be found as refractory as ever when the question of the test should come on.*

On the road the royal train was joined by two courtiers who in temper and opinions differed widely from each other. Penn was at Chester on a pastoral, or, to speak more correctly, on a political, tour. The chief object of his expedition was to induce the Dissenters, throughout England, to support the government. His popularity and authority among his brethren had greatly declined since he had become a tool of the King and of the Jesuits.† He was, however, most graciously received by James, and, on the Sunday, was permitted to harangue in the tennis-court, while Cartwright preached in the Cathedral, and while the King heard mass at an altar which had been decked in the Shire Hall. It is said, indeed, that His Majesty deigned to look into the tennis-court and to listen with decency to his friend's melodious eloquence.‡

The furious Tyrconnel had crossed the sea from Dublin to give an account of his administration. All the most respectable English Roman Catholics looked coldly on him as an enemy of their race and a scandal to their religion. But he was cordially welcomed by his master, and dismissed with assurances of undiminished confidence and steady support. James expressed his delight at learning that in a short time

---

* See the London Gazette, from August 18 to September 1, 1687; Barillon, September $\frac{19}{29}$.

† Penn, chef des Quakers, qu'on sait être dans les intérêts du Roi d'Angleterre, est si fort décrié parmi ceux de son parti qu'ils n'ont plus aucune confiance en lui."—Bonrepaux to Seignelay, Sept. $\frac{12}{22}$, 1687. The evidence of Gerard Croese is to the same effect. "Etiam Quakeri Pennum non amplius, ut ante, ita amabant ac magnifaciebant, quidam aversabantur ac fugiebant."—Historia Quakeriana, lib. ii., 1695. As to Penn's tour, Van Citters wrote on Oct. $\frac{4}{14}$, 1687, "Dat den bekenden Arch-Quaker Pen door het Laut op reyse was, om die van syne gesintheyt, en andere soo veel doenlyck, tot des Conings partie en Sinnelyckheyt te winnen."

‡ Cartwright's Diary, Aug. 30, 1687; Clarkson's Life of William Penn.

the whole government of Ireland would be in Roman Catholic hands. The English colonists had already been stripped of all political power. Nothing remained but to strip them of their property; and this last outrage was deferred only till the co-operation of an Irish Parliament should have been secured.*

From Cheshire the King turned southward, and, in the full belief that the Fellows of Magdalene College, however mutinous they might be, would not dare to disobey a command uttered by his own lips, directed his course toward Oxford. By the way he made some little excursions to places which peculiarly interested him, as a King, a brother, and a son. He visited the hospitable roof of Boscobel, and the remains of the oak so conspicuous in the history of his house. He rode over the field of Edgehill, where the Cavaliers first crossed swords with the soldiers of the Parliament. On the third of September he dined in great state at the palace of Woodstock, an ancient and renowned mansion, of which not a stone is now to be seen, but of which the site is still marked on the turf of Blenheim Park by two sycamores which grow near the stately bridge. In the evening he reached Oxford. He was received there with the wonted honors. The students in their academical garb were ranged to welcome him on the right hand and on the left, from the entrance of the city to the great gate of Christ Church. He lodged at the deanery, where, among other accommodations, he found a chapel fitted up for the celebration of the mass.†

The King at Oxford.

On the day after his arrival, the Fellows of Magdalene College were ordered to attend him. When they appeared before him, he treated them with an insolence such as had never been shown to their predecessors

He reprimands the Fellows of Magdalene.

---

* London Gazette, Sept. 5; Sheridan MS.; Barillon, Sept. $\frac{6}{16}$, 1687. "Le Roi son maître," says Barillon, "a témoigné une grande satisfaction des mesures qu'il a prises, et a autorisé ce qu'il a fait en faveur des Catholiques. Il les établit dans les emplois et les charges, en sorte que l'autorité se trouvera bientôt entre leurs mains. Il reste encore beaucoup de choses à faire en ce pays là pour retirer les biens injustement ôtés aux Catholiques. Mais cela ne peut s'exécuter qu'avec le tems et dans l'assemblée d'un parlement en Irlande."

† London Gazette of Sept. 5 and Sept. 8, 1687.

by the Puritan visitors. "You have not dealt with me like gentlemen," he exclaimed. "You have been unmannerly as well as undutiful." They fell on their knees and tendered a petition. He would not look at it. "Is this your Church of England loyalty? I could not have believed that so many clergymen of the Church of England would have been concerned in such a business. Go home. Get you gone. I am King, I will be obeyed. Go to your chapel this instant; and admit the Bishop of Oxford. Let those who refuse look to it. They shall feel the whole weight of my hand. They shall know what it is to incur the displeasure of their Sovereign." The Fellows, still kneeling before him, again offered him their petition. He angrily flung it down. "Get you gone, I tell you. I will receive nothing from you till you have admitted the Bishop."

They retired and instantly assembled in their chapel. The question was propounded whether they would comply with His Majesty's command. Smith was absent. Charnock alone answered in the affirmative. The other Fellows who were at the meeting declared that in all things lawful they were ready to obey the King, but that they would not violate their statutes and their oaths.

The King, greatly incensed and mortified by his defeat, quitted Oxford and rejoined the Queen at Bath. His obstinacy and violence had brought him into an embarrassing position. He had trusted too much to the effect of his frowns and angry tones, and had rashly staked, not merely the credit of his administration, but his personal dignity, on the issue of the contest. Could he yield to subjects whom he had menaced with raised voice and furious gestures? Yet could he venture to eject in one day a crowd of respectable clergymen from their homes, because they had discharged what the whole nation regarded as a sacred duty? Perhaps there might be an escape from this dilemma. Perhaps the college might still be terrified, caressed, or bribed into submission. The agency *Penn attempts* of Penn was employed. He had too much good *to mediate.* feeling to approve of the violent and unjust proceedings of the government, and even ventured to express part of what he thought. James was, as usual, obstinate in the wrong. The courtly Quaker, therefore, did his best to seduce the college from the path of right. He first tried intimidation. Ruin, he said, impended over the society. The King was highly incensed. The case might be a hard one. Most people thought it so. But every child knew that His Majesty loved to have his own way, and could not bear to be thwarted. Penn, therefore, exhorted the Fellows not to rely on the goodness of their cause, but to submit, or at least to temporize.*

* See Penn's Letter to Bailey, one of the Fellows of the College, in the Impartial Relation printed at Oxford in 1688. It has lately been asserted that Penn most certainly did not write this letter. Now, the evidence which proves the letter to be his is irresistible. Bailey, to whom the letter was addressed, ascribed it to Penn, and sent an answer to Penn. In a very short time both the letter and the answer appeared in print. Many thousands of copies were circulated. Penn was pointed out to the whole world as the author of the letter; and it is not pretended that he met this public accusation with a public contradiction. Everybody therefore believed, and was perfectly warranted in believing, that he was the author. The letter was repeatedly quoted as his, during his own lifetime, not merely in fugitive pamphlets, such as the History of the Ecclesiastical Commission, published in 1711, but in grave and elaborate books which were meant to descend to posterity. Boyer, in his History of William the Third, printed immediately after that King's death, and reprinted in 1703, pronounced the letter to be Penn's, and added some severe reflections on the writer. Kennet, in the bulky History of England published in 1706, a history which had a large sale and produced a great sensation, adopted the very words of Boyer. When these works appeared, Penn was not only alive, but in the full enjoyment of his faculties. He cannot have been ignorant of the charge brought against him by writers of so much note; and it was not his practice to hold his peace when unjust charges were brought against him even by obscure scribblers. In 1695, a pamphlet on the Exclusion Bill was falsely imputed to him in an anonymous libel. Contemptible as was the quarter from which the calumny proceeded, he hastened to vindicate himself. His denial, distinct, solemn, and indignant, speedily came forth in print. Is it possible to doubt that he would, if he could, have confounded Boyer and Kennet by a similar denial? He however silently suffered them to tell the whole nation, during many years, that this letter was written by " William Penn, the head of the Quakers, or, as some then thought, an ambitious, crafty Jesuit, who under a phanatical outside, promoted King James's designs." He died without attempting to clear himself. In the year of his death appeared Eachard's huge volume, containing the History of England from the Restoration to the Revolution; and Eachard, though often differing with Boyer and Kennet, agreed with them in unhesitatingly ascribing the letter to Penn.

Such is the evidence on one side. I am not aware that any evidence deserving a serious answer has been produced on the other (1857).

Such counsel came strangely from one who had himself been expelled from the University for raising a riot about the surplice, who had run the risk of being disinherited rather than take off his hat to the princes of the blood, and who had been more than once sent to prison for haranguing in conventicles. He did not succeed in frightening the Magdalene men. In answer to his alarming hints he was reminded that in the last generation thirty-four out of the forty Fellows had cheerfully left their beloved cloisters and gardens, their hall and their chapel, and had gone forth not knowing where they should find a meal or a bed, rather than violate the oath of allegiance. The King now wished them to violate another oath. He should find that the old spirit was not extinct.

Then Penn tried a gentler tone. He had an interview with Hough and with some of the Fellows, and, after many professions of sympathy and friendship, began to hint at a compromise. The King could not bear to be crossed. The college must give way. Parker must be admitted. But he was in very bad health. All his preferments would soon be vacant. "Doctor Hough," said Penn, "may then be Bishop of Oxford. How should you like that, gentlemen?"* Penn

---

* Here again I have been accused of calumniating Penn; and some show of a case has been made out by suppression amounting to falsification. It is asserted that Penn did not "begin to hint at a compromise;" and in proof of this assertion, a few words, quoted from the letter in which Hough gives an account of the interview, are printed in italics. These words are, "I thank God, he did not offer any proposal by way of accommodation." These words, taken by themselves, undoubtedly seem to prove that Penn did not begin to hint at a compromise. But their effect is very different indeed when they are read in connection with words which immediately follow, without the intervention of a full stop, but which have been carefully suppressed. The whole sentence runs thus: "I thank God, he did not offer any proposal by way of accommodation; only once, upon the mention of the Bishop of Oxford's indisposition, he said, smiling, 'If the Bishop of Oxford die, Dr. Hough may be made Bishop. What think you of that, gentlemen?'" Can anything be clearer than that the latter part of the sentence limits the general assertion contained in the former part? Everybody knows that *only* is perpetually used as synonymous with *except that*. Instances will readily occur to all who are well acquainted with the English Bible, a book from the authority of which there is no appeal when the question is about the force of an English word. We read in the Book of Genesis, to go no farther, that *every* living thing was destroyed; and Noah *only* remained, and they that were with him in the ark; and that Joseph

had passed his life in declaiming against a hireling ministry. He held that he was bound to refuse the payment of tithes, and this even when he had bought land chargeable with tithes, and had been allowed the value of the tithes in the purchase-money. According to his own principles, he would have committed a great sin if he had interfered for the purpose of obtaining a benefice on the most honorable terms for the most pious divine. Yet to such a degree had his manners been corrupted by evil communications, and his understanding obscured by inordinate zeal for a single object, that he did not scruple to become a broker in simony of a peculiarly discreditable kind, and to use a bishopric as a bait to tempt a divine to perjury. Hough replied with civil contempt that he wanted nothing from the crown but common justice. "We stand," he said, "on our statutes and our oaths: but, even setting aside our statutes and oaths, we feel that we have our religion to defend. The Papists have robbed us of University College. They have robbed us of Christ Church. The fight is now for Magdalene. They will soon have all the rest."

Penn was foolish enough to answer that he really believed that the Papists would now be content. "University," he said, "is a pleasant college. Christ Church is a noble place. Magdalene is a fine building. The situation is convenient. The walks by the river are delightful. If the Roman Catholics are reasonable they will be satisfied with these." This absurd avowal would alone have made it impossible for Hough and his brethren to yield.* The negotiation was broken off;

---

bought *all* the land of Egypt for Pharaoh; *only* the land of the priests bought he not. The defenders of Penn reason exactly like a commentator who should construe these passages to mean that Noah was drowned in the flood, and that Joseph bought the land of the priests for Pharaoh (1857).

* I will give one other specimen of the arts which are thought legitimate where the fame of Penn is concerned. To vindicate the language which he held on this occasion, if we suppose him to have meant what he said, is plainly impossible. We are therefore told that he was in a merry mood; that his benevolent heart was so much exhilarated by the sight of several pious and learned men who were about to be reduced to beggary for observing their oaths and adhering to their religion, that he could not help joking; and that it would be most unjust to treat his charm-

and the King hastened to make the disobedient know, as he had threatened, what it was to incur his displeasure.

A special commission was directed to Cartwright, Bishop of Chester, to Wright, Chief-justice of the King's Bench, and to Sir Thomas Jenner, a Baron of the Exchequer, appointing them to exercise visitatorial jurisdiction over the college. On the twentieth of October they arrived at Oxford, escorted by three troops of cavalry with drawn swords. On the following morning the Commissioners took their seats in the hall of Magdalene. Cartwright pronounced a loyal oration, which, a few years before, would have called forth the acclamations of an Oxonian audience, but which was now heard with sullen indignation. A long dispute followed. The President defended his rights with skill, temper, and resolution. He professed great respect for the royal authority: but he steadily maintained that he had by the laws of England a freehold interest in the house and revenues annexed to the Presidency. Of that interest he could not be deprived by an arbitrary mandate of the Sovereign. "Will you submit," said the Bishop, "to our visitation?" "I submit to it," said Hough with great dexterity, "so far as it is consistent with the laws, and no further." "Will you deliver up the key of your lodgings?" said Cartwright. Hough remained silent. The question was repeated; and Hough returned a mild but resolute refusal. The Commissioners pronounced him an intruder, and charged the Fellows to assist at the admission of the Bishop of Oxford. Charnock eagerly promised obedience: Smith returned an evasive answer: but the great body of the members of the college firmly declared that they still regarded Hough as their rightful head.

Special Ecclesiastical Commissioners sent to Oxford.

---

ing facetiousness as a crime. In order to make out this defence—a poor defence even if made out—the following words are quoted, as part of Hough's letter, "He had a mind to droll upon us." This is given as a positive assertion made by Hough. The context is carefully suppressed. My readers will, I believe, be surprised when they learn that Hough's words really are these: "When I heard him talk at this rate, I concluded he was either off his guard, or had a mind to droll upon us."

And now Hough himself craved permission to address a few words to the Commissioners. They consented with much civility, perhaps expecting from the calmness and suavity of his manner that he would make some concession. "My Lords," said he, "you have this day deprived me of my freehold: I hereby protest against all your proceedings as illegal, unjust, and null; and I appeal from you to our Sovereign Lord the King in his courts of justice." A loud murmur of applause arose from the gownsmen who filled the hall. The Commissioners were furious. Search was made for the offenders, but in vain. Then the rage of the whole board was turned against Hough. "Do not think to huff us, sir," cried Jenner, punning on the President's name. "I will uphold His Majesty's authority," said Wright, "while I have breath in my body. All this comes of your popular protest. You have broken the peace. You shall answer it in the King's Bench. I bind you over in one thousand pounds to appear there next term. I will see whether the civil power cannot manage you. If that is not enough, you shall have the military too." In truth Oxford was in a state which made the Commissioners not a little uneasy. The soldiers were ordered to have their carbines loaded. It was said that an express was sent to London for the purpose of hastening the arrival of more troops. No disturbance, however, took place. The Bishop of Oxford was quietly installed by proxy: but only two members of Magdalene College attended the ceremony. Many signs showed that the spirit of resistance had spread to the common people. The porter of the college threw down his keys. The butler refused to scratch Hough's name out of the buttery book, and was instantly dismissed. No blacksmith could be found in the whole city who would force the lock of the President's lodgings. It was necessary for the Commissioners to employ their own servants, who broke open the door with iron bars. The sermons which on the following Sunday were preached in the University Church were full of reflections such as stung Cartwright to the quick, though such as he could not discreetly resent.

Protest of Hough.

Parker.

And here, if James had not been infatuated, the matter might have stopped. The Fellows in general were not inclined to carry their resistance farther. They were of opinion that, by refusing to assist in the admission of the intruder, they had sufficiently proved their respect for their statutes and oaths, and that, since he was now in actual possession, they might justifiably submit to him as their head, till he should be removed by sentence of a competent court. Only one Fellow, Doctor Fairfax, refused to yield even to this extent. The Commissioners would gladly have compromised the dispute on these terms; and during a few hours there was a truce which many thought likely to end in an amicable arrangement: but soon all was again in confusion. The Fellows found that the popular voice loudly accused them of pusillanimity. The townsmen already talked ironically of a Magdalene conscience, and exclaimed that the brave Hough and the honest Fairfax had been betrayed and abandoned. Still more annoying were the sneers of Obadiah Walker and his brother renegades. This, then, said those apostates, was the end of all the big words in which the society had declared itself resolved to stand by its lawful President and by its Protestant faith. While the Fellows, bitterly annoyed by the public censure, were regretting the modified submission which they had consented to make, they learned that this submission was by no means satisfactory to the King. It was not enough, he said, that they offered to obey the Bishop of Oxford as President in fact. They must distinctly admit the Commission and all that had been done under it to be legal: they must acknowledge that they had acted undutifully: they must declare themselves penitent: they must promise to behave better in future, must implore his Majesty's pardon, and must lay themselves at his feet. Two Fellows, of whom the King had no complaint to make, Charnock and Smith, were excused from the obligation of making these degrading apologies.

Even James never committed a grosser error. *The Fellows, already angry with themselves for having conceded so much, and galled by the censure of the world, eagerly caught at the opportunity which was now offered them of regaining the public esteem. With one voice they declared that they would never ask pardon for being in the right, or admit that the visitation of their college and the deprivation of their President had been legal.

Then the King, as he had threatened, laid on them the whole weight of his hand. They were by one sweeping edict condemned to expulsion. Yet this punishment was not deemed sufficient. It was known that many noblemen and gentlemen who possessed church patronage would be disposed to provide for men who had suffered so much for the laws of England and for the Protestant religion. The High Commission therefore pronounced the ejected Fellows incapable of ever holding any ecclesiastical preferment. Such of them as were not yet in holy orders were pronounced incapable of receiving the clerical character. James might enjoy the thought that he had reduced many of them from a situation in which they were surrounded by comforts, and had before them the fairest professional prospects, to hopeless indigence.

Ejection of the Fellows.

But all these severities produced an effect directly the opposite of that which he had anticipated. The spirit of Englishmen, that sturdy spirit which no King of the House of Stuart could ever be taught by experience to understand, swelled up high and strong against injustice. Oxford, the quiet seat of learning and loyalty, was in a state resembling that of the City of London on the morning after the attempt of Charles the First to seize the five members. The Vicechancellor had been asked to dine with the Commissioners on the day of the expulsion. He refused. "My taste," he said, "differs from that of Colonel Kirke. I cannot eat my meals with appetite under a gallows." The scholars refused to pull off their caps to the new rulers of Magdalene College. Smith was nicknamed Doctor Roguery, and was publicly insulted in a coffee-house. When Charnock summoned the Demies to perform their academical exercises before him, they answered that they were deprived of their lawful governors and would submit to no usurped authority. They assembled apart both for study and for divine service. Attempts were made to corrupt them by offers of the lucrative fellowships which had just been declared vacant: but one undergraduate after another manfully answered that his conscience would not suffer him to profit by injustice. One lad who was induced to take a fellowship was turned out of the hall by the rest. Youths were invited from other colleges, but with small success. The richest foundation in the kingdom seemed to have lost all attractions for needy students. Meanwhile, in London and all over the country money was collected for the support of the ejected Fellows. The Princess of Orange, to the great joy of all Protestants, subscribed two hundred pounds. Still, however, the King held on his course. The expulsion of the Fellows was soon followed by the expulsion of a crowd of Demies. All this time the new President was fast sinking under bodily and mental disease. He had made a last feeble effort to serve the government by publishing, at the very time when the college was in a state of open rebellion against his authority, a defence of the Declaration of Indulgence, or rather a defence of the doctrine of transubstantiation. This piece called forth many answers, and particularly one from Burnet, written with extraordinary vigor and acrimony. A few weeks after the expulsion of the Demies, Parker died in the house of which he had violently taken possession. Men said that his heart was broken by remorse and shame. He lies in the beautiful antechapel of the college; but no monument marks his grave.

Then the King's plan was carried into full effect. The college was turned into a Popish seminary. Bonaventure Giffard, the Roman Catholic Bishop of Madura, was appointed President. The Roman Catholic service was performed in the chapel. In one day twelve Roman Catholics were admitted Fellows. Some servile Protestants applied for fellowships, but met with refusals. Smith, an enthusiast in loyalty, but still a sincere member of the Anglican Church, could not bear to see the altered aspect of the house. He absented himself: he was ordered to return

<small>Magdalene College turned into a Popish seminary.</small>

into residence : he disobeyed : he was expelled ; and the work of spoliation was complete.*

The nature of the academical system of England is such that no event which seriously affects the interests and honor of either University can fail to excite a strong feeling throughout the country. Every successive blow, therefore, which fell on Magdalene College, was felt to the extremities of the kingdom. In the coffee-houses of London, in the Inns of Court, in the closes of all the Cathedral towns, in parsonages and manor-houses scattered over the remotest shires, pity for the sufferers and indignation against the government went on growing. The protest of Hough was everywhere applauded; the forcing of his door was everywhere mentioned with abhorrence; and at length the sentence of deprivation fulminated against the Fellows dissolved those ties, once so close and dear, which had bound the Church of England to the House of Stuart. Bitter resentment and cruel apprehension took the place of love and confidence. There was no prebendary, no rector, no vicar, whose mind was not haunted by the thought that, however quiet his temper, however obscure his situation, he might, in a few months, be driven from his dwelling by an arbitrary edict to beg in a ragged cassock with his wife and children, while his freehold, secured to him by laws of immemorial antiquity and by the royal word, was occupied by some apostate. This, then, was the reward of that heroic loyalty never once found wanting through the vicissitudes of fifty tempestuous years. It was for this that the clergy had endured spoliation and persecution in the cause of Charles the First. It was for this that they had supported Charles the Second in his hard contest with the Whig opposition. It was for this that they had stood in the front of the battle against those who sought to despoil James of his birthright. To their fidelity alone their

<small>Resentment of the clergy.</small>

---

* Proceedings against Magdalene College, in Oxon., for not electing Anthony Farmer president of the said College, in the Collection of State Trials; Luttrell's Diary, June 15, 17, Oct. 24, Dec. 10, 1687; Smith's Narrative; Letter of Dr. Richard Rawlinson, dated Oct. 31, 1687; Reresby's Memoirs; Burnet, i., 699; Cartwright's Diary; Van Citters, $\frac{\text{Oct. 25, Oct. 28,}}{\text{Nov. 4, Nov. 7,}}$ Nov. $\frac{8}{18}, \frac{18}{28}$, 1687.

oppressor owed the power which he was now employing to their ruin. They had long been in the habit of recounting in acrimonious language all that they had suffered at the hand of the Puritan in the day of his power. Yet for the Puritan there was some excuse. He was an avowed enemy: he had wrongs to avenge; and even he, while remodelling the ecclesiastical constitution of the country, and ejecting all who would not subscribe his Covenant, had not been altogether without compassion. He had at least granted to those whose benefices he seized a pittance sufficient to support life. But the hatred felt by the King toward that Church which had saved him from exile and placed him on a throne was not to be so easily satiated. Nothing but the utter ruin of his victims would content him. It was not enough that they were expelled from their homes and stripped of their revenues. They found every walk of life toward which men of their habits could look for a subsistence closed against them with malignant care, and nothing left to them but the precarious and degrading resource of alms.

The Anglican clergy, therefore, and that portion of the laity which was strongly attached to Protestant episcopacy, now regarded the King with those feelings which injustice aggravated by ingratitude naturally excites. Yet had the Churchman still many scruples of conscience and honor to surmount before he could bring himself to oppose the government by force. He had been taught that passive obedience was enjoined without restriction or exception by the divine law. He had professed this opinion ostentatiously. He had treated with contempt the suggestion that an extreme case might possibly arise which would justify a people in drawing the sword against regal tyranny. Both principle and shame, therefore, restrained him from imitating the example of the rebellious Roundheads, while any hope of a peaceful and legal deliverance remained; and such a hope might reasonably be cherished as long as the Princess of Orange stood next in succession to the crown. If he would but endure with patience this trial of his faith, the laws of nature would soon do for him what he could not, without sin and dishonor, do for himself. The wrongs of the Church would be redressed: her property and dignity would be fenced by new guarantees; and those wicked courtiers who had, in the day of her adversity, injured and insulted her would be signally punished.

The event to which the Church of England looked forward as an honorable and peaceful termination of her troubles was one of which even the most reckless members of the Jesuitical cabal could not think without painful apprehensions. If their master should die, leaving them no better security against the penal laws than a Declaration which the general voice of the nation pronounced to be a nullity, if a Parliament, animated by the same spirit which had prevailed in the Parliaments of Charles the Second, should assemble round the throne of a Protestant sovereign, was it not probable that a terrible retribution would be exacted, that the old laws against Popery would be rigidly enforced, and that new laws still more severe would be added to the statute-book? The evil counsellors had long been tormented by these gloomy apprehensions, and some of them had contemplated strange and desperate remedies. James had scarcely mounted the throne when it began to be whispered about Whitehall that, if the Lady Anne would turn Roman Catholic, it might not be impossible, with the help of Lewis, to transfer to her the birthright of her elder sister. At the French embassy this scheme was warmly approved; and Bonrepaux gave it as his opinion that the assent of James would be easily obtained.* Soon, however, it became manifest that Anne was unalterably attached to the Established Church. All thought of making her Queen was therefore relinquished. Nevertheless, a small knot of fanatics still continued to cherish a wild hope that they might be able to change the order of succession. The plan formed by these men was set forth in a minute of which a rude French translation has been preserved. It was to be hoped, they said, that the King might be able to establish the true faith without resorting to

Schemes of the Jesuitical cabal respecting the succession.

* " Quand on connoit le dedans de cette cour aussi intimement que je la connois, on peut croire que sa Majesté Britannique donnera volontiers dans ces sortes de projets."—Bonrepaux to Seignelay, March $\frac{18}{28}$, 1686.

extremities; but in the worst event, he might leave his crown at the disposal of Lewis. It was better for Englishmen to be the vassals of France than the slaves of the Devil.* This extraordinary document was handed about from Jesuit to Jesuit, and from courtier to courtier, till some eminent Roman Catholics, in whom bigotry had not extinguished patriotism, furnished the Dutch Ambassador with a copy. He put the paper into the hands of James. James, greatly agitated, pronounced it a vile forgery contrived by some pamphleteer in Holland. The Dutch minister resolutely answered that he could prove the contrary by the testimony of several distinguished members of His Majesty's own Church; nay, that there would be no difficulty in pointing out the writer, who, after all, had written only what many priests and many busy politicians said every day in the galleries of the palace. The King did not think it expedient to ask who the writer was, but, abandoning the charge of forgery, protested, with great vehemence and solemnity, that no thought of disinheriting his eldest daughter had ever crossed his mind. "Nobody," he said, "ever dared to hint such a thing to me. I never would listen to it. God does not command us to propagate the true religion by injustice; and this would be the foulest, the most unnatural injustice."† Notwithstanding all these professions, Barillon, a few days later, reported to his court that James had begun to listen to suggestions respecting a change in the order of succession, that the question was doubtless a delicate one, but that there was reason to hope that, with time and management, a way might be found to settle the crown on some Roman Catholic to the exclusion of the two princesses.‡

* "Que, quand pour établir la religion Catholique et pour la confirmer icy, il (James) devroit se rendre en quelque façon dépendant de la France, et mettre la décision de la succession à la couronne entre les mains de ce monarque là, qu'il seroit obligé de le faire, parcequ'il vaudroit mieux pour ses sujets qu'ils devinssent vassaux du Roy de France, étant Catholiques, que de demeurer comme esclaves du Diable." This paper is in the archives of both France and Holland.

† Van Citters, Aug. $\frac{6}{16}$, $\frac{17}{27}$, 1686; Barillon, Aug. $\frac{19}{29}$.

‡ Barillon, Sept. $\frac{13}{23}$, 1686. "La succession est une matière fort délicate à traiter. Je sais pourtant qu'on en parle au Roy d'Angleterre, et qu'on ne désespère pas avec le temps de trouver des moyens pour faire passer la couronne sur la tête d'un héritier Catholique."

II.—19

During many months this subject continued to be discussed by the fiercest and most extravagant Papists about the court; and candidates for the regal office were actually named.*

It is not probable, however, that James ever meant to take a course so insane. He must have known that England would never bear for a single day the yoke of a usurper who was also a Papist, and that any attempt to set aside the Lady Mary would have been withstood to the death, both by all those who had supported the Exclusion Bill, and by all those who had opposed it. There is, however, no doubt that the King was an accomplice in a plot less absurd, but not less unjustifiable, against the rights of his children. Tyrconnel had, with his master's approbation, made arrangements for separating Ireland from the empire, and for placing her under the protection of Lewis, as soon as the crown should devolve on a Protestant sovereign. Bonrepaux had been consulted, had imparted the design to his court, and had been instructed to assure Tyrconnel that France would lend effectual aid to the accomplishment of this great project.† These transactions, which, though perhaps not in all parts accurately known at the Hague, were strongly suspected there, must not be left out of the account if we would pass a just judgment on the course taken a few months later by the Princess of Orange. Those who pronounced her guilty of a breach of filial duty must admit that her fault was at least greatly extenuated by her wrongs. If, to serve the cause of her religion, she broke through the most sacred ties of consanguinity, she only followed her father's

Marginal note: Scheme of James and Tyrconnel for preventing the Princess of Orange from succeeding to the kingdom of Ireland.

---

* Bonrepaux, July $\frac{11}{21}$, 1687.

† Bonrepaux to Seignelay, $\frac{\text{Aug. 25,}}{\text{Sept. 4,}}$ 1687. I will quote a few words from this most remarkable despatch: ' Je sçay bien certainement que l'intention du Roy d'Angleterre est de faire perdre ce royaume (Ireland) à son successeur et de le fortifier en sorte que tous ses sujets Catholiques y puissent avoir un asile assuré. Son projet est de mettre les choses en cet estat dans le cours de cinq années." In the Secret Consults of the Romish Party in Ireland, printed in 1690, there is a passage which shows that his negotiation had not been kept strictly secret. "Though the King kept it private from most of his council, yet certain it is that he had promised the French King the disposal of that government and kingdom when things had attained to that growth as to be fit to bear it."

example. She did not assist to depose him until he had conspired to disinherit her.

Scarcely had Bonrepaux been informed that Lewis had resolved to assist the enterprise of Tyrconnel when all thoughts of that enterprise were abandoned. James had caught the first glimpse of a hope which delighted and elated him. The Queen was with child.

The Queen pregnant.

Before the end of October, 1687, the great news began to be whispered. It was observed that Her Majesty had absented herself from some public ceremonies, on the plea of indisposition. It was said that many relics, supposed to possess extraordinary virtue, had been hung about her. Soon the story made its way from the palace to the coffee-houses of the capital, and spread fast over the country. By a very small minority the rumor was welcomed with joy. The great body of the nation listened with mingled derision and fear. There was indeed nothing very extraordinary in what had happened. The King had but just completed his fifty-fourth year. The Queen was in the summer of life. She had already borne four children who had died young; and long afterward she was delivered of another child whom nobody had any interest in treating as suppositious, and who was, therefore, never said to be so. As, however, five years had elapsed since her last pregnancy, the people, under the influence of that delusion which leads men to believe what they wish, had ceased to entertain any apprehension that she would give an heir to the throne. On the other hand, nothing seemed more natural and probable than that the Jesuits should have contrived a pious fraud. It was certain that they must consider the accession of the Princess of Orange as one of the greatest calamities which could befall their Church. It was equally certain that they would not be very scrupulous about doing whatever might be necessary to save their Church from a great calamity. In books written by eminent members of the Society, and licensed by its rulers, it was distinctly laid down that means even more shocking to all notions of justice and humanity than the introduction of a spurious heir into a family might lawfully be employed for

General incredulity.

ends less important than the conversion of a heretical kingdom. It had got abroad that some of the King's advisers, and even the King himself, had meditated schemes for defrauding the Lady Mary, either wholly or in part, of her rightful inheritance. A suspicion, not indeed well founded, but by no means so absurd as is commonly supposed, took possession of the public mind. The folly of some Roman Catholics confirmed the vulgar prejudice. They spoke of the auspicious event as strange, as miraculous, as an exertion of the same Divine power which had made Sarah proud and happy in Isaac, and had given Samuel to the prayers of Hannah. Mary's mother, the Duchess of Modena, had lately died. A short time before her death, she had, it was said, implored the Virgin of Loretto, with fervent vows and rich offerings, to bestow a son on James. The King himself had, in the preceding August, turned aside from his progress to visit the Holy Well, and had there besought Saint Winifred to obtain for him that boon without which his great designs for the propagation of the true faith could be but imperfectly executed. The imprudent zealots who dwelt on these tales foretold with confidence that the unborn infant would be a boy, and offered to back their opinion by laying twenty guineas to one. Heaven, they affirmed, would not have interfered but for a great end. One fanatic announced that the Queen would give birth to twins, of whom the elder would be King of England, and the younger Pope of Rome. Mary could not conceal the delight with which she heard this prophecy; and her ladies found that they could not gratify her more than by talking of it. The Roman Catholics would have acted more wisely if they had spoken of the pregnancy as of a natural event, and if they had borne with moderation their unexpected good fortune. Their insolent triumph excited the popular indignation. Their predictions strengthened the popular suspicions. From the Prince and Princess of Denmark down to porters and laundresses nobody alluded to the promised birth without a sneer. The wits of London described the new miracle in rhymes which, it may well be supposed, were not the most delicate. The rough country squires roared with laughter if they met with any person simple enough to believe that the Queen was really likely to be again a mother. A royal proclamation appeared commanding the clergy to read a form of prayer and thanksgiving which had been prepared for this joyful occasion by Crewe and Sprat. The clergy obeyed: but it was observed that the congregations made no responses and showed no signs of reverence. Soon in all the coffee-houses was handed about a brutal lampoon on the courtly prelates whose pens the King had employed. Mother East had also her full share of abuse. Into that homely monosyllable our ancestors had degraded the name of the great house of Este which reigned at Modena.*

The new hope which elated the King's spirits was mingled with many fears. Something more than the birth of a Prince of Wales was necessary to the success of the plans formed by the Jesuitical party. It was not very likely that James would live till his son should be of age to exercise the regal functions. The law had made no provision for the case of a minority. The reigning sovereign was not competent to make provision for such a case by will. The legislature only could supply the defect. If James should die before the defect had been supplied, leaving a successor of tender years, the supreme power would undoubtedly devolve on Protestants. Those Tories who held most firmly the doctrine that nothing could justify them in resisting their liege lord, would have no scruple about drawing their swords against a Popish woman who should dare to usurp the guardianship of the realm and of the infant sovereign. The result of a contest could scarcely be matter of doubt. The Prince of Orange, or his wife, would be Regent. The young King would be placed in the hands of heretical instructors, whose arts might speedily efface from his mind the impressions which might have been made on it in the nursery. He might prove another Edward the Sixth;

---

* Van Citters, $\frac{\text{Oct. 28,}}{\text{Nov. 7,}} \frac{\text{Nov. 22,}}{\text{Dec. 2,}}$ 1687; the Princess Anne to the Princess of Orange, March 14 and 20, 168$\frac{7}{8}$; Barillon, Dec. $\frac{1}{11}$, 1687; Revolution Politics; the song "Two Toms and a Nat;" Johnstone, April 4, 1688; Secret Consults of the Romish Party in Ireland, 1690.

and the blessing granted to the intercession of the Virgin Mother and of Saint Winifred might be turned into a curse.* This was a danger against which nothing but an Act of Parliament could be a security; and how was such an act to be obtained? Everything seemed to indicate that, if the Houses were convoked, they would come up to Westminster animated by the spirit of 1640. The event of the country elections could hardly be doubted. The whole body of freeholders high and low, clerical and lay, was strongly excited against the government. In the great majority of those towns where the right of voting depended on the payment of local taxes, or on the occupation of a tenement, no courtly candidate could dare to show his face. A very large part of the House of Commons was returned by members of municipal corporations. These corporations had recently been remodelled for the purpose of destroying the influence of the Whigs and Dissenters. More than a hundred constituent bodies had been deprived of their charters by tribunals devoted to the crown, or had been induced to avert compulsory disfranchisement by voluntary surrender. Every Mayor, every Alderman, every Town Clerk, from Berwick to Helstone, was a Tory and a Churchman: but Tories and Churchmen were now no longer devoted to the Sovereign. The new municipalities were more unmanageable than the old municipalities had ever been, and would undoubtedly return representatives whose first act would be to impeach all the Popish Privy Councillors, and all the members of the High Commission.

[Marginal note: Feeling of the constituent bodies, and of the Peers.]

In the Lords the prospect was scarcely less gloomy than in the Commons. Among the temporal peers it was certain that there would be an immense majority against the King's measures; and on that episcopal bench, which seven years before

---

* The King's uneasiness on this subject is strongly described by Ronquillo, Dec. $\frac{12}{22}$, 1687. "Un Principe de Vales y un Duque de York y otro di Lochaosterna (Lancaster, I suppose) no bastan á reducir la gente; porque el Rey tiene 54 años, y vendrá á morir, dejando los hijos pequeños, y que entonces el reyno se apoderará dellos, y los nombrará tutor, y los educará en la religion protestante, contra la disposicion que dejare el Rey, y la autoridad de la Reyna."

had unanimously supported him against those who had attempted to deprive him of his birthright, he could now look for support only to four or five sycophants despised by their profession and by their country.*

To all men not utterly blinded by passion these difficulties appeared insuperable. The most unscrupulous slaves of power showed signs of uneasiness. Dryden muttered that the King would only make matters worse by trying to mend them, and sighed for the golden days of the careless and good-natured Charles.† Even Jeffreys wavered. As long as he was poor, he was perfectly ready to face obloquy and public hatred for lucre. But he had now, by corruption and extortion, accumulated great riches; and he was more anxious to secure them than to increase them. His slackness drew on him a sharp reprimand from the royal lips. In dread of being deprived of the Great Seal, he promised whatever was required of him: but Barillon, in reporting this circumstance to Lewis, remarked that the King of England could place little reliance on any man who had anything to lose.‡

Nevertheless James determined to persevere. The sanction of a Parliament was necessary to his system. The sanction of a free and lawful Parliament it was evidently impossible to obtain: but it might not be altogether impossible to bring together by corruption, by intimidation, by violent exertions of prerogative, by fraudulent distortions of law, an assembly which might call itself a Parliament, and might be willing to register any edict

James determines to pack a Parliament.

---

* Three lists framed at this time are extant; one in the French archives, the other two in the archives of the Portland family. In these lists every peer is entered under one of three heads, For the Repeal of the Test, Against the Repeal, and Doubtful. According to one list the numbers were, 31 for, 86 against, and 20 doubtful; according to another, 33 for, 87 against, and 19 doubtful; according to the third, 35 for, 92 against, and 10 doubtful. Copies of the three lists are among the Mackintosh MSS.

† There is in the British Museum a letter of Dryden to Etherege, dated Feb., 1688. I do not remember to have seen it in print. "Oh," says Dryden, "that our monarch would encourage noble idleness by his own example, as he of blessed memory did before him. For my mind misgives me that he will not much advance his affairs by stirring." ‡ Barillon, $\frac{\text{Aug. 29,}}{\text{Sept. 8,}}$ 1687.

of the Sovereign. Returning officers must be appointed who would avail themselves of the slightest pretence to declare the King's friends duly elected. Every placeman, from the highest to the lowest, must be made to understand that, if he wished to retain his office, he must at this conjuncture support the throne by his vote and interest. The High Commission meanwhile would keep its eye on the clergy. The boroughs, which had just been remodelled to serve one turn, might be remodelled again to serve another. By such means the King hoped to obtain a majority in the House of Commons. The Upper House would then be at his mercy. He had undoubtedly by law the power of creating peers without limit; and this power he was fully determined to use. He did not wish, and indeed no sovereign can wish, to make the highest honor which is in the gift of the crown worthless. He cherished the hope that, by calling up some heirs-apparent to the assembly in which they must ultimately sit, and by conferring English titles on some Scotch and Irish Lords, he might be able to secure a majority without ennobling new men in such numbers as to bring ridicule on the coronet and the ermine. But there was no extremity to which he was not prepared to go in case of necessity. When in a large company an opinion was expressed that the peers would prove intractable, "Oh, silly," cried Sunderland, turning to Churchill; "your troop of guards shall be called up to the House of Lords."*

Having determined to pack a Parliament, James set himself energetically and methodically to the work. A proclamation appeared in the Gazette, announcing that the King had determined to revise the Commissions of Peace and of Lieutenancy, and to retain in public employment only such gentlemen as should be disposed to support his policy.† A committee of seven Privy Councillors sat at Whitehall, for the purpose of regulating — such was the phrase — the municipal corporations. In this committee Jeffreys alone repre-

---

* Told by Lord Bradford, who was present, to Dartmouth; note on Burnet, i., 755. † London Gazette, Dec. 12, 1687.

sented the Protestant interest. Powis alone represented the moderate Roman Catholics. All the other members belonged to the Jesuitical faction. Among them was Petre, who had just been sworn of the Council. Till he took his seat at the board, his elevation had been kept a profound secret from everybody but Sunderland. The public indignation at this new violation of the law was clamorously expressed; and it was remarked that the Roman Catholics were even louder in censure than the Protestants. The vain and ambitious Jesuit was now charged with the business of destroying and reconstructing half the constituent bodies in the kingdom. Under the Committee of Privy Councillors a subcommittee consisting of bustling agents less eminent in rank was intrusted with the management of details. Local subcommittees of regulators all over the country corresponded with the central board at Westminster.*

<small>The Board of Regulators.</small>

The persons on whom James chiefly relied for assistance in his new and arduous enterprise were the Lords-lieutenants. Every Lord-lieutenant received written orders directing him to go down immediately into his county. There he was to summon before him all his deputies, and all the Justices of the Peace, and to put to them a series of interrogatories framed for the purpose of ascertaining how they would act at a general election. He was to take down the answers in writing, and to transmit them to the government. He was to furnish a list of such Roman Catholics, and such Protestant Dissenters, as might be best qualified for the bench and for commands in the militia. He was also to examine into the state of all the boroughs in his county, and to make such reports as might be necessary to guide the operations of the board of regulators. It was intimated to him that he must himself perform these duties, and that he could not be permitted to delegate them to any other person.†

The first effect produced by these orders would have at once sobered a prince less infatuated than James. Half the

---

* Bonrepaux to Seignelay, November $\frac{14}{24}$; Van Citters, November $\frac{15}{25}$; Lords' Journals, December 20, 1689. † Van Citters, $\frac{\text{Oct. 28,}}{\text{Nov. 7,}}$ 1687.

Lords-lieutenants of England peremptorily refused to stoop to the odious service which was required of them. They were immediately dismissed. All those who incurred this glorious disgrace were peers of high consideration; and all had hitherto been regarded as firm supporters of monarchy. Some names in the list deserve especial notice.

Many Lords-lieutenants dismissed.

The noblest subject in England, and indeed, as Englishmen loved to say, the noblest subject in Europe, was Aubrey de Vere, twentieth and last of the old Earls of Oxford. He derived his title, through an uninterrupted male descent, from a time when the families of Howard and Seymour were still obscure, when the Nevilles and Percies enjoyed only a provincial celebrity, and when even the great name of Plantagenet had not yet been heard in England. One chief of the house of De Vere had held high command at Hastings: another had marched, with Godfrey and Tancred, over heaps of slaughtered Moslem, to the sepulchre of Christ. The first Earl of Oxford had been minister of Henry Beauclerc. The third Earl had been conspicuous among the Lords who extorted the Great Charter from John. The seventh Earl had fought bravely at Cressy and Poictiers. The thirteenth Earl had, through many vicissitudes of fortune, been the chief of the party of the Red Rose, and had led the van on the decisive day of Bosworth. The seventeenth Earl had shone at the court of Elizabeth, and had won for himself an honorable place among the early masters of English poetry. The nineteenth Earl had fallen in arms for the Protestant religion and for the liberties of Europe under the walls of Maestricht. His son Aubrey, in whom closed the longest and most illustrious line of nobles that England has seen, a man of loose morals, but of inoffensive temper and of courtly manners, was Lord-lieutenant of Essex, and Colonel of the Blues. His nature was not factious; and his interest inclined him to avoid a rupture with the court; for his estate was encumbered, and his military command lucrative. He was summoned to the royal closet, and an explicit declaration of his intentions was demanded from him. "Sir," answered Ox-

The Earl of Oxford.

ford, "I will stand by Your Majesty against all enemies to the last drop of my blood. But this is matter of conscience, and I cannot comply." He was instantly deprived of his lieutenancy and of his regiment.*

Inferior in antiquity and splendor to the house of De Vere, but to the house of De Vere alone, was the house of Talbot. The Earl of Shrewsbury. Ever since the reign of Edward the Third, the Talbots had sat among the peers of the realm. The earldom of Shrewsbury had been bestowed, in the fifteenth century, on John Talbot, the antagonist of the Maid of Orleans. He had been long remembered by his countrymen with tenderness and reverence as one of the most illustrious of those warriors who had striven to erect a great English empire on the Continent of Europe. The stubborn courage which he had shown in the midst of disasters had made him an object of interest greater than more fortunate captains had inspired; and his death had furnished a singularly touching scene to our early stage. His posterity had, during two centuries, flourished in great honor. The head of the family at the time of the Restoration was Francis, the eleventh Earl, a Roman Catholic. His death had been attended by circumstances such as, even in those licentious times which immediately followed the downfall of the Puritan tyranny, had moved men to horror and pity. The Duke of Buckingham in the course of his vagrant amours was for a moment attracted by the Countess of Shrewsbury. She was easily won. Her Lord challenged the gallant, and fell. Some said that the abandoned woman witnessed the combat in man's attire, and others that she clasped her victorious lover to her bosom while his shirt was still dripping with the blood of her husband. The honors of the murdered man descended to his infant son Charles. As the orphan grew up to man's estate, it was generally acknowledged that of the young nobility of

---

* Halstead's Succinct Genealogy of the Family of Vere, 1685; Collins's Historical Collections. See in the Lords' Journals, and in Jones's Reports, the proceedings respecting the earldom of Oxford, in March and April, $162\frac{5}{6}$. The exordium of the speech of Lord Chief-justice Crewe is among the finest specimens of the ancient English eloquence. Van Citters, Feb. $\frac{7}{17}$, 1688.

England none had been so richly gifted by nature. His person was pleasing, his temper singularly sweet, his parts such as, if he had been born in a humble rank, might well have raised him to civil greatness. All these advantages he had so improved that, before he was of age, he was allowed to be one of the finest gentlemen and finest scholars of his time. His learning is proved by notes which are still extant in his handwriting on books in almost every department of literature. He spoke French like a gentleman of Lewis's bedchamber, and Italian like a citizen of Florence. It was impossible that a youth of such parts should not be anxious to understand the grounds on which his family had refused to conform to the religion of the state. He studied the disputed points closely, submitted his doubts to priests of his own faith, laid their answers before Tillotson, weighed the arguments on both sides long and attentively, and, after an investigation which occupied two years, declared himself a Protestant. The Church of England welcomed the illustrious convert with delight. His popularity was great, and became greater when it was known that royal solicitations and promises had been vainly employed to seduce him back to the superstition which he had abjured. The character of the young Earl did not, however, develop itself in a manner quite satisfactory to those who had borne the chief part in his conversion. His morals by no means escaped the contagion of fashionable libertinism. In truth the shock which had overturned his early prejudices had at the same time unfixed all his opinions, and left him to the unchecked guidance of his feelings. But, though his principles were unsteady, his impulses were so generous, his temper so bland, his manners so gracious and easy, that it was impossible not to love him. He was early called the King of Hearts, and never, through a long, eventful, and checkered life, lost his right to that name.*

Shrewsbury was Lord-lieutenant of Staffordshire and col-

---

* Coxe's Shrewsbury Correspondence; Mackay's Memoirs; Life of Charles Duke of Shrewsbury, 1718; Burnet, i., 762; Birch's Life of Tillotson, where the reader will find a letter from Tillotson to Shrewsbury, which seems to me a model of serious, friendly, and gentlemanlike reproof.

onel of one of the regiments of horse which had been raised in consequence of the Western insurrection. He now refused to act under the board of regulators, and was deprived of both his commissions.

None of the English nobles enjoyed a larger measure of public favor than Charles Sackville, Earl of Dorset. He was indeed a remarkable man. In his youth he had been one of the most notorious libertines of the wild time which followed the Restoration. He had been the terror of the City watch, had passed many nights in the round-house, and had at least once occupied a cell in Newgate. His passion for Betty Morrice, and for Nell Gwynn, who called him her Charles the First, had given no small amusement and scandal to the town.* Yet, in the midst of follies and vices, his courageous spirit, his fine understanding, and his natural goodness of heart, had been conspicuous. Men said that the excesses in which he indulged were common between him and the whole race of gay young Cavaliers, but that his sympathy with human suffering, and the generosity with which he made reparation to those whom his freaks had injured, were all his own. His associates were astonished by the distinction which the public made between him and them. "He may do what he chooses," said Wilmot; "he is never in the wrong." The judgment of the world became still more favorable to Dorset when he had been sobered by time and marriage. His graceful manners, his brilliant conversation, his soft heart, his open hand, were universally praised. No day passed, it was said, in which some distressed family had not reason to bless his name. And yet, with all his good-nature, such was the keenness of his wit that scoffers whose sarcasm all the town feared stood in craven fear of the sarcasm of Dorset. All political parties esteemed and caressed him: but politics were not much to his taste. Had he been driven by necessity to exert himself, he would probably have

_{The Earl of Dorset.}

---

* The King was only Nell's Charles III. Whether Dorset or Major Charles Hart had the honor of being her Charles I. is a point open to dispute. But the evidence in favor of Dorset's claim seems to me to preponderate. See the suppressed passage of Burnet, i., 263, and Pepys's Diary, Oct. 26, 1667.

risen to the highest posts in the state: but he was born to rank so high and wealth so ample that many of the motives which impel men to engage in public affairs were wanting to him. He took just so much part in parliamentary and diplomatic business as sufficed to show that he wanted nothing but inclination to rival Danby and Sunderland, and turned away to pursuits which pleased him better. Like many other men who, with great natural abilities, are constitutionally and habitually indolent, he became an intellectual voluptuary, and a master of all those pleasing branches of knowledge which can be acquired without severe application. He was allowed to be the best judge of painting, of sculpture, of architecture, of acting, that the court could show. On questions of polite learning his decisions were regarded at all the coffee-houses as without appeal. More than one clever play which had failed on the first representation was supported by his single authority against the whole clamor of the pit, and came forth successful from the second trial. The delicacy of his taste in French composition was extolled by Saint Evremond and La Fontaine. Such a patron of letters England had never seen. His bounty was bestowed with equal judgment and liberality, and was confined to no sect or faction. Men of genius, estranged from each other by literary jealousy or by difference of political opinion, joined in acknowledging his impartial kindness. Dryden owned that he had been saved from ruin by Dorset's princely generosity. Yet Montague and Prior, who had keenly satirized Dryden, were introduced by Dorset into public life; and the best comedy of Dryden's mortal enemy, Shadwell, was written at Dorset's country seat. The munificent Earl might, if such had been his wish, have been the rival of those of whom he was content to be the benefactor. For the verses which he occasionally composed, unstudied as they are, exhibit the traces of a genius which, assiduously cultivated, would have produced something great. In the small volume of his works may be found songs which have the easy vigor of Suckling, and little satires which sparkle with wit as splendid as that of Butler.*

---

* Pepys's Diary; Prior's Dedication of his Poems to the Duke of Dorset; John-

Dorset was Lord-lieutenant of Sussex; and to Sussex the board of regulators looked with great anxiety: for in no other county, Cornwall and Wiltshire excepted, were there so many small boroughs. He was ordered to repair to his post. No person who knew him expected that he would obey. He gave such an answer as became him, and was informed that his services were no longer needed. The interest which his many noble and amiable qualities inspired was heightened when it was known that he had received by the post an anonymous billet telling him that, if he did not promptly comply with the King's wishes, all his wit and popularity should not save him from assassination. A similar warning was sent to Shrewsbury. Threatening letters were then much more rare than they afterward became. It is therefore not strange that the people, excited as they were, should have been disposed to believe that the best and noblest Englishmen were really marked out for Popish daggers.* Just when these letters were the talk of all London, the mutilated corpse of a noted Puritan was found in the streets. It was soon discovered that the murderer had acted from no religious or political motive. But the first suspicions of the populace fell on the Papists. The mangled remains were carried in procession to the house of the Jesuits in the Savoy; and during a few hours the fear and rage of the populace were scarcely less violent than on the day when Godfrey was borne to the grave.†

The other dismissions must be more concisely related. The Duke of Somerset, whose regiment had been taken from him some months before, was now turned out of the lord-lieu-

---

son's Life of Dorset; Dryden's Essay on Satire, and Dedication of the Essay on Dramatic Poesy. The affection of Dorset for his wife and his strict fidelity to her are mentioned with great contempt by that profligate coxcomb Sir George Etherege in his letters from Ratisbon, December $\frac{9}{19}$, 1687, and January $\frac{16}{26}$, 1688. See also Shadwell's Dedication of the Squire of Alsatia; Burnet, i., 264; Mackay's Characters. Some parts of Dorset's character are well touched in his epitaph, written by Pope:

               "Yet soft his nature, though severe his lay;"
and again:
       "Blest courtier, who could king and country please,
       Yet sacred keep his friendship and his ease."

* Barillon, Jan. $\frac{9}{19}$, 1688; Van Citters, $\frac{\text{Jan. 31.}}{\text{Feb. 10.}}$ † Adda, Feb. $\frac{3}{13}$, $\frac{10}{20}$, 1688.

tenancy of the East Riding of Yorkshire. The North Riding was taken from Viscount Fauconberg, Shropshire from Viscount Newport, and Lancashire from the Earl of Derby, grandson of that gallant Cavalier who had faced death so bravely, both on the field of battle and on the scaffold, for the House of Stuart. The Earl of Pembroke, who had recently served the crown with fidelity and spirit against Monmouth, was displaced in Wiltshire, the Earl of Rutland in Leicestershire, the Earl of Bridgewater in Buckinghamshire, the Earl of Thanet in Cumberland, the Earl of Northampton in Warwickshire, the Earl of Abingdon in Oxfordshire, and the Earl of Scarsdale in Derbyshire. Scarsdale was also deprived of a regiment of cavalry, and of an office in the household of the Princess of Denmark. She made a struggle to retain his services, and yielded only to a peremptory command of her father. The Earl of Gainsborough was ejected, not only from the lieutenancy of Hampshire, but also from the government of Portsmouth and the rangership of the New Forest, two places for which he had, only a few months before, given five thousand pounds.*

The King could not find Lords of great note, or indeed Protestant Lords of any sort, who would accept the vacant offices. It was necessary to assign two shires to Jeffreys, a new man whose landed property was small, and two to Preston, who was not even an English peer. The other counties which had been left without governors were intrusted, with scarcely an exception, to known Roman Catholics, or to courtiers who had secretly promised the King to declare themselves Roman Catholics as soon as they could do so with prudence.

At length the new machinery was put in action; and soon from every corner of the realm arrived the news of complete and hopeless failure. The catechism by which the Lords-lieutenants had been directed to test the sentiments of the country gentlemen consisted of three questions. Every magistrate and Deputy Lieutenant was to be asked, first, whether, if he should be chosen to serve

<small>Questions put to the Magistrates.</small>

---

* Barillon, Dec. $\frac{5}{15}$, $\frac{8}{18}$, $\frac{12}{22}$, 1687; Van Citters, $\frac{\text{Nov. 29}}{\text{Dec. 9,}}$ Dec. $\frac{2}{12}$.

in Parliament, he would vote for a bill framed on the principles of the Declaration of Indulgence; secondly, whether, as an elector, he would support candidates who would engage to vote for such a bill; and, thirdly, whether, in his private capacity, he would aid the King's benevolent designs by living in friendship with people of all religious persuasions.*

As soon as the questions got abroad, a form of answer, drawn up with admirable skill, was circulated all over the kingdom, and was generally adopted. It was to the following effect: "As a member of the House of Commons, should I have the honor of a seat there, I shall think it my duty carefully to weigh such reasons as may be adduced in debate for and against a Bill of Indulgence, and then to vote according to my conscientious conviction. As an elector, I shall give my support to candidates whose notions of the duty of a representative agree with my own. As a private man, it is my wish to live in peace and charity with everybody." This answer, far more provoking than a direct refusal, because slightly tinged with a sober and decorous irony which could not well be resented, was all that the emissaries of the court could extract from most of the country gentlemen. Arguments, promises, threats, were tried in vain. The Duke of Norfolk, though a Protestant, and though dissatisfied with the proceedings of the government, had consented to become its agent in two counties. He went first to Surrey, where he soon found that nothing could be done.† He then repaired to Norfolk, and returned to inform the King that, of seventy gentlemen who bore office in that great province, only six had held out hopes that they should support the policy of the court.‡ The Duke of Beaufort, whose authority extended over four English shires and over the whole principality of Wales, came up to Whitehall with an account not less discouraging.§ Rochester was Lord-lieutenant of Hertfordshire. All his little stock of virtue had been expended in his struggle against the strong

---

* Van Citters, $\frac{\text{Oct. 28,}}{\text{Nov. 7,}}$ 1687; Lonsdale's Memoirs.

† Van Citters, $\frac{\text{Nov. 22,}}{\text{Dec. 2,}}$ 1687. ‡ Ibid., $\frac{\text{Dec. 27,}}{\text{Jan. 6,}}$ 168⅞. § Ibid.

temptation to sell his religion for lucre. He was still bound to the court by a pension of four thousand pounds a year; and in return for this pension he was willing to perform any service, however illegal or degrading, provided only that he were not required to go through the forms of a reconciliation with Rome. He had readily undertaken to manage his county; and he exerted himself, as usual, with indiscreet heat and violence. But his anger was thrown away on the sturdy squires to whom he addressed himself. They told him with one voice that they would send up no man to Parliament who would vote for taking away the safeguards of the Protestant religion.* The same answer was given to the Chancellor in Buckinghamshire.† The gentry of Shropshire, assembled at Ludlow, unanimously refused to fetter themselves by the pledge which the King demanded of them.‡ The Earl of Yarmouth reported from Wiltshire that, of sixty magistrates and Deputy Lieutenants with whom he had conferred, only seven had given favorable answers, and that even those seven could not be trusted.§ The renegade Peterborough made no progress in Northamptonshire.‖ His brother renegade, Dover, was equally unsuccessful in Cambridgeshire.¶ Preston brought cold news from Cumberland and Westmoreland. Dorsetshire and Huntingdonshire were animated by the same spirit. The Earl of Bath, after a long canvass, returned from the West with gloomy tidings. He had been authorized to make the most tempting offers to the inhabitants of that region. In particular he had promised that, if proper respect were shown to the royal wishes, the trade in tin should be freed from the oppressive restrictions under which it lay. But this lure, which at another time would have proved irresistible, was now slighted. All the Justices and Deputy Lieutenants of Devonshire and Cornwall, without a single dissenting voice, declared that they would put life and property in

---

* Rochester's offensive warmth on this occasion is twice noticed by Johnstone, November 25 and December 8, 1687. His failure is mentioned by Van Citters, December $\frac{6}{16}$.

† Van Citters, Dec. $\frac{6}{16}$, 1687.

‡ Ibid., Dec. $\frac{20}{30}$, 1687.

§ Ibid., $\frac{\text{March 30,}}{\text{April 9,}}$ 1687.

‖ Ibid., $\frac{\text{Nov. 22,}}{\text{Dec. 2,}}$ 1687.

¶ Ibid., Nov. $\frac{15}{25}$, 1687.

jeopardy for the King, but that the Protestant religion was dearer to them than either life or property. "And, sir," said Bath, "if Your Majesty should dismiss all these gentlemen, their successors would give exactly the same answer."* If there was any district in which the government might have hoped for success, that district was Lancashire. Considerable doubts had been felt as to the result of what was passing there. In no part of the realm had so many opulent and honorable families adhered to the old religion. The heads of many of those families had already, by virtue of the dispensing power, been made Justices of the Peace and intrusted with commands in the militia. Yet from Lancashire the new Lord-lieutenant, himself a Roman Catholic, reported that two-thirds of his deputies and of the magistrates were opposed to the court.† But the proceedings in Hampshire wounded the King's pride still more deeply. Arabella Churchill had, more than twenty years before, borne him a son, widely renowned, at a later period, as one of the most skilful captains of Europe. The youth, named James Fitzjames, had as yet given no promise of the eminence which he afterward attained: but his manners were so gentle and inoffensive that he had no enemy except Mary of Modena, who had long hated the child of the concubine with the bitter hatred of a childless wife. A small part of the Jesuitical faction had, before the pregnancy of the Queen was announced, seriously thought of setting him up as a competitor of the Princess of Orange.‡ When it is remembered how signally Monmouth, though believed by the populace to be legitimate, and though the champion of the national religion, had failed in a similar competition, it must seem extraordinary that any man should have been so much blinded by fanaticism as to think of placing on the throne one who was universally known to be a Popish bastard. It does not appear that this absurd design was ever countenanced by the King. The boy, however, was acknowledged;

---

* Van Citters, April $\frac{10}{20}$, 1688.
† The anxiety about Lancashire is mentioned by Van Citters, in a despatch dated Nov. $\frac{18}{28}$, 1687; the result in a despatch dated four days later.
‡ Bonrepaux, July $\frac{11}{21}$, 1687.

and whatever distinctions a subject, not of the royal blood, could hope to attain were bestowed on him. He had been created Duke of Berwick; and he was now loaded with honorable and lucrative employments, taken from those noblemen who had refused to comply with the royal commands. He succeeded the Earl of Oxford as Colonel of the Blues, and the Earl of Gainsborough as Lord-lieutenant of Hampshire, Ranger of the New Forest, and Governor of Portsmouth. On the frontier of Hampshire Berwick expected to have been met, according to custom, by a long cavalcade of baronets, knights, and squires: but not a single person of note appeared to welcome him. He sent out letters commanding the attendance of the gentry: but only five or six paid the smallest attention to his summons. The rest did not wait to be dismissed. They declared that they would take no part in the civil or military government of their county while the King was represented there by a Papist, and voluntarily laid down their commissions.*

Sunderland, who had been named Lord-lieutenant of Warwickshire in the room of the Earl of Northampton, found some excuse for not going down to face the indignation and contempt of the gentry of that shire; and his plea was the more readily admitted because the King had by that time begun to feel that the spirit of the rustic gentry was not to be bent.†

It is to be observed that those who displayed this spirit were not the old enemies of the House of Stuart. The Commissions of Peace and Lieutenancy had long been carefully purged of all republican names. The persons from whom the court had in vain attempted to extract any promise of support were, with scarcely an exception, Tories. The elder among them could still show scars given by the swords of Roundheads, and receipts for plate sent to Charles the First in his distress. The younger had adhered firmly to James against Shaftesbury and Monmouth. Such were the men who were now turned out of office in a mass by the very prince to

---

* Van Citters, Feb. $\tfrac{3}{13}$, 1688.   † Ibid., April $\tfrac{5}{15}$, 1688.

whom they had given such signal proofs of fidelity. Dismission, however, only made them more resolute. It had become a sacred point of honor among them to stand stoutly by one another in this crisis. There could be no doubt that, if the suffrage of the freeholders were fairly taken, not a single knight of the shire favorable to the policy of the government would be returned. Men therefore asked one another, with no small anxiety, whether the suffrages were likely to be fairly taken. The list of the sheriffs for the new year was impatiently expected. It appeared while the Lord-lieutenants were still engaged in their canvass, and was received with a general cry of alarm and indignation. Most of the functionaries who were to preside at the county elections were either Roman Catholics or Protestant Dissenters who had expressed their approbation of the Indulgence.* For a time the most gloomy apprehensions prevailed: but soon they began to subside. There was good reason to believe that there was a point beyond which the King could not reckon on the support even of those sheriffs who were members of his own Church. Between the Roman Catholic courtier and the Roman Catholic country gentleman there was very little sympathy. That cabal which domineered at Whitehall consisted partly of fanatics, who were ready to break through all rules of morality and to throw the world into confusion for the purpose of propagating their religion, and partly of hypocrites who, for lucre, had apostatized from the faith in which they had been brought up, and who now overacted the zeal characteristic of neophytes. Both the fanatical and the hypocritical courtiers were generally destitute of all English feeling. In some of them devotion to their Church had extinguished every national sentiment. Some were Irishmen, whose patriotism consisted in mortal hatred of the Saxon conquerors of Ireland. Some, again, were traitors, who received regular hire from a foreign power. Some had passed a great part of their lives abroad, and either were mere cosmopolites, or felt a positive

List of Sheriffs.

Character of the Roman Catholic country gentlemen.

---

* London Gazette, Dec. 5, 1687; Van Citters, Dec. $\tfrac{8}{18}$.

distaste for the manners and institutions of the country which was now subjected to their rule. Between such men and the lord of a Cheshire or Staffordshire manor who adhered to the old Church there was scarcely anything in common. He was neither a fanatic nor a hypocrite. He was a Roman Catholic because his father and grandfather had been so; and he held his hereditary faith, as men generally hold a hereditary faith, sincerely, but with little enthusiasm. In all other points he was a mere English squire, and, if he differed from the neighboring squires, differed from them by being somewhat more simple and clownish than they. The disabilities under which he lay had prevented his mind from expanding to the standard, moderate as that standard was, which the minds of Protestant country gentlemen then ordinarily attained. Excluded, when a boy, from Eton and Westminster, when a youth, from Oxford and Cambridge, when a man, from Parliament and from the bench of justice, he generally vegetated as quietly as the elms of the avenue which led to his ancestral grange. His cornfields, his dairy, and his ciderpress, his greyhounds, his fishing-rod, and his gun, his ale and his tobacco, occupied almost all his thoughts. With his neighbors, in spite of his religion, he was generally on good terms. They knew him to be unambitious and inoffensive. He was almost always of a good old family. He was always a Cavalier. His peculiar notions were not obtruded, and caused no annoyance. He did not, like a Puritan, torment himself and others with scruples about everything that was pleasant. On the contrary, he was as keen a sportsman, and as jolly a boon companion, as any man who had taken the oath of supremacy and the declaration against transubstantiation. He met his brother squires at the cover, was in with them at the death, and, when the sport was over, took them home with him to a venison pasty and to October four years in bottle. The oppressions which he had undergone had not been such as to impel him to any desperate resolution. Even when his Church was barbarously persecuted, his life and property were in little danger. The most impudent false-witnesses could hardly venture to shock the common-sense of mankind by accusing him of being a conspirator. The Papists whom Oates selected for attack were peers, prelates, Jesuits, Benedictines, a busy political agent, a lawyer in high practice. The Roman Catholic country gentleman, protected by his obscurity, by his peaceable demeanor, and by the good-will of those among whom he lived, carted his hay or filled his bag with game unmolested, while Coleman and Langhorne, Whitbread and Pickering, Archbishop Plunkett and Lord Stafford, died by the halter or the axe. An attempt was indeed made by a knot of villains to bring home a charge of treason to Sir Thomas Gascoigne, an aged Roman Catholic baronet of Yorkshire: but twelve gentlemen of the West Riding, who knew his way of life, could not be convinced that their honest old acquaintance had hired cutthroats to murder the King, and, in spite of charges which did very little honor to the bench, found a verdict of Not Guilty. Sometimes, indeed, the head of an old and respectable provincial family might reflect with bitterness that he was excluded, on account of his religion, from places of honor and authority which men of humbler descent and less ample estate were thought competent to fill: but he was little disposed to risk land and life in a struggle against overwhelming odds; and his honest English spirit would have shrunk with horror from means such as were contemplated by the Petres and Tyrconnels. Indeed he would have been as ready as any of his Protestant neighbors to gird on his sword, and to put pistols in his holsters, for the defence of his native land against an invasion of French or Irish Papists. Such was the general character of the men to whom James now looked as to his most trustworthy instruments for the conduct of county elections. He soon found that they were not inclined to throw away the esteem of their neighbors, and to endanger their heads and their estates, by rendering him an infamous and criminal service. Several of them refused to be sheriffs. Of those who accepted the shrievalty many declared that they would discharge their duty as fairly as if they were members of the Established Church, and would return no candidate who had not a real majority.*

---

* About twenty years before this time a Jesuit had noticed the retiring character

If the King could place little confidence even in his Roman Catholic sheriffs, still less could he rely on the Puritans. Since the publication of the Declaration several months had elapsed, months crowded with important events, months of unintermitted controversy. Discussion had opened the eyes of many Dissenters: but the acts of the government, and especially the severity with which Magdalene College had been treated, had done more than even the pen of Halifax to alarm and to unite all classes of Protestants. Most of those sectaries who had been induced to express gratitude for the Indulgence were now ashamed of their error, and were desirous of making atonement by casting in their lot with the great body of their countrymen.

Feeling of the Dissenters.

In consequence of this change in the feeling of the Nonconformists, the government found almost as great difficulty in the towns as in the counties. When the regulators began their work, they had taken it for granted that every Dissenter who had availed himself of the Indulgence would be favorable to the King's policy. They were therefore confident that they should be able to fill all the municipal offices in the kingdom with stanch friends. In the

Regulation of corporations.

---

of the Roman Catholic country gentlemen of England. "La nobiltà Inglese, senon è legata in servigio di Corte, ò in opera di maestrato, vive, e gode il più dell' anno alla campagna, ne' suoi palagi e poderi, dove son liberi e padroni; e ciò tanto più sollecitamente i Cattolici quanto più utilmente, si come meno osservati colià."—L'Inghilterra descritta dal P. Daniello Bartoli, Roma, 1667.

"Many of the Popish sheriffs," Johnstone wrote, "have estates, and declare that whoever expects false returns from them will be disappointed. The Popish gentry that live at their houses in the country are much different from those that live here in town. Several of them have refused to be sheriffs or deputy-lieutenants" (Dec. 8, 1687).

Ronquillo says the same. "Algunos Catolicos que fueron nombrados por sherifes se han excusado," Jan. $\frac{9}{19}$, 1688. He some months later assured his court that the Catholic country gentlemen would willingly consent to a compromise of which the terms should be that the penal laws should be abolished and the test retained. "Estoy informado," he says, "que los Catolicos de las provincias no lo reprueban, pues no pretendiendo oficios, y siendo solo algunos de la Corte los provechosos, les parece que mejoran su estado, quedando seguros ellos y sus descendientes en la religion, en la quietud, y en la seguridad de sus haciendas." $\frac{\text{July 23,}}{\text{Aug. 2,}}$ 1688.

new charters a power had been reserved to the crown of dismissing magistrates at pleasure. This power was now exercised without limit. It was by no means equally clear that James had the power of appointing magistrates; but, whether it belonged to him or not, he determined to assume it. Everywhere, from the Tweed to the Land's End, Tory functionaries were ejected; and the vacant places were filled with Presbyterians, Independents, and Baptists. In the new charter of the City of London the crown had reserved the power of displacing the masters, wardens, and assistants of all the companies. Accordingly more than eight hundred citizens of the first consideration, all of them members of that party which had opposed the Exclusion Bill, were turned out of office by a single edict. In a short time appeared a supplement to this long list.* But scarcely had the new office-bearers been sworn in when it was discovered that they were as unmanageable as their predecessors. At Newcastle on Tyne the regulators appointed a Roman Catholic mayor and Puritan aldermen. No doubt was entertained that the municipal body, thus remodelled, would vote an address promising to support the King's measures. The address, however, was negatived. The Mayor went up to London in a fury, and told the King that the Dissenters were all knaves and rebels, and that in the whole corporation the government could not reckon on more than four votes.† At Reading twenty-four Tory aldermen were dismissed. Twenty-four new aldermen were appointed. Twenty-three of these immediately declared against the Indulgence, and were dismissed in their turn.‡ In the course of a few days the borough of Yarmouth was governed by three different sets of magistrates, all equally hostile to the court.§ These are mere examples of what was passing all over the kingdom. The Dutch Ambassador informed the States that in many towns the public functionaries had, within one month, been changed twice, and even

---

* Privy Council Book, Sept. 25, 1687; Feb. 21, 168⅞.
† Records of the Corporation, quoted in Brand's History of Newcastle; Johnstone, Feb. 21, 168⅞.
‡ Johnstone, Feb. 21, 168⅞. § Van Citters, Feb. $\frac{14}{24}$, 1688.

thrice, and yet changed in vain.* From the records of the Privy Council it appears that the number of regulations, as they were called, exceeded two hundred.† The regulators, indeed, found that, in not a few places, the change had been for the worse. The discontented Tories, even while murmuring against the King's policy, had constantly expressed respect for his person and his office, and had disclaimed all thought of resistance. Very different was the language of some of the new members of corporations. It was said that old soldiers of the Commonwealth, who, to their own astonishment and that of the public, had been made aldermen, gave the agents of the court very distinctly to understand that blood should flow before Popery and arbitrary power were established in England.‡

The regulators found that little or nothing had been gained by what had as yet been done. There was one way, and one way only, in which they could hope to effect their object. The charters of the boroughs must be resumed; and other charters must be granted confining the elective franchise to very small constituent bodies appointed by the sovereign.§

But how was this plan to be carried into effect? In a few of the new charters, indeed, a right of revocation had been reserved to the crown; but the rest James could get into his hands only by voluntary surrender on the part of corporations, or by judgment of a court of law. Few corporations were now disposed to surrender their charters voluntarily; and such judgments as would suit the purposes of the government were hardly to be expected even from such a slave as Wright. The writs of Quo Warranto which had been brought a few years before for the purpose of crushing the Whig party had been condemned by every impartial man. Yet those writs had at least the semblance of justice; for they were brought against ancient municipal bodies; and there

---

* Van Citters, May $\frac{1}{11}$, 1688.

† In the margin of the Privy Council Book may be observed the words "Second regulation," and "Third regulation," when a corporation had been remodelled more than once.

‡ Johnstone, May 23, 1688.   § Ibid., Feb. 21, 1688.

were few ancient municipal bodies in which some abuse, sufficient to afford a pretext for a penal proceeding, had not grown up in the course of ages. But the corporations now to be attacked were still in the innocence of infancy. The oldest among them had not completed its fifth year. It was impossible that many of them should have committed offences meriting disfranchisement. The Judges themselves were uneasy. They represented that what they were required to do was in direct opposition to the plainest principles of law and justice: but all remonstrance was vain. The boroughs were commanded to surrender their charters. Few complied; and the course which the King took with those few did not encourage others to trust him. In several towns the right of voting was taken away from the commonalty, and given to a very small number of persons, who were required to bind themselves by oath to support the candidates recommended by the government. At Tewkesbury, for example, the franchise was confined to thirteen persons. Yet even this number was too large. Hatred and fear had spread so widely through the community that it was scarcely possible to bring together in any town, by any process of packing, thirteen men on whom the court could absolutely depend. It was rumored that the majority of the new constituent body of Tewkesbury was animated by the same sentiment which was general throughout the nation, and would, when the decisive day should arrive, send true Protestants to Parliament. The regulators in great wrath threatened to reduce the number of electors to three.* Meanwhile the great majority of the boroughs firmly refused to give up their privileges. Barnstaple, Winchester, and Buckingham distinguished themselves by the boldness of their opposition. At Oxford the motion that the city should resign its franchises to the King was negatived by eighty votes to two.† The Temple and Westminster Hall were in a ferment with the sudden rush of business from all corners of the kingdom. Every lawyer in high practice was overwhelmed with the briefs from corporations. Ordinary

---

* Johnstone, Feb. 21, 1688. † Van Citters, March $\frac{20}{30}$, 1688.

litigants complained that their business was neglected.* It was evident that a considerable time must elapse before judgment could be given in so great a number of important cases. Tyranny could ill brook this delay. Nothing was omitted which could terrify the refractory boroughs into submission. At Buckingham some of the municipal officers had spoken of Jeffreys in language which was not laudatory. They were prosecuted, and were given to understand that no mercy should be shown to them unless they would ransom themselves by surrendering their charter.† At Winchester still more violent measures were adopted. A large body of troops was marched into the town for the sole purpose of burdening and harassing the inhabitants.‡ The town continued resolute: and the public voice loudly accused the King of imitating the worst crimes of his brother of France. The dragonnades, it was said, had begun. There was indeed reason for alarm. It had occurred to James that he could not more effectually break the spirit of an obstinate town than by quartering soldiers on the inhabitants. He must have known that this practice had sixty years before excited formidable discontents, and had been solemnly pronounced illegal by the Petition of Right, a statute scarcely less venerated by Englishmen than the Great Charter. But he hoped to obtain from the courts of law a declaration that even the Petition of Right could not control the prerogative. He actually consulted the Chief-justice of the King's Bench on this subject:§ but the result of the consultation remained secret; and in a very few weeks the aspect of affairs became such that a fear stronger than the fear of the royal displeasure began to impose some restraint on the most servile magistrates.

While the Lords-lieutenants were questioning the Justices of the Peace, while the regulators were remodelling the boroughs, all the public departments were subjected to a strict inquisition. The palace was first purified. Every battered old Cavalier, who, in re-

Inquisition in all the public departments.

---

* Van Citters, May $\frac{1}{11}$, 1688.
‡ Ibid., May $\frac{1}{11}$, 1688.

† Ibid., $\frac{May\ 22}{June\ 1}$, 1688.
§ Ibid., May $\frac{18}{28}$, 1688.

turn for blood and lands lost in the royal cause, had obtained some small place under the Keeper of the Wardrobe or the Master of the Harriers, was called upon to choose between the King and the Church. The Commissioners of Customs and Excise were ordered to attend His Majesty at the Treasury. There he demanded from them a promise to support his policy, and directed them to require a similar promise from all their subordinates.* One custom-house officer notified his submission to the royal will in a way which excited both merriment and compassion. " I have," he said, " fourteen reasons for obeying His Majesty's commands, a wife and thirteen young children."† Such reasons were indeed cogent; yet there were not a few instances in which, even against such reasons, religious and patriotic feelings prevailed.

There is ground to believe that the government at this time seriously meditated a blow which would have reduced many thousands of families to beggary, and would have disturbed the whole social system of every part of the country. No wine, beer, or coffee could be sold without a license. It was rumored that every person holding such a license would shortly be required to enter into the same engagements which had been imposed on public functionaries, or to relinquish his trade.‡ It seems certain that, if such a step had been taken, the houses of entertainment and of public resort all over the kingdom would have been at once shut up by hundreds. What effect such an interference with the comfort of all ranks would have produced must be left to conjecture. The resentment excited by grievances is not always proportioned to their dignity; and it is by no means improbable that the resumption of licenses might have done what the resumption of charters had failed to do. Men of fashion would have missed the chocolate-house in Saint James's Street, and men of business the coffee-pot round which they were accus-

---

* Van Citters, April $\frac{6}{16}$, 1688; Treasury Letter Book, March 14, 168$\frac{7}{8}$; Ronquillo, April $\frac{16}{23}$.

† Ibid., May $\frac{18}{28}$, 1688   ‡ Ibid., May $\frac{18}{28}$, 1688.

tomed to smoke and talk politics in Change Alley. Half the clubs would have been wandering in search of shelter. The traveller at nightfall would have found the inn where he had expected to sup and lodge deserted. The clown would have regretted the hedge ale-house, where he had been accustomed to take his pot on the bench before the door in summer, and at the chimney-corner in winter. The nation might, perhaps, on such provocation, have risen in general rebellion without waiting for the help of foreign allies.

It was not to be expected that a prince who required all the humblest servants of the government to support his policy on pain of dismission would continue to employ an Attorney-general whose aversion to that policy was no secret. Sawyer had been suffered to retain his situation more than a year and a half after he had declared against the dispensing power. This extraordinary indulgence he owed to the extreme difficulty which the government found in supplying his place. It was necessary, for the protection of the pecuniary interests of the crown, that at least one of the two chief law officers should be a man of ability and knowledge; and it was by no means easy to induce any barrister of ability and knowledge to put himself in peril by committing every day acts which the next Parliament would probably treat as high crimes and misdemeanors. It had been impossible to procure a better Solicitor-general than Powis, a man who indeed stuck at nothing, but who was incompetent to perform the ordinary duties of his post. In these circumstances it was thought desirable that there should be a division of labor. An attorney, the value of whose professional talents was much diminished by his conscientious scruples, was coupled with a solicitor whose want of scruples made some amends for his want of talents. When the government wished to enforce the law, recourse was had to Sawyer. When the government wished to break the law, recourse was had to Powis. This arrangement lasted till the King was able to obtain the services of an advocate at once baser than Powis and abler than Sawyer.

No barrister living had opposed the court with more viru-

Dismission of Sawyer.

lence than William Williams. He had distinguished himself
Williams Solic- in the late reign as a Whig and an Exclusionist.
itor-general. When faction was at the height, he had been chosen
Speaker of the House of Commons. After the prorogation of
the Oxford Parliament, he had commonly been counsel for
the most noisy demagogues who had been accused of sedition.
He was allowed to possess both parts and learning. His chief
faults were supposed to be rashness and party spirit. It was
not yet suspected that he had faults compared with which
rashness and party spirit might well pass for virtues. The
government sought occasion against him, and easily found it.
He had published, by order of the House of Commons, a narrative which Dangerfield had written. This narrative, if
published by a private man, would undoubtedly have been a
seditious libel. A criminal information was filed in the King's
Bench against Williams: he pleaded the privileges of Parliament in vain: he was convicted and sentenced to a fine of ten
thousand pounds. A large part of this sum he actually paid:
for the rest he gave a bond. The Earl of Peterborough, who
had been injuriously mentioned in Dangerfield's narrative, was
encouraged, by the success of the criminal information, to bring
a civil action, and to demand large damages. Williams was
driven to extremity. At this juncture a way of escape presented itself. It was indeed a way which, to a man of strong
principles or high spirit, would have been more dreadful than
beggary, imprisonment, or death. He might sell himself to
that government of which he had been the enemy and the
victim. He might offer to go on the forlorn hope in every
assault on those liberties and on that religion for which he
had professed an inordinate zeal. He might expiate his
Whiggism by performing services from which bigoted Tories,
stained with the blood of Russell and Sidney, shrank in horror. The bargain was struck. The debt still due to the
crown was remitted. Peterborough was induced, by royal
mediation, to compromise his action. Sawyer was dismissed.
Powis became Attorney-general. Williams was made Solicitor, received the honor of knighthood, and was soon a favorite. Though in rank he was only the second law officer of

the crown, his abilities, knowledge, and energy were such that he completely threw his superior into the shade.*

Williams had not been long in office when he was required to bear a chief part in the most memorable state trial recorded in the British annals.

On the twenty-seventh of April, 1688, the King put forth a second Declaration of Indulgence. In this paper he recited at length the Declaration of the preceding April. His past life, he said, ought to have convinced his people that he was not a person who could easily be induced to depart from any resolution which he had formed. But, as designing men had attempted to persuade the world that he might be prevailed on to give way in this matter, he thought it necessary to proclaim that his purpose was immutably fixed, that he was resolved to employ those only who were prepared to concur in his design, and that he had, in pursuance of that resolution, dismissed many of his disobedient servants from civil and military employments. He announced that he meant to hold a Parliament in November at the latest; and he exhorted his subjects to choose representatives who would assist him in the great work which he had undertaken.†

Second Declaration of Indulgence.

This Declaration at first produced little sensation. It contained nothing new; and men wondered that the King should think it worth while to publish a solemn manifesto merely for the purpose of telling them that he had not changed his mind.‡ Perhaps James was nettled by the indifference with which the announcement of his fixed resolution was received by the public, and thought that his dignity and authority would suffer unless he without delay did something novel and striking. On the fourth of May, accord-

The clergy ordered to read it.

---

* London Gazette, December 15, 1687. See the proceedings against Williams in the Collection of State Trials. "Ha hecho," says Ronquillo, "grande susto el haber nombrado el abogado Williams, que fue el orador y el mas arrabiado de toda la casa des comunes en los ultimos terribles parlamentos del Rey difunto." $\frac{\text{Nov. 27,}}{\text{Dec. 7,}}$ 1687.

† London Gazette, April 30, 1688; Barillon, $\frac{\text{April 26.}}{\text{May 6.}}$

‡ Van Citters, May $\frac{1}{11}$, 1688.

ingly, he made an Order in Council that his Declaration of the preceding week should be read, on two successive Sundays, at the time of divine service, by the officiating ministers of all the churches and chapels of the kingdom. In London and in the suburbs the reading was to take place on the twentieth and twenty-seventh of May, in other parts of England on the third and tenth of June. The Bishops were directed to distribute copies of the Declaration through their respective dioceses.*

When it is considered that the clergy of the Established Church, with scarcely an exception, regarded the Indulgence as a violation of the laws of the realm, as a breach of the plighted faith of the King, and as a fatal blow levelled at the interest and dignity of their own profession, it will scarcely admit of doubt that the Order in Council was intended to be felt by them as a cruel affront. It was popularly believed that Petre had avowed this intention in a coarse metaphor borrowed from the rhetoric of the East. He would, he said, make them eat dirt, the vilest and most loathsome of all dirt. But, tyrannical and malignant as the mandate was, would the Anglican priesthood refuse to obey? The King's temper was arbitrary and severe. The proceedings of the Ecclesiastical Commission were as summary as those of a court-martial. Whoever ventured to resist might in a week be ejected from his parsonage, deprived of his whole income, pronounced incapable of holding any other spiritual preferment, and left to beg from door to door. If, indeed, the whole body offered a united opposition to the royal will, it was probable that even James would scarcely venture to punish ten thousand delinquents at once. But there was not time to form an extensive combination. The Order in Council was gazetted on the seventh of May. On the twentieth the Declaration was to be read in all the pulpits of London and the neighborhood. By no exertion was it possible in that age to ascertain within a fortnight the intentions of one-tenth part of the parochial ministers who were scattered over the kingdom. It was not

---

* London Gazette, May 7, 1688.

II.—21

easy to collect in so short a time the sense even of the episcopal order. It might also well be apprehended that, if the clergy refused to read the Declaration, the Protestant Dissenters would misinterpret the refusal, would despair of obtaining any toleration from the members of the Church of England, and would throw their whole weight into the scale of the court.

The clergy therefore hesitated; and this hesitation may well be excused: for some eminent laymen, who possessed a large share of the public confidence, were disposed to recommend submission. They thought that a general opposition could hardly be expected, and that a partial opposition would be ruinous to individuals, and of little advantage to the Church and to the nation. Such was the opinion given at this time by Halifax and Nottingham. The day drew near; and still there was no concert and no formed resolution.*

<small>They hesitate.</small>

At this conjuncture the Protestant Dissenters of London won for themselves a title to the lasting gratitude of their country. They had hitherto been reckoned by the government as part of its strength. A few of their most active and noisy preachers, corrupted by the favors of the court, had got up addresses in favor of the King's policy. Others, estranged by the recollection of many cruel wrongs both from the Church of England and from the House of Stuart, had seen with resentful pleasure the tyrannical prince and the tyrannical hierarchy separated by a bitter enmity, and bidding against each other for the help of sects lately persecuted and despised. But this feeling, however natural, had been indulged long enough. The time had come when it was necessary to make a choice; and the Non-conformists of the City, with a noble spirit, arrayed themselves side by side with the members of the Church in defence of the fundamental laws of the realm. Baxter, Bates, and Howe distinguished themselves by their efforts to bring about this coalition: but the generous enthusiasm which pervaded the whole Puritan body made the task easy. The zeal of the flocks outran that of the pastors. Those Presbyterian and

<small>Patriotism of the Protestant Non-conformists of London.</small>

---

* Johnstone, May 27, 1688.

Independent teachers who showed an inclination to take part with the King against the ecclesiastical establishment received distinct notice that, unless they changed their conduct, their congregations would neither hear them nor pay them. Alsop, who had flattered himself that he should be able to bring over a great body of his disciples to the royal side, found himself on a sudden an object of contempt and abhorrence to those who had lately revered him as their spiritual guide, sank into a deep melancholy, and hid himself from the public eye. Deputations waited on several of the London clergy imploring them not to judge of the dissenting body from the servile adulation which had lately filled the London Gazette, and exhorting them, placed as they were in the van of this great fight, to play the men for the liberties of England and for the faith delivered to the Saints. These assurances were received with joy and gratitude. Yet there was still much anxiety and much difference of opinion among those who had to decide whether, on Sunday the twentieth, they would or would not obey the King's command. The London clergy, then universally acknowledged to be the flower of their profession, held a meeting.

Consultation of the London clergy.

Fifteen Doctors of Divinity were present. Tillotson, Dean of Canterbury, the most celebrated preacher of the age, came thither from a sick-bed. Sherlock, Master of the Temple, Patrick, Dean of Peterborough and Rector of Saint Paul's, Covent Garden, and Stillingfleet, Archdeacon of London and Dean of Saint Paul's Cathedral, attended. The general feeling of the assembly seemed to be that it was, on the whole, advisable to obey the Order in Council. The dispute began to wax warm, and might have produced fatal consequences, if it had not been brought to a close by the firmness and wisdom of Doctor Edward Fowler, Vicar of Saint Giles's, Cripplegate, one of a small but remarkable class of divines who united that love of civil liberty which belonged to the school of Calvin with the theology of the school of Arminius.* Standing up, Fowler spoke thus: "I must be

---

* That very remarkable man, the late Alexander Knox, whose eloquent conver-

plain. The question is so simple that argument can throw no new light on it, and can only beget heat. Let every man say Yes or No. But I cannot consent to be bound by the vote of the majority. I shall be sorry to cause a breach of unity. But this Declaration I cannot in conscience read." Tillotson, Patrick, Sherlock, and Stillingfleet declared that they were of the same mind. The majority yielded to the authority of a minority so respectable. A resolution by which all present pledged themselves to one another not to read the Declaration was then drawn up. Patrick was the first who set his hand to it; Fowler was the second. The paper was sent round the city, and was speedily subscribed by eighty-five incumbents.*

Meanwhile several of the Bishops were anxiously deliberating as to the course which they should take. On the twelfth of May a grave and learned company was assembled round the table of the Primate at Lambeth. Compton, Bishop of London, Turner, Bishop of Ely, White, Bishop of Peterborough, and Tenison, Rector of Saint Martin's Parish, were among the guests. The Earl of Clarendon, a zealous and uncompromising friend of the Church, had been invited. Cartwright, Bishop of Chester, intruded himself on the meeting, probably as a spy. While he remained, no confidential communication could take place: but, after his departure, the great question of which all minds were full was propounded and discussed. The general opinion was that the Declaration ought not to be read. Letters were forthwith written to several of the most respectable prelates of the province of Canterbury, entreating them to come up without delay to London, and to strengthen the hands of their metropolitan at this conjuncture.† As there was little doubt that these letters would

---

sation and elaborate letters had a great influence on the minds of his contemporaries, learned, I suspect, much of his theological system from Fowler's writings. Fowler's book on the Design of Christianity was assailed by John Bunyan with a ferocity which nothing can justify, but which the birth and breeding of the honest tinker in some degree excuse.

* Johnstone, May 23, 1688. There is a satirical poem on this meeting entitled the Clerical Cabal. † Clarendon's Diary, May 22, 1688.

be opened if they passed through the office in Lombard Street, they were sent by horsemen to the nearest country post-towns on the different roads. The Bishop of Winchester, whose loyalty had been so signally proved at Sedgemoor, though suffering from indisposition, resolved to set out in obedience to the summons, but found himself unable to bear the motion of a coach. The letter addressed to William Lloyd, Bishop of Norwich, was, in spite of all precautions, detained by a postmaster; and that prelate, inferior to none of his brethren in courage and in zeal for the common cause of his order, did not reach London in time.* His namesake, William Lloyd, Bishop of Saint Asaph, a pious, honest, and learned man, but of slender judgment, and half crazed by his persevering endeavors to extract from the Book of Daniel and from the Revelations some information about the Pope and the King of France, hastened to the capital, and arrived on the sixteenth.† On the following day came the excellent Ken, Bishop of Bath and Wells, Lake, Bishop of Chichester, and Sir John Trelawney, Bishop of Bristol, a baronet of an old and honorable Cornish family.

On the eighteenth a meeting of prelates and of other eminent divines was held at Lambeth. Tillotson, Tenison, Stillingfleet, Patrick, and Sherlock were present. Prayers were solemnly read before the consultation began.

Consultation at Lambeth Palace.

After long deliberation, a petition embodying the general sense was written by the Archbishop with his own hand. It was not drawn up with much felicity of style. Indeed, the cumbrous and inelegant structure of the sentences brought on Sancroft some raillery, which he bore with less patience than he showed under much heavier trials. But in substance nothing could be more skilfully framed than this memorable document. All disloyalty, all intolerance, was earnestly disclaimed. The King was assured that the Church still was, as she had ever been, faithful to the throne. He was assured also that the Bishops would, in proper place and time,

---

* Extracts from Tanner MSS. in Howell's State Trials; Life of Prideaux; Clarendon's Diary, May 16, 1688.

† Clarendon's Diary, May 16 and 17, 1688.

as Lords of Parliament and members of the Upper House of Convocation, show that they by no means wanted tenderness for the conscientious scruples of Dissenters. But Parliament had, both in the late and in the present reign, pronounced that the sovereign was not constitutionally competent to dispense with statutes in matters ecclesiastical. The Declaration was therefore illegal; and the petitioners could not, in prudence, honor, or conscience, be parties to the solemn publishing of an illegal Declaration in the house of God, and during the time of divine service.

This paper was signed by the Archbishop and by six of his suffragans, Lloyd of Saint Asaph, Turner of Ely, Lake of Chichester, Ken of Bath and Wells, White of Peterborough, and Trelawney of Bristol. The Bishop of London, being under suspension, did not sign.

It was now late on Friday evening; and on Sunday morning the Declaration was to be read in the churches of London.

Petition of the seven Bishops presented to the King. It was necessary to put the paper into the King's hands without delay. The six Bishops crossed the river to Whitehall. The Archbishop, who had long been forbidden the court, did not accompany them. Lloyd, leaving his five brethren at the House of Lord Dartmouth in the vicinity of the palace, went to Sunderland, and begged that minister to read the petition, and to ascertain when the King would be willing to receive it. Sunderland, afraid of compromising himself, refused to look at the paper, but went immediately to the royal closet. James directed that the Bishops should be admitted. He had heard from his tool Cartwright that they were disposed to obey the royal mandate, but that they wished for some little modifications in form, and that they meant to present a humble request to that effect. His Majesty was therefore in very good humor. When they knelt before him, he graciously told them to rise, took the paper from Lloyd, and said, "This is my Lord of Canterbury's hand." "Yes, sir, his own hand," was the answer. James read the petition: he folded it up; and his countenance grew dark. "This," he said, "is a great surprise to me. I did not expect this from your Church, especially from some of you. This is a standard of rebellion." The Bishops broke out into passionate professions of loyalty: but the King, as usual, repeated the same words over and over. "I tell you, this is a standard of rebellion." "Rebellion!" cried Trelawney, falling on his knees. "For God's sake, sir, do not say so hard a thing of us. No Trelawney can be a rebel. Remember that my family has fought for the crown. Remember how I served Your Majesty when Monmouth was in the West." "We put down the last rebellion," said Lake: "we shall not raise another." "We rebel!" exclaimed Turner; "we are ready to die at Your Majesty's feet." "Sir," said Ken, in a more manly tone, "I hope that you will grant to us that liberty of conscience which you grant to all mankind." Still James went on. "This is rebellion. This is a standard of rebellion. Did ever a good Churchman question the dispensing power before? Have not some of you preached for it and written for it? It is a standard of rebellion. I will have my Declaration published." "We have two duties to perform," answered Ken, "our duty to God, and our duty to Your Majesty. We honor you: but we fear God." "Have I deserved this?" said the King, more and more angry: "I who have been such a friend to your Church? I did not expect this from some of you. I will be obeyed. My Declaration shall be published. You are trumpeters of sedition. What do you do here? Go to your dioceses; and see that I am obeyed. I will keep this paper. I will not part with it. I will remember you that have signed it." "God's will be done," said Ken. "God has given me the dispensing power," said the King, "and I will maintain it. I tell you that there are still seven thousand of your Church who have not bowed the knee to Baal." The Bishops respectfully retired.* That very evening the document which they had put into the hands of the King appeared word for word in print, was laid on the tables of all the coffee-houses, and was cried about the streets. Everywhere the people rose from their beds, and came out to stop the hawkers. It was said that the printer cleared a thou-

* Sancroft's Narrative, printed from the Tanner MSS.; Van Citters, $\frac{\text{May 22,}}{\text{June 1,}}$ 1688.

sand pounds in a few hours by this penny broadside. This is probably an exaggeration; but it is an exaggeration which proves that the sale was enormous. How the petition got abroad is still a mystery. Sancroft declared that he had taken every precaution against publication, and that he knew of no copy except that which he had himself written, and which James had taken out of Lloyd's hand. The veracity of the Archbishop is beyond all suspicion. But it is by no means improbable that some of the divines who assisted in framing the petition may have remembered so short a composition accurately, and may have sent it to the press. The prevailing opinion, however, was that some person about the King had been indiscreet or treacherous.* Scarcely less sensation was produced by a short letter which was written with great power of argument and language, printed secretly, and largely circulated on the same day by the post and by the common carriers. A copy was sent to every clergyman in the kingdom. The writer did not attempt to disguise the danger which those who disobeyed the royal mandate would incur: but he set forth in a lively manner the still greater danger of submission. "If we read the Declaration," said he, "we fall to rise no more. We fall unpitied and despised. We fall amidst the curses of a nation whom our compliance will have ruined." Some thought that this paper came from Holland. Others attributed it to Sherlock. But Prideaux, Dean of Norwich, who was a principal agent in distributing it, believed it to be the work of Halifax.

The conduct of the prelates was rapturously extolled by the general voice: but some murmurs were heard. It was said that such grave men, if they thought themselves bound in conscience to remonstrate with the King, ought to have remonstrated earlier. Was it fair to leave him in the dark till within thirty-six hours of the time fixed for the reading of the Declaration? Even if he wished to revoke the Order in Council, it was too late to do so. The inference seemed to be that the petition was intended, not to move the royal mind,

---

* Burnet, i., 741; Revolution Politics· Higgins's Short View.

but merely to inflame the discontents of the people.* These complaints were utterly groundless. The King had laid on the Bishops a command new, surprising, and embarrassing. It was their duty to communicate with each other, and to ascertain as far as possible the sense of the profession of which they were the heads before they took any step. They were dispersed over the whole kingdom. Some of them were distant from others a full week's journey. James allowed them only a fortnight to inform themselves, to meet, to deliberate, and to decide; and he surely had no right to think himself aggrieved because that fortnight was drawing to a close before he learned their decision. Nor is it true that they did not leave him time to revoke his order if he had been wise enough to do so. He might have called together his Council on Saturday morning, and before night it might have been known throughout London and the suburbs that he had yielded to the entreaties of the fathers of the Church. The Saturday, however, passed over without any sign of relenting on the part of the government; and the Sunday arrived, a day long remembered.

In the City and Liberties of London were about a hundred parish churches. In only four of these was the Order in Council obeyed. At Saint Gregory's the Declaration was read by a divine of the name of Martin. As soon as he uttered the first words, the whole congregation rose and withdrew. At Saint Matthew's, in Friday Street, a wretch named Timothy Hall, who had disgraced his gown by acting as broker for the Duchess of Portsmouth in the sale of pardons, and who now had hopes of obtaining the vacant bishopric of Oxford, was in like manner left alone in his church. At Sergeant's Inn, in Chancery Lane, the clerk pretended that he had forgotten to bring a copy; and the Chief-justice of the King's Bench, who had attended in order to see that the royal mandate was obeyed, was forced to content himself with this excuse. Samuel Wesley, the father of John and Charles Wesley, a curate in

The London clergy disobey the royal order.

---

* Life of James the Second, ii., 155

London, took for his text that day the noble answer of the three Jews to the Chaldean tyrant: "Be it known unto thee, O King, that we will not serve thy gods, nor worship the golden image which thou hast set up." Even in the chapel of Saint James's Palace the officiating minister had the courage to disobey the order. The Westminster boys long remembered what took place that day in the Abbey. Sprat, Bishop of Rochester, officiated there as Dean. As soon as he began to read the Declaration, murmurs and the noise of people crowding out of the choir drowned his voice. He trembled so violently that men saw the paper shake in his hand. Long before he had finished, the place was deserted by all but those whose situation made it necessary for them to remain.*

Never had the Church been so dear to the nation as on the afternoon of that day. The spirit of dissent seemed to be extinct. Baxter from his pulpit pronounced a eulogium on the Bishops and parochial clergy. The Dutch minister, a few hours later, wrote to inform the States-general that the Anglican priesthood had risen in the estimation of the public to an incredible degree. The universal cry of the Non-conformists, he said, was that they would rather continue to lie under the penal statutes than separate their cause from that of the prelates.†

Another week of anxiety and agitation passed away. Sunday came again. Again the churches of the capital were thronged by hundreds of thousands. The Declaration was read nowhere except at the very few places where it had been read the week before. The minister who had officiated at the chapel in Saint James's Palace had been turned out of his situation: a more obsequious divine appeared with the paper in his hand: but his agitation was so great that he could not articulate. In truth, the feeling of the whole nation had now become such as none but the very best and noblest, or the very worst and basest, of mankind could without much discomposure encounter.‡

---

* Van Citters, May 22, June 1, 1688; Burnet, i., 740; and Lord Dartmouth's note; Southey's Life of Wesley.

† Van Citters, May 22, June 1, 1688.

‡ Ibid., May 29, June 8, 1688.

Even the King stood aghast for a moment at the violence of the tempest which he had raised. What step was he next to take? He must either advance or recede: and it was impossible to advance without peril, or to recede without humiliation. At one moment he determined to put forth a second order enjoining the clergy in high and angry terms to publish his Declaration, and menacing every one who should be refractory with instant suspension. This order was drawn up and sent to the press, then recalled, then a second time sent to the press, then recalled a second time.* A different plan was suggested by some of those who were for rigorous measures. The prelates who had signed the petition might be cited before the Ecclesiastical Commission and deprived of their sees. But to this course strong objections were urged in Council. It had been announced that the Houses would be convoked before the end of the year. The Lords would assuredly treat the sentence of deprivation as a nullity, would insist that Sancroft and his fellow-petitioners should be summoned to Parliament, and would refuse to acknowledge a new Archbishop of Canterbury or a new Bishop of Bath and Wells. Thus the session, which at best was likely to be sufficiently stormy, would commence with a deadly quarrel between the crown and the peers. If, therefore, it was thought necessary to punish the Bishops, the punishment ought to be inflicted according to the known course of English law. Sunderland had from the beginning objected, as far as he dared, to the Order in Council. He now suggested a course which, though not free from inconveniences, was the most prudent and the most dignified that a series of errors had left open to the government. The King might with grace and majesty announce to the world that he was deeply hurt by the undutiful conduct of the Church of England; but that he could not forget all the services rendered by that Church, in trying times, to his father, to his brother, and to himself; that, as a friend to the liberty of conscience, he was unwilling to deal severely with men

---

* Van Citters, $\frac{\text{May 29,}}{\text{June 8,}}$ 1688.

whom conscience, ill informed indeed, and unreasonably scrupulous, might have prevented from obeying his commands; and that he would therefore leave the offenders to that punishment which their own reflections would inflict whenever they should calmly compare their recent acts with the loyal doctrines of which they had so loudly boasted. Not only Powis and Bellasyse, who had always been for moderate counsels, but even Dover and Arundell, leaned toward this proposition. Jeffreys, on the other hand, maintained that the government would be disgraced if such transgressors as the seven Bishops were suffered to escape with a mere reprimand. He did not, however, wish them to be cited before the Ecclesiastical Commission, in which he sat as chief, or rather as sole judge. For the load of public hatred under which he already lay was too much even for his shameless forehead and obdurate heart; and he shrank from the responsibility which he would have incurred by pronouncing an illegal sentence on the rulers of the Church and the favorites of the nation. He therefore recommended a criminal information. It was accordingly resolved that the Archbishop and the six other petitioners should be brought before the Court of King's Bench on a charge of seditious libel. That they would be convicted it was scarcely possible to doubt. The Judges and their officers were tools of the court. Since the old charter of the City of London had been forfeited, scarcely one prisoner whom the government was bent on bringing to punishment had been absolved by a jury. The refractory prelates would probably be condemned to ruinous fines and to long imprisonment, and would be glad to ransom themselves by serving, both in and out of Parliament, the designs of the Sovereign.*

It is determined to prosecute the Bishops for a libel.

On the twenty-seventh of May it was notified to the Bishops that on the eighth of June they must appear before the King in Council. Why so long an interval was allowed we are not informed. Perhaps James hoped that some of the offenders,

---

* Barillon, $\frac{May 24,}{June 3,}$ $\frac{May 31,}{June 10,}$ 1688; Van Citters, July $\frac{1}{11}$; Adda, $\frac{May 25,}{June 4,}$ $\frac{May 30,}{June 9,}$ June $\frac{1}{11}$; Life of James the Second, ii., 158.

terrified by his displeasure, might submit before the day fixed for the reading of the Declaration in their dioceses, and might, in order to make their peace with him, persuade their clergy to obey his order. If such was his hope, it was signally disappointed. Sunday the third of June came; and all parts of England followed the example of the capital. Already the Bishops of Norwich, Gloucester, Salisbury, Winchester, and Exeter had signed copies of the petition in token of their approbation. The Bishop of Worcester had refused to distribute the Declaration among his clergy. The Bishop of Hereford had distributed it: but it was generally understood that he was overwhelmed by remorse and shame for having done so. Not one parish priest in fifty complied with the Order in Council. In the great diocese of Chester, including the county of Lancaster, only three clergymen could be prevailed on by Cartwright to obey the King. In the diocese of Norwich are many hundreds of parishes. In only four of these was the Declaration read. The courtly Bishop of Rochester could not overcome the scruples of the minister of the ordinary of Chatham, who depended on the government for bread. There is still extant a pathetic letter which this honest priest sent to the Secretary of the Admiralty. "I cannot," he wrote, "reasonably expect Your Honor's protection. God's will be done. I must choose suffering rather than sin."*

On the evening of the eighth of June the seven prelates, furnished by the ablest lawyers in England with full advice, repaired to the palace, and were called into the Council-chamber. Their petition was lying on the table. The Chancellor took the paper up, showed it to the Archbishop, and said, "Is this the paper which Your Grace wrote, and which the six Bishops present delivered to His Majesty?" Sancroft looked at the paper, turned to the King, and spoke thus: "Sir, I stand here a culprit. I never was so before. Once I little thought that I ever should be so. Least of all could I think that I should be charged with

<small>They are examined by the Privy Council.</small>

---

* Burnet, i., 740; Life of Prideaux; Van Citters, June $\frac{12}{22}$, $\frac{15}{25}$, 1688; Tanner MSS.; Life and Correspondence of Pepys.

any offence against my King: but, since I am so unhappy as to be in this situation, Your Majesty will not be offended if I avail myself of my lawful right to decline saying anything which may criminate me." "This is mere chicanery," said the King. "I hope that Your Grace will not do so ill a thing as to deny your own hand." "Sir," said Lloyd, whose studies had been much among the casuists, "all divines agree that a person situated as we are may refuse to answer such a question." The King, as slow of understanding as quick of temper, could not comprehend what the prelates meant. He persisted, and was evidently becoming very angry. "Sir," said the Archbishop, "I am not bound to accuse myself. Nevertheless, if Your Majesty positively commands me to answer, I will do so in the confidence that a just and generous prince will not suffer what I say in obedience to his orders to be brought in evidence against me." "You must not capitulate with your Sovereign," said the Chancellor. "No," said the King; "I will not give any such command. If you choose to deny your own hands, I have nothing more to say to you."

The Bishops were repeatedly sent out into the antechamber, and repeatedly called back into the Council-room. At length James positively commanded them to answer the question. He did not expressly engage that their confession should not be used against them. But they, not unnaturally, supposed that, after what had passed, such an engagement was implied in his command. Sancroft acknowledged his handwriting; and his brethren followed his example. They were then interrogated about the meaning of some words in the petition, and about the letter which had been circulated with so much effect all over the kingdom: but their language was so guarded that nothing was gained by the examination. The Chancellor then told them that a criminal information would be exhibited against them in the Court of King's Bench, and called upon them to enter into recognizances. They refused. They were peers of parliament, they said. They were advised by the best lawyers in Westminster Hall that no peer could be required to enter into a recognizance in a case of libel; and they should not think themselves justified in relinquishing the privilege of their order. The King was so absurd as to think himself personally affronted because they chose, on a legal question, to be guided by legal advice. "You believe everybody," he said, "rather than me." He was indeed mortified and alarmed. For he had gone so far that, if they persisted, he had no choice left but to send them to prison; and, though he by no means foresaw all the consequences of such a step, he foresaw, probably, enough to disturb him. They were resolute. A warrant was therefore made out directing the Lieutenant of the Tower to keep them in safe custody, and a barge was manned to convey them down the river.*

They are committed to the Tower.

It was known all over London that the Bishops were before the Council. The public anxiety was intense. A great multitude filled the courts of Whitehall and all the neighboring streets. Many people were in the habit of refreshing themselves at the close of a summer day with the cool air of the Thames; but on this evening the whole river was alive with wherries. When the Seven came forth under a guard, the emotions of the people broke through all restraint. Thousands fell on their knees and prayed aloud for the men who had, with the Christian courage of Ridley and Latimer, confronted a tyrant inflamed by all the bigotry of Mary. Many dashed into the stream, and, up to their waists in ooze and water, cried to the holy fathers to bless them. All down the river, from Whitehall to London Bridge, the royal barge passed between lines of boats, from which arose a shout of "God bless Your Lordships." The King, in great alarm, gave orders that the garrison of the Tower should be doubled, that the Guards should be held ready for action, and that two companies should be detached from every regiment in the kingdom, and sent up instantly to London. But the force on which he relied as the means of coercing the people shared all the feelings of the people. The very sentinels who were posted at the Traitors' Gate reverently asked for a blessing from the martyrs whom they were to guard. Sir Edward

---

* Sancroft's Narrative, printed from the Tanner MSS

Hales was Lieutenant of the Tower. He was little inclined to treat his prisoners with kindness. For he was an apostate from that Church for which they suffered; and he held several lucrative posts by virtue of that dispensing power against which they had protested. He learned with indignation that his soldiers were drinking the health of the Bishops. He ordered his officers to see that it was done no more. But the officers came back with a report that the thing could not be prevented, and that no other health was drunk in the garrison. Nor was it only by carousing that the troops showed their reverence for the fathers of the Church. There was such a show of devotion throughout the Tower that pious men thanked God for bringing good out of evil, and for making the persecution of His faithful servants the means of saving many souls. All day the coaches and liveries of the first nobles of England were seen round the prison gates. Thousands of humbler spectators constantly covered Tower Hill.* But among the marks of public respect and sympathy which the prelates received there was one which more than all the rest enraged and alarmed the King. He learned that a deputation of ten Non-conformist ministers had visited the Tower. He sent for four of these persons, and himself upbraided them. They courageously answered that they thought it their duty to forget past quarrels, and to stand by the men who stood by the Protestant religion.†

Scarcely had the gates of the Tower been closed on the prisoners when an event took place which increased the public excitement. It had been announced that the Queen did not expect to be confined till July. But, on the day after the Bishops had appeared before the Council, it was observed that the King seemed to be anxious about her state. In the evening, however, she sat playing cards at Whitehall till near midnight. Then she was carried in a sedan to Saint James's Palace, where apartments had been very hastily fitted up for her reception. Soon messen-

Birth of the Pretender.

---

* Burnet, i., 741; Van Citters, June $\frac{8}{18}$, $\frac{12}{22}$, 1688; Luttrell's Diary, June 8; Evelyn's Diary; Letter of Dr. Nalson to his wife, dated June 14, and printed from the Tanner MSS.; Reresby's Memoirs.   † Reresby's Memoirs.

gers were running about in all directions to summon physicians and priests, Lords of the Council, and Ladies of the Bedchamber. In a few hours many public functionaries and women of rank were assembled in the Queen's room. There, on the morning of Sunday, the tenth of June, a day long kept sacred by the too faithful adherents of a bad cause, was born the most unfortunate of princes, destined to seventy-seven years of exile and wandering, of vain projects, of honors more galling than insults, and of hopes such as make the heart sick.

The calamities of the poor child had begun before his birth. The nation over which, according to the ordinary course of succession, he would have reigned, was fully persuaded that his mother was not really pregnant.

<small>He is generally believed to be supposititious.</small>

By whatever evidence the fact of his birth had been proved, a considerable number of people would probably have persisted in maintaining that the Jesuits had practised some skilful sleight of hand; and the evidence, partly from accident, partly from gross mismanagement, was really open to some objections. Many persons of both sexes were in the royal bedchamber when the child first saw the light; but none of them enjoyed any large measure of public confidence. Of the Privy Councillors present half were Roman Catholics; and those who called themselves Protestants were generally regarded as traitors to their country and their God. Many of the women in attendance were French, Italian, and Portuguese. Of the English ladies some were Papists, and some were the wives of Papists. Some persons who were peculiarly entitled to be present, and whose testimony would have satisfied all minds accessible to reason, were absent; and for their absence the King was held responsible. The Princess Anne was, of all the inhabitants of the island, the most deeply interested in the event. Her sex and her experience qualified her to act as the guardian of her sister's birthright and her own. She had conceived strong suspicions, which were daily confirmed by circumstances trifling or imaginary. She fancied that the Queen carefully shunned her scrutiny, and ascribed to guilt a reserve which was perhaps the effect

II.—22

of delicacy.* In this temper Anne had determined to be present and vigilant when the critical day should arrive. But she had not thought it necessary to be at her post a month before that day, and had, in compliance, it was said, with her father's advice, gone to drink the Bath waters. Sancroft, whose great place made it his duty to attend, and on whose probity the nation placed entire reliance, had a few hours before been sent to the Tower by James. The Hydes were the proper protectors of the rights of the two Princesses. The Dutch Ambassador might be regarded as the representative of William, who, as first prince of the blood and consort of the King's eldest daughter, had a deep interest in what was passing. James never thought of summoning any member, male or female, of the family of Hyde; nor was the Dutch Ambassador invited to be present.

Posterity has fully acquitted the King of the fraud which his people imputed to him. But it is impossible to acquit him of folly and perverseness such as explain and excuse the error of his contemporaries. He was perfectly aware of the suspicions which were abroad.† He ought to have known that those suspicions would not be dispelled by the evidence of members of the Church of Rome, or of persons who, though they might call themselves members of the Church of England, had shown themselves ready to sacrifice the interests of the Church of England in order to obtain his favor. That he was taken by surprise is true. But he had twelve hours to make his arrangements. He found no difficulty in crowding Saint James's Palace with bigots and sycophants on whose word the nation placed no reliance. It would have been quite as easy to procure the attendance of some eminent persons whose attachment to the Princesses and to the established religion was unquestionable.

At a later period, when he had paid dearly for his foolhardy contempt of public opinion, it was the fashion at Saint Germain's to excuse him by throwing the blame on others. Some

---

* Correspondence between Anne and Mary, in Dalrymple; Clarendon's Diary, Oct. 31, 1688.

† This is clear from Clarendon's Diary, Oct. 31, 1688.

Jacobites charged Anne with having purposely kept out of the way. Nay, they were not ashamed to say that Sancroft had provoked the King to send him to the Tower, in order that the evidence which was to confound the calumnies of the malcontents might be defective.* The absurdity of these imputations is palpable. Could Anne or Sancroft possibly have foreseen that the Queen's calculations would turn out to be erroneous by a whole month? Had those calculations been correct, Anne would have been back from Bath, and Sancroft would have been out of the Tower, in ample time for the birth. At all events, the maternal uncles of the King's daughters were neither at a distance nor in a prison. The same messenger who summoned the whole bevy of renegades, Dover, Peterborough, Murray, Sunderland, and Mulgrave, could just as easily have summoned Clarendon. If they were Privy Councillors, so was he. His house was in Jermyn Street, not two hundred yards from the chamber of the Queen. Yet he was left to learn at Saint James's Church, from the agitation and whispers of the congregation, that his niece had ceased to be heiress presumptive of the crown.† Was it a disqualification that he was the near kinsman of the Princesses of Orange and Denmark? Or was it a disqualification that he was unalterably attached to the Church of England?

The cry of the whole nation was that an imposture had been practised. Papists had, during some months, been predicting, from the pulpit and through the press, in prose and verse, in English and Latin, that a Prince of Wales would be given to the prayers of the Church; and they had now accomplished their own prophecy. Every witness who could not be corrupted or deceived had been studiously excluded. Anne had been tricked into visiting Bath. The Primate had, on the very day preceding that which had been fixed for the villany, been sent to prison in defiance of the rules of law and of the privileges of peerage. Not a single man or woman who had the smallest interest in detecting the fraud had been

---

* Life of James the Second, ii., 159, 160.
† Clarendon's Diary, June 10, 1688.

suffered to be present. The Queen had been removed suddenly and at the dead of night to Saint James's Palace, because that building, less commodious for honest purposes than Whitehall, had some rooms and passages well suited for the purpose of the Jesuits. There, amidst a circle of zealots who thought nothing a crime that tended to promote the interests of their Church, and of courtiers who thought nothing a crime that tended to enrich and aggrandize themselves, a new-born child had been introduced, by means of a warming-pan, into the royal bed, and then handed round in triumph, as heir of three kingdoms. Heated by such suspicions, suspicions unjust, it is true, but not altogether unnatural, men thronged more eagerly than ever to pay their homage to the saintly victims of the tyrant, who, having long foully injured his people, had now filled up the measure of his iniquities by more foully injuring his children.*

The Prince of Orange, not himself suspecting any trick, and not aware of the state of public feeling in England, ordered prayers to be said under his own roof for his little brother-in-law, and sent Zulestein to London with a formal message of congratulation. Zulestein, to his amazement, found all the people whom he met open-mouthed about the infamous fraud just committed by the Jesuits, and saw every hour some fresh pasquinade on the pregnancy and the delivery. He soon wrote to the Hague that not one person in ten believed the child to have been born of the Queen.†

The demeanor of the seven prelates meanwhile strengthened the interest which their situation excited. On the evening of the Black Friday, as it was called, on which they were committed, they reached their prison just at the hour of divine service. They instantly hastened to the chapel. It

---

* Johnstone gives in a very few words an excellent summary of the case against the King. "The generality of people conclude all this a trick; because they say the reckoning is changed, the Princess sent away, none of the Clarendon family nor the Dutch Ambassador sent for, the suddenness of the thing, the sermons, the confidence of the priests, the hurry" (June 13, 1688).

† Ronquillo, $\frac{\text{July 26.}}{\text{Aug. 5.}}$ Ronquillo adds, that what Zulestein said of the state of public opinion was strictly true.

chanced that in the second lesson were these words: "In all things approving ourselves as the ministers of God, in much patience, in afflictions, in distresses, in stripes, in imprisonments." All zealous Churchmen were delighted by this coincidence, and remembered how much comfort a similar coincidence had given, near forty years before, to Charles the First at the time of his death.

On the evening of the next day, Saturday, the ninth, a letter came from Sunderland enjoining the chaplain of the Tower to read the Declaration during divine service on the following morning. As the time fixed by the Order in Council for the reading in London had long expired, this proceeding of the government could be considered only as a personal insult of the meanest and most childish kind to the venerable prisoners. The chaplain refused to comply: he was dismissed from his situation; and the chapel was shut up.*

The Bishops edified all who approached them by the firmness and cheerfulness with which they endured confinement, by the modesty and meekness with which they received the applauses and blessings of the whole nation, and by the loyal attachment which they professed for the persecutor who sought their destruction. They remained only a week in custody. On Friday the fifteenth of June, the first day of term, they were brought before the King's Bench. An immense throng awaited their coming. From the landing-place to the Court of Requests they passed through a lane of spectators who blessed and applauded them. "Friends," said the prisoners as they passed, "honor the King; and remember us in your prayers." These humble and pious expressions moved the hearers, even to tears. When at length the procession had made its way through the crowd into the presence of the Judges, the Attorney-general exhibited the information which he had been commanded to prepare, and moved that the defendants might be ordered to plead. The counsel on the other side objected that the Bishops had been unlawfully

<small>The Bishops brought before the King's Bench and bailed.</small>

---

* Van Citters, June $\frac{12}{22}$, 1688; Luttrell's Diary, June 18.

committed, and were therefore not regularly before the court. The question whether a peer could be required to enter into recognizances on a charge of libel was argued at great length, and decided by a majority of the Judges in favor of the crown. The prisoners then pleaded Not Guilty. That day fortnight, the twenty-ninth of June, was fixed for their trial. In the mean time they were allowed to be at large on their own recognizances. The crown lawyers acted prudently in not requiring sureties. For Halifax had arranged that twenty-one temporal peers of the highest consideration should be ready to put in bail, three for each defendant; and such a manifestation of the feeling of the nobility would have been no slight blow to the government. It was also known that one of the most opulent Dissenters of the City had begged that he might have the honor of giving security for Ken.

The Bishops were now permitted to depart to their own homes. The common people, who did not understand the nature of the legal proceedings which had taken place in the King's Bench, and who saw that their favorites had been brought to Westminster Hall in custody and were suffered to go away in freedom, imagined that the good cause was prospering. Loud acclamations were raised. The steeples of the churches sent forth joyous peals. Sprat was amazed to hear the bells of his own Abbey ringing merrily. He promptly silenced them; but his interference caused much angry muttering. The Bishops found it difficult to escape from the importunate crowd of their well-wishers. Lloyd was detained in Palace Yard by admirers who struggled to touch his hands and to kiss the skirt of his robe, till Clarendon, with some difficulty, rescued him and conveyed him home by a by-path. Cartwright, it is said, was so unwise as to mingle with the crowd. A person who saw his episcopal habit asked and received his blessing. A by-stander cried out, "Do you know who blessed you?" "Surely," said he who had just been honored by the benediction, "it was one of the seven." "No," said the other; "it is the Popish Bishop of Chester." "Popish dog!" cried the enraged Protestant; "take your blessing back again."

Such was the concourse, and such the agitation, that the Dutch Ambassador was surprised to see the day close without an insurrection. The King had been anxious and irritable. In order that he might be ready to suppress any disturbance, he had passed the morning in reviewing several battalions of infantry in Hyde Park. It is, however, by no means certain that his troops would have stood by him if he had needed their services. When Sancroft reached Lambeth, in the afternoon, he found the Foot Guards who were quartered in that suburb assembled before the gate of his palace. They formed in two lines on his right and left, and asked his benediction as he went through them. He with difficulty prevented them from lighting a bonfire in honor of his return to his dwelling. There were, however, many bonfires that evening in the City. Two Roman Catholics, who were so indiscreet as to beat some boys for joining in these rejoicings, were seized by the mob, stripped naked, and ignominiously branded.*

Sir Edward Hales now came to demand fees from those who had lately been his prisoners. They refused to pay anything for a detention which they regarded as illegal to an officer whose commission was, on their principles, a nullity. The Lieutenant hinted very intelligibly that, if they came into his hands again, they should be put into heavy irons and should lie on bare stones. "We are under our King's displeasure," was the answer; "and most deeply do we feel it: but a fellow-subject who threatens us does but lose his breath." It is easy to imagine with what indignation the people, excited as they were, must have learned that a renegade from the Protestant faith, who held a command in defiance of the fundamental laws of England, had dared to menace divines of venerable age and dignity with all the barbarities of Lollard's Tower.†

Before the day of trial the agitation had spread to the farthest corners of the island. From Scotland the Bishops received letters assuring them of the sympathy of the Presby-

---

* For the events of this day see the State Trials; Clarendon's Diary; Luttrell's Diary; Van Citters, June $\frac{15}{25}$; Johnstone, June 18; Revolution Politics.

† Johnstone, June 18, 1688; Evelyn's Diary, June 29.

terians of that country, so long and so bitterly hostile to prelacy.* The people of Cornwall, a fierce, bold, and athletic race, among whom there was a stronger provincial feeling than in any other part of the realm, were greatly moved by the danger of Trelawney, whom they reverenced less as a ruler of the Church than as the head of an honorable house, and the heir through twenty descents of ancestors who had been of great note before the Normans had set foot on English ground. All over the country the peasants chanted a ballad of which the burden is still remembered:

Agitation of the public mind.

> "And shall Trelawney die, and shall Trelawney die?
> Then thirty thousand Cornish boys will know the reason why."

The miners from their caverns re-echoed the song with a variation:

> "Then twenty thousand underground will know the reason why."†

The rustics in many parts of the country loudly expressed a strange hope which had never ceased to live in their hearts. Their Protestant Duke, their beloved Monmouth, would suddenly appear, would lead them to victory, and would tread down the King and the Jesuits under his feet.‡

The ministers were appalled. Even Jeffreys would gladly have retraced his steps. He charged Clarendon with friendly messages to the Bishops, and threw on others the blame of the prosecution which he had himself recommended. Sunderland again ventured to recommend concession. The late auspicious birth, he said, had given the King an excellent opportunity of withdrawing from a position full of danger and inconvenience without incurring the reproach of timidity or of caprice. On such happy occasions it had been usual for sovereigns to make the hearts of subjects glad by acts of clemency; and nothing could be more advantageous to the Prince

---

* Tanner MSS.

† This fact was communicated to me in the most obliging manner by the Reverend R. S. Hawker, of Morwenstow, in Cornwall.

‡ Johnstone, June 18, 1688.

of Wales than that he should, while still in his cradle, be the peace-maker between his father and the agitated nation. But the King's resolution was fixed. "I will go on," he said. "I have been only too indulgent.. Indulgence ruined my father."* The artful minister found that his advice had been formerly taken only because it had been shaped to suit the royal temper, and that, from the moment at which he began to counsel well, he began to counsel in vain. He had shown some signs of slackness in the proceeding against Magdalene College. He had recently attempted to convince the King that Tyrconnel's scheme of confiscating the property of the English colonists in Ireland was full of danger, and had, with the help of Powis and Bellasyse, so far succeeded that the execution of the design had been postponed for another year. But this timidity and scrupulosity had excited disgust and suspicion in the royal mind.† The day of retribution had arrived. Sunderland was in the same situation in which his rival Rochester had been some months before. Each of the two statesmen in turn experienced the misery of clutching with an agonizing grasp power which was perceptibly slipping away. Each in turn saw his suggestions scornfully rejected. Both endured the pain of reading displeasure and distrust in the countenance and demeanor of their master; yet both were by their country held responsible for those crimes and errors from which they had vainly endeavored to dissuade him. While he suspected them of trying to win popularity at the expense of his authority and dignity, the public voice loudly accused them of trying to win his favor at the expense of their own honor and of the general weal. Yet, in spite of mortifications and humiliations, they both clung to office with the gripe of drowning men. Both attempted to propitiate the King by affecting a willingness to be reconciled to his Church. But there was a point at which Rochester was determined to stop. He went

Uneasiness of Sunderland.

---

* Adda, $\frac{\text{June 29,}}{\text{July 9,}}$ 1688.

† Sunderland's own narrative is, of course, not to be implicitly trusted. But he vouched Godolphin as a witness of what took place respecting the Irish Act of Settlement.

to the verge of apostasy: but there he recoiled: and the world, in consideration of the firmness with which he refused to take the final step, granted him a liberal amnesty for all former compliances. Sunderland, less scrupulous and less sensible of shame, resolved to atone for his late moderation, and to recover the royal confidence, by an act which, to a mind impressed with the importance of religious truth, must have appeared to be one of the most flagitious of crimes, and which even men of the world regard as the last excess of baseness. About a week before the day fixed for the great trial, it was publicly announced that he was a Papist. The King talked with delight of this triumph of divine grace. Courtiers and envoys kept their countenances as well as they could while the renegade protested that he had been long convinced of the impossibility of finding salvation out of the communion of Rome, and that his conscience would not let him rest till he had renounced the heresies in which he had been brought up. The news spread fast. At all the coffee-houses it was told how the prime minister of England, his feet bare, and a taper in his hand, had repaired to the royal chapel and knocked humbly for admittance; how a priestly voice from within had demanded who was there; how Sunderland had made answer that a poor sinner who had long wandered from the true Church entreated her to receive and to absolve him; how the doors were opened; and how the neophyte partook of the holy mysteries.*

He professes himself a Roman Catholic.

This scandalous apostasy could not but heighten the interest with which the nation looked forward to the day when the fate of the seven brave confessors of the English Church was to be decided. To pack a jury was now the great object of the King. The crown lawyers were ordered to make strict inquiry as to the sentiments of the persons who were registered in the freeholders' book. Sir Samuel Astry, clerk of the crown, whose duty it was, in

Trial of the Bishops.

---

* Barillon, $\frac{\text{June 21, June 28}}{\text{July 1, July 8}}$, 1688; Adda, $\frac{\text{June 29}}{\text{July 9}}$; Van Citters, $\frac{\text{June 26}}{\text{July 6}}$; Johnstone, July 2, 1688; The Converts, a poem.

cases of this description, to select the names, was summoned to the palace, and had an interview with James in the presence of the Chancellor.* Sir Samuel seems to have done his best. For among the forty-eight persons whom he nominated were said to be several servants of the King, and several Roman Catholics.† But as the counsel for the Bishops had a right to strike off twelve, these persons were removed. The crown lawyers also struck off twelve. The list was thus reduced to twenty-four. The first twelve who answered to their names were to try the issue.

On the twenty-ninth of June, Westminster Hall, Old and New Palace Yard, and all the neighboring streets to a great distance were thronged with people. Such an auditory had never before and has never since been assembled in the Court of King's Bench. Thirty-five temporal peers of the realm were counted in the crowd.‡

All the four Judges of the Court were on the bench. Wright, who presided, had been raised to his high place over the heads of many abler and more learned men solely on account of his unscrupulous servility. Allibone was a Papist, and owed his situation to that dispensing power, the legality of which was now in question. Holloway had hitherto been a serviceable tool of the government. Even Powell, whose character for honesty stood high, had borne a part in some proceedings which it is impossible to defend. He had, in the great case of Sir Edward Hales, with some hesitation, it is true, and after some delay, concurred with the majority of the bench, and had thus brought on his character a stain which his honorable conduct on this day completely effaced.

The counsel were by no means fairly matched. The government had required from its law officers services so odious and disgraceful that all the ablest jurists and advocates of the Tory party had, one after another, refused to comply, and had been dismissed from their employments. Sir Thomas Powis, the Attorney-general, was scarcely of the third rank in his

---

* Clarendon's Diary, June 21, 1688.   † Van Citters, $\frac{\text{June 26}}{\text{July 6}}$, 1688.
‡ Johnstone, July 2, 1688.

profession. Sir William Williams, the Solicitor-general, had great abilities and dauntless courage: but he wanted discretion; he loved wrangling: he had no command over his temper; and he was hated and despised by all political parties. The most conspicuous assistants of the Attorney and Solicitor were Sergeant Trinder, a Roman Catholic, and Sir Bartholomew Shower, Recorder of London, who had some legal learning, but whose fulsome apologies and endless repetitions were the jest of Westminster Hall. The government had wished to secure the services of Maynard: but he had plainly declared that he could not in conscience do what was asked of him.*

On the other side were arrayed almost all the eminent forensic talents of the age. Sawyer and Finch, who, at the time of the accession of James, had been Attorney and Solicitor-general, and who, during the persecution of the Whigs in the late reign, had served the crown with but too much vehemence and success, were of counsel for the defendants. With them were joined two persons who, since age had diminished the activity of Maynard, were reputed the two best lawyers that could be found in the Inns of Court; Pemberton, who had, in the time of Charles the Second, been Chief-justice of the King's Bench, who had been removed from his high place on account of his humanity and moderation, and who had resumed his practice at the bar; and Pollexfen, who had long been at the head of the Western circuit, and who, though he had incurred much unpopularity by holding briefs for the crown at the Bloody Assizes, and particularly by appearing against Alice Lisle, was known to be at heart a Whig, if not a Republican. Sir Creswell Levinz was also there, a man of great knowledge and experience, but of singularly timid nature. He had been removed from the bench some years before, because he was afraid to serve the purposes of the government. He was now afraid to appear as the advocate of the Bishops, and had at first refused to receive their retainer: but it had been intimated to him by the whole body of attorneys who

---

* Johnstone, July 2, 1688.

employed him that, if he declined this brief, he should never have another.*

Sir George Treby, an able and zealous Whig, who had been Recorder of London under the old charter, was on the same side. Sir John Holt, a still more eminent Whig lawyer, was not retained for the defence, in consequence, it should seem, of some prejudice conceived against him by Sancroft, but was privately consulted on the case by the Bishop of London.† The junior counsel for the Bishops was a young barrister named John Somers. He had no advantage of birth or fortune; nor had he yet had any opportunity of distinguishing himself before the eyes of the public; but his genius, his industry, his great and various accomplishments, were well known to a small circle of friends; and, in spite of his Whig opinions, his pertinent and lucid mode of arguing and the constant propriety of his demeanor had already secured to him the ear of the Court of King's Bench. The importance of obtaining his services had been strongly represented to the Bishops by Johnstone; and Pollexfen, it is said, had declared that no man in Westminster Hall was so well qualified to treat a historical and constitutional question as Somers.

The jury was sworn. It consisted of persons of highly respectable station. The foreman was Sir Roger Langley, a baronet of old and honorable family. With him were joined a knight and ten esquires, several of whom are known to have been men of large possessions. There were some Non-conformists in the number; for the Bishops had wisely resolved not to show any distrust of the Protestant Dissenters. One name excited considerable alarm, that of Michael Arnold. He was brewer to the palace; and it was apprehended that the government counted on his voice. The story goes that he complained bitterly of the position in which he found himself. "Whatever I do," he said, "I am sure to be half ruined.

* Johnstone, July 2, 1688. The editor of Levinz's Reports expresses great wonder that, after the Revolution, Levinz was not replaced on the bench. The facts related by Johnstone may perhaps explain the seeming injustice.

† I draw this inference from a letter of Compton to Sancroft, dated the 12th of June.

If I say Not Guilty, I shall brew no more for the King; and if I say Guilty, I shall brew no more for anybody else."*

The trial then commenced, a trial which, even when coolly perused after the lapse of more than a century and a half, has all the interest of a drama. The advocates contended on both sides with far more than professional keenness and vehemence; the audience listened with as much anxiety as if the fate of every one of them was to be decided by the verdict: and the turns of fortune were so sudden and amazing that the multitude repeatedly passed in a single minute from anxiety to exultation, and back again from exultation to still deeper anxiety.

The information charged the Bishops with having written or published, in the county of Middlesex, a false, malicious, and seditious libel. The Attorney and Solicitor first tried to prove the writing. For this purpose several persons were called to speak to the hands of the Bishops. But the witnesses were so unwilling that hardly a single plain answer could be extracted from any of them. Pemberton, Pollexfen, and Levinz contended that there was no evidence to go to the jury. Two of the Judges, Holloway and Powell, declared themselves of the same opinion; and the hopes of the spectators rose high. All at once the crown lawyers announced their intention to take another line. Powis, with shame and reluctance which he could not dissemble, put into the witness-box Blathwayt, a clerk of the Privy Council, who had been present when the King interrogated the Bishops. Blathwayt swore that he had heard them own their signatures. His testimony was decisive. "Why," said Judge Holloway to the Attorney, "when you had such evidence, did you not produce it at first, without all this waste of time?" It soon appeared why the counsel for the crown had been unwilling, without absolute necessity, to resort to this mode of proof. Pemberton stopped Blathwayt, subjected him to a searching cross-examination, and insisted upon having all that had passed between the King and the defendants fully related. "That is

---

* Revolution Politics.

a pretty thing indeed," cried Williams. "Do you think," said Powis, "that you are at liberty to ask our witnesses any impertinent question that comes into your heads?" The advocates of the Bishops were not men to be so put down. "He is sworn," said Pollexfen, "to tell the truth and the whole truth; and an answer we must and will have." The witness shuffled, equivocated, pretended to misunderstand the questions, implored the protection of the court. But he was in hands from which it was not easy to escape. At length the Attorney again interposed. "If," he said, "you persist in asking such a question, tell us, at least, what use you mean to make of it." Pemberton, who, through the whole trial, did his duty manfully and ably, replied without hesitation: "My Lords, I will answer Mr. Attorney. I will deal plainly with the court. If the Bishops owned this paper under a promise from His Majesty that their confession should not be used against them, I hope that no unfair advantage will be taken of them." "You put on His Majesty what I dare hardly name," said Williams. "Since you will be so pressing, I demand, for the King, that the question may be recorded." "What do you mean, Mr. Solicitor?" said Sawyer, interposing. "I know what I mean," said the apostate: "I desire that the question may be recorded in court." "Record what you will. I am not afraid of you, Mr. Solicitor," said Pemberton. Then came a loud and fierce altercation, which Wright could with difficulty quiet. In other circumstances, he would probably have ordered the question to be recorded, and Pemberton to be committed. But on this great day the unjust Judge was overawed. He often cast a side glance toward the thick rows of Earls and Barons by whom he was watched, and before whom, in the next Parliament, he might stand at the bar. He looked, a by-stander said, as if all the peers present had halters in their pockets.* At length Blathwayt was forced to give a full account of what had passed. It appeared that the King had entered into no express covenant with

---

* This is the expression of an eye-witness. It is in a news-letter in the Mackintosh Collection.

the Bishops. But it appeared also that the Bishops might not unreasonably think that there was an implied engagement. Indeed, from the unwillingness of the crown lawyers to put the Clerk of the Council into the witness-box, and from the vehemence with which they objected to Pemberton's cross-examination, it is plain that they were themselves of this opinion.

However, the handwriting was now proved. But a new and serious objection was raised. It was not sufficient to prove that the Bishops had written the alleged libel. It was necessary to prove also that they had written it in the county of Middlesex. And not only was it out of the power of the Attorney and Solicitor to prove this, but it was in the power of the defendants to prove the contrary. For it so happened that Sancroft had never once left the palace at Lambeth from the time when the Order in Council appeared till after the petition was in the King's hands. The whole case for the prosecution had therefore completely broken down; and the audience, with great glee, expected a speedy acquittal.

The crown lawyers then changed their ground again, abandoned altogether the charge of writing a libel, and undertook to prove that the Bishops had published a libel in the county of Middlesex. The difficulties were great. The delivery of the petition to the King was undoubtedly, in the eye of the law, a publication. But how was this delivery to be proved? No person had been present at the audience in the royal closet, except the King and the defendants. The King could not well be sworn. It was therefore only by the admissions of the defendants that the fact of publication could be established. Blathwayt was again examined, but in vain. He well remembered, he said, that the Bishops owned their hands: but he did not remember that they owned the paper which lay on the table of the Privy Council to be the same paper which they had delivered to the King, or that they were even interrogated on that point. Several other official men who had been in attendance on the Council were called, and among them Samuel Pepys, Secretary of the Admiralty; but none of them could remember that anything was said about the delivery. It was to no purpose that Williams put leading questions till the counsel on the other side declared that such twisting, such wire-drawing, was never seen in a court of justice, and till Wright himself was forced to admit that the Solicitor's mode of examination was contrary to all rule. As witness after witness answered in the negative, roars of laughter and shouts of triumph, which the Judges did not even attempt to silence, shook the hall.

It seemed that at length this hard fight had been won. The case for the crown was closed. Had the counsel for the Bishops remained silent, an acquittal was certain; for nothing which the most corrupt and shameless Judge could venture to call legal evidence of publication had been given. The Chief-justice was beginning to charge the jury, and would undoubtedly have directed them to acquit the defendants; but Finch, too anxious to be perfectly discreet, interfered, and begged to be heard. "If you will be heard," said Wright, "you shall be heard; but you do not understand your own interests." The other counsel for the defence made Finch sit down, and begged the Chief-justice to proceed. He was about to do so, when a messenger came to the Solicitor-general with news that Lord Sunderland could prove the publication, and would come down to the court immediately. Wright maliciously told the counsel for the defence that they had only themselves to thank for the turn which things had taken. The countenances of the great multitude fell. Finch was, during some hours, the most unpopular man in the country. Why could he not sit still, as his betters, Sawyer, Pemberton, and Pollexfen, had done? His love of meddling, his ambition to make a fine speech, had ruined everything.

Meanwhile the Lord President was brought in a sedan chair through the hall. Not a hat moved as he passed; and many voices cried out "Popish dog!" He came into court pale and trembling, with eyes fixed on the ground, and gave his evidence in a faltering voice. He swore that the Bishops had informed him of their intention to present a petition to the King, and that they had been admitted into the royal closet for that purpose. This circumstance, coupled with the

II.—23

circumstance that, after they left the closet, there was in the King's hands a petition signed by them, was such proof as might reasonably satisfy a jury of the fact of the publication.

Publication in Middlesex was then proved. But was the paper thus published a false, malicious, and seditious libel? Hitherto the matter in dispute had been whether a fact which everybody well knew to be true could be proved according to technical rules of evidence; but now the contest became one of deeper interest. It was necessary to inquire into the limits of prerogative and liberty, into the right of the King to dispense with statutes, into the right of the subject to petition for the redress of grievances. During three hours the counsel for the petitioners argued with great force in defence of the fundamental principles of the constitution, and proved from the journals of the House of Commons that the Bishops had affirmed no more than the truth when they represented to the King that the dispensing power which he claimed had been repeatedly declared illegal by Parliament. Somers rose last. He spoke little more than five minutes: but every word was full of weighty matter; and when he sat down his reputation as an orator and a constitutional lawyer was established. He went through the expressions which were used in the information to describe the offence imputed to the Bishops, and showed that every word, whether adjective or substantive, was altogether inappropriate. The offence imputed was a false, a malicious, a seditious libel. False the paper was not; for every fact which it set forth had been shown from the journals of Parliament to be true. Malicious the paper was not; for the defendants had not sought an occasion of strife, but had been placed by the government in such a situation that they must either oppose themselves to the royal will, or violate the most sacred obligations of conscience and honor. Seditious the paper was not; for it had not been scattered by the writers among the rabble, but delivered privately into the hands of the King alone; and a libel it was not, but a decent petition such as, by the laws of England, nay, by the laws of imperial Rome, by the laws of all civilized states, a subject who thinks himself aggrieved may with propriety present to the sovereign.

The Attorney replied shortly and feebly. The Solicitor spoke at great length and with great acrimony, and was often interrupted by the clamors and hisses of the audience. He went so far as to lay it down that no subject or body of subjects, except the Houses of Parliament, had a right to petition the King. The galleries were furious; and the Chief-justice himself stood aghast at the effrontery of this venal turncoat.

At length Wright proceeded to sum up the evidence. His language showed that the awe in which he stood of the government was tempered by the awe with which the audience, so numerous, so splendid, and so strongly excited, had impressed him. He said that he would give no opinion on the question of the dispensing power; that it was not necessary for him to do so; that he could not agree with much of the Solicitor's speech; that it was the right of the subject to petition; but that the particular petition before the court was improperly worded, and was, in the contemplation of law, a libel. Allibone was of the same mind, but, in giving his opinion, showed such gross ignorance of law and history as brought on him the contempt of all who heard him. Holloway evaded the question of the dispensing power, but said that the petition seemed to him to be such as subjects who think themselves aggrieved are entitled to present, and therefore no libel. Powell took a bolder course. He avowed that, in his judgment, the Declaration of Indulgence was a nullity, and that the dispensing power, as lately exercised, was utterly inconsistent with all law. If these encroachments of prerogative were allowed, there was an end of Parliaments. The whole legislative authority would be in the King. "That issue, gentlemen," he said, "I leave to God and to your consciences."*

It was dark before the jury retired to consider of their verdict. The night was a night of intense anxiety. Some let-

---

* See the proceedings in the Collection of State Trials. I have taken some touches from Johnstone, and some from Van Citters.

ters are extant which were despatched during that period of suspense, and which have therefore an interest of a peculiar kind. "It is very late," wrote the Papal Nuncio; "and the decision is not yet known. The Judges and the culprits have gone to their own homes. The jury remain together. To-morrow we shall learn the event of this great struggle."

The solicitor for the Bishops sat up all night with a body of servants on the stairs leading to the room where the jury was consulting. It was absolutely necessary to watch the officers who watched the doors; for those officers were supposed to be in the interest of the crown, and might, if not carefully observed, have furnished a courtly juryman with food, which would have enabled him to starve out the other eleven. Strict guard was therefore kept. Not even a candle to light a pipe was permitted to enter. Some basins of water for washing were suffered to pass at about four in the morning. The jurymen, raging with thirst, soon lapped up the whole. Great numbers of people walked the neighboring streets till dawn. Every hour a messenger came from Whitehall to know what was passing. Voices, high in altercation, were repeatedly heard within the room: but nothing certain was known.*

At first, nine were for acquitting and three for convicting. Two of the minority soon gave way: but Arnold was obstinate. Thomas Austin, a country gentleman of great estate, who had paid close attention to the evidence and speeches, and had taken full notes, wished to argue the question. Arnold declined. He was not used, he doggedly said, to reasoning and debating. His conscience was not satisfied; and he should not acquit the Bishops. "If you come to that," said Austin, "look at me. I am the largest and strongest of the twelve; and before I find such a petition as this a libel, here I will stay till I am no bigger than a tobacco-pipe." It was six in the morning before Arnold yielded. It was soon known that the jury were agreed: but what the verdict would be was still a secret.†

---

* Johnstone, July 2, 1688; Letter from Mr. Ince to the Archbishop, dated at six o'clock in the morning; Tanner MSS.; Revolution Politics.

† Johnstone, July 2, 1688.

At ten the court again met. The crowd was greater than ever. The jury appeared in their box; and there was a breathless stillness.

Sir Samuel Astry spoke. "Do you find the defendants, or any of them, guilty of the misdemeanor whereof they are impeached, or not guilty?" Sir Roger Langley answered, "Not Guilty." As the words were uttered, Halifax sprang up and waved his hat. At that signal, benches and galleries raised a shout. In a moment ten thousand persons, who crowded the great hall, replied with a still louder shout, which made the old oaken roof crack; and in another moment the innumerable throng without set up a third huzza, which was heard at Temple Bar. The boats which covered the Thames gave an answering cheer. A peal of gunpowder was heard on the water, and another, and another; and so, in a few moments, the glad tidings went flying past the Savoy and the Friars to London Bridge, and to the forest of masts below. As the news spread, streets and squares, market-places and coffee-houses, broke forth into acclamations. Yet were the acclamations less strange than the weeping. For the feelings of men had been wound up to such a point that at length the stern English nature, so little used to outward signs of emotion, gave way, and thousands sobbed aloud for very joy. Meanwhile, from the outskirts of the multitude, horsemen were spurring off to bear along all the great roads intelligence of the victory of our Church and nation. Yet not even that astounding explosion could awe the bitter and intrepid spirit of the Solicitor. Striving to make himself heard above the din, he called on the Judges to commit those who had violated, by clamor, the dignity of a court of justice. One of the rejoicing populace was seized. But the tribunal felt that it would be absurd to punish a single individual for an offence common to hundreds of thousands, and dismissed him with a gentle reprimand.*

---

* State Trials; Oldmixon, 739; Clarendon's Diary, June 25, 1688; Johnstone, July 2; Van Citters, July $\frac{8}{13}$; Adda, July $\frac{6}{16}$; Luttrell's Diary; Barillon, July $\frac{2}{12}$.

It was vain to think of passing at that moment to any other business. Indeed the roar of the multitude was such that, during half an hour, scarcely a word could be heard in the court. Williams got to his coach amidst a tempest of hisses and curses. Cartwright, whose curiosity was ungovernable, had been guilty of the folly and indecency of coming to Westminster in order to hear the decision. He was recognized by his sacerdotal garb and by his corpulent figure, and was hooted through the hall. "Take care," said one, "of the wolf in sheep's clothing." "Make room," cried another, "for the man with the Pope in his belly."*

The acquitted prelates took refuge in the nearest chapel from the crowd which implored their blessing. Many churches were open on that morning throughout the capital; and many pious persons repaired thither. The bells of all the parishes of the City and liberties were ringing. The jury meanwhile could scarcely make their way out of the hall. They were forced to shake hands with hundreds. "God bless you!" cried the people; "God prosper your families! you have done like honest good-natured gentlemen: you have saved us all to-day." As the noblemen who had attended to support the good cause drove off, they flung from their carriage windows handfuls of money, and bade the crowd drink to the health of the King, the Bishops, and the jury.†

---

* Van Citters, July $\frac{3}{13}$. The gravity with which he tells the story has a comic effect. "Den Bisschop van Chester, wie seer de partie van het hof houdt, om te voldoen aan syne gewoone nieusgierigheyt, hem op dien tyt in Westminster Hall mede hebbende laten vinden, in het uytgaan doorgaans was uytgekreten voor een grypende wolf in schaaps kleederen; en hy synde een heer van hooge stature en vollyvig, spotsgewyse alomme geroepen was dat men voor hem plaats moeste maken, om te laten passen, gelyck ook geschiede, om dat soo sy uytschreeuwden en hem in het aansigt seyden, hy den Paus in syn buyck hadde."

† Luttrell; Van Citters, July $\frac{3}{13}$, 1688. "Soo syn in tegendeel gedagte jurys met de uyterste acclamatie en alle teyckenen van genegenheyt en danckbaarheyt in het door passeren van de gemeente ontvangen. Honderden vielen haar om den hals met alle bedenckelycke wewensch van segen en geluck over hare persoonen en familien, om dat sy haar so heusch en eerlyck buyten verwagtinge als het ware in desen gedragen hadden. Veele van de grooten en kleynen adel wierpen in het wegryden handen vol gelt onder de armen luyden, om op de gesontheyt van den Coning, der Heeren Prelaten, en de Jurys te drincken."

The Attorney went with the tidings to Sunderland, who happened to be conversing with the Nuncio. "Never," said Powis, "within man's memory, have there been such shouts and such tears of joy as to-day."* The King had that morning visited the camp on Hounslow Heath. Sunderland instantly sent a courier thither with the news. James was in Lord Feversham's tent when the express arrived. He was greatly disturbed, and exclaimed in French, "So much the worse for them." He soon set out for London. While he was present, respect prevented the soldiers from giving a loose to their feelings; but he had scarcely quitted the camp when he heard a great shouting behind him. He was surprised, and asked what that uproar meant. "Nothing," was the answer: "the soldiers are glad that the Bishops are acquitted." "Do you call that nothing?" said James. And then he repeated, "So much the worse for them."†

He might well be out of temper. His defeat had been complete and most humiliating. Had the prelates escaped on account of some technical defect in the case for the crown, had they escaped because they had not written the petition in Middlesex, or because it was impossible to prove, according to the strict rules of law, that they had delivered to the King the paper for which they were called in question, the prerogative would have suffered no shock. Happily for the country, the fact of publication had been fully established. The counsel for the defence had therefore been forced to attack the dispensing power. They had attacked it with great learning, eloquence, and boldness. The advocates of the government had been by universal acknowledgment overmatched in the contest. Not a single Judge had ventured to declare that the Declaration of Indulgence was legal. One Judge had in the strongest terms pronounced it illegal. The language of the whole town was that the dispensing power had received a

---

* " Mi trovava con Milord Sunderland la stessa mattina, quando venne l'Avvocato Generale a rendergli conto del successo, e disse, che mai più a memoria d' huomini si era sentito un applauso, mescolato di voci e lagrime di giubilo, egual a quello che veniva egli di vedere in quest' occasione."—Adda, July $\frac{6}{16}$, 1688.

† Burnet, i., 744; Van Citters, July $\frac{3}{13}$, 1688.

fatal blow. Finch, who had the day before been universally reviled, was now universally applauded. He had been unwilling, it was said, to let the case be decided in a way which would have left the great constitutional question still doubtful. He had felt that a verdict which should acquit his clients, without condemning the Declaration of Indulgence, would be but half a victory. It is certain that Finch deserved neither the reproaches which had been cast on him while the event was doubtful, nor the praises which he received when it had proved happy. It was absurd to blame him because, during the short delay which he occasioned, the crown lawyers unexpectedly discovered new evidence. It was equally absurd to suppose that he deliberately exposed his clients to risk, in order to establish a general principle; and still more absurd was it to praise him for what would have been a gross violation of professional duty.

That joyful day was followed by a not less joyful evening. The Bishops, and some of their most respectable friends, in vain exerted themselves to prevent tumultuous demonstrations of public feeling. Never within the memory of the oldest, not even on that night on which it was known through London that the army of Scotland had declared for a free Parliament, had the streets been in such a glare with bonfires. Round every bonfire crowds were drinking good health to the Bishops and confusion to the Papists. The windows were lighted with rows of candles. Each row consisted of seven; and the taper in the centre, which was taller than the rest, represented the Primate. The noise of rockets, squibs, and fire-arms was incessant. One huge pile of fagots blazed right in front of the great gate at Whitehall. Others were lighted before the doors of Roman Catholic peers. Lord Arundell of Wardour wisely quieted the mob with a little money: but at Salisbury House in the Strand an attempt at resistance was made. Lord Salisbury's servants sallied out and fired; but they killed only the unfortunate beadle of the parish, who had come thither to put out the fire; and they were soon routed and driven back into the house. None of the spectacles of that night interested the common people so much as one with which they had, a few years before, been familiar, and which they now, after a long interval, enjoyed once more — the burning of the Pope. This once familiar pageant is known to our generation only by descriptions and engravings. A figure, by no means resembling those rude representations of Guy Faux which are still paraded on the fifth of November, but made of wax with some skill, and adorned at no small expense with robes and a tiara, was mounted on a chair resembling that in which the Bishops of Rome are still, on some great festivals, borne through Saint Peter's Church to the high altar. His Holiness was generally accompanied by a train of Cardinals and Jesuits. At his ear stood a buffoon disguised as a devil, with horns and tail. No rich and zealous Protestant grudged his guinea on such an occasion, and, if rumor could be trusted, the cost of the procession was sometimes not less than a thousand pounds. After the Pope had been borne some time in state over the heads of the multitude, he was committed to the flames with loud acclamations. In the time of the popularity of Oates and Shaftesbury, this show was exhibited annually in Fleet Street before the windows of the Whig Club on the anniversary of the birth of Queen Elizabeth. Such was the celebrity of these grotesque rites, that Barillon once risked his life in order to peep at them from a hiding-place.* But, from the day when the Rye-house Plot was discovered, till the day of the acquittal of the Bishops, the ceremony had been disused. Now, however, several Popes made their appearance in different parts of London. The Nuncio was much shocked; and the King was more hurt by this insult to his Church than by all the other affronts which he had received. The magistrates, however, could do nothing. The Sunday had dawned, and the bells of the parish churches were ringing for early prayers, before the fires began to languish and the crowds to disperse. A proclamation was speedily put forth against the

* See a very curious narrative published, among other papers, in 1710, by Danby, then Duke of Leeds. There is an amusing account of the ceremony of burning a Pope in North's Examen, 570. See also the note on the Epilogue to the Tragedy of Œdipus in Scott's edition of Dryden.

rioters. Many of them, mostly young apprentices, were apprehended; but the bills were thrown out at the Middlesex sessions. The Justices, many of whom were Roman Catholics, expostulated with the grand jury, and sent them three or four times back, but to no purpose.*

Peculiar state of public feeling at this time. Meanwhile the glad tidings were flying to every part of the kingdom, and were everywhere received with rapture. Gloucester, Bedford, and Lichfield were among the places which were distinguished by peculiar zeal: but Bristol and Norwich, which stood nearest to London in population and wealth, approached nearest to London in enthusiasm on the joyful occasion.

The prosecution of the Bishops is an event which stands by itself in our history. It was the first and the last occasion on which two feelings of tremendous potency, two feelings which have generally been opposed to each other, and either of which, when strongly excited, has sufficed to convulse the state, were united in perfect harmony. Those feelings were love of the Church and love of freedom. During many generations every violent outbreak of High-church feeling, with one exception, has been unfavorable to civil liberty; every violent outbreak of zeal for liberty, with one exception, has been unfavorable to the authority and influence of the prelacy and the priesthood. In 1688 the cause of the hierarchy was for a moment that of the popular party. More than nine thousand clergymen, with the Primate and his most respectable suffragans at their head, offered themselves to endure bonds and the spoiling of their goods for the great fundamental principle of our free constitution. The effect was a coalition which included the most zealous Cavaliers, the most zealous Republicans, and all the intermediate sections of the community. The spirit which had supported Hampden in the preceding generation, the spirit which, in the succeeding generation, supported Sacheverell, combined to support the Archbishop, who was Hampden and Sacheverell in one. Those classes of society which

---

* Reresby's Memoirs; Van Citters, July $\frac{3}{13}$, 1688; Adda, July $\frac{6}{16}$; Barillon, July $\frac{2}{12}$; Luttrell's Diary; News-letter of July 4; Oldmixon, 739; Ellis Correspondence.

are most deeply interested in the preservation of order, which in troubled times are generally most ready to strengthen the hands of government, and which have a natural antipathy to agitators, followed, without scruple, the guidance of a venerable man, the first peer of the Parliament, the first minister of the Church, a Tory in politics, a saint in manners, whom tyranny had in his own despite turned into a demagogue. Many, on the other hand, who had always abhorred episcopacy, as a relic of Popery, and as an instrument of arbitrary power, now asked on bended knees the blessing of a prelate who was ready to wear fetters and to lay his aged limbs on bare stones rather than betray the interests of the Protestant religion, and set the prerogative above the laws. With love of the Church and with love of freedom was mingled, at this great crisis, a third feeling which is among the most honorable peculiarities of our national character. An individual oppressed by power, even when destitute of all claim to public respect and gratitude, generally finds strong sympathy among us. Thus, in the time of our grandfathers, society was thrown into confusion by the persecution of Wilkes. We have ourselves seen the nation roused to madness by the wrongs of Queen Caroline. It is probable, therefore, that, even if no great political or religious interest had been staked on the event of the proceeding against the Bishops, England would not have seen, without strong emotions of pity and anger, old men of stainless virtue pursued by the vengeance of a harsh and inexorable prince who owed to their fidelity the crown which he wore.

Actuated by these sentiments, our ancestors arrayed themselves against the government in one huge and compact mass. All ranks, all parties, all Protestant sects, made up that vast phalanx. In the van were the Lords Spiritual and Temporal. Then came the landed gentry and the clergy, both the Universities, all the Inns of Court, merchants, shopkeepers, farmers, the porters who plied in the streets of the great towns, the peasants who ploughed the fields. The league against the King included the very foremost men who manned his ships, the very sentinels who guarded his palace. The names of Whig and Tory were for a moment forgotten. The old Exclusionist took the old Abhorrer by the hand. Episcopalians, Presbyterians, Independents, Baptists, forgot their long feud, and remembered only their common Protestantism and their common danger. Divines bred in the school of Laud talked loudly, not only of toleration, but of comprehension. The Archbishop, soon after his acquittal, put forth a pastoral letter which is one of the most remarkable compositions of that age. He had, from his youth up, been at war with the Non-conformists, and had repeatedly assailed them with unjust and unchristian asperity. His principal work was a hideous caricature of the Calvinistic theology.* He had drawn up for the thirtieth of January and for the twenty-ninth of May forms of prayer which reflected on the Puritans in language so strong that the government had thought fit to soften it down. But now his heart was melted and opened. He solemnly enjoined the Bishops and clergy to have a very tender regard to their brethren the Protestant Dissenters, to visit them often, to entertain them hospitably, to discourse with them civilly, to persuade them, if it might be, to conform to the Church, but, if that were found impossible, to join them heartily and affectionately in exertions for the blessed cause of the Reformation.†

Many pious persons in subsequent years remembered that time with bitter regret. They described it as a short glimpse of a golden age between two iron ages. Such lamentation, though natural, was not reasonable. The coalition of 1688 was produced, and could be produced, only by tyranny which approached to insanity, and by danger which threatened at

---

* The Fur Prædestinatus.

† This document will be found in the first of the twelve collections of papers relating to the affairs of England, printed at the end of 1688 and the beginning of 1689. It was put forth on the 26th of July, not quite a month after the trial. Lloyd of Saint Asaph about the same time told Henry Wharton that the bishops purposed to adopt an entirely new policy toward the Protestant Dissenters: " Omni modo curaturos ut ecclesia sordibus et corruptelis penitus exueretur; ut sectariis reformatis reditus in ecclesiæ sinum exoptati occasio ac ratio concederetur, si qui sobrii et pii essent; ut pertinacibus interim jugum levaretur, extinctis penitus legibus mulctatoriis."—Excerpta ex Vita H. Wharton.

once all the great institutions of the country. If there has never since been similar union, the reason is that there has never since been similar misgovernment. It must be remembered that, though concord is in itself better than discord, discord may indicate a better state of things than is indicated by concord. Calamity and peril often force men to combine. Prosperity and security often encourage them to separate.

CHAPTER IX.

THE acquittal of the Bishops was not the only event which makes the thirtieth of June, 1688, a great epoch in history. On that day, while the bells of a hundred churches were ringing, while multitudes were busied, from Hyde Park to Mile End, in piling fagots and dressing Popes for the rejoicings of the night, was despatched from London to the Hague an instrument scarcely less important to the liberties of England than the Great Charter.

The prosecution of the Bishops, and the birth of the Prince of Wales, had produced a great revolution in the feelings of many Tories. At the very moment at which their Church was suffering the last excess of injury and insult, they were compelled to renounce the hope of peaceful deliverance. Hitherto they had flattered themselves that the trial to which their loyalty was subjected would, though severe, be temporary, and that their wrongs would shortly be redressed without any violation of the ordinary rule of succession. A very different prospect was now before them. As far as they could look forward they saw only misgovernment, such as that of the last three years, extending through ages. The cradle of the heir-apparent of the crown was surrounded by Jesuits. Deadly hatred of that Church of which he would one day be the head would be studiously instilled into his infant mind, would be the guiding principle of his life, and would be bequeathed by him to his posterity. This vista of calamities had no end. It stretched beyond the life of the youngest man living, beyond the eighteenth century. None could say how many generations of Protestant Englishmen might have to bear oppression, such as, even when it had been believed to be short, had been found almost insupportable. Was there, then, no

Change in the opinion of the Tories concerning the lawfulness of resistance.

remedy? One remedy there was, quick, sharp, and decisive, a remedy which the Whigs had been but too ready to employ, but which had always been regarded by the Tories as, in all cases, unlawful.

The greatest Anglican doctors of that age had maintained that no breach of law or contract, no excess of cruelty, rapacity, or licentiousness, on the part of a rightful king, could justify his people in withstanding him by force. Some of them had delighted to exhibit the doctrine of non-resistance in a form so exaggerated as to shock common-sense and humanity. They frequently and emphatically remarked that Nero was at the head of the Roman government when Saint Paul inculcated the duty of obeying magistrates. The inference which they drew was that, if an English king should, without any law but his own pleasure, persecute his subjects for not worshipping idols, should fling them to the lions in the Tower, should wrap them up in pitched cloth and set them on fire to light up Saint James's Park, and should go on with these massacres till whole towns and shires were left without one inhabitant, the survivors would still be bound meekly to submit, and to be torn in pieces or roasted alive without a struggle. The arguments in favor of this proposition were futile indeed: but the place of sound argument was amply supplied by the omnipotent sophistry of interest and of passion. Many writers have expressed wonder that the high-spirited Cavaliers of England should have been zealous for the most slavish theory that has ever been known among men. The truth is that this theory at first presented itself to the Cavalier as the very opposite of slavish. Its tendency was to make him not a slave but a freeman and a master. It exalted him by exalting one whom he regarded as his protector, as his friend, as the head of his beloved party and of his more beloved Church. When Republicans were dominant, the Royalist had endured wrongs and insults which the restoration of the legitimate government had enabled him to retaliate. Rebellion was therefore associated in his imagination with subjection and degradation, and monarchical authority with liberty and ascendency. It had never crossed his imagination that a time might come when a king, a Stuart, would persecute the most loyal of the clergy and gentry with more than the animosity of the Rump or the Protector. That time had, however, arrived. It was now to be seen how the patience which Churchmen professed to have learned from the writings of Paul would stand the test of a persecution by no means so severe as that of Nero. The event was such as everybody who knew anything of human nature would have predicted. Oppression speedily did what philosophy and eloquence would have failed to do. The system of Filmer might have survived the attacks of Locke; but it never recovered from the death-blow given by James.

That logic, which, while it was used to prove that Presbyterians and Independents ought to bear imprisonment and confiscation with meekness, had been pronounced unanswerable, seemed to be of very little force when the question was whether Anglican Bishops should be imprisoned, and the revenues of Anglican colleges confiscated. It had been often repeated, from the pulpits of all the cathedrals of the land, that the apostolical injunction to obey the civil magistrate was absolute and universal, and that it was impious presumption in man to limit a precept which had been promulgated without any limitation in the word of God. Now, however, divines, whose sagacity had been sharpened by the imminent danger in which they stood of being turned out of their livings and prebends to make room for Papists, discovered flaws in the reasoning which had formerly seemed so convincing. The ethical parts of Scripture were not to be construed like Acts of Parliament, or like the casuistical treatises of the schoolmen. What Christian really turned the left cheek to the ruffian who had smitten the right? What Christian really gave his cloak to the thieves who had taken his coat away? Both in the Old and in the New Testament general rules were perpetually laid down unaccompanied by the exceptions. Thus there was a general command not to kill, unaccompanied by any reservation in favor of the warrior who kills in defence of his king and country. There was a general command not to swear, unaccompanied by any reservation in favor of the witness who swears to speak the truth before a judge. Yet the lawfulness of defensive war and of judicial oaths was disputed only by a few obscure sectaries, and was positively affirmed in the articles of the Church of England. All the arguments which showed that the Quaker, who refused to bear arms, or to kiss the Gospels, was unreasonable and perverse, might be turned against those who denied to subjects the right of resisting extreme tyranny by force. If it was contended that the texts which prohibited homicide, and the texts which prohibited swearing, though generally expressed, must be construed in subordination to the great commandment by which every man is enjoined to promote the welfare of his neighbors, and would, when so construed, be found not to apply to cases in which homicide or swearing might be absolutely necessary to protect the dearest interests of society, it was not easy to deny that the texts which prohibited resistance ought to be construed in the same manner. If the ancient people of God had been directed sometimes to destroy human life, and sometimes to bind themselves by oaths, they had also been directed sometimes to resist wicked princes. If early fathers of the Church had occasionally used language which seemed to imply that they disapproved of all resistance, they had also occasionally used language which seemed to imply that they disapproved of all war and of all oaths. In truth the doctrine of passive obedience, as taught at Oxford in the reign of Charles the Second, can be deduced from the Bible only by a mode of interpretation which would irresistibly lead us to the conclusions of Barclay and Penn.

It was not merely by arguments drawn from the letter of Scripture that the Anglican theologians had, during the years which immediately followed the Restoration, labored to prove their favorite tenet. They had attempted to show that, even if revelation had been silent, reason would have taught wise men the folly and wickedness of all resistance to established government. It was universally admitted that such resistance was, except in extreme cases, unjustifiable. And who would undertake to draw the line between extreme cases and ordinary cases? Was there any government in the world under

II.—24

which there were not to be found some discontented and factious men who would say, and perhaps think, that their grievances constituted an extreme case? If, indeed, it were possible to lay down a clear and accurate rule which might forbid men to rebel against Trajan, and yet leave them at liberty to rebel against Caligula, such a rule might be highly beneficial. But no such rule had ever been, or ever would be, framed. To say that rebellion was lawful under some circumstances, without accurately defining those circumstances, was to say that every man might rebel whenever he thought fit; and a society in which every man rebelled whenever he thought fit would be more miserable than a society governed by the most cruel and licentious despot. It was, therefore, necessary to maintain the great principle of non-resistance in all its integrity. Particular cases might doubtless be put in which resistance would benefit a community: but it was, on the whole, better that the people should patiently endure a bad government than that they should relieve themselves by violating a law on which the security of all government depended.

Such reasoning easily convinced a dominant and prosperous party, but could ill bear the scrutiny of minds strongly excited by royal injustice and ingratitude. It is true that to trace the exact boundary between rightful and wrongful resistance is impossible: but this impossibility arises from the nature of right and wrong, and is found in every part of ethical science. A good action is not distinguished from a bad action by marks so plain as those which distinguish a hexagon from a square. There is a frontier where virtue and vice fade into each other. Who has ever been able to define the exact boundary between courage and rashness, between prudence and cowardice, between frugality and avarice, between liberality and prodigality? Who has ever been able to say how far mercy to offenders ought to be carried, and where it ceases to deserve the name of mercy and becomes a pernicious weakness? What casuist, what law-giver, has ever been able nicely to mark the limits of the right of self-defence? All our jurists hold that a certain quantity of risk to life or limb justifies a man in shooting or stabbing an assailant: but they have long given up in despair the attempt to describe, in precise words, that quantity of risk. They only say that it must be, not a slight risk, but a risk such as would cause serious apprehension to a man of firm mind; and who will undertake to say what is the precise amount of apprehension which deserves to be called serious, or what is the precise texture of mind which deserves to be called firm? It is doubtless to be lamented that the nature of words and the nature of things do not admit of more accurate legislation: nor can it be denied that wrong will often be done when men are judges in their own cause, and proceed instantly to execute their own judgment. Yet who would on that account interdict all self-defence? The right which a people has to resist a bad government bears a close analogy to the right which an individual, in the absence of legal protection, has to slay an assailant. In both cases the evil must be grave. In both cases all regular and peaceable modes of defence must be exhausted before the aggrieved party resorts to extremities. In both cases an awful responsibility is incurred. In both cases the burden of the proof lies on him who has ventured on so desperate an expedient: and, if he fails to vindicate himself, he is justly liable to the severest penalties. But in neither case can we absolutely deny the existence of the right. A man beset by assassins is not bound to let himself be tortured and butchered without using his weapons because nobody has ever been able precisely to define the amount of danger which justifies homicide; nor is a society bound to endure passively all that tyranny can inflict because nobody has ever been able precisely to define the amount of misgovernment which justifies rebellion.

But could the resistance of Englishmen to such a prince as James be properly called rebellion? The thorough-paced disciples of Filmer, indeed, maintained that there was no difference whatever between the polity of our country and that of Turkey, and that, if the King did not confiscate the contents of all the tills in Lombard Street, and send mutes with bowstrings to Sancroft and Halifax, this was only because His Majesty was too gracious to use the whole power which he derived from Heaven. But the great body of Tories, though, in the heat of conflict, they might occasionally use language which seemed to indicate that they approved of these extravagant doctrines, heartily abhorred despotism. The English government was, in their view, a limited monarchy. Yet how can a monarchy be said to be limited, if force is never to be employed, even in the last resort, for the purpose of maintaining the limitations? In Muscovy, where the sovereign was, by the constitution of the state, absolute, it might perhaps be, with some color of truth, contended that, whatever excesses he might commit, he was still entitled to demand, on Christian principles, the obedience of his subjects. But here prince and people were alike bound by the laws. It was therefore James who incurred the woe denounced against those who insult the powers that be. It was James who was resisting the ordinance of God, who was mutinying against that legitimate authority to which he ought to have been subject, not only for wrath, but also for conscience' sake, and who was, in the true sense of the words of Jesus, withholding from Cæsar the things which were Cæsar's.

Moved by such considerations as these, the ablest and most enlightened Tories began to admit that they had overstrained the doctrine of passive obedience. The difference between these men and the Whigs as to the reciprocal obligations of kings and subjects was now no longer a difference of principle. There still remained, it is true, many historical controversies between the party which had always maintained the lawfulness of resistance and the new converts. The memory of the blessed Martyr was still as much revered as ever by those old Cavaliers who were ready to take arms against his degenerate son. They still spoke with abhorrence of the Long Parliament, of the Rye-house Plot, and of the Western insurrection. But, whatever they might think about the past, the view which they took of the present was altogether Whiggish; for they now held that extreme oppression might justify resistance, and they held that the oppression which the nation suffered was extreme.*

---

* This change in the opinion of a section of the Tory party is well illustrated

It must not, however, be supposed that all the Tories renounced, even at that conjuncture, a tenet which they had from childhood been taught to regard as an essential part of Christianity, which they had professed during many years with ostentatious vehemence, and which they had attempted to propagate by persecution. Many were kept steady to their old creed by conscience, and many by shame. But the greater part, even of those who still continued to pronounce all resistance to the sovereign unlawful, were disposed, in the event of a civil conflict, to remain neutral. No provocation should drive them to rebel: but, if rebellion broke forth, it did not appear that they were bound to fight for James the Second as they would have fought for Charles the First. The Christians of Rome had been forbidden by Saint Paul to resist the government of Nero: but there was no reason to believe that the Apostle, if he had been alive when the Legions and the Senate rose up against that wicked Emperor, would have commanded the brethren to fly to arms in support of tyranny. The duty of the persecuted Church was clear: she must suffer patiently, and commit her cause to God. But, if God, whose providence perpetually educes good out of evil, should be pleased, as oftentimes he had been pleased, to redress her wrongs by the instrumentality of men whose angry passions her lessons had not been able to tame, she might gratefully accept from him a deliverance which her principles did not permit her to achieve for herself. Most of those Tories, therefore, who still sincerely disclaimed all thought of attacking the government, were yet by no means inclined to defend it, and perhaps, while glorying in their own scruples, secretly rejoiced that everybody was not so scrupulous as themselves.

The Whigs saw that their time was come. Whether they should draw the sword against the government had, during six or seven years, been, in their view, merely a question of prudence; and prudence itself now urged them to take a bold course.

---

by a little tract published at the beginning of 1689, and entitled "A Dialogue between Two Friends, wherein the Church of England is vindicated in joining with the Prince of Orange."

In May, before the birth of the Prince of Wales, and while it was still uncertain whether the Declaration would or would not be read in the churches, Edward Russell had repaired to the Hague. He had strongly represented to the Prince of Orange the state of the public mind, and had advised His Highness to appear in England at the head of a strong body of troops, and to call the people to arms.

<small>Russell proposes to the Prince of Orange a descent on England.</small>

William had seen, at a glance, the whole importance of the crisis. "Now or never," he exclaimed, in Latin, to Van Dykvelt.* To Russell he held more guarded language, admitted that the distempers of the state were such as required an extraordinary remedy, but spoke with earnestness of the chance of failure, and of the calamities which failure might bring on Britain and on Europe. He knew well that many who talked in high language about sacrificing their lives and fortunes for their country would hesitate when the prospect of another Bloody Circuit was brought close to them. He wanted, therefore, to have, not vague professions of good-will, but distinct invitations and promises of support subscribed by powerful and eminent men. Russell remarked that it would be dangerous to intrust the design to a great number of persons. William assented, and said that a few signatures would be sufficient, if they were the signatures of statesmen who represented great interests.†

With this answer Russell returned to London, where he found the excitement greatly increased and daily increasing. The imprisonment of the Bishops and the delivery of the Queen made his task easier than he could have anticipated. He lost no time in collecting the voices of the chiefs of the opposition. His principal coadjutor in this work was Henry Sidney, brother of Algernon. It is remarkable that both Edward Russell and Henry Sidney had been in the household of James, that both had, partly on public and partly on private grounds, become his enemies, and

<small>Henry Sidney.</small>

---

* "Aut nunc, aut nunquam."—Witsen MS. quoted by Wagenaar, Book IX.
† Burnet, i., 763.

that both had to avenge the blood of near kinsmen who had, in the same year, fallen victims to his implacable severity. Here the resemblance ends. Russell, with considerable abilities, was proud, acrimonious, restless, and violent. Sidney, with a sweet temper and winning manners, seemed to be deficient in capacity and knowledge, and to be sunk in voluptuousness and indolence. His face and form were eminently handsome. In his youth he had been the terror of husbands; and even now, at near fifty, he was the favorite of women and the envy of younger men. He had formerly resided at the Hague in a public character, and had then succeeded in obtaining a large share of William's confidence. Many wondered at this: for it seemed that between the most austere of statesmen and the most dissolute of idlers there could be nothing in common. Swift, many years later, could not be convinced that one whom he had known only as an illiterate and frivolous old rake could really have played a great part in a great revolution. Yet a less acute observer than Swift might have been aware that there is a certain tact, resembling an instinct, which is often wanting to great orators and philosophers, and which is often found in persons who, if judged by their conversation or by their writings, would be pronounced simpletons. Indeed, when a man possesses this tact, it is in some sense an advantage to him that he is destitute of those more showy talents which would make him an object of admiration, of envy, and of fear. Sidney was a remarkable instance of this truth. Incapable, ignorant, and dissipated as he seemed to be, he understood, or rather felt, with whom it was necessary to be reserved, and with whom he might safely venture to be communicative. The consequence was, that he did what Mordaunt, with all his vivacity and invention, or Burnet, with all his multifarious knowledge and fluent elocution, never could have done.*

With the old Whigs there could be no difficulty. In their opinion there had been scarcely a moment, during many

---

* Sidney's Diary and Correspondence, edited by Mr. Blencowe; Mackay's Memoirs with Swift's note; Burnet, i., 763.

years, at which the public wrongs would not have justified resistance. Devonshire, who might be regarded as their chief, had private as well as public wrongs to revenge. He went into the scheme with his whole heart, and answered for his party.*

Devonshire.

Russell opened the design to Shrewsbury. Sidney sounded Halifax. Shrewsbury took his part with a courage and decision which, at a later period, seemed to be wanting to his character. He at once agreed to set his estate, his honors, and his life on the stake. But Halifax received the first hint of the project in a way which showed that it would be useless, and perhaps hazardous, to be explicit. He was, indeed, not the man for such an enterprise. His intellect was inexhaustibly fertile of distinctions and objections, his temper calm and unadventurous. He was ready to oppose the court to the utmost in the House of Lords and by means of anonymous writings: but he was little disposed to exchange his lordly repose for the insecure and agitated life of a conspirator, to be in the power of accomplices, to live in constant dread of warrants and King's messengers, nay, perhaps to end his days on a scaffold, or to live on alms in some back street of the Hague. He therefore let fall some words which plainly indicated that he did not wish to be privy to the intentions of his more daring and impetuous friends. Sidney understood him, and said no more.†

Shrewsbury.
Halifax.

The next application was made to Danby, and had far better success. Indeed, for his bold and active spirit the danger and the excitement, which were insupportable to the more delicately organized mind of Halifax, had a strong fascination. The different characters of the two statesmen were legible in their faces. The brow, the eye, and the mouth of Halifax indicated a powerful intellect and an exquisite sense of the ludicrous; but the expression was that of a sceptic, of a voluptuary, of a man not likely to venture his all on a single hazard, or to be a martyr in any

Danby.

---

* Burnet, i., 764; Letter in cipher to William, dated June 18, 1688, in Dalrymple.
† Ibid.; Letter in cipher to William, dated June 18, 1688.

cause. To those who are acquainted with his countenance it will not seem wonderful that the writer in whom he most delighted was Montaigne.* Danby was a skeleton; and his meagre and wrinkled, though handsome and noble, face strongly expressed both the keenness of his parts and the restlessness of his ambition. Already he had once risen from obscurity to the height of power. He had then fallen headlong from his elevation. His life had been in danger. He had passed years in a prison. He was now free: but this did not content him; he wished to be again great. Attached as he was to the Anglican Church, hostile as he was to the French ascendency, he could not hope to be great in a court swarming with Jesuits and obsequious to the House of Bourbon. But, if he bore a chief part in a revolution which should confound all the schemes of the Papists, which should put an end to the long vassalage of England, and which should transfer the regal power to an illustrious pair whom he had united, he might emerge from his eclipse with new splendor. The Whigs, whose animosity had nine years before driven him from office, would, on his auspicious reappearance, join their acclamations to the acclamations of his old friends the Cavaliers. Already there had been a complete reconciliation between him and one of the most distinguished of those who had formerly been managers of his impeachment, the Earl of Devonshire. The two noblemen had met at a village in the Peak, and had exchanged assurances of good-will. Devonshire had frankly owned that the Whigs had been guilty of a great injustice, and had declared that they were now convinced of their error. Danby, on his side, had also recantations to make. He had once held, or pretended to hold, the doctrine of passive obedience in the largest sense. Under his administration, and with his sanction, a law had been proposed which, if it had been passed, would have excluded from Parliament and office all who refused to declare on oath that they thought resistance in every case unlawful. But his vig-

* As to Montaigne, see Halifax's Letter to Cotton. I am not sure that the head of Halifax in Westminster Abbey does not give a more lively notion of him than any painting or engraving that I have seen.

orous understanding, now thoroughly awakened by anxiety for the public interests and for his own, was no longer to be duped, if indeed it ever had been duped, by such childish fallacies. He at once gave in his own adhesion to the conspiracy. He then exerted himself to obtain the concurrence of Compton, the suspended Bishop of London, and succeeded without difficulty. No prelate had been so insolently and unjustly treated by the government as Compton; nor had any prelate so much to expect from a revolution: for he had directed the education of the Princess of Orange, and was supposed to possess a large share of her confidence. He had, like his brethren, strongly maintained, as long as he was not oppressed, that it was a crime to resist oppression; but, since he had stood before the High Commission, a new light had broken in upon his mind.*

Bishop Compton.

Both Danby and Compton were desirous to secure the assistance of Nottingham. The whole plan was opened to him; and he approved of it. But in a few days he began to be unquiet. His mind was not sufficiently powerful to emancipate itself from the prejudices of education. He went about from divine to divine, proposing in general terms hypothetical cases of tyranny, and inquiring whether in such cases resistance would be lawful. The answers which he obtained increased his distress. He at length told his accomplices that he could go no farther with them. If they thought him capable of betraying them, they might stab him; and he should hardly blame them; for, by drawing back after going so far, he had given them a kind of right over his life. They had, however, he assured them, nothing to fear from him: he would keep their secret: he could not help wishing them success; but his conscience would not suffer him to take an active part in a rebellion. They heard his confession with suspicion and disdain. Sidney, whose notions of a conscientious scruple were extremely vague, informed the Prince that Nottingham had taken fright. It is due to Nottingham, how-

Nottingham.

---

* See Danby's Introduction to the papers which he published in 1710; Burnet, i., 764.

ever, to say that the general tenor of his life justifies us in believing his conduct on this occasion to have been perfectly honest, though most unwise and irresolute.*

The agents of the Prince had more complete success with Lord Lumley, who knew himself to be, in spite of the emi-
<small>Lumley.</small> nent service which he had performed at the time of the Western insurrection, abhorred at Whitehall, not only as a heretic but as a renegade, and who was therefore more eager than most of those who had been born Protestants to take arms in defence of Protestantism.†

During June the meetings of those who were in the secret were frequent. At length, on the last day of the month, the
<small>Invitation to William despatched.</small> day on which the Bishops were pronounced not guilty, the decisive step was taken. A formal invitation, transcribed by Sidney, but drawn up by some person better skilled than Sidney in the art of composition, was despatched to the Hague. In this paper William was assured that nineteen-twentieths of the English people were desirous of a change, and would willingly join to effect it, if only they could obtain the help of such a force from abroad as might secure those who should rise in arms from the danger of being dispersed and slaughtered before they could form themselves into anything like military order. If His Highness would appear in the island at the head of some troops, tens of thousands would hasten to his standard. He would soon find himself at the head of a force greatly superior to the whole regular army of England. Nor could that army be implicitly depended on by the government. The officers were discontented; and the common soldiers shared that aversion to Popery which was general in the class from which they were taken. In the navy Protestant feeling was still stronger. It was important to take some decisive step while things were in this state. The enterprise would be far more arduous if it were deferred till the King, by remodelling boroughs and regiments, had procured a Parliament and

---

* Burnet, i., 764; Sidney to the Prince of Orange, June 30, 1688, in Dalrymple.
† Burnet, i., 763; Lumley to William, May 31, 1688, in Dalrymple.

an army on which he could rely. The conspirators, therefore, implored the Prince to come among them with as little delay as possible. They pledged their honor that they would join him; and they undertook to secure the co-operation of as large a number of persons as could safely be trusted with so momentous and perilous a secret. On one point they thought it their duty to remonstrate with His Highness. He had not taken advantage of the opinion which the great body of the English people had formed touching the late birth. He had, on the contrary, sent congratulations to Whitehall, and had thus seemed to acknowledge that the child who was called Prince of Wales was rightful heir of the throne. This was a grave error, and had damped the zeal of many. Not one person in a thousand doubted that the boy was supposititious; and the Prince would be wanting to his own interests if the suspicious circumstances which had attended the Queen's confinement were not put prominently forward among his reasons for taking arms.*

This paper was signed in cipher by the seven chiefs of the conspiracy—Shrewsbury, Devonshire, Danby, Lumley, Compton, Russell, and Sidney. Herbert undertook to be their messenger. His errand was one of no ordinary peril. He assumed the garb of a common sailor, and in this disguise reached the Dutch coast in safety, on the Friday after the trial of the Bishops. He instantly hastened to the Prince. Bentinck and Van Dykvelt were summoned, and several days were passed in deliberation. The first result of this deliberation was that the prayer for the Prince of Wales ceased to be read in the Princess's chapel.†

From his wife William had no opposition to apprehend. Her understanding had been completely subjugated by his; and, what is more extraordinary, he had won her entire affection. He was to her in the place of the parents whom she had lost by death and by estrangement, of the children who had been denied to her prayers, and of the

<small>Conduct of Mary.</small>

---

* See the invitation at length in Dalrymple.
† Sidney's Letter to William, June 30, 1688; Avaux Neg., July $\frac{10}{20}$, $\frac{12}{22}$.

country from which she was banished. His empire over her heart was divided only with her God. To her father she had probably never been attached: she had quitted him young: many years had elapsed since she had seen him; and no part of his conduct to her, since her marriage, had indicated tenderness on his part, or had been calculated to call forth tenderness on hers. He had done all in his power to disturb her domestic happiness, and had established a system of spying, eavesdropping, and tale-bearing under her roof. He had a far greater revenue than any of his predecessors had ever possessed, and allowed to her younger sister thirty or forty thousand pounds a year:* but the heiress presumptive of his throne had never received from him the smallest pecuniary assistance, and was scarcely able to make that appearance which became her high rank among European princesses. She had ventured to intercede with him on behalf of her old friend and preceptor, Compton, who, for refusing to commit an act of flagitious injustice, had been suspended from his episcopal functions; but she had been ungraciously repulsed.† From the day on which it had become clear that she and her husband were determined not to be parties to the subversion of the English constitution, one chief object of the politics of James had been to injure them both. He had recalled the British regiments from Holland. He had conspired with Tyrconnel and with France against Mary's rights, and had made arrangements for depriving her of one at least of the three crowns to which, at his death, she would have been entitled. It was believed by the great body of his people, and by many persons high in rank and distinguished by abilities, that he had introduced a supposititious Prince of Wales into the royal family in order to deprive her of a magnificent inheritance; and there is no reason to doubt that she partook of the prevailing suspicion. That she should love such a father was impossible. Her religious principles, indeed, were so strict that she would probably have tried to perform what she considered as her duty, even to a father whom she did not

---

* Bonrepaux, July $\frac{18}{28}$, 1687. † Birch's Extracts, in the British Museum.

love. On the present occasion, however, she judged that the claim of James to her obedience ought to yield to a claim more sacred. And indeed all divines and publicists agree in this, that, when the daughter of a prince of one country is married to a prince of another country, she is bound to forget her own people and her father's house, and, in the event of a rupture between her husband and her parents, to side with her husband. This is the undoubted rule even when the husband is in the wrong; and to Mary the enterprise which William meditated appeared not only just, but holy.

But, though she carefully abstained from doing or saying anything that could add to his difficulties, those difficulties were serious indeed. They were in truth but imperfectly understood even by some of those who invited him over, and have been but imperfectly described by some of those who have written the history of his expedition.

Difficulties of William's enterprise.

The obstacles which he might expect to encounter on English ground, though the least formidable of the obstacles which stood in the way of his design, were yet serious. He felt that it would be madness in him to imitate the example of Monmouth, to cross the sea with a few British adventurers, and to trust to a general rising of the population. It was necessary, and it was pronounced necessary by all those who invited him over, that he should carry an army with him. Yet who could answer for the effect which the appearance of such an army might produce? The government was indeed justly odious. But would the English people, altogether unaccustomed to the interference of Continental powers in English disputes, be inclined to look with favor on a deliverer who was surrounded by foreign soldiers? If any part of the royal forces resolutely withstood the invaders, would not that part soon have on its side the patriotic sympathy of millions? A defeat would be fatal to the whole undertaking. A bloody victory gained in the heart of the island by the mercenaries of the States-general over the Coldstream Guards and the Buffs would be almost as great a calamity as a defeat. Such a victory would be the most cruel wound ever inflicted on the national pride of one of the proudest of nations. The crown so won would never be worn in peace or security. The hatred with which the High Commission and the Jesuits were regarded would give place to the more intense hatred which would be inspired by the alien conquerors; and many, who had hitherto contemplated the power of France with dread and loathing, would say that, if a foreign yoke must be borne, there was less ignominy in submitting to France than in submitting to Holland.

These considerations might well have made William uneasy, even if all the military means of the United Provinces had been at his absolute disposal. But in truth it seemed very doubtful whether he would be able to obtain the assistance of a single battalion. Of all the difficulties with which he had to struggle, the greatest, though little noticed by English historians, arose from the constitution of the Batavian republic. No great society has ever existed during a long course of years under a polity so inconvenient. The States-general could not make war or peace, could not conclude any alliance or levy any tax, without the consent of the States of every province. The States of a province could not give such consent without the consent of every municipality which had a share in the representation. Every municipality was, in some sense, a sovereign state, and, as such, claimed the right of communicating directly with foreign ambassadors, and of concerting with them the means of defeating schemes on which other municipalities were intent. In some town councils the party, which had, during several generations, regarded the influence of the Stadtholders with jealousy, had great power. At the head of this party were the magistrates of the noble city of Amsterdam, which was then at the height of prosperity. They had, ever since the peace of Nimeguen, kept up a friendly correspondence with Lewis through the instrumentality of his able and active envoy, the Count of Avaux. Propositions brought forward by the Stadtholder as indispensable to the security of the commonwealth, sanctioned by all the provinces except Holland, and sanctioned by seventeen of the eighteen town councils of Holland, had repeatedly been negatived by the single voice of Amsterdam. The only constitutional remedy in such cases was that deputies from the cities which were agreed should pay a visit to the city which dissented, for the purpose of expostulation. The number of deputies was unlimited: they might continue to expostulate as long as they thought fit; and meanwhile all their expenses were defrayed by the obstinate community which refused to yield to their arguments. This absurd mode of coercion had once been tried with success on the little town of Gorkum, but was not likely to produce much effect on the mighty and opulent Amsterdam, renowned throughout the world for its haven bristling with innumerable masts, its canals bordered by stately mansions, its gorgeous hall of state, walled, roofed, and floored with polished marble, its warehouses filled with the most costly productions of Ceylon and Surinam, and its Exchange resounding with the endless hubbub of all the languages spoken by civilized men.*

The disputes between the majority which supported the Stadtholder and the minority headed by the magistrates of Amsterdam had repeatedly run so high that bloodshed had seemed to be inevitable. On one occasion the Prince had attempted to bring the refractory deputies to punishment as traitors. On another occasion the gates of Amsterdam had been barred against him, and troops had been raised to defend the privileges of the municipal council. That the rulers of this great city would ever consent to an expedition offensive in the highest degree to Lewis whom they courted, and likely to aggrandize the House of Orange which they abhorred, was not likely. Yet, without their consent, such an expedition could not legally be undertaken. To quell their opposition by main force was a course from which, in different circumstances, the resolute and daring Stadtholder would not have shrunk. But at that moment it was most important that he should carefully avoid every act which could be represented as tyrannical. He could not venture to violate the fundamental laws of Holland at the very moment at which

---

* Avaux Neg., $\frac{\text{Oct. 29,}}{\text{Nov. 8,}}$ 1683.

he was drawing the sword against his father-in-law for violating the fundamental laws of England. The violent subversion of one free constitution would have been a strange prelude to the violent restoration of another.*

There was yet another difficulty which has been too little noticed by English writers, but which was never for a moment absent from William's mind. In the expedition which he meditated he could succeed only by appealing to the Protestant feeling of England, and by stimulating that feeling till it became, for a time, the dominant and almost the exclusive sentiment of the nation. This would indeed have been a very simple course, had the end of all his politics been to effect a revolution in our island and to reign there. But he had in view an ulterior end which could be obtained only by the help of princes sincerely attached to the Church of Rome. He was desirous to unite the Empire, the Catholic King, and the Holy See, with England and Holland, in a league against the French ascendency. It was therefore necessary that, while striking the greatest blow ever struck in defence of Protestantism, he should yet contrive not to lose the goodwill of governments which regarded Protestantism as a deadly heresy.

Such were the complicated difficulties of this great undertaking. Continental statesmen saw a part of those difficulties, British statesmen another part. One capacious and powerful mind alone took them all in at one view, and determined to surmount them all. It was no easy thing to subvert the English government by means of a foreign army without galling the national pride of Englishmen. It was no easy thing to obtain from that Batavian faction which regarded France with partiality, and the House of Orange with aversion, a decision in favor of an expedition which would confound all the schemes of France, and raise the House of Orange to the height of greatness. It was no easy thing to lead enthusiastic Protestants on a crusade against Popery

---

* As to the relation in which the Stadtholder and the City of Amsterdam stood toward each other, see Avaux, *passim*.

II.—25

with the good wishes of almost all Popish governments and of the Pope himself. Yet all these things William effected. All his objects, even those which appeared most incompatible with each other, he attained completely and at once. The whole history of ancient and of modern times records no other such triumph of statesmanship.

The task would indeed have been too arduous even for such a statesman as the Prince of Orange, had not his chief adversaries been at this time smitten with an infatuation such as by many men not prone to superstition was ascribed to the special judgment of God. Not only was the King of England, as he had ever been, stupid and perverse: but even the counsel of the politic King of France was turned into foolishness. Whatever wisdom and energy could do William did. Those obstacles which no wisdom or energy could have overcome, his enemies themselves studiously removed.

On the great day on which the Bishops were acquitted, and on which the invitation was despatched to the Hague, James Conduct of James after the trial of the Bishops. returned from Hounslow to Westminster in a gloomy and unquiet mood. He made an effort that afternoon to appear cheerful:* but the bonfires, the rockets, and above all the waxen Popes who were blazing in every quarter of London, were not likely to soothe him. Those who saw him on the morrow could easily read in his face and demeanor the violent emotions which disturbed his mind.† During some days he appeared so unwilling to talk about the trial that even Barillon could not venture to introduce the subject.‡

Soon it began to be clear that defeat and mortification had only hardened the King's heart. Almost the first words which he uttered when he learned that the objects of his revenge had escaped him were, "So much the worse for them." In a few days these words, which he, according to his fashion, repeated many times, were fully explained. He blamed himself, not for having prosecuted the Bishops, but for having prosecuted them before a tribunal where questions of fact

---

* Adda, July $\frac{6}{16}$, 1688.   † Reresby's Memoirs.   ‡ Barillon, July $\frac{2}{12}$, 1688.

were decided by juries, and where established principles of law could not be utterly disregarded even by the most servile Judges. This error he determined to repair. Not only the seven prelates who had signed the petition, but the whole Anglican clergy, should have reason to curse the day on which they had triumphed over their Sovereign. Within a fortnight after the trial an order was made, enjoining all Chancellors of dioceses and all Archdeacons to make a strict inquisition throughout their respective jurisdictions, and to report to the High Commission, within five weeks, the names of all such rectors, vicars, and curates as had omitted to read the Declaration.* The King anticipated with delight the terror with which the offenders would learn that they were to be cited before a court which would give them no quarter.† The number of culprits was little, if at all, short of ten thousand: and, after what had passed at Magdalene College, every one of them might reasonably expect to be interdicted from all his spiritual functions, ejected from his benefice, declared incapable of holding any other preferment, and charged with the costs of the proceedings which had reduced him to beggary.

Such was the persecution with which James, smarting from his great defeat in Westminster Hall, resolved to harass the clergy. Meanwhile he tried to show the lawyers, by a prompt and large distribution of rewards and punishments, that strenuous and unblushing servility, even when least successful, was a sure title to his favor, and that whoever, after years of obsequiousness, ventured to deviate but for one moment into courage and honesty was guilty of an unpardonable offence. The violence and audacity which the apostate Williams had exhibited throughout the trial of the Bishops had made him hateful to the whole nation.‡ He was recompensed with a baronetcy. Holloway

Dismissions and promotions.

---

* London Gazette of July 16, 1688. The order bears date July 12.
† Barillon's own phrase, July $\frac{6}{16}$, 1688.
‡ In one of the numerous ballads of that time are the following lines:
"Both our Britons are fooled,
Who the laws overruled,
And next parliament each will be plaguily schooled."
The two Britons are Jeffreys and Williams, who were both natives of Wales.

and Powell had raised their character by declaring that, in their judgment, the petition was no libel. They were dismissed from their situations.* The fate of Wright seems to have been, during some time, in suspense. He had indeed summed up against the Bishops: but he had suffered their counsel to question the dispensing power. He had pronounced the petition a libel: but he had carefully abstained from pronouncing the Declaration legal; and, through the whole proceeding, his tone had been that of a man who remembered that a day of reckoning might come. He had indeed strong claims to indulgence: for it was hardly to be expected that any human impudence would hold out without flagging through such a task, in the presence of such a bar and of such an auditory. The members of the Jesuitical cabal, however, blamed his want of spirit: the Chancellor pronounced him a beast; and it was generally believed that a new Chief-justice would be appointed.† But no change was made. It would indeed have been no easy matter to supply Wright's place. The many lawyers who were far superior to him in parts and learning were, with scarcely an exception, hostile to the designs of the government: and the very few lawyers who surpassed him in turpitude and effrontery were, with scarcely an exception, to be found only in the lowest ranks of the profession, and would have been incompetent to conduct the ordinary business of the Court of King's Bench. Williams, it is true, united all the qualities which James required in a magistrate. But the services of Williams were needed at the bar; and, had he been removed thence, the crown would have been left without the help of any advocate even of the third rate.

Nothing had amazed or mortified the King more than the enthusiasm which the Dissenters had shown in the cause of the Bishops. Penn, who, though he had himself sacrificed wealth and honors to his conscientious scruples, seems to have imagined that nobody but himself had a conscience, imputed

---

* London Gazette, July 9, 1688.
† Ellis Correspondence, July 10, 1688; Clarendon's Diary, Aug. 3, 1688.

the discontent of the Puritans to envy and dissatisfied ambition. They had not had their share of the benefits promised by the Declaration of Indulgence: none of them had been admitted to any high and honorable post; and therefore it was not strange that they were jealous of the Roman Catholics. Accordingly, within a week after the great verdict had been pronounced in Westminster Hall, Silas Titus, a noted Presbyterian, a vehement Exclusionist, and a manager of Stafford's impeachment, was invited to occupy a seat in the Privy Council. He was one of the persons on whom the opposition had most confidently reckoned. But the honor now offered to him, and the hope of obtaining a large sum due to him from the crown, overcame his virtue, and, to the great disgust of all classes of Protestants, he was sworn in.*

<small>Proceedings of the High Commission. Sprat resigns his seat.</small>
The vindictive designs of the King against the Church were not accomplished. Almost all the Archdeacons and diocesan Chancellors refused to furnish the information which was required. The day on which it had been intended that the whole body of the priesthood should be summoned to answer for the crime of disobedience arrived. The High Commission met. It appeared that scarcely one ecclesiastical officer had sent up a return. At the same time a paper of grave import was delivered to the board. It came from Sprat, Bishop of Rochester. During two years, supported by the hope of an archbishopric, he had been content to bear the reproach of persecuting that Church which he was bound by every obligation of conscience and honor to defend. But his hope had been disappointed. He saw that, unless he abjured his religion, he had no chance of sitting on the metropolitan throne of York. He was too good-natured to find any pleasure in tyranny, and too discerning not to see the signs of the coming retribution. He therefore determined to resign his odious functions; and he communicated his determination to his colleagues in a letter written, like all his prose compositions, with great propri-

---

* London Gazette, July 9, 1688; Adda, July $\frac{13}{23}$; Evelyn's Diary, July 12; Johnstone, Dec. $\frac{8}{18}$, 1687, Feb. $\frac{6}{16}$, 1688.

ety and dignity of style. It was impossible, he said, that he could any longer continue to be a member of the Commission. He had himself, in obedience to the royal command, read the Declaration: but he could not presume to condemn thousands of pious and loyal divines who had taken a different view of their duty; and, since it was resolved to punish them for acting according to their conscience, he must declare that he would rather suffer with them than be accessary to their sufferings.

The Commissioners read and stood aghast. The very faults of their colleague, the known laxity of his principles, the known meanness of his spirit, made his defection peculiarly alarming. A government must be indeed in danger when men like Sprat address it in the language of Hampden. The tribunal, lately so insolent, became on a sudden strangely tame. The ecclesiastical functionaries who had defied its authority were not even reprimanded. It was not thought safe to hint any suspicion that their disobedience had been intentional. They were merely enjoined to have their reports ready in four months. The Commission then broke up in confusion. It had received a death-blow.*

While the High Commission shrank from a conflict with the Church, the Church, conscious of its strength, and animated by a new enthusiasm, invited, by a series of defiances, the attack of the High Commission. Soon after the acquittal of the Bishops, the venerable Ormond, the most illustrious of the Cavaliers of the great civil war, sank under his infirmities. The intelligence of his death was conveyed with speed to Oxford. Instantly the University, of which he had long been Chancellor, met to name a successor. One party was for the eloquent and accomplished Halifax, another for the grave and orthodox Nottingham. Some mentioned the Earl of Abingdon, who resided near them, and had recently been turned out of the lieutenancy of the county for refusing to join with the King against the established religion. But the majority, consisting of a hundred and eighty graduates, voted for the young Duke

<small>Discontent of the clergy.</small>

<small>Transactions at Oxford.</small>

---

* Sprat's Letters to the Earl of Dorset; London Gazette, Aug. 23, 1688.

of Ormond, grandson of their late head, and son of the gallant Ossory. The speed with which they came to this resolution was caused by their apprehension that, if there were a delay even of a day, the King would attempt to force on them some chief who would betray their rights. The apprehension was reasonable: for, only two hours after they had separated, came a mandate from Whitehall requiring them to choose Jeffreys. Happily the election of young Ormond was already complete and irrevocable.* A few weeks later the infamous Timothy Hall, who had distinguished himself among the clergy of London by reading the Declaration, was rewarded with the Bishopric of Oxford, which had been vacant since the death of the not less infamous Parker. Hall came down to his see: but the Canons of his Cathedral refused to attend his installation: the University refused to create him a doctor: not a single one of the academic youth applied to him for holy orders: no cap was touched to him; and, in his palace, he found himself alone.†

Soon afterward a living which was in the gift of Magdalene College, Oxford, became vacant. Hough and his ejected brethren assembled and presented a clerk: and the Bishop of Gloucester, in whose diocese the living lay, instituted their presentee without hesitation.‡

The gentry were not less refractory than the clergy. The assizes of that summer wore all over the country an aspect never before known. The Judges, before they set out on their circuits, had been summoned into the King's presence, and had been directed by him to impress on the grand jurors and magistrates, throughout the kingdom, the duty of electing such members of Parliament as would support his policy. They obeyed his commands, harangued vehemently against the clergy, reviled the seven Bishops, called the memorable petition a factious libel, criticised with great asperity Sancroft's style, which was indeed open to crit-

Discontent of the gentry.

---

* London Gazette, July 26, 1688; Adda, $\frac{\text{July 27}}{\text{Aug. 6}}$; News-letter in the Mackintosh Collection, July 25; Ellis Correspondence, July 28, 31; Wood's Fasti Oxonienses.
† Wood's Athenæ Oxonienses; Luttrell's Diary, Aug. 23, 1688.
‡ Ronquillo, Sept. $\frac{17}{27}$, 1688; Luttrell's Diary, Sept. 6.

icism, and pronounced that His Grace ought to be whipped by Doctor Busby for writing bad English. But the only effect of these indecent declamations was to increase the public discontent. All the marks of respect which had usually been shown to the judicial office and to the royal commission were withdrawn. The old custom was that men of good birth and estate should ride in the train of the Sheriff when he escorted the Judges to the county-town: but such a procession could now with difficulty be formed in any part of the kingdom. The successors of Powell and Holloway, in particular, were treated with marked indignity. The Oxford circuit had been allotted to them; and they had expected to be greeted in every shire by a cavalcade of the loyal gentry. But as they approached Wallingford, where they were to open their commission for Berkshire, the Sheriff alone came forth to meet them. As they approached Oxford, the eminently loyal capital of an eminently loyal province, they were again welcomed by the Sheriff alone.*

The army was scarcely less disaffected than the clergy or the gentry. The garrison of the Tower had drunk the health of the imprisoned Bishops. The Foot Guards stationed at Lambeth had, with every mark of reverence, welcomed the Primate back to his palace. Nowhere had the news of the acquittal been received with more clamorous delight than at Hounslow Heath. In truth, the great force which the King had assembled for the purpose of overawing his mutinous capital had become more mutinous than the capital itself, and was more dreaded by the court than by the citizens. Early in August, therefore, the camp was broken up, and the troops were sent to quarters in different parts of the country.†

<small>Discontent of the army.</small>

James flattered himself that it would be easier to deal with separate battalions than with many thousands of men collected in one mass. The first experiment was tried on Lord Lichfield's regiment of infantry, now called the Twelfth of the

* Ellis Correspondence, August 4, 7, 1688; Bishop Sprat's relation of the Conference of November 6, 1688.
† Luttrell's Diary, August 8, 1688.

Line. That regiment was probably selected because it had been raised, at the time of the Western insurrection, in Staffordshire, a province where the Roman Catholics were more numerous and powerful than in almost any other part of England. The men were drawn up in the King's presence. Their major informed them that His Majesty wished them to subscribe an engagement, binding them to assist in carrying into effect his intentions concerning the test, and that all who did not choose to comply must quit the service on the spot. To the King's great astonishment, whole ranks instantly laid down their pikes and muskets. Only two officers and a few privates, all Roman Catholics, obeyed his command. He remained silent for a short time. Then he bade the men take up their arms. "Another time," he said, with a gloomy look, "I shall not do you the honor to consult you."*

It was plain that, if he determined to persist in his designs, he must remodel his army. Yet materials for that purpose he could not find in our island. The members of his Church, even in the districts where they were most numerous, were a small minority of the people. Hatred of Popery had spread through all classes of his Protestant subjects, and had become the ruling passion even of ploughmen and artisans. But there was another part of his dominions where a very different spirit animated the great body of the population. There was no limit to the number of Roman Catholic soldiers whom the good pay and quarters of England would attract across St. George's Channel. Tyrconnel had been, during some time, employed in forming out of the peasantry of his country a military force on which his master might depend. Already Papists, of Celtic blood and speech, composed almost the whole army of Ireland. Barillon earnestly and repeatedly advised James to bring over that army for the purpose of coercing the English.†

James wavered. He wished to be surrounded by troops

---

* This is told us by three writers who could well remember that time—Kennet, Eachard, and Oldmixon. See also the Caveat against the Whigs.

† Barillon, $\frac{\text{Aug. 23,}}{\text{Sept. 2,}}$ 1688; September $\frac{3}{13}, \frac{6}{16}, \frac{8}{18}$.

on whom he could rely: but he dreaded the explosion of national feeling which the appearance of a great Irish force on English ground must produce. At last, as usually happens when a weak man tries to avoid opposite inconveniences, he took a course which united them all. He brought over Irishmen, not indeed enough to hold down the single city of London, or the single county of York, but more than enough to excite the alarm and rage of the whole kingdom, from Northumberland to Cornwall. Battalion after battalion, raised and trained by Tyrconnel, landed on the western coast and moved toward the capital; and Irish recruits were imported in considerable numbers, to fill up vacancies in the English regiments.*

Irish troops brought over.

Public indignation.

Of the many errors which James committed, none was more fatal than this. Already he had alienated the hearts of his people by violating their laws, confiscating their estates, and persecuting their religion. Of those who had once been most zealous for monarchy, he had already made many rebels in heart. Yet he might still, with some chance of success, have appealed to the patriotic spirit of his subjects against an invader. For they were a race insular in temper as well as in geographical position. Their national antipathies were, indeed, in that age, unreasonably and unamiably strong. Never had the English been accustomed to the control or interference of any stranger. The appearance of a foreign army on their soil might impel them to rally even round a King whom they had no reason to love. William might perhaps have been unable to overcome this difficulty: but James removed it. Not even the arrival of a brigade of Lewis's musketeers would have excited such resentment and shame as our ancestors felt when they saw armed columns of Papists, just arrived from Dublin, moving in military pomp along the highroads. No man of English blood then regarded the aboriginal Irish as his countrymen. They did not belong to our branch of the great human family. They were distinguished from us by more than one moral and intellectual peculiarity,

---

* Luttrell's Diary, Aug. 27, 1688.

which the difference of situation and of education, great as that difference was, did not seem altogether to explain. They had an aspect of their own, a mother-tongue of their own. When they talked English their pronunciation was ludicrous; and their phraseology was grotesque, as is always the phraseology of those who think in one language and express their thoughts in another. They were therefore foreigners; and of all foreigners they were the most hated and despised: the most hated, for they had, during five centuries, always been our enemies; the most despised, for they were our vanquished, enslaved, and despoiled enemies. The Englishman felt proud when he compared his own fields with the desolate bogs whence the Rapparees issued forth to rob and murder, and his own dwelling with the hovels where the peasants and the hogs of the Shannon wallowed in filth together. He was a member of a society, far inferior, indeed, in wealth and civilization, to the society in which we live, but still one of the wealthiest and most highly civilized societies that the world had then seen: the Irish were almost as rude as the savages of Labrador. He was a freeman: the Irish were the hereditary serfs of his race. He worshipped God after a pure and rational fashion: the Irish were sunk in idolatry and superstition. He knew that great numbers of Irish had repeatedly fled before a small English force, and that the whole Irish population had been held down by a small English colony; and he very complacently inferred that he was naturally a being of a higher order than the Irishman: for it is thus that a dominant race always explains its ascendency and excuses its tyranny. That in vivacity, humor, and eloquence the Irish stand high among the nations of the world is now universally acknowledged. That, when well disciplined, they are excellent soldiers has been proved on a hundred fields of battle. Yet it is certain that, in the seventeenth century, they were generally despised in our island as both a stupid and a cowardly people. And these were the men who were to hold England down by main force while her civil and ecclesiastical constitution was destroyed. The blood of the whole nation boiled at the thought. To be conquered by Frenchmen or by Spaniards would have seemed comparatively a tolerable fate. With Frenchmen and Spaniards we had been accustomed to treat on equal terms. We had sometimes envied their prosperity, sometimes dreaded their power, sometimes congratulated ourselves on their friendship. In spite of our unsocial pride, we admitted that they were great nations, and that they could boast of men eminent in the arts of war and peace. But to be subjugated by an inferior caste was a degradation beyond all other degradation. The English felt as the white inhabitants of Charleston and New Orleans would feel if those towns were occupied by negro garrisons. The real facts would have been sufficient to excite uneasiness and indignation: but the real facts were lost amidst a crowd of wild rumors which flew without ceasing from coffee-house to coffee-house and from ale-bench to ale-bench, and became more wonderful and terrible at every stage of the progress. The number of the Irish troops who had landed on our shores might justly excite serious apprehensions as to the King's ulterior designs: but it was magnified tenfold by the public apprehensions. It may well be supposed that the rude kern of Connaught, placed, with arms in his hands, among a foreign people whom he hated, and by whom he was hated in turn, was guilty of some excesses. These excesses were exaggerated by report; and, in addition to the outrages which the stranger had really committed, all the offences of his English comrades were set down to his account. From every corner of the kingdom a cry arose against the foreign barbarians who forced themselves into private houses, seized horses and wagons, extorted money, and insulted women. These men, it was said, were the sons of those who, forty-seven years before, had massacred Protestants by tens of thousands. The history of the rebellion of 1641, a history which, even when soberly related, might well move pity and horror, and which had been frightfully distorted by national and religious antipathies, was now the favorite topic of conversation. Hideous stories of houses burned with all the inmates, of women and young children butchered, of near relations compelled by torture to be the murderers of each other, of corpses outraged and mutilated, were told and heard with full belief and intense interest. Then it was added that the dastardly savages, who had by surprise committed all these cruelties on an unsuspecting and defenceless colony, had, as soon as Oliver came among them on his great mission of vengeance, flung down their arms in panic terror, and sunk, without trying the chances of a single pitched field, into that slavery which was their fit portion. Many signs indicated that another great spoliation and slaughter of the Saxon settlers was meditated by the Lord-lieutenant. Already thousands of Protestant colonists, flying from the injustice and insolence of Tyrconnel, had raised the indignation of the mother country by describing all that they had suffered, and all that they had, with too much reason, feared. How much the public mind had been excited by the complaints of these fugitives had recently been shown in a manner not to be mistaken. Tyrconnel had transmitted for the royal approbation the heads of a bill repealing the law by which half the soil of Ireland was held, and he had sent to Westminster, as his agents, two of his Roman Catholic countrymen who had lately been raised to high judicial office: Nugent, Chief-justice of the Irish Court of King's Bench, a personification of all the vices and weaknesses which the English then imagined to be characteristic of the Popish Celt, and Rice, a Baron of the Irish Exchequer, who, in abilities and attainments, was perhaps the foremost man of his race and religion. The object of the mission was well known: and the two Judges could not venture to show themselves in the streets. If ever they were recognized, the rabble shouted, "Room for the Irish Ambassadors;" and their coach was escorted with mock solemnity by a train of ushers and harbingers bearing sticks with potatoes stuck on the points.*

So strong and general, indeed, was at that time the aversion of the English to the Irish, that the most distinguished Roman Catholics partook of it. Powis and Bellasyse expressed, in coarse and acrimonious language, even at the

---

* King's State of the Protestants of Ireland; Secret Consults of the Romish Party in Ireland.

Council-board, their antipathy to the aliens.* Among English Protestants that antipathy was far stronger; and perhaps it was strongest in the army. Neither officers nor soldiers were disposed to bear patiently the preference shown by their master to a foreign and a subject race. The Duke of Berwick, who was Colonel of the Eighth Regiment of the Line, then quartered at Portsmouth, gave orders that thirty men just arrived from Ireland should be enlisted. The English soldiers declared that they would not serve with these intruders. John Beaumont, the Lieutenant-colonel, in his own name and in the name of five of the Captains, protested to the Duke's face against this insult to the English army and nation. "We raised the regiment," he said, "at our own charges to defend His Majesty's crown in a time of danger. We had then no difficulty in procuring hundreds of English recruits. We can easily keep every company up to its full complement without admitting Irishmen. We therefore do not think it consistent with our honor to have these strangers forced on us; and we beg that we may either be permitted to command men of our own nation or to lay down our commissions." Berwick sent to Windsor for directions. The King, greatly exasperated, instantly despatched a troop of horse to Portsmouth with orders to bring the six refractory officers before him. A council of war sat on them. They refused to make any submission; and they were sentenced to be cashiered, the highest punishment which a court-martial was then competent to inflict. The whole nation applauded the disgraced officers; and the prevailing sentiment was stimulated by an unfounded rumor that, while under arrest, they had been treated with cruelty.†

---

* Secret Consults of the Romish Party in Ireland.

† History of the Desertion, 1689; compare the first and second editions; Barillon, Sept. $\frac{8}{18}$, 1688; Van Citters of the same date; Life of James the Second, ii., 168. The compiler of the last mentioned work says that Churchill moved the court to sentence the six officers to death. This story does not appear to have been taken from the King's papers. I therefore regard it as one of the thousand fictions invented at Saint Germains for the purpose of blackening a character which was black enough without such daubing. That Churchill may have affected great indignation on this occasion, in order to hide the treason which he meditated,

Public feeling did not then manifest itself by those signs with which we are familiar—by large meetings, and by vehement harangues. Nevertheless it found a vent. Thomas Wharton, who, in the last Parliament, had represented Buckinghamshire, and who had long been conspicuous both as a libertine and as a Whig, had written a satirical ballad on the administration of Tyrconnel. In this little poem an Irishman congratulates a brother Irishman, in a barbarous jargon, on the approaching triumph of Popery and of the Milesian race. The Protestant heir will be excluded. The Protestant officers will be broken. The Great Charter and the praters who appealed to it will be hanged in one rope. The good Talbot will shower commissions on his countrymen, and will cut the throats of the English. These verses, which were in no respect above the ordinary standard of street poetry, had for burden some gibberish which was said to have been used as a watchword by the insurgents of Ulster in 1641. The verses and the tune caught the fancy of the nation. From one end of England to the other all classes were constantly singing this idle rhyme. It was especially the delight of the English army. More than seventy years after the Revolution, Sterne delineated, with exquisite skill, a veteran who had fought at the Boyne and at Namur. One of the characteristics of the good old soldier is his trick of whistling Lillibullero.*

Wharton afterward boasted that he had sung a King out of three kingdoms. But in truth the success of Lillibullero was the effect, and not the cause, of that excited state of public feeling which produced the Revolution.

While James was thus raising against himself all those national feelings which, but for his own folly, might have saved

---

is highly probable. But it is impossible to believe that a man of his sense would have urged the members of a council of war to inflict a punishment which was notoriously beyond their competence.

* The song of Lillibullero is among the State Poems. In Percy's Relics the first part will be found, but not the second part, which was added after William's landing. In the Examiner, and in several pamphlets of 1712, Wharton is mentioned as the author.

his throne, Lewis was in another way exerting himself not less effectually to facilitate the enterprise which William meditated.

The party in Holland which was favorable to France was a minority, but a minority strong enough, according to the constitution of the Batavian federation, to prevent the Stadtholder from striking any great blow. To keep that minority steady was an object to which, if the court of Versailles had been wise, every other object would at that conjuncture have been postponed. Lewis, however, had during some time labored, as if of set purpose, to estrange his Dutch friends; and he at length, though not without difficulty, succeeded in forcing them to become his enemies at the precise moment at which their help would have been invaluable to him.

<small>Politics of the United Provinces.</small>

There were two subjects on which the people of the United Provinces were peculiarly sensitive, religion and trade; and both their religion and their trade the French King had assailed. The persecution of the Huguenots, and the revocation of the Edict of Nantes, had everywhere moved the grief and indignation of Protestants. But in Holland these feelings were stronger than in any other country; for many persons of Dutch birth, confiding in the repeated and solemn declarations of Lewis that the toleration granted by his grandfather should be maintained, had, for commercial purposes, settled in France, and a large proportion of the settlers had been naturalized there. Every post now brought to Holland the tidings that these persons were treated with extreme rigor on account of their religion. Dragoons, it was reported, were quartered on one. Another had been held naked before a fire till he was half roasted. All were forbidden, under the severest penalties, to celebrate the rites of their religion, or to quit the country into which they had, under false pretences, been decoyed. The partisans of the House of Orange exclaimed against the cruelty and perfidy of the tyrant. The opposition was abashed and dispirited. Even the town council of Amsterdam, though strongly attached to the French interest and to the Arminian theology,

<small>Errors of the French King.</small>

and though little inclined to find fault with Lewis or to sympathize with the Calvinists whom he persecuted, could not venture to oppose itself to the general sentiment; for in that great city there was scarcely one wealthy merchant who had not some kinsman or friend among the sufferers. Petitions numerously and respectably signed were presented to the Burgomasters, imploring them to make strong representations to Avaux. There were even suppliants who made their way into the Stadthouse, flung themselves on their knees, described with tears and sobs the lamentable condition of those whom they most loved, and besought the intercession of the magistrates. The pulpits resounded with invectives and lamentations. The press poured forth heart-rending narratives and stirring exhortations. Avaux saw the whole danger. He reported to his court that even the well-intentioned—for so he always called the enemies of the House of Orange—either partook of the public feeling or were overawed by it; and he suggested the policy of making some concession to their wishes. The answers which he received from Versailles were cold and acrimonious. Some Dutch families, indeed, which had not been naturalized in France, were permitted to return to their country. But to those natives of Holland who had obtained letters of naturalization Lewis refused all indulgence. No power on earth, he said, should interfere between him and his subjects. These people had chosen to become his subjects; and how he treated them was a matter with which no neighboring state had anything to do. The magistrates of Amsterdam naturally resented the scornful ingratitude of the potentate whom they had strenuously and unscrupulously served against the general sense of their own countrymen. Soon followed another provocation which they felt even more keenly. Lewis began to make war on their trade. He first put forth an edict prohibiting the importation of herrings into his dominions. Avaux hastened to inform his court that this step had excited great alarm and indignation, that sixty thousand persons in the United Provinces subsisted by the herring fishery, and that some strong measures of retaliation would probably be adopted by the

II.—26

States. The answer which he received was that the King was determined, not only to persist, but also to increase the duties on many of those articles in which Holland carried on a lucrative commerce with France. The consequence of these errors, errors committed in defiance of repeated warnings, and, as it should seem, in the mere wantonness of self-will, was that now, when the voice of a single powerful member of the Batavian federation might have averted an event fatal to all the politics of Lewis, no such voice was raised. The Envoy, with all his skill, vainly endeavored to rally the party by the help of which he had, during several years, held the Stadtholder in check. The arrogance and obstinacy of the master counteracted all the efforts of the servant. At length Avaux was compelled to send to Versailles the alarming tidings that no reliance could be placed on Amsterdam, so long devoted to the French cause, that some of the well-intentioned were alarmed for their religion, that others were alarmed for their trade, and that the few whose inclinations were unchanged could not venture to utter what they thought. The fervid eloquence of preachers who declaimed against the horrors of the French persecution, and the lamentations of bankrupts who ascribed their ruin to the French decrees, had wrought up the people to such a temper that no citizen could declare himself favorable to France without imminent risk of being flung into the nearest canal. Men remembered that, only fifteen years before, the most illustrious chief of the party adverse to the House of Orange had been torn to pieces by an infuriated mob in the very precinct of the palace of the States-general. A similar fate might not improbably befall those who should, at this crisis, be accused of serving the purposes of France against their native land, and against the reformed religion.*

* See the Negotiations of the Count of Avaux. It would be almost impossible for me to cite all the passages which have furnished me with materials for this part of my narrative. The most important will be found under the following dates: 1685, Sept. 20, Sept. 24, Oct. 5, Dec. 20; 1686, Jan. 3, Nov. 22; 1687, Oct. 2, Nov. 6, Nov. 19; 1688, July 29, Aug. 20. Lord Lonsdale, in his Memoirs, justly remarks that, but for the mismanagement of Lewis, the City of Amsterdam would have prevented the Revolution.

While Lewis was thus forcing his friends in Holland to become, or to pretend to become, his enemies, he was laboring with not less success to remove all the scruples which might have prevented the Roman Catholic princes of the continent from countenancing William's designs. A new quarrel had arisen between the court of Versailles and the Vatican, a quarrel in which the injustice and insolence of the French King were perhaps more offensively displayed than in any other transaction of his reign.

<small>His quarrel with the Pope concerning franchises.</small>

It had long been the rule at Rome that no officer of justice or finance could enter the dwelling inhabited by the minister who represented a Catholic state. In process of time not only the dwelling, but a large precinct round it, was held inviolable. It was a point of honor with every Ambassador to extend as widely as possible the limits of the region which was under his protection. At length half the city consisted of privileged districts, within which the Papal government had no more power than within the Louvre or the Escurial. Every asylum was thronged with contraband traders, fraudulent bankrupts, thieves, and assassins. In every asylum were collected magazines of stolen or smuggled goods. From every asylum ruffians sallied forth nightly to plunder and stab. In no town of Christendom, consequently, was law so impotent and wickedness so audacious as in the ancient capital of religion and civilization. On this subject Innocent felt as became a priest and a prince. He declared that he would receive no Ambassador who insisted on a right so destructive of order and morality. There was at first much murmuring; but his resolution was so evidently just that all governments but one speedily acquiesced. The Emperor, highest in rank among Christian monarchs, the Spanish court, distinguished among all courts by sensitiveness and pertinacity on points of etiquette, renounced the odious privilege. Lewis alone was impracticable. What other sovereigns might choose to do, he said, was nothing to him. He therefore sent a mission to Rome, escorted by a great force of cavalry and infantry. The Ambassador marched to his palace as a general marches in triumph through a conquered town. The house was strongly guarded. Round the limits of the protected district sentinels paced the rounds day and night, as on the walls of a fortress. The Pope was unmoved. "They trust," he cried, "in chariots and in horses; but we will remember the name of the Lord our God." He betook himself to his spiritual weapons, and laid the region garrisoned by the French under an interdict.*

This dispute was at the height when another dispute arose, in which the Germanic body was as deeply concerned as the Pope.

Cologne and the surrounding district were governed by an Archbishop, who was an elector of the Empire. The right of choosing this great prelate belonged, under certain limitations, to the Chapter of the Cathedral. The Archbishop was also Bishop of Liege, of Munster, and of Hildesheim. His dominions were extensive, and included several strong fortresses, which in the event of a campaign on the Rhine would be of the highest importance. In time of war he could bring twenty thousand men into the field. Lewis had spared no effort to gain so valuable an ally, and had succeeded so well that Cologne had been almost separated from Germany, and had become an outwork of France. Many ecclesiastics devoted to the court of Versailles had been brought into the Chapter, and Cardinal Furstemberg, a mere creature of that court, had been appointed Coadjutor.

The Archbishopric of Cologne.

In the summer of the year 1688 the archbishopric became vacant. Furstemberg was the candidate of the House of Bourbon. The enemies of that house proposed the young Prince Clement of Bavaria. Furstemberg was already a bishop, and therefore could not be moved to another diocese except by a special dispensation from the Pope, or by a postulation, in which it was necessary that two-thirds of the Chapter of Cologne should join. The Pope would grant no dispensation to a creature of France. The Emperor induced more than a third part of the Chapter to vote for the Bavarian prince. Meanwhile, in the Chapters of Liege, Munster, and

---

* Professor Von Ranke, Die Römischen Päpste, Book VIII.; Burnet, i., 759.

Hildesheim, the majority was adverse to France. Lewis saw, with indignation and alarm, that an extensive province which he had begun to regard as a fief of his crown was about to become, not merely independent of him, but hostile to him. In a paper written with great acrimony he complained of the injustice with which France was on all occasions treated by that See which ought to extend a parental protection to every part of Christendom. Many signs indicated his fixed resolution to support the pretensions of his candidate by arms against the Pope and the Pope's confederates.*

Thus Lewis, by two opposite errors, raised against himself at once the resentment of both the religious parties between which Western Europe was divided. Having alienated one great section of Christendom by persecuting the Huguenots, he alienated another by insulting the Holy See. These faults he committed at a conjuncture at which no fault could be committed with impunity, and under the eye of an opponent second in vigilance, sagacity, and energy to no statesman whose memory history has preserved. William saw with stern delight his adversaries toiling to clear away obstacle after obstacle from his path. While they raised against themselves the enmity of all sects, he labored to conciliate all. The great design which he meditated he with exquisite skill presented to different governments in different lights; and it must be added that, though those lights were different, none of them was false. He called on the princes of Northern Germany to rally round him in a defence of the common cause of all reformed Churches. He set before the two heads of the House of Austria the danger with which they were threatened by French ambition, and the necessity of rescuing England from vassalage and of uniting her to the European confederacy.† He disclaimed,

Skilful management of William.

---

* Burnet, i., 758; Lewis's paper bears date $\frac{\text{Aug. 27,}}{\text{Sept. 6,}}$ 1688. It will be found in the Recueil des Traités, vol. iv., No. 219.

† For the consummate dexterity with which he exhibited two different views of his policy to two different parties he was afterward bitterly reviled by the court of Saint Germains. "Licet Fœderatis publicus ille prædo haud aliud aperte proponat nisi ut Gallici imperii exuberans amputetur potestas, veruntamen sibi et suis ex

and with truth, all bigotry. The real enemy, he said, of the British Roman Catholics was that short-sighted and headstrong monarch who, when he might easily have obtained for them a legal toleration, had trampled on law, liberty, property, in order to raise them to an odious and precarious ascendency. If the misgovernment of James were suffered to continue, it must produce, at no remote time, a popular outbreak, which might be followed by a barbarous persecution of the Papists. The Prince declared that to avert the horrors of such a persecution was one of his chief objects. If he succeeded in his design, he would use the power which he must then possess, as head of the Protestant interest, to protect the members of the Church of Rome. Perhaps the passions excited by the tyranny of James might make it impossible to efface the penal laws from the statute-book: but those laws should be mitigated by a lenient administration. No class would really gain more by the proposed expedition than those peaceable and unambitious Roman Catholics who merely wished to follow their callings and to worship their Maker without molestation. The only losers would be the Tyrconnels, the Dovers, the Albevilles, and other political adventurers, who, in return for flattery and evil counsel, had obtained from their credulous master governments, regiments, and embassies.

While William exerted himself to enlist on his side the sympathies both of Protestants and of Roman Catholics, he His military and naval preparations. exerted himself with not less vigor and prudence to provide the military means which his undertaking required. He could not make a descent on England without the sanction of the United Provinces. If he asked for that sanction before his design was ripe for execution, his intentions might possibly be thwarted by the faction hostile to his house, and would certainly be divulged to the whole world. He therefore determined to make his preparations with all speed, and, when they were complete, to

---

hæretica fæce complicibus, ut pro comperto habemus, longe aliud promittit, nempe ut, exciso vel enervato Francorum regno, ubi Catholicarum partium summum jam robur situm est, hæretica ipsorum pravitas per orbem Christianum universum prævaleat."—Letter of James to the Pope, written in 1689.

seize some favorable moment for requesting the consent of the federation. It was observed by the agents of France that he was more busy than they had ever known him. Not a day passed on which he was not seen spurring from his villa to the Hague. He was perpetually closeted with his most distinguished adherents. Twenty-four ships of war were fitted out for sea in addition to the ordinary force which the commonwealth maintained. There was, as it chanced, an excellent pretence for making this addition to the marine: for some Algerine corsairs had recently dared to show themselves in the German Ocean. A camp was formed near Nimeguen. Many thousands of troops were assembled there. In order to strengthen this army the garrisons were withdrawn from the strongholds in Dutch Brabant. Even the renowned fortress of Bergopzoom was left almost defenceless. Field-pieces, bombs, and tumbrels from all the magazines of the United Provinces were collected at the head-quarters. All the bakers of Rotterdam toiled day and night to make biscuit. All the gun-makers of Utrecht were found too few to execute the orders for pistols and muskets. All the saddlers of Amsterdam were hard at work on harness and holsters. Six thousand sailors were added to the naval establishment. Seven thousand new soldiers were raised. They could not, indeed, be formally enlisted without the sanction of the federation; but they were well drilled, and kept in such a state of discipline that they might without difficulty be distributed into regiments within twenty-four hours after that sanction should be obtained. These preparations required ready money: but William had, by strict economy, laid up against a great emergency a treasure amounting to about two hundred and fifty thousand pounds sterling. What more was wanting was supplied by the zeal of his partisans. Great quantities of gold— not less, it was said, than a hundred thousand guineas—came to him from England. The Huguenots, who had carried with them into exile large quantities of the precious metals, were eager to lend him all that they possessed; for they fondly hoped that, if he succeeded, they should be restored to the country of their birth; and they feared that, if he failed, they should scarcely be safe even in the country of their adoption.*

<small>He receives numerous assurances of support from England.</small> Through the latter part of July and the whole of August the preparations went on rapidly, yet too slowly for the vehement spirit of William. Meanwhile the intercourse between England and Holland was active. The ordinary modes of conveying intelligence and passengers were no longer thought safe. A light bark of marvellous speed constantly ran backward and forward between Schevening and the eastern coast of our island.† By this vessel William received a succession of letters from persons of high note in the Church, the state, and the army. Two of the seven prelates who had signed the memorable petition, Lloyd, Bishop of Saint Asaph, and Trelawney, Bishop of Bristol, had, during their residence in the Tower, reconsidered the doctrine of non-resistance, and were ready to welcome an armed deliverer. A brother of the Bishop of Bristol, Colonel Charles Trelawney, who commanded one of the Tangier regiments, now known as the Fourth of the Line, signified his readiness to draw his sword for the Protestant religion. Similar assurances arrived from the savage Kirke. Churchill, in a letter written with a certain elevation of language, which was the sure mark that he was going to commit a baseness, declared that he was determined to perform his duty to heaven and to his country, and that he put his honor absolutely into the hands of the Prince of Orange. William doubtless read these words with one of those bitter and cynical smiles which gave his face its least pleasing expression. It was not his business to take care of the honor of other men; nor had the most rigid casuists pronounced it unlawful in a general to invite, to use, and to reward the services of deserters whom he could not but despise.‡

Churchill's letter was brought by Sidney, whose situation in England had become hazardous, and who, having taken many precautions to hide his track, had passed over to Hol-

---

* Avaux Neg., August $\frac{9}{12}, \frac{10}{20}, \frac{11}{21}, \frac{14}{24}, \frac{16}{26}, \frac{17}{27}, \frac{\text{Aug. 23,}}{\text{Sept. 2,}}$ 1688.
† Avaux Neg., September $\frac{4}{14}$, 1688.
‡ Burnet, i., 765; Churchill's letter bears date Aug. 4, 1688.

land about the middle of August.* About the same time Shrewsbury and Edward Russell crossed the German Ocean in a boat which they had hired with great secrecy, and appeared at the Hague. Shrewsbury brought with him twelve thousand pounds, which he had raised by a mortgage on his estates, and which he lodged in the bank of Amsterdam.† Devonshire, Danby, and Lumley remained in England, where they undertook to rise in arms as soon as the Prince should set foot on the island.

There is reason to believe that, at this conjuncture, William first received assurances of support from a very different quarter. Part of the history of Sunderland's intrigues is covered with an obscurity which it is not probable that any inquirer will ever succeed in penetrating: but, though it is impossible to discover the whole truth, it is easy to detect some palpable fictions. The Jacobites, for obvious reasons, affirmed that the revolution of 1688 was the result of a plot concerted long before. Sunderland they represented as the chief conspirator. He had, they averred, in pursuance of his great design, incited his too confiding master to dispense with statutes, to create an illegal tribunal, to confiscate freehold property, and to send the fathers of the Established Church to a prison. This romance rests on no evidence, and, though it has been repeated down to our time, seems hardly to deserve confutation. No fact is more certain than that Sunderland opposed some of the most imprudent steps which James took, and in particular the prosecution of the Bishops, which really brought on the decisive crisis. But, even if this fact were not established, there would still remain one argument sufficient to decide the controversy. What conceivable motive had Sunderland to wish for a revolution? Under the existing system he was at the height of dignity and prosperity. As President of the Council he took precedence of the whole temporal peerage. As principal Secretary of State he was the most active and powerful member of the

---

* William to Bentinck, August $\frac{17}{27}$, 1688.
† Memoirs of the Duke of Shrewsbury, 1718.

cabinet. He might look forward to a dukedom. He had obtained the garter lately worn by the brilliant and versatile Buckingham, who, having squandered away a princely fortune and a vigorous intellect, had sunk into the grave deserted, contemned, and broken-hearted.* Money, which Sunderland valued more than honors, poured in upon him in such abundance that, with ordinary management, he might hope to become, in a few years, one of the wealthiest subjects in Europe. The direct emolument of his posts, though considerable, was a very small part of what he received. From France alone he drew a regular stipend of near six thousand pounds a year, besides large occasional gratuities. He had bargained with Tyrconnel for five thousand a year, or fifty thousand pounds down, from Ireland. What sums he made by selling places, titles, and pardons, can only be conjectured, but must have been enormous. James seemed to take a pleasure in loading with wealth one whom he regarded as his own convert. All fines, all forfeitures went to Sunderland. On every grant toll was paid to him. If any suitor ventured to ask any favor directly from the King, the answer was, "Have you spoken to my Lord President?" One bold man ventured to say that the Lord President got all the money of the court. "Well," replied His Majesty; "he deserves it all."† We shall scarcely overrate the amount of the minister's gains, if we put them at thirty thousand pounds a year: and it must be remembered that fortunes of thirty thousand pounds a year were in his time rarer than fortunes of a hundred thousand pounds a year now are. It is probable that there was then not one peer of the realm whose private income equalled Sunderland's official income.

What chance was there that, in a new order of things, a man so deeply implicated in illegal and unpopular acts, a

---

* London Gazette, April 25, 28, 1687.

† Secret Consults of the Romish Party in Ireland. This account is strongly confirmed by what Bonrepaux wrote to Seignelay, Sept. $\frac{12}{22}$, 1687. "Il (Sunderland) amassera beaucoup d'argent, le roi son maître lui donnant la plus grande partie de celui qui provient des confiscations ou des accommodemens que ceux qui ont encouru des peines font pour obtenir leur grâce."

member of the High Commission, a renegade whom the multitude, in places of general resort, pursued with the cry of Popish dog, would be greater and richer? What chance that he would even be able to escape condign punishment?

He had undoubtedly been long in the habit of looking forward to the time when William and Mary might be, in the ordinary course of nature and law, at the head of the English government, and had probably attempted to make for himself an interest in their favor, by promises and services which, if discovered, would not have raised his credit at Whitehall. But it may with confidence be affirmed that he had no wish to see them raised to power by a revolution, and that he did not at all foresee such a revolution when, toward the close of June, 1688, he solemnly joined the communion of the Church of Rome.

Scarcely, however, had he, by that inexpiable crime, made himself an object of hatred and contempt to the whole nation, when he learned that the civil and ecclesiastical polity of England would shortly be vindicated by foreign and domestic arms. From that moment all his plans seem to have undergone a change. Fear bowed down his whole soul, and was so written in his face that all who saw him could read.* It could hardly be doubted that, if there were a revolution, the evil counsellors who surrounded the throne would be called to a strict account: and among those counsellors he stood in the foremost rank. The loss of his places, his salaries, his pensions, was the least that he had to dread. His patrimonial mansion and woods at Althorpe might be confiscated. He might lie many years in a prison. He might end his days in a foreign land, a pensioner on the bounty of France. Even this was not the worst. Visions of an innumerable crowd covering Tower Hill and shouting with savage joy at the sight of the apostate, of a scaffold hung with black, of Burnet reading the prayer for the departing, and of Ketch leaning on the axe with which Russell and Monmouth had been mangled in so butcherly a fashion, began to haunt the unhappy

---

* Adda says that Sunderland's terror was visible. $\frac{\text{Oct. 26,}}{\text{Nov. 5,}}$ 1688.

statesman. There was yet one way in which he might escape, a way more terrible to a noble spirit than a prison or a scaffold. He might still, by a well-timed and useful treason, earn his pardon from the foes of the government. It was in his power to render to them at this conjuncture services beyond all price: for he had the royal ear: he had great influence over the Jesuitical cabal; and he was blindly trusted by the French Ambassador. A channel of communication was not wanting, a channel worthy of the purpose which it was to serve. The Countess of Sunderland was an artful woman, who, under a show of devotion which imposed on some grave men, carried on, with great activity, both amorous and political intrigues.* The handsome and dissolute Henry Sidney had long been her favorite lover. Her husband was well pleased to see her thus connected with the court of the Hague. Whenever he wished to transmit a secret message to Holland, he spoke to his wife: she wrote to Sidney; and Sidney communicated her letter to William. One of her communications was intercepted, and carried to James. She vehemently protested that it was a forgery. Her husband, with characteristic ingenuity, defended himself by representing that it was quite impossible for any man to be so base as to do what he was in the habit of doing. "Even if this is Lady Sunderland's hand," he said, "that is no affair of mine. Your Majesty knows my domestic misfortunes. The footing on which my wife and Mr. Sidney are is but too public. Who can believe that I would make a confidant of the man who has injured my honor in the tenderest point, of the man whom, of all others, I ought most to hate?"† This defence was thought satisfactory: and secret intelligence was still transmitted from the wittol to the adulteress, from the adulteress to the gallant, and from the gallant to the enemies of James.

It is highly probable that the first decisive assurances of Sunderland's support were conveyed orally by Sidney to Wil-

---

* Compare Evelyn's account of her with what the Princess of Denmark wrote about her to the Hague, and with her own letters to Henry Sidney.
† Bonrepaux to Seignelay, July $\frac{11}{21}$, 1688.

liam about the middle of August. It is certain that, from that time till the expedition was ready to sail, a most significant correspondence was kept up between the Countess and her lover. A few of her letters, partly written in cipher, are still extant. They contain professions of good-will and promises of service mingled with earnest entreaties for protection. The writer intimates that her husband will do all that his friends at the Hague can wish: she supposes that it will be necessary for him to go into temporary exile: but she hopes that his banishment will not be perpetual, and that his patrimonial estate will be spared; and she earnestly begs to be informed in what place it will be best for him to take refuge till the first fury of the storm is over.*

The help of Sunderland was most welcome. For, as the time of striking the great blow drew near, the anxiety of William became intense. From common eyes his feelings were concealed by the icy tranquillity of his demeanor: but his whole heart was open to Bentinck. The preparations were not quite complete. The design was already suspected, and could not be long concealed. The King of France or the city of Amsterdam might still frustrate the whole plan. If Lewis were to send a great force into Brabant, if the faction which hated the Stadtholder were to raise its head, all was over. "My sufferings, my disquiet," the Prince wrote, "are dreadful. I hardly see my way. Never in my life did I so much feel the need of God's guidance."† Bentinck's wife was at this time dangerously ill; and both the friends were painfully anxious about her. "God support you," William wrote, "and enable you to bear your part in a work on which, as far as human beings can see, the welfare of his Church depends."‡

_{Anxiety of William.}

It was indeed impossible that a design so vast as that which had been formed against the King of England should remain during many weeks a secret. No art could prevent intelli-

---

* See her letters in the Sidney Diary and Correspondence lately published. Mr. Fox, in his copy of Barillon's despatches, marked the 30th of August, N.S., 1688, as the date from which it was quite certain that Sunderland was playing false. † August $\frac{19}{29}$, 1688. ‡ September $\frac{4}{14}$, 1688.

gent men from perceiving that William was making great
military and naval preparations, and from suspecting the object with which those preparations were
made. Early in August hints that some great event
was approaching were whispered up and down London. The
weak and corrupt Albeville was then on a visit to England,
and was, or affected to be, certain that the Dutch government
entertained no design unfriendly to James. But, during the
absence of Albeville from his post, Avaux performed, with
eminent skill, the duties both of French and English Ambassador to the States, and supplied Barillon as well as Lewis
with ample intelligence. Avaux was satisfied that a descent
on England was in contemplation, and succeeded in convincing his master of the truth. Every courier who arrived
at Westminster, either from the Hague or from Versailles,
brought earnest warnings.* But James was under a delusion
which appears to have been artfully encouraged by Sunderland. The Prince of Orange, said the cunning minister, would
never dare to engage in an expedition beyond sea, leaving
Holland defenceless. The States, remembering what they
had suffered and what they had been in danger of suffering
during the great agony of 1672, would never incur the risk
of again seeing an invading army encamped on the plain between Utrecht and Amsterdam. There was doubtless much
discontent in England: but the interval was immense between
discontent and rebellion. Men of rank and fortune were not
disposed lightly to hazard their honors, their estates, and their
lives. How many eminent Whigs had held high language
when Monmouth was in the Netherlands! And yet, when
he set up his standard, what eminent Whig had joined it? It
was easy to understand why Lewis affected to give credit to
these idle rumors. He doubtless hoped to frighten the King
of England into taking the French side in the dispute about
Cologne. By such reasoning James was easily lulled into
stupid security.† The alarm and indignation of Lewis in-

Warnings conveyed to James.

---

* Avaux, July $\frac{19}{29}$, $\frac{\text{July }31}{\text{Aug. }10}$, August $\frac{11}{21}$, 1688; Lewis to Barillon, August $\frac{2}{12}$, $\frac{16}{26}$.

† Barillon, Aug. $\frac{20}{30}$, $\frac{\text{Aug. }23}{\text{Sept. }2}$, 1688; Adda, $\frac{\text{Aug. }24}{\text{Sept. }3}$; Life of James, ii., 177, Orig. Mem.

creased daily. The style of his letters became sharp and vehement.* He could not understand, he wrote, this lethargy on the eve of a terrible crisis. Was the King bewitched? Were his ministers blind? Was it possible that nobody at Whitehall was aware of what was passing in England and on the Continent? Such foodhardy security could scarcely be the effect of mere improvidence. There must be foul play. James was evidently in bad hands. Barillon was earnestly cautioned not to repose implicit confidence in the English ministers: but he was cautioned in vain. On him, as on James, Sunderland had cast a spell which no exhortation could break.

Lewis bestirred himself vigorously. Bonrepaux, who was far superior to Barillon in shrewdness, and who had always disliked and distrusted Sunderland, was despatched to London with an offer of naval assistance. Avaux was at the same time ordered to declare to the States-general that France had taken James under her protection. A large body of troops was held in readiness to march toward the Dutch frontier. This bold attempt to save the infatuated tyrant in his own despite was made with the full concurrence of Skelton, who was now Envoy from England to the court of Versailles.

Exertions of Lewis to save James.

Avaux, in conformity with his instructions, demanded an audience of the States. It was readily granted. The assembly was unusually large. The general belief was that some overture respecting commerce was about to be made; and the President brought a written answer framed on that supposition. As soon as Avaux began to disclose his errand, signs of uneasiness were discernible. Those who were believed to enjoy the confidence of the Prince of Orange cast down their eyes. The agitation became great when the envoy announced that his master was strictly bound by the ties of friendship and alliance to His Britannic Majesty, and that any attack on England would be considered as a declaration of war against France. The President, completely taken by surprise, stammered out a few evasive phrases; and the conference termi-

---

* Lewis to Barillon, Sept. $\frac{3}{13}$, $\frac{8}{18}$, $\frac{11}{21}$, 1688.

nated. It was at the same time notified to the States that Lewis had taken under his protection Cardinal Furstemberg and the Chapter of Cologne.*

The Deputies were in great agitation. Some recommended caution and delay. Others breathed nothing but war. Fagel spoke vehemently of the French insolence, and implored his brethren not to be daunted by threats. The proper answer to such a communication, he said, was to levy more soldiers, and to equip more ships. A courier was instantly despatched to recall William from Minden, where he was holding a consultation of high moment with the Elector of Brandenburg.

But there was no cause for alarm. James was bent on ruining himself; and every attempt to stop him only made him James frustrates them. rush more eagerly to his doom. When his throne was secure, when his people were submissive, when the most obsequious of Parliaments was eager to anticipate all his reasonable wishes, when foreign kingdoms and commonwealths paid emulous court to him, when it depended only on himself whether he would be the arbiter of Christendom, he had stooped to be the slave and the hireling of France. And now when, by a series of crimes and follies, he had succeeded in alienating his neighbors, his subjects, his soldiers, his sailors, his children, and had left himself no refuge but the protection of France, he was taken with a fit of pride, and determined to assert his independence. That help which, when he did not want it, he had accepted with ignominious tears, he now, when it was indispensable to him, threw contemptuously away. Having been abject when he might with propriety have been punctilious in maintaining his dignity, he became ungratefully haughty at a moment when haughtiness must bring on him at once derision and ruin. He resented the friendly intervention which might have saved him. Was ever King so used? Was he a child, or an idiot, that others must think for him? Was he a petty prince, a Cardinal Furstemberg, who must fall if not upheld by a powerful patron? Was he to be degraded in the estimation of all Eu-

---

* Avaux, $\frac{\text{Aug. 23, Aug. 30,}}{\text{Sept. 2, Sept. 9,}}$ 1688.

rope, by an ostentatious patronage which he had never asked? Skelton was recalled to answer for his conduct, and, as soon as he arrived, was committed prisoner to the Tower. Van Citters was well received at Whitehall, and had a long audience. He could, with more truth than diplomatists on such occasions think at all necessary, disclaim, on the part of the States-general, any hostile project. For the States-general had as yet no official knowledge of the design of William; nor was it by any means impossible that they might, even now, refuse to sanction that design. James declared that he gave not the least credit to the rumors of a Dutch invasion, and that the conduct of the French government had surprised and annoyed him. Middleton was directed to assure all the foreign ministers that there existed no such alliance between France and England as the court of Versailles had, for its own ends, pretended. To the Nuncio the King said that the designs of Lewis were palpable and should be frustrated. This officious protection was at once an insult and a snare. "My good brother," said James, "has excellent qualities; but flattery and vanity have turned his head."* Adda, who was much more anxious about Cologne than about England, encouraged this strange delusion. Albeville, who had now returned to his post, was commanded to give friendly assurances to the States-general, and to add some high language, which might have been becoming in the mouth of Elizabeth or Oliver. "My master," he said, "is raised, alike by his power and by his spirit, above the position which France affects to assign to him. There is some difference between a King of England and an Archbishop of Cologne." The reception of Bonrepaux at Whitehall was cold. The naval succors which he offered were not absolutely declined: but he was forced to return without having settled anything; and the envoys, both of the United Provinces and of the House of Austria, were informed that his mission had been disagreeable to the King and had produced no result. After the Revolution Sunderland boasted, and probably with truth, that he

---

* "Che l'adulazione e la vanità gli avevano tornato il capo."—Adda, $\frac{\text{Aug. 31,}}{\text{Sept. 10,}}$ 1688.

had induced his master to reject the proffered assistance of France.*

The perverse folly of James naturally excited the indignation of his powerful neighbor. Lewis complained that, in return for the greatest service which he could render to the English government, that government had given him the lie in the face of all Christendom. He justly remarked that what Avaux had said, touching the alliance between France and Great Britain, was true according to the spirit, though, perhaps, not according to the letter. There was not, indeed, a treaty digested into articles, signed, sealed, and ratified: but assurances equivalent in the estimation of honorable men to such a treaty had, during some years, been frequently exchanged between the two courts. Lewis added that, high as was his own place in Europe, he should never be so absurdly jealous of his dignity as to see an insult in any act prompted by friendship. But James was in a very different situation, and would soon learn the value of that aid which he had so ungraciously rejected.†

Yet, notwithstanding the stupidity and ingratitude of James, it would have been wise in Lewis to persist in the resolution which had been notified to the States-general. Avaux, whose sagacity and judgment made him an antagonist worthy of William, was decidedly of this opinion. The first object of the French government, so the skilful envoy reasoned, ought to be to prevent the intended descent on England. The way to prevent that descent was to invade the Spanish Netherlands, and to menace the Batavian frontier. The Prince of Orange, indeed, was so bent on his darling enterprise that he would persist, even if the white flag were flying on the walls of Brussels. He had actually said that, if the Spaniards could only manage to keep Ostend, Mons, and

---

* Van Citters, Sept. $\frac{11}{21}$, 1688; Avaux, Sept. $\frac{17}{27}$, $\frac{\text{Sept. 27}}{\text{Oct. 7}}$; Barillon, $\frac{\text{Sept. 23}}{\text{Oct. 3}}$; Wagenaar, Book LX.; Sunderland's Apology. It has been often asserted that James declined the help of a French army. The truth is that no such army was offered. Indeed, the French troops would have served James much more effectually by menacing the frontiers of Holland than by crossing the Channel.

† Lewis to Barillon, Sept. $\frac{20}{30}$, 1688.

Namur till the next spring, he would then return from England with a force which would soon recover all that had been lost. But, though such was the Prince's opinion, it was not the opinion of the States. They would not readily consent to send their Captain-general and the flower of their army across the German Ocean, while a formidable enemy threatened their own territory.*

Lewis admitted the force of these reasonings : but he had already resolved on a different line of action. Perhaps he had been provoked by the discourtesy and wrongheadedness of the English government, and indulged his temper at the expense of his interest. Perhaps he was misled by the counsels of his minister of war, Louvois, whose influence was great, and who regarded Avaux with no friendly feeling. It was determined to strike in a quarter remote from Holland a great and unexpected blow. Lewis suddenly withdrew his troops from Flanders, and poured them into Germany. One army, placed under the nominal command of the Dauphin, but really directed by the Duke of Duras and by Vauban, the father of the science of fortification, invested Philipsburg. Another, led by the Marquess of Boufflers, seized Worms, Mentz, and Treves. A third, commanded by the Marquess of Humieres, entered Bonn. All down the Rhine, from Baden to Cologne, the French arms were victorious. The news of the fall of Philipsburg reached Versailles on All-saints-day, while the court was listening to a sermon in the chapel. The King made a sign to the preacher to stop, announced the good news to the congregation, and, kneeling down, returned thanks to God for this great success. The audience wept for joy.† The tidings were eagerly welcomed by the sanguine and susceptible people of France. Poets celebrated the triumphs of their magnificent patron. Orators extolled from the pulpit the wisdom and magnanimity of the eldest son of the Church. The Te Deum was sung with unwonted pomp; and the solemn notes of the organ were mingled with the clash of the cym-

<small>*margin: The French armies invade Germany.*</small>

---

* Avaux, $\frac{\text{Sept. 27,}}{\text{Oct. 7,}}$ Oct. $\frac{4}{14}$, 1688.   † Madame de Sévigné, $\frac{\text{Oct. 24,}}{\text{Nov. 3,}}$ 1688.

bal and the blast of the trumpet. But there was little cause for rejoicing. The great statesman who was at the head of the European coalition smiled inwardly at the misdirected energy of his foe. Lewis had indeed, by his promptitude, gained some advantages on the side of Germany: but those advantages would avail little if England, inactive and inglorious under four successive kings, should suddenly resume her old rank in Europe. A few weeks would suffice for the enterprise on which the fate of the world depended; and for a few weeks the United Provinces were in security.

William now urged on his preparations with indefatigable activity, and with less secrecy than he had hitherto thought necessary. Assurances of support came pouring in daily from foreign courts. Opposition had become extinct at the Hague. It was in vain that Avaux, even at this last moment, exerted all his skill to reanimate the faction which had contended against three generations of the House of Orange. The chiefs of that faction, indeed, still regarded the Stadtholder with no friendly feeling. They had reason to fear that, if he prospered in England, he would become absolute master of Holland. Nevertheless, the errors of the court of Versailles, and the dexterity with which he had availed himself of those errors, made it impossible to continue the struggle against him. He saw that the time had come for demanding the sanction of the States. Amsterdam was the head-quarters of the party hostile to his line, his office, and his person; and even from Amsterdam he had at this moment nothing to apprehend. Some of the chief functionaries of that city had been repeatedly closeted with him, with Van Dykvelt, and with Bentinck, and had been induced to promise that they would promote, or at least that they would not oppose, the great design: some were exasperated by the commercial edicts of Lewis: some were in deep distress for kinsmen and friends who were harassed by the French dragoons; some shrank from the responsibility of causing a schism which might be fatal to the Batavian federation; and some were afraid of the common people, who, stimulated by the exhortations of zealous preach-

<small>William obtains the sanction of the States-general to his expedition.</small>

ers, were ready to execute summary justice on any traitor who should, at this crisis, be false to the Protestant cause. The majority, therefore, of that town council which had long been devoted to France pronounced in favor of William's undertaking. Thenceforth all fear of opposition in any part of the United Provinces was at an end; and the full sanction of the federation to his enterprise was, in secret sittings, formally given.*

The Prince had already fixed upon a general well qualified to be second in command. This was indeed no light matter. A random shot or the dagger of an assassin might in a moment leave the expedition without a head. It was necessary that a successor should be ready to fill the vacant place. Yet it was impossible to make choice of any Englishman without giving offence either to the Whigs or to the Tories; nor had any Englishman then living shown that he possessed the military skill necessary for the conduct of a campaign. On the other hand, it was not easy to assign pre-eminence to a foreigner without wounding the national sensibility of the haughty islanders. One man there was, and only one, in Europe, to whom no objection could be found—Frederic, Count of Schomberg, a German, sprung from a noble house of the Palatinate. He was generally esteemed the greatest living master of the art of war. His rectitude and piety, tried by strong temptations and never found wanting, commanded general respect and confidence. Though a Protestant, he had been, during many years, in the service of Lewis, and had, in spite of the ill offices of the Jesuits, extorted from his employer, by a series of great actions, the staff of a Marshal of France. When persecution began to rage, the brave veteran steadfastly refused to purchase the royal favor by apostasy, resigned, without one murmur, all his honors and commands, quitted his adopted country forever, and took refuge at the court of Berlin. He had long passed his seventieth year: but both his mind and his body

_{Schomberg.}

---

* Witsen MS. quoted by Wagenaar; Lord Lonsdale's Memoirs; Avaux, Oct. $\frac{4}{14}$, $\frac{5}{15}$, 1688. The formal declaration of the States-general, dated Oct. $\frac{18}{28}$, will be found in the Recueil des Traités, vol. iv., No. 252.

were still in full vigor. He had been in England, and was much loved and honored there. He had, indeed, a recommendation of which very few foreigners could then boast; for he spoke our language, not only intelligibly, but with grace and purity. He was, with the consent of the Elector of Brandenburg, and with the warm approbation of the chiefs of all the English parties, appointed William's lieutenant.*

And now the Hague was crowded with British adventurers of all the various factions which the tyranny of James had united in a strange coalition—old royalists who had shed their blood for the throne, old agitators of the army of the Parliament, Tories who had been persecuted in the days of the Exclusion Bill, Whigs who had fled to the Continent for their share in the Rye-house Plot.

<small>British adventurers at the Hague.</small>

Conspicuous in this great assemblage were Charles Gerard, Earl of Macclesfield, an ancient Cavalier who had fought for Charles the First and had shared the exile of Charles the Second; Archibald Campbell, who was the eldest son of the unfortunate Argyle, but had inherited nothing except an illustrious name and the inalienable affection of a numerous clan; Charles Paulet, Earl of Wiltshire, heir-apparent of the Marquisate of Winchester; and Peregrine Osborne, Lord Dumblane, heir-apparent of the Earldom of Danby. Mordaunt, exulting in the prospect of adventures irresistibly attractive to his fiery nature, was among the foremost volunteers. Fletcher of Saltoun had learned, while guarding the frontier of Christendom against the infidels, that there was once more a hope of deliverance for his country, and had hastened to offer the help of his sword. Sir Patrick Hume, who had, since his flight from Scotland, lived humbly at Utrecht, now emerged from his obscurity: but, fortunately, his eloquence could, on this occasion, do little mischief; for the Prince of Orange was by no means disposed to be the lieutenant of a debating society such as that which had ruined the enterprise of Argyle. The subtle and restless Wildman, who had some time before found

---

* Abrégé de la Vie de Frédéric Duc de Schomberg, 1690; Sidney to William, June 30, 1688; Burnet, i., 677.

England an unsafe residence, and had escaped to Germany, repaired from his retreat to the Prince's court. There, too, was Carstairs, a Presbyterian minister from Scotland, who in craft and courage had no superior among the politicians of his age. He had been intrusted some years before by Fagel with important secrets, and had resolutely kept them in spite of the most horrible torments which could be inflicted by boot and thumb-screw. His rare fortitude had earned for him as large a share of the Prince's confidence and esteem as was granted to any man except Bentinck.* Ferguson could not remain quiet when a revolution was preparing. He secured for himself a passage in the fleet, and made himself busy among his fellow-emigrants: but he found himself generally distrusted and despised. He had been a great man in the knot of ignorant and hot-headed outlaws who had urged the feeble Monmouth to destruction: but there was no place for a low-minded agitator, half maniac and half knave, among the grave statesmen and generals who partook the cares of the resolute and sagacious William.

The difference between the expedition of 1685 and the expedition of 1688 was sufficiently marked by the difference between the manifestoes which the leaders of those expeditions published. For Monmouth Ferguson had scribbled an absurd and brutal libel about the burning of London, the strangling of Godfrey, the butchering of Essex, and the poisoning of Charles. The Declaration of William was drawn up by the Grand Pensionary Fagel, who was highly renowned as a publicist. Though weighty and learned, it was, in its original form, much too prolix: but it was abridged and translated into English by Burnet, who well understood the art of popular composition. It began by a solemn preamble, setting forth that, in every community, the strict observance of law was necessary alike to the happiness of nations and to the security of governments. The Prince of Orange had therefore seen with deep concern that the fundamental laws of a kingdom, with which he was by blood and

<small>William's Declaration.</small>

---

* Burnet, i., 584; Mackay's Memoirs.

by marriage closely connected, had, by the advice of evil counsellors, been grossly and systematically violated. The power of dispensing with Acts of Parliament had been strained to such a point that the whole legislative authority had been transferred to the crown. Decisions at variance with the spirit of the constitution had been obtained from the tribunals by turning out judge after judge, till the bench had been filled with men ready to obey implicitly the directions of the government. Notwithstanding the King's repeated assurances that he would maintain the established religion, persons notoriously hostile to that religion had been promoted, not only to civil offices, but also to ecclesiastical benefices. The government of the Church had, in defiance of express statutes, been intrusted to a new court of High Commission; and in that court an avowed Papist had a seat. Good subjects, for refusing to violate their duty and their oaths, had been ejected from their property, in contempt of the Great Charter of the liberties of England. Meanwhile persons who could not legally set foot on the island had been placed at the head of seminaries for the corruption of youth. Lieutenants, Deputy Lieutenants, Justices of the Peace, had been dismissed in multitudes for refusing to support a pernicious and unconstitutional policy. The franchises of almost every borough in the realm had been invaded. The courts of justice were in such a state that their decisions, even in civil matters, had ceased to inspire confidence, and that their servility in criminal cases had brought on the kingdom the stain of innocent blood. All these abuses, loathed by the English nation, were to be defended, it seemed, by an army of Irish Papists. Nor was this all. The most arbitrary princes had never accounted it an offence in a subject modestly and peaceably to represent his grievances and to ask for relief. But supplication was now treated as a high misdemeanor in England. For no crime but that of offering to the Sovereign a petition drawn up in the most respectful terms, the fathers of the Church had been imprisoned and prosecuted; and every judge who had given his voice in their favor had instantly been turned out. The calling of a free and lawful Parliament might indeed be an effectual remedy for all these evils: but such a Parliament, unless the whole spirit of the administration was changed, the nation could not hope to see. It was evidently the intention of the court to bring together, by means of regulated corporations and of Popish returning officers, a body which would be a House of Commons in name alone. Lastly, there were circumstances which raised a grave suspicion that the child who was called Prince of Wales was not really born of the Queen. For these reasons the Prince, mindful of his near relation to the royal house, and grateful for the affection which the English people had ever shown to his beloved wife and to himself, had resolved, in compliance with the request of many Lords Spiritual and Temporal, and of many other persons of all ranks, to go over at the head of a force sufficient to repel violence. He abjured all thought of conquest. He protested that, while his troops remained in the island, they should be kept under the strictest restraints of discipline, and that, as soon as the nation had been delivered from tyranny, they should be sent back. His single object was to have a free and legal Parliament assembled: and to the decision of such a Parliament he solemnly pledged himself to leave all questions both public and private.

As soon as copies of this Declaration were handed about the Hague, signs of dissension began to appear among the English. Wildman, indefatigable in mischief, prevailed on some of his countrymen, and, among others, on the headstrong and volatile Mordaunt, to declare that they would not take up arms on such grounds. The paper had been drawn up merely to please the Cavaliers and the parsons. The injuries of the Church and the trial of the Bishops had been put too prominently forward; and nothing had been said of the tyrannical manner in which the Tories, before their rupture with the court, had treated the Whigs. Wildman then brought forward a counter-project, prepared by himself, which, if it had been adopted, would have disgusted all the Anglican clergy and four-fifths of the landed aristocracy. The leading Whigs strongly opposed him. Russell in particular declared that, if such an insane course were taken, there would be an end of the coalition from which alone the nation could expect deliverance. The dispute was at length settled by the authority of William, who, with his usual good-sense, determined that the manifesto should stand nearly as Fagel and Burnet had framed it.*

While these things were passing in Holland, James had at length become sensible of his danger. Intelligence which could not be disregarded came pouring in from various quarters. At length a despatch from Albeville removed all doubts.

<small>James roused to a sense of his danger.</small> It is said that when the King had read it, the blood left his cheeks, and he remained some time speechless.† He might, indeed, well be appalled. The first easterly wind would bring a hostile armament to the shores of his realm. All Europe, one single power alone excepted, was impatiently waiting for the news of his downfall. The help of that single power he had madly rejected. Nay, he had requited with insult the friendly intervention which might have saved him. The French armies which, but for his own folly, might have been employed in overawing the States-general, were besieging Philipsburg or garrisoning Mentz. In a few days he might have to fight, on English ground, for his crown and for the birthright of his infant son.

<small>His naval means.</small> His means were, indeed, in appearance great. The navy was in a much more efficient state than at the time of his accession; and the improvement is partly to be attributed to his own exertions. He had appointed no Lord High Admiral or Board of Admiralty, but had kept the chief direction of maritime affairs in his own hands, and had been strenuously assisted by Pepys. It is a proverb that the eye of a master is more to be trusted than that of a deputy: and, in an age of corruption and peculation, a department on which a sovereign, even of very slender capacity, bestows close personal attention is likely to be comparatively free from abuses. It would have been easy to find an abler minister of marine than James; but it would not have been easy to find, among the public men of that age, any minister of

---

* Burnet, i., 775, 780. † Eachard's History of the Revolution, ii., 2.

marine, except James, who would not have embezzled stores, taken bribes from contractors, and charged the crown with the cost of repairs which had never been made. The King was, in truth, almost the only person who could be trusted not to rob the King. There had therefore been, during the last three years, much less waste and pilfering in the dockyards than formerly. Ships had been built which were fit to go to sea. An excellent order had been issued increasing the allowances of captains, and at the same time strictly forbidding them to carry merchandise from port to port without the royal permission. The effect of these reforms was already perceptible; and James found no difficulty in fitting out, at short notice, a considerable fleet. Thirty ships of the line, all third-rates and fourth-rates, were collected in the Thames, under the command of Lord Dartmouth. The loyalty of Dartmouth was not suspected; and he was thought to have as much professional skill and knowledge as any of the patrician sailors who, in that age, rose to the highest naval commands without a regular naval training, and who were at once flag-officers on the sea and colonels of infantry on shore.*

<small>His military means.</small> The regular army had, during some years, been the largest that any King of England had ever commanded, and was now rapidly augmented. New companies were incorporated with the existing regiments. Commissions for the raising of fresh regiments were issued. Four thousand men were added to the English establishment. Three thousand were sent for with all speed from Ireland. As many more were ordered to march southward from Scotland. James estimated the force with which he should be able to meet the invaders at near forty thousand troops, exclusive of the militia.†

The navy and army were therefore far more than sufficient

---

* Pepys's Memoirs relating to the Royal Navy, 1690; Life of James the Second, ii., 186, Orig. Mem.; Adda, $\frac{\text{Sept. 21}}{\text{Oct. 1}}$; Van Citters, $\frac{\text{Sept. 21}}{\text{Oct. 1}}$.

† Life of James the Second, ii., 186, Orig. Mem.; Adda, $\frac{\text{Sept. 22}}{\text{Oct. 2}}$; Van Citters, $\frac{\text{Sept. 21}}{\text{Oct. 1}}$.

to repel a Dutch invasion. But could the navy, could the army, be trusted? Would not the trainbands flock by thousands to the standard of the deliverer? The party which had, a few years before, drawn the sword for Monmouth would undoubtedly be eager to welcome the Prince of Orange. And what had become of the party which had, during seven and forty years, been the bulwark of monarchy? Where were now those gallant gentlemen who had ever been ready to shed their blood for the crown? Outraged and insulted, driven from the bench of justice, and deprived of all military command, they saw the peril of their ungrateful sovereign with undisguised delight. Where were those priests and prelates who had, from ten thousand pulpits, proclaimed the duty of obeying the anointed delegate of God? Some of them had been imprisoned: some had been plundered: all had been placed under the iron rule of the High Commission, and were in hourly fear lest some new freak of tyranny should deprive them of their freeholds and leave them without a morsel of bread. That Churchmen would even now so completely forget the doctrine which had been their peculiar boast as to join in active resistance seemed incredible. But could their oppressor expect to find among them the spirit which, in the preceding generation, had triumphed over the armies of Essex and Waller, and had yielded only after a desperate struggle to the genius and vigor of Cromwell? The tyrant was overcome by fear. He ceased to repeat that concession had always ruined princes, and sullenly owned that he must stoop to court the Tories once more.* There is reason to believe that Halifax was, at this time, invited to return to office, and that he was not unwilling to do so. The part of mediator between the throne and the nation was, of all parts, that for which he was best qualified, and of which he was most ambitious. How the negotiation with him was broken off is not known: but it is not improbable that the question of the dispensing power was the

He attempts to conciliate his subjects.

---

* Adda, $\frac{\text{Sept. 28,}}{\text{Oct. 8,}}$ 1688. This despatch describes strongly James's dread of a universal defection of his subjects.

insurmountable difficulty. His hostility to the dispensing power had caused his disgrace three years before: nothing that had since happened had been of a nature to change his views; and James was fully determined to make no concession on that point.* As to other matters His Majesty was less pertinacious. He put forth a proclamation in which he solemnly promised to protect the Church of England and to maintain the Act of Uniformity. He declared himself willing to make great sacrifices for the sake of concord. He would no longer insist that Roman Catholics should be admitted into the House of Commons; and he trusted that his people would justly appreciate such a proof of his disposition to meet their wishes. Three days later he notified his intention to replace all the magistrates and deputy-lieutenants who had been dismissed for refusing to support his policy. On the day after the appearance of this notification Compton's suspension was taken off.†

At the same time the King gave an audience to all the Bishops who were then in London. They had requested admittance to his presence for the purpose of tendering their counsel in this emergency. The Primate was spokesman. He respectfully asked that the administration might be put into the hands of persons duly qualified, that all acts done under pretence of the dispensing power might be revoked, that the Ecclesiastical Commission might be annulled, that the wrongs of Magdalene College might be redressed, and that the old franchises of the municipal corporations might be restored. He hinted very intelligibly that there was one most desirable event which would completely secure the throne and quiet the distracted realm. If His Majesty would reconsider the points in dispute between the Churches of Rome and England, perhaps, by the divine blessing on the arguments which the Bishops wished to lay before him, he might be convinced that it was his duty to return

_{He gives audience to the Bishops.}

---

* All the scanty light which we have respecting this negotiation is derived from Reresby. His informant was a lady whom he does not name, and who certainly was not to be implicitly trusted.

† London Gazette, Sept. 24, 27, Oct. 1, 1688.

to the religion of his father and of his grandfather. Thus far, Sancroft said, he had spoken the sense of his brethren. There remained a subject on which he had not taken counsel with them, but to which he thought it his duty to advert. He was, indeed, the only man of his profession who could advert to that subject without being suspected of an interested motive. The metropolitan see of York had been three years vacant. The Archbishop implored the King to fill it speedily with a pious and learned divine, and added that such a divine might without difficulty be found among those who then stood in the royal presence. The King commanded himself sufficiently to return thanks for this unpalatable counsel, and promised to consider what had been said.* Of the dispensing power he would not yield one tittle. No unqualified person was removed from any civil or military office. But some of Sancroft's suggestions were adopted. Within forty-eight hours the Court of High Commission was abolished.† It was determined that the charter of the City of London, which had been forfeited six years before, should be restored; and the Chancellor was sent in state to carry back the venerable parchment to Guildhall.‡ A week later the public was informed that the Bishop of Winchester, who was by virtue of his office Visitor of Magdalene College, had it in charge from the King to correct whatever was amiss in that society. It was not without a long struggle and a bitter pang that James stooped to this last humiliation. Indeed, he did not yield till the Vicar Apostolic Leyburn, who seems to have behaved on all occasions like a wise and honest man, declared that in his judgment the ejected President and Fellows had been wronged, and that, on religious as well as on political grounds, restitution ought to be made to them.§ In a few days ap-

---

* Tanner MSS.; Burnet, i., 784. Burnet has, I think, confounded this audience with an audience which took place a few weeks later.

† London Gazette, Oct. 8, 1688.   ‡ Ibid.

§ London Gazette, Oct. 15, 1688; Adda, Oct. $\frac{12}{22}$. The Nuncio, though generally an enemy to violent courses, seems to have opposed the restoration of Hough, probably from regard for the interests of Giffard and the other Roman Catholics who were quartered in Magdalene College. Leyburn declared himself " nel sentimento che fosse stato uno spoglio, e che il possesso in cui si trovano ora li Cattolici fosse

peared a proclamation restoring the forfeited franchises of all the municipal corporations.*

James flattered himself that concessions so great, made in the short space of a month, would bring back to him the hearts of his people. Nor can it be doubted that such concessions, if they had been made before there was reason to expect an invasion from Holland, would have done much to conciliate the Tories. But gratitude is not to be expected by rulers who give to fear what they have refused to justice. During three years the King had been proof to all argument and to all entreaty. Every minister who had dared to raise his voice in favor of the civil and ecclesiastical constitution of the realm had been disgraced. A Parliament eminently loyal had ventured to protest gently and respectfully against a violation of the fundamental laws of England, and had been sternly reprimanded, prorogued, and dissolved. Judge after judge had been stripped of the ermine for declining to give decisions opposed to the whole common and statute law. The most respectable Cavaliers had been excluded from all share in the government of their counties for refusing to betray the public liberties. Scores of clergymen had been deprived of their livelihood for observing their oaths. Prelates, to whose steadfast fidelity the King owed the crown which he wore, had on their knees besought him not to command them to violate the laws of God and of the land. Their modest petition had been treated as a seditious libel. They had been browbeaten, threatened, imprisoned, prosecuted, and had narrowly escaped utter ruin. Then at length the nation, finding that right was borne down by might, and that even supplication was regarded as a crime, began to think of trying the chances of war. The oppressor learned that an armed deliverer was at hand, and would be eagerly welcomed by Whigs and Tories, Dissenters and Churchmen. All was immediately changed. That government which had requited constant and zealous

_{His concessions ill received.}

---

violento ed illegale, onde non era privar questi di un dritto acquisto, ma rendere agli altri quello che era stato levato con violenza."

* London Gazette, Oct. 18, 1688.

service with spoliation and persecution, that government which to weighty reasons and pathetic entreaties had replied only by injuries and insults, became in a moment strangely gracious. Every Gazette now announced the removal of some grievance. It was then evident that on the equity, the humanity, the plighted word of the King, no reliance could be placed, and that he would govern well only so long as he was under the strong dread of resistance. His subjects were therefore by no means disposed to restore to him a confidence which he had justly forfeited, or to relax the pressure which had wrung from him the only good acts of his whole reign. The general impatience for the arrival of the Dutch became every day stronger. The gales which at this time blew obstinately from the west, and which at once prevented the Prince's armament from sailing and brought fresh Irish regiments from Dublin to Chester, were bitterly cursed and reviled by the common people. The weather, it was said, was Popish.* Crowds stood in Cheapside gazing intently at the weather-cock on the graceful steeple of Bow Church, and praying for a Protestant wind.†

The general feeling was strengthened by an event which, though merely accidental, was not unnaturally ascribed to the perfidy of the King. The Bishop of Winchester announced that, in obedience to the royal commands, he designed to restore the ejected members of Magdalene College. He fixed the twenty-first of October for this ceremony, and on the twentieth went down to Oxford. The whole University was in expectation. The expelled Fellows had arrived from all parts of the kingdom, eager to take possession of their beloved home. Three hundred gentlemen on horseback escorted the Visitor to his lodgings. As he passed, the bells rang, and the High Street was crowded with shouting spectators. He retired to rest. The next morning a joyous crowd assembled at the gates of Magdalene: but the Bishop did not make his

---

* "Vento Papista," says Adda, $\frac{\text{Oct. 24,}}{\text{Nov. 3,}}$ 1688.

† The expression Protestant wind seems to have been first applied to the wind which kept Tyrconnel, during some time, from taking possession of the government of Ireland. See the first part of Lillibullero.

appearance; and soon it was known that he had been roused from his bed by a royal messenger, and had been directed to repair immediately to Whitehall. This strange disappointment caused much wonder and anxiety: but in a few hours came news which, to minds disposed, not without reason, to think the worst, seemed completely to explain the King's change of purpose. The Dutch armament had put out to sea, and had been driven back by a storm. The disaster was exaggerated by rumor. Many ships, it was said, had been lost. Thousands of horses had perished. All thought of a design on England must be relinquished, at least for the present year. Here was a lesson for the nation. While James expected immediate invasion and rebellion, he had given orders that reparation should be made to those whom he had unlawfully despoiled. As soon as he found himself safe, those orders had been revoked. This imputation, though at that time generally believed, and though, since that time, repeated by writers who ought to have been well informed, was without foundation. It is certain that the mishap of the Dutch fleet could not, by any mode of communication, have been known at Westminster till some hours after the Bishop of Winchester had received the summons which called him away from Oxford. The King, however, had little right to complain of the suspicions of his people. If they sometimes, without severely examining evidence, ascribed to his dishonest policy what was really the effect of accident or inadvertence, the fault was his own. That men who are in the habit of breaking faith should be distrusted when they mean to keep it is part of their just and natural punishment.*

It is remarkable that James, on this occasion, incurred one unmerited imputation solely in consequence of his eagerness to clear himself from another imputation equally unmerited. The Bishop of Winchester had been hastily summoned from Oxford to attend an extraordinary meeting of the Privy Council, or rather an assembly of Notables, which had been

---

* All the evidence on this point is collected in Howell's edition of the State Trials.

II.—28

convoked at Whitehall. With the Privy Councillors were joined, in this solemn sitting, all the Peers Spiritual and Temporal who chanced to be in or near the capital, the Judges, the crown lawyers, the Lord Mayor and the Aldermen of the City of London. A hint had been given to Petre that he would do well to absent himself. In truth, few of the Peers would have chosen to sit with him. Near the head of the board a chair of state was placed for the Queen-dowager. The Princess Anne had been requested to attend, but had excused herself on the plea of delicate health.

James informed this great assembly that he thought it necessary to produce proofs of the birth of his son. The arts of bad men had poisoned the public mind to such an extent that very many believed the Prince of Wales to be a supposititious child. But Providence had graciously ordered things so that scarcely any prince had ever come into the world in the presence of so many witnesses. Those witnesses then appeared and gave their evidence. After all the depositions had been taken, James with great solemnity declared that the imputation thrown on him was utterly false, and that he would rather die a thousand deaths than wrong any of his children.

Proofs of the birth of the Prince of Wales submitted to the Privy Council.

All who were present appeared to be satisfied. The evidence was instantly published, and was allowed by judicious and impartial persons to be decisive.* But the judicious are always a minority; and scarcely anybody was then impartial. The whole nation was convinced that all sincere Papists thought it a duty to perjure themselves whenever they could, by perjury, serve the interests of their Church. Men who, having been bred Protestants, had for the sake of lucre pretended to be converted to Popery, were, if possible, less trustworthy than sincere Papists. The depositions of all who belonged to these two classes were therefore regarded as mere nullities. Thus the weight of the testimony on which James had relied was greatly reduced. What remained was malig-

---

* The evidence will be found, with much illustrative matter, in Howell's edition of the State Trials.

nantly scrutinized. To every one of the few Protestant witnesses who had said anything material some exception was taken. One was notoriously a greedy sycophant. Another had not indeed yet apostatized, but was nearly related to an apostate. The people asked, as they had asked from the first, why, if all was right, the King, knowing, as he knew, that many doubted the reality of his wife's pregnancy, had not taken care that the birth should be more satisfactorily proved. Was there nothing suspicious in the false reckoning, in the sudden change of abode, in the absence of the Princess Anne and of the Archbishop of Canterbury? Why was no prelate of the Established Church in attendance? Why was not the Dutch Ambassador summoned? Why, above all, were not the Hydes, loyal servants of the crown, faithful sons of the Church, and natural guardians of the interest of their nieces, suffered to mingle with the crowd of Papists which was assembled in and near the royal bedchamber? Why, in short, was there, in the long list of assistants, not a single name which commanded public confidence and respect? The true answer to these questions was that the King's understanding was weak, that his temper was despotic, and that he had willingly seized an opportunity of manifesting his contempt for the opinion of his subjects. But the multitude, not contented with this explanation, attributed to deep-laid villany what was really the effect of folly and perverseness. Nor was this opinion confined to the multitude. The Lady Anne, at her toilette, on the morning after the Council, spoke of the investigation with such scorn as emboldened the very tirewomen who were dressing her to put in their jests. Some of the Lords who had heard the examination, and had appeared to be satisfied, were really unconvinced. Lloyd, Bishop of Saint Asaph, whose piety and learning commanded general respect, continued to the end of his life to believe that a fraud had been practised.

The depositions taken before the Council had not been many hours in the hands of the public when it was noised abroad that Sunderland had been dismissed from all his places. The news of his disgrace seems to have

Disgrace of Sunderland.

taken the politicians of the coffee-houses by surprise, but did not astonish those who had observed what was passing in the palace. Treason had not been brought home to him by legal, or even by tangible, evidence: but there was a strong suspicion among those who watched him closely that, through some channel or other, he was in communication with the enemies of that government in which he occupied so high a place. He, with unabashed forehead, imprecated on his own head all evil here and hereafter if he was guilty. His only fault, he protested, was that he had served the crown too well. Had he not given hostages to the royal cause? Had he not broken down every bridge by which he could, in case of a disaster, effect his retreat? Had he not gone all lengths in favor of the dispensing power, sat in the High Commission, signed the warrant for the commitment of the Bishops, appeared as a witness against them, at the hazard of his life, amidst the hisses and curses of the thousands who filled Westminster Hall? Had he not given the last proof of fidelity by renouncing his religion, and publicly joining a Church which the nation detested? What had he to hope from a change? What had he not to dread? These arguments, though plausible, and though set off by the most insinuating address, could not remove the impression which whispers and reports arriving at once from a hundred different quarters had produced. The King became daily colder and colder. Sunderland attempted to support himself by the Queen's help, obtained an audience of Her Majesty, and was actually in her apartment when Middleton entered, and, by the King's orders, demanded the seals. That evening the fallen minister was for the last time closeted with the Prince whom he had flattered and betrayed. The interview was a strange one. Sunderland acted calumniated virtue to perfection. He regretted not, he said, the Secretaryship of State or the Presidency of the Council, if only he retained his Sovereign's esteem. "Do not, sir, do not make me the most unhappy gentleman in your dominions, by refusing to declare that you acquit me of disloyalty." The King hardly knew what to believe. There was no positive proof of guilt; and the energy and pathos with which Sunderland lied might have imposed on a keener understanding than that with which he had to deal. At the French embassy his professions still found credit. There he declared that he should remain a few days in London, and show himself at court. He would then retire to his country-seat at Althorpe, and try to repair his dilapidated fortunes by economy. If a revolution should take place he must fly to France. His ill-requited loyalty had left him no other place of refuge.*

The seals which had been taken from Sunderland were delivered to Preston. The same Gazette which announced this change contained the official intelligence of the disaster which had befallen the Dutch fleet.† That disaster was serious, though far less serious than the King and his few adherents, misled by their wishes, were disposed to believe.

On the sixteenth of October, according to the English reckoning, was held a solemn sitting of the States of Holland.
<small>William takes leave of the States of Holland.</small> The Prince came to bid them farewell. He thanked them for the kindness with which they had watched over him when he was left an orphan child, for the confidence which they had reposed in him during his administration, and for the assistance which they had granted to him at this momentous crisis. He entreated them to believe that he had always meant and endeavored to promote the interest of his country. He was now quitting them, perhaps never to return. If he should fall in defence of the reformed religion and of the independence of Europe, he commended his beloved wife to their care. The Grand Pensionary answered in a faltering voice; and in all that grave senate there was none who could refrain from shedding tears. But the iron stoicism of William never gave way; and he stood among his weeping friends calm and austere, as if he had been about to leave them only for a short visit to his hunting-grounds at Loo.‡

* Barillon, Oct. $\frac{8}{18}, \frac{15}{25}, \frac{18}{28}, \frac{Oct.\ 25}{Nov.\ 4}, \frac{Oct.\ 27}{Nov.\ 6}, \frac{Oct.\ 29}{Nov.\ 8}$, 1688; Adda, $\frac{Oct.\ 26}{Nov.\ 5}$.

† London Gazette, Oct 29, 1688.

‡ Register of the Proceedings of the States of Holland and West Friesland; Burnet, i., 782.

The deputies of the principal towns accompanied him to his yacht. Even the representatives of Amsterdam, so long the chief seat of opposition to his administration, joined in paying him this compliment. Public prayers were offered for him on that day in all the churches of the Hague.

In the evening he arrived at Helvoetsluys and went on board of a frigate called the Brill. His flag was immediately hoisted. It displayed the arms of Nassau quartered with those of England. The motto, embroidered in letters three feet long, was happily chosen. The House of Orange had long used the elliptical device, "I will maintain." The ellipsis was now filled up with words of high import, "The liberties of England and the Protestant religion."

He embarks and sails.

The Prince had not been many hours on board when the wind became fair. On the nineteenth the armament put out to sea, and traversed, before a strong breeze, about half the distance between the Dutch and English coasts. Then the wind changed, blew hard from the west, and swelled into a violent tempest. The ships, scattered and in great distress, regained the shore of Holland as they best might. The Brill reached Helvoetsluys on the twenty-first. The Prince's fellow-passengers had observed with admiration that neither peril nor mortification had for one moment disturbed his composure. He now, though suffering from sea-sickness, refused to go on shore: for he conceived that, by remaining on board, he should in the most effectual manner notify to Europe that the late misfortune had only delayed for a very short time the execution of his purpose. In two or three days the fleet reassembled. One vessel only had been cast away. Not a single soldier or sailor was missing. Some horses had perished: but this loss the Prince with great expedition repaired; and, before the London Gazette had spread the news of his mishap, he was again ready to sail.*

He is driven back by a storm.

---

* London Gazette, October 29, 1688; Burnet, i., 782; Bentinck to his wife, October $\frac{21}{31}$, $\frac{\text{Oct. 22, Oct. 24, Oct. 27,}}{\text{Nov. 1, Nov. 3, Nov. 6,}}$ 1688.

His Declaration preceded him only by a few hours. On the first of November it began to be mentioned in mysterious whispers by the politicians of London, was passed secretly from man to man, and was slipped into the boxes of the post-office. One of the agents was arrested, and the packets of which he was in charge were carried to Whitehall. The King read, and was greatly troubled. His first impulse was to hide the paper from all human eyes. He threw into the fire every copy which had been brought to him, except one; and that one he would scarcely trust out of his own hands.*

His Declaration arrives in England.

The paragraph in the manifesto which disturbed him most was that in which it was said that some of the Peers, Spiritual and Temporal, had invited the Prince of Orange to invade England. Halifax, Clarendon, and Nottingham were then in London. They were immediately summoned to the palace and interrogated. Halifax, though conscious of innocence, refused at first to make any answer. "Your Majesty asks me," said he, "whether I have committed high treason. If I am suspected, let me be brought before my peers. And how can Your Majesty place any dependence on the answer of a culprit whose life is at stake? Even if I had invited His Highness over, I should without scruple plead Not Guilty." The King declared that he did not at all consider Halifax as a culprit, and that he had asked the question as one gentleman asks another who has been calumniated whether there be the least foundation for the calumny. "In that case," said Halifax, "I have no objection to aver, as a gentleman speaking to a gentleman, on my honor, which is as sacred as my oath, that I have not invited the Prince of Orange over."† Clarendon and Nottingham said the same. The King was still more anxious to ascertain the temper of the Prelates. If they were hostile to him, his throne was indeed in danger. But it could not be. There was something monstrous in the supposition that any Bishop

James questions the Lords.

---

* Van Citters, Nov. $\frac{2}{12}$, 1688; Adda, Nov. $\frac{2}{12}$.

† Ronquillo, Nov. $\frac{12}{22}$, 1688. "Estas respuestas," says Ronquillo, "son ciertas, aunque mas las encubrian en la corte."

of the Church of England could rebel against his Sovereign. Compton was called into the royal closet, and was asked whether he believed that there was the slightest ground for the Prince's assertion. The Bishop was in a strait; for he was himself one of the seven who had signed the invitation; and his conscience, not a very enlightened conscience, would not suffer him, it seems, to utter a direct falsehood. "Sir," he said, "I am quite confident that there is not one of my brethren who is not as guiltless as myself in this matter." The equivocation was ingenious: but whether the difference between the sin of such an equivocation and the sin of a lie be worth any expense of ingenuity may perhaps be doubted. The King was satisfied. "I fully acquit you all," he said. "But I think it necessary that you should publicly contradict the slanderous charge brought against you in the Prince's Declaration." The Bishop very naturally begged that he might be allowed to read the paper which he was required to contradict: but the King would not suffer him to look at it.

On the following day appeared a proclamation threatening with the severest punishment all who should circulate, or who should even dare to read, William's manifesto.* The Primate and the few Spiritual Peers who happened to be then in London had orders to wait upon the King. Preston was in attendance with the Prince's Declaration in his hand. "My Lords," said James, "listen to this passage. It concerns you." Preston then read the sentence in which the Spiritual Peers were mentioned. The King proceeded: "I do not believe one word of this: I am satisfied of your innocence: but I think it fit to let you know of what you are accused."

The Primate, with many dutiful expressions, protested that the King did him no more than justice. "I was born in Your Majesty's allegiance. I have repeatedly confirmed that allegiance by my oath. I can have but one king at one time. I have not invited the Prince over; and I do not believe that a single one of my brethren has done so." "I am sure I have not," said Crewe of Durham. "Nor I," said Cart-

---

* London Gazette, Nov. 5, 1688. The Proclamation is dated November 2.

wright of Chester. Crewe and Cartwright might well be believed; for both had sat in the Ecclesiastical Commission. When Compton's turn came, he parried the question with an adroitness which a Jesuit might have envied. "I gave Your Majesty my answer yesterday."

James repeated again and again that he fully acquitted them all. Nevertheless it would, in his judgment, be for his service and for their own honor that they should publicly vindicate themselves. He therefore required them to draw up a paper setting forth their abhorrence of the Prince's design. They remained silent: their silence was supposed to imply consent; and they were suffered to withdraw.*

Meanwhile the fleet of William was on the German Ocean. It was on the evening of Thursday the first of November that he put to sea the second time. The wind blew fresh from the east. The armament, during twelve hours, held a course toward the north-west. The light vessels sent out by the English Admiral for the purpose of obtaining intelligence brought back news which confirmed the prevailing opinion that the enemy would try to land in Yorkshire. All at once, on a signal from the Prince's ship, the whole fleet tacked, and made sail for the British Channel. The same breeze which favored the voyage of the invaders prevented Dartmouth from coming out of the Thames. His ships were forced to strike yards and topmasts; and two of his frigates, which had gained the open sea, were shattered by the violence of the weather and driven back into the river.†

William sets sail the second time.

The Dutch fleet ran fast before the gale, and reached the Straits at about ten in the morning of Saturday, the third of November. William himself, in the Brill, led the way. More than six hundred vessels, with canvas spread to a favorable wind, followed in his train. The transports were in the centre. The men-of-war, more than fifty in number, formed

---

* Tanner MSS.

† Burnet, i., 787; Rapin; Whittle's Exact Diary; Expedition of the Prince of Orange to England, 1688; History of the Desertion, 1688; Dartmouth to James, Nov. 5, 1688, in Dalrymple.

an outer rampart. Herbert, with the title of Lieutenant Admiral General, commanded the whole fleet. His post was in the rear, and many English sailors, inflamed against Popery, and attracted by high pay, served under him. It was not without great difficulty that the Prince had prevailed on some Dutch officers of high reputation to submit to the authority of a stranger. But the arrangement was eminently judicious. There was in the King's fleet much discontent, and an ardent zeal for the Protestant faith. But within the memory of old mariners the Dutch and English navies had thrice, with heroic spirit and various fortune, contended for the empire of the sea. Our sailors had not forgotten the broom with which Tromp had threatened to sweep the Channel, or the fire which De Ruyter had lighted in the dockyards of the Medway. Had the rival nations been once more brought face to face on the element of which both claimed the sovereignty, all other thoughts might have given place to mutual animosity. A bloody and obstinate battle might have been fought. Defeat would have been fatal to William's enterprise. Even victory would have deranged all his deeply meditated schemes of policy. He therefore wisely determined that the pursuers, if they overtook him, should be hailed in their own mother-tongue, and adjured, by an admiral under whom they had served, and whom they esteemed, not to fight against old messmates for Popish tyranny. Such an appeal might possibly avert a conflict. If a conflict took place, one English commander would be opposed to another; nor would the pride of the islanders be wounded by learning that Dartmouth had been compelled to strike to Herbert.*

Happily William's precautions were not necessary. Soon

---

* Avaux, July $\frac{12}{22}$, Aug. $\frac{14}{24}$, 1688. On this subject, Mr. De Jonge, who is connected by affinity with the descendants of the Dutch Admiral Evertsen, has kindly communicated to me some interesting information derived from family papers. In a letter to Bentinck, dated Sept. $\frac{6}{16}$, 1688, William insists strongly on the importance of avoiding an action, and begs Bentinck to represent this to Herbert. "Ce n'est pas le tems de faire voir sa bravoure, ni de se battre si l'on le peut éviter. Je luy l'ai déjà dit: mais il sera nécessaire que vous le répétiez, et que vous le luy fassiez bien comprendre."

after mid-day he passed the Straits. His fleet spread to within a league of Dover on the north, and of Calais on the south. The men-of-war on the extreme right and left saluted both fortresses at once. The troops appeared under arms on the decks. The flourish of trumpets, the clash of cymbals, and the rolling of drums were distinctly heard at once on the English and French shores. An innumerable company of gazers blackened the white beach of Kent. Another mighty multitude covered the coast of Picardy. Rapin de Thoyras, who, driven by persecution from his country, had taken service in the Dutch army, and now went with the Prince to England, described the spectacle, many years later, as the most magnificent and affecting that was ever seen by human eyes. At sunset the armament was off Beachy Head. Then the lights were kindled. The sea was in a blaze for many miles. But the eyes of all the steersmen were directed throughout the night to three huge lanterns which flamed on the stern of the Brill.*

He passes the Straits.

Meanwhile a courier had been riding post from Dover Castle to Whitehall with news that the Dutch had passed the Straits and were steering westward. It was necessary to make an immediate change in all the military arrangements. Messengers were despatched in every direction. Officers were roused from their beds at dead of night. At three on the Sunday morning there was a great muster by torch-light in Hyde Park. The King had sent several regiments northward in the expectation that William would land in Yorkshire. Expresses were despatched to recall them. All the forces except those which were necessary to keep the peace of the capital were ordered to move to the West. Salisbury was appointed as the place of rendezvous; but, as it was thought possible that Portsmouth might be the first point of attack, three battalions of Guards and a strong body of cavalry set out for that fortress. In a few hours it was known that Portsmouth was safe; and these troops then re-

---

* Rapin's History; Whittle's Exact Diary. I have seen a contemporary Dutch chart of the order in which the fleet sailed.

ceived orders to change their route and to hasten to Salisbury.*

When Sunday the fourth of November dawned, the cliffs of the Isle of Wight were full in view of the Dutch armament. That day was the anniversary both of William's birth and of his marriage. Sail was slackened during part of the morning; and divine service was performed on board of the ships. In the afternoon and through the night the fleet held on its course. Torbay was the place where the Prince intended to land. But the morning of Monday the fifth of November was hazy. The pilot of the Brill could not discern the sea marks, and carried the fleet too far to the west. The danger was great. To return in the face of the wind was impossible. Plymouth was the next port. But at Plymouth a garrison had been posted under the command of the Earl of Bath. The landing might be opposed; and a check might produce serious consequences. There could be little doubt, moreover, that by this time the royal fleet had got out of the Thames and was hastening full sail down the Channel. Russell saw the whole extent of the peril, and exclaimed to Burnet, "You may go to prayers, Doctor. All is over." At that moment the wind changed: a soft breeze sprang up from the south: the mist dispersed: the sun shone forth; and, under the mild light of an autumnal noon, the fleet turned back, passed round the lofty cape of Berry Head, and rode safe in the harbor of Torbay.†

Since William looked on that harbor its aspect has greatly changed. The amphitheatre which surrounds the spacious basin now exhibits everywhere the signs of prosperity and civilization. At the north-eastern extremity has sprung up a great watering-place, to which strangers are attracted from the most remote parts of our island by the Italian softness of the air: for in that climate the myrtle flourishes unsheltered; and even the winter is milder than the Northumbrian April. The inhabitants are about

He lands at Torbay.

* Adda, Nov. $\frac{5}{15}$, 1688; News-letter in the Mackintosh Collection; Van Citters, Nov. $\frac{6}{16}$.

† Burnet, i., 788; Extracts from the Legge Papers in the Mackintosh Collection.

ten thousand in number. The newly built churches and chapels, the baths and libraries, the hotels and public gardens, the infirmary and the museum, the white streets, rising terrace above terrace, the gay villas peeping from the midst of shrubberies and flower-beds, present a spectacle widely different from any that in the seventeenth century England could show. At the opposite end of the bay lies, sheltered by Berry Head, the stirring market-town of Brixham, the wealthiest seat of our fishing trade. A pier and a haven were formed there at the beginning of the present century, but have been found insufficient for the increasing traffic. The population is about six thousand souls. The shipping amounts to more than two hundred sail. The tonnage exceeds many times the tonnage of the port of Liverpool under the kings of the House of Stuart. But Torbay, when the Dutch fleet cast anchor there, was known only as a haven where ships sometimes took refuge from the tempests of the Atlantic. Its quiet shores were undisturbed by the bustle either of commerce or of pleasure; and the huts of ploughmen and fishermen were thinly scattered over what is now the site of crowded marts and of luxurious pavilions.

The peasantry of the coast of Devonshire remembered the name of Monmouth with affection, and held Popery in detestation. They therefore crowded down to the sea-side with provisions and offers of service. The disembarkation instantly commenced. Sixty boats conveyed the troops to the coast. Mackay was sent on shore first with the British regiments. The Prince soon followed. He landed where the quay of Brixham now stands. The whole aspect of the place has been altered. Where we now see a port crowded with shipping, and a market-place swarming with buyers and sellers, the waves then broke on a desolate beach; but a fragment of the rock on which the deliverer stepped from his boat has been carefully preserved, and is set up as an object of public veneration in the centre of that busy wharf.

As soon as the Prince had planted his foot on dry ground he called for horses. Two beasts, such as the small yeomen of that time were in the habit of riding, were procured from the neighboring village. William and Schomberg mounted and proceeded to examine the country.

As soon as Burnet was on shore he hastened to the Prince. An amusing dialogue took place between them. Burnet poured forth his congratulations with genuine delight, and then eagerly asked what were His Highness's plans. Military men are seldom disposed to take counsel with gownsmen on military matters; and William regarded the interference of unprofessional advisers, in questions relating to war, with even more than the disgust ordinarily felt by soldiers on such occasions. But he was at that moment in an excellent humor, and, instead of signifying his displeasure by a short and cutting reprimand, graciously extended his hand, and answered his chaplain's question by another question: "Well, Doctor, what do you think of predestination now?" The reproof was so delicate that Burnet, whose perceptions were not very fine, did not perceive it. He answered with great fervor that he should never forget the signal manner in which Providence had favored their undertaking.*

During the first day the troops who had gone on shore had many discomforts to endure. The earth was soaked with rain. The baggage was still on board of the ships. Officers of high rank were compelled to sleep in wet clothes on the wet ground: the Prince himself had no better quarters than a hut afforded. His banner was displayed on the thatched roof; and some bedding brought from the Brill was spread for him on the floor.† There was some difficulty about landing the horses; and it seemed probable that this operation would occupy several days. But on the following morning the prospect cleared. The wind was gentle. The water in the bay was as even as glass. Some fishermen pointed out a place where the ships could be brought within sixty feet of the beach. This was done; and in three hours many hundreds of horses swam safely to shore.

---

* I think that nobody who compares Burnet's account of this conversation with Dartmouth's can doubt that I have correctly represented what passed.

† I have seen a contemporary Dutch print of the disembarkation. Some men are bringing the Prince's bedding into the hut on which his flag is flying.

The disembarkation had hardly been effected when the wind rose again, and swelled into a fierce gale from the west. The enemy coming in pursuit down the Channel had been stopped by the same change of weather which enabled William to land. During two days the King's fleet lay on an unruffled sea in sight of Beachy Head. At length Dartmouth was able to proceed. He passed the Isle of Wight, and one of his ships came in sight of the Dutch top-masts in Torbay. Just at this moment he was encountered by the tempest, and compelled to take shelter in the harbor of Portsmouth.* At that time James, who was not incompetent to form a judgment on a question of seamanship, declared himself perfectly satisfied that his admiral had done all that man could do, and had yielded only to the irresistible hostility of the winds and waves. At a later period the unfortunate prince began, with little reason, to suspect Dartmouth of treachery, or at least of slackness.†

The weather had indeed served the Protestant cause so well that some men of more piety than judgment fully believed the ordinary laws of nature to have been suspended for the preservation of the liberty and religion of England. Exactly a hundred years before, they said, the Armada, invincible by man, had been scattered by the wrath of God. Civil freedom and divine truth were again in jeopardy; and again the obedient elements had fought for the good cause. The wind had blown strong from the east while the Prince wished to sail down the Channel, had turned to the south when he wished to enter Torbay, had sunk to a calm during the disembarkation, and, as soon as the disembarkation was completed, had risen to a storm, and had met the pursuers in the face. Nor did men omit to remark that, by an extraordinary coincidence, the Prince had reached our shores on a day on which the Church of England commemorated, by prayer and thanksgiving, the wonderful escape of the royal House and of the

---

* Burnet, i., 789; Legge Papers.
† On Nov. 9, James wrote to Dartmouth thus: "Nobody could work otherwise than you did. I am sure all knowing seamen must be of the same mind." But see the Life of James, ii., 207, Orig. Mem.

three Estates from the blackest plot ever devised by Papists. Carstairs, whose suggestions were sure to meet with attention from the Prince, recommended that, as soon as the landing had been effected, public thanks should be offered to God for the protection so conspicuously accorded to the great enterprise. This advice was taken, and with excellent effect. The troops, taught to regard themselves as favorites of heaven, were inspired with new courage; and the English people formed the most favorable opinion of a general and an army so attentive to the duties of religion.

On Tuesday, the sixth of November, William's army began to march up the country. Some regiments advanced as far as Newton Abbot. A stone, set up in the midst of that little town, still marks the spot where the Prince's Declaration was solemnly read to the people. The movements of the troops were slow: for the rain fell in torrents; and the roads of England were then in a state which seemed frightful to persons accustomed to the excellent communications of Holland. William took up his quarters, during two days, at Ford, a seat of the ancient and illustrious family of Courtenay, in the neighborhood of Newton Abbot. He was magnificently lodged and feasted there: but it is remarkable that the owner of the house, though a strong Whig, did not choose to be the first to put life and fortune in peril, and cautiously abstained from doing anything which, if the King should prevail, could be treated as a crime.

Exeter, in the mean time, was greatly agitated. Lamplugh, the bishop, as soon as he heard that the Dutch were at
<small>He enters Exeter.</small> Torbay, set off in terror for London. The Dean fled from the deanery. The magistrates were for the King, the body of the inhabitants for the Prince. Everything was in confusion when, on the morning of Thursday, the eighth of November, a body of troops, under the command of Mordaunt, appeared before the city. With Mordaunt came Burnet, to whom William had intrusted the duty of protecting the clergy of the Cathedral from injury and insult.* The Mayor and Aldermen had ordered the gates

---

* Burnet, i., 790.

to be closed, but yielded on the first summons. The deanery was prepared for the reception of the Prince. On the following day, Friday the ninth, he arrived. The magistrates had been pressed to receive him in state at the entrance of the city, but had steadfastly refused. The pomp of that day, however, could well spare them. Such a sight had never been seen in Devonshire. Many of the citizens went forth half a day's journey to meet the champion of their religion. All the neighboring villages poured forth their inhabitants. A great crowd, consisting chiefly of young peasants, brandishing their cudgels, had assembled on the top of Haldon Hill, whence the army, marching from Chudleigh, first descried the rich valley of the Exe, and the two massive towers rising from the cloud of smoke which overhung the capital of the West. The road, all down the long descent, and through the plain to the banks of the river, was lined, mile after mile, with spectators. From the West Gate to the Cathedral Close, the pressing and shouting on each side was such as reminded Londoners of the crowds on the Lord-Mayor's Day. The houses were gayly decorated. Doors, windows, balconies, and roofs were thronged with gazers. An eye accustomed to the pomp of war would have found much to criticise in the spectacle; for several toilsome marches in the rain, through roads where one who travelled on foot sank at every step up to the ankles in clay, had not improved the appearance either of the men or of their accoutrements. But the people of Devonshire, altogether unused to the splendor of well-ordered camps, were overwhelmed with delight and awe. Descriptions of the martial pageant were circulated all over the kingdom. They contained much that was well fitted to gratify the vulgar appetite for the marvellous. For the Dutch army, composed of men who had been born in various climates, and had served under various standards, presented an aspect at once grotesque, gorgeous, and terrible to islanders who had, in general, a very indistinct notion of foreign countries. First rode Macclesfield at the head of two hundred gentlemen, mostly of English blood, glittering in helmets and cuirasses, and mounted on Flemish war-horses. Each was attended by a negro, brought from the sugar plantations on the coast of Guiana. The citizens of Exeter, who had never seen so many specimens of the African race, gazed with wonder on those black faces set off by embroidered turbans and white feathers. Then, with drawn broadswords, came a squadron of Swedish horsemen in black armor and fur cloaks. They were regarded with a strange interest; for it was rumored that they were natives of a land where the ocean was frozen and where the night lasted through half the year, and that they had themselves slain the huge bears whose skins they wore. Next, surrounded by a goodly company of gentlemen and pages, was borne aloft the Prince's banner. On its broad folds the crowd which covered the roofs and filled the windows read with delight that memorable inscription, "The Protestant religion and the liberties of England." But the acclamations redoubled when, attended by forty running footmen, the Prince himself appeared, armed on back and breast, wearing a white plume and mounted on a white charger. With how martial an air he curbed his horse, how thoughtful and commanding was the expression of his ample forehead and falcon eye, may still be seen on the canvas of Kneller. Once those grave features relaxed into a smile. It was when an ancient woman, perhaps one of the zealous Puritans who, through twenty-eight years of persecution, had waited with firm faith for the consolation of Israel, perhaps the mother of some rebel who had perished in the carnage of Sedgemoor, or in the more fearful carnage of the Bloody Circuit, broke from the crowd, rushed through the drawn swords and curvetting horses, touched the hand of the deliverer, and cried out that now she was happy. Near to the Prince was one who divided with him the gaze of the multitude. That, men said, was the great Count Schomberg, the first soldier in Europe, since Turenne and Condé were gone, the man whose genius and valor had saved the Portuguese monarchy on the field of Montes Claros, the man who had earned a still higher glory by resigning the truncheon of a Marshal of France for the sake of the true religion. It was not forgotten that the two heroes who, indissolubly united by their common Protestantism, were entering Exeter together, had twelve years before been opposed to each other under the walls of Maestricht, and that the energy of the young Prince had not then been found a match for the cool science of the veteran who now rode in friendship by his side. Then came a long column of the whiskered infantry of Switzerland, distinguished in all the Continental wars of two centuries by pre-eminent valor and discipline, but never till that week seen on English ground. And then marched a succession of bands designated, as was the fashion of that age, after their leaders, Bentinck, Solmes, and Ginkell, Talmash and Mackay. With peculiar pleasure Englishmen might look on one gallant regiment which still bore the name of the honored and lamented Ossory. The effect of the spectacle was heightened by the recollection of more than one renowned event in which the warriors now pouring through the West Gate had borne a share. For they had seen service very different from that of the Devonshire militia or of the camp at Hounslow. Some of them had repelled the fiery onset of the French on the field of Seneff; and others had crossed swords with the infidels in the cause of Christendom on that great day when the siege of Vienna was raised. The very senses of the multitude were fooled by imagination. News-letters conveyed to every part of the kingdom fabulous accounts of the size and strength of the invaders. It was affirmed that they were, with scarcely an exception, above six feet high, and that they wielded such huge pikes, swords, and muskets as had never before been seen in England. Nor did the wonder of the population diminish when the artillery arrived, twenty-one heavy pieces of brass cannon, which were with difficulty tugged along by sixteen cart-horses to each. Much curiosity was excited by a strange structure mounted on wheels. It proved to be a movable smithy, furnished with all tools and materials necessary for repairing arms and carriages. But nothing caused so much astonishment as the bridge of boats, which was laid with great speed on the Exe for the conveyance of wagons, and afterward as speedily taken to pieces and carried away. It was made, if report said true, after a pattern contrived by the Christians who were warring against the Great Turk on the Danube. The foreigners inspired as much good-will as admiration. Their politic leader took care to distribute the quarters in such a manner as to cause the smallest possible inconvenience to the inhabitants of Exeter and of the neighboring villages. The most rigid discipline was maintained. Not only were pillage and outrage effectually prevented, but the troops were required to demean themselves with civility toward all classes. Those who had formed their notions of an army from the conduct of Kirke and his Lambs were amazed to see soldiers who never swore at a landlady or took an egg without paying for it. In return for this moderation the people furnished the troops with provisions in great abundance and at reasonable prices.*

Much depended on the course which, at this great crisis, the clergy of the Church of England might take; and the members of the Chapter of Exeter were the first who were called upon to declare their sentiments. Burnet informed the Canons, now left without a head by the flight of the Dean, that they could not be permitted to use the prayer for the Prince of Wales, and that a solemn service must be performed

---

* See Whittle's Diary, the Expedition of His Highness, and the Letter from Exon published at the time. I have myself seen two manuscript news-letters describing the pomp of the Prince's entrance into Exeter. A few months later a bad poet wrote a play, entitled "The late Revolution." One scene is laid at Exeter. "Enter battalions of the Prince's army, on their march into the city, with colors flying, drums beating, and the citizens shouting." A nobleman named Misopapas says,

"Can you guess, my lord,
How dreadful guilt and fear has represented
Your army to the court? Your number and your stature
Are both advanced; all six foot high at least,
In bearskins clad, Swiss, Swedes, and Brandenburghers."

In a song which appeared just after the entrance into Exeter, the Irish are described as mere dwarfs in comparison of the giants whom William commanded:

"Poor Berwick, how will thy dear joys
Oppose this famed viaggio?
Thy tallest sparks will be mere toys
To Brandenburgh and Swedish boys,
Coraggio! Coraggio!"

Addison alludes, in the Freeholder, to the extraordinary effect which these romantic stories produced.

in honor of the safe arrival of the Prince. The Canons did not choose to appear in their stalls; but some of the choristers and prebendaries attended. William repaired in military state to the Cathedral. As he passed under the gorgeous screen, that renowned organ, scarcely surpassed by any of those which are the boast of his native Holland, gave out a peal of triumph. He mounted the Bishop's seat, a stately throne rich with the carving of the fifteenth century. Burnet stood below; and a crowd of warriors and nobles appeared on the right hand and on the left. The singers, robed in white, sang the Te Deum. When the chant was over, Burnet read the Prince's Declaration: but, as soon as the first words were uttered, prebendaries and singers crowded in all haste out of the choir. At the close Burnet cried in a loud voice, "God save the Prince of Orange!" and many fervent voices answered, "Amen."*

On Sunday, the eleventh of November, Burnet preached before the Prince in the Cathedral, and dilated on the signal mercy vouchsafed by God to the English Church and nation. At the same time a singular event happened in a humbler place of worship. Ferguson resolved to preach at the Presbyterian meeting-house. The minister and elders would not consent: but the turbulent and half-witted knave, fancying that the times of Fleetwood and Harrison were come again, forced the door, went through the congregation sword in hand, mounted the pulpit, and there poured forth a fiery invective against the King. The time for such follies had gone by; and this exhibition excited nothing but derision and disgust.†

<small>Conversation of the King with the Bishops.</small> While these things were passing in Devonshire the ferment was great in London. The Prince's Declaration, in spite of all precautions, was now in every man's hands. On the sixth of November, James, still uncertain on what part of the coast the invaders had landed, summoned the Primate and three other Bishops, Compton of

---

* Expedition of the Prince of Orange; Oldmixon, 755; Whittle's Diary; Eachard, iii., 911; London Gazette, Nov. 15, 1688.

† London Gazette, Nov. 15, 1688; Expedition of the Prince of Orange.

London, White of Peterborough, and Sprat of Rochester, to a conference in the closet. The King listened graciously while the prelates made warm professions of loyalty, and assured them that he did not suspect them. "But where," said he, "is the paper that you were to bring me?" "Sir," answered Sancroft, "we have brought no paper. We are not solicitous to clear our fame to the world. It is no new thing to us to be reviled and falsely accused. Our consciences acquit us: Your Majesty acquits us; and we are satisfied." "Yes," said the King; "but a declaration from you is necessary to my service." He then produced a copy of the Prince's manifesto. "See," he said, "how you are mentioned here." "Sir," answered one of the Bishops, "not one person in five hundred believes this manifesto to be genuine." "No!" cried the King, fiercely: "then those five hundred would bring the Prince of Orange to cut my throat." "God forbid!" exclaimed the prelates in concert. But the King's understanding, never very clear, was now quite bewildered. One of his peculiarities was that, whenever his opinion was not adopted, he fancied that his veracity was questioned. "This paper not genuine!" he exclaimed, turning over the leaves with his hands. "Am I not worthy to be believed? Is my word not to be taken?" "At all events, sir," said one of the Bishops, "this is not an ecclesiastical matter. It lies within the sphere of the civil power. God has intrusted Your Majesty with the sword: and it is not for us to invade your functions." Then the Archbishop, with that gentle and temperate malice which inflicts the deepest wounds, declared that he must be excused from setting his hand to any political document. "I and my brethren, sir," he said, "have already smarted severely for meddling with affairs of state; and we shall be very cautious how we do so again. We once subscribed a petition of the most harmless kind: we presented it in the most respectful manner; and we found that we had committed a high offence. We were saved from ruin only by the merciful protection of God. And, sir, the ground then taken by Your Majesty's Attorney and Solicitor was that, out of Parliament, we were private men, and that it was criminal presumption in private men to meddle with politics. They attacked us so fiercely that for my part I gave myself over for lost." "I thank you for that, my Lord of Canterbury," said the King: "I should have hoped that you would not have thought yourself lost by falling into my hands." Such a speech might have become the mouth of a merciful sovereign, but it came with a bad grace from a prince who had burned a woman alive for harboring one of his flying enemies, from a prince round whose knees his own nephew had clung in vain agonies of supplication. The Archbishop was not to be so silenced. He resumed his story, and recounted the insults which the creatures of the court had offered to the Church of England, among which some ridicule thrown on his own style occupied a conspicuous place. The King had nothing to say but that there was no use in repeating old grievances, and that he had hoped that these things had been quite forgotten. He, who never forgot the smallest injury that he had suffered, could not understand how others should remember for a few weeks the most deadly injuries that he had inflicted.

At length the conversation came back to the point from which it had wandered. The King insisted on having from the Bishops a paper declaring their abhorrence of the Prince's enterprise. They, with many professions of the most submissive loyalty, pertinaciously refused. The Prince, they said, asserted that he had been invited by temporal as well as by spiritual peers. The imputation was common. Why should not the purgation be common also? "I see how it is," said the King. "Some of the temporal peers have been with you, and have persuaded you to cross me in this matter." The Bishops solemnly averred that it was not so. But it would, they said, seem strange that, on a question involving grave political and military considerations, the temporal peers should be entirely passed over, and the prelates alone should be required to take a prominent part. "But this," said James, "is my method. I am your King. It is for me to judge what is best. I will go my own way; and I call on you to assist me." The Bishops assured him that they would assist him in their proper department, as Christian ministers with their prayers, and as peers of the realm with their advice in his Parliament. James, who wanted neither the prayers of heretics nor the advice of Parliaments, was bitterly disappointed. After a long altercation, "I have done," he said; "I will urge you no further. Since you will not help me, I must trust to myself and to my own arms."*

The Bishops had hardly left the royal presence, when a courier arrived with the news that on the preceding day the Prince of Orange had landed in Devonshire. During the following week London was violently agitated. On Sunday, the eleventh of November, a rumor was circulated that knives, gridirons, and caldrons, intended for the torturing of heretics, were concealed in the monastery which had been established under the King's protection at Clerkenwell. Great multitudes assembled round the building, and were about to demolish it, when a military force arrived. The crowd was dispersed, and several of the rioters were slain. An inquest sat on the bodies, and came to a decision which strongly indicated the temper of the public mind. The jury found that certain loyal and well disposed persons, who had gone to put down the meetings of traitors and public enemies at a mass-house, had been wilfully murdered by the soldiers; and this strange verdict was signed by all the jurors. The ecclesiastics at Clerkenwell, naturally alarmed by these symptoms of popular feeling, were desirous to place their property in safety. They succeeded in removing most of their furniture before any report of their intentions got abroad. But at length the suspicions of the rabble were excited. The last two carts were stopped in Holborn, and all that they contained was publicly burned in the middle of the street. So great was the alarm among the Catholics that all their places of worship were closed, except those which belonged to the royal family and to foreign Ambassadors. †

<small>Disturbances in London.</small>

---

* Life of James, ii., 210, Orig. Mem.; Sprat's Narrative; Van Citters, Nov. $\frac{6}{16}$, 1688.

† Luttrell's Diary; News-letter in the Mackintosh Collection; Adda, Nov. $\frac{16}{26}$, 1688.

On the whole, however, things as yet looked not unfavorable for James. The invaders had been more than a week on English ground. Yet no man of note had joined them. No rebellion had broken out in the north or the east. No servant of the crown appeared to have betrayed his trust. The royal army was assembling fast at Salisbury, and, though inferior in discipline to that of William, was superior in numbers.

The Prince was undoubtedly surprised and mortified by the slackness of those who had invited him to England. By the common people of Devonshire, indeed, he had been received with every sign of good-will: but no nobleman, no gentleman of high consideration, had yet repaired to his quarters. The explanation of this singular fact is probably to be found in the circumstance that he had landed in a part of the island where he had not been expected. His friends in the north had made their arrangements for a rising, on the supposition that he would be among them with an army. His friends in the west had made no arrangements at all, and were naturally disconcerted at finding themselves suddenly called upon to take the lead in a movement so important and perilous. They had also fresh in their recollection, and, indeed, full in their sight, the disastrous consequences of rebellion — gibbets, heads, mangled quarters, families still in deep mourning for brave sufferers who had loved their country well but not wisely. After a warning so terrible and so recent, some hesitation was natural. It was equally natural, however, that William, who, trusting to promises from England, had put to hazard not only his own fame and fortunes but also the prosperity and independence of his native land, should feel deeply mortified. He was, indeed, so indignant, that he talked of falling back to Torbay, re-embarking his troops, returning to Holland, and leaving those who had betrayed him to the fate which they deserved. At length, on Monday, the twelfth of November, a gentleman named Burrington, who resided in the neighborhood of Crediton, joined the Prince's standard, and his example was followed by several of his neighbors.

Men of rank begin to repair to the Prince.

Men of higher consequence had already set out from different parts of the country for Exeter. The first of these was John Lord Lovelace, distinguished by his taste, by his magnificence, and by the audacious and intemperate vehemence of his Whiggism. He had been five or six times arrested for political offences. The last crime laid to his charge was that he had contemptuously denied the validity of a warrant signed by a Roman Catholic Justice of the Peace. He had been brought before the Privy Council and strictly examined, but to little purpose. He resolutely refused to criminate himself; and the evidence against him was insufficient. He was dismissed; but, before he retired, James exclaimed in great heat, "My Lord, this is not the first trick that you have played me." "Sir," answered Lovelace, with undaunted spirit, "I never played any trick to Your Majesty, or to any other person. Whoever has accused me to Your Majesty of playing tricks is a liar."* Lovelace had subsequently been admitted into the confidence of those who planned the Revolution. His mansion, built by his ancestors out of the spoils of Spanish galleons from the Indies, rose on the ruins of a house of Our Lady in that beautiful valley through which the Thames, not yet defiled by the precincts of a great capital, nor rising and falling with the flow and ebb of the sea, rolls under woods of beech round the gentle hills of Berkshire. Beneath the stately saloon, adorned by Italian pencils, was a subterraneous vault, in which the bones of ancient monks had sometimes been found. In this dark chamber some zealous and daring opponents of the government had held many midnight conferences during that anxious time when England was impatiently expecting the Protestant wind.† The season for action had now arrived. Lovelace, with seventy followers, well armed and mounted, quitted his dwelling, and directed his course westward. He reached Gloucestershire without difficulty. But Beaufort, who governed that county, was exerting all his great authority and in-

---

* Johnstone, Feb. 27, 1688; Van Citters of the same date.
† Lysons, Magna Britannia, Berkshire.

fluence in support of the crown. The militia had been called out. A strong party had been posted at Cirencester. When Lovelace arrived there he was informed that he could not be suffered to pass. It was necessary for him either to relinquish his undertaking or to fight his way through. He resolved to force a passage; and his friends and tenants stood gallantly by him. A sharp conflict took place. The militia lost an officer and six or seven men; but at length the followers of Lovelace were overpowered: he was made a prisoner, and sent to Gloucester Castle.*

Others were more fortunate. On the day on which the skirmish took place at Cirencester, Richard Savage, Lord Colchester, son and heir of the Earl Rivers, and father, by a lawless amour, of that unhappy poet whose misdeeds and misfortunes form one of the darkest portions of literary history, came with between sixty and seventy horse to Exeter. With him arrived the bold and turbulent Thomas Wharton. A few hours later came Edward Russell, son of the Earl of Bedford, and brother of the virtuous nobleman whose blood had been shed on the scaffold. Another arrival still more important was speedily announced. Colchester, Wharton, and Russell belonged to that party which had been constantly opposed to the court. James Bertie, Earl of Abingdon, had, on the contrary, been regarded as a supporter of arbitrary government. He had been true to James in the days of the Exclusion Bill. He had, as Lord-lieutenant of Oxfordshire, acted with vigor and severity against the adherents of Monmouth, and had lighted bonfires to celebrate the defeat of Argyle. But dread of Popery had driven him into opposition and rebellion. He was the first peer of the realm who made his appearance at the quarters of the Prince of Orange.†

But the King had less to fear from those who openly arrayed themselves against his authority, than from the dark conspiracy which had spread its ramifications through his

---

* London Gazette, Nov. 15, 1688; Luttrell's Diary.
† Burnet, i., 790; Life of William, 1703.

army and his family. Of that conspiracy Churchill, unrivalled in sagacity and address, endowed by nature with a certain cool intrepidity which never failed him either in fighting or lying, high in military rank, and high in the favor of the Princess Anne, must be regarded as the soul. It was not yet time for him to strike the decisive blow. But even thus early he inflicted, by the instrumentality of a subordinate agent, a wound, serious if not deadly, on the royal cause.

Edward Viscount Cornbury, eldest son of the Earl of Clarendon, was a young man of slender abilities, loose principles, and violent temper. He had been early taught to consider his relationship to the Princess Anne as the groundwork of his fortunes, and had been exhorted to pay her assiduous court. It had never occurred to his father that the hereditary loyalty of the Hydes could run any risk of contamination in the household of the King's favorite daughter: but in that household the Churchills held absolute sway; and Cornbury became their tool. He commanded one of the regiments of dragoons which had been sent westward. Such dispositions had been made that, on the fourteenth of November, he was, during a few hours, the senior officer at Salisbury, and all the troops assembled there were subject to his authority. It seems extraordinary that, at such a crisis, the army on which everything depended should have been left, even for a moment, under the command of a young colonel, who had neither abilities nor experience. There can be little doubt that so strange an arrangement was the result of deep design, and as little doubt to what head and to what heart the design is to be imputed.

Desertion of Cornbury.

Suddenly three of the regiments of cavalry which had assembled at Salisbury were ordered to march westward. Cornbury put himself at their head, and conducted them first to Blandford and thence to Dorchester. From Dorchester, after a halt of an hour or two, they set out for Axminster. Some of the officers began to be uneasy, and demanded an explanation of these strange movements. Cornbury replied that he had instructions to make a night attack on some troops which the Prince of Orange had posted at Honiton. But suspicion was awake. Searching questions were put, and were evasively answered. At last Cornbury was pressed to produce his orders. He perceived, not only that it would be impossible for him to carry over all the three regiments, as he had hoped, but that he was himself in a situation of considerable peril. He accordingly stole away with a few followers to the Dutch quarters. Most of his troops returned to Salisbury: but some who had been detached from the main body, and who had no suspicion of the designs of their commander, proceeded to Honiton. There they found themselves in the midst of a large force which was fully prepared to receive them. Resistance was impossible. Their leader pressed them to take service under William. A gratuity of a month's pay was offered to them, and was by most of them accepted.*

The news of these events reached London on the fifteenth. James had been on the morning of that day in high goodhumor. Bishop Lamplugh had just presented himself at court on his arrival from Exeter, and had been most graciously received. "My Lord," said the King, "you are a genuine old Cavalier." The archbishopric of York, which had now been vacant more than two years and a half, was immediately bestowed on Lamplugh as the reward of loyalty. That afternoon, just as the King was sitting down to dinner, arrived an express with the tidings of Cornbury's defection. James turned away from his untasted meal, swallowed a crust of bread and a glass of wine, and retired to his closet. He afterward learned that, as he was rising from table, several of the Lords in whom he reposed the greatest confidence were shaking hands and congratulating each other in the adjoining gallery. When the news was carried to the Queen's apartments she and her ladies broke out into tears and loud cries of sorrow.†

The blow was indeed a heavy one. It was true that the direct loss to the crown and the direct gain to the invaders

---

* Life of James, ii., 215, Orig. Mem.; Burnet, i., 790; Clarendon's Diary, Nov. 15, 1688; London Gazette, Nov. 17.

† Life of James, ii., 218; Clarendon's Diary, Nov. 15, 1688; Van Citters, Nov. $\frac{16}{26}$.

hardly amounted to two hundred men and as many horses. But where could the King henceforth expect to find those sentiments in which consists the strength of states and of armies? Cornbury was the heir of a house conspicuous for its attachment to monarchy. His father Clarendon, his uncle Rochester, were men whose loyalty was supposed to be proof to all temptation. What must be the strength of that feeling against which the most deeply rooted hereditary prejudices were of no avail, of that feeling which could reconcile a young officer of high birth to desertion, aggravated by breach of trust and by gross falsehood? That Cornbury was not a man of brilliant parts or enterprising temper made the event more alarming. It was impossible to doubt that he had in some quarter a powerful and artful prompter. Who that prompter was soon became evident. In the mean time no man in the royal camp could feel assured that he was not surrounded by traitors. Political rank, military rank, the honor of a nobleman, the honor of a soldier, the strongest professions, the purest Cavalier blood, could no longer afford security. Every man might reasonably doubt whether every order which he received from his superior was not meant to serve the purposes of the enemy. That prompt obedience without which an army is merely a rabble was necessarily at an end. What discipline could there be among soldiers who had just been saved from a snare by refusing to follow their commanding officer on a secret expedition, and by insisting on a sight of his orders?

Cornbury was soon kept in countenance by a crowd of deserters superior to him in rank and capacity: but during a few days he stood alone in his shame, and was bitterly reviled by many who afterward imitated his example and envied his dishonorable precedence. Among these was his own father. The first outbreak of Clarendon's rage and sorrow was highly pathetic. "Oh God!" he ejaculated, "that a son of mine should be a rebel!" A fortnight later he made up his mind to be a rebel himself. Yet it would be unjust to pronounce him a mere hypocrite. In revolutions men live fast: the experience of years is crowded into hours; old habits of thought and action are violently broken; and novelties, which at first sight inspire dread and disgust, become in a few days familiar, endurable, attractive. Many men of far purer virtue and higher spirit than Clarendon were prepared, before that memorable year ended, to do what they would have pronounced wicked and infamous when it began.

The unhappy father composed himself as well as he could, and sent to ask a private audience of the King. It was granted. James said, with more than his usual graciousness, that he from his heart pitied Cornbury's relations, and should not hold them at all accountable for the crime of their unworthy kinsman. Clarendon went home, scarcely daring to look his friends in the face. Soon, however, he learned with surprise that the act, which had, as he at first thought, forever dishonored his family, was applauded by some persons of high station. His niece, the Princess of Denmark, asked him why he shut himself up. He answered that he had been overwhelmed with confusion by his son's villany. Anne seemed not at all to understand this feeling. "People," she said, "are very uneasy about Popery. I believe that many of the army will do the same."*

And now the King, greatly disturbed, called together the principal officers who were still in London. Churchill, who was about this time promoted to the rank of Lieutenant-general, made his appearance with that bland serenity which neither peril nor infamy could ever disturb. The meeting was attended by Henry Fitzroy, Duke of Grafton, whose audacity and activity made him conspicuous among the natural children of Charles the Second. Grafton was colonel of the first regiment of Foot Guards. He seems to have been at this time completely under Churchill's influence, and was prepared to desert the royal standard as soon as the favorable moment should arrive. Two other traitors were in the circle, Kirke and Trelawney, who commanded those two fierce and lawless bands then known as the Tangier regiments. Both of them had, like the other Protestant officers of the army, long seen with extreme displeasure the partiality which the King

---

* Clarendon's Diary, Nov. 15, 16, 17, 20, 1688.

had shown to members of his own Church; and Trelawney remembered with bitter resentment the persecution of his brother the Bishop of Bristol. James addressed the assembly in language worthy of a better man and of a better cause. It might be, he said, that some of the officers had conscientious scruples about fighting for him. If so, he was willing to receive back their commissions. But he adjured them as gentlemen and soldiers not to imitate the shameful example of Cornbury. All seemed moved; and none more than Churchill. He was the first to vow with well feigned enthusiasm that he would shed the last drop of his blood in the service of his gracious master: Grafton was loud and forward in similar protestations; and the example was followed by Kirke and Trelawney.*

Deceived by these professions, the King prepared to set out for Salisbury. Before his departure he was informed that a considerable number of peers, temporal and spiritual, desired to be admitted to an audience. They came, with Sancroft at their head, to present a petition, praying that a free and legal Parliament might be called, and that a negotiation might be opened with the Prince of Orange.

Petition of the Lords for a Parliament.

The history of this petition is curious. The thought seems to have occurred at once to two great chiefs of parties who had long been rivals and enemies, Rochester and Halifax. They both, independently of one another, consulted the Bishops. The Bishops warmly approved the suggestion. It was then proposed that a general meeting of peers should be called to deliberate on the form of an address to the King. It was term time; and in term time men of rank and fashion then lounged every day in Westminster Hall as they now lounge in the clubs of Pall Mall and Saint James's Street. Nothing could be easier than for the Lords who assembled there to step aside into some adjoining room and to hold a consultation. But unexpected difficulties arose. Halifax became first cold and then adverse. It was his nature to dis-

---

* Life of James, ii., 219, Orig. Mem.

cover objections to everything; and on this occasion his sagacity was quickened by rivalry. The scheme, which he had approved while he regarded it as his own, began to displease him as soon as he found that it was also the scheme of Rochester, by whom he had been long thwarted and at length supplanted, and whom he disliked as much as it was in his easy nature to dislike anybody. Nottingham was at that time much under the influence of Halifax. They both declared that they would not join in the address if Rochester signed it. Clarendon expostulated in vain. "I mean no disrespect," said Halifax, "to my Lord Rochester: but he has been a member of the Ecclesiastical Commission: the proceedings of that court must soon be the subject of a very serious inquiry; and it is not fit that one who has sat there should take any part in our petition." Nottingham, with strong expressions of personal esteem for Rochester, avowed the same opinion. The authority of the two dissentient Lords prevented several other noblemen from subscribing the address; but the Hydes and the Bishops persisted. Nineteen signatures were procured; and the petitioners waited in a body on the King.*

He received their address ungraciously. He assured them, indeed, that he passionately desired the meeting of a free Parliament; and he promised them, on the faith of a King, that he would call one as soon as the Prince of Orange should have left the island. "But how," said he, "can a Parliament be free when an enemy is in the kingdom, and can return near a hundred votes?" To the prelates he spoke with peculiar acrimony. "I could not," he said, "prevail on you the other day to declare against this invasion: but you are ready enough to declare against me. Then you would not meddle with politics. You have no scruple about meddling now. You have excited this rebellious temper among your flocks; and now you foment it. You would be better employed in teaching them how to obey than in teaching me how to govern." He was much incensed against his nephew Grafton, whose signature stood next to that of Sancroft, and said to

---

* Clarendon's Diary, from Nov. 8 to Nov. 17, 1688.

the young man, with great asperity, "You know nothing about religion: you care nothing about it; and yet, forsooth, you must pretend to have a conscience." "It is true, sir," answered Grafton, with impudent frankness, "that I have very little conscience: but I belong to a party which has a great deal."*

Bitter as was the King's language to the petitioners, it was far less bitter than that which he held after they had withdrawn. He had done, he said, far too much already in the hope of satisfying an undutiful and ungrateful people. He had always hated the thought of concession: but he had suffered himself to be talked over; and now he, like his father before him, had found that concession only made subjects more encroaching. He would yield nothing more, not an atom; and, after his fashion, he vehemently repeated many times, "Not an atom." Not only would he make no overtures to the invaders, but he would receive none. If the Dutch sent flags of truce, the first messenger should be dismissed without an answer; the second should be hanged.†

The King goes to Salisbury. In such a mood James set out for Salisbury. His last act before his departure was to appoint a Council of five Lords to represent him in London during his absence. Of the five, two were Papists, and by law incapable of office. Joined with them was Jeffreys, a Protestant, indeed, but more detested by the nation than any Papist. To the other two members of this board, Preston and Godolphin, no serious objection could be made. On the day on which the King left London the Prince of Wales was sent to Portsmouth. That fortress was strongly garrisoned, and was under the government of Berwick. The fleet commanded by Dartmouth lay close at hand: and it was supposed that, if things went ill, the royal infant would, without difficulty, be conveyed from Portsmouth to France.‡

---

* Life of James, ii., 212, Orig. Mem.; Clarendon's Diary, Nov. 17, 1688; Van Citters, Nov. $\frac{20}{30}$; Burnet, i., 791; Some Reflections upon the most Humble Petition to the King's most Excellent Majesty, 1688; Modest Vindication of the Petition; First Collection of Papers relating to English Affairs, 1688.

† Adda, Nov. $\frac{19}{29}$, 1688.   ‡ Life of James, 220, 221.

On the nineteenth James reached Salisbury, and took up his quarters in the episcopal palace. Evil news was now fast pouring in upon him from all sides. The western counties had at length risen. As soon as the news of Cornbury's desertion was known, many wealthy land-owners took heart and hastened to Exeter. Among them was Sir William Portman of Bryanstone, one of the greatest men in Dorsetshire, and Sir Francis Warre of Hestercombe, whose interest was great in Somersetshire.* But the most important of the new-comers was Seymour, who had recently inherited a baronetcy which added nothing to his dignity, and who, in birth, in political influence, and in parliamentary abilities, was beyond comparison the foremost among the Tory gentlemen of England. At his first audience he is said to have exhibited his characteristic pride in a way which surprised and amused the Prince. "I think, Sir Edward," said William, meaning to be very civil, "that you are of the family of the Duke of Somerset." "Pardon me, sir," said Sir Edward, who never forgot that he was the head of the elder branch of the Seymours: "the Duke of Somerset is of my family."†

Seymour.

The quarters of William now began to present the appearance of a court. More than sixty men of rank and fortune were lodged at Exeter; and the daily display of rich liveries, and of coaches drawn by six horses, in the Cathedral Close, gave to that quiet precinct something of the splendor and gayety of Whitehall. The common people were eager to take arms; and it would have been easy to form many battalions of infantry. But Schomberg, who thought little of soldiers fresh from the plough, maintained that, if the expedition could not succeed without such help, it would not succeed at all; and William, who had as much professional feeling as Schomberg, concurred in this opinion. Commissions, therefore, for raising new regiments

Court of William at Exeter.

---

* Eachard's History of the Revolution.
† Seymour's reply to William is related by many writers. It much resembles a story which is told of the Manriquez family. They, it is said, took for their device the words, "Nos no descendemos de los Reyes; sino los Reyes descienden de nos."—Carpentariana.

were very sparingly given; and none but picked recruits were enlisted.

It was now thought desirable that the Prince should give a public reception to the whole body of noblemen and gentlemen who had assembled at Exeter. He addressed them in a short but dignified and well-considered speech. He was not, he said, acquainted with the faces of all whom he saw. But he had a list of their names, and knew how high they stood in the estimation of their country. He gently chid their tardiness, but expressed a confident hope that it was not yet too late to save the kingdom. "Therefore," he said, "gentlemen, friends, and fellow-Protestants, we bid you and all your followers most heartily welcome to our court and camp."*

Seymour, a keen politician, long accustomed to the tactics of faction, saw in a moment that the party which had begun to rally round the Prince stood in need of organization. It was as yet, he said, a mere rope of sand: no common object had been publicly and formally avowed: nobody was pledged to anything. As soon as the assembly at the deanery broke up, he sent for Burnet, and suggested that an association should be formed, and that all the English adherents of the Prince should put their hands to an instrument binding them to be true to their leader and to each other. Burnet carried the suggestion to the Prince and to Shrewsbury, by both of whom it was approved. A meeting was held in the Cathedral. A short paper drawn up by Burnet was produced, approved, and eagerly signed. The subscribers engaged to pursue in concert the objects set forth in the Prince's Declaration; to stand by him and by each other; to take signal vengeance on all who should make any attempt on his person; and, even if such an attempt should unhappily succeed, to persist in their undertaking till the liberties and the religion of the nation should be effectually secured.†

About the same time a messenger arrived at Exeter from the Earl of Bath, who commanded at Plymouth. Bath de-

---

* Fourth Collection of Papers, 1688; Letter from Exon; Burnet, i., 792.

† Burnet, i., 792; History of the Desertion; Second Collection of Papers, 1688.

clared that he placed himself, his troops, and the fortress which he governed at the Prince's disposal. The invaders, therefore, had now not a single enemy in their rear.*

While the West was thus rising to confront the King, the North was all in a flame behind him. On the sixteenth, Delamere took arms in Cheshire. He convoked his tenants, called upon them to stand by him, promised that, if they fell in the cause, their leases should be renewed to their children, and exhorted every one who had a good horse either to take the field or to provide a substitute.† He appeared at Manchester with fifty men armed and mounted, and his force had trebled before he reached Boaden Downs.

<small>Northern insurrection.</small>

The neighboring counties were violently agitated. It had been arranged that Danby should seize York, and that Devonshire should appear at Nottingham. At Nottingham no resistance was anticipated. But at York there was a small garrison under the command of Sir John Reresby. Danby acted with rare dexterity. A meeting of the gentry and freeholders of Yorkshire had been summoned for the twenty-second of November to address the King on the state of affairs. All the Deputy Lieutenants of the three Ridings, several noblemen, and a multitude of opulent esquires and substantial yeomen, had been attracted to the provincial capital. Four troops of militia had been drawn out under arms to preserve the public peace. The Common Hall was crowded with freeholders, and the discussion had begun, when a cry was suddenly raised that the Papists were up, and were slaying the Protestants. The Papists of York were much more likely to be employed in seeking for hiding-places than in attacking enemies who outnumbered them in the proportion of a hundred to one. But at that time no story of Popish atrocity could be so wild and marvellous as not to find ready belief. The meeting separated in dismay. The whole city was in confusion. At this moment Danby, at the head of about a

---

* Letter of Bath to the Prince of Orange, Nov. 18, 1688; Dalrymple.
† First Collection of Papers, 1688; London Gazette, Nov. 22.

hundred horsemen, rode up to the militia, and raised the cry
"No Popery! A free Parliament! The Protestant religion!" The militia echoed the shout. The garrison was instantly surprised and disarmed. The governor was placed under arrest. The gates were closed. Sentinels were posted everywhere. The populace was suffered to pull down a Roman Catholic chapel; but no other harm appears to have been done. On the following morning the Guildhall was crowded with the first gentlemen of the shire, and with the principal magistrates of the city. The Lord Mayor was placed in the chair. Danby proposed a Declaration setting forth the reasons which had induced the friends of the constitution and of the Protestant religion to rise in arms. This Declaration was eagerly adopted, and received in a few hours the signatures of six peers, of five baronets, of six knights, and of many gentlemen of high consideration.*

Devonshire meantime, at the head of a great body of friends and dependents, quitted the palace which he was rearing at Chatsworth, and appeared in arms at Derby. There he formally delivered to the municipal authorities a paper setting forth the reasons which had moved him to this enterprise. He then proceeded to Nottingham, which soon became the head-quarters of the Northern insurrection. Here a proclamation was put forth couched in bold and severe terms. The name of rebellion, it was said, was a bugbear which could frighten no reasonable man. Was it rebellion to defend those laws and that religion which every king of England bound himself by oath to maintain? How that oath had lately been observed was a question on which, it was to be hoped, a free Parliament would soon pronounce. In the mean time, the insurgents declared that they held it to be not rebellion, but legitimate self-defence, to resist a tyrant who knew no law but his own will. The Northern rising became every day more formidable. Four powerful and wealthy earls—Manchester, Stamford, Rutland, and Chesterfield—repaired to

---

* Reresby's Memoirs; Life of James, ii., 231, Orig. Mem.

Nottingham, and were joined by Lord Cholmondeley and by Lord Grey de Ruthyn.*

All this time the hostile armies in the south were approaching each other. The Prince of Orange, when he learned that the King had arrived at Salisbury, thought it time to leave Exeter. He placed that city and the surrounding country under the government of Sir Edward Seymour, and set out on Wednesday the twenty-first of November, escorted by many of the most considerable gentlemen of the western counties, for Axminster, where he remained several days.

The King was eager to fight; and it was obviously his interest to do so. Every hour took away something from his own strength, and added something to the strength of his enemies. It was most important, too, that his troops should be blooded. A great battle, however it might terminate, could not but injure the Prince's popularity. All this William perfectly understood, and determined to avoid an action as long as possible. It is said that, when Schomberg was told that the enemy were advancing and were determined to fight, he answered, with the composure of a tactician confident in his skill, "That will be just as we may choose." It was, however, impossible to prevent all skirmishing between the advanced guards of the armies. William was desirous that in such skirmishing nothing might happen which could wound the pride or rouse the vindictive feelings of the nation which he meant to deliver. He therefore, with admirable prudence, placed his British regiments in the situations where there was most risk of collision. The outposts of the royal army were Irish. The consequence was that, in the little combats of this short campaign, the invaders had on their side the hearty sympathy of all Englishmen.

The first of these encounters took place at Wincanton. Mackay's regiment, composed of British soldiers, lay near a body of the King's Irish troops, commanded by their countryman, the gallant Sarsfield. Mackay

<small>Skirmish at Wincanton.</small>

---

* Cibber's Apology; History of the Desertion; Luttrell's Diary; Second Collection of Papers, 1688.

sent out a small party under a lieutenant, named Campbell, to procure horses for the baggage. Campbell found what he wanted at Wincanton, and was just leaving that town on his return when a strong detachment of Sarsfield's troops approached. The Irish were four to one: but Campbell resolved to fight it out to the last. With a handful of resolute men he took his stand in the road. The rest of his soldiers lined the hedges which overhung the highway on the right and on the left. The enemy came up. "Stand!" cried Campbell; "for whom are you?" "I am for King James," answered the leader of the other party. "And I for the Prince of Orange," cried Campbell. "We will prince you!" answered the Irishman, with a curse. "Fire!" exclaimed Campbell; and a sharp fire was instantly poured in from both the hedges. The King's troops received three well-aimed volleys before they could make any return. At length they succeeded in carrying one of the hedges; and would have overpowered the little band which was opposed to them, had not the country people, who mortally hated the Irish, given a false alarm that more of the Prince's troops were coming up. Sarsfield recalled his men and fell back; and Campbell proceeded on his march unmolested with the baggage-horses. This affair, creditable undoubtedly to the valor and discipline of the Prince's army, was magnified by report into a victory won against great odds by British Protestants over Popish barbarians who had been brought from Connaught to oppress our island.*

A few hours after this skirmish an event took place which put an end to all risk of a more serious struggle between the armies. Churchill and some of his principal accomplices were assembled at Salisbury. Two of the conspirators, Kirke and Trelawney, had proceeded to Warminster, where their regiments were posted. All was ripe for the execution of the long-meditated treason.

Churchill advised the King to visit Warminster, and to inspect the troops stationed there. James assented; and his

---

* Whittle's Diary; History of the Desertion; Luttrell's Diary.

coach was at the door of the episcopal palace when his nose began to bleed violently. He was forced to postpone his expedition and to put himself under medical treatment. Three days elapsed before the hemorrhage was entirely subdued: and during those three days alarming rumors reached his ears.

It was impossible that a conspiracy so widely spread as that of which Churchill was the head could be kept altogether secret. There was no evidence which could be laid before a jury or a court-martial; but strange whispers wandered about the camp. Feversham, who held the chief command, reported that there was a bad spirit in the army. It was hinted to the King that some who were near his person were not his friends, and that it would be a wise precaution to send Churchill and Grafton under a guard to Portsmouth. James rejected this counsel. A propensity to suspicion was not among his vices. Indeed the confidence which he reposed in professions of fidelity and attachment were such as might rather have been expected from a good-hearted and inexperienced stripling than from a politician who was far advanced in life, who had seen much of the world, who had suffered much from villanous arts, and whose own character was by no means a favorable specimen of human nature. It would be difficult to mention any other man who, having himself so little scruple about breaking faith with his neighbors, was so slow to believe that his neighbors could break faith with him. Nevertheless the reports which he had received of the state of his army disturbed him greatly. He was now no longer impatient for a battle. He even began to think of retreating. On the evening of Saturday, the twenty-fourth of November, he called a council of war. The meeting was attended by those officers against whom he had been most earnestly cautioned. Feversham expressed an opinion that it was desirable to fall back. Churchill argued on the other side. The consultation lasted till midnight. At length the King declared that he had decided for a retreat. Churchill saw or imagined that he was distrusted, and, though gifted with a rare self-command, could not conceal his uneasiness.

Desertion of Churchill and Grafton.

Before the day broke he fled to the Prince's quarters, accompanied by Grafton.*

Churchill left behind him a letter of explanation. It was written with that decorum which he never failed to preserve in the midst of guilt and dishonor. He acknowledged that he owed everything to the royal favor. Interest, he said, and gratitude impelled him in the same direction. Under no other government could he hope to be so great and prosperous as he had been; but all such considerations must yield to a paramount duty. He was a Protestant; and he could not conscientiously draw his sword against the Protestant cause. As to the rest, he would ever be ready to hazard life and fortune in defence of the sacred person and of the lawful rights of his gracious master.†

Next morning all was confusion in the royal camp. The King's friends were in dismay. His enemies could not conceal their exultation. The consternation of James was increased by news which arrived on the same day from Warminster. Kirke, who commanded at that post, had refused to obey orders which he had received from Salisbury. There could no longer be any doubt that he too was in league with the Prince of Orange. It was rumored that he had actually gone over with all his troops to the enemy: and the rumor, though false, was during some hours fully believed.‡ A new light flashed on the mind of the unhappy King. He thought that he understood why he had been pressed, a few days before, to visit Warminster. There he would have found himself helpless, at the mercy of the conspirators, and in the vicinity of the hostile outposts. Those who might have attempted to defend him would have been easily overpowered. He would have been carried a prisoner to the head-quarters of the invading army. Perhaps some still blacker treason might have been committed; for men who have once engaged in a

---

* Life of James, ii., 222, Orig. Mem.; Barillon, $\frac{\text{Nov. 21,}}{\text{Dec. 1,}}$ 1688; Sheridan MS.
† First Collection of Papers, 1688.
‡ Letter from Middleton to Preston, dated Salisbury, Nov. 25. "Villany upon villany," says Middleton, "the last still greater than the former." Life of James, ii., 224, 225, Orig. Mem.

wicked and perilous enterprise are no longer their own masters, and are often impelled, by a fatality which is part of their just punishment, to crimes such as they would at first have shuddered to contemplate. Surely it was not without the special intervention of some guardian saint that a king devoted to the Catholic Church had, at the very moment when he was blindly hastening to captivity, perhaps to death, been suddenly arrested by what he had then thought a disastrous malady.

All these things confirmed James in the resolution which he had taken on the preceding evening. Orders were given for an immediate retreat. Salisbury was in an uproar. The camp broke up with the confusion of a flight. No man knew whom to trust or whom to obey. The material strength of the army was little diminished: but its moral strength had been destroyed. Many whom shame would have restrained from leading the way to the Prince's quarters were eager to imitate an example which they never would have set; and many, who would have stood by their King while he appeared to be resolutely advancing against the invaders, felt no inclination to follow a receding standard.*

<small>Retreat of the royal army from Salisbury.</small>

James went that day as far as Andover. He was attended by his son-in-law Prince George, and by the Duke of Ormond. Both were among the conspirators, and would probably have accompanied Churchill, had he not, in consequence of what had passed at the council of war, thought it expedient to take his departure suddenly. The impenetrable stupidity of Prince George served his turn on this occasion better than cunning would have done. It was his habit, when any news was told him, to exclaim in French, "Est-il-possible?" "Is it possible?" This catchword was now of great use to him. "Est-il-possible?" he cried, when he had been made to understand that Churchill and Grafton were missing. And when the ill tidings came from Warminster, he again ejaculated, "Est-il-possible?"

---

* History of the Desertion; Luttrell's Diary.

Prince George and Ormond were invited to sup with the King at Andover. The meal must have been a sad one. The King was overwhelmed by his misfortunes. His son-in-law was the dullest of companions. "I have tried Prince George sober," said Charles the Second; "and I have tried him drunk; and, drunk or sober, there is nothing in him."* Ormond, who was through life taciturn and bashful, was not likely to be in high spirits at such a moment. At length the repast terminated. The King retired to rest. Horses were in waiting for the Prince and Ormond, who, as soon as they left the table, mounted and rode off. They were accompanied by the Earl of Drumlanrig, eldest son of the Duke of Queensberry. The defection of this young nobleman was no insignificant event. For Queensberry was the head of the Protestant Episcopalians of Scotland, a class compared with whom the bitterest English Tories might be called Whiggish; and Drumlanrig himself was Lieutenant-colonel of Dundee's regiment, a band more detested by the Whigs than even Kirke's lambs. This fresh calamity was announced to the King on the following morning. He was less disturbed by the news than might have been expected. The shock which he had undergone twenty-four hours before had prepared him for almost any disaster; and it was impossible to be seriously angry with Prince George, who was hardly an accountable being, for having yielded to the arts of such a tempter as Churchill. "What!" said James, "is Est-il-possible gone too? After all, a good trooper would have been a greater loss."† In truth the King's whole anger seems, at this time, to have been concentrated, and not without cause, on one object. He set off for London, breathing vengeance against Churchill, and learned, on arriving, a new crime of the arch-deceiver. The Princess Anne had been some hours missing.

Anne, who had no will but that of the Churchills, had been induced by them to notify under her own hand to William, a week before, her approbation of his enterprise. She assured

Desertion of Prince George and Ormond.

---

* Dartmouth's note on Burnet, i., 643.

† Clarendon's Diary, Nov. 26; Life of James, ii., 224. Prince George's letter to the King has often been printed.

him that she was entirely in the hands of her friends, and
<small>Flight of the Princess Anne.</small> that she would remain in the palace, or take refuge in the City, as they might determine.* On Sunday, the twenty-fifth of November, she, and those who thought for her, were under the necessity of coming to a sudden resolution. That afternoon a courier from Salisbury brought tidings that Churchill had disappeared, that he had been accompanied by Grafton, that Kirke had proved false, and that the royal forces were in full retreat. There was, as usually happened when great news, good or bad, arrived in town, an immense crowd that evening in the galleries of Whitehall. Curiosity and anxiety sat on every face. The Queen broke forth into natural expressions of indignation against the chief traitor, and did not altogether spare his too partial mistress. The sentinels were doubled round that part of the palace which Anne occupied. The Princess was in dismay. In a few hours her father would be at Westminster. It was not likely that he would treat her personally with severity; but that he would permit her any longer to enjoy the society of her friend was not to be hoped. It could hardly be doubted that Sarah would be placed under arrest, and would be subjected to a strict examination by shrewd and rigorous inquisitors. Her papers would be seized. Perhaps evidence affecting her life might be discovered. If so, the worst might well be dreaded. The vengeance of the implacable King knew no distinction of sex. For offences much smaller than those which might probably be brought home to Lady Churchill he had sent women to the scaffold and the stake. Strong affection braced the feeble mind of the Princess. There was no tie which she would not break, no risk which she would not run, for the object of her idolatrous affection. "I will jump out of the window," she cried, "rather than be found here by my father." The favorite undertook to manage an escape. She communicated in all haste with some of the chiefs of the conspiracy. In a few hours everything was arranged. That evening Anne retired to her chamber as usual. At dead of

---

* The letter, dated Nov. 18, will be found in Dalrymple.

night she rose, and, accompanied by her friend Sarah and two other female attendants, stole down the back stairs in a dressing-gown and slippers. The fugitives gained the open street unchallenged. A hackney-coach was in waiting for them there. Two men guarded the humble vehicle. One of them was Compton, Bishop of London, the Princess's old tutor: the other was the magnificent and accomplished Dorset, whom the extremity of the public danger had roused from his luxurious repose. The coach drove instantly to Aldersgate Street, where the town residence of the Bishops of London then stood, within the shadow of their Cathedral. There the Princess passed the night. On the following morning she set out for Epping Forest. In that wild tract Dorset possessed a venerable mansion, which has long since been destroyed. In his hospitable dwelling, the favorite resort, during many years, of wits and poets, the fugitives made a short stay. They could not safely attempt to reach William's quarters; for the road thither lay through a country occupied by the royal forces. It was therefore determined that Anne should take refuge with the Northern insurgents. Compton wholly laid aside, for the time, his sacerdotal character. Danger and conflict had rekindled in him all the military ardor which he had felt twenty-eight years before, when he rode in the Life Guards. He preceded the Princess's carriage in a buff coat and jack-boots, with a sword at his side and pistols in his holsters. Long before she reached Nottingham, she was surrounded by a body-guard of gentlemen who volunteered to escort her. They invited the Bishop to act as their colonel; and he consented with an alacrity which gave great scandal to rigid Churchmen, and did not much raise his character even in the opinion of Whigs.*

When, on the morning of the twenty-sixth, Anne's apartment was found empty, the consternation was great in Whitehall. While the Ladies of her Bedchamber ran up and

---

* Clarendon's Diary, Nov. 25, 26, 1688; Van Citters, $\frac{\text{Nov. 26}}{\text{Dec. 6}}$; Ellis Correspondence, Dec. 19; Duchess of Marlborough's Vindication; Burnet, i., 792; Compton to the Prince of Orange, Dec. 2, 1688, in Dalrymple. The Bishop's military costume is mentioned in innumerable pamphlets and lampoons.

down the courts of the palace, screaming and wringing their hands, while Lord Craven, who commanded the Foot Guards, was questioning the sentinels in the gallery, while the Chancellor was sealing up the papers of the Churchills, the Princess's nurse broke into the royal apartments crying out that the dear lady had been murdered by the Papists. The news flew to Westminster Hall. There the story was that Her Highness had been hurried away by force to a place of confinement. When it could no longer be denied that her flight had been voluntary, numerous fictions were invented to account for it. She had been grossly insulted: she had been threatened: nay, though she was in that situation in which woman is entitled to peculiar tenderness, she had been beaten by her cruel step-mother. The populace, which years of misrule had made suspicious and irritable, was so much excited by these calumnies that the Queen was scarcely safe. Many Roman Catholics, and some Protestant Tories whose loyalty was proof to all trials, repaired to the palace that they might be in readiness to defend her in the event of an outbreak. In the midst of this distress and terror arrived the news of Prince George's flight. The courier who brought these evil tidings was fast followed by the King himself. The evening was closing in when James arrived, and was informed that his daughter had disappeared. After all that he had suffered, this affliction forced a cry of misery from his lips. "God help me!" he said; "my own children have forsaken me!"*

That evening he sat in Council with his principal ministers till a late hour. It was determined that he should summon all the Lords, Spiritual and Temporal, who were then in London, to attend him on the following day, and that he should solemnly ask their advice. Accordingly, on the afternoon of Tuesday, the twenty-seventh, the Lords met in the dining-room of the palace. The assembly consisted of nine prelates and between thirty and forty noblemen, all Protestants. The two Secretaries of

Council of Lords held by James.

---

* Dartmouth's note on Burnet, i., 792; Van Citters, $\frac{\text{Nov. 26,}}{\text{Dec. 6,}}$ 1688; Life of James, ii., 226, Orig. Mem.; Clarendon's Diary, Nov. 26; Revolution Politics.

State, Middleton and Preston, though not peers of England, were in attendance. The King himself presided. The traces of severe bodily and mental suffering were discernible in his countenance and deportment. He opened the proceedings by referring to the petition which had been put into his hands just before he set out for Salisbury. The prayer of that petition was that he would convoke a free Parliament. Situated as he then was, he had not, he said, thought it right to comply. But, during his absence from London, great changes had taken place. He had also observed that his people everywhere seemed anxious that the Houses should meet. He had therefore commanded the attendance of his faithful Peers, in order to ask their counsel.

For a time there was silence. Then Oxford, whose pedigree, unrivalled in antiquity and splendor, gave him a kind of primacy in the meeting, said that, in his opinion, those Lords who had signed the petition to which His Majesty had referred ought now to explain their views.

These words called up Rochester. He defended the petition, and declared that he still saw no hope for the throne or the country but in a Parliament. He would not, he said, venture to affirm that, in so disastrous an extremity, even that remedy would be efficacious: but he had no other remedy to propose. He added that it might be advisable to open a negotiation with the Prince of Orange. Jeffreys and Godolphin followed; and both declared that they agreed with Rochester.

Then Clarendon rose, and, to the astonishment of all, who remembered his loud professions of loyalty, and the agony of shame and sorrow into which he had been thrown, only a few days before, by the news of his son's defection, broke forth into a vehement invective against tyranny and Popery. "Even now," he said, "His Majesty is raising in London a regiment into which no Protestant is admitted." "That is not true!" cried James, in great agitation, from the head of the board. Clarendon persisted, and left this offensive topic only to pass to a topic still more offensive. He accused the unfortunate King of pusillanimity. Why retreat from Salisbury? Why not try the event of a battle? Could people be blamed for submitting to the invader when they saw their sovereign run away at the head of his army? James felt these insults keenly, and remembered them long. Indeed, even Whigs thought the language of Clarendon indecent and ungenerous. Halifax spoke in a very different tone. During several years of peril he had defended with admirable ability the civil and ecclesiastical constitution of his country against the prerogative. But his serene intellect, singularly unsusceptible of enthusiasm, and singularly averse to extremes, began to lean toward the cause of royalty at the very moment at which those noisy Royalists who had lately execrated the Trimmers as little better than rebels, were everywhere rising in rebellion. It was his ambition to be, at this conjuncture, the peace-maker between the throne and the nation. His talents and character fitted him for that office; and, if he failed, the failure is to be ascribed to causes against which no human skill could contend, and chiefly to the folly, faithlessness, and obstinacy of the Prince whom he tried to save.

Halifax now gave utterance to much unpalatable truth, but with a delicacy which brought on him the reproach of flattery from spirits too abject to understand that what would justly be called flattery when offered to the powerful is a debt of humanity to the fallen. With many expressions of sympathy and deference, he declared it to be his opinion that the King must make up his mind to great sacrifices. It was not enough to convoke a Parliament or to open a negotiation with the Prince of Orange. Some at least of the grievances of which the nation complained should be instantly redressed without waiting till redress was demanded by the Houses, or by the captain of the hostile army. Nottingham, in language equally respectful, declared that he agreed with Halifax. The chief concessions which these Lords pressed the King to make were three. He ought, they said, forthwith to dismiss all Roman Catholics from office, to separate himself wholly from France, and to grant an unlimited amnesty to those who were in arms against him. The last of these propositions, it should

II.—31

seem, admitted of no dispute. For, though some of those who were banded together against the King had acted toward him in a manner which might not unreasonably excite his bitter resentment, it was more likely that he would soon be at their mercy than that they would ever be at his. It would have been childish to open a negotiation with William, and yet to denounce vengeance against men whom William could not without infamy abandon. But the clouded understanding and implacable temper of James held out long against the arguments of those who labored to convince him that it would be wise to pardon offences which he could not punish. "I cannot do it," he exclaimed: "I must make examples; Churchill above all; Churchill, whom I raised so high. He, and he alone, has done all this. He has corrupted my army. He has corrupted my child. He would have put me into the hands of the Prince of Orange, but for God's special providence. My Lords, you are strangely anxious for the safety of traitors. None of you troubles himself about my safety." In answer to this burst of impotent anger, those who had recommended the amnesty represented with profound respect, but with firmness, that a prince attacked by powerful enemies can be safe only by conquering or by conciliating. "If Your Majesty, after all that has happened, has still any hope of safety in arms we have done: but if not, you can be safe only by regaining the affections of your people." After a long and animated debate the King broke up the meeting. "My Lords," he said, "you have used great freedom: but I do not take it ill of you. I have made up my mind on one point—I shall call a Parliament. The other suggestions which have been offered are of grave importance: and you will not be surprised that I take a night to reflect on them before I decide."*

---

* Life of James, ii., 236, Orig. Mem.; Burnet, i., 794; Luttrell's Diary; Clarendon's Diary, Nov. 27, 1688; Van Citters, $\frac{\text{Nov. 27,}}{\text{Dec. 7,}}$ and $\frac{\text{Nov. 30.}}{\text{Dec. 10.}}$

Van Citters evidently had his intelligence from one of the Lords who were present. As the matter is important, I will give two short passages from his despatches. The king said, "Dat het by na voor hem unmogelyck was te pardoneren persoonen wie so hoog in syn reguarde schuldig stonden, vooral seer uytvarende

At first James seemed disposed to make excellent use of the time which he had taken for consideration. The Chancellor was directed to issue writs convoking a Parliament for the thirteenth of January. Halifax was sent for to the closet, had a long audience, and spoke with much more freedom than he had thought it decorous to use in the presence of a large assembly. He was informed that he had been appointed a Commissioner to treat with the Prince of Orange. With him were joined Nottingham and Godolphin. The King declared that he was prepared to make great sacrifices for the sake of peace. Halifax answered that great sacrifices would doubtless be required. "Your Majesty," he said, must not expect that those who have the power in their hands will consent to any terms which would leave the laws at the mercy of the prerogative." With this distinct explanation of his views, he accepted the Commission which the King wished him to undertake.* The concessions which a few hours before had been so obstinately refused were now made in the most liberal manner. A proclamation was put forth by which the King not only granted a free pardon to all who were in rebellion against him, but declared them eligible to be members of the approaching Parliament. It was not even required as a condition of eligibility that they should lay down their arms. The same Gazette which announced that the Houses were about to meet contained a notification that Sir Edward Hales, who, as a Papist, as a renegade, as the foremost champion of the dispensing

He appoints Commissioners to treat with William.

---

jegens den Lord Churchill, wien hy hadde groot gemaakt, en nogtans meynde de eenigste oorsake van alle dese desertie en van de retraite van hare Coninglycke Hoogheden te wesen." One of the Lords, probably Halifax or Nottingham, "seer hadde geurgeert op de securiteyt van de lords die nu met syn Hoogheyt geengageert staan. Soo hoor ick," says Van Citters, "dat syn Majesteyt onder anderen soude gesegt hebben; 'Men spreekt al voor de securiteyt voor andere, en niet voor de myne.' Waar op een der Pairs resolut dan met groot respect soude geantwoordt hebben dat, soo syne Majesteyt's wapenen in staat waren om hem te connen mainteneren, dat dan sulk syne securiteyte koude wesen; soo niet, en soo de difficulteyt dan nog te surmonteren was, dat het den moeste geschieden door de meeste condescendance, en hoe meer die was, en hy genegen om aan de natic contentement te geven, dat syne securiteyt ook des te grooter soude wesen."

* Letter of the Bishop of Saint Asaph to the Prince of Orange, Dec. 17, 1688.

power, and as the harsh jailer of the Bishops, was one of the most unpopular men in the realm, had ceased to be Lieutenant of the Tower, and had been succeeded by his late prisoner, Bevil Skelton, who, though he held no high place in the esteem of his countrymen, was at least not disqualified by law for public trust.*

But these concessions were meant only to blind the Lords and the nation to the King's real designs. He had secretly <small>The negotiation a feint.</small> determined that, even in this extremity, he would yield nothing. On the very day on which he issued the proclamation of amnesty, he fully explained his intentions to Barillon. "This negotiation," said James, "is a mere feint. I must send Commissioners to my nephew, that I may gain time to ship off my wife and the Prince of Wales. You know the temper of my troops. None but the Irish will stand by me; and the Irish are not in sufficient force to resist the enemy. A Parliament would impose on me conditions which I could not endure. I should be forced to undo all that I have done for the Catholics, and to break with the King of France. As soon, therefore, as the Queen and my child are safe, I will leave England, and take refuge in Ireland, in Scotland, or with your master."†

Already James had made preparations for carrying this scheme into effect. Dover had been sent to Portsmouth with instructions to take charge of the Prince of Wales; and Dartmouth, who commanded the fleet there, had been ordered to obey Dover's directions in all things concerning the royal infant, and to have a yacht manned by trusty sailors in readiness to sail for France at a moment's notice.‡ The King now sent positive orders that the child should instantly be conveyed to the nearest Continental port.§ Next to the Prince of Wales the chief object of anxiety was the Great Seal. To that symbol of kingly authority our jurists have always ascribed a peculiar and almost mysterious importance. It is

---

* London Gazette, Nov. 29, Dec. 3, 1688; Clarendon's Diary, Nov. 29, 30.
† Barillon, December $\frac{1}{11}$, 1688.
‡ James to Dartmouth, Nov. 25, 1688. The letters are in Dalrymple.
§ James to Dartmouth, Dec. 1, 1688.

held that, if the Keeper of the Seal should affix it, without taking the royal pleasure, to a patent of peerage or to a pardon, though he may be guilty of a high offence, the instrument cannot be questioned by any court of law, and can be annulled only by an Act of Parliament. James seems to have been afraid that his enemies might get this organ of his will into their hands, and might thus give a legal validity to acts which might affect him injuriously. Nor will his apprehensions be thought unreasonable when it is remembered that, exactly a hundred years later, the Great Seal of a King was used, with the assent of the Lords and the Commons, and with the approbation of many great statesmen and lawyers, for the purpose of transferring his prerogatives to his son. Lest the talisman which possessed such formidable powers should be abused, James determined that it should be kept within a few yards of his own closet. Jeffreys was therefore ordered to quit the costly mansion which he had lately built in Duke Street, and to take up his residence in a small apartment at Whitehall.*

The King had made all his preparations for flight, when an unexpected impediment compelled him to postpone the execution of his design. His agents at Portsmouth began to entertain scruples. Even Dover, though a member of the Jesuitical cabal, showed signs of hesitation. Dartmouth was still less disposed to comply with the royal wishes. He was zealous for the crown, and had done all that he could do, with a disaffected fleet, and in the face of an adverse wind, to prevent the Dutch from landing in England: but he was also zealous for the Established Church, and was by no means friendly to the policy of that government of which he was the defender. The mutinous temper of the officers and men under his command had caused him much anxiety; and he had been greatly relieved by the news that a free Parliament had been convoked, and that Commissioners had been named to treat with the Prince of Orange. The joy was clamorous throughout the fleet. An address, warmly thanking the King for these

---

* Luttrell's Diary.

gracious concessions to public feeling, was drawn up on board of the flag-ship. The Admiral signed first. Thirty-eight Captains wrote their names under his. This paper on its way to Whitehall crossed the messenger who brought to Portsmouth the order that the Prince of Wales should instantly be conveyed to France. Dartmouth learned, with bitter grief and resentment, that the free Parliament, the general amnesty, the negotiation, were all parts of a great fraud on the nation, and that in this fraud he was expected to be an accomplice. His conduct on this occasion was the most honorable part of a not very honorable life. In a sensible and spirited letter he declared that he had already carried his obedience to the farthest point to which a Protestant and an Englishman could go. To put the heir-apparent of the British crown into the hands of Lewis would be nothing less than treason against the monarchy. The nation, already too much alienated from the Sovereign, would be roused to madness. The Prince of Wales would either not return at all, or would return attended by a French army. If His Royal Highness remained in the island, the worst that could be apprehended was that he would be brought up a member of the national Church; and that he might be so brought up ought to be the prayer of every loyal subject. Dartmouth concluded by declaring that he would risk his life in defence of the throne, but that he would be no party to the transporting of the Prince into France.*

Dartmouth refuses to send the Prince of Wales into France.

This letter deranged all the projects of James. He learned, too, that he could not on this occasion expect from his Admiral even passive obedience. For Dartmouth had gone so far as to station several sloops at the mouth of the harbor of Portsmouth, with orders to suffer no vessel to pass out unexamined. A change of plan was necessary. The child must

---

* Second Collection of Papers, 1688; Dartmouth's Letters, dated December 3, 1688, will be found in Dalrymple; Life of James, ii., 233, Orig. Mem. James accuses Dartmouth of having got up an address from the fleet demanding a Parliament. This is a mere calumny. The address is one of thanks to the King for having called a Parliament, and was framed before Dartmouth had the least suspicion that His Majesty was deceiving the nation.

be brought back to London, and sent thence to France. An interval of some days must elapse before this could be done. During that interval the public mind must be amused by the hope of a Parliament and the semblance of a negotiation. Writs were sent out for the elections. Trumpeters went backward and forward between the capital and the Dutch head-quarters. At length passes for the King's Commissioners arrived; and the three Lords set out on their embassy.

They left the capital in a state of fearful distraction. The passions which, during three troubled years, had been gradu-
Agitation of London. ally gathering force, now, emancipated from the restraint of fear, and stimulated by victory and sympathy, showed themselves without disguise, even in the precincts of the royal dwelling. The grand jury of Middlesex found a bill against the Earl of Salisbury for turning Papist.* The Lord Mayor ordered the houses of the Roman Catholics of the city to be searched for arms. The mob broke into the house of one respectable merchant who held the unpopular faith, in order to ascertain whether he had not run a mine from his cellars under the neighboring parish church, for the purpose of blowing up parson and congregation.† The hawkers bawled about the streets a hue-and-cry after Father Petre, who had withdrawn himself, and not before it was time, from his apartments in Whitehall.‡ Wharton's celebrated song, with many additional verses, was chanted more loudly than ever in all the streets of the capital. The very sentinels who guarded the palace hummed, as they paced their rounds,

<blockquote>"The English confusion to Popery drink,
Lillibullero bullen a la."</blockquote>

The secret presses of London worked without ceasing. Many papers daily came into circulation by means which the magistracy could not discover, or would not check. One
Forged proclamation. of these has been preserved from oblivion by the skilful audacity with which it was written, and by the im-

---

* Luttrell's Diary. † Adda, Dec. $\frac{7}{17}$, 1688.

‡ The Nuncio says, "Se lo avesse fatto prima di ora, per il Rè ne sarebbe stato meglio."

mense effect which it produced. It purported to be a supplemental declaration under the hand and seal of the Prince of Orange: but it was written in a style very different from that of his genuine manifesto. Vengeance alien from the usages of Christian and civilized nations was denounced against all Papists who should dare to espouse the royal cause. They should be treated, not as soldiers or gentlemen, but as freebooters. The ferocity and licentiousness of the invading army, which had hitherto been restrained with a strong hand, should be let loose on them. Good Protestants, and especially those who inhabited the capital, were adjured, as they valued all that was dear to them, and commanded, on peril of the Prince's highest displeasure, to seize, disarm, and imprison their Roman Catholic neighbors. This document, it is said, was found by a Whig bookseller one morning under his shop door. He made haste to print it. Many copies were dispersed by the post, and passed rapidly from hand to hand. Discerning readers had no difficulty in pronouncing it a forgery devised by some unquiet and unprincipled adventurer, such as, in troubled times, are always busied in the foulest and darkest offices of faction. But the multitude was completely duped. Indeed, to such a height had national and religious feeling been excited against the Irish Papists, that most of those who believed the spurious proclamation to be genuine were inclined to applaud it as a seasonable exhibition of vigor. When it was known that no such document had really proceeded from William, men asked anxiously what impostor had so daringly and so successfully personated His Highness. Some suspected Ferguson, others Johnson. At length, after the lapse of twenty-seven years, Hugh Speke avowed the forgery, and demanded from the House of Brunswick a reward for so eminent a service rendered to the Protestant religion. He asserted, in the tone of a man who conceives himself to have done something eminently virtuous and honorable, that, when the Dutch invasion had thrown Whitehall into consternation, he had offered his services to the court, had pretended to be estranged from the Whigs, and had promised to act as a spy upon them; that he had thus obtained admittance to the royal closet, had vowed fidelity, had been promised large pecuniary rewards, and had procured blank passes which enabled him to travel backward and forward across the hostile lines. All these things he protested that he had done solely in order that he might, unsuspected, aim a deadly blow at the government, and produce a violent outbreak of popular feeling against the Roman Catholics. The forged proclamation he claimed as one of his contrivances: but whether his claim were well founded may be doubted. He delayed to make it so long that we may reasonably suspect him of having waited for the death of those who could confute him; and he produced no evidence but his own.*

While these things happened in London, every post from every part of the country brought tidings of some new insurrection. Lumley had seized Newcastle. The inhabitants had welcomed him with transport. The statue of the King, which stood on a lofty pedestal of marble, had been pulled down and hurled into the Tyne. The third of December was long remembered at Hull as the Town-taking Day. That place had a garrison commanded by Lord Langdale, a Roman Catholic. The Protestant officers concerted with the magistracy a plan of revolt: Langdale and his adherents were arrested; and soldiers and citizens united in declaring for the Protestant religion and a free Parliament.†

Risings in various parts of the country.

The Eastern counties were up. The Duke of Norfolk, attended by three hundred gentlemen armed and mounted, appeared in the stately market-place of Norwich. The Mayor and Aldermen met him there, and engaged to stand by him against Popery and arbitrary power.‡ Lord Herbert of Cherbury and Sir Edward Harley took up arms in Worcestershire.§ Bristol, the second city of the realm, opened its gates

---

* See the Secret History of the Revolution, by Hugh Speke, 1715. In the London Library is a copy of this rare work, with a manuscript note which seems to be in Speke's own hand.

† Brand's History of Newcastle; Tickell's History of Hull.

‡ An account of what passed at Norwich may still be seen in several collections on the original broadside. See also the Fourth Collection of Papers, 1688.

§ Life of James, ii., 233; MS. Memoir of the Harley family in the Mackintosh Collection.

to Shrewsbury. Trelawney, the Bishop, who had entirely unlearned in the Tower the doctrine of non-resistance, was the first to welcome the Prince's troops. Such was the temper of the inhabitants that it was thought unnecessary to leave any garrison among them.* The people of Gloucester rose and delivered Lovelace from confinement. An irregular army soon gathered round him. Some of his horsemen had only halters for bridles. Many of his infantry had only clubs for weapons. But this force, such as it was, marched unopposed through counties once devoted to the House of Stuart, and at length entered Oxford in triumph. The magistrates came in state to welcome the insurgents. The University itself, exasperated by recent injuries, was little disposed to pass censures on rebellion. Already some of the Heads of Houses had despatched one of their number to assure the Prince of Orange that they were cordially with him, and that they would gladly coin their plate for his service. The Whig chief, therefore, rode through the capital of Toryism amidst general acclamation. Before him the drums beat Lillibullero. Behind him came a long stream of horse and foot. The whole High Street was gay with orange ribbons. For already the orange ribbon had the double signification which, after the lapse of one hundred and sixty years, it still retains. Already it was the emblem to the Protestant Englishman of civil and religious freedom, to the Roman Catholic Celt of subjugation and persecution.†

While foes were thus rising up all round the King, friends were fast shrinking from his side. The idea of resistance had become familiar to every mind. Many, who had been struck with horror when they heard of the first defections, now blamed themselves for having been so slow to discern the signs of the times. There was no longer any difficulty or danger in repairing to William. The King, in calling on the nation to elect representatives, had, by implication, authorized

---

* Van Citters, Dec. $\frac{9}{19}$, 1688; Letter of the Bishop of Bristol to the Prince of Orange, Dec. 5, 1688, in Dalrymple.

† Van Citters, $\frac{\text{Nov. 27,}}{\text{Dec. 7,}}$ 1688; Clarendon's Diary, Dec. 11; Song on Lord Lovelace's entry into Oxford, 1688; Burnet, i., 793.

all men to repair to the places where they had votes or interest; and many of those places were already occupied by invaders or insurgents. Clarendon eagerly caught at this opportunity of deserting the falling cause. He knew that his speech in the council of Peers had given deadly offence; and he was mortified by finding that he was not to be one of the royal Commissioners. He had estates in Wiltshire; and he determined that his son, the son of whom he had lately spoken with grief and horror, should be a candidate for that county. Under pretence of looking after the election, Clarendon set out for the West. He was speedily followed by the Earl of Oxford, and by others who had hitherto disclaimed all connection with the Prince's enterprise.*

By this time the invaders, steadily though slowly advancing, were within seventy miles of London. Though midwinter was approaching, the weather was fine; the way was pleasant; and the turf of Salisbury Plain seemed luxuriously smooth to men who had been toiling through the miry ruts of the Devonshire and Somersetshire highways. The route of the army lay close by Stonehenge; and regiment after regiment halted to examine that mysterious ruin, celebrated all over the Continent as the greatest wonder of our island. William entered Salisbury with the same military pomp which he had displayed at Exeter, and was lodged there in the palace which the King had occupied a few days before.†

The Prince's train was now swelled by the Earls of Clarendon and Oxford, and by other men of high rank, who had, *Clarendon joins the Prince at Salisbury.* till within a few days, been considered as zealous Royalists. Van Citters also made his appearance at the Dutch head-quarters. He had been during some weeks almost a prisoner in his house near Whitehall, under the constant observation of relays of spies. Yet, in spite of those spies, or perhaps by their help, he had succeeded in obtaining full and accurate intelligence of all that passed in the palace; and now, full fraught with valuable informa-

---

* Clarendon's Diary, Dec. 2, 3, 4, 5, 1688.
† Whittle's Exact Diary; Eachard's History of the Revolution.

tion about men and things, he came to assist the deliberations of William.*

Thus far the Prince's enterprise had prospered beyond the anticipations of the most sanguine. And now, according to the general law which governs human affairs, prosperity began to produce disunion. The Englishmen assembled at Salisbury were divided into two parties. One party consisted of Whigs who had always regarded the doctrines of passive obedience and of indefeasible hereditary right as slavish superstitions. Many of them had passed years in exile. All had been long shut out from participation in the favors of the crown. They now exulted in the near prospect of greatness and of vengeance. Burning with resentment, flushed with victory and hope, they would hear of no compromise. Nothing less than the deposition of their enemy would content them; nor can it be disputed that herein they were perfectly consistent. They had exerted themselves, nine years earlier, to exclude him from the throne, because they thought it likely that he would be a bad king. It could therefore scarcely be expected that they would willingly leave him on the throne, now that he had turned out a far worse king than any reasonable man could have anticipated.

Dissension in the Prince's camp.

On the other hand, not a few of William's followers were zealous Tories, who had, till very recently, held the doctrine of non-resistance in the most absolute form, but whose faith in that doctrine had, for a moment, given way to the strong passions excited by the ingratitude of the King and by the peril of the Church. No situation could be more painful or perplexing than that of the old Cavalier who found himself in arms against the throne. The scruples which had not prevented him from repairing to the Dutch camp began to torment him cruelly as soon as he was there. His mind misgave him that he had committed a crime. At all events, he had exposed himself to reproach, by acting in diametrical opposition to the professions of his whole life. He felt insurmount-

---

* Van Citters, Nov. $\frac{20}{30}$, Dec. $\frac{9}{19}$, 1688.

able disgust for his new allies. They were people whom, ever since he could remember, he had been reviling and persecuting—Presbyterians, Independents, Anabaptists, old soldiers of Cromwell, brisk boys of Shaftesbury, accomplices in the Ryehouse Plot, captains of the Western insurrection. He naturally wished to find out some salvo which might soothe his conscience, which might vindicate his consistency, and which might put a distinction between him and the crew of schismatical rebels whom he had always despised and abhorred, but with whom he was now in danger of being confounded. He therefore disclaimed with vehemence all thought of taking the crown from that anointed head which the ordinance of heaven and the fundamental laws of the realm had made sacred. His dearest wish was to see a reconciliation effected on terms which would not lower the royal dignity. He was no traitor. He was not, in truth, resisting the kingly authority. He was in arms only because he was convinced that the best service which could be rendered to the throne was to rescue His Majesty, by a little gentle coercion, from the hands of wicked counsellors.

The evils which the mutual animosity of these factions tended to produce were, to a great extent, averted by the ascendency and by the wisdom of the Prince. Surrounded by eager disputants, officious advisers, abject flatterers, vigilant spies, malicious tale-bearers, he remained serene and inscrutable. He preserved silence while silence was possible. When he was forced to speak, the earnest and peremptory tone in which he uttered his well-weighed opinions soon silenced everybody else. Whatever some of his too-zealous adherents might say, he uttered not a word indicating any design on the English crown. He was doubtless well aware that between him and that crown were still interposed obstacles which no prudence might be able to surmount, and which a single false step would make insurmountable. His only chance of obtaining the splendid prize was not to seize it rudely, but to wait till, without any appearance of exertion or stratagem on his part, his secret wish should be accomplished by the force of circumstances, by the blunders of his opponents, and by the free choice of the Estates of the Realm. Those who ventured to interrogate him learned nothing, and yet could not accuse him of shuffling. He quietly referred them to his Declaration, and assured them that his views had undergone no change since that instrument had been drawn up. So skilfully did he manage his followers that their discord seems rather to have strengthened than to have weakened his hands: but it broke forth with violence when his control was withdrawn, interrupted the harmony of convivial meetings, and did not respect even the sanctity of the house of God. Clarendon, who tried to hide from others and from himself, by an ostentatious display of loyal sentiments, the plain fact that he was a rebel, was shocked to hear some of his new associates laughing over their wine at the royal amnesty which had just been graciously offered to them. They wanted no pardon, they said. They would make the King ask pardon before they had done with him. Still more alarming and disgusting to every good Tory was an incident which happened at Salisbury Cathedral. As soon as the officiating minister began to read the collect for the King, Burnet, among whose many good qualities self-command and a fine sense of the becoming cannot be reckoned, rose from his knees, sat down in his stall, and uttered some contemptuous noises which disturbed the devotions of the congregation.*

In a short time the factions which divided the Prince's camp had an opportunity of measuring their strength. The royal Commissioners were on their way to him. Several days had elapsed since they had been appointed; and it was thought strange that, in a case of such urgency, there should be such delay. But in truth neither James nor William was desirous that negotiations should speedily commence; for James wished only to gain time sufficient for sending his wife and son into France; and the position of William became every day more commanding. At length the Prince caused it to be notified to the Commissioners that he would meet them at Hungerford. He probably selected this place because, lying

---

* Clarendon's Diary, Dec. 6, 7, 1688.

at an equal distance from Salisbury and from Oxford, it was well situated for a rendezvous of his most important adherents. At Salisbury were those noblemen and gentlemen who had accompanied him from Holland or had joined him in the West; and at Oxford were many chiefs of the Northern insurrection.

Late on Thursday, the sixth of December, he reached Hungerford. The little town was soon crowded with men of rank and note who came thither from opposite quarters. The Prince was escorted by a strong body of troops.

<small>The Prince reaches Hungerford.</small>

The northern Lords brought with them hundreds of irregular cavalry, whose accoutrements and horsemanship moved the mirth of men accustomed to the splendid aspect and exact movements of regular armies.*

While the Prince lay at Hungerford a sharp encounter took place between two hundred and fifty of his troops and six hundred Irish who were posted at Reading. The superior discipline of the invaders was signally proved on this occasion. Though greatly outnumbered, they, at one onset, drove the King's forces in confusion through the streets of the town into the market-place. There the Irish attempted to rally; but, being vigorously attacked in front, and fired upon at the same time by the inhabitants from the windows of the neighboring houses, they soon lost heart, and fled, with the loss of their colors and of fifty men. Of the conquerors, only five fell. The satisfaction which this news gave to the Lords and gentlemen who had joined William was unmixed. There was nothing in what had happened to gall their national feelings. The Dutch had not beaten the English, but had assisted an English town to free itself from the insupportable dominion of the Irish.†

<small>Skirmish at Reading.</small>

On the morning of Saturday, the eighth of December, the King's Commissioners reached Hungerford. The Prince's body-guard was drawn up to receive them with military respect. Bentinck welcomed them, and proposed to conduct them immediately to his mas-

<small>The King's Commissioners arrive at Hungerford.</small>

---

* Clarendon's Diary, Dec. 7, 1688.
† History of the Desertion; Van Citters, Dec. $\frac{9}{19}$, 1688; Exact Diary; Oldmixon, 760.

ter. They expressed a hope that the Prince would favor them with a private audience; but they were informed that he had resolved to hear them and answer them in public. They were ushered into his bedchamber, where they found him surrounded by a crowd of noblemen and gentlemen. Halifax, whose rank, age, and abilities entitled him to precedence, was spokesman. The proposition which the Commissioners had been instructed to make was that the points in dispute should be referred to the Parliament, for which the writs were already sealing, and that in the mean time the Prince's army would not come within thirty or forty miles of London. Halifax, having explained that this was the basis on which he and his colleagues were prepared to treat, put into William's hand a letter from the King, and retired. William opened the letter, and seemed unusually moved. It was the first letter which he had received from his father-in-law since they had become avowed enemies. Once they had been on good terms and had written to each other familiarly; nor had they, even when they had begun to regard each other with suspicion and aversion, banished from their correspondence those forms of kindness which persons nearly related by blood and marriage commonly use. The letter which the Commissioners had brought was drawn up by a secretary in diplomatic form and in the French language. "I have had many letters from the King," said William, "but they were all in English, and in his own hand." He spoke with a sensibility which he was little in the habit of displaying. Perhaps he thought at that moment how much reproach his enterprise, just, beneficent, and necessary as it was, must bring on him and on the wife who was devoted to him. Perhaps he repined at the hard fate which had placed him in such a situation that he could fulfil his public duties only by breaking through domestic ties, and envied the happier condition of those who are not responsible for the welfare of nations and Churches. But such thoughts, if they rose in his mind, were firmly suppressed. He requested the Lords and gentlemen whom he had convoked on this occasion to consult together, unrestrained by his presence, as to

Negotiation.

the answer which ought to be returned. To himself, however, he reserved the power of deciding in the last resort, after hearing their opinion. He then left them, and retired to Littlecote Hall, a manor-house situated about two miles off, and renowned down to our own times, not more on account of its venerable architecture and furniture than on account of a horrible and mysterious crime which was perpetrated there in the days of the Tudors.*

Before he left Hungerford, he was told that Halifax had expressed a great desire to see Burnet. In this desire there was nothing strange; for Halifax and Burnet had long been on terms of friendship. No two men, indeed, could resemble each other less. Burnet was utterly destitute of delicacy and tact. Halifax's taste was fastidious, and his sense of the ludicrous morbidly quick. Burnet viewed every act and every character through a medium distorted and colored by party spirit. The tendency of Halifax's mind was always to see the faults of his allies more strongly than the faults of his opponents. Burnet was, with all his infirmities, and through all the vicissitudes of a life passed in circumstances not very favorable to piety, a sincerely pious man. The sceptical and sarcastic Halifax lay under the imputation of infidelity. Halifax, therefore, often incurred Burnet's indignant censure; and Burnet was often the butt of Halifax's keen and polished pleasantry. Yet they were drawn to each other by a mutual attraction, liked each other's conversation, appreciated each other's abilities, interchanged opinions freely, and interchanged also good offices in perilous times. It was not, however, merely from personal regard that Halifax now wished to see his old acquaintance. The Commissioners must have been anxious to know what was the Prince's real aim. He had refused to see them in private; and little could be learned from what he might say in a formal and public interview. Almost all those who were admitted to his confidence were men taciturn and impenetrable as himself. Burnet was the only exception. He was notoriously garrulous and indiscreet.

---

* See a very interesting note on the fifth canto of Sir Walter Scott's Rokeby.

II.—32

Yet circumstances had made it necessary to trust him; and he would doubtless, under the dexterous management of Halifax, have poured out secrets as fast as words. William knew this well, and, when he was informed that Halifax was asking for the Doctor, could not refrain from exclaiming, "If they get together there will be fine tattling." Burnet was forbidden to see the Commissioners in private: but he was assured in very courteous terms that his fidelity was regarded by the Prince as above all suspicion; and, that there might be no ground for complaint, the prohibition was made general.

That afternoon the noblemen and gentlemen whose advice William had asked met in the great room of the principal inn at Hungerford. Oxford was placed in the chair; and the King's overtures were taken into consideration. It soon appeared that the assembly was divided into two parties, a party anxious to come to terms with the King, and a party bent on his destruction. The latter party had the numerical superiority: but it was observed that Shrewsbury, who of all the English nobles was supposed to enjoy the largest share of William's confidence, though a Whig, sided on this occasion with the Tories. After much altercation the question was put. The majority was for rejecting the proposition which the royal Commissioners had been instructed to make. The resolution of the assembly was reported to the Prince at Littlecote. On no occasion during the whole course of his eventful life did he show more prudence and self-command. He could not wish the negotiation to succeed. But he was far too wise a man not to know that, if unreasonable demands made by him should cause it to fail, public feeling would no longer be on his side. He therefore overruled the opinion of his too eager followers, and declared his determination to treat on the basis proposed by the King. Many of the Lords and gentlemen assembled at Hungerford remonstrated: a whole day was spent in bickering: but William's purpose was immovable. He declared himself willing to refer all the questions in dispute to the Parliament which had just been summoned, and not to advance within forty miles of London. On his side he made some demands which even those who were least disposed to commend him allowed to be moderate. He insisted that the existing statutes should be obeyed till they should be altered by competent authority, and that all persons who held offices without a legal qualification should be forthwith dismissed. The deliberations of the Parliament, he justly conceived, could not be free if it was to sit surrounded by Irish regiments while he and his army lay at a distance of several marches. He therefore thought it reasonable that, since his troops were not to advance within forty miles of London on the west, the King's troops should fall back as far to the east. There would thus be, round the spot where the Houses were to meet, a wide circle of neutral ground. Within that circle, indeed, there were two fastnesses of great importance to the people of the capital—the Tower, which commanded their dwellings, and Tilbury Fort, which commanded their maritime trade. It was impossible to leave their places ungarrisoned. William, therefore, proposed that they should be temporarily intrusted to the care of the City of London. It might possibly be convenient that, when the Parliament assembled, the King should repair to Westminster with a body-guard. The Prince announced that, in that case, he should claim the right of repairing thither with an equal number of soldiers. It seemed to him just that, while military operations were suspended, both the armies should be considered as alike engaged in the service of the English nation, and should be alike maintained out of the English revenue. Lastly, he required some guarantee that the King would not take advantage of the armistice for the purpose of introducing a French force into England. The point where there was most danger was Portsmouth. The Prince did not insist that this important fortress should be delivered up to him, but proposed that it should, during the truce, be under the government of an officer in whom both himself and James could confide.

The propositions of William were framed with a punctilious fairness, such as might have been expected rather from a disinterested umpire pronouncing an award than from a victorious prince dictating to a helpless enemy. No fault could be found with them by the partisans of the King. But among the Whigs there was much murmuring. They wanted no reconciliation with their old master. They thought themselves absolved from all allegiance to him. They were not disposed to recognize the authority of a Parliament convoked by his writ. They were averse to an armistice; and they could not conceive why, if there was to be an armistice, it should be an armistice on equal terms. By all the laws of war the stronger party had a right to take advantage of his strength; and what was there in the character of James to justify any extraordinary indulgence? Those who reasoned thus little knew from how elevated a point of view, and with how discerning an eye, the leader whom they censured contemplated the whole situation of England and Europe. They were eager to ruin James, and would therefore either have refused to treat with him on any conditions, or have imposed on him conditions insupportably hard. To the success of William's vast and profound scheme of policy it was necessary that James should ruin himself by rejecting conditions ostentatiously liberal. The event proved the wisdom of the course which the majority of the Englishmen at Hungerford were inclined to condemn.

On Sunday, the ninth of December, the Prince's demands were put in writing, and delivered to Halifax. The Commissioners dined at Littlecote. A splendid assemblage had been invited to meet them. The old hall, hung with coats of mail which had seen the wars of the Roses, and with portraits of gallants who had adorned the court of Philip and Mary, was now crowded with peers and generals. In such a throng a short question and answer might be exchanged without attracting notice. Halifax seized this opportunity, the first which had presented itself, of extracting all that Burnet knew or thought. "What is it that you want?" said the dexterous diplomatist: "do you wish to get the King into your power?" "Not at all," said Burnet: "we would not do the least harm to his person." "And if he were to go away?" said Halifax. "There is nothing," said Burnet, "so much to be wished." There can be no doubt that Burnet expressed the general sentiment of the Whigs in the Prince's camp. They were all desirous that James should fly from the country: but only a few of the wisest among them understood how important it was that his flight should be ascribed by the nation to his own folly and perverseness, and not to harsh usage and well-grounded apprehension. It seems probable that, even in the extremity to which he was now reduced, all his enemies united would have been unable to effect his complete overthrow had he not been his own worst enemy: but while his Commissioners were laboring to save him, he was laboring as earnestly to make all their efforts useless.*

His plans were at length ripe for execution. The pretended negotiation had answered its purpose. On the same day on which the three Lords reached Hungerford the Prince of Wales arrived at Westminster. It had been intended that he should come over London Bridge; and some Irish troops were sent to Southwark to meet him. But they were received by a great multitude with such hooting and execration that they thought it advisable to retire with all speed. The poor child crossed the Thames at Kingston, and was brought into Whitehall so privately that many believed him to be still at Portsmouth.†

<small>The Queen and the Prince of Wales sent to France.</small>

To send him and the Queen out of the country without delay was now the first object of James. But who could be trusted to manage the escape? Dartmouth was accounted the most loyal of Protestant Tories; and Dartmouth had refused. Dover was a creature of the Jesuits; and even Dover had hesitated. It was not very easy to find an Englishman of rank and honor who would undertake to place the heir-apparent of the English crown in the hands of the King of France. In these circumstances, James bethought him of

---

* My account of what passed at Hungerford is taken from Clarendon's Diary, December 8, 9, 1688; Burnet, i., 794; the Paper delivered to the Prince by the Commissioners, and the Prince's Answer; Sir Patrick Hume's Diary; Van Citters, December $\frac{9}{19}$.

† Life of James, ii., 237. Burnet, strange to say, had not heard, or had forgotten, that the Prince was brought back to London: i., 796.

a French nobleman who then resided in London, Antonine, Count of Lauzun. Of this man it has been said that his life was stranger than the dreams of other people. At an early age he had been the intimate associate of Lewis, and had been encouraged to expect the highest employments under the French crown. Then his fortunes had undergone an eclipse. Lewis had driven from him the friend of his youth with bitter reproaches, and had, it was said, scarcely refrained from adding blows. The fallen favorite had been sent prisoner to a fortress: but he had emerged from his confinement, had again enjoyed the smiles of his master, and had gained the heart of one of the greatest ladies in Europe, Anna Maria, daughter of Gaston, Duke of Orleans, granddaughter of King Henry the Fourth, and heiress of the immense domains of the House of Montpensier. The lovers were bent on marriage. The royal consent was obtained. During a few hours Lauzun was regarded by the court as an adopted member of the House of Bourbon. The portion which the princess brought with her might well have been an object of competition to sovereigns; three great dukedoms, an independent principality with its own mint and with its own tribunals, and an income greatly exceeding the whole revenue of the kingdom of Scotland. But this splendid prospect had been overcast. The match had been broken off. The aspiring suitor had been, during many years, shut up in a remote castle. At length Lewis relented. Lauzun was forbidden to appear in the royal presence, but was allowed to enjoy liberty at a distance from the court. He visited England, and was well received at the palace of James and in the fashionable circles of London; for in that age the gentlemen of France were regarded throughout Europe as models of grace; and many chevaliers and viscounts, who had never been admitted to the interior circle at Versailles, found themselves objects of general curiosity and admiration at Whitehall. Lauzun was in every respect the man for the present emergency. He had courage and a sense of honor, had been accustomed to eccentric adventures, and, with the keen observation and ironical pleasantry of a finished man of the world, had a strong propensity to knight-errantry. All his national feelings and all his personal interests impelled him to undertake the adventure from which the most devoted subjects of the English crown seemed to shrink. As the guardian, at a perilous crisis, of the Queen of Great Britain and of the Prince of Wales, he might return with honor to his native land: he might once more be admitted to see Lewis dress and dine, and might, after so many vicissitudes, recommence, in the decline of life, the strangely fascinating chase of royal favor.

Animated by such feelings, Lauzun eagerly accepted the high trust which was offered to him. The arrangements for the flight were promptly made: a vessel was ordered to be in readiness at Gravesend: but to reach Gravesend was not easy. The City was in a state of extreme agitation. The slightest cause sufficed to bring a crowd together. No foreigner could appear in the streets without risk of being stopped, questioned, and carried before a magistrate as a Jesuit in disguise. It was, therefore, necessary to take the road on the south of the Thames. No precaution which could quiet suspicion was omitted. The King and Queen retired to rest as usual. When the palace had been some time profoundly quiet, James rose and called a servant who was in attendance. "You will find," said the King, "a man at the door of the antechamber: bring him hither." The servant obeyed, and Lauzun was ushered into the royal bedchamber. "I confide to you," said James, "my Queen and my son; everything must be risked to carry them into France." Lauzun, with a truly chivalrous spirit, returned thanks for the dangerous honor which had been conferred on him, and begged permission to avail himself of the assistance of his friend Saint Victor, a gentleman of Provence, whose courage and faith had been often tried. The services of so valuable an assistant were readily accepted. Lauzun gave his hand to Mary. Saint Victor wrapped up in his warm cloak the ill-fated heir of so many kings. The party stole down the back stairs, and embarked in an open skiff. It was a miserable voyage. The night was bleak; the rain fell; the wind roared; the water was rough; at length the boat reached Lambeth; and the fugitives landed near an inn, where a coach and horses were in waiting. Some time elapsed before the horses could be harnessed. Mary, afraid that her face might be known, would not enter the house. She remained with her child, cowering for shelter from the storm under the tower of Lambeth Church, and distracted by terror whenever the hostler approached her with his lantern. Two of her women attended her, one who gave suck to the Prince, and one whose office was to rock his cradle; but they could be of little use to their mistress; for both were foreigners who could hardly speak the English language, and who shuddered at the rigor of the English climate. The only consolatory circumstance was that the little boy was well, and uttered not a single cry. At length the coach was ready. Saint Victor followed it on horseback. The fugitives reached Gravesend safely, and embarked in the yacht which waited for them. They found there Lord Powis and his wife. Three Irish officers were also on board. These men had been sent thither in order that they might assist Lauzun in any desperate emergency; for it was thought not impossible that the captain of the ship might prove false; and it was fully determined that, on the first suspicion of treachery, he should be stabbed to the heart. There was, however, no necessity for violence. The yacht proceeded down the river with a fair wind; and Saint Victor, having seen her under sail, spurred back with the good news to Whitehall.*

On the morning of Monday, the tenth of December, the King learned that his wife and son had begun their voyage with a fair prospect of reaching their destination. About the same time a courier arrived at the palace with despatches from Hungerford. Had James been a little more discerning, or a little less obstinate, those despatches would have induced him to reconsider all his plans. The Commissioners wrote hopefully. The conditions proposed by the conqueror were

---

* Life of James, ii., 246; Père d'Orléans, Révolutions d'Angleterre, xi.; Madame de Sévigné, Dec. $\frac{14}{24}$, 1688; Dangeau, Mémoires, Dec. $\frac{18}{28}$. As to Lauzun, see the Memoirs of Mademoiselle and of the Duke of Saint Simon, and the Characters of Labruyère.

strangely liberal. The King himself could not refrain from exclaiming that they were more favorable than he could have expected. He might indeed not unreasonably suspect that they had been framed with no friendly design: but this mattered nothing; for, whether they were offered in the hope that, by closing with them, he would lay the ground for a happy reconciliation, or, as is more likely, in the hope that, by rejecting them, he would exhibit himself to the whole nation as utterly unreasonable and incorrigible, his course was equally clear. In either case his policy was to accept them promptly and to observe them faithfully.

But it soon appeared that William had perfectly understood the character with which he had to deal, and, in offering those terms which the Whigs at Hungerford had censured as too indulgent, had risked nothing.

The King's preparations for flight.

The solemn farce by which the public had been amused since the retreat of the royal army from Salisbury was prolonged during a few hours. All the Lords who were still in the capital were invited to the palace that they might be informed of the progress of the negotiation which had been opened by their advice. Another meeting of Peers was appointed for the following day. The Lord Mayor and the Sheriffs of London were summoned to attend the King. He exhorted them to perform their duties vigorously, and owned that he had thought it expedient to send his wife and child out of the country, but assured them that he would himself remain at his post. While he uttered this unkingly and unmanly falsehood, his fixed purpose was to depart before daybreak. Already he had intrusted his most valuable movables to the care of several foreign ambassadors. His most important papers had been deposited with the Tuscan minister. But before the flight there was still something to be done. The tyrant pleased himself with the thought that he might avenge himself on a people who had been impatient of his despotism by inflicting on them, at parting, all the evils of anarchy. He ordered the Great Seal and the writs for the new Parliament to be brought to his apartment. The writs he threw into the fire. Some which had been already sent out he annulled by an instrument drawn up in legal form. To Feversham he wrote a letter which could be understood only as a command to disband the army. Still, however, he concealed, even from his chief ministers, his intention of absconding. Just before he retired he directed Jeffreys to be in the closet early on the morrow, and, while stepping into bed, whispered to Mulgrave that the news from Hungerford was highly satisfactory. Everybody withdrew except the Duke of Northumberland. This young man, a natural son of Charles the Second by the Duchess of Cleveland, commanded a troop of Life Guards, and was a Lord of the Bedchamber. It seems to have been then the custom of the court that, in the Queen's absence, a Lord of the Bedchamber should sleep on a pallet in the King's room; and it was Northumberland's turn to perform this duty.

At three in the morning of Tuesday, the eleventh of December, James rose, took the Great Seal in his hand, laid His flight. his commands on Northumberland not to open the door of the bedchamber till the usual hour, and disappeared through a secret passage, the same passage probably through which Huddleston had been brought to the bedside of the late King. Sir Edward Hales was in attendance with a hackney-coach. James was conveyed to Millbank, where he crossed the Thames in a small wherry. As he passed Lambeth, he flung the Great Seal into the midst of the stream, where, after many months, it was accidentally caught by a fishing-net and dragged up.

At Vauxhall he landed. A carriage and horses had been stationed there for him; and he immediately took the road toward Sheerness, where a hoy belonging to the Customhouse had been ordered to await his arrival.*

---

* History of the Desertion; Life of James, ii., 251, Orig. Mem.; Mulgrave's Account of the Revolution; Burnet, i., 795.

CHAPTER X.

The flight of James known.

NORTHUMBERLAND strictly obeyed the injunction which had been laid on him, and did not open the door of the royal apartment till it was broad day. The antechamber was filled with courtiers who came to make their morning bow and with Lords who had been summoned to council. The news of James's flight passed in an instant from the galleries to the streets; and the whole capital was in commotion.

Great agitation.

It was a terrible moment. The King was gone. The Prince had not arrived. No Regency had been appointed. The Great Seal, essential to the administration of ordinary justice, had disappeared. It was soon known that Feversham had, on the receipt of the royal order, instantly disbanded his forces. What respect for law or property was likely to be found among soldiers, armed and congregated, emancipated from the restraints of discipline, and destitute of the necessaries of life? On the other hand, the populace of London had, during some weeks, shown a strong disposition to turbulence and rapine. The urgency of the crisis united for a short time all who had any interest in the peace of society. Rochester had till that day adhered firmly to the royal cause. He now saw that there was only one way of averting general confusion. "Muster your troop of Guards," he said to Northumberland; "and declare for the Prince of Orange." The advice was promptly followed. The principal officers of the army who were then in London held a meeting at Whitehall, and resolved that they would submit to William's authority, and would, till his pleasure should be known, keep their men together, and assist the civil power to preserve order.*

---

* History of the Desertion; Mulgrave's Account of the Revolution; Eachard's History of the Revolution.

Who was to supply, at that awful crisis, the place of the King? In the days of the Plantagenets, if a suspension of the regal functions took place, the Lords Spiritual and Temporal generally assumed the supreme executive power. It was by the Lords that provision was made for the government of the kingdom during the minority of Henry the Third and during the absence of Edward the First. Both when Henry the Sixth succeeded to the crown in his infancy, and when many years later he sank into imbecility, the Lords took upon themselves to administer the government in his stead till the legislature had appointed a Protector. Whether our old Barons and Prelates, in acting for a king who could not act for himself, exercised a strictly legal right, or committed an irregularity which only extreme necessity could excuse, is a question which has been much debated. But the morning of the eleventh of December, 1688, was not a time for controversy. It was necessary to the public safety that there should be a provisional government; and the eyes of men naturally turned to the magnates of the realm. Most of the Peers who were in the capital repaired to Guildhall, and were received there with all honor by the magistracy of the City. The extremity of the danger drew Sancroft forth from his palace. He took the chair; and, under his presidency, the new Archbishop of York, five Bishops, and twenty-two temporal Lords determined to draw up, subscribe, and publish a Declaration. By this instrument they declared that they were firmly attached to the religion and constitution of their country, and that they had cherished the hope of seeing grievances redressed and tranquillity restored by the Parliament which the King had lately summoned, but that this hope had been extinguished by his flight. They had therefore determined to join with the Prince of Orange, in order that the freedom of the nation might be vindicated, that the rights of the Church might be secured, that a just liberty of conscience might be given to Dissenters, and that the Protestant interest throughout the world might be strengthened. Till His Highness should arrive, they were prepared to take on themselves the responsibility of giving

The Lords meet at Guildhall.

such directions as might be necessary for the preservation of order. A deputation was instantly sent to lay this Declaration before the Prince, and to inform him that he was impatiently expected in London.*

The Lords then proceeded to deliberate on the course which it was necessary to take for the prevention of tumult. They sent for the two Secretaries of State. Middleton refused to submit to what he regarded as an illegitimate authority: but Preston, astounded by his master's flight, and not knowing what to expect or whither to turn, obeyed the summons. A message was sent to Skelton, who was Lieutenant of the Tower, requesting his attendance at Guildhall. He came, and was told that his services were no longer wanted, and that he must instantly deliver up his keys. He was succeeded by Lord Lucas. At the same time the Peers ordered a letter to be written to Dartmouth, enjoining him to refrain from all hostile operations against the Dutch fleet, and to displace all the Popish officers who held commands under him.†

The part taken in these proceedings by Sancroft, and by some other persons who had, up to that day, been strictly faithful to the principle of passive obedience, deserves especial notice. To usurp the command of the military and naval forces of the state, to remove the officers whom the King had set over his castles and his ships, and to prohibit his Admiral from giving battle in defence of the royal cause, was surely nothing less than rebellion. Yet several honest and able Tories of the school of Filmer persuaded themselves that they could do all these things without incurring the guilt of resisting their Sovereign. The distinction which they took was, at least, ingenious. Government, they said, is the ordinance of God. Hereditary monarchical government is eminently the ordinance of God. While the King commands what is lawful, we must obey him actively. When he commands what is unlawful, we must obey him passively. In no extremity are we justified in withstanding him by force. But, if he

---

* London Gazette, Dec. 13, 1688.

† Life of James, ii., 259; Mulgrave's Account of the Revolution; Legge Papers in the Mackintosh Collection.

chooses to resign his office, his rights over us are at an end. While he governs us, though he may govern us ill, we are bound to submit: but, if he refuses to govern us at all, we are not bound to remain forever without a government. Anarchy is not the ordinance of God; nor will he impute it to us as a sin that, when a prince, whom, in spite of extreme provocations, we have never ceased to honor and obey, has departed we know not whither, leaving no vicegerent, we take the only course which can prevent the entire dissolution of society. Had our Sovereign remained among us, we were ready, little as he deserved our love, to die at his feet. Had he, when he quitted us, appointed a regency to govern us with vicarious authority during his absence, to that regency alone should we have looked for direction. But he has disappeared, having made no provision for the preservation of order or the administration of justice. With him, and with his Great Seal, has vanished the whole machinery by which a murderer can be punished, by which the right to an estate can be decided, by which the effects of a bankrupt can be distributed. His last act has been to free thousands of armed men from the restraints of military discipline, and to place them in such a situation that they must plunder or starve. Yet a few hours, and every man's hand will be against his neighbor. Life, property, female honor, will be at the mercy of every lawless spirit. We are at this moment actually in that state of nature about which theorists have written so much; and in that state we have been placed, not by our fault, but by the voluntary defection of him who ought to have been our protector. His defection may be justly called voluntary: for neither his life nor his liberty was in danger. His enemies had just consented to treat with him on a basis proposed by himself, and had offered immediately to suspend all hostile operations, on conditions which he could not deny to be liberal. In such circumstances it is that he has abandoned his trust. We retract nothing. We are in nothing inconsistent. We still assert our old doctrines without qualification. We still hold that it is in all cases sinful to resist the magistrate: but we say that there is no longer any magistrate to resist. He who was the magistrate, after long abusing his powers, has at last abdicated them. The abuse did not give us a right to depose him: but the abdication gives us a right to consider how we may best supply his place.

It was on these grounds that the Prince's party was now swollen by many adherents who had previously stood aloof from it. Never, within the memory of man, had there been so near an approach to entire concord among all intelligent Englishmen as at this conjuncture; and never had concord been more needed. All those evil passions which it is the office of government to restrain, and which the best governments restrain but imperfectly, were on a sudden emancipated from control; avarice, licentiousness, revenge, the hatred of sect to sect, the hatred of nation to nation. On such occasions it will ever be found that the human vermin, which, neglected by ministers of state and ministers of religion, barbarous in the midst of civilization, heathen in the midst of Christianity, burrows, among all physical and all moral pollution, in the cellars and garrets of great cities, will at once rise into a terrible importance. So it was now in London. When the night, the longest night, as it chanced, of the year approached, forth came from every den of vice, from the bear-garden at Hockley, and from the labyrinth of tippling-houses and brothels in the Friars, thousands of house-breakers and highwaymen, cut-purses and ring-droppers. With these were mingled thousands of idle apprentices, who wished merely for the excitement of a riot. Even men of peaceable and honest habits were impelled by religious animosity to join the lawless part of the population. For the cry of No Popery, a cry which has more than once endangered the existence of London, was the signal for outrage and rapine. First the rabble fell on the Roman Catholic places of worship. The buildings were demolished. Benches, pulpits, confessionals, breviaries were heaped up and set on fire. A great mountain of books and furniture blazed on the site of the convent at Clerkenwell. Another pile was kindled before the ruins of the Franciscan house in Lincoln's Inn Fields. The chapel in Lime Street, the chapel in Bucklersbury, were

Riots in London.

pulled down. The pictures, images, and crucifixes were carried along the streets in triumph, amidst lighted tapers torn from the altars. The procession bristled thick with swords and staves, and on the point of every sword and of every staff was an orange. The King's printing-house, whence had issued, during the preceding three years, innumerable tracts in defence of Papal supremacy, image-worship, and monastic vows, was—to use a coarse metaphor which then, for the first time, came into fashion—completely gutted. The vast stock of paper, much of which was still unpolluted by types, furnished an immense bonfire. From monasteries, temples, and public offices, the fury of the multitude turned to private dwellings. Several houses were pillaged and destroyed: but the smallness of the booty disappointed the plunderers; and soon a rumor was spread that the most valuable effects of the Papists had been placed under the care of the foreign ambassadors. To the savage and ignorant populace the law of nations and the risk of bringing on their country the just vengeance of all Europe were as nothing. The houses of the ambassadors were besieged. A great crowd assembled before Barillon's door, in Saint James's Square. He, however, fared better than might have been expected. For, though the government which he represented was held in abhorrence, his liberal housekeeping and exact payments had made him personally popular. Moreover, he had taken the precaution of asking for a guard of soldiers; and, as several men of rank, who lived near him, had done the same, a considerable force was collected in the square. The rioters, therefore, when they were assured that no arms or priests were concealed under his roof, left him unmolested. The Venetian Envoy was protected by a detachment of troops: but the mansions occupied by the ministers of the Elector Palatine and of the Grand Duke of Tuscany were destroyed. One precious box the Tuscan minister was able to save from the marauders. It contained nine volumes of memoirs, written in the hand of James himself. These volumes reached France in safety, and, after the lapse of more than a century, perished there in the havoc of a revolution far more terrible than that from which they had escaped. But some fragments still remain, and, though grievously mutilated, and embedded in masses of childish fiction, well deserve to be attentively studied.*

The rich plate of the Chapel Royal had been deposited at Wild House, near Lincoln's Inn Fields, the residence of the Spanish ambassador Ronquillo. Ronquillo, conscious that he and his court had not deserved ill of the English nation, had thought it unnecessary to ask for soldiers: but the mob was not in a mood to make nice distinctions. The name of Spain had long been associated in the public mind with the Inquisition and the Armada, with the cruelties of Mary and the plots against Elizabeth. Ronquillo had also made himself many enemies among the common people by availing himself of his privilege to avoid the necessity of paying his debts. His house was therefore sacked without mercy; and a noble library, which he had collected, perished in the flames. His only comfort was that the host in his chapel was rescued from the same fate.†

<small>The Spanish ambassador's house sacked.</small>

---

* I take this opportunity of giving an explanation which well-informed persons may think superfluous. Several critics have complained that I treat the Saint Germains Life of James the Second sometimes as a work of the highest authority, and sometimes as a mere romance. They seem to imagine that the book is all from the same hand, and ought either to be uniformly quoted with respect or uniformly thrown aside with contempt. The truth is that part of the Life is of the very highest authority, and that the rest is the work of an ignorant and silly compiler, and is of no more value than any common Jacobite pamphlet. Those passages which were copied from the Memoirs written by James, and those passages which were carefully revised by his son, are among the most useful materials for history. They contain the testimony of witnesses, who were undoubtedly under a strong bias, and for whose bias large allowance ought to be made, but who had the best opportunities of learning the truth. The interstices between these precious portions of the narrative are sometimes filled with trash. Whoever will take the trouble to examine the references in my notes will see that I have constantly borne in mind the distinction which I have now pointed out. Surely I may cite, as of high authority, an account of the last moments of Charles the Second, which was written by his brother, or an account of the plottings of Penn, of Dartmouth, and of Churchill, which was corrected by the hand of the Pretender, and yet may, with perfect consistency, reject the fables of a nameless scribbler who makes Argyle, with all his cavalry, swim across the Clyde at a place where the Clyde is more than four miles wide (1857).

† London Gazette, Dec. 13, 1688; Barillon, Dec. $\frac{14}{24}$; Van Citters, same date; Luttrell's Diary; Life of James, ii., 256, Orig. Mem.; Ellis Correspondence, Dec. 13;

The morning of the twelfth of December rose on a ghastly sight. The capital in many places presented the aspect of a city taken by storm. The Lords met at Whitehall, and exerted themselves to restore tranquillity. The trainbands were ordered under arms. A body of cavalry was kept in readiness to disperse tumultuous assemblages. Such atonement as was at that moment possible was made for the gross insults which had been offered to foreign governments. A reward was promised for the discovery of the property taken from Wild House; and Ronquillo, who had not a bed or an ounce of plate left, was splendidly lodged in the deserted palace of the kings of England. A sumptuous table was kept for him; and the yeomen of the guard were ordered to wait in his antechamber with the same observance which they were in the habit of paying to the Sovereign. These marks of respect soothed even the punctilious pride of the Spanish court, and averted all danger of a rupture.*

In spite, however, of the well-meant efforts of the provisional government, the agitation grew hourly more formidable. It was heightened by an event which, even at this distance of time, can hardly be related without a feeling of vindictive pleasure. A scrivener who lived at Wapping, and whose trade was to furnish the seafaring men there with money at high interest, had some time before lent a sum on bottomry. The debtor applied to equity for relief against his own bond; and the case came before Jeffreys. The counsel for the borrower, having little else to say, said that the lender was a Trimmer. The Chancellor instantly fired. "A Trimmer! where is he? Let me see him. I have

<small>Arrest of Jeffreys.</small>

Consultation of the Spanish Council of State, Jan. $\frac{19}{29}$, 1689. It appears that Ronquillo complained bitterly to his government of his losses; "Sirviendole solo de consuelo el haber tenido prevencion de poder consumir El Santisimo."

* London Gazette, Dec. 13, 1688; Luttrell's Diary; Mulgrave's Account of the Revolution; Consultation of the Spanish Council of State, Jan. $\frac{19}{29}$, 1689. Something was said about reprisals: but the Spanish council treated the suggestion with contempt. "Habiendo sido este hecho por un furor de pueblo, sin consentimiento del gobierno, y antes contra su voluntad, como lo ha mostrado la satisfaccion que le han dado y le han prometido, parece que no hay juicio humano que puede aconsejar que se pase á semejante remedio."

heard of that kind of monster. What is it made like?" The unfortunate creditor was forced to stand forth. The Chancellor glared fiercely on him, stormed at him, and sent him away half dead with fright. "While I live," the poor man said, as he tottered out of the court, "I shall never forget that terrible countenance." And now the day of retribution had arrived. The Trimmer was walking through Wapping, when he saw a well-known face looking out of the window of an ale-house. He could not be deceived. The eyebrows, indeed, had been shaved away. The dress was that of a common sailor from Newcastle, and was black with coal-dust: but there was no mistaking the savage eye and mouth of Jeffreys. The alarm was given. In a moment the house was surrounded by hundreds of people shaking bludgeons and bellowing curses. The fugitive's life was saved by a company of the trainbands; and he was carried before the Lord Mayor. The Mayor was a simple man who had passed his whole life in obscurity, and was bewildered by finding himself an important actor in a mighty revolution. The events of the last twenty-four hours, and the perilous state of the city which was under his charge, had disordered his mind and his body. When the great man, at whose frown, a few days before, the whole kingdom had trembled, was dragged into the justice-room begrimed with ashes, half dead with fright, and followed by a raging multitude, the agitation of the unfortunate Mayor rose to the height. He fell into fits, and was carried to his bed, whence he never rose. Meanwhile the throng without was constantly becoming more numerous and more savage. Jeffreys begged to be sent to prison. An order to that effect was procured from the Lords who were sitting at Whitehall; and he was conveyed in a carriage to the Tower. Two regiments of militia were drawn out to escort him, and found the duty a difficult one. It was repeatedly necessary for them to form, as if for the purpose of repelling a charge of cavalry, and to present a forest of pikes to the mob. The thousands who were disappointed of their revenge pursued the coach, with howls of rage, to the gate of the Tower, brandishing cudgels, and holding up halters full in the prisoner's view.

The wretched man meantime was in convulsions of terror. He wrung his hands: he looked wildly out, sometimes at one window, sometimes at the other, and was heard even above the tumult, crying "Keep them off, gentlemen! For God's sake, keep them off!" At length, having suffered far more than the bitterness of death, he was safely lodged in the fortress where some of his most illustrious victims had passed their last days, and where his own life was destined to close in unspeakable ignominy and horror.*

All this time an active search was making after Roman Catholic priests. Many were arrested. Two Bishops, Ellis and Leyburn, were sent to Newgate. The Nuncio, who had little reason to expect that either his spiritual or his political character would be respected by the multitude, made his escape, disguised as a lackey, in the train of the minister of the Duke of Savoy.†

Another day of agitation and alarm closed, and was followed by a night the strangest and most terrible that England had ever seen. Early in the evening an attack was made by the rabble on a stately house which had been built a few months before for Lord Powis, which, in the reign of George the Second, was the residence of the Duke of Newcastle, and which is still conspicuous at the north-western angle of Lincoln's Inn Fields. Some troops were sent thither: the mob was dispersed, tranquillity seemed to be restored, and the citizens were retiring quietly to their beds. Just at this time arose a whisper which swelled fast into a fearful clamor, passed in an hour from Piccadilly to Whitechapel, and spread into every street and alley of the capital. It was said that the Irish whom Feversham had let loose were marching on London and massacring every man, woman, and child on the road. At one in the morning the drums of the militia beat to arms. Everywhere terrified women were weeping and

The Irish Night.

---

* North's Life of Guildford, 220; Jeffreys's Elegy; Luttrell's Diary; Oldmixon, 762. Oldmixon was in the crowd, and was, I doubt not, one of the most furious there. He tells the story well. Ellis Correspondence; Burnet, i., 797, and Onslow's note.

† Adda, Dec. $\frac{9}{19}$; Van Citters, Dec. $\frac{18}{28}$.

wringing their hands, while their fathers and husbands were equipping themselves for fight. Before two the capital wore a face of stern preparedness which might well have daunted a real enemy, if such an enemy had been approaching. Candles were blazing at all the windows. The public places were as bright as at noonday. All the great avenues were barricaded. More than twenty thousand pikes and muskets lined the streets. The late daybreak of the winter solstice found the whole City still in arms. During many years the Londoners retained a vivid recollection of what they called the Irish Night. When it was known that there had been no danger, attempts were made to discover the origin of the rumor which had produced so much agitation. It appeared that some persons who had the look and dress of clowns just arrived from the country had first spread the report in the suburbs a little before midnight: but whence these men came, and by whom they were employed, remained a mystery. And soon news arrived from many quarters which bewildered the public mind still more. The panic had not been confined to London. The cry that disbanded Irish soldiers were coming to murder the Protestants had, with malignant ingenuity, been raised at once in many places widely distant from each other. Great numbers of letters, skilfully framed for the purpose of frightening ignorant people, had been sent by stage-coaches, by wagons, and by the post, to various parts of England. All these letters came to hand almost at the same time. In a hundred towns at once the populace was possessed with the belief that armed barbarians were at hand, bent on perpetrating crimes as foul as those which had disgraced the rebellion of Ulster. No Protestant would find mercy. Children would be compelled by torture to murder their parents. Babes would be stuck on pikes, or flung into the blazing ruins of what had lately been happy dwellings. Great multitudes assembled with weapons: the people in some places began to pull down bridges, and to throw up barricades: but soon the excitement went down. In many districts those who had been so foully imposed upon learned with delight, alloyed by shame, that there was not a single Popish soldier within a week's march. There were places, indeed, where some straggling bands of Irish made their appearance and demanded food: but it can scarcely be imputed to them as a crime that they did not choose to die of hunger; and there is no evidence that they committed any wanton outrage. In truth, they were much less numerous than was commonly supposed; and their spirit was cowed by finding themselves left on a sudden, without leaders or provisions, in the midst of a mighty population which felt toward them as men feel toward a drove of wolves. Of all the subjects of James none had more reason to execrate him than these unfortunate members of his church and defenders of his throne.*

It is honorable to the English character that, notwithstanding the aversion with which the Roman Catholic religion and the Irish race were then regarded, notwithstanding the anarchy which was the effect of the flight of James, notwithstanding the artful machinations which were employed to scare the multitude into cruelty, no atrocious crime was perpetrated at this conjuncture. Much property, indeed, was destroyed and carried away. The houses of many Roman Catholic gentlemen were attacked. Parks were ravaged. Deer were slain and stolen. Some venerable specimens of the domestic architecture of the Middle Ages bear to this day the marks of the popular violence. The roads were in many places made impassable by a self-appointed police, which stopped every traveller till he proved that he was not a Papist. The Thames was infested by a set of pirates who, under pretence of searching for arms or delinquents, rummaged every boat that passed. Obnoxious persons were insulted and hustled. Many persons who were not obnoxious were glad to ransom their persons and effects by bestowing some guineas on the zealous Protestants who had, without any legal authority, assumed the office of inquisitors. But in all this confusion, which lasted several days and extended over many counties, not a single Roman Catholic lost his life. The mob

* Van Citters, Dec. $\frac{14}{24}$, 1688; Luttrell's Diary; Ellis Correspondence; Oldmixon, 761; Speke's Secret History of the Revolution; Life of James, ii., 257; Eachard's History of the Revolution; History of the Desertion.

showed no inclination to blood, except in the case of Jeffreys; and the hatred which that bad man inspired had more affinity with humanity than with cruelty.*

Many years later Hugh Speke affirmed that the Irish Night was his work, that he had prompted the rustics who raised London, and that he was the author of the letters which had spread dismay through the country. His assertion is not intrinsically improbable: but it rests on no evidence except his own word. He was a man quite capable of committing such a villany, and quite capable also of falsely boasting that he had committed it.†

At London William was impatiently expected: for it was not doubted that his vigor and ability would speedily restore order and security. There was, however, some delay for which the Prince cannot justly be blamed. His original intention had been to proceed from Hungerford to Oxford, where he was assured of an honorable and affectionate reception: but the arrival of the deputation from Guildhall induced him to change his intention and to hasten directly toward the capital. On the way he learned that Feversham, in pursuance of the King's orders, had dismissed the royal army, and that thousands of soldiers, freed from restraint and destitute of necessaries, were scattered over the counties through which the road to London lay. It was, therefore, impossible for William to proceed slenderly attended without great danger, not only to his own person, about which he was not much in the habit of being solicitous, but also to the great interests which were under his care. It was necessary that he should regulate his own movements by the movements of his troops; and troops could then move but slowly along the highways of England in midwinter. He was, on this occasion, a little moved from his ordinary composure. "I am not to be thus dealt with," he exclaimed, with bitterness; "and that my Lord Feversham shall find." Prompt and judicious measures were taken to remedy the evils which James had caused. Churchill and Grafton were intrusted with the task of reassembling the

---

* Life of James, ii., 258. † Secret History of the Revolution.

dispersed army and bringing it into order. The English soldiers were invited to resume their military character. The Irish were commanded to deliver up their arms on pain of being treated as banditti, but were assured that, if they would submit quietly, they should be supplied with necessaries.*

The Prince's orders were carried into effect with scarcely any opposition, except from the Irish soldiers who had been in garrison at Tilbury. One of these men snapped a pistol at Grafton. It missed fire, and the assassin was instantly shot dead by an Englishman. About two hundred of the unfortunate strangers made a gallant attempt to return to their own country. They seized a richly laden East Indiaman which had just arrived in the Thames, and tried to procure pilots by force at Gravesend. No pilot, however, was to be found; and they were under the necessity of trusting to their own skill in navigation. They soon ran their ship aground, and, after some bloodshed, were compelled to lay down their arms.†

William had now been five weeks on English ground; and during the whole of that time his good fortune had been uninterrupted. His own prudence and firmness had been conspicuously displayed, and yet had done less for him than the folly and pusillanimity of others. And now, at the moment when it seemed that his plans were about to be crowned with entire success, they were disconcerted by one of those strange incidents which so often confound the most exquisite devices of human policy.

On the morning of the thirteenth of December the people of London, not yet fully recovered from the agitation of the Irish Night, were surprised by a rumor that the King had been detained, and was still in the island. The report gathered strength during the day, and was fully confirmed before the evening.

The King detained near Sheerness.

James had travelled with relays of coach-horses along the southern shore of the Thames, and on the morning of the

---

* Clarendon's Diary, December 13, 1688; Van Citters, December $\frac{14}{24}$; Eachard's History of the Revolution.

† Van Citters, Dec. $\frac{14}{24}$, 1688; Luttrell's Diary.

twelfth had reached Emley Ferry near the island of Sheppey. There lay the hoy in which he was to sail. He went on board: but the wind blew fresh; and the master would not venture to put to sea without more ballast. A tide was thus lost. Midnight was approaching before the vessel began to float. By that time the news that the King had disappeared, that the country was without a government, and that London was in confusion, had travelled fast down the Thames, and wherever it spread had produced outrage and misrule. The rude fishermen of the Kentish coast eyed the hoy with suspicion and with cupidity. It was whispered that some persons in the garb of gentlemen had gone on board of her in great haste. Perhaps they were Jesuits: perhaps they were rich. Fifty or sixty boatmen, animated at once by hatred of Popery and by love of plunder, boarded the hoy just as she was about to make sail. The passengers were told that they must go on shore and be examined by a magistrate. The King's appearance excited suspicion. "It is Father Petre," cried one ruffian; "I know him by his lean jaws." "Search the hatchet-faced old Jesuit!" became the general cry. He was rudely pulled and pushed about. His money and watch were taken from him. He had about him his coronation ring, and some other trinkets of great value: but these escaped the search of the robbers, who, indeed, were so ignorant of jewellery that they took his diamond buckles for bits of glass.

At length the prisoners were put on shore and carried to an inn. A crowd had assembled there to see them; and James, though disguised by a wig of different shape and color from that which he usually wore, was at once recognized. For a moment the rabble seemed to be overawed: but the exhortations of their chiefs revived their courage; and the sight of Hales, whom they well knew and bitterly hated, inflamed their fury. His park was in the neighborhood; and at that very moment a band of rioters was employed in pillaging his house and shooting his deer. The multitude assured the King that they would not hurt him: but they refused to let him depart. It chanced that the Earl of Winchelsea, a Protestant, but a zealous royalist, head of the

Finch family, and a kinsman of Nottingham, was then at Canterbury. As soon as he learned what had happened he hastened to the coast, accompanied by some Kentish gentlemen. By their intervention the King was removed to a more convenient lodging: but he was still a prisoner. The mob kept constant watch round the house to which he had been carried; and some of the ringleaders lay at the door of his bedroom. His demeanor meantime was that of a man, all the nerves of whose mind had been broken by the load of misfortunes. Sometimes he spoke so haughtily that the rustics who had charge of him were provoked into making insolent replies. Then he betook himself to supplication. "Let me go," he cried; "get me a boat. The Prince of Orange is hunting for my life. If you do not let me fly now, it will be too late. My blood will be on your heads. He that is not with me is against me." On this last text he preached a sermon half an hour long. He harangued on a strange variety of subjects, on the disobedience of the fellows of Magdalene College, on the miracles wrought by Saint Winifred's Well, on the disloyalty of the black-coats, and on the virtues of a piece of the true cross which he had unfortunately lost. "What have I done?" he demanded of the Kentish squires who attended him. "Tell me the truth. What error have I committed?" Those to whom he put these questions were too humane to return the answer which must have risen to their lips, and listened to his wild talk in pitying silence.*

When the news that he had been stopped, insulted, roughly handled, and plundered, and that he was still a prisoner in the hands of rude churls, reached the capital, many passions were roused. Rigid Churchmen, who had, a few hours before, begun to think that they were freed from their allegiance to him, now felt misgivings. He had not quitted his kingdom. He had not consummated his abdication. If he should resume his regal office, could they, on their principles, refuse to pay him obedience? Enlightened statesmen foresaw with

---

* Life of James, ii., 251, Orig. Mem.; Letter printed in Tindal's Continuation of Rapin. This curious letter is in the Harl. MSS., 6852.

concern that all the disputes which his flight had for a moment set at rest would be revived and exasperated by his return. Some of the common people, though still smarting from recent wrongs, were touched with compassion for a great prince outraged by ruffians, and were willing to entertain a hope, more honorable to their good-nature than to their discernment, that he might even now repent of the errors which had brought on him so terrible a punishment.

From the moment when it was known that the King was still in England, Sancroft, who had hitherto acted as chief of the Provisional Government, absented himself from the sittings of the Peers. Halifax, who had just returned from the Dutch head-quarters, was placed in the chair. His sentiments had undergone a great change in a few hours. Both public and private feelings now impelled him to join the Whigs. Those who candidly examine the evidence which has come down to us will be of opinion that he accepted the office of royal Commissioner in the sincere hope of effecting an accommodation between the King and the Prince on fair terms. The negotiation had commenced prosperously: the Prince had offered terms which the King could not but acknowledge to be fair: the eloquent and ingenious Trimmer might flatter himself that he should be able to mediate between infuriated factions, to dictate a compromise between extreme opinions, to secure the liberties and religion of his country, without exposing her to the risks inseparable from a change of dynasty and a disputed succession. While he was pleasing himself with thoughts so agreeable to his temper, he learned that he had been deceived, and had been used as an instrument for deceiving the nation. His mission to Hungerford had been a fool's errand. The King had never meant to abide by the terms which he had instructed his Commissioners to propose. He had charged them to declare that he was willing to submit all the questions in dispute to the Parliament which he had summoned; and, while they were delivering his message, he had burned the writs, made away with the seal, let loose the army, suspended the administration of justice, dissolved the government, and fled from the capital. Halifax saw that an amicable arrangement was no longer possible. He also felt, it may be suspected, the vexation natural to a man widely renowned for wisdom, who finds that he has been duped by an understanding immeasurably inferior to his own, and the vexation natural to a great master of ridicule, who finds himself placed in a ridiculous situation. His judgment and his resentment alike induced him to relinquish the schemes of reconciliation on which he had hitherto been intent, and to place himself at the head of those who were bent on raising William to the throne.*

A journal of what passed in the Council of Lords while Halifax presided is still extant in his own handwriting.† No precaution, which seemed necessary for the prevention of outrage and robbery, was omitted. The Peers took on themselves the responsibility of giving orders that, if the rabble rose again, the soldiers should fire with bullets. Jeffreys was brought to Whitehall and interrogated as to what had become of the Great Seal and the writs. At his own earnest request he was remanded to the Tower, as the only place where his life could be safe; and he retired thanking and blessing those who had given him the protection of a prison. A Whig nobleman moved that Oates should be set at liberty; but this motion was overruled.‡

The business of the day was nearly over, and Halifax was about to rise, when he was informed that a messenger from Sheerness was in attendance. No occurrence could be more perplexing or annoying. To do anything, to do nothing, was to incur a grave responsibility. Halifax, wishing probably to obtain time for communication with the Prince, would have adjourned the meeting: but Mulgrave begged the Lords to

---

* Reresby was told, by a lady whom he does not name, that the King had no intention of withdrawing till he received a letter from Halifax, who was then at Hungerford. The letter, she said, informed His Majesty that, if he stayed, his life would be in danger. This was certainly a fiction. The King, before the Commissioners left London, had told Barillon that their embassy was a mere feint, and had expressed a full resolution to leave the country. It is clear from Reresby's own narrative that Halifax thought himself shamefully used.

† Harl. MS., 255.   ‡ Halifax MS.; Van Citters, Dec. $\frac{18}{28}$, 1688.

keep their seats, and introduced the messenger. The man told his story with many tears, and produced a letter written in the King's hand, and addressed to no particular person, but imploring the aid of all good Englishmen.*

Such an appeal it was hardly possible to disregard. The Lords ordered Feversham to hasten with a troop of the Life Guards to the place where the King was detained, and to set His Majesty at liberty.

The Lords order him to be set at liberty.

Already Middleton and a few other adherents of the royal cause had set out to assist and comfort their unhappy master. They found him strictly confined, and were not suffered to enter his presence till they had delivered up their swords. The concourse of people about him was by this time immense. Some Whig gentlemen of the neighborhood had brought a large body of militia to guard him. They had imagined most erroneously that by detaining him they were ingratiating themselves with his enemies, and were greatly disturbed when they learned that the treatment which the King had undergone was disapproved by the Provisional Government in London, and that a body of cavalry was on the road to release him. Feversham soon arrived. He had left his troop at Sittingbourne: but there was no occasion to use force. The King was suffered to depart without opposition, and was removed by his friends to Rochester, where he took some rest, which he greatly needed. He was in a pitiable state. Not only was his understanding, which had never been very clear, altogether bewildered: but the personal courage which, when a young man, he had shown in several battles, both by sea and by land, had forsaken him. The rough corporal usage which he had now, for the first time, undergone, seems to have discomposed him more than any other event of his checkered life. The desertion of his army, of his favorites, of his family, affected him less than the indignities which he had suffered when his hoy was boarded. The remembrance of those indignities continued long to rankle in his heart, and showed itself, after the lapse of more than three

---

* Mulgrave's Account of the Revolution.

years, in a way which moved all Europe to contemptuous mirth.

Yet, had he possessed an ordinary measure of good sense, he would have seen that those who had detained him had unintentionally done him a great service. The events which had taken place during his absence from his capital ought to have convinced him that, if he had succeeded in escaping, he never would have returned. In his own despite he had been saved from ruin. He had another chance, a last chance. Great as his offences had been, to dethrone him, while he remained in his kingdom and offered to assent to such conditions as a free Parliament might impose, would have been almost impossible.

During a short time he seemed disposed to remain. He sent Feversham from Rochester with a letter to William. The substance of the letter was that His Majesty was on his way back to Whitehall, that he wished to have a personal conference with the Prince, and that Saint James's Palace should be fitted up for His Highness.*

William was now at Windsor. He had learned with deep mortification the events which had taken place on the coast of Kent. Just before the news arrived, those who approached him had observed that his spirits were unusually high. He had, indeed, reason to rejoice. A vacant throne was before him. All parties, it seemed, would, with one voice, invite him to mount it. On a sudden his prospects were overcast. The abdication, it appeared, had not been completed. A large proportion of his own followers would have scruples about deposing a King who remained among them, who invited them to represent their grievances in a parliamentary way, and who promised full redress. It was necessary that the Prince should examine his new position, and should determine on a new line of action. No course was open to him which was altogether free from objections, no course which would place him in a situation so advantageous as that which he had occupied a few hours before.

William's embarrassment.

---

* Life of James, ii., 261, Orig. Mem.

Yet something might be done. The King's first attempt to escape had failed. What was now most to be desired was that he should make a second attempt with better success. He must be at once frightened and enticed. The liberality with which he had been treated in the negotiation at Hungerford, and which he had requited by a breach of faith, would now be out of season. No terms of accommodation must be proposed to him. If he should propose terms he must be coldly answered. No violence must be used toward him, or even threatened. Yet it might not be impossible, without either using or threatening violence, to make so weak a man uneasy about his personal safety. He would soon be eager to fly. All facilities for flight must then be placed within his reach; and care must be taken that he should not again be stopped by any officious blunderer.

Such was William's plan; and the ability and determination with which he carried it into effect present a strange contrast to the folly and cowardice with which he had to deal. He soon had an excellent opportunity of commencing his system of intimidation. Feversham arrived at Windsor with James's letter. The messenger had not been very judiciously selected. It was he who had disbanded the royal army. To him primarily were to be imputed the confusion and terror of the Irish Night. His conduct was loudly blamed by the public. William had been provoked into muttering a few words of menace; and a few words of menace from William's lips generally meant something. Feversham was asked for his safe-conduct. He had none. By coming without one into the midst of a hostile camp, he had, according to the laws of war, made himself liable to be treated with the utmost severity. William refused to see him, and ordered him to be put under arrest.* Zulestein was instantly despatched to inform James that the Prince declined the proposed conference, and desired that His Majesty would remain at Rochester.

<small>Arrest of Feversham.</small>

But it was too late. * James was already in London. He

---

* Clarendon's Diary, Dec. 16, 1688; Burnet, i., 800.

had hesitated about the journey, and had, at one time, determined to make another attempt to reach the Continent. But at length he yielded to the urgency of friends who were wiser than himself, and set out for Whitehall. He arrived there on the afternoon of Sunday, the sixteenth of December. He had been apprehensive that the common people, who, during his absence, had given so many proofs of their aversion to Popery, would offer him some affront. But the very violence of the recent outbreak had produced a remission. The storm had spent itself. Good humor and pity had succeeded to fury. In no quarter was any disposition shown to insult the King. Some cheers were raised as his coach passed through the City. The bells of some churches were rung; and a few bonfires were lighted in honor of his return.* His feeble mind, which had just before been sunk in despondency, was extravagantly elated by these unexpected signs of popular good-will and compassion. He entered his dwelling in high spirits. It speedily resumed its old aspect. Roman Catholic priests, who had, during the preceding week, been glad to hide themselves from the rage of the multitude in vaults and cocklofts, now came forth from their lurking-places, and demanded possession of their old apartments in the palace. Grace was said at the royal table by a Jesuit. The Irish brogue, then the most hateful of all sounds to English ears, was heard everywhere in the courts and galleries. The King himself had resumed all his old haughtiness. He held a Council, his last Council, and, even in that extremity, summoned to the board persons not legally qualified to sit there. He expressed high displeasure at the

Arrival of James in London.

---

* Life of James, ii., 262, Orig. Mem.; Burnet, i., 799. In the History of the Desertion (1689) it is affirmed that the shouts on this occasion were uttered merely by some idle boys, and that the great body of the people looked on in silence. Oldmixon, who was in the crowd, says the same; and Ralph, whose prejudices were very different from Oldmixon's, tells us that the information which he had received from a respectable eye-witness was to the same effect. The truth probably is that the signs of joy were in themselves slight, but seemed extraordinary because a violent explosion of public indignation had been expected. Barillon mentions that there had been acclamations and some bonfires, but adds, "Le peuple dans le fond est pour le Prince d'Orange" (December $\frac{17}{27}$, 1688).

conduct of those Lords who, during his absence, had dared to take the administration on themselves. It was their duty, he conceived, to let society be dissolved, to let the houses of ambassadors be pulled down, to let London be set on fire, rather than assume the functions which he had thought fit to abandon. Among those whom he thus censured were some nobles and prelates who, in spite of all his errors, had been constantly true to him, and who, even after this provocation, never could be induced by hope or fear to transfer their allegiance from him to any other sovereign.*

But his courage was soon cast down. Scarcely had he entered his palace when Zulestein was announced. William's cold and stern message was delivered. The King still pressed for a personal conference with his nephew. "I would not have left Rochester," he said, "if I had known that he wished me not to do so: but, since I am here, I hope that he will come to Saint James's." "I must plainly tell Your Majesty," said Zulestein, "that His Highness will not come to London while there are any troops here which are not under his orders." The King, confounded by this answer, remained silent. Zulestein retired; and soon a gentleman entered the bedchamber with the news that Feversham had been put under arrest.† James was greatly disturbed. Yet the recollection of the applause with which he had been greeted still buoyed up his spirits. A wild hope rose in his mind. He fancied that London, so long the stronghold of Protestantism and Whiggism, was ready to take arms in his defence. He sent to ask the Common Council whether, if he took up his residence in the City, they would engage to defend him against the Prince. But the Common Council had not forgotten the seizure of the charter and the judicial murder of Cornish, and refused to give the pledge which was demanded. Then the King's heart again sank within him. Where, he asked, was he to look for protection? He might as well have Dutch troops about him as his own Life Guards. As to the citizens, he

---

* London Gazette, Dec. 16, 1688; Mulgrave's Account of the Revolution; History of the Desertion; Burnet, i., 799; Evelyn's Diary, Dec. 13, 17, 1688.
† History of James, ii., 262, Orig. Mem.

II.—34

now understood what their huzzas and bonfires were worth. Nothing remained but flight; and yet, he said, he knew that there was nothing which his enemies so much desired as that he would fly.*

<small>Consultation at Windsor.</small> While he was in this state of trepidation, his fate was the subject of grave deliberation at Windsor. The court of William was now crowded to overflowing with eminent men of all parties. Most of the chiefs of the Northern insurrection had joined him. Several of the Lords, who had, during the anarchy of the preceding week, taken upon themselves to act as a Provisional Government, had, as soon as the King returned, quitted London for the Dutch head-quarters. One of these was Halifax. William had welcomed him with great satisfaction, but had not been able to suppress a sarcastic smile at seeing the ingenious and accomplished politician, who had aspired to be the umpire in that great contention, forced to abandon the middle course and to take a side. Among those who, at this conjuncture, repaired to Windsor were some men who had purchased the favor of James by ignominious services, and who were now impatient to atone, by betraying their master, for the crime of having betrayed their country. Such a man was Titus, who had sat at the Council-board in defiance of law, and who had labored to unite the Puritans with the Jesuits in a league against the constitution. Such a man was Williams, who had been converted by interest from a demagogue into a champion of prerogative, and who was now ready for a second apostasy. These men the Prince, with just contempt, suffered to wait at the door of his apartment in vain expectation of an audience.†

On Monday, the seventeenth of December, all the Peers who were at Windsor were summoned to a solemn consultation at the Castle. The subject proposed for deliberation was what should be done with the King. William did not think it advisable to be present during the discussion. He retired; and Halifax was called to the chair. On one point the Lords

---

* Barillon, Dec. $\frac{17}{27}$, 1688; Life of James, ii., 271.
† Mulgrave's Account of the Revolution; Clarendon's Diary, Dec. 16, 1688.

were agreed. The King could not be suffered to remain where he was. That one prince should fortify himself in Whitehall and the other in Saint James's, that there should be two hostile garrisons within an area of a hundred acres, was universally felt to be inexpedient. Such an arrangement could scarcely fail to produce suspicions, insults, and bickerings which might end in blood. The assembled Lords, therefore, thought it advisable that James should be sent out of London. Ham, which had been built and decorated by Lauderdale, on the banks of the Thames, out of the plunder of Scotland and the bribes of France, and which was regarded as the most luxurious of villas, was proposed as a convenient retreat. When the Lords had come to this conclusion, they requested the Prince to join them. Their opinion was then communicated to him by Halifax. William listened and approved. A short message to the King was drawn up. "Whom," said William, "shall we send with it?" "Ought it not," said Halifax, " to be conveyed by one of Your Highness's officers?" "Nay, my Lord," answered the Prince; "by your favor, it is sent by the advice of your Lordships, and some of you ought to carry it." Then, without pausing to give time for remonstrance, he appointed Halifax, Shrewsbury, and Delamere to be the messengers.*

The resolution of the Lords appeared to be unanimous. But there were in the assembly those who by no means approved of the decision in which they affected to concur, and who wished to see the King treated with a severity which they did not venture openly to recommend. It is a remarkable fact that the chief of this party was a peer who had been a vehement Tory, and who afterward died a Nonjuror, Clarendon. The rapidity with which, at this crisis, he went backward and forward from extreme to extreme, might seem incredible to people living in quiet times, but will not surprise those who have had an opportunity of watching the course of revolutions. He knew that the asperity with which he had, in the royal presence, censured the whole system of govern-

---

* Burnet, i., 800; Clarendon's Diary, Dec. 17, 1688; Van Citters, Dec. $\frac{18}{28}$, 1688.

ment, had given mortal offence to his old master. On the other hand, he might, as the uncle of the Princesses, hope to be great and rich in the new world which was about to commence. The English colony in Ireland regarded him as a friend and patron; and he felt that on the confidence and attachment of that great interest much of his importance depended. To such considerations as these the principles, which he had, during his whole life, ostentatiously professed, now gave way. He repaired to the Prince's closet, and represented the danger of leaving the King at liberty. The Protestants of Ireland were in extreme peril. There was only one way to secure their estates and their lives; and that was to keep His Majesty close prisoner. It might not be prudent to shut him up in an English castle. But he might be sent across the sea and confined in the fortress of Breda till the affairs of the British Islands were settled. If the Prince were in possession of such a hostage, Tyrconnel would probably lay down the sword of state; and the English ascendency would be restored in Ireland without a blow. If, on the other hand, James should escape to France and make his appearance at Dublin, accompanied by a foreign army, the consequences must be disastrous. William owned that there was great weight in these reasons; but it could not be. He knew his wife's temper, and he knew that she never would consent to such a step. Indeed, it would not be for his own honor to treat his vanquished kinsman so ungraciously. Nor was it quite clear that generosity might not be the best policy. Who could say what effect such severity as Clarendon recommended might produce on the public mind of England? Was it impossible that the loyal enthusiasm, which the King's misconduct had extinguished, might revive as soon as it was known that he was within the walls of a foreign fortress? On these grounds William determined not to subject his father-in-law to personal restraint; and there can be little doubt that the determination was wise.*

---

* Burnet, i., 800; Conduct of the Duchess of Marlborough; Mulgrave's Account of the Revolution. Clarendon says nothing of this under the proper date; but see his Diary, August 19, 1689.

James, while his fate was under discussion, remained at Whitehall, fascinated, as it seemed, by the greatness and nearness of the danger, and unequal to the exertion of either struggling or flying. In the evening news came that the Dutch had occupied Chelsea and Kensington. The King, however, prepared to go to rest as usual. The Coldstream Guards were on duty at the palace. They were commanded by William, Earl of Craven, an aged man who, more than fifty years before, had been distinguished in war and love, who had led the forlorn hope at Creutznach with such courage that he had been patted on the shoulder by the great Gustavus, and who was believed to have won from a thousand rivals the heart of the unfortunate Queen of Bohemia. Craven was now in his eightieth year; but time had not tamed his spirit.*

It was past ten o'clock when he was informed that three battalions of the Prince's foot, mingled with some troops of horse, were pouring down the long avenue of Saint James's Park, with matches lighted, and in full readiness for action. Count Solmes, who commanded the foreigners, said that his orders were to take military possession of the posts round Whitehall, and exhorted Craven to retire peaceably. Craven swore that he would rather be cut in pieces: but when the King, who was undressing himself, learned what was passing, he forbade the stout old soldier to attempt a resistance which must have been ineffectual. By eleven the Coldstream Guards had withdrawn; and Dutch sentinels were pacing the rounds on every side of the palace. Some of the King's attendants asked whether he would venture to lie down surrounded by enemies. He answered that they could hardly use him worse than his own subjects had done, and, with the apathy of a man stupefied by disasters, went to bed and to sleep.†

Scarcely was the palace again quiet when it was again

margin note: The Dutch troops occupy Whitehall.

---

* Harte's Life of Gustavus Adolphus.

† Life of James, ii., 264, mostly from Orig. Mem.; Mulgrave's Account of the Revolution; Rapin de Thoyras. It must be remembered that in these events Rapin was himself an actor.

roused. A little after midnight the three Lords arrived from Windsor. Middleton was called up to receive them. They informed him that they were charged with an errand which did not admit of delay. The King was awakened from his first slumber; and they were ushered into his bedchamber. They delivered into his hand the letter with which they had been intrusted, and informed him that the Prince would be at Westminster in a few hours, and that His Majesty would do well to set out for Ham before ten in the morning. James made some difficulties. He did not like Ham. It was a pleasant place in the summer, but cold and comfortless at Christmas, and was, moreover, unfurnished. Halifax answered that furniture should be instantly sent in. The three messengers retired, but were speedily followed by Middleton, who told them that the King would greatly prefer Rochester to Ham. They answered that they had not authority to accede to His Majesty's wish, but that they would instantly send off an express to the Prince, who was to lodge that night at Sion House. A courier started immediately, and returned before daybreak with William's consent. That consent, indeed, was most gladly given: for there could be no doubt that Rochester had been named because it afforded facilities for flight; and that James might fly was the first wish of his nephew.*

On the morning of the eighteenth of December, a rainy and stormy morning, the royal barge was early at Whitehall stairs: and round it were eight or ten boats filled with Dutch soldiers. Several noblemen and gentlemen attended the King to the water-side. It is said, and may well be believed, that many tears were shed. For even the most zealous friend of liberty could scarcely have seen, unmoved, the sad and ignominious close of a dynasty which might have been so great. Shrewsbury did all in his power to soothe the fallen Sovereign. Even the bitter and vehement Delamere was softened. But it was observed that Hal-

---

* Life of James, ii., 265, Orig. Mem.; Mulgrave's Account of the Revolution; Burnet, i., 801; Van Citters, Dec. $\frac{18}{28}$, 1688.

ifax, who was generally distinguished by his tenderness to the vanquished, was, on this occasion, less compassionate than his two colleagues. The mock embassy to Hungerford was doubtless still rankling in his mind.*

While the King's barge was slowly working its way on rough waves down the river, brigade after brigade of the Prince's troops marched into London from the west. It had been wisely determined that the duty of the capital should be chiefly done by the British soldiers in the service of the States-general. The three English regiments were quartered in and round the Tower, the three Scotch regiments in Southwark.†

In defiance of the weather a great multitude assembled between Albemarle House and Saint James's Palace to greet the Prince. Every hat, every cane, was adorned with an orange ribbon. The bells were ringing all over London. Candles for an illumination were disposed in the windows. Fagots for bonfires were heaped up in the streets. William, however, who had no taste for crowds and shouting, took the road through the Park. Before nightfall he arrived at Saint James's in a light carriage, accompanied by Schomberg. In a short time all the rooms and staircases in the palace were thronged by those who came to pay their court. Such was the press, that men of the highest rank were unable to elbow their way into the presence-chamber.‡ While Westminster was in this state of excitement, the Common Council was preparing at Guildhall an address of thanks and congratulation. The Lord Mayor was unable to preside. He had never held up his head since the Chancellor had been dragged into the justice-room in the garb of a collier. But the Aldermen and the other officers of the corporation were in their places. On the following day the magistrates of the City went in state to pay their

Arrival of William at St. James's.

---

* Van Citters, Dec. $\frac{18}{28}$, 1688; Evelyn's Diary, same date; Life of James, ii., 266, 267, Orig. Mem.

† Van Citters, December $\frac{18}{28}$, 1688.

‡ Luttrell's Diary; Evelyn's Diary; Clarendon's Diary, December 18, 1688; Revolution Politics.

duty to their deliverer. Their gratitude was eloquently expressed by their Recorder, Sir George Treby. Some princes of the House of Nassau, he said, had been the chief officers of a great republic. Others had worn the imperial crown. But the peculiar title of that illustrious line to the public veneration was this, that God had set it apart and consecrated it to the high office of defending truth and freedom against tyrants from generation to generation. On the same day all the prelates who were in town, Sancroft excepted, waited on the Prince in a body. Then came the clergy of London, the foremost men of their profession in knowledge, eloquence, and influence, with their Bishop at their head. With them were mingled some eminent dissenting ministers, whom Compton, much to his honor, treated with marked courtesy. A few months earlier, or a few months later, such courtesy would have been considered by many Churchmen as treason to the Church. Even then it was but too plain to a discerning eye that the armistice to which the Protestant sects had been forced would not long outlast the danger from which it had sprung. About a hundred Non-conformist divines, resident in the capital, presented a separate address. They were introduced by Devonshire, and were received with every mark of respect and kindness. The lawyers paid their homage, headed by Maynard, who, at ninety years of age, was as alert and clear-headed as when he stood up in Westminster Hall to accuse Strafford. "Mr. Sergeant," said the Prince, "you must have survived all the lawyers of your standing." "Yes, sir," said the old man, "and, but for Your Highness, I should have survived the laws too."*

But, though the addresses were numerous and full of eulogy, though the acclamations were loud, though the illuminations were splendid, though Saint James's Palace was too small for the crowd of courtiers, though the theatres were every night, from the pit to the ceiling, one blaze of orange ribbons, William felt that the difficulties of his enterprise were

---

* Fourth Collection of Papers relating to the present juncture of affairs in England, 1688; Burnet, i., 802, 803; Calamy's Life and Times of Baxter, Chap. xiv.

but beginning. He had pulled a government down. The far harder task of reconstruction was now to be performed. From the moment of his landing till he reached London, he had exercised the authority which, by the laws of war, acknowledged throughout the civilized world, belongs to the commander of an army in the field. It was now necessary that he should exchange the character of a general for that of a magistrate; and this was no easy task. A single false step might be fatal; and it was impossible to take any step without offending prejudices and rousing angry passions.

Some of the Prince's advisers pressed him to assume the crown at once as his own by right of conquest, and then, as <small>He is advised to assume the crown by right of conquest.</small> King, to send out, under his Great Seal, writs calling a Parliament. This course was strongly recommended by some eminent lawyers. It was, they said, the shortest way to what could otherwise be attained only through innumerable difficulties and disputes. It was in strict conformity with the auspicious precedent set after the battle of Bosworth by Henry the Seventh. It would also quiet the scruples which many respectable people felt as to the lawfulness of transferring allegiance from one ruler to another. Neither the law of England nor the Church of England recognized any right in subjects to depose a sovereign. But no jurist, no divine, had ever denied that a nation, overcome in war, might, without sin, submit to the decision of the God of battles. Thus, after the Chaldean conquest, the most pious and patriotic Jews did not think that they violated their duty to their native King by serving with loyalty the new master whom Providence had set over them. The three confessors, who were marvellously preserved in the furnace, held high office in the province of Babylon. Daniel was minister successively of the Assyrian who subjugated Judea, and of the Persian who subjugated Assyria. Nay, Jesus himself, who was, according to the flesh, a prince of the House of David, had, by commanding his countrymen to pay tribute to Cæsar, pronounced that foreign conquest annuls hereditary right, and is a legitimate title to dominion. It was therefore probable that great numbers of Tories, though they could not, with a clear conscience, choose a king for themselves, would accept, without hesitation, a king given to them by the event of war.*

On the other side, however, there were reasons which greatly preponderated. The Prince could not claim the crown as won by his sword without a gross violation of faith. In his Manifesto he had declared that he had no design of conquering England; that those who imputed to him such a design foully calumniated, not only himself, but the patriotic noblemen and gentlemen who had invited him over; that the force which he brought with him was evidently inadequate to an enterprise so arduous; and that it was his full resolution to refer all the public grievances, and all his own pretensions, to a free Parliament. For no earthly object could it be right or wise that he should forfeit his word so solemnly pledged in the face of all Europe. Nor was it certain that, by calling himself a conqueror, he would have removed the scruples which made rigid Churchmen unwilling to acknowledge him as king. For, call himself what he might, all the world knew that he was not really a conqueror. It was notoriously a mere fiction to say that this great kingdom, with a mighty fleet on the sea, with a regular army of forty thousand men, and with a militia of a hundred and fifty thousand men, had been, without one siege or battle, reduced to the state of a province by fifteen thousand invaders. Such a fiction was not likely to quiet consciences really sensitive; but it could scarcely fail to gall the national pride, already sore and irritable. The English soldiers were in a temper which required the most delicate management. They were conscious that, in the late campaign, their part had not been brilliant. Captains and privates were alike impatient to prove that they had not given way before an inferior force from want of courage. Some Dutch officers had been indiscreet enough to boast, at a tavern over their wine, that they had driven the King's army before them. This insult had raised among the English troops a ferment which, but for the Prince's prompt interference,

---

* Burnet, i., 803.

would probably have ended in a terrible slaughter.* What, in such circumstances, was likely to be the effect of a proclamation announcing that the commander of the foreigners considered the whole island as lawful prize of war?

It was also to be remembered that, by putting forth such a proclamation, the Prince would at once abrogate all the rights of which he had declared himself the champion. For the authority of a foreign conqueror is not circumscribed by the customs and statutes of the conquered nation, but is, by its own nature, despotic. Either, therefore, it was not competent to William to declare himself King, or it was competent to him to declare the Great Charter and the Petition of Right nullities, to abolish trial by jury, and to raise taxes without the consent of Parliament. He might, indeed, re-establish the ancient constitution of the realm. But, if he did so, he did so in the exercise of an arbitrary discretion. English liberty would thenceforth be held by a base tenure. It would be, not, as heretofore, an immemorial inheritance, but a recent gift which the generous master who had bestowed it might, if such had been his pleasure, have withheld.

William, therefore, righteously and prudently determined to observe the promises contained in his Declaration, and to leave to the legislature the office of settling the government. So carefully did he avoid whatever looked like usurpation, that he would not, without some semblance of parliamentary authority, take upon himself even to convoke the Estates of the Realm, or to direct the executive administration during the elections. Authority strictly parliamentary there was none in the State: but it was possible to bring together, in a few hours, an assembly which would be regarded by the nation with a large portion of the respect due to a Parliament. One Chamber might be formed of the numerous Lords Spiritual and Temporal who were then in London, and another of old members of the House of Commons and of the magistrates of the City. The scheme was ingenious and was promptly executed. The

He calls together the Lords and the members of the Parliaments of Charles II.

---

* Gazette de France, $\frac{\text{Jan. 26,}}{\text{Feb. 5,}}$ 1689.

Peers were summoned to Saint James's on the twenty-first of December. About seventy attended. The Prince requested them to consider the state of the country, and to lay before him the result of their deliberations. Shortly after appeared a notice inviting all gentlemen who had sat in the House of Commons during the reign of Charles the Second to attend His Highness on the morning of the twenty-sixth. The Aldermen of London were also summoned; and the Common Council was requested to send a deputation.*

It has often been asked, in a reproachful tone, why the invitation was not extended to the members of the Parliament which had been dissolved in the preceding year. The answer is obvious. One of the chief grievances of which the nation complained was the manner in which that Parliament had been elected. The majority of the burgesses had been returned by constituent bodies remodelled in a manner which was generally regarded as illegal, and which the Prince had, in his Declaration, condemned. James himself had, just before his downfall, consented to restore the old municipal franchises. It would surely have been the height of inconsistency in William, after taking up arms for the purpose of vindicating the invaded charters of corporations, to recognize persons chosen in defiance of those charters as the legitimate representatives of the towns of England.

On Saturday, the twenty-second, the Lords met in their own house. That day was employed in settling the order of proceeding. A clerk was appointed; and, as no confidence could be placed in any of the twelve Judges, some sergeants and barristers of great note were requested to attend, for the purpose of giving advice on legal points. It was resolved that on the Monday the state of the kingdom should be taken into consideration.†

The interval between the sitting of Saturday and the sitting of Monday was anxious and eventful. A strong party among the Peers still cherished the hope that the constitution and

---

* History of the Desertion; Clarendon's Diary, Dec. 21, 1688; Burnet, i., 803, and Onslow's note.

† Clarendon's Diary, Dec. 21, 1688; Van Citters, same date.

religion of England might be secured without the deposition of the King. This party resolved to move a solemn address to him, imploring him to consent to such terms as might remove the discontents and apprehensions which his past conduct had excited. Sancroft, who, since the return of James from Kent to Whitehall, had taken no part in public affairs, determined to come forth from his retreat on this occasion, and to put himself at the head of the Royalists. Several messengers were sent to Rochester with letters for the King. He was assured that his interests would be strenuously defended, if only he could, at this last moment, make up his mind to renounce designs abhorred by his people. Some respectable Roman Catholics followed him, in order to implore him, for the sake of their common faith, not to carry the vain contest further.*

The advice was good; but James was in no condition to take it. His understanding had always been dull and feeble; and, such as it was, womanish tremors and childish fancies now disabled him from using it. He was aware that his flight was the thing which his adherents most dreaded and which his enemies most desired. Even if there had been serious personal risk in remaining, the occasion was one on which he ought to have thought it infamous to flinch: for the question was whether he and his posterity should reign on an ancestral throne, or should be vagabonds and beggars. But in his mind all other feelings had given place to a craven fear for his life. To the earnest entreaties and unanswerable arguments of the agents whom his friends had sent to Rochester, he had only one answer. His head was in danger. In vain he was assured that there was no ground for such an apprehension, that common sense, if not principle, would restrain his kinsman from incurring the guilt and shame of regicide and parricide, and that many, who never would consent to depose their Sovereign while he remained on English ground, would think themselves absolved from their allegiance by his desertion. Fright overpowered every other feeling. James determined to depart;

---

* Clarendon's Diary, Dec. 21, 22, 1688; Life of James, ii., 268, 270, Orig. Mem.

and it was easy for him to do so. He was negligently guarded: all persons were suffered to repair to him: vessels ready to put to sea lay at no great distance; and their boats might come close to the garden of the house in which he was lodged. Had he been wise, the pains which his keepers took to facilitate his escape would have sufficed to convince him that he ought to stay where he was. In truth, the snare was so ostentatiously exhibited that it could impose on nothing but folly bewildered by terror.

The arrangements were expeditiously made. On the evening of Saturday the twenty-second the King assured some of the gentlemen, who had been sent to him from London with intelligence and advice, that he would see them again in the morning. He went to bed, rose at dead of night, and, attended by Berwick, stole out at a back door, and went through the garden to the shore of the Medway. A small skiff was in waiting. Soon after the dawn of Sunday the fugitives were on board of a smack which was running down the Thames.*

Flight of James from Rochester.

That afternoon the tidings of the flight reached London. The King's adherents were confounded. The Whigs could not conceal their joy. The good news encouraged the Prince to take a bold and important step. He was informed that communications were passing between the French embassy and the party hostile to him. It was well known that at that embassy all the arts of corruption were well understood; and there could be little doubt that, at such a juncture, neither intrigues nor pistoles would be spared. Barillon was most desirous to remain a few days longer in London, and for that end omitted no art which could conciliate the victorious party. In the streets he quieted the populace, who looked angrily at his coach, by throwing money among them. At his table he publicly drank the health of the Prince of Orange. But William was not to be so cajoled. He had not, indeed, taken on himself to exercise regal authority: but he was a general: and, as such, he was not bound to tolerate, within the territory of

---

* Clarendon, Dec. 23, 1688; Life of James, ii., 271, 273, 275, Orig. Mem.

which he had taken military occupation, the presence of one whom he regarded as a spy. Before that day closed Barillon was informed that he must leave England within twenty-four hours. He begged hard for a short delay: but minutes were precious; the order was repeated in more peremptory terms; and he unwillingly set off for Dover. That no mark of contempt and defiance might be omitted, he was escorted to the coast by one of his Protestant countrymen whom persecution had driven into exile. So bitter was the resentment excited by the French ambition and arrogance that even those Englishmen who were not generally disposed to take a favorable view of William's conduct loudly applauded him for retorting with so much spirit the insolence with which Lewis had, during many years, treated every court in Europe.

On Monday the Lords met again. Halifax was chosen to preside. The Primate was absent, the Royalists sad and gloomy, the Whigs eager and in high spirits. It was known that James had left a letter behind him. Some of his friends moved that it might be produced, in the faint hope that it might contain propositions which might furnish a basis for a happy settlement. On this motion the previous question was put and carried. Godolphin, who was known not to be unfriendly to his old master, uttered a few words which were decisive. "I have seen the paper," he said; "and I grieve to say that there is nothing in it which will give your Lordships any satisfaction." In truth it contained no expression of regret for past errors: it held out no hope that those errors would in future be avoided; and it threw the blame of all that had happened on the malice of William and on the blindness of a nation deluded by the specious names of religion and property. None ventured to propose that a negotiation should be opened with a prince whom the most rigid discipline of adversity seemed only to have made more obstinate in wrong. Something was said about inquiring into the birth of the Prince of Wales: but the Whig peers treated the suggestion with disdain. "I did

Debates and resolutions of the Lords.

---

* Van Citters, Jan. $\frac{1}{11}$, 1689; Witsen MS. quoted by Wagenaar, Book LX.

not expect, my Lords," exclaimed Philip Lord Wharton, an old Roundhead, who had commanded a regiment against Charles the First at Edgehill, "I did not expect to hear anybody at this time of day mention the child who was called Prince of Wales; and I hope that we have now heard the last of him." After long discussion it was resolved that two addresses should be presented to William. One address requested him to take on himself provisionally the administration of the government; the other recommended that he should, by circular letters subscribed with his own hand, invite all the constituent bodies of the kingdom to send up representatives to Westminster. At the same time the Peers took upon themselves to issue an order banishing all Papists, except a few privileged persons, from London and the vicinity.*

The Lords presented their addresses to the Prince on the following day, without waiting for the issue of the deliberations of the commoners whom he had called together. It seems, indeed, that the hereditary nobles were disposed at this moment to be punctilious in asserting their dignity, and were unwilling to recognize a co-ordinate authority in an assembly unknown to the law. They conceived that they were a real House of Lords. The other Chamber they despised as only a mock House of Commons. William, however, wisely excused himself from coming to any decision till he had ascertained the sense of the gentlemen who had formerly been honored with the confidence of the counties and towns of England.†

<small>Debates and resolutions of the commoners summoned by the Prince.</small>
The commoners who had been summoned met in Saint Stephen's Chapel, and formed a numerous assembly. They placed in the chair Henry Powle, who had represented Cirencester in several Parliaments, and had been eminent among the supporters of the Exclusion Bill.

Addresses were proposed and adopted similar to those which the Lords had already presented. No difference of opinion appeared on any serious question; and some feeble

---

* Halifax's notes; Lansdowne MS., 255; Clarendon's Diary, December 24, 1688; London Gazette, December 31. † Van Citters, $\frac{\text{Dec. 25,}}{\text{Jan. 4,}}$ 168$\frac{8}{9}$.

attempts which were made to raise a debate on points of form were put down by the general contempt. Sir Robert Sawyer declared that he could not conceive how it was possible for the Prince to administer the government without some distinguishing title, such as Regent or Protector. Old Maynard, who, as a lawyer, had no equal, and who was also a politician versed in the tactics of revolutions, was at no pains to conceal his disdain for so puerile an objection, taken at a moment when union and promptitude were of the highest importance. "We shall sit here very long," he said, "if we sit till Sir Robert can conceive how such a thing is possible;" and the assembly thought the answer as good as the cavil deserved.*

The resolutions of the meeting were communicated to the Prince. He forthwith announced his determination to comply with the joint request of the two Chambers which he had called together, to issue letters summoning a Convention of the Estates of the Realm, and, till the Convention should meet, to take on himself the executive administration.†

<small>A Convention called.</small>

He had undertaken no light task. The whole machine of government was disordered. The Justices of the Peace had abandoned their functions. The officers of the revenue had ceased to collect the taxes. The army which Feversham had disbanded was still in confusion, and ready to break out into mutiny. The fleet was in a scarcely less alarming state. Large arrears of pay were due to the civil and military servants of the crown; and only forty thousand pounds remained in the Exchequer. The Prince addressed himself with vigor to the work of restoring order. He published a proclamation by which all magistrates were continued in office, and another containing orders for the collection of the revenue.‡ The new modelling of the

<small>Exertions of the Prince to restore order.</small>

---

* The objector was designated in contemporary books and pamphlets only by his initials; and these were sometimes misinterpreted. Eachard attributes the cavil to Sir Robert Southwell. But I have little doubt that Oldmixon is right in putting it into the mouth of Sawyer.

† History of the Desertion; Life of William, 1703; Van Citters, $\frac{\text{Dec. 28,}}{\text{Jan. 7,}}$ 168⅞.

‡ London Gazette, Jan. 3, 7, 168⅞.

II.—35

army went rapidly on. Many of the noblemen and gentlemen who had been removed from the command of the English regiments were reappointed. A way was found of employing the thousands of Irish soldiers whom James had brought into England. They could not safely be suffered to remain in a country where they were objects of religious and national animosity. They could not safely be sent home to re-enforce the army of Tyrconnel. It was therefore determined that they should be conveyed to the Continent, where they might, under the banners of the House of Austria, render indirect but effectual service to the cause of the English constitution and of the Protestant religion. Dartmouth was removed from his command; and the navy was conciliated by assurances that every sailor should speedily receive his due. The City of London undertook to extricate the Prince from his financial difficulties. The Common Council, by a unanimous vote, engaged to find him two hundred thousand pounds. It was thought a great proof, both of the wealth and of the public spirit of the merchants of the capital, that in forty-eight hours the whole sum was raised on no security but the Prince's word. A few weeks before, James had been unable to procure a much smaller loan, though he had offered to pay higher interest, and to pledge valuable property.*

His tolerant policy. In a very few days the confusion, which the invasion, the insurrection, the flight of James, and the suspension of all regular government had produced, was at an end, and the kingdom wore again its accustomed aspect. There was a general sense of security. Even the classes which were most obnoxious to public hatred, and which had most reason to apprehend persecution, were protected by the politic clemency of the conqueror. Persons deeply implicated in the illegal transactions of the late reign not only walked the streets in safety, but offered themselves as candidates for seats in the Convention. Mulgrave was received not ungra-

---

* London Gazette, January 10, 17, 168$\frac{8}{9}$; Luttrell's Diary; Legge Papers; Van Citters, January $\frac{1}{11}$, $\frac{4}{14}$, $\frac{11}{21}$, 1689; Ronquillo, January $\frac{15}{25}$, $\frac{\text{Feb. 23}}{\text{Mar. 5}}$; Consultation of the Spanish Council of State, $\frac{\text{Mar. 26.}}{\text{April 5.}}$

ciously at Saint James's. Feversham was released from arrest, and was permitted to resume the only office for which he was qualified, that of keeping the bank at the Queen-Dowager's basset-table. But no body of men had so much reason to feel grateful to William as the Roman Catholics. It would not have been safe to rescind formally the severe resolutions which the Peers had passed against the professors of a religion generally abhorred by the nation: but, by the prudence and humanity of the Prince, those resolutions were practically annulled. On his line of march from Torbay to London, he had given orders that no outrage should be committed on the persons or dwellings of Papists. He now renewed those orders, and directed Burnet to see that they were strictly obeyed. A better choice could not have been made; for Burnet was a man of such generosity and good-nature, that his heart always warmed toward the unhappy; and at the same time his known hatred of Popery was a sufficient guarantee to the most zealous Protestants that the interests of their religion would be safe in his hands. He listened kindly to the complaints of the Roman Catholics, procured passports for those who wished to go beyond sea, and went himself to Newgate to visit the prelates who were imprisoned there. He ordered them to be removed to a more commodious apartment and supplied with every indulgence. He solemnly assured them that not a hair of their heads should be touched, and that, as soon as the Prince could venture to act as he wished, they should be set at liberty. The Spanish minister reported to his government, and, through his government, to the Pope, that no Catholic need feel any scruple of conscience on account of the late revolution in England, that for the danger to which the members of the true Church were exposed James alone was responsible, and that William alone had saved them from a sanguinary persecution.*

---

* Burnet, i., 802; Ronquillo, Jan. $\frac{2}{12}$, Feb. $\frac{8}{18}$, 1689. The originals of these despatches were intrusted to me by the kindness of the late Lady Holland and of the present Lord Holland. From the latter despatch I will quote a very few words: "La tema de S. M. Britanica á seguir imprudentes consejos perdió á los Catolicos aquella quietud en que les dexó Carlos segundo. V. E. asegure á su Santidad que mas sacaré del Principe para los Catolicos que pudiera sacar del Rey."

There was, therefore, little alloy to the satisfaction with which the princes of the House of Austria and the Sovereign Pontiff learned that the long vassalage of England was at an end. When it was known at Madrid that William was in the full career of success, a single voice in the Spanish Council of State faintly expressed regret that an event which, in a political point of view, was most auspicious, should be prejudicial to the interests of the true Church.* But the tolerant policy of the Prince soon quieted all scruples, and his elevation was seen with scarcely less satisfaction by the bigoted Grandees of Castile than by the English Whigs.

Satisfaction of Roman Catholic powers.

With very different feelings had the news of this great revolution been received in France. The politics of a long, eventful, and glorious reign had been confounded in a day. England was again the England of Elizabeth and of Cromwell; and all the relations of all the states of Christendom were completely changed by the sudden introduction of this new power into the system. The Parisians could talk of nothing but what was passing in London. National and religious feeling impelled them to take the part of James. They knew nothing of the English constitution. They abominated the English Church. Our revolution appeared to them, not as the triumph of public liberty over despotism, but as a frightful domestic tragedy in which a venerable and pious Servius was hurled from his throne by a Tarquin, and crushed under the chariot-wheels of a Tullia. They cried shame on the traitorous captains, execrated the unnatural daughters, and regarded William with a mortal loathing, tempered, however, by the respect which valor, capacity, and success seldom fail to inspire.† The Queen, ex-

State of feeling in France.

---

* On December $\frac{13}{23}$, 1688, the Admiral of Castile gave his opinion thus: "Esta materia es de calidad que no puede dexar de padecer nuestra sagrada religion ó él servicio de V. M.; porque, si el Principe de Orange tiene buenos successos, nos aseguraremos de Franceses, pero peligrará la religion." The Council was much pleased on February $\frac{16}{26}$, by a letter of the Prince, in which he promised "que los Catolicos que se portaren con prudencia no sean molestados, y gocen libertad de conciencia, por ser contra su dictamen el forzar ni castigar por esta razon á nadie."

† In the chapter of La Bruyère, entitled "Sur les Jugemens," is a passage which

posed to the night wind and rain, with the infant heir of three crowns clasped to her breast, the King stopped, robbed, and outraged by ruffians, were objects of pity and of romantic interest to all France. But Lewis saw with peculiar emotion the calamities of the House of Stuart. All the selfish and all the generous parts of his nature were moved alike. After many years of prosperity he had at length met with a great check. He had reckoned on the support or neutrality of England. He had now nothing to expect from her but energetic and pertinacious hostility. A few weeks earlier he might not unreasonably have hoped to subjugate Flanders and to give law to Germany. At present he might think himself fortunate if he should be able to defend his own frontiers against a confederacy such as Europe had not seen during many ages. From this position, so new, so embarrassing, so alarming, nothing but a counter-revolution or a civil war in the British Islands could extricate him. He was therefore impelled by ambition and by fear to espouse the cause of the fallen dynasty. And it is but just to say that motives nobler than ambition or fear had a large share in determining his course. His heart was naturally compassionate; and this was an occasion which could not fail to call forth all his compassion. His situation had prevented his good feelings from fully developing themselves. Sympathy is rarely strong where there is a great inequality of condition; and he was raised so high above the mass of his fellow-creatures that their distresses excited in him only a languid pity, such as that with which we regard the sufferings of the inferior animals, of a famished redbreast or of an overdriven post-horse. The devastation of the Palatinate and the persecution of the Huguenots had therefore given him no uneasiness which pride and bigotry could not effectually soothe. But all the tenderness of which he was capable was called forth by the misery of a great King who had a few weeks ago been served on the knee by Lords, and who was now a destitute exile. With that tenderness

---

deserves to be read, as showing in what light our revolution appeared to a Frenchman of distinguished abilities.

was mingled, in the soul of Lewis, a not ignoble vanity. He would exhibit to the world a pattern of munificence and courtesy. He would show mankind what ought to be the bearing of a perfect gentleman in the highest station and on the greatest occasion; and, in truth, his conduct was marked by a chivalrous generosity and urbanity, such as had not embellished the annals of Europe since the Black Prince had stood behind the chair of King John at the supper on the field of Poitiers.

As soon as the news that the Queen of England was on the French coast had been brought to Versailles, a palace was prepared for her reception. Carriages and troops of guards were despatched to await her orders. Workmen were employed to mend the Calais road, that her journey might be easy. Lauzun was not only assured that his past offences were forgiven for her sake, but was honored with a friendly letter in the handwriting of Lewis. Mary was on the road toward the French court when news came that her husband had, after a rough voyage, landed safe at the little village of Ambleteuse. Persons of high rank were instantly despatched from Versailles to greet and escort him. Meanwhile Lewis, attended by his family and his nobility, went forth in state to receive the exiled Queen. Before his gorgeous coach went the Swiss halberdiers. On each side of it and behind it rode the Body Guards, with cymbals clashing and trumpets pealing. After the King, in a hundred carriages, each drawn by six horses, came the most splendid aristocracy of Europe, all feathers, ribbons, jewels, and embroidery. Before the procession had gone far it was announced that Mary was approaching. Lewis alighted and advanced on foot to meet her. She broke forth into passionate expressions of gratitude. "Madam," said her host, "it is but a melancholy service that I am rendering you to-day. I hope that I may be able hereafter to render you services greater and more pleasing." He embraced the little Prince of Wales, and made the Queen seat herself in the royal state-coach, on the right hand. The cavalcade then turned toward Saint Germains.

Reception of the Queen of England in France.

At Saint Germains, on the verge of a forest swarming with beasts of chase, and on the brow of a hill which looks down on the windings of the Seine, Francis the First had built a castle, and Henry the Fourth had constructed a noble terrace. Of the residences of the French Kings none stood in a more salubrious air or commanded a fairer prospect. The huge size and venerable age of the trees, the beauty of the gardens, the abundance of the springs, were widely famed. Lewis the Fourteenth had been born there, had, when a young man, held his court there, had added several stately pavilions to the mansion of Francis, and had completed the terrace of Henry. Soon, however, the magnificent King conceived an inexplicable disgust for his birthplace. He quitted Saint Germains for Versailles, and expended sums almost fabulous in the vain attempt to create a paradise on a spot singularly sterile and unwholesome, all sand or mud, without wood, without water, and without game. Saint Germains had now been selected to be the abode of the royal family of England. Sumptuous furniture had been hastily sent in. The nursery of the Prince of Wales had been carefully furnished with everything that an infant could require. One of the attendants presented to the Queen the key of a superb casket which stood in her apartment. She opened the casket, and found in it six thousand pistoles.

Arrival of James at Saint Germains.

On the following day James arrived at Saint Germains. Lewis was already there to welcome him. The unfortunate exile bowed so low that it seemed as if he was about to embrace the knees of his protector. Lewis raised him, and embraced him with brotherly tenderness. The two Kings then entered the Queen's room. "Here is a gentleman," said Lewis to Mary, "whom you will be glad to see." Then, after entreating his guests to visit him next day at Versailles, and to let him have the pleasure of showing them his buildings, pictures, and plantations, he took the unceremonious leave of an old friend.

In a few hours the royal pair were informed that, as long as they would do the King of France the favor to accept of his hospitality, forty-five thousand pounds sterling a year would be paid them from his treasury. Ten thousand pounds sterling were sent for outfit.

The liberality of Lewis, however, was much less rare and admirable than the exquisite delicacy with which he labored to soothe the feelings of his guests, and to lighten the almost intolerable weight of the obligations which he laid upon them. He who had hitherto, on all questions of precedence, been sensitive, litigious, insolent, who had been more than once ready to plunge Europe into war rather than concede the most frivolous point of etiquette, was now punctilious indeed, but punctilious for his unfortunate friends against himself. He gave orders that Mary should receive all the marks of respect that had ever been paid to his own deceased wife. A question was raised whether the Princes of the House of Bourbon were entitled to be indulged with chairs in the presence of the Queen. Such trifles were serious matters at the old court of France. There were precedents on both sides: but Lewis decided the point against his own blood. Some ladies of illustrious rank omitted the ceremony of kissing the hem of Mary's robe. Lewis remarked the omission, and noticed it in such a voice and with such a look that the whole peerage was ever after ready to kiss her shoe. When Esther, just written by Racine, was acted at Saint Cyr, Mary had the seat of honor. James was at her right hand. Lewis modestly placed himself on the left. Nay, he was well pleased that, in his own palace, an outcast living on his bounty should assume the title of King of France, should, as King of France, quarter the lilies with the English lions, and should, as King of France, dress in violet on days of court mourning.

The demeanor of the French nobility on public occasions was absolutely regulated by their sovereign: but it was beyond even his power to prevent them from thinking freely, and from expressing what they thought, in private circles, with the keen and delicate wit characteristic of their nation and of their order. Their opinion of Mary was favorable. They found her person agreeable and her deportment dignified: they respected her courage and her maternal affection; and they pitied her ill-fortune. But James they regarded with extreme contempt. They were disgusted by his insensibility, by the cool way in which he talked to everybody of his ruin, and by the childish pleasure which he took in the pomp and luxury of Versailles. This strange apathy they attributed, not to philosophy or religion, but to stupidity and meanness of spirit, and remarked that nobody who had had the honor to hear His Britannic Majesty tell his own story could wonder that he was at Saint Germains and his son-in-law at Saint James's.*

In the United Provinces the excitement produced by the tidings from England was even greater than in France. This was the moment at which the Batavian federation reached the highest point of power and glory. From the day on which the expedition sailed, the anxiety of the whole Dutch nation had been intense. Never had there been such crowds in the churches. Never had the enthusiasm of the preachers been so ardent. The inhabitants of the Hague could not be restrained from insulting Albeville. His house was so closely beset by the populace, day and night, that scarcely any person ventured to visit him; and he was afraid that his chapel would be burned to the ground.† As mail after mail arrived with news of the Prince's progress, the spirits of his countrymen rose higher and higher; and when at length it was known that he had, on the invitation of the Lords and of an assembly of eminent commoners, taken on himself the executive administration, a general cry of pride and joy rose from all the Dutch factions. An extraordinary mission was, with great speed, despatched to congratulate him. Dykvelt, whose adroitness and intimate knowledge of English politics made his assistance, at such a conjuncture, peculiarly valuable, was one of the Ambassadors; and with him was joined Nicholas Witsen, a Burgomaster of Amsterdam, who seems to have been selected for the purpose of proving to all Europe that the long feud between the

Sidenote: State of feeling in the United Provinces.

---

* My account of the reception of James and his wife in France is taken chiefly from the letters of Madame de Sévigné and the Memoirs of Dangeau.

† Albeville to Preston, $\frac{\text{Nov. 23,}}{\text{Dec. 3,}}$ 1688, in Mackintosh Collection.

House of Orange and the chief city of Holland was at an end. On the eighth of January Dykvelt and Witsen made their appearance at Westminster. William talked to them with a frankness and an effusion of heart which seldom appeared in his conversations with Englishmen. His first words were, "Well, and what do our friends at home say now?" In truth, the only applause by which his stoical nature seems to have been strongly moved was the applause of his dear native country. Of his immense popularity in England he spoke with cold disdain, and predicted, too truly, the reaction which followed. "Here," said he, "the cry is all Hosanna to-day, and will, perhaps, be Crucify to-morrow."*

Election of members to serve in the Convention.
On the following day the first members of the Convention were chosen. The City of London led the way, and elected, without any contest, four great merchants who were zealous Whigs. The King and his adherents had hoped that many returning officers would treat the Prince's letter as a nullity; but the hope was disappointed. The elections went on rapidly and smoothly. There were scarcely any contests; for the nation had, during more than a year, been kept in constant expectation of a Parliament. Writs, indeed, had been issued and recalled. Some constituent bodies had, under those writs, actually proceeded to the choice of representatives. There was scarcely a county in which the gentry and yeomanry had not, many months before, fixed upon candidates, good Protestants, whom no exertions must be spared to carry, in defiance of the King and of the Lord-lieutenant; and these candidates were now generally returned without opposition.

The Prince gave strict orders that no person in the public

* "'Tis hier nu Hosanna: maar 't zal, veelligt, haast Kruist hem, kruist hem, zyn."—Witsen MS. in Wagenaar, Book LXI. It is an odd coincidence that, a very few years before, Richard Duke, a Tory poet, once well known, but now scarcely remembered, except by Johnson's biographical sketch, had used exactly the same illustration about James:

"Was not of old the Jewish rabble's cry,
Hosanna first, and after crucify?"—*The Review.*

Despatch of the Dutch Ambassadors Extraordinary, Jan. $\frac{8}{18}$, 1689; Van Citters, same date.

service should, on this occasion, practise those arts which had brought so much obloquy on the late government. He especially directed that no soldiers should be suffered to appear in any town where an election was going on.* His admirers were able to boast, and his enemies seem not to have been able to deny, that the sense of the constituent bodies was fairly taken. It is true that he risked little. The party which was attached to him was triumphant, enthusiastic, full of life and energy. The party from which alone he could expect serious opposition was disunited and disheartened, out of humor with itself, and still more out of humor with its natural chief. A great majority, therefore, of the shires and boroughs returned Whig members.

It was not over England alone that William's guardianship now extended. Scotland had risen on her tyrants. All the regular soldiers by whom she had long been held down had been summoned by James to his help against the Dutch invaders, with the exception of a very small force, which, under the command of the Duke of Gordon, a great Roman Catholic lord, garrisoned the Castle of Edinburgh. Every mail which had gone northward during the eventful month of November had carried news which stirred the passions of the oppressed Scots. While the event of the military operations was still doubtful, there were disturbances at Edinburgh; and those disturbances became more formidable after James had retreated from Salisbury. Great crowds assembled at first by night, and then by broad daylight. Popes were publicly burned: loud shouts were raised for a free Parliament: placards were stuck up setting prices on the heads of the ministers of the crown. Among those ministers, Perth, as filling the great place of Chancellor, as standing high in the royal favor, as an apostate from the reformed faith, and as the man who had first introduced the thumb-screw into the jurisprudence of his country, was the most detested. His nerves were weak: his spirit was abject; and the only courage which he possessed was that evil cour-

Affairs of Scotland.

---

* London Gazette, Jan. 7, 1688⅘.

age which braves infamy, and which looks steadily on the torments of others. His post, at such a time, was at the head of the Council-board: but his heart failed him; and he determined to take refuge at his country-seat from the danger which, as he judged by the looks and the cries of the fierce and resolute populace of Edinburgh, was not remote. A strong guard escorted him safe to Castle Drummond: but scarcely had he departed when the city rose up. A few troops tried to suppress the insurrection, but were overpowered. The Palace of Holyrood, which had been turned into a Roman Catholic seminary and printing-house, was stormed and sacked. Huge heaps of Popish books, beads, crucifixes, and pictures were burned in the High Street. In the midst of the agitation came down the tidings of the King's flight. The members of the government gave up all thought of contending with the popular fury, and changed sides with a promptitude then common among Scottish politicians. The Privy Council, by one proclamation, ordered that all Papists should be disarmed, and by another invited Protestants to muster for the defence of pure religion. The nation had not waited for the call. Town and country were already up in arms for the Prince of Orange. Nithisdale and Clydesdale were the only regions in which there was the least chance that the Roman Catholics would make head; and both Nithisdale and Clydesdale were soon occupied by bands of armed Presbyterians. Among the insurgents were some fierce and moody men who had formerly disowned Argyle, and who were now equally eager to disown William. His Highness, they said, was plainly a malignant. There was not a word about the Covenant in his Declaration. The Dutch were a people with whom no true servant of the Lord would unite. They consorted with Lutherans: and a Lutheran was as much a child of perdition as a Jesuit. The general voice of the kingdom, however, effectually drowned the growl of this hateful faction.*

The commotion soon reached the neighborhood of Castle

---

* The Sixth Collection of Papers, 1689; Wodrow, III., xii., 4, App. 150, 151; Faithful Contendings Displayed; Burnet, i., 804.

Drummond. Perth found that he was no longer safe among his own servants and tenants. He gave himself up to an agony as bitter as that into which his merciless tyranny had often thrown better men. He wildly tried to find consolation in the rites of his new Church. He importuned his priests for comfort, prayed, confessed, and communicated: but his faith was weak; and he owned that, in spite of all his devotions, the strong terrors of death were upon him. At this time he learned that he had a chance of escaping on board of a ship which lay off Brentisland. He disguised himself as well as he could, and, after a long and difficult journey by unfrequented paths over the Ochill mountains, which were then deep in snow, he succeeded in embarking: but, in spite of all his precautions, he had been recognized, and the alarm had been given. As soon as it was known that the cruel renegade was on the waters, and that he had gold with him, persuers, inflamed at once by hatred and by avarice, were on his track. A skiff, commanded by an old buccaneer, overtook the flying vessel and boarded her. Perth was dragged out of the hold on deck in woman's clothes, stripped, hustled, and plundered. Bayonets were held to his breast. Begging for life with unmanly cries, he was hurried to the shore, and flung into the common jail of Kirkaldy. Thence, by order of the Council over which he had lately presided, and which was filled with men who had been partakers in his guilt, he was removed to Stirling Castle. It was on a Sunday, during the time of public worship, that he was conveyed, under a guard, to his place of confinement: but even rigid Puritans forgot the sanctity of the day. The churches poured forth their congregations as the torturer passed by, and the noise of threats, execrations, and screams of hatred accompanied him to the gate of his prison.*

Several eminent Scotsmen were in London when the Prince arrived there; and many others now hastened thither to pay their court to him. On the seventh of January he requested

---

* Perth to Lady Errol, Dec. 29, 1688; to Melfort, Dec. 21, 1688; Sixth Collection of Papers, 1689.

them to attend him at Whitehall. The assemblage was large and respectable. The Duke of Hamilton and his eldest son, the Earl of Arran, the chiefs of a house of almost regal dignity, appeared at the head of the procession. They were accompanied by thirty Lords and about eighty gentlemen of note. William desired them to consult together, and to let him know in what way he could best promote the welfare of their country. He then withdrew, and left them to deliberate unrestrained by his presence. They repaired to the Council-chamber, and put Hamilton into the chair. Though there seems to have been little difference of opinion, their debates lasted three days, a fact which is sufficiently explained by the circumstance that Sir Patrick Hume was one of the debaters. Arran ventured to recommend a negotiation with the King. But this motion was ill received by the mover's father and by the whole assembly, and did not even find a seconder. At length resolutions were carried closely resembling the resolutions which the English Lords and Commoners had presented to the Prince a few days before. He was requested to call together a Convention of the Estates of Scotland, to fix the fourteenth of March for the day of meeting, and, till that day, to take on himself the civil and military administration. To this request he acceded; and thenceforth the government of the whole island was in his hands.*

The decisive moment approached; and the agitation of the public mind rose to the height. Knots of politicians were whispering and consulting in every part of London. The coffee-houses were in a ferment. The presses were hard at work. Of the pamphlets which appeared at that time enough may still be collected to form several volumes; and from those pamphlets it is not difficult to gather a correct notion of the state of parties.

State of parties in England.

There was a very small faction which wished to recall James without stipulations. There was also a very small faction which wished to set up a commonwealth, and to intrust the administration to a council of state under the presidency

---

* Burnet, i., 805; Sixth Collection of Papers, 1689.

of the Prince of Orange. But these extreme opinions were generally held in abhorrence. Nineteen-twentieths of the nation consisted of persons in whom love of hereditary monarchy and love of constitutional freedom were combined, though in different proportions, and who were equally opposed to the total abolition of the kingly office and to the unconditional restoration of the King.

But, in the wide interval which separated the bigots who still clung to the doctrines of Filmer from the enthusiasts who still dreamed the dreams of Harrington, there was room for many shades of opinion. If we neglect minute subdivisions, we shall find that the great majority of the nation and of the Convention was divided into four bodies. Three of these bodies consisted of Tories. The Whig party formed the fourth.

The amity of the Whigs and Tories had not survived the peril which had produced it. On several occasions, during the Prince's march from the West, dissension had appeared among his followers. While the event of his enterprise was doubtful, that dissension had, by his skilful management, been easily quieted. But, from the day on which he entered Saint James's palace in triumph, such management could no longer be practised. His victory, by relieving the nation from the strong dread of Popish tyranny, had deprived him of half his influence. Old antipathies, which had slept when Bishops were in the Tower, when Jesuits were at the Council-board, when loyal clergymen were deprived of their bread by scores, when loyal gentlemen were put out of the commission of the peace by hundreds, were again strong and active. The Royalist shuddered at the thought that he was allied with all that from his youth up he had most hated, with old parliamentary Captains who had stormed his country house, with old parliamentary Commissioners who had sequestrated his estate, with men who had plotted the Rye-house butchery and headed the Western rebellion. That beloved Church, too, for whose sake he had, after a painful struggle, broken through his allegiance to the throne, was she really in safety? Or had he rescued her from one enemy only that she might be exposed to another? The Popish priests, indeed, were in exile, in hiding, or in prison. No Jesuit or Benedictine who valued his life now dared to show himself in the habit of his order. But the Presbyterian and Independent teachers went in long procession to salute the chief of the government, and were as graciously received as the true successors of the Apostles. Some schismatics avowed the hope that every fence which excluded them from ecclesiastical preferment would soon be levelled; that the Articles would be softened down; that the Liturgy would be garbled; that Christmas would cease to be a feast; that Good-Friday would cease to be a fast; that canons on whom no Bishop had ever laid his hand would, without the sacred vestment of white linen, distribute, in the choirs of Cathedrals, the eucharistic bread and wine to communicants lolling on benches. The Prince, indeed, was not a fanatical Presbyterian; but he was at best a Latitudinarian. He had no scruple about communicating in the Anglican form; but he cared not in what form other people communicated. His wife, it was to be feared, had imbibed too much of his spirit. Her conscience was under the direction of Burnet. She heard preachers of different Protestant sects. She had recently said that she saw no essential difference between the Church of England and the other reformed Churches.* It was necessary, therefore, that the Cavaliers should, at this conjuncture, follow the example set by their fathers in 1641, should draw off from Roundheads and sectaries, and should, in spite of all the faults of the hereditary monarch, uphold the cause of hereditary monarchy.

The body which was animated by these sentiments was large and respectable. It included about one-half of the House of Lords, about one-third of the House of Commons, a majority of the country gentlemen, and at least nine-tenths of the clergy; but it was torn by dissensions, and beset on every side by difficulties.

One section of this great party, a section which was especially strong among divines, and of which Sherlock was the

---

* Albeville, Nov. $\frac{6}{19}$, 1688.

chief organ, wished that a negotiation should be opened with James, and that he should be invited to return to Whitehall on such conditions as might fully secure the civil and ecclesiastical constitution of the realm.* It is evident that this plan, though strenuously supported by the clergy, was altogether inconsistent with the doctrines which the clergy had been teaching during many years. It was, in truth, an attempt to make a middle way where there was no room for a middle way, to effect a compromise between two things which do not admit of compromise, resistance and non-resistance. The Tories had formerly taken their stand on the principle of non-resistance. But that ground most of them had now abandoned, and were not disposed again to occupy. The Cavaliers of England had, as a class, been so deeply concerned, directly or indirectly, in the late rising against the King, that they could not, for very shame, talk at that moment about the sacred duty of obeying Nero; nor, indeed, were they disposed to recall the prince under whose misgovernment they had suffered so much, without exacting from him terms which might make it impossible for him again to abuse his power. They were, therefore, in a false position. Their old theory, sound or unsound, was at least complete and coherent. If that theory were sound, the King ought to be immediately invited back, and permitted, if such were his pleasure, to put Seymour and Danby, the Bishop of London and the Bishop of Bristol, to death for high treason, to re-establish the Ecclesiastical Commission, to fill the Church with Popish dignitaries, and to place the army under the command of Popish officers. But if, as the Tories themselves now seemed to confess, that theory was unsound, why treat with the King? If it was admitted that he might lawfully be excluded till he gave satisfactory guarantees for the security of the constitution in Church and State, it was not easy to deny that he might lawfully be excluded forever. For what satisfactory guarantee could he give? How was it

---

* See the pamphlet entitled Letter to a Member of the Convention, and the answer, 1689; Burnet, i., 809.

possible to draw up an Act of Parliament in language clearer than the language of the Acts of Parliament which required that the Dean of Christ Church should be a Protestant? How was it possible to put any promise into words stronger than those in which James had repeatedly declared that he would strictly respect the legal rights of the Anglican clergy? If law or honor could have bound him, he would never have been forced to fly from his kingdom. If neither law nor honor could bind him, could he safely be permitted to return?

It is probable, however, that, in spite of these arguments, a motion for opening a negotiation with James would have been made in the Convention, and would have been supported by the great body of Tories, had he not been, on this as on every other occasion, his own worst enemy. Every post which arrived from Saint Germains brought intelligence which damped the ardor of his adherents. He did not think it worth his while to feign regret for his past errors, or to promise amendment. He put forth a manifesto, telling his people that it had been his constant care to govern them with justice and moderation, and that they had been cheated into ruin by imaginary grievances.* The effect of his folly and obstinacy was that those who were most desirous to see him restored to his throne on fair conditions felt that, by proposing at that moment to treat with him, they should injure the cause which they wished to serve. They therefore determined to coalesce with another body of Tories of whom Sancroft was the chief. Sancroft fancied that he had found out a device by which provision might be made for the government of the country without recalling James, and yet without despoiling him of his crown. This device was a Regency. The most uncompromising of those divines who had inculcated the doctrine of passive obedience had never maintained that such obedience was due to a babe or to a madman. It was universally acknowledged that, when the rightful sovereign was intellectually incapable of performing his office, a deputy might be appointed to act in his stead, and

<small>Sancroft's plan.</small>

---

* Letter to the Lords of the Council, Jan. $\frac{4}{14}$, $168\frac{8}{9}$; Clarendon's Diary, Jan. $\frac{9}{15}$.

that any person who should resist the deputy, and should plead as an excuse for doing so the command of a prince who was in the cradle, or who was raving, would justly incur the penalties of rebellion. Stupidity, perverseness, and superstition — such was the reasoning of the Primate — had made James as unfit to rule his dominions as any child in swaddling-clothes, or as any maniac who was grinning and chattering in the straw of Bedlam. That course must, therefore, be taken which had been taken when Henry the Sixth was an infant, and again when he became lethargic. James could not be King in effect: but he must still continue to be King in semblance. Writs must still run in his name. His image and superscription must still appear on the coin and on the Great Seal. Acts of Parliament must still be called from the years of his reign. But the administration must be taken from him and confided to a Regent named by the Estates of the Realm. In this way, Sancroft gravely maintained, the people would remain true to their allegiance: the oaths of fealty which they had sworn to their King would be strictly observed; and the most orthodox Churchmen might, without any scruple of conscience, take office under the Regent.*

---

* It seems incredible that any man should really have been imposed upon by such nonsense. I therefore think it right to quote Sancroft's words, which are still extant in his own handwriting:

"The political capacity or authority of the King, and his name in the government, are perfect, and cannot fail; but his person being human and mortal, and not otherwise privileged than the rest of mankind, is subject to all the defects and failings of it. He may therefore be incapable of directing the government and dispensing the public treasure, &c., either by absence, by infancy, lunacy, deliracy, or apathy, whether by nature or casual infirmity, or, lastly, by some invincible prejudices of mind, contracted and fixed by education and habit, with unalterable resolutions superinduced, in matters wholly inconsistent and incompatible with the laws, religion, peace, and true policy of the kingdom. In all these cases (I say) there must be some one or more persons appointed to supply such defect, and vicariously to him, and by his power and authority, to direct public affairs. And this done, I say further, that all proceedings, authorities, commissions, grants, &c., issued as formerly, are legal and valid to all intents, and the people's allegiance is the same still, their oaths and obligations no way thwarted. * * * So long as the government moves by the King's authority, and in his name, all those sacred ties and settled forms of proceedings are kept, and no man's conscience burdened with anything he needs scruple to undertake."—Tanner MSS.; Doyly's Life of

The opinion of Sancroft had great weight with the whole Tory party, and especially with the clergy. A week before the day for which the Convention had been summoned, a grave party assembled at Lambeth Palace, heard prayers in the chapel, dined with the Primate, and then consulted on the state of public affairs. Four suffragans of the Archbishop, who had shared his perils and his glory in the preceding summer, were present. The Earls of Clarendon and Ailesbury represented the Tory laity. The unanimous sense of the meeting appeared to be that those who had taken the oath of allegiance to James might justifiably withdraw their obedience from him, but could not with a safe conscience call any other by the name of King.*

Danby's plan. Thus two sections of the Tory party, a section which looked forward to an accommodation with James, and a section which was opposed to any such accommodation, agreed in supporting the plan of Regency. But a third section, which, though not very numerous, had great weight and influence, recommended a very different plan. The leaders of this small band were Danby and the Bishop of London in the House of Lords, and Sir Robert Sawyer in the House of Commons. They conceived that they had found out a way of effecting a complete revolution under strictly legal forms. It was contrary to all principle, they said, that the King should be deposed by his subjects; nor was it necessary to depose him. He had himself, by his flight, abdicated his power and dignity. A demise had actually taken place. All constitutional lawyers held that the throne of England could not be one moment vacant. The next heir had, therefore, succeeded. Who, then, was the next heir? As to the infant who had been carried into France, his entrance into the world had been attended by many suspicious circumstances. It was due to the other members of the royal family and to the nation that all doubts should be cleared up. An investigation had been solemnly demanded, in the name of the Prin-

---

Sancroft. It was not altogether without reason that the creatures of James made themselves merry with the good Archbishop's English.

* Evelyn, Jan. 15, 168$\frac{8}{9}$.

cess of Orange by her husband, and would have been instituted if the parties who were accused of fraud had not taken a course which, in any ordinary case, would have been considered as a decisive proof of guilt. They had not chosen to await the issue of a solemn parliamentary proceeding: they had stolen away into a foreign country: they had carried with them the child: they had carried with them all those French and Italian women of the bedchamber who, if there had been foul play, must have been privy to it, and who ought therefore to have been subjected to a rigorous cross-examination. To admit the boy's claim without inquiry was impossible; and those who called themselves his parents had made inquiry impossible. Judgment must therefore go against him by default. If he was wronged, he was wronged, not by the nation, but by those whose strange conduct at the time of his birth had justified the nation in demanding investigation, and who had then avoided investigation by flight. He might therefore, with perfect equity, be considered as a pretender. And thus the crown had legally devolved on the Princess of Orange. She was actually Queen Regnant. The Houses had nothing to do but to proclaim her. She might, if such were her pleasure, make her husband her first minister, and might even, with the consent of Parliament, bestow on him the title of King.

The persons who preferred this scheme to any other were few; and it was certain to be opposed, both by all who still bore any good-will to James, and by all the adherents of William. Yet Danby, confident in his own knowledge of parliamentary tactics, and well aware how much, when great parties are nearly balanced, a small flying squadron can effect, was not without hopes of being able to keep the event of the contest in suspense till both Whigs and Tories, despairing of complete victory, and afraid of the consequences of delay, should suffer him to act as umpire. Nor is it impossible that he might have succeeded if his efforts had been seconded, nay, if they had not been counteracted, by her whom he wished to raise to the height of human greatness. Quick-sighted as he was and versed in affairs, he was altogether ignorant of the character of Mary, and of the feeling with which she regarded her husband; nor was her old preceptor, Compton, better informed. William's manners were dry and cold: his constitution was infirm, and his temper by no means bland: he was not a man who would commonly be thought likely to inspire a fine young woman of twenty-six with a violent passion. It was known that he had not always been strictly constant to his wife; and tale-bearers had reported that she did not live happily with him. The most acute politicians, therefore, never suspected that, with all his faults, he had obtained such an empire over her heart as princes the most renowned for their success in gallantry, Francis the First and Henry the Fourth, Lewis the Fourteenth and Charles the Second, had never obtained over the heart of any woman, and that the three kingdoms of her forefathers were valuable in her estimation chiefly because, by bestowing them on him, she could prove to him the intensity and disinterestedness of her affection. Danby, in profound ignorance of her sentiments, assured her that he would defend her rights, and that, if she would support him, he hoped to place her alone on the throne.*

The course of the Whigs, meanwhile, was simple and consistent. Their doctrine was that the foundation of our government was a contract expressed on one side by the oath of allegiance, and on the other by the coronation oath, and that the duties imposed by this contract were mutual. They held that a sovereign who grossly abused his power might lawfully be withstood and dethroned by his people. That James had grossly abused his power was not disputed; and the whole Whig party was ready to pronounce that he had forfeited it. Whether the Prince of Wales was suppositious, was a point not worth discussing. There were now far stronger reasons than any which could be drawn from the circumstances of his birth for excluding him from the throne. A child, brought to the royal couch in a warming-pan, might possibly prove a good King of England. But

The Whig plan.

---

* Clarendon's Diary, December 24, 1688; Burnet, i., 819; Proposals humbly offered in behalf of the Princess of Orange, January 28, 168$\frac{8}{9}$.

there could be no such hope for a child educated by a father who was the most stupid and obstinate of tyrants, in a foreign country, the seat of despotism and superstition; in a country where the last traces of liberty had disappeared; where the States-general had ceased to meet; where parliaments had long registered without one remonstrance the most oppressive edicts of the sovereign; where valor, genius, learning, seemed to exist only for the purpose of aggrandizing a single man; where adulation was the main business of the press, the pulpit, and the stage; and where one chief subject of adulation was the barbarous persecution of the Reformed Church. Was the boy likely to learn, under such tuition and in such a situation, respect for the institutions of his native land? Could it be doubted that he would be brought up to be the slave of the Jesuits and the Bourbons, and that he would be, if possible, more bitterly prejudiced than any preceding Stuart against the laws of England?

Nor did the Whigs think that, situated as the country then was, a departure from the ordinary rule of succession was in itself an evil. They were of opinion that, till that rule had been broken, the doctrines of indefeasible hereditary right and passive obedience would be pleasing to the court, would be inculcated by the clergy, and would retain a strong hold on the public mind. The notion would still prevail that the kingly office is the ordinance of God in a sense different from that in which all government is his ordinance. It was plain that, till this superstition was extinct, the constitution could never be secure. For a really limited monarchy cannot long exist in a society which regards monarchy as something divine, and the limitations as mere human inventions. Royalty, in order that it might exist in perfect harmony with our liberties, must be unable to show any higher or more venerable title than that by which we hold our liberties. The King must be henceforth regarded as a magistrate, a great magistrate indeed, and highly to be honored, but subject, like all other magistrates, to the law, and deriving his power from heaven in no other sense than that in which the Lords and the Commons may be said to derive their power from heaven.

The best way of effecting this salutary change would be to interrupt the course of descent. Under sovereigns who would consider it as little short of high treason to preach non-resistance and the patriarchal theory of government, under sovereigns whose authority, springing from resolutions of the two Houses, could never rise higher than its source, there would be little risk of oppression such as had compelled two generations of Englishmen to rise in arms against two generations of Stuarts. On these grounds the Whigs were prepared to declare the throne vacant, to fill it by election, and to impose on the prince of their choice such conditions as might secure the country against misgovernment.

The time for the decision of these great questions had now arrived. At break of day, on the twenty-second of January, the House of Commons was crowded with knights and burgesses. On the benches appeared many faces which had been well known in that place during the reign of Charles the Second, but had not been seen there under his successor. Most of those Tory squires, and of those needy retainers of the court, who had been returned in multitudes to the Parliament of 1685, had given place to the men of the old country party, the men who had driven the Cabal from power, who had carried the Habeas Corpus Act, and who had sent up the Exclusion Bill to the Lords. Among them was Powle, deeply read in the history and law of Parliament, and distinguished by the species of eloquence which is required when grave questions are to be solemnly brought under the notice of senates, and Sir Thomas Littleton, versed in European politics, and gifted with a vehement and piercing logic which had often, when, after a long sitting, the candles had been lighted, roused the languishing House, and decided the event of the debate. There, too, was William Sacheverell, an orator whose great parliamentary abilities were, many years later, a favorite theme of old men who lived to see the conflicts of Walpole and Pulteney.* With these eminent persons were joined Sir Robert Clayton, the wealthiest merchant

Meeting of the Convention. Leading members of the House of Commons.

---

* Burnet, i., 389; and the notes of Speaker Onslow.

of London, whose palace in the Old Jewry surpassed in splendor the aristocratical mansions of Lincoln's Inn Fields and Covent Garden, whose villa among the Surrey hills was described as a garden of Eden, whose banquets vied with those of kings, and whose judicious munificence, still attested by numerous public monuments, had obtained for him in the annals of the City a place second only to that of Gresham. In the Parliament which met at Oxford in 1681, Clayton had, as member for the capital, and at the request of his constituents, moved for leave to bring in the Bill of Exclusion, and had been seconded by Lord Russell. In 1685, the City, deprived of its franchises and governed by the creatures of the court, had returned four Tory representatives. But the old charter had now been restored; and Clayton had been again chosen by acclamation.* Nor must John Birch be passed over. He had begun life as a carter, but had, in the civil wars, left his team, had turned soldier, had risen to the rank of colonel in the army of the Commonwealth, had, in high fiscal offices, shown great talents for business, had sat many years in Parliament, and, though retaining to the last the rough manners and plebeian dialect of his youth, had, by strong sense and mother-wit, gained the ear of the Commons, and was regarded as a formidable opponent by the most accomplished debaters of his time.† These were the most conspicuous among the veterans who now, after a long seclusion, returned to public life. But they were all speedily thrown into the shade by two younger Whigs, who, on this great day, took their seats for the first time, who soon rose to the highest honors of the State, who weathered together the fiercest storms of faction, and who, having been long and widely renowned as statesmen, as orators, and as munificent patrons of genius and learning, died, within a few months of each other, soon after the accession of the House of Brunswick. These were Charles Montague and John Somers.

One other name must be mentioned, a name then known

---

* Evelyn's Diary, September 26, 1672, October 12, 1679, July 13, 1700; Seymour's Survey of London.

† Burnet, i., 388; and Speaker Onslow's note.

only to a small circle of philosophers, but now pronounced beyond the Ganges and the Mississippi with reverence exceeding that which is paid to the memory of the greatest warriors and rulers. Among the crowd of silent members appeared the majestic forehead and pensive face of Isaac Newton. The renowned University on which his genius had already begun to impress a peculiar character, still plainly discernible after the lapse of more than a hundred and sixty years, had sent him to the Convention; and he sat there, in his modest greatness, the unobtrusive but unflinching friend of civil and religious freedom.

The first act of the Commons was to choose a Speaker; and the choice which they made indicated in a manner not to be mistaken their opinion touching the great questions which they were about to decide. Down to the very eve of the meeting, it had been understood that Seymour would be placed in the chair. He had formerly sat there during several years. He had great and various titles to consideration — descent, fortune, knowledge, experience, eloquence. He had long been at the head of a powerful band of members from the Western counties. Though a Tory, he had in the last Parliament headed, with conspicuous ability and courage, the opposition to Popery and arbitrary power. He had been among the first gentlemen who had repaired to the Dutch head-quarters at Exeter, and had been the author of that Association by which the Prince's adherents had bound themselves to stand or fall together. But, a few hours before the Houses met, a rumor was spread that Seymour was against declaring the throne vacant. As soon, therefore, as the benches had filled, the Earl of Wiltshire, who represented Hampshire, stood up, and proposed that Powle should be Speaker. Sir Vere Fane, member for Kent, seconded the motion. A plausible objection might have been raised; for it was known that a petition was about to be presented against Powle's return: but the general cry of the House called him to the chair; and the Tories thought it prudent to acquiesce.* The mace was then laid on the

Choice of a Speaker.

---

* Van Citters, $\frac{\text{Jan. 22,}}{\text{Feb. 1,}}$ 1689; Grey's Debates.

table; the list of members was called over; and the names of the defaulters were noted.

Meanwhile the Peers, about a hundred in number, had met, had chosen Halifax to be their Speaker, and had appointed several eminent lawyers to perform the functions which, in regular Parliaments, belong to the Judges. There was, in the course of that day, frequent communication between the Houses. They joined in requesting that the Prince would continue to administer the government till he should hear further from them, in expressing to him their gratitude for the deliverance which he, under God, had wrought for the nation, and in directing that the thirty-first of January should be observed as a day of thanksgiving for that deliverance.*

Thus far no difference of opinion had appeared: but both sides were preparing for the conflict. The Tories were strong in the Upper House, and weak in the Lower; and they knew that, at such a conjuncture, the House which should be the first to come to a resolution would have a great advantage over the other. There was not the least chance that the Commons would send up to the Lords a vote in favor of the plan of Regency: but, if such a vote were sent down from the Lords to the Commons, it was not absolutely impossible that many even of the Whig representatives of the people might be disposed to acquiesce rather than take the grave responsibility of causing discord and delay at a crisis which required union and expedition. The Commons had determined that, on Monday the twenty-eighth of January, they would take into consideration the state of the nation. The Tory Lords therefore proposed, on Friday the twenty-fifth, to enter instantly on the great business for which they had been called together. But their motives were clearly discerned and their tactics frustrated by Halifax, who, ever since his return from Hungerford, had seen that the settlement of the government could be effected on Whig principles only, and who had therefore, for the time, allied himself closely with

---

* Lords' and Commons' Journals, Jan. 22, 1688; Van Citters's despatch and Clarendon's Diary of the same date.

the Whigs. Devonshire moved that Tuesday the twenty-ninth should be the day. "By that time," he said, with more truth than discretion, "we may have some lights from below which may be useful for our guidance." His motion was carried; but his language was severely censured by some of his brother peers as derogatory to their order.*

On the twenty-eighth the Commons resolved themselves into a Committee of the whole House. A member who had, more than thirty years before, been one of Cromwell's Lords, Richard Hampden, son of the illustrious leader of the Roundheads, and father of the unhappy man who had, by large bribes and degrading submissions, narrowly escaped with life from the vengeance of James, was placed in the chair, and the great debate began.

Debate on the state of the nation.

It was soon evident that an overwhelming majority considered James as no longer King. Gilbert Dolben, son of a late Archbishop of York, was the first who declared himself to be of that opinion. He was supported by many members, particularly by the bold and vehement Wharton; by Sawyer, whose steady opposition to the dispensing power had, in some measure, atoned for old offences; by Maynard, whose voice, though so feeble with age that it could not be heard on distant benches, still commanded the respect of all parties; and by Somers, whose luminous eloquence and varied stores of knowledge were on that day exhibited, for the first time, within the walls of Parliament. The unblushing forehead and voluble tongue of Sir William Williams were found on the same side. Already he had been deeply concerned in the excesses both of the worst of oppositions and of the worst of governments. He had persecuted innocent Papists and innocent Protestants. He had been the patron of Oates and the tool of Petre. His name was associated with seditious violence which was remembered with regret and shame by all respectable Whigs, and with freaks of despotism abhorred by all respectable Tories. How men live under such infamy it is not easy to understand: but even such infamy was not

---

* Lords' Journals, Jan. 25, 168⅜; Clarendon's Diary, Jan. 23, 25.

enough for Williams. He was not ashamed to attack the fallen master to whom he had hired himself out for work which no honest man in the Inns of Court would undertake, and from whom he had, within six months, accepted a baronetcy as the reward of servility.

Only three members ventured to oppose themselves to what was evidently the general sense of the assembly. Sir Christopher Musgrave, a Tory gentleman of great weight and ability, hinted some doubts. Heneage Finch let fall some expressions which were understood to mean that he wished a negotiation to be opened with the King. This suggestion was so ill received that he made haste to explain it away. He protested that he had been misapprehended. He was convinced that, under such a prince, there could be no security for religion, liberty, or property. To recall King James, or to treat with him, would be a fatal course; but many who would never consent that he should exercise the regal power had conscientious scruples about depriving him of the royal title. There was one expedient which would remove all difficulties—a Regency. This proposition found so little favor that Finch did not venture to demand a division. Richard Fanshaw, Viscount Fanshaw of the kingdom of Ireland, said a few words in behalf of James, and recommended an adjournment; but the recommendation was met by a general outcry. Member after member stood up to represent the importance of despatch. Every moment, it was said, was precious: the public anxiety was intense: trade was suspended. The minority sullenly submitted, and suffered the predominant party to take its own course.

What that course would be was not perfectly clear. For the majority was made up of two classes. One class consisted of eager and vehement Whigs, who, if they had been able to take their own course, would have given to the proceedings of the Convention a decidedly revolutionary character. The other class admitted that a revolution was necessary, but regarded it as a necessary evil, and wished to disguise it, as much as possible, under the show of legitimacy. The former class demanded a distinct recognition of the right of subjects to dethrone bad princes. The latter class desired to rid the country of one bad prince, without promulgating any doctrine which might be abused for the purpose of weakening the just and salutary authority of future monarchs. The former class dwelt chiefly on the King's misgovernment; the latter on his flight. The former class considered him as having forfeited his crown; the latter as having resigned it. It was not easy to draw up any form of words which would please all whose assent it was important to obtain; but at length, out of many suggestions offered from different quarters, a resolution was framed which gave general satisfaction. It was moved that King James the Second, having endeavored to subvert the constitution of the kingdom by breaking the original contract between King and people, and, by the advice of Jesuits and other wicked persons, having violated the fundamental laws, and having withdrawn himself out of the kingdom, had abdicated the government, and that the throne had thereby become vacant.

<small>Resolution declaring the throne vacant.</small>

This resolution has been many times subjected to criticism as minute and severe as was ever applied to any sentence written by man; and perhaps there never was a sentence written by man which would bear such criticism less. That a King, by grossly abusing his power, may forfeit it, is true. That a King who absconds without making any provision for the administration, and leaves his people in a state of anarchy, may, without any violent straining of language, be said to have abdicated his functions, is also true. But no accurate writer would affirm that long-continued misgovernment and desertion, added together, make up an act of abdication. It is evident, too, that the mention of the Jesuits and other evil advisers of James weakens, instead of strengthening, the case against him. For it is a well-known maxim of English law that, when a king is misled by pernicious counsel, his counsellors, and not himself, ought to be held accountable for his errors. It is idle, however, to examine these memorable words as we should examine a chapter of Aristotle or of Hobbes. Such words are to be considered, not as words, but as deeds. If they effect that which they are intended to effect, they are rational, though they may be contradictory. If they fail of attaining their end, they are absurd, though they carry demonstration with them. Logic admits of no compromise. The essence of politics is compromise. It is therefore not strange that some of the most important and most useful political instruments in the world should be among the most illogical compositions that ever were penned. The object of Somers, of Maynard, and of the other eminent men who shaped this celebrated motion was, not to leave to posterity a model of definition and partition, but to make the restoration of a tyrant impossible, and to place on the throne a sovereign under whom law and liberty might be secure. This object they attained by using language which, in a philosophical treatise, would justly be reprehended as inexact and confused. They cared little whether their major agreed with their conclusion, if the major secured two hundred votes, and the conclusion two hundred more. In fact, the one beauty of the resolution is its inconsistency. There was a phrase for every subdivision of the majority. The mention of the original contract gratified the disciples of Sidney. The word abdication conciliated politicians of a more timid school. There were doubtless many fervent Protestants who were pleased with the censure cast on the Jesuits. To the real statesman the single important clause was that which declared the throne vacant; and, if that clause could be carried, he cared little by what preamble it might be introduced. The force which was thus united made all resistance hopeless. The motion was adopted by the Committee without a division. It was ordered that the report should be instantly made. Powle returned to the chair: the mace was laid on the table: Hampden brought up the resolution: the House instantly agreed to it, and ordered him to carry it to the Lords.*

On the following morning the Lords assembled early. The benches both of the spiritual and of the temporal peers

---

* Commons' Journals, Jan. 28, 168$\frac{8}{9}$; Grey's Debates; Van Citters, $\frac{\text{Jan. 29.}}{\text{Feb. 8.}}$ If the report in Grey's Debates be correct, Van Citters must have been misinformed as to Sawyer's speech.

were crowded. Hampden appeared at the bar, and put the resolution of the Commons into the hands of Halifax. The Upper House then resolved itself into a committee, and Danby took the chair.

It is sent up to the Lords.

The discussion was soon interrupted by the reappearance of Hampden with another message. The House resumed, and was informed that the Commons had just voted it inconsistent with the safety and welfare of this Protestant nation to be governed by a Popish King. To this resolution, irreconcilable as it obviously was with the doctrine of indefeasible hereditary right, the Peers gave an immediate and unanimous assent. The principle which was thus affirmed has always, down to our own time, been held sacred by all Protestant statesmen, and has never been considered by any reasonable Roman Catholic as objectionable. If, indeed, our sovereigns were, like the Presidents of the United States, mere civil functionaries, it would not be easy to vindicate such a restriction. But the headship of the English Church is annexed to the English crown; and there is no intolerance in saying that a Church ought not to be subjected to a head who regards her as schismatical and heretical.*

After this short interlude the Lords again went into committee. The Tories insisted that their plan should be discussed before the vote of the Commons which declared the throne vacant was considered. This was conceded to them; and the question was put whether a Regency, exercising kingly power during the life of James, in his name, would be the best expedient for preserving the laws and liberties of the nation?

Debate in the Lords on the plan of Regency.

The contest was long and animated. The chief speakers in favor of a Regency were Rochester and Nottingham. Halifax and Danby led the other side. The Primate, strange to say, did not make his appearance, though earnestly importuned by the Tory peers to place himself at their head. His absence drew on him many contumelious censures; nor have even his eulogists been able to find any explanation of it which raises

---

* Lords' and Commons' Journals, Jan. 29, 168$\frac{8}{9}$.

his character.* The plan of Regency was his own. He had, a few days before, in a paper written with his own hand, pronounced that plan to be clearly the best that could be adopted. The deliberations of the Lords who supported that plan had been carried on under his roof. His situation made it his clear duty to declare publicly what he thought. Nobody can suspect him of personal cowardice or of vulgar cupidity. It was probably from a nervous fear of doing wrong that, at this great conjuncture, he did nothing: but he should have known that, situated as he was, to do nothing was to do wrong. A man who is too scrupulous to take on himself a grave responsibility at an important crisis, ought to be too scrupulous to accept the place of first minister of the Church and first peer of the Parliament.

It is not strange, however, that Sancroft's mind should have been ill at ease; for he could hardly be blind to the obvious truth that the scheme which he had recommended to his friends was utterly inconsistent with all that he and his brethren had been teaching during many years. That the King had a divine and indefeasible right to the regal power, and that the regal power, even when most grossly abused, could not, without sin, be resisted, was the doctrine in which the Anglican Church had long gloried. Did this doctrine, then, really mean only that the King had a divine and indefeasible right to have his effigy and name cut on a seal which was to be daily employed in despite of him for the purpose of commissioning his enemies to levy war on him, and of sending his friends to the gallows for obeying him? Did the whole duty of a good subject consist in using the word King? If so, Fairfax and Cromwell at Naseby had performed all the duty of good subjects. For Charles had been designated as King even by the generals who commanded against him. Nothing in the conduct of the Long Parliament had been more severely blamed by the Church than the ingenious device of using his name against himself. Every one of her ministers had been required to sign a declaration condemning

---

* Clarendon's Diary, Jan. 21, 168⅜; Burnet, i., 810; Doyly's Life of Sancroft.

as traitorous the fiction by which the authority of the sovereign had been separated from his person.* Yet this traitorous fiction was now considered by the Primate and by many of his suffragans as the only basis on which they could, in strict conformity with Christian principles, erect a government.

The distinction which Sancroft had borrowed from the Roundheads of the preceding generation subverted from the foundation that system of politics which the Church and the Universities pretended to have learned from Saint Paul. The Holy Spirit, it had been a thousand times repeated, had commanded the Romans to be subject to Nero. The meaning of the precept now appeared to be only that the Romans were to call Nero Augustus. They were perfectly at liberty to chase him beyond the Euphrates, to leave him a pensioner on the bounty of the Parthians, to withstand him by force if he attempted to return, to punish all who aided him or corresponded with him, and to transfer the Tribunitian power and the Consular power, the Presidency of the Senate and the command of the Legions, to Galba or Vespasian.

The analogy which the Archbishop imagined that he had discovered between the case of a wrong-headed king and the case of a lunatic king will not bear a moment's examination. It was plain that James was not in that state of mind in which, if he had been a country gentleman or a merchant, any tribunal would have held him incapable of executing a contract or a will. He was of unsound mind only as all bad kings are of unsound mind; as Charles the First had been of unsound mind when he went to seize the five members; as Charles the Second had been of unsound mind when he concluded the treaty of Dover. If this sort of mental unsoundness did not justify subjects in withdrawing their obedience from princes, the plan of a Regency was evidently indefensible. If this sort of mental unsoundness did justify subjects in withdrawing their obedience from princes, the doctrine of non-resistance was completely given up; and all that any moderate Whig had ever contended for was fully admitted.

---

* See the Act of Uniformity.

As to the oath of allegiance about which Sancroft and his disciples were so anxious, one thing at least is clear, that, whoever might be right, they were wrong. The Whigs held that, in the oath of allegiance, certain conditions were implied, that the King had violated these conditions, and that the oath had therefore lost its force. But, if the Whig doctrine were false, if the oath were still binding, could men of sense really believe that they escaped the guilt of perjury by voting for a Regency? Could they affirm that they bore true allegiance to James, while they were, in defiance of his protestations made before all Europe, authorizing another person to receive the royal revenues, to summon and prorogue Parliaments, to create Dukes and Earls, to name Bishops and Judges, to pardon offenders, to command the forces of the State, and to conclude treaties with foreign powers? Had Pascal been able to find, in all the folios of the Jesuitical casuists, a sophism more contemptible than that which now, as it seemed, sufficed to quiet the consciences of the fathers of the Anglican Church?

Nothing could be more evident than that the plan of Regency could be defended only on Whig principles. Between the rational supporters of that plan and the majority of the House of Commons there could be no dispute as to the question of right. All that remained was a question of expediency. And would any statesman seriously contend that it was expedient to constitute a government with two heads, and to give to one of those heads regal power without regal dignity, and to the other regal dignity without regal power? It was notorious that such an arrangement, even when made necessary by the infancy or insanity of a prince, had serious disadvantages. That times of Regency were times of weakness, of trouble, and of disaster, was a truth proved by the whole history of England, of France, and of Scotland, and had almost become a proverb. Yet, in a case of infancy or of insanity, the King was at least passive. He could not actively counterwork the Regent. What was now proposed was that England should have two first magistrates, of ripe age and sound mind, waging with each other an irreconcilable war.

It was absurd to talk of leaving James merely the kingly name, and depriving him of all the kingly power. For the name was a part of the power. The word King was a word of conjuration. It was associated in the minds of many Englishmen with the idea of a mysterious character derived from above, and in the minds of almost all Englishmen with the idea of legitimate and venerable authority. Surely, if the title carried with it such power, those who maintained that James ought to be deprived of all power could not deny that he ought to be deprived of the title.

And how long was the anomalous government planned by the genius of Sancroft to last? Every argument which could be urged for setting it up at all might be urged with equal force for retaining it to the end of time. If the boy who had been carried into France was really born of the Queen, he would hereafter inherit the divine and indefeasible right to be called King. The same right would very probably be transmitted from Papist to Papist through the whole of the eighteenth and nineteenth centuries. Both the Houses had unanimously resolved that England should not be governed by a Papist. It might well be, therefore, that, from generation to generation, regents would continue to administer the government in the name of vagrant and mendicant kings. There was no doubt that the Regents must be appointed by Parliament. The effect, therefore, of this contrivance, a contrivance intended to preserve unimpaired the sacred principle of hereditary monarchy, would be that the monarchy would become really elective.

Another unanswerable reason was urged against Sancroft's plan. There was in the statute-book a law which had been passed soon after the close of the long and bloody contest between the Houses of York and Lancaster, and which had been framed for the purpose of averting calamities such as the alternate victories of those Houses had brought on the nobility and gentry of the realm. By this law it was provided that no person should, by adhering to a King in possession, incur the penalties of treason. When the regicides were brought to trial after the Restoration, some of them insisted that their case lay within the equity of this act. They had obeyed, they said, the government which was in possession, and were, therefore, not traitors. The Judges admitted that this would have been a good defence if the prisoners had acted under the authority of a usurper who, like Henry the Fourth and Richard the Third, bore the regal title, but declared that such a defence could not avail men who had indicted, sentenced, and executed one who, in the indictment, in the sentence, and in the death-warrant, was designated as King. It followed, therefore, that whoever should support a regent in opposition to James would run great risk of being hanged, drawn, and quartered, if ever James should recover supreme power; but that no person could, without such a violation of law as Jeffreys himself would hardly venture to commit, be punished for siding with a king who was reigning, though wrongfully, at Whitehall, against a rightful king who was in exile at Saint Germains.*

It should seem that these arguments admit of no reply; and they were doubtless urged with force by Danby, who had a wonderful power of making every subject which he treated clear to the dullest mind, and by Halifax, who, in fertility of thought and brilliancy of diction, had no rival among the orators of that age. Yet so numerous and powerful were the Tories in the Upper House that, notwithstanding the weakness of their case, the defection of their leader, and the ability of their opponents, they very nearly carried the day. A hundred Lords divided. Forty-nine voted for a Regency, fifty-one against it. In the minority were the natural children of Charles, the brothers-in-law of James, the Dukes of Somerset and Ormond, the Archbishop of York, and eleven Bishops. No prelate voted in the majority except Compton and Trelawney.†

It was near nine in the evening before the House rose.

---

* Stat. 2 Hen. 7, c. 1; Lord Coke's Institutes, Part III., Chap. i.; Trial of Cook for high-treason, in the Collection of State Trials; Burnet, i., 813; and Swift's note.

† Lords' Journals, January 29, 168$\frac{8}{9}$; Clarendon's Diary; Evelyn's Diary; Van Citters; Eachard's History of the Revolution; Burnet, i., 813; History of the Reestablishment of the Government, 1689. The numbers of the Contents and Not Contents are not given in the journals, and are differently reported by different writers. I have followed Clarendon, who took the trouble to make out lists of the majority and minority.

The following day was the thirtieth of January, the anniversary of the death of Charles the First. The great body of the Anglican clergy had, during many years, thought it a sacred duty to inculcate on that day the doctrines of non-resistance and passive obedience. Their old sermons were now of little use; and many divines were even in doubt whether they could venture to read the whole Liturgy. The Lower House had declared that the throne was vacant. The Upper had not yet expressed any opinion. It was therefore not easy to decide whether the prayers for the sovereign ought to be used. Every officiating minister took his own course. In most of the churches of the capital the petitions for James were omitted: but at Saint Margaret's, Sharp, Dean of Norwich, who had been requested to preach before the Commons, not only read to their faces the whole service as it stood in the book, but, before his sermon, implored, in his own words, a blessing on the King, and, toward the close of his discourse, declaimed against the Jesuitical doctrine that princes might lawfully be deposed by their subjects. The Speaker, that very afternoon, complained to the House of this affront. "You pass a vote one day," he said, "and on the next day it is contradicted from the pulpit in your own hearing." Sharp was strenuously defended by the Tories, and had friends even among the Whigs: for it was not forgotten that he had incurred serious danger in the evil times by the courage with which, in defiance of the royal injunction, he had preached against Popery. Sir Christopher Musgrave very ingeniously remarked that the House had not ordered the resolution which declared the throne vacant to be published. Sharp, therefore, was not only not bound to know anything of that resolution, but could not have taken notice of it without a breach of privilege for which he might have been called to the bar and reprimanded on his knees. The majority felt that it was not wise at that conjuncture to quarrel with the clergy; and the subject was suffered to drop.*

---

* Grey's Debates; Evelyn's Diary; Life of Archbishop Sharp, by his son; Apology for the New Separation, in a letter to Dr. John Sharp, Archbishop of York, 1691.

While the Commons were discussing Sharp's sermon, the Lords had again gone into a committee on the state of the nation, and had ordered the resolution which pronounced the throne vacant to be read clause by clause.

The first expression on which a debate arose was that which recognized the original contract between king and people. It was not to be expected that the Tory peers would suffer a phrase which contained the quintessence of Whiggism to pass unchallenged. A division took place; and it was determined by fifty-three votes to forty-six that the words should stand.

The severe censure passed by the Commons on the administration of James was next considered, and was approved without one dissentient voice. Some verbal objections were made to the proposition that James had abdicated the government. It was urged that he might more correctly be said to have deserted it. This amendment was adopted, it should seem, with scarcely any debate, and without a division. By this time it was late, and the Lords again adjourned.*

Up to this moment the small body of peers which was under the guidance of Danby had acted in firm union with Halifax and the Whigs. The effect of this union had been that the plan of Regency had been rejected, and the doctrine of the original contract affirmed.

Schism between the Whigs and the followers of Danby.

The proposition that James had ceased to be King had been the rallying-point of the two parties which had made up the majority. But from that point their path diverged. The next question to be decided was whether the throne was vacant; and this was a question not merely verbal, but of grave practical importance. If the throne was vacant, the Estates of the Realm might place William in it. If it was not vacant, he could succeed to it only after his wife, after Anne, and after Anne's posterity.

It was, according to the followers of Danby, an established maxim that our country could not be, even for a moment, without a rightful prince. The man might die; but the magistrate was immortal. The man might abdicate; but the mag-

---

* Lords' Journals, Jan. 30, 168⅜; Clarendon's Diary.

istrate was irremovable. If, these politicians said, we once admit that the throne is vacant, we admit that it is elective. The sovereign whom we may place on it will be a sovereign, not after the English, but after the Polish, fashion. Even if we choose the very person who would reign by right of birth, still that person will reign not by right of birth, but in virtue of our choice, and will take as a gift what ought to be regarded as an inheritance. That salutary reverence with which the blood-royal and the order of primogeniture have hitherto been regarded will be greatly diminished. Still more serious will the evil be, if we not only fill the throne by election, but fill it with a prince who has doubtless the qualities of a great and good ruler, and who has wrought a wonderful deliverance for us, but who is not first, nor even second, in the order of succession. If we once say that merit, however eminent, shall be a title to the crown, we disturb the very foundations of our polity, and furnish a precedent of which every ambitious warrior or statesman who may have rendered any great service to the public will be tempted to avail himself. This danger we avoid if we logically follow out the principles of the constitution to their consequences. There has been a demise of the crown. At the instant of the demise the next heir became our lawful sovereign. We consider the Princess of Orange as next heir; and we hold that she ought, without any delay, to be proclaimed, what she already is, our Queen.

The Whigs answered that it was idle to apply ordinary rules to a country in a state of revolution, that the great question now depending was not to be decided by the saws of pedantic Templars, and that, if it were to be so decided, such saws might be quoted on one side as well as the other. If it were a legal maxim that the throne could never be vacant, it was also a legal maxim that a living man could have no heir. James was still living. How, then, could the Princess of Orange be his heir? The truth was that the laws of England had made full provision for the succession when the power of a sovereign and his natural life terminated together, but had made no provision for the very rare cases in which his power terminated before the close of his natural life; and with one of those very rare cases the Convention had now to deal. That James no longer filled the throne both Houses had pronounced. Neither common law nor statute law designated any person as entitled to fill the throne between his demise and his decease. It followed that the throne was vacant, and that the Houses might invite the Prince of Orange to fill it. That he was not next in order of birth was true; but this was no disadvantage: on the contrary, it was a positive recommendation. Hereditary monarchy was a good political institution, but was by no means more sacred than other good political institutions. Unfortunately, bigoted and servile theologians had turned it into a religious mystery, almost as awful and as incomprehensible as transubstantiation itself. To keep the institution, and yet to get rid of the abject and noxious superstitions with which it had of late years been associated, and which had made it a curse instead of a blessing to society, ought to be the first object of English statesmen; and that object would be best attained by slightly deviating for a time from the general rule of descent, and then returning to it.

Many attempts were made to prevent an open breach between the party of the Prince and the party of the Princess.

Meeting at the Earl of Devonshire's. A great meeting was held at the Earl of Devonshire's house, and the dispute was warm. Halifax was the chief speaker for William, Danby for Mary. Of the mind of Mary Danby knew nothing. She had been some time expected in London, but had been detained in Holland, first by masses of ice which had blocked up the rivers, and, when the thaw came, by strong westerly winds. Had she arrived earlier, the dispute would probably have been at once quieted. Halifax, on the other side, had no authority to say anything in William's name. The Prince, true to his promise that he would leave the settlement of the government to the Convention, had maintained an impenetrable reserve, and had not suffered any word, look, or gesture, indicative either of satisfaction or of displeasure, to escape him. One of his countrymen, who had a large share of his confidence, had been invited to the meeting, and was earnestly pressed by the Peers to give them some information. He long excused himself. At last he so far yielded to their urgency as to say, "I can only guess at His Highness's mind. If you wish to know what I guess, I guess that he would not like to be his wife's gentleman usher; but I know nothing." "I know something now, however," said Danby. "I know enough, and too much." He then departed; and the assembly broke up.*

On the thirty-first of January the debate which had terminated thus in private was publicly renewed in the House of Peers. That day had been fixed for the national thanksgiving. An office had been drawn up for the occasion by several Bishops, among whom were Ken and Sprat. It is perfectly free both from the adulation and from the malignity by which such compositions were in that age too often deformed, and sustains, better perhaps than any occasional service which has been framed during two centuries, a comparison with that great model of chaste, lofty, and pathetic eloquence, the Book of Common Prayer. The Lords went in the morning to Westminster Abbey. The Commons had desired Burnet to preach before them at Saint Margaret's. He was not likely to fall into the same error which had been committed in the same place on the preceding day. His vigorous and animated discourse doubtless called forth the loud hums of his auditors. It was not only printed by command of the House, but was translated into French for the edification of foreign Protestants.† The day closed with the festivities usual on such occasions. The whole town shone bright with fireworks and bonfires: the roar of guns and the pealing of bells lasted till the night was far spent: but, before the lights were extinct and the streets silent, an event had taken place which threw a damp on the public joy.

---

* Dartmouth's note on Burnet, i., 393. Dartmouth says that it was from Fagel that the Lords extracted the hint. This was a slip of the pen very pardonable in a hasty marginal note; but Dalrymple and others ought not to have copied so palpable a blunder. Fagel died in Holland, on the 5th of December, 1688, when William was at Salisbury and James at Whitehall. The real person was, I suppose, Zulestein or Dykvelt.

† Both the service and Burnet's sermon are still to be found in our great libraries, and will repay the trouble of perusal.

The Peers had repaired from the Abbey to their house, and had resumed the discussion on the state of the nation. The last words of the resolution of the Commons were taken into consideration; and it soon became clear that the majority was not disposed to assent to those words. To near fifty Lords who held that the regal title still belonged to James were now added seven or eight who held that it had already devolved on Mary. The Whigs, finding themselves outnumbered, tried to compromise the dispute. They proposed to omit the words which pronounced the throne vacant, and simply to declare the Prince and Princess King and Queen. It was manifest that such a declaration implied, though it did not expressly affirm, all that the Tories were unwilling to concede. For nobody could pretend that William had succeeded to the regal office by right of birth. To pass a resolution acknowledging him as King was therefore an act of election; and how could there be an election without a vacancy? The proposition of the Whig Lords was rejected by fifty-two votes to forty-seven. The question was then put whether the throne was vacant. The Contents were only forty-one: the Non-contents fifty-five. Of the minority thirty-six protested.

During the two following days London was in an unquiet and anxious state. The Tories began to hope that they might be able again to bring forward their favorite plan of Regency with better success. Perhaps the Prince himself, when he found that he had no chance of wearing the crown, might prefer Sancroft's scheme to Danby's. It was better, doubtless, to be a king than to be a regent: but it was better to be a regent than to be a gentleman usher. On the other side, the lower and fiercer class of Whigs, the old emissaries of Shaftesbury, the old associates of College, began to stir in the City. Crowds assembled in Palace Yard, and held threatening language. Lord Lovelace, who was suspected of having encouraged these assemblages, informed

---

* Lords' Journals, Jan. 31, 168$\frac{8}{9}$.

the Peers that he was charged with a petition requesting them instantly to declare the Prince and Princess of Orange King and Queen. He was asked by whom the petition was signed. "There are no hands to it yet," he answered; "but, when I bring it here next, there shall be hands enough." This menace alarmed and disgusted his own party. The leading Whigs were, in truth, even more anxious than the Tories that the deliberations of the Convention should be perfectly free, and that it should not be in the power of any adherent of James to allege that either House had acted under force. A petition, similar to that which had been intrusted to Lovelace, was brought into the House of Commons, but was contemptuously rejected. Maynard was foremost in protesting against the attempt of the rabble in the streets to overawe the Estates of the Realm. William sent for Lovelace, expostulated with him strongly, and ordered the magistrates to act with vigor against all unlawful assemblies.* Nothing in the history of our revolution is more deserving of admiration and of imitation than the manner in which the two parties in the Convention, at the very moment at which their disputes ran highest, joined like one man to resist the dictation of the mob of the capital.

But, though the Whigs were fully determined to maintain order and to respect the freedom of debate, they were equally determined to make no concession. On Saturday, the second of February, the Commons, without a division, resolved to adhere to their resolution as it originally stood. James, as usual, came to the help of his enemies. A letter from him to the Convention had just arrived in London. It had been transmitted to Preston by the apostate Melfort, who was now high in favor at Saint Germains. The name of Melfort was an abomination to every Churchman. That he was still a confidential minister was alone sufficient to prove that his master's folly and perverseness were incurable. No member of either House vent-

Letter of James to the Convention.

* Van Citters, Feb. $\frac{5}{15}$, 1689; Clarendon's Diary, Feb. 2. The story is greatly exaggerated in the work entitled Revolution Politics, an eminently absurd book, yet of some value as a record of the foolish reports of the day. Grey's Debates.

ured to propose that a paper which came from such a quarter should be read. The contents, however, were well known to all the town. His Majesty exhorted the Lords and Commons not to despair of his clemency, and graciously assured them that he would pardon those who had betrayed him, some few excepted, whom he did not name. How was it possible to do anything for a prince who, vanquished, deserted, banished, living on alms, told those who were the arbiters of his fate that, if they would set him on his throne again, he would hang only a few of them?*

Debates. The contest between the two branches of the legislature lasted some days longer. On Monday, the fourth of February, the Peers resolved that they would insist on their amendments: but a protest to which thirty-nine names were subscribed was entered on the journals.† On the following day the Tories determined to try their strength in the Lower House. They mustered there in great force. *Negotiations.* A motion was made to agree to the amendments of the Lords. Those who were for the plan of Sancroft and those who were for the plan of Danby divided together; but they were beaten by two hundred and eighty-two votes to a hundred and fifty-one. The House than resolved to request a free conference with the Lords.‡

At the same time strenuous efforts were making without the walls of Parliament to bring the dispute between the two branches of the legislature to a close. Burnet *Letter of the Princess of Orange to Danby.* thought that the importance of the crisis justified him in publishing the great secret which the Princess had confided to him. He knew, he said, from her own lips,

---

* The letter of James, dated $\frac{\text{Jan. 24,}}{\text{Feb. 3,}}$ 1689, will be found in Kennet. It is most disingenuously garbled in his Life. See Clarendon's Diary, Feb. 2, 4; Grey's Debates; Lords' Journals, Feb. 2, 4, 168$\frac{8}{9}$.

† It has been asserted by several writers, and, among others, by Ralph and by M. Mazure, that Danby signed this protest. This is a mistake. Probably some person who examined the journals before they were printed mistook Derby for Danby. Lords' Journals, Feb. 4, 168$\frac{8}{9}$. Evelyn, a few days before, wrote Derby, by mistake, for Danby. Diary, Jan. 29, 168$\frac{8}{9}$.

‡ Commons' Journals, Feb. 5, 168$\frac{8}{9}$.

that it had long been her full determination, even if she came to the throne in the regular course of descent, to surrender her power, with the sanction of Parliament, into the hands of her husband. Danby received from her an earnest, and almost angry, reprimand. She was, she wrote, the Prince's wife; she had no other wish than to be subject to him: the most cruel injury that could be done to her would be to set her up as his competitor; and she never could regard any person who took such a course as her true friend.* The Tories had still one hope. Anne might insist on her own rights, and on those of her children. No effort was spared to stimulate her ambition, and to alarm her conscience. Her uncle Clarendon was especially active. A few weeks only had elapsed since the hope of wealth and greatness had impelled him to belie the boastful professions of his whole life, to desert the royal cause, to join with the Wildmans and Fergusons, nay, to propose that the King should be sent a prisoner to a foreign land and immured in a fortress begirt by pestilential marshes. The lure which had produced this strange transformation was the Viceroyalty of Ireland. Soon, however, it appeared that the proselyte had little chance of obtaining the splendid prize on which his heart was set. He found that others were consulted on Irish affairs. His advice was never asked, and, when obtrusively and importunately offered, was coldly received. He repaired many times to Saint James's Palace, but could scarcely obtain a word or a look. One day the Prince was writing: another day he wanted fresh air, and must ride in the Park: on a third he was closeted with officers on military business, and could see nobody. Clarendon saw that he was not likely to gain anything by the sacrifice of his principles, and determined to take them back again. In December ambition had converted him into a rebel. In January disappointment reconverted him into a Royalist. The uneasy consciousness that he had not been a consistent Tory gave a peculiar acrimony to his Toryism.†

The Princess Anne acquiesces in the Whig plan.

---

* Burnet, i., 819.
† Clarendon's Diary, Jan. 1, 4, 8, 9, 10, 11, 12, 13, 14, 168$\frac{8}{9}$; Burnet, i., 807.

In the House of Lords he had done all in his power to prevent a settlement. He now exerted, for the same end, all his influence over the Princess Anne. But his influence over her was small indeed when compared with that of the Churchills, who wisely called to their help two powerful allies, Tillotson, who, as a spiritual director, had, at that time, immense authority, and Lady Russell, whose noble and gentle virtues, proved by the most cruel of all trials, had gained for her the reputation of a saint. The Princess of Denmark, it was soon known, was willing that William should reign for life; and it was evident that to defend the cause of the daughters of James against themselves was a hopeless task.*

And now William thought that the time had come when he ought to explain himself. He accordingly sent for Halifax, Danby, Shrewsbury, and some other political leaders of great note, and with that air of stoical apathy under which he had, from a boy, been in the habit of concealing his strongest emotions, addressed to them a few deeply meditated and weighty words.

William explains his views.

He had hitherto, he said, remained silent: he had used neither solicitation nor menace: he had not even suffered a hint of his opinions or wishes to get abroad: but a crisis had now arrived at which it was necessary for him to declare his intentions. He had no right and no wish to dictate to the Convention. All that he claimed was the privilege of declining any office which he felt that he could not hold with honor to himself and with benefit to the public.

A strong party was for a Regency. It was for the Houses to determine whether such an arrangement would be for the interest of the nation. He had a decided opinion on that point; and he thought it right to say distinctly that he would not be Regent.

Another party was for placing the Princess on the throne, and for giving to him, during her life, the title of King, and such a share in the administration as she might be pleased to

---

* Clarendon's Diary, Feb. 5, 168⅜; Duchess of Marlborough's Vindication; Mulgrave's Account of the Revolution.

allow him. He could not stoop to such a post. He esteemed the Princess as much as it was possible for man to esteem woman: but not even from her would he accept a subordinate and a precarious place in the government. He was so made that he could not submit to be tied to the apron-strings even of the best of wives. He did not desire to take any part in English affairs; but, if he did consent to take a part, there was one part only which he could usefully or honorably take. If the Estates offered him the crown for life, he would accept it. If not, he should, without repining, return to his native country. He concluded by saying that he thought it reasonable that the Lady Anne and her posterity should be preferred in the succession to any children whom he might have by any other wife than the Lady Mary.*

The meeting broke up; and what the Prince had said was in a few hours known all over London. That he must be King was now clear. The only question was whether he should hold the regal dignity alone or conjointly with the Princess. Halifax and a few other politicians, who saw in a strong light the danger of dividing the supreme executive authority, thought it desirable that, during William's life, Mary should be only Queen Consort and a subject. But this arrangement, though much might doubtless be said for it in argument, shocked the general feeling even of those Englishmen who were most attached to the Prince. His wife had given an unprecedented proof of conjugal submission and affection; and the very least return that could be made to her would be to bestow on her the dignity of Queen Regnant. William Harbord, one of the most zealous of the Prince's adherents, was so much exasperated that he sprang out of the bed to which he was confined by gout, and vehemently declared that he never would have drawn a sword in His High-

---

* Burnet, i., 820. Burnet says that he has not related the events of this stirring time in chronological order. I have, therefore, been forced to arrange them by guess; but I think that I can scarcely be wrong in supposing that the letter of the Princess of Orange to Danby arrived, and that the Prince's explanation of his views was given, between Thursday, the 31st of January, and Wednesday, the 6th of February.

ness's cause if he had foreseen that so shameful an arrangement would be made. No person took the matter up so eagerly as Burnet. His blood boiled at the wrong done to his kind patroness. He expostulated vehemently with Bentinck, and begged to be permitted to resign the chaplainship. "While I am His Highness's servant," said the brave and honest divine, "it would be unseemly in me to oppose any plan which may have his countenance. I therefore desire to be set free, that I may fight the Princess's battle with every faculty that God has given me." Bentinck prevailed on Burnet to defer an open declaration of hostilities till William's resolution should be distinctly known. In a few hours the scheme which had excited so much resentment was entirely given up; and all those who considered James as no longer King were agreed as to the way in which the throne must be filled. William and Mary must be King and Queen. The heads of both must appear together on the coin: writs must run in the names of both: both must enjoy all the personal dignities and immunities of royalty: but the administration, which could not be safely divided, must belong to William alone.*

And now the time arrived for the free conference between the Houses. The managers for the Lords, in their robes, took their seats along one side of the table in the Painted Chamber: but the crowd of members of the House of Commons on the other side was so great that the gentlemen who were to argue the question in vain tried to get through. It was not without much difficulty and long delay that the Sergeant-at-arms was able to clear a passage.†

The conference between the Houses.

At length the discussion began. A full report of the speeches on both sides has come down to us. There are few students of history who have not taken up that report with eager curiosity and laid it down with disappointment. The question between the Houses was argued on both sides as a question of law. The objections which the Lords made to the resolution of the Commons were verbal and technical,

---

* Mulgrave's Account of the Revolution.
† Commons' Journals, Feb. 6, 168⅘.

II.—38

and were met by verbal and technical answers. Somers vindicated the use of the word abdication by quotations from Grotius and Brissonius, Spigelius and Bartolus. When he was challenged to show any authority for the proposition that England could be without a sovereign, he produced the Parliament roll of the year 1399, in which it was expressly set forth that the kingly office was vacant during the interval between the resignation of Richard the Second and the enthroning of Henry the Fourth. The Lords replied by producing the Parliament roll of the first year of Edward the Fourth, from which it appeared that the record of 1399 had been solemnly annulled. They therefore maintained that the precedent on which Somers relied was no longer valid. Treby then came to Somers's assistance, and laid on the table the Parliament roll of the first year of Henry the Seventh, which repealed the act of Edward the Fourth, and consequently restored the validity of the record of 1399. After a colloquy of several hours the disputants separated.* The Lords assembled in their own house. It was well understood that they were about to yield, and that the conference had been a mere form. The friends of Mary had found that, by setting her up as her husband's rival, they had deeply displeased her. Some of the Peers who had formerly voted for a Regency had determined to absent themselves or to support the resolution of the Lower House. Their opinion, they said, was unchanged: but any government was better than no government; and the country could not bear a prolongation of this agony of suspense. Even Nottingham, who, in the Painted Chamber, had taken the lead against the Commons, declared that, though his own conscience would not suffer him to give way, he was glad that the consciences of other men were less squeamish. Several Lords who had not yet voted in the Convention had been induced to attend; Lord Lexington, who had just hurried over from the Continent; the Earl of Lincoln, who was half mad; the Earl of Carlisle, who limped

---

* See the Lords' and Commons' Journals of Feb. 6, 168$\frac{8}{9}$, and the Report of the Conference.

in on crutches; and the Bishop of Durham, who had been in hiding and had intended to fly beyond sea, but had received an intimation that, if he would vote for the settling of the government, his conduct in the Ecclesiastical Commission should not be remembered against him. Danby, desirous to heal the schism which he had caused, exhorted the House, in a speech distinguished by even more than his usual ability, not to persevere in a contest which might be fatal to the state. He was strenuously supported by Halifax. The spirit of the opposite party was quelled. When the question was put whether King James had abdicated the government, only three Lords said Not Content. On the question whether the throne was vacant, a division was demanded. The Contents were sixty-two; the Non-contents forty-seven. It was immediately proposed and carried, without a division, that the Prince and Princess of Orange should be declared King and Queen of England.*

The Lords yield.

Nottingham then moved that the wording of the oaths of allegiance and supremacy should be altered in such a way that they might be conscientiously taken by persons who, like himself, disapproved of what the Convention had done, and yet fully purposed to be loyal and dutiful subjects of the new sovereigns. To his proposition no objection was made. Indeed there can be little doubt that there was an understanding on this subject between the Whig leaders and those Tory Lords whose votes had turned the scale on the last division. The new oaths were sent down to the Commons, together with the resolution that the Prince and Princess should be declared King and Queen.†

It was now known to whom the crown would be given. On what conditions it should be given, still remained to be decided. The Commons had appointed a committee to consider what steps it might be advisable to take, in order to secure law and liberty against the ag-

New laws proposed for the security of liberty.

---

* Lords' Journals, February 6, 168⅜; Clarendon's Diary; Burnet, i., 822, and Dartmouth's note; Van Citters, February $\frac{8}{18}$. I have followed Clarendon as to the numbers. Some writers make the majority smaller, and some larger.

‡ Lords' Journals, Feb. 6, 7, 168⅜; Clarendon's Diary.

gressions of future sovereigns; and the committee had made a report.* This report recommended, first, that those great principles of the constitution which had been violated by the dethroned King should be solemnly asserted; and, secondly, that many new laws should be enacted, for the purpose of curbing the prerogative and purifying the administration of justice. Most of the suggestions of the committee were excellent; but it was utterly impossible that the Houses could, in a month, or even in a year, deal properly with matters so numerous, so various, and so important. It was proposed, among other things, that the militia should be remodelled, that the power which the sovereign possessed of proroguing and dissolving Parliaments should be restricted; that the duration of Parliaments should be limited; that the royal pardon should no longer be pleadable to a parliamentary impeachment; that toleration should be granted to Protestant Dissenters; that the crime of high-treason should be more precisely defined; that trials for high-treason should be conducted in a manner more favorable to innocence; that the Judges should hold their places for life; that the mode of appointing Sheriffs should be altered; that juries should be nominated in such a way as might exclude partiality and corruption; that the practice of filing criminal informations in the King's Bench should be abolished; that the Court of Chancery should be reformed; that the fees of public functionaries should be regulated; and that the law of Quo Warranto should be amended. It was evident that cautious and deliberate legislation on these subjects must be the work of more than one laborious session; and it was equally evident that hasty and crude legislation on subjects so grave could not but produce new grievances, worse than those which it might remove. If the committee meant to give a list of the reforms which ought to be accomplished before the throne was filled, the list was absurdly long. If, on the other hand, the committee meant to give a list of all the reforms which the legislature would do well to make in proper season, the list was strangely imper-

---

* Commons' Journals, Jan. 29, Feb. 2, 168⅜.

fect. Indeed, as soon as the report had been read, member after member rose to suggest some addition. It was moved and carried that the selling of offices should be prohibited, that the Habeas Corpus Act should be made more efficient, and that the law of Mandamus should be revised. One gentleman fell on the chimneymen, another on the excisemen; and the House resolved that the malpractices of both chimneymen and excisemen should be restrained. It is a most remarkable circumstance that, while the whole political, military, judicial, and fiscal system of the kingdom was thus passed in review, not a single representative of the people proposed the repeal of the statute which subjected the press to a censorship. It was not yet understood, even by the most enlightened men, that the liberty of discussion is the chief safeguard of all other liberties.*

Disputes and compromise. The House was greatly perplexed. Some orators vehemently said that too much time had already been lost, and that the government ought to be settled without the delay of a day. Society was unquiet: trade was languishing: the English colony in Ireland was in imminent danger of perishing: a foreign war was impending: the exiled King might, in a few weeks, be at Dublin with a French army, and from Dublin he might soon cross to Chester. Was it not insanity, at such a crisis, to leave the throne unfilled, and, while the very existence of Parliaments was in jeopardy, to waste time in debating whether Parliaments should be prorogued by the sovereign or by themselves? On the other side it was asked whether the Convention could think that it had fulfilled its mission by merely pulling down one prince and putting up another. Surely now or never was the time to secure public liberty by such fences as might effectually prevent the encroachments of prerogative.† There was doubtless great weight in what was urged on both sides. The able chiefs of the Whig party, among whom Somers was fast rising to ascendency, proposed a middle course. The House had, they said, two objects in view, which ought to be

---

* Commons' Journals, Feb. 2, 168⅔. † Grey's Debates; Burnet, i., 822.

kept distinct. One object was to secure the old polity of the realm against illegal attacks: the other was to improve that polity by legal reforms. The former object might be attained by solemnly putting on record, in the resolution which called the new sovereigns to the throne, the claim of the English nation to its ancient franchises, so that the King might hold his crown, and the people their privileges, by one and the same title-deed. The latter object would require a whole volume of elaborate statutes. The former object might be attained in a day; the latter, scarcely in five years. As to the former object, all parties were agreed: as to the latter, there were innumerable varieties of opinion. No member of either House would hesitate for a moment to vote that the King could not levy taxes without the consent of Parliament: but it would be hardly possible to frame any new law of procedure in cases of high-treason which would not give rise to long debate, and be condemned by some persons as unjust to the prisoner, and by others as unjust to the crown. The business of an extraordinary convention of the Estates of the Realm was not to do the ordinary work of Parliaments, to regulate the fees of masters in Chancery, and to provide against the exactions of gaugers, but to put right the great machine of government. When this had been done, it would be time to inquire what improvement our institutions needed: nor would anything be risked by delay; for no sovereign who reigned merely by the choice of the nation could long refuse his assent to any improvement which the nation, speaking through its representatives, demanded.

On these grounds the Commons wisely determined to postpone all reforms till the ancient constitution of the kingdom should have been restored in all its parts, and forthwith to fill the throne without imposing on William and Mary any other obligation than that of governing according to the existing laws of England. In order that the questions which had been in dispute between the Stuarts and the nation might never again be stirred, it was determined that the instrument by which the Prince and Princess of Orange were called to the throne, and by which the order of succession was settled, should set forth, in the most distinct and solemn manner, the fundamental principles of the constitution. This instrument, known by the name of the Declaration of Right, was prepared by a committee, of which Somers was chairman. The fact that the low-born young barrister was appointed to so honorable and important a post in a Parliament filled with able and experienced men, only ten days after he had spoken in the House of Commons for the first time, sufficiently proves the superiority of his abilities. In a few hours the Declaration was framed and approved by the Commons. The Lords assented to it with some amendments of no great importance.*

<small>The Declaration of Right.</small>

The Declaration began by recapitulating the crimes and errors which had made a revolution necessary. James had invaded the province of the legislature; had treated modest petitioning as a crime; had oppressed the Church by means of an illegal tribunal; had, without the consent of Parliament, levied taxes and maintained a standing army in time of peace; had violated the freedom of election, and perverted the course of justice. Proceedings which could lawfully be questioned only in Parliament had been made the subjects of prosecution in the King's Bench. Partial and corrupt juries had been returned: excessive bail had been required from prisoners: excessive fines had been imposed: barbarous and unusual punishments had been inflicted: the estates of accused persons had been granted away before conviction. He, by whose authority these things had been done, had abdicated the government. The Prince of Orange, whom God had made the glorious instrument of delivering the nation from superstition and tyranny, had invited the Estates of the Realm to meet and to take counsel together for the securing of religion, of law, and of freedom. The Lords and Commons, having deliberated, had resolved that they would first, after the example of their ancestors, assert the ancient rights and liberties of England. Therefore it was declared that the dispensing power, as lately assumed and exercised, had no legal existence;

---

* Commons' Journals, Feb. 4, 8, 11, 12; Lords' Journals, Feb. 9, 11, 12, 168$\frac{8}{9}$.

that, without grant of Parliament, no money could be exacted by the sovereign from the subject; that, without consent of Parliament, no standing army could be kept up in time of peace. The right of subjects to petition, the right of electors to choose representatives freely, the right of the legislature to freedom of debate, the right of the nation to a pure and merciful administration of justice according to the spirit of our mild laws, were solemnly affirmed. All these things the Convention claimed, as the undoubted inheritance of Englishmen. Having thus vindicated the principles of the constitution, the Lords and Commons, in the entire confidence that the deliverer would hold sacred the laws and liberties which he had saved, resolved that William and Mary, Prince and Princess of Orange, should be declared King and Queen of England for their joint and separate lives, and that, during their joint lives, the administration of the government should be in the Prince alone. After them the crown was settled on the posterity of Mary, then on Anne and her posterity, and then on the posterity of William.

By this time the wind had ceased to blow from the west. The ship in which the Princess of Orange had embarked lay Arrival of Mary. off Margate on the eleventh of February, and, on the following morning, anchored at Greenwich.* She was received with many signs of joy and affection: but her demeanor shocked the Tories, and was not thought faultless even by the Whigs. A young woman, placed, by a destiny as mournful and awful as that which brooded over the fabled houses of Labdacus and Pelops, in such a situation that she could not, without violating her duty to her God, her husband, and her country, refuse to take her seat on the throne from which her father had just been hurled, should have been sad, or at least serious. Mary was not merely in high, but in extravagant, spirits. She entered Whitehall, it was asserted, with a girlish delight at being mistress of so fine a house, ran about the rooms, peeped into the closets, and examined the quilt of the state bed, without seeming to remember by whom

---

* London Gazette, Feb. 14, 168$\frac{8}{9}$; Van Citters, Feb. $\frac{12}{22}$.

those magnificent apartments had last been occupied. Burnet, who had, till then, thought her an angel in human form, could not, on this occasion, refrain from blaming her. He was the more astonished because, when he took leave of her at the Hague, she had, though fully convinced that she was in the path of duty, been deeply dejected. To him, as to her spiritual guide, she afterward explained her conduct. William had written to inform her that some of those who had tried to separate her interest from his still continued their machinations: they gave it out that she thought herself wronged: and, if she wore a gloomy countenance, the report would be confirmed. He therefore entreated her to make her first appearance with an air of cheerfulness. Her heart, she said, was far indeed from cheerful; but she had done her best; and, as she was afraid of not sustaining well a part which was uncongenial to her feelings, she had overacted it. Her deportment was the subject of much spiteful prose and verse: it lowered her in the opinion of some whose esteem she valued; nor did the world know, till she was beyond the reach of praise and censure, that the conduct which had brought on her the reproach of levity and insensibility was really a signal instance of that perfect disinterestedness and self-devotion of which man seems to be incapable, but which is sometimes found in woman.*

Tender and acceptance of the crown.
On the morning of Wednesday, the thirteenth of February, the court of Whitehall and all the neighboring streets were filled with gazers. The magnificent Banqueting-house, the masterpiece of Inigo, embellished by masterpieces of Rubens, had been prepared for a great ceremony. The walls were lined by the yeomen of the guard. Near the northern door, on the right hand, a large number of Peers had assembled. On the left were the Commons with their Speaker, attended by the mace. The southern door opened: and the Prince and Princess of Orange, side by side, entered, and took their place under the canopy of state.

---

* Duchess of Marlborough's Vindication; Review of the Vindication; Burnet, i., 781, 825, and Dartmouth's note; Evelyn's Diary, Feb. 21, 168⅜.

Both Houses approached, bowing low. William and Mary advanced a few steps. Halifax on the right, and Powle on the left, stood forth; and Halifax spoke. The Convention, he said, had agreed to a resolution which he prayed Their Highnesses to hear. They signified their assent; and the clerk of the House of Lords read, in a loud voice, the Declaration of Right. When he had concluded, Halifax, in the name of all the Estates of the Realm, requested the Prince and Princess to accept the crown.

William, in his own name and in that of his wife, answered that the crown was, in their estimation, the more valuable because it was presented to them as a token of the confidence of the nation. "We thankfully accept," he said, "what you have offered us." Then, for himself, he assured them that the laws of England, which he had once already vindicated, should be the rules of his conduct, that it should be his study to promote the welfare of the kingdom, and that, as to the means of doing so, he should constantly recur to the advice of the Houses, and should be disposed to trust their judgment rather than his own.* These words were received with a shout of joy which was heard in the streets below, and was instantly answered by huzzas from many thousands of voices. The Lords and Commons then reverently retired from the Banqueting-house and went in procession to the great gate of Whitehall, where the heralds and pursuivants were waiting in their gorgeous tabards. All the space as far as Charing Cross was one sea of heads. The kettle-drums struck up; the trumpets pealed; and Garter King at Arms, in a loud voice, proclaimed the Prince and Princess of Orange King and Queen of England, charged all Englishmen to bear, from that moment, true allegiance to the new sovereigns, and besought God, who had already wrought so signal a deliverance for our Church and na-

<small>William and Mary proclaimed.</small>

---

* Lords' and Commons' Journals, Feb. 14, 168$\frac{8}{9}$; Van Citters, Feb. $\frac{15}{25}$. Van Citters puts into William's mouth stronger expressions of respect for the authority of Parliament than appear in the journals; but it is clear from what Powle said that the report in the journals was not strictly accurate.

tion, to bless William and Mary with a long and happy reign.*

Thus was consummated the English Revolution. When we compare it with those revolutions which have, during the last sixty years, overthrown so many ancient governments, we cannot but be struck by its peculiar character. Why that character was so peculiar is sufficiently obvious, and yet seems not to have been always understood either by eulogists or by censors.

Peculiar character of the English Revolution.

The Continental revolutions of the eighteenth and nineteenth centuries took place in countries where all trace of the limited monarchy of the Middle Ages had long been effaced. The right of the prince to make laws and to levy money had, during many generations, been undisputed. His throne was guarded by a great regular army. His administration could not, without extreme peril, be blamed even in the mildest terms. His subjects held their personal liberty by no other tenure than his pleasure. Not a single institution was left which had, within the memory of the oldest man, afforded efficient protection to the subject against the utmost excess of tyranny. Those great councils which had once curbed the regal power had sunk into oblivion. Their composition and their privileges were known only to antiquaries. We cannot wonder, therefore, that, when men who had been thus ruled succeeded in wresting supreme power from a government which they had long in secret hated, they should have been impatient to demolish and unable to construct, that they should have been fascinated by every specious novelty, that they should have proscribed every title, ceremony, and phrase associated with the old system, and that, turning away with disgust from their own national precedents and traditions, they should have sought for principles of government in the writings of theorists, or aped, with ignorant and ungraceful affectation, the patriots of Athens and Rome. As little can we wonder that the violent action of the revolutionary spirit

---

* London Gazette, Feb. 14, 168$\frac{8}{9}$; Lords' and Commons' Journals, Feb. 13; Van Citters, Feb. $\frac{15}{25}$; Evelyn, Feb. 21.

should have been followed by reaction equally violent, and that confusion should speedily have engendered despotism sterner than that from which it had sprung.

Had we been in the same situation; had Strafford succeeded in his favorite scheme of Thorough; had he formed an army as numerous and as well disciplined as that which, a few years later, was formed by Cromwell; had a series of judicial decisions, similar to that which was pronounced by the Exchequer Chamber in the case of ship-money, transferred to the crown the right of taxing the people; had the Star Chamber and the High Commission continued to fine, mutilate, and imprison every man who dared to raise his voice against the government; had the press been as completely enslaved here as at Vienna or at Naples; had our Kings gradually drawn to themselves the whole legislative power; had six generations of Englishmen passed away without a single session of Parliament; and had we then at length risen up in some moment of wild excitement against our masters, what an outbreak would that have been! With what a crash, heard and felt to the farthest ends of the world, would the whole vast fabric of society have fallen! How many thousands of exiles, once the most prosperous and the most refined members of this great community, would have begged their bread in Continental cities, or have sheltered their heads under huts of bark in the uncleared forests of America! How often should we have seen the pavement of London piled up in barricades, the houses dinted with bullets, the gutters foaming with blood! How many times should we have rushed wildly from extreme to extreme, sought refuge from anarchy in despotism, and been again driven by despotism into anarchy! How many years of blood and confusion would it have cost us to learn the very rudiments of political science! How many childish theories would have duped us! How many rude and ill-poised constitutions should we have set up, only to see them tumble down! Happy would it have been for us if a sharp discipline of half a century had sufficed to educate us into a capacity of enjoying true freedom.

These calamities our Revolution averted. It was a revolution strictly defensive, and had prescription and legitimacy on its side. Here, and here only, a limited monarchy of the thirteenth century had come down unimpaired to the seventeenth century. Our parliamentary institutions were in full vigor. The main principles of our government were excellent. They were not, indeed, formally and exactly set forth in a single written instrument: but they were to be found scattered over our ancient and noble statutes; and, what was of far greater moment, they had been engraven on the hearts of Englishmen during four hundred years. That, without the consent of the representatives of the nation, no legislative act could be passed, no tax imposed, no regular soldiery kept up; that no man could be imprisoned, even for a day, by the arbitrary will of the sovereign; that no tool of power could plead the royal command as a justification for violating any right of the humblest subject, were held, both by Whigs and Tories, to be fundamental laws of the realm. A realm of which these were the fundamental laws stood in no need of a new constitution.

But, though a new constitution was not needed, it was plain that changes were required. The misgovernment of the Stuarts, and the troubles which that misgovernment had produced, sufficiently proved that there was somewhere a defect in our polity; and that defect it was the duty of the Convention to discover and to supply.

Some questions of great moment were still open to dispute. Our constitution had begun to exist in times when statesmen were not much accustomed to frame exact definitions. Anomalies, therefore, inconsistent with its principles and dangerous to its very existence, had sprung up almost imperceptibly, and not having, during many years, caused any serious inconvenience, had gradually acquired the force of prescription. The remedy for these evils was to assert the rights of the people in such language as should terminate all controversy, and to declare that no precedent could justify any violation of those rights.

When this had been done it would be impossible for our rulers to misunderstand the law: but, unless something more were done, it was by no means improbable that they might violate it. Unhappily the Church had long taught the nation that hereditary monarchy, alone among our institutions, was divine and inviolable; that the right of the House of Commons to a share in the legislative power was a right merely human, but that the right of the King to the obedience of his people was from above; that the Great Charter was a statute which might be repealed by those who had made it, but that the rule which called the princes of the blood-royal to the throne in order of succession was of celestial origin, and that any Act of Parliament inconsistent with that rule was a nullity. It is evident that, in a society in which such superstitions prevail, constitutional freedom must ever be insecure. A power which is regarded merely as the ordinance of man cannot be an efficient check on a power which is regarded as the ordinance of God. It is vain to hope that laws, however excellent, will permanently restrain a King who, in his own opinion, and in the opinion of a great part of his people, has an authority infinitely higher in kind than the authority which belongs to those laws. To deprive royalty of these mysterious attributes, and to establish the principle that Kings reigned by a right in no respect differing from the right by which freeholders chose knights of the shire, or from the right by which Judges granted writs of Habeas Corpus, was absolutely necessary to the security of our liberties.

Thus the Convention had two great duties to perform. The first was to clear the fundamental laws of the realm from ambiguity. The second was to eradicate from the minds, both of the governors and of the governed, the false and pernicious notion that the royal prerogative was something more sublime and holy than those fundamental laws. The former object was attained by the solemn recital and claim with which the Declaration of Right commences; the latter by the resolution which pronounced the throne vacant, and invited William and Mary to fill it.

The change seems small. Not a single flower of the crown was touched. Not a single new right was given to the people. The whole English law, substantive and adjective, was, in the judgment of all the greatest lawyers, of Holt and Treby, of Maynard and Somers, almost exactly the same after the Revolution as before it. Some controverted points had been decided according to the sense of the best jurists; and there had been a slight deviation from the ordinary course of succession. This was all; and this was enough.

As our Revolution was a vindication of ancient rights, so it was conducted with strict attention to ancient formalities. In almost every word and act may be discerned a profound reverence for the past. The Estates of the Realm deliberated in the old halls and according to the old rules. Powle was conducted to his chair between his mover and his seconder with the accustomed forms. The Sergeant with his mace brought up the messengers of the Lords to the table of the Commons; and the three obeisances were duly made. The conference was held with all the antique ceremonial. On one side of the table, in the Painted Chamber, the managers for the Lords sat covered and robed in ermine and gold. The managers for the Commons stood bareheaded on the other side. The speeches present an almost ludicrous contrast to the revolutionary oratory of every other country. Both the English parties agreed in treating with solemn respect the ancient constitutional traditions of the State. The only question was, in what sense those traditions were to be understood. The assertors of liberty said not a word about the natural equality of men and the inalienable sovereignty of the people, about Harmodius or Timoleon, Brutus the elder or Brutus the younger. When they were told that, by the English law, the crown, at the moment of a demise, must descend to the next heir, they answered that, by the English law, a living man could have no heir. When they were told that there was no precedent for declaring the throne vacant, they produced from among the records in the Tower a roll of parchment, near three hundred years old, on which, in quaint characters and barbarous Latin, it was recorded that the Estates of the Realm had declared vacant the throne of a perfidious and tyrannical Plantagenet. When at length the dispute had been accommodated, the new sovereigns were proclaimed with the old pageantry. All the fantastic pomp of heraldry was there—Clarencieux and Norroy, Portcullis and Rouge Dragon, the trumpets, the banners, the grotesque coats embroidered with lions and lilies. The title of King of France, assumed by the conqueror of Cressy, was not omitted in the royal style. To us, who have lived in the year 1848, it may seem almost an abuse of terms to call a proceeding conducted with so much deliberation, with so much sobriety, and with such minute attention to prescriptive etiquette, by the terrible name of Revolution.

And yet this revolution, of all revolutions the least violent, has been of all revolutions the most beneficent. It finally decided the great question whether the popular element which had, ever since the age of Fitzwalter and De Montfort, been found in the English polity, should be destroyed by the monarchical element, or should be suffered to develop itself freely, and to become dominant. The strife between the two principles had been long, fierce, and doubtful. It had lasted through four reigns. It had produced seditions, impeachments, rebellions, battles, sieges, proscriptions, judicial massacres. Sometimes liberty, sometimes loyalty, had seemed to be on the point of perishing. During many years one-half of the energy of England had been employed in counteracting the other half. The executive power and the legislative power had so effectually impeded each other that the state had been of no account in Europe. The King at Arms, who proclaimed William and Mary before Whitehall Gate, did in truth announce that this great struggle was over; that there was entire union between the throne and the Parliament; that England, long dependent and degraded, was again a power of the first rank; that the ancient laws by which the prerogative was bounded would thenceforth be held as sacred as the prerogative itself, and would be followed out to all their consequences; that the executive administration would be conducted in conformity with the sense of the representatives of the nation; and that no reform, which the two Houses should, after mature deliberation, propose, would be obstinately withstood by the sovereign. The Declaration of Right, though it made nothing law which had not been law before, contained the germ of the law which gave religious freedom to the Dissenter, of the law which secured the independence of the Judges, of the law which limited the duration of Parliaments, of the law which placed the liberty of the press under the protection of juries, of the law which prohibited the slave-trade, of the law which abolished the sacramental test, of the law which relieved the Roman Catholics from civil disabilities, of the law which reformed the representative system, of every good law which has been passed during more than a century and a half, of every good law which may hereafter, in the course of ages, be found necessary to promote the public weal, and to satisfy the demands of public opinion.

The highest eulogy which can be pronounced on the Revolution of 1688 is this, that it was our last revolution. Several generations have now passed away since any wise and patriotic Englishman has meditated resistance to the established government. In all honest and reflecting minds there is a conviction, daily strengthened by experience, that the means of affecting every improvement which the constitution requires may be found within the constitution itself.

Now, if ever, we ought to be able to appreciate the whole importance of the stand which was made by our forefathers against the House of Stuart.* All around us the world is convulsed by the agonies of great nations. Governments which lately seemed likely to stand during ages have been on a sudden shaken and overthrown. The proudest capitals of Western Europe have streamed with civil blood. All evil passions, the thirst of gain and the thirst of vengeance, the antipathy of class to class, the antipathy of race to race, have broken loose from the control of divine and human laws. Fear and anxiety have clouded the faces and depressed the hearts of millions. Trade has been suspended, and industry paralyzed. The rich have become poor; and the poor have become poorer. Doctrines hostile to all sciences, to all arts, to all industry, to all domestic charities, doctrines which, if carried into effect, would, in thirty years, undo all that thirty

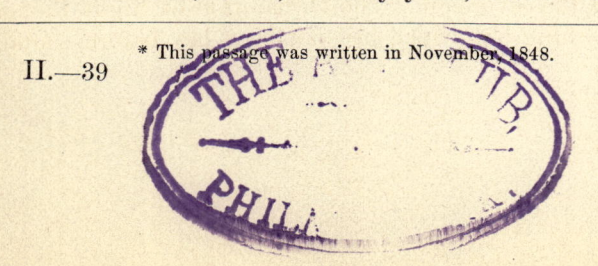

---

* This passage was written in November, 1848.

centuries have done for mankind, and would make the fairest provinces of France and Germany as savage as Congo or Patagonia, have been avowed from the tribune and defended by the sword. Europe has been threatened with subjugation by barbarians, compared with whom the barbarians who marched under Attila and Alboin were enlightened and humane. The truest friends of the people have with deep sorrow owned that interests more precious than any political privileges were in jeopardy, and that it might be necessary to sacrifice even liberty in order to save civilization. Meanwhile, in our island the regular course of government has never been for a day interrupted. The few bad men who longed for license and plunder have not had the courage to confront for one moment the strength of a loyal nation, rallied in firm array round a parental throne. And if it be asked what has made us to differ from others, the answer is that we never lost what others are wildly and blindly seeking to regain. It is because we had a preserving revolution in the seventeenth century that we have not had a destroying revolution in the nineteenth. It is because we have had freedom in the midst of servitude that we have order in the midst of anarchy. For the authority of law, for the security of property, for the peace of our streets, for the happiness of our homes, our gratitude is due, under Him who raises and pulls down nations at his pleasure, to the Long Parliament, to the Convention, and to William of Orange.

END OF VOL. II.